The Irish Dominicans, 1536–1641

THOMAS S. FLYNN, O.P.

The Irish Dominicans 1536–1641

FOUR COURTS PRESS

The typesetting for this book
(in 10.5 on 12 Plantin)
was produced by
Seton Music Graphics, Bantry, Co. Cork for
FOUR COURTS PRESS LTD
Kill Lane, Blackrock, Co. Dublin.

A catalogue record for this book
is available from the British Library.

ISBN 1-85182-122-8

Printed in Ireland by Colour Books Ltd, Dublin

Sacrum memoriae
dilectissimi ac admirabilis patris
MICHAELIS FRANCISCI FLYNN,
Ph.C., M.P.S.I. (1910–1958)
de Rehillensi agro in Tipperaria meridionali
qui in Collegio Sanctissimae et Individuae Trinitatis
Universitatis almae Dublinensis
operam assidue dedit studiis atque bonae amicorum conversationi
deinde in Artes feliciter admissus est,
anno salutis millesimo nongentesimo vigesimo nono.

Matri amabilissimi
MARGARITAE JOSEPHINAE
gratulationes quoque maximae
in octogesimo hoc anno sexto natalicio
pia cum gratiarum actione
hic iterum referuntur.

Contents

List of Illustrations

MAP

CREDITS

Illustrations nos. 1, 2, 4 and 5: Archivio Segreto Vaticano; no. 3: Carte Collection, Bodleian Library, Oxford; nos. 6–16: Commissioners of Public Works, Ireland. Table 6 is courtesy of Dr K.W. Nicholls, University College, Cork. The map is adapted from D.D.C. Pochin Mould, *The Irish Dominicans* (Dublin, 1957).

Foreword

Religious developments in early modern Ireland have given rise to lively debate in recent years as historians have thought again about the reasons for the failure of Protestantism to make significant progress. The results have been inconclusive, not least because of an inability to shake off an old habit of circular thought which has continued to frame the question in terms of deciding whether Protestantism failed because Catholicism succeeded, or Catholicism succeeded because Protestantism failed. The exchange has served to show two things: that the question is unanswerable in the present state of knowledge, and that both processes need to be examined independently before their reciprocity can be understood. In short, what is needed is more research. The present volume exemplifies how that need can be fulfilled.

Dr Flynn's work is important not only because the religious orders were central both to the religious life of pre-Reformation Ireland and to the Counter-Reformation, and their survival and revival is a large part of the story that needs to be recovered, but also because it demonstrates so clearly what the task involves and the extent of the benefits to be gained. As may be inferred from the bibliography, the history of the religious orders is not easy to reconstruct. The evidence is widely scattered, sometimes in inhospitable archives, often buried in vast collections without adequate finding aids, and written in a variety of languages and hands. Its investigation requires patience and resource as well as technical skills of an unusually high order. The rewards are of two kinds. There is the satisfaction of retrieving people and events from oblivion and placing on record a continuous account of individual and collective achievement: this is in the nature of a duty that we owe to our predecessors. In this context, Dr Flynn's study is a genuine work of *pietas*, all the more so because it is informed throughout by an overriding objective concern to discover and tell the truth. There is also the larger benefit of contributing additional understanding to the whole process of the survival and regeneration of Catholicism in Ireland in the post-Reformation period. The themes which emerge herein are representative: the tenuous existence during the later sixteenth century and the confident revival of the seventeenth; the importance of the continental dimension in sustaining and transforming the effort; the confused rivalries as the orders competed among themselves and with the parochial clergy for position; the importance of capturing bishoprics and sources of support in Rome and elsewhere. In their richness and complexity, these themes confirm that there is much more to the Counter-Reformation than the contest with Protestantism.

It is a matter of pride to recall that this work began as a doctoral thesis under my supervision, and of satisfaction to record that the pupil has become the master.

Aidan Clarke
Professor of Modern History
Trinity College
Dublin

Preface

The object of this study is to trace the changing fortunes of the Irish Dominicans from their definitive establishment as an independent corporate body in 1536 through the gradual but systematic destruction of their houses and community existence in the sixteenth century to exciting fresh beginnings in the first decades of the seventeenth. The period from 1536 to 1641 marked the painful but ultimately successful transition from late medieval Christianity to the militant Counter-Reformation Catholicism of early modern Ireland. For the Irish Dominicans it was the most critical century of their existence; several other religious orders, planted in Ireland for centuries, failed to survive the vicissitudes of the sixteenth century and disappeared forever from the Irish religious scene. The Dominicans adapted themselves to many radical changes—religious, social, political and cultural—and were successfully restored as a flourishing province before the onset of further misfortunes with the rebellion of 1641.

By no accident, this study concerns 'The Irish Dominicans' rather than 'The Dominicans in Ireland'. The fact that the Order maintained its continuity in Ireland during two very disturbed centuries was almost entirely due to its sustained contact with the religious and cultural wellsprings of continental Europe. The European-based revival of the province began about the year 1600; the Dominican houses of Spain, Portugal, Italy, France and Flanders became the chosen centres of spiritual and intellectual renewal which in turn inspired a remarkable resurgence of the Order in Ireland, thereafter depending on Irish Dominican colleges and other *studia generalia* in Europe to supply the necessary trained personnel. The unfolding of the historical experience of one major religious order—in so far as that is now possible—has the further advantage of throwing some incidental light on other religious orders, on diocesan history, and on the restructured Irish Church as a whole, besides explaining some of the complexities of the multi-dimensional reality of Irish life in the period chosen for this study. Thus in its own modest way the work may be incorporated as another missing piece into the incomplete mosaic of Irish history, secular as well as ecclesiastical, in the century (1536–1641) now recognised as the first phase of modern Irish history.

This book is a thoroughly revised and amplified version of a Ph.D. thesis presented at Trinity College, Dublin, in 1988.

St John's College
Oxford
20 October 1993

Acknowledgements

I am deeply indebted to the following archives and libraries to which I was granted access with permission to copy, photocopy or microfilm material for this study when requested.

The Department of Manuscripts, the Department of Early Printed Books and the Berkeley Library of Trinity College, Dublin; the National Library of Ireland; the Public Record Office of Ireland; the Royal Irish Academy Library, Dublin; the Franciscan Library and Archives, Dún Mhuire, Killiney, Co. Dublin; the Archives of the Irish Dominican province; the library of University College, Dublin; the Dublin Corporation Gilbert Library; the Russell Library and the library of St Patrick's College, Maynooth, Co. Kildare; the Catholic Central Library, Merrion Square, Dublin.

The Archives Générales du Royaume Belgique, Brussels, for the use of transcripts; the Archiepiscopal Archives of Mechelen/Malines.

The British Library; the Public Record Office, London; Westminster Cathedral Archives; the Bodleian Library, Oxford; Sheffield City Library.

The Archives de la région Aquitaine et du département de la Gironde, Bordeaux; the Archives départementales de la Haute-Garonne, Toulouse.

The General Archives of the Dominican Order, Rome; the Archives of the Congregation de Propaganda Fide, Rome; the Secret Archives of the Vatican; the Vatican Library; the Archivio di Santa Maria sopra Minerva, Rome; the Archives of the Irish Franciscans, St Isidore's, Rome; the Roman Archive of the Society of Jesus; the Archivio del Vicariato di Roma; the Casanatensian Library, Rome; the Dominican Provincial Archive, Bologna; the Biblioteca Fabroniana, Pistoia; the Archivio Mediceo, Florence. The following Italian state archives, of which the most important were inspected and all of whom co-operated by correspondence: Alessandria, Ancona, Arezzo, Bologna, Brescia, Cagliari, Casale Monferato, Cesena, Como, Cremona, Faenza, Fermo, Ferrara, Florence, Forlì, Genoa, Lucca, Mantua, Milan, Modena, Naples, Parma, Pavia, Perugia, Piacenza, Pisa, Pistoia, Ravenna, Reggio Emilia, Rimini, Rome, Turin, Venice, Verona and Vicenza.

The Arquivo Nacional da Torre do Tombo, Lisbon; the Biblioteca Nacional, Lisbon; the Biblioteca da Ajuda, Lisbon; the Arquivo do Patriarcado, Lisbon; and the Arquivo da Universidade, Coimbra; the Archive of the Portuguese Dominican province, Oporto.

The Archivo General de Simancas (Valladolid); the Archivo Histórico Nacional, Madrid; the Biblioteca Nacional, Madrid; the Real Academia de la Historia, Madrid; the Archivo Universitario, Salamanca; the Archivo General de Indias, Seville; the Archivo de la Santa Iglesia Catedral, Seville; the Biblioteca Colombina, Seville; the Biblioteca Universitaria, Seville; the Archivo de Protocolos, Seville; the Archivo de la Real Chancillería of Granada and Valladolid; the Archivo Histórico Provincial y Universitario, Valladolid; the Archivo del Reino de Valencia, Valencia; the Biblioteca General de la Universidad, Valencia; the Archivo de la Corona de Aragón, Barcelona; the Biblioteca de la Universidad, Barcelona; the Biblioteca de la Universidad, Zaragoza; the Archivo Particular de la Familia Medina-Sidonia, Sanlúcar de Barrameda. The following Spanish municipal and provincial archives who co-operated by correspondence or were visited by me personally: Alicante, Almagro, Avila, Ayerbe, Bádajoz, Barcelona, Bilbao, Burgos, Cádiz, Cuenca, Huesca, Jerez de la Frontera, León, Lérida (Lleida), Málaga, Orihuela, Palencia, Pamplona, Plasencia, Puerto de Santa María, Sanlúcar de Barrameda, Segovia, Seville, Talavera de la Reina, Tarragona, Toro, Trujillo, Valladolid, Valencia, Vitoria, Xátiva, Zamora and Zaragoza; also the following cathedral or cathedral chapter and diocesan archives: Barcelona, Burgos, Evora (Portugal), Granada, León, Málaga, Pamplona, Salamanca, Santander, Segovia, Seville, Valencia, Valladolid, Zamora, Zaragoza; and finally the archives of the Dominican provinces of Spain (Salamanca), Andalucía (Seville) and Aragón (Torrente, Valencia).

Among the many people who assisted or encouraged my research, I should like to thank very warmly the following: Dr Micheline Kerney Walsh, sometime archivist of the Overseas Archives of University College, Dublin, who first set me on the road to Simancas and Spain; Revd Manuel Gonçalves da Costa, Lamego, Portugal; Sor Agueda Rodriguez Cruz, O.P., Salamanca; Revd Miguel Itza Urlézaga, O.P., Salamanca; Revd Javier Serra, Valencia; Revd Fernando Aporta García, O.P., Seville; Dr and Mrs Manuel Augusto Rodrigues, Coimbra University, and those communities of Dominican men and women of the Iberian peninsula who so kindly received me; Revd Dr Benignus Millett, O.F.M., Killiney, Co. Dublin; tá buíochas ar leith ag dul don Athair Oirmhinneach Seanán Mac Conchra, O.P., fíor-chara dílis a chuir ar mo mhisneach mé an saothar seo a thabhairt chun críche; Revd Albert J. Loomie, S.J., Fordham University, New York; Dr Geoffrey Parker, C. E. Nowell Distinguished Professor of History at the University of Illinois at Urbana–Champaign

(U.S.A.); Revd Liam Swords, Via degli Ibernesi, Rome; Miss Íde Ní Thuama and Mrs Siobhán O'Rafferty, Royal Irish Academy Library, Dublin; and Miss Joan Phillips, formerly of the Ancient Monuments section, Board of Public Works.

To the supervisor of my thesis, Professor Aidan Clarke, President of the Royal Irish Academy, sometime Vice-Provost, and Erasmus Smith Professor of Modern History, Trinity College, Dublin, I should like to pay a special tribute. He it was who encouraged me to begin my researches while I was still at Rome and long before I became his graduate student in Dublin. I particularly appreciated the graciousness he showed at every stage of my work, his conscientious direction of the thesis in its various stages of evolution, and the exacting scholarly standards he demanded.

I must also express my indebtedness to the following: Mrs Penelope Woods, librarian of the Russell Library, St Patrick's College, Maynooth, and Dr Colm Lennon, Lecturer in Modern Irish History, Maynooth, who read my work and made valuable suggestions for its improvement; Mr Colm H. Croker, my copy-editor, whose expertise has significantly enhanced my work; Brother Martin Cogan, O.P., St Mary's Priory, Tallaght, who most patiently and generously placed his computer, time and technical skills at my disposal.

Finally, I wish to place on record my deep gratitude to my beloved mother, Mrs Margaret Flynn, and to my brother, Mr Michael F. Flynn, B.SC. (Pharm.), PH.C., M.P.S.I., for financial support throughout all the years of my researches; to Dr W. A. Watts, former Provost of Trinity College and chairman of the board of the Grace Lawless Lee Fund, who awarded me grants for the ever-increasing expenses of continental research in 1985 and 1986; and to the Irish Dominican province, who provided a generous subsidy towards publication.

Historiography and Sources

No scientific or comprehensive study of the Irish Dominicans in the sixteenth or seventeenth centuries has ever been attempted. Sir James Ware, the seventeenth-century antiquarian and ecclesiastical historian, compiled the first reliable but incomplete account of Irish Dominican foundations in his *De Hiberniae et Antiquitatibus eius Disquisitiones* . . . (London 1654; 2nd ed., 1658). Ware did not comment, however, on the post-suppression history of the Dominicans, although he was in personal contact with the friars of his time and had access to some of their medieval annals and other records no longer extant. John O'Heyne's *Epilogus Chronologicus* (Louvain 1706) deals almost exclusively with the Irish province in the second half of the seventeenth century and is not always dependable. The author is at his best when reminiscing about fellow Dominicans and people he actually knew. In his monumental *Hibernia Dominicana* (Cologne 1762; supplement 1772) Bishop Thomas Burke, O.P., of Ossory concentrates heavily on the medieval history of convents and houses, biographies of provincials, Dominican bishops and Dominicans martyred for the Catholic faith. While he had access at second hand to the Roman archives of the Order, but not to those of Corpo Santo College, Lisbon, before its destruction in the earthquake of 1755, he certainly utilised those of Holy Cross College, Louvain, since lost during the French invasion of 1794. Though he was painstaking in his researches and generally reliable in the assertions and conclusions he presented in his polished Latin prose, Burke too stands in need of correction. Neither his purpose nor his method lent themselves to a systematic study of the province as such, not even for his own times. And great archives, such as those of the Vatican and the Spanish government, while closed to him, are now open to all. Mervyn Archdall's *Monasticon Hibernicum* (Dublin 1786) relies very heavily on the works of his antiquarian predecessors Ware, Alemand and Harris. Notwithstanding many inaccuracies, his work has the value of citing many documentary sources now lost or destroyed, such as the offices of the Chief Remembrancer and of the Auditor General of Ireland in relation to the possessions of suppressed religious houses.

At the beginning of this century Ambrose Coleman, O.P., made a thorough study of the calendared editions of the Irish State Papers and administrative legal documents. He also had recourse to some manuscript sources in Britain and Ireland. The fruits of this patiently collated material appeared as an appendix to his edition of O'Heyne (Dundalk 1902). Despite the value of Coleman's work, it drew nothing from the prime continental manuscript sources. Daphne D. C. Pochin Mould's eminently readable *The Irish Dominicans* (Dublin 1957) provides an excellent summary of the Order's more than seven-hundred-year history in Ireland and abroad. Her book owed much to the advice and scattered but valuable researches of the late Luke Taheney, O.P., who tirelessly pieced together well-known and not so well-known fragments of the Irish Dominican past. In 1961–2 Hugh Fenning, O.P., wrote a series of popular articles entitled 'Irish Dominican Letters' for the now defunct *Irish Rosary* magazine on specific topics and personalities of the period 1553–1627. The Dominican section in Aubrey Gwynn's and Neville Hadcock's *Medieval Religious Houses: Ireland* (London 1970 represents a succinct and updated version of Coleman, but is flawed by many factual inaccuracies; notwithstanding the printed assurance that it had been scrutinised before publication by Hugh Fenning, O.P., he never saw either the text or the proofs.

⋆

The primary sources for the present study proved to be very widely scattered, assorted, and of unequal value when critically assessed. Space here allows only brief comments where necessary on some of the more significant and recurring printed and manuscript material. Dr Ciarán Brady, in a bibliographical survey of Tudor politics and government in Ireland published in *Natives and Newcomers: Essays on the Making of Irish Colonial Society* (Dublin 1986), has pointed out that the calendared editions of the Irish State Papers, especially for the period 1509–1603, are seriously inadequate and sometimes misleading. One senses an even more serious defect traceable to administrative officialdom of the sixteenth and seventeenth centuries: the deliberate destruction of records relating to the actual execution of religious policy, as also to the interrogation and treatment of Catholic dissenters, including imprisoned friars whose shadows flit in and out of the selectively preserved records.

Archdeacon John Lynch's *De Praesulibus Hiberniae*, compiled in exile at Saint-Malo *c.*1670, is without doubt particularly valuable as a repository of oral source material not only on the Catholic bishops but also on the broader sweep of sixteenth- and seventeenth-century Catholic Ireland. However, owing to uncritical use of his sources, in particular oral information, and perhaps even more to his inability to verify their accuracy, one is left in serious doubt as to their veracity and evidential reliability.

Hence his work has to be handled with critical discrimination. This criticism, however, is not to disclaim the sometimes confused or hidden truth and validity of his statements and judgements. As history is not simply a question of verifiable fact, but readily admits the human element of how it was recorded by those who heard, saw and felt the historical experience, the strong oral element in Lynch has its value and awaits proper elucidation by future historians and researchers. In the present context his book provided valuable biographical details on four Irish Dominican bishops for which one would look elsewhere in vain.

By far the most important contribution to the meagre Dominican historiography of the period is Hugh Fenning's article 'Irish Material in the Registers of the Dominican Masters General (1390–1649)' in *Archivum Fratrum Praedicatorum* (1969). Here the author published, in the original Latin, all entries concerning the Irish Dominicans up to 1649 from the extant registers in the general archives of the Order.

Turning to other Roman archival sources, the most notable is that of Propaganda Fide, the congregation charged in 1622 with worldwide missionary work. The archive is replete with prime documentation on the Irish diocesan and regular clergy. All the letters and reports, including those from Ireland, received by Propaganda before 1669 were bound up in 417 volumes, without much regard for chronology or provenance. Each volume has a contemporary but unreliable index.

The Secret Archives of the Vatican remain the most challenging and formidable ecclesiastical archive, a veritable uncharted *mare magnum* as far as Irish documentation is concerned. The indispensable guide in English to the numerous collections is L. E. Boyle's *A Survey of the Vatican Archives and its Medieval Holdings* (Toronto 1972). A thorough inspection of certain sections of the daunting *Regesta Supplicationum* or *Suppliche* series yielded a fruitful harvest even for the specialised subject-matter of the Irish Dominicans. Approximately 2,585 volumes span the years 1536–1641, each volume consisting of 300 paper folios (r v) measuring 16 × 13 inches. From the mid-sixteenth century there is a continuing high incidence of Irish petitions (*supplicationes, suppliche*) to the Apostolic Datary. Regrettably, access to the independent archive of the Congregation for the Doctrine of the Faith (founded originally as the Sacred Congregation of the Universal Inquisition in 1542 and later known as the Congregation of the Holy Office) is still arrogantly and unjustifiably refused to researchers and historians. Worse still, there is no reliable inventory of this archive which belongs to what was the most important and powerful Roman congregation until the present century.

In Spain the greatest treasure-house of archival documentation for European history as a whole in the sixteenth and seventeenth centuries is that of Simancas (south of Valladolid) founded by Charles I of Spain (the Emperor Charles v) in the years 1540–45. In this archive, housed in the splendid fifteenth-century *castillo* of the Admirals of Castille, there is a vast quantity of material as yet untapped or unused on all aspects of Irish history. A significant but by no means complete body of the documentation relating to Irish political and military history is already on microfilm in the National Library of Ireland. Nothing comparable has been done for the abundant Irish ecclesiastical documentation, most of which is to be found scattered in the immense State Papers section (approximately 8,500 bundles or *legajos*), especially within the sub-section designated *Negocios de 'partes'* (approximately 650 *legajos*).

The archives of religious orders of men which were confiscated in the 1830s have been virtually centralised in the *sección de clero* of the Archivo Histórico Nacional of Madrid. Serious losses had already been occasioned by the Peninsular War and by the destruction and dispersal of material in the aftermath of the *exclaustración*. While the bulk of the large corpus of Dominican archival material housed there (largely account books, property deeds and a host of legal documents relating to benefactions, etc.) is preponderantly of economic interest, there are some registers such as profession books, with a small number of Irish Dominican entries. The State Paper section too has items relating to Irish Dominican history and far more for the history of Ireland itself. Apart from the State Papers of Spain and the remnants of former Dominican archives, two other collections proved useful to this study: the *libros de matriculas* of Salamanca University, and the Gayangos manuscripts in the Biblioteca Nacional of Madrid. The former list Irish students of arts and theology at Salamanca from the late sixteenth century to 1695, while the latter contain a particularly important letter bearing on the foundation of an Irish Dominican college within the dominions of Spain.

In Portugal the policy of *exclaustración* of religious and secularisation of their property (1832–5) had even more disastrous consequences for existing Dominican archives than in Spain. In Lisbon the principal state archive is Torre do Tombo, adjacent to the parliament building. Here historical investigation is rendered extremely difficult owing to the inadequacies of handwritten inventories and to internal archival confusion. In the reserved manuscripts (*reservados*) section of the Biblioteca Nacional, Lisbon, there is a surprising amount of material of Irish interest, including seventeenth-century descriptions of the church and college of Corpo Santo. In the archives of the Lisbon patriarchate (*patriarcado*) there is an incomplete series of ordination registers from the 1580s to the nineteenth century. There is a major problem in disentangling Irish Dominican entries from the Portuguese because the surnames and nationality of religious ordinands were seldom noted.

Documents of the years 1626–30 in the Archives Générales du Royaume de Belgique, Brussels, reflect the serious psychological and economic pressures under which the first Irish Dominicans laboured while establishing a college at Louvain. The most valuable French source is the profession book of Toulouse, which names five of the first Irishmen professed with the Dominicans of France (1603–10).

In England the Carte manuscript collection in the Bodleian Library, Oxford, and the manuscript collections of the British Library, London, contributed significant biographical information on David Brown and Cormac O'Fergus, two key Dominican personalities in sixteenth-century Ireland. In both libraries invaluable manuscript sources for Irish history, including the Bodleian's Carte collection, still remain uncalendared and unpublished. A calendar of some of the material of Irish interest in the Carte collection was prepared and published by C. W. Russell and J. P. Prendergast in 1871, and this was supplemented by a further manuscript calendar prepared by Russell which is now in the Russell Library, St Patrick's College, Maynooth.

⋆

The Irish Dominicans, 1536–1641 is primarily a documentary history and not a purely analytical study. The sheer dearth of native sources compelled the author to rely heavily on prime continental archival documentation. The fruit of these researches have been brought to light for the first time in this study. Close adherence to documentary evidence therefore dictated the author's methodology in his attempts to bring sixteenth- and seventeenth-century Irish Dominicans authentically out of the darkness and into the light of early modern Irish history. Valuable archival material relating to the Irish Dominicans for the second half of the seventeenth century was also uncovered in Spain, Portugal and Italy and noted for future publication.

NOTE ON DATING

During the period 1582–1752 there was a discrepancy between the official calendar used in Ireland and England (the Julian or old-style calendar) and that used over most of continental Europe (the Gregorian or new-style calendar). The Julian calendar was ten days behind the Gregorian calendar in the years 1582–1700. To avoid as far as possible inconsistencies in dating, the accepted modern practice has been adopted in this work. The Julian or old-style (o.s.) calendar is followed for events occurring in Ireland or England, while the Gregorian or new-style (n.s.) calendar is accepted for events recorded in the states of Catholic Europe.

Abbreviations

AFP	*Archivum Fratrum Praedicatorum*
AGOP	Archivum Generale Ordinis Praedicatorum (Rome)
AGRB	Archives Générales du Royaume de Belgique (Brussels)
AGS	Archivo General de Simancas (Valladolid)
AHN	Archivo Histórico Nacional (Madrid)
ANTT	Arquivo Nacional da Torre do Tombo (Lisbon)
APF	Archivum Sacrae Congregationis de Propaganda Fide (Rome)
ARSI	Archivum Romanum Societatis Iesu (Rome)
ASV	Archivio Segreto Vaticano
AUS	Archivo Universitario de Salamanca
Anal. Hib.	*Analecta Hibernica*
Archiv. Hib.	*Archivium Hibernica*
BAV	Biblioteca Apostolica Vaticana
BL	British Library (London)
Bibl. Nac. (Lisbon)	Biblioteca Nacional (Lisbon)
Bibl. Nac. (Madrid)	Biblioteca Nacional (Madrid)
Bodl.	Bodleian Library (Oxford)
Brady, *Ep. Succ.*	W. M. Brady (ed.), *The Episcopal Succession in England, Scotland and Ireland, 1400–1875*, 3 vols, Rome 1876–7
Bullarium Ord. Praed.	*Bullarium Ordinis FF. Praedicatorum*, ed. Antoine Bremond, 8 vols, Rome 1729–40
Burke, *Hib. Dom.*	Thomas Burke, *Hibernia Dominicana*, Cologne 1762; supplement, 1772
Cal. Carew MSS	*Calendar of the Carew Manuscripts*, 6 vols, London 1867–73
Cal. Pat. Rolls Ire., Hen. VIII*–Eliz.*	*Calendar of Patent and Close Rolls of Chancery in Ireland, Henry* VIII *to 18th Elizabeth*, ed. James Morrin, Dublin 1861

Cal. Pat. Rolls Ire., Eliz.	*Calendar of Patent and Close Rolls of Chancery in Ireland, Elizabeth, 19th year to end of reign*, ed. James Morrin, Dublin 1862
Cal. Pat. Rolls Ire., Jas I	*Irish Patent Rolls of James I: Facsimile of the Irish Record Commissioners' Calendar prepared prior to 1830*, with foreword by M. C. Griffith, Dublin 1966
Cal. Pat. Rolls Ire. [1603–10]	*Calendar of the Patent and Close Rolls, Chancery, Ireland* [1603–10], n.p., n.d.
Cal. S.P. Ire., 1509–73 [etc.]	*Calendar of State Papers relating to Ireland, 1509–73* [etc.], 24 vols, London 1860–1911
Cal. S.P. Ire., Hen. VIII	*Calendar of State Papers, Ireland, Henry VIII*, 11 vols, London 1830–52
Cal. S.P. Rome	*Calendar of State Papers relating to English Affairs, preserved principally at Rome*, 2 vols, London 1916–26
Collect. Hib.	*Collectania Hibernica*
Eubel, *Hier. Cath.*	C. Eubel and P. Gauchat (eds), *Hierarchia Catholica Medii Aevi et Recentioris Aetatis*, Münster 1898–
FLK	Franciscan Library, Killiney, Co. Dublin
Fenning, *Irish material*	Hugh Fenning (ed.), 'Irish Material in the Registers of the Dominican Masters General (1390–1649)' in *AFP*, 39 (1969)
Fiants Ire., Hen. VIII—Eliz.	'Calendar to Fiants of the Reign of Henry VIII—Elizabeth I' in *Reports of the Deputy Keeper of the Public Records in Ireland*, 7–22, Dublin 1875–90
HMC	Historical Manuscripts Commission
IER	*Irish Ecclesiastical Record*
Ir. Cath. Hist. Comm. Proc.	*Proceedings of the Irish Catholic Historical Committee*, Dublin 1955–
Ir. Theol. Quart.	*Irish Theological Quarterly*
Jn. Ecc. Hist.	*Journal of Ecclesiastical History*
Lynch, *De Praesulibus Hib.*	John Lynch, *De Praesulibus Hiberniae Potissimis Catholicae Religionis in Hibernia, Serendae, Propagandae, et Conservandae Authoribus*, ed J. F. O'Doherty, 2 vols, Dublin 1944

Moran, *Spicil. Ossor.*	P. F. Moran (ed.), *Spicilegium Ossoriense, being a Collection of Original Letters and Papers Illustrative of the History of the Irish Church from the Reformation to the year 1800*, 3 vols, Dublin 1874–84
NHI, iii	T. W. Moody, F. X. Martin and F. J. Byrne (eds), *A New History of Ireland*, vol. iii: *Early Modern Ireland, 1534–1691*, Oxford 1976
NHI, ix	—— (eds), *A New History of Ireland*, ix: *Maps, Genealogies, Lists*, Oxford 1984
NLI	National Library of Ireland (Dublin)
O'Heyne, *Epil. Chron.*	John O'Heyne, *Epilogus Chronologicus exponens succincte Conventus et Fundationes Sacri Ordinis Praedicatorum in Regno Hyberniae*, Louvain 1706; ed. and trans. Ambrose Coleman, Dundalk 1902
PRO	Public Record Office (London)
PROI	Public Record Office of Ireland (Dublin)
RIA Proc.	*Proceedings of the Royal Irish Academy*
RSAI Jn.	*Journal of the Royal Society of Antiquaries of Ireland*
Reichert, *MOPH*	B. M. Reichert (ed.), *Monumenta Ordinis Fratrum Praedicatorum Historica: Acta Capitulorum Generalium . . . 1220–1844*, 9 vols, Rome 1898–1904
SOCG	Scritture Originali riferite nelle Congregazioni Generali di Propaganda Fide (AFP)
TA	Irish Dominican Provincial Archives (St Mary's Priory, Tallaght, Co. Dublin)
TCD	Trinity College, Dublin
Wadding Papers	*Wadding Papers, 1614–1638*, ed. Brendan Jennings, Dublin 1953

Ancient Dominican Foundations with date of foundation: Cashel 1243
Post-Reformation houses of refuge and other sites: Boula
Dominican foundations at which part of the pre-Reformation buildings survive:
Present Dominican houses: WATERFORD 1226
Coleraine 1244
Derry 1274
Newtownards 1244
ULSTER
Gola
Castlewellan
Moneyscalp
NEWRY 1871
Carlingford 1305
DUNDALK
SLIGO 1252
Rathfran 1274
Cloonymeaghan 1488
Ballindoon 1507
Burrishoole 1486
Strade 1252
Clonshanville 14th. cent.
Urlar 1434
Tulsk 1448
Longford c.1420
DROGHEDA 1224
Trim 1263
CONNACHT
Roscommon 1253
Kilcommoc
Mary Hill
Donore
Mullingar 1237
DUBLIN 1224
Tombeola 1427
LEINSTER
TALLAGHT 1856
GALWAY 1488
Athenry 1241
Yeomanstown
Naas 1356
Boula
NEWBRIDGE
Kilcorban
Lorrha 1269
Portumna 1414
ATHY 1253
Aghaboe 1382
ARKLOW 1264
KILKENNY 1225
LIMERICK 1227
Cashel 1243
MUNSTER
Rosbercon 1267
Kilmallock 1291
Clonmel
TRALEE 1243
WATERFORD 1226
Glanworth 1475
? Castlelyons
Youghal 1268
CORK 1229
0
50
Miles

INTRODUCTION

Hibernia Dominicana: The M
Legacy of Division, 1224–1

THE IRISH VICARIATE: ANGLO-IRISH AND GAELIC IRISH, 1224–1400

In 1216 the Order of Friars Preachers or Dominicans received papal approval from Innocent III shortly after the closure of the great reform council of the Lateran. Impelled by its multinational composition as much as by its universal preaching mandate, the Order swiftly established itself in the towns and cities of medieval Europe. The Dominicans first reached Ireland in 1224 from England,[1] where communities had been formed at Oxford (1221) and London (1223), and in that same year made two foundations in the flourishing towns of Dublin and Drogheda. Arriving in the wake of the Anglo-Norman invasion and conquest of Ireland, it was quite natural that these French-speaking Dominicans should find their first patrons within the Anglo-Norman lordships of Leinster and their enclaves in Munster, Connacht and Ulster. Initially the Dominicans must have been viewed as part of the spiritual wing of Norman civilisation and colonisation, but they rather quickly distanced themselves from that image and became highly esteemed by the leading Irish families as well.

The politico-cultural theatre in Ireland, therefore, largely determined the foundation of the first houses or convents of the Dominicans by Anglo-Norman magnates within their general sphere of influence, which was more extensive than what later emerged as the area of the Pale. Within a short time houses were established through the generous patronage of local lords within the Gaelic Irish territories. Racial division within the medieval Irish Church, stemming from the conflicts and complexities of the two *naciones* or *linque* (to use medieval terminology),[2] Irish and English, was dominant until challenged and mitigated by the fifteenth-century Observant movement and later by the irrepressible tide of religious developments in the sixteenth and seventeenth centuries. The

1 BL, Cotton MS Vesp. B. XI, f. 137; 'Annals of Multyfarnham (*Annales de Monte Fernandi*)' in *Tracts relating to Ireland*, ed. A Smith, Dublin 1843, 12.
2 J. A. Watt, *The Church and the Two Nations in Medieval Ireland*, Cambridge 1970, ix.

ming of the four major orders of friars (Dominicans, Franciscans, Augustinians and Carmelites) to Ireland was of immense significance in the process of changing the old ecclesiastical order and in affording new expressions of Irish Christianity. Nonetheless, as in many similar promising developments, the spirit and vision of the friars was seriously disrupted and damaged by national hatreds and discords.[3] Sadly, medieval divisions within the Irish Church continued unabated and weakened resistance in the face of the Tudor ecclesiastical revolution, of which the suppression of the religious houses was but a symptom.

The first wave of Dominican expansion in Ireland resulted in the founding of twenty-four houses. Chronologically the list runs: Dublin (1224), Drogheda (1224), Kilkenny (1225), Waterford (1226), Limerick (1227), Cork (1229), Mullingar (1237), Athenry (1241), Cashel (1243), Tralee (1243), Newtownards (1244), Coleraine (1244), Sligo (1252), Strade (1252), Athy (1253), Roscommon (1253), Trim (1263), Arklow (1264), Rosbercon (1267), Youghal (1268), Lorrha (1269), Derry (1274), Rathfran (1274) and Kilmallock (1291).

All but five of these houses had Anglo-Norman founders. In 1275 the Irish houses were constituted a vicariate, made subject to English jurisdiction, and were henceforth ruled by a vicar provincial appointed by the provincial of England. Its 'chapters' assembled regularly, though scarcely any records of their deliberations have survived. In spite of the rapid spread of the Order, serious difficulties arose in the administration of the Irish vicariate. In 1314 the Master General (*Magister Generalis*), Berengar de Landorra, on the conclusion of the Order's general chapter held at London, issued a letter amounting to a statute for the Irish Dominicans. The letter defined with considerable precision the status of the Irish vicariate and its government. The most important provisions dealt with the appointment of a vicar with plenary powers selected from among the Irish conventual priors, the extent of his jurisdiction, and arrangements for the studies of Irish students. The Irish vicariate had the right to send two students to Oxford, two to Cambridge, two to London, one to Paris, and others by quota to continental universities. Expenses were to be defrayed at the rate which obtained in English houses. Irish students in England were to enjoy the privileges accorded to foreign students. Those considered suitable might be promoted to the degree of bachelor or master of theology. Finally, the vicariate was granted the right to send two delegates annually to the general chapter of the Order.[4] In effect this

3 Ibid., 176.

4 The text of the letter is in Burke, *Hib. Dom.*, 49–50; D. D. C. Pochin Mould, *The Irish Dominicans*, Dublin 1957, 245–7. See also W. A. Hinnebusch, 'Foreign Dominican Students and Professors at the Oxford Blackfriars' in A. B. Emden *et al.* (eds), *Oxford Studies presented to Daniel Callus*, Oxford 1964, 114.

letter constituted Ireland as a distinct province, but owing to English intransigence the title and full juridical recognition was withheld; nor is there any evidence that Irish delegates ever attended a general chapter in an official capacity after 1314.

The general chapter of Carcassonne (1378) witnessed a fresh attempt to secure final approval for the separation of Ireland from the English province. Legislation for the setting up of an autonomous Irish province had been introduced at Florence (1374), approved at Bourges (1376) and accepted at Carcassonne on the eve of the Western Schism.[5] The English Dominicans quickly appealed the decisions of Carcassonne with reference to Ireland and succeeded in having them revoked by Urban VI on 25 August 1379. Under pressure from the English king, Richard II, this ruling was confirmed and given legal force by Boniface IX in the bull *Ex injuncto nobis desuper* of 20 February 1397.[6] This papal decision ran entirely contrary to normal Dominican legislative procedures and practice; legally the general chapter of the Order could not act with regard to Ireland as long as the decision of Boniface IX remained in force. Thus the nascent Irish Dominican province ceased to exist. It seems that the impetus for an independent province had the support of Dominicans of English and Irish origin alike. The fettered vicariate of Ireland, ever conscious of its insecurity, sought and obtained confirmation of its existing rights and status, as enshrined in the charter of Master Berengar de Landorra, from the same Pope Boniface in the decree *Sacrae religionis* (21 February 1400).[7]

THE OBSERVANT AND SEPARATIST MOVEMENTS, 1390–1536

In the last decades of the calamitous fourteenth century a spiritual resurgence and sense of genuine reform swept through the orders of friars in continental Europe, notably the Franciscans, Dominicans and Augustinians. While inspired by diverse antecedents, and independent in external forms, the reform manifested a fervour and vitality reminiscent of the original spirit of the orders. In the fourteenth and early fifteenth centuries currents of reform and stricter religious observance—perhaps in Ireland accepted more on a personal than an institutional level—exercised very considerable influence in living and preaching the standards of European Christianity.

The Dominican Observant reform movement in an Irish context was first mentioned in 1390. Drogheda was designated as a convent of regular

5 Reichert, *MOPH*, iv, 427, 442.
6 Text in Burke, *Hib. Dom.*, 57–8.
7 Ibid., 58–9.

observance for those who had accepted the reform as vigorously promoted by Raymund of Capua, Master of the Order.[8] Whether or not this aspiration was ever realised at Drogheda or elsewhere is not known. Source material for a study of the Irish Dominican reform is extremely sparse and certainly inadequate for making definitive judgements on the history of its progress or its spiritual impact on the several groupings of Irish and Anglo-Irish Dominicans.

In the extant registers of the Masters General, practically the sole source of information, almost one hundred years (1390–1484) are passed over in silence as far as the affairs of the Observant reform in Ireland are concerned. What is known is that a further spate of Irish Dominican foundations took place in the late fourteenth and fifteenth centuries, principally in the west of Ireland: Cloonshanville (late fourteenth century); Portumna (1414); Longford (1420); Toombeola (1427); Urlar (1434); Tulsk (1448); Burrishoole (1486); Galway (1488); Clooneymeaghan (1488); and Ballindoon (1507). Of these, Portumna and Longford were founded specifically as houses of observance. In contrast to their thirteenth-century brethren, who concentrated on installing themselves in or close to cities and towns, the Observants for the most part withdrew to the countryside and places of seclusion. On the whole these small Connacht foundations are thought to have been affected to a greater or lesser extent by the reform ideals: a return to the strict observance of the rule and constitutions and to the solemn celebration of the liturgy according to the Dominican rite and ceremonies. The objective of the Dominicans established at Portumna was thus expressed in 1420: 'Certain brethren had chosen this site as a place remote from the noise and turmoil of the world, in order that they might serve the Most High in a life of regular observance.'[9] There is no proof that all the Connacht houses accepted the reform programme. What is undeniable is that the Observant movement in Ireland sprang mostly from a Gaelic Irish environment and would later infiltrate Anglo-Irish areas. As the reform gained momentum it became the religious expression of a Gaelic Irish political and cultural revival. The emergence of this revival coincided with the decline of English interest and authority in Irish affairs. Furthermore, the currents of religious reform in Italy and the Low Countries impinged more on Gaelic Ireland, which long since had been accustomed to direct recourse to Rome in ecclesiastical matters. This strategy whereby Irish ecclesiastics obtained independent papal judgements and decisions

8 H. Fenning (ed.), 'Irish Material in the Registers of the Dominican Masters General (1390–1649)' in *AFP*, 39 (1969), 254. In this work the author calendared all the Irish Dominican entries in the original Latin text. Henceforth cited as Fenning, *Irish material*.

9 Cited in J. A. Watt, *The Church in Medieval Ireland*, Dublin 1972, 194.

served increasingly to circumvent and counterbalance the power of the English political and ecclesiastical structures in Ireland. The Observant Dominicans of Connacht desired very strongly to be autonomous in government, and indeed spearheaded an attempt to obtain a fully independent province of Ireland.

At the general chapter of the Order in 1484 the Irish representatives successfully petitioned for the foundation of an autonomous province. An outstanding personality of that period, Master Maurice Ó Mocháin,[10] was appointed first provincial of the new province. Maurice Ó Mocháin was educated as a Dominican in the English houses of Salisbury, Worcester and finally at Oxford, where he was permitted in 1474 to sit for the Order's highest theology degree of Master of Sacred Theology.[11] 'Though his career can be known to us only in the barest outline, he exemplifies that transcendence of the barriers between Gaelic and English traditions which was the characteristic strength of the Observant movement as a whole.'[12] In 1488 a fresh reform initiative was undertaken by Ó Mocháin when he was given authority by the Master of the Order to introduce the reform in the convents of Drogheda, Coleraine, Cork, Youghal, and others at his discretion.[13] Unexpectedly the English Dominicans in 1491 objected to the independent Irish province, in virtue of the papal bull of 1397. For a second time the newly founded Irish province was reduced to the status of a vicariate. Ó Mocháin declined to continue as vicar and simply resigned the office.[14] Not until 1536 would the seemingly irreversible decision of that papal bull be finally rescinded by Paul III in favour of the Irish province.

While the surviving registers show that the central Roman administration of the Dominican Order consistently supported and assisted the reform movement in Ireland, its progress there depended on the dedicated leadership of a select number of Dominicans. From the 1480s Maurice Ó Mocháin was the indefatigable promoter of Dominican

10 The Ó Mocháin family name is variously anglicised O'Mochane, O'Moghane, O'Moughan, O'Moone, Moane, Moghan, Moughan, Mohan, Moohan, Moon, Moone, Maughan and Vaughan. It is also rendered Morall from the Latinised version Moralis. The two principal branches of the family were located in Connacht: (1) that of Cinél Ianna in the counties of Galway and Clare, diocese of Kilmacduagh; (2) an important ecclesiastical family—a branch of the Uí Fiachrach—who were erenaghs of Killaraght (barony of Coolavin), Co. Sligo, hereditary keepers of the cross of St Attracta and renowned as patrons of learning. See P. Woulfe, *Sloinnte Gaedhael is Gall: Irish Names and Surnames*, Dublin 1923, 617–18.

11 A. B. Emden, *A Survey of Dominicans in England: based on the ordination lists in episcopal registers (1268 to 1538)*, Rome 1967, 177–8, 209, 406.

12 Watt, *The Church in Medieval Ireland*, 198.

13 Fenning, *Irish material*, 261.

14 Ibid., 263.

reform. His reform of Youghal was approved in 1493, when he was also reappointed vicar of the province and commissioned to proceed with the reform of whichever houses desired it.[15] Having served several terms as vicar provincial, he was relieved of the general government of the Irish vicariate in 1496, but at the same time was nominated vicar of the reformed houses.[16] By this time the Observant reform had been introduced into some of the houses of the Anglo-Irish zones of influence, and this tended to foster unity among the Gaelic Irish and the Anglo-Irish. Altogether less fettered to English interests and better organised were the Irish Franciscan and Augustinian Observant brethren, whose antecedents and progress are well documented.[17]

The establishment of a distinct congregation of Dominican Observant brethren was a logical objective, arising from their desire to safeguard their spirit of reform and their own particular interests. The Irish Dominicans, like those of Scotland who became independent in 1481, had been in contact with the reformed congregation of Holland from as early as 1501. In 1503 John de Bauffremez, the vicar of the congregation of Holland, was made vicar of the reformed houses of Ireland and of those to be reformed in the future. Two years later John Quin was confirmed in the office of vicar of the Irish Observant congregation.[18]

Up to the close of the fifteenth century the Irish Dominicans seem to have belonged to two distinct vicariates, one for the English Pale and Anglo-Irish houses, the other for the Irish houses in the remainder of the country. However, with the emergence of the reformed houses and the growth of the Observant movement, a third vicar was appointed by the Master of the Order. By 1509 a very tangled triple jurisdiction operated in Ireland. In that year Thomas de Vio Cajetano, the Master General of the Dominicans, knew only that there were three vicars with corresponding jurisdictions: the vicar of Ireland of the English provincial, the vicar of three reformed houses, and the vicar of the entire Irish nation who had been appointed in 1503. All three vicars were ordered to clarify their appointments and their authority and to compile lists of houses under their respective jurisdictions.[19] The general chapter held in 1518 recognised

15 Ibid.
16 Ibid., 264.
17 For comparison with the more prolific Franciscan and Augustinian Observant reform movements see P. Conlan, *Franciscan Ireland*, Mullingar 1988, 21–5; F. X. Martin, 'The Augustinian Reform Movement in the Fifteenth Century' in J. A. Watt, J. B. Morall and F. X. Martin (eds), *Medieval Studies presented to Aubrey Gwynn, S.J.*, Dublin 1961, 230–64; Watt, *The Church in Medieval Ireland*, 193–202. For the Carmelites see P. O'Dwyer, *The Irish Carmelites*, Dublin 1988, 55–75.
18 Fenning, *Irish material*, 265.
19 Ibid., 267.

only two groups of Dominicans in Ireland: the congregation of the reform and the vicariate of the English province.[20] By 1529 all previous jurisdictions had coalesced into two bodies: Conventual and Observant Dominicans, each with their own vicar.[21]

On the eve of the suppression of religious houses in Ireland the Observant reform movement was gaining ground among the Augustinians, Dominicans and Franciscans. Only three or four Dominican houses were Observant at the beginning of the sixteenth century (Youghal, Drogheda, Kilkenny and Cork), and even these were mixed communities.[22] Others still were designated for reform, but there is no proof that strict observance was established in them.[23] On the other hand, both Portumna and Longford had been expressly founded as houses of the reform, and the Observant movement was gathering momentum in Connacht by 1500. Although the movement was more widespread and better documented for the Augustinians and Franciscans, as already noted (note 17), the impetus of reform was far more influential among the Dominicans than the small number of their Observant communities would suggest.

The Observant movement had shallow roots among the friars in England. Long before 1500 the English Dominicans were already in decline and subservient to the crown. By the 1520s the universities of Oxford and Cambridge had been infiltrated by the rising intellectual tide of continental Protestantism, facilitated by the invention of printing and the consequent influx of Lutheran books. The Protestant revolution was primarily one of doctrine and morals rather than administration and structural reorganisation. The principal tenets of Protestant doctrinal reform: the biblical doctrine of grace, the uniqueness of Christ's atonement, the priesthood of all believers, the primacy of individual private judgement and the doctrine of justification by faith alone were openly debated and frequently accepted by representatives of the orders of friars, studying or lecturing at English or Scottish universities. In Ireland, however, there were no predisposing factors for the reception of the Protestant intellectual challenge; moreover, lacking universities and for the most part uninfluenced by the Protestant reform movement, the country was not confronted by intense intellectual debate of the primary doctrinal issues as highlighted by early continental Protestantism.

By way of contrast, the orders of Irish friars were experiencing vigorous currents of internal religious reform and spiritual renewal. The Observant friars were increasingly viewed as exemplary for personal holiness, pastoral

20 Reichert, *MOPH*, ix, 174.
21 Fenning, *Irish material*, 269–70.
22 Watt, *The Church in Medieval Ireland*, 197–8.
23 According to Burke, Limerick and other unnamed houses were reformed in 1504. *Hib. Dom.*, 213.

devotion and learning.[24] Their involvement with all social classes, particularly as spiritual and moral guides, added to the high esteem in which they were held. An early sixteenth-century moralist singled out 'the poor friars beggars' for praise because they alone attended to the preaching of the Word of God in both English and Irish districts.[25] The process of suppression in Ireland would be quite unlike the similar programme set in train in England. There were unexpected repercussions and a quite different response not only to the suppression itself, but also to the Catholic reform movements thrown up by the Reformation era.

The Irish houses of thc Observants proved to be agents of ongoing reform and played a significant role in cutting across the Gaelic Irish and Anglo-Irish divide. Most importantly, the Observant movement provided a line of communication with reforming continental Catholicism before the emergence of the distinctively Protestant manifesto and the later Tridentine plan of reform. The Dominican stream of this movement would soon be instrumental in resuscitating the Order in the southern lands of Desmond. Later it was to maintain a fragile but persistent Dominican presence on the western seaboard during the troubled and dangerous years of Elizabeth's reign until fresh beginnings became feasible in the seventeenth century.

DAVID BROWN AND THE RE-ESTABLISHMENT OF THE IRISH PROVINCE, 1536

In the year 1536 two Irish Dominicans of exceptional stature quite unexpectedly made their appearance in the Irish ecclesiastical world. One of these was Quentin Cogly, who was appointed Bishop of Dromore in that year and whose vigorous campaign against the Anglican Reformation is described in the following chapter. The other was Master David Brown, an Anglo-Irishman by birth and education, who was made prior provincial of the Irish province, newly established, and inquisitor of the island of Ireland during a visit to Rome in the summer of that year.[26] The latter part of his career as provincial, which spanned over twenty eventful years, is dealt with in Chapter 2.

This Master David, the first true provincial of the Irish Dominicans, is identical with the David Brown who accompanied the provincial of England and was styled definitor for England (*magister socius Angliae*) at

24 M. Piò, *Delle Nobile e Generosa Progenie del P.S. Domenico in Italia*, Bologna 1615, 440.

25 *Cal. S.P. Ire., Hen. VIII*, iii, pt 3, p. 15.

26 Fenning, *Irish material*, 270.

the general chapter of the Order of 1515.[27] The student rolls of Cambridge University attest that he became a bachelor of divinity there in the academic year 1513–14.[28] It is very likely that he was the person surnamed Brown admitted to lecture on the *Sentences* of Peter Lombard at Cambridge in 1515.[29] Thomas Quirke, Dominican prior of Limerick in 1627, who had access to medieval house records, informed Sir James Ware, the historian and antiquarian, that David Brown was a most distinguished *filius* of the convent of Tralee, and that he had obtained his doctorate of theology in the presence of Cardinal Thomas de Vio Cajetano (better known as Cajetan, the famous theologian and Thomist). More correctly, it was at the general chapter of Naples in 1515, over which Cajetan presided as Master of the Order, that David Brown was conferred with the mastership in theology. Subsequently, as a royal agent of Henry VIII, he was sent to Italy on unspecified diplomatic business, possibly to Rome in relation to the king's divorce petition. After the suppression of the religious houses in England he returned to Ireland, his native land, where he ended his days.[30]

In the register of Master General Jean du Feynier, David Brown's visit to Rome in 1536 is recorded in an extremely terse and factual way.[31] It is clear that his objective in travelling to Rome was to secure the establishment of the Irish Dominican province and that he succeeded in doing so. It was not, however, accomplished in the normal Dominican constitutional way, namely by decision of the Master General or by approval of a general chapter, the legislative body of the Order.

In May 1536 a general chapter met at Lyons, but its proceedings had no reference to Ireland, nor was the English province officially represented. At Rome, perhaps with the active support of the Master General, David Brown obtained an audience with Pope Paul III. Brown's status as a former English diplomat in Italy may have more readily gained him the ear of the Pope. In all likelihood he presented an account of the precarious position of the Order in Ireland and made his plea for the restoration of a separate province, severing its links with England. Whatever the exact role played by David Brown, it is certain that the Irish Dominican province was unambiguously and permanently established in 1536 through the personal initiative of Paul III, thus annulling the bull of Boniface IX, *Ex injuncto nobis desuper* of 1397. This ruling was later

27 Reichert, *MOPH*, ix, 124, 145.

28 J. and J. A. Venn, *Alumni Cantabrigienses*, i, Cambridge 1922, 232.

29 W. Gumbley, *The Cambridge Dominicans*, Oxford 1938, 33.

30 BL, Add. MSS (Milles Collection), 4793, f. 6r. A thorough search of English State Papers for the reign of Henry VIII and other contemporary documentation has not revealed any reference to Brown or his earlier career.

31 Fenning, *Irish material*, 270.

accepted by the Master of the Order and ratified by the general chapter of 1558.[32]

Thus the legacy of medieval Irish Dominican divisions was overcome in principle, enabling the remaining obstacles to fraternal unity to be slowly and painfully surmounted in the course of the next century. Almost certainly the papal Chancery or another Roman curial body drew up a document at the bidding of Paul III, reversing the judgement of Boniface IX, canonically erecting the Irish province, spelling out its more important rights and privileges, and placing the disparate groups, Anglo-Irish and Gaelic Irish, Observants and Conventuals, under the direct supervision and jurisdiction of David Brown. Several painstaking searches in the Vatican archives have failed to locate a copy of this epoch-making document; such documents were not, however, systematically registered in the papal Chancery or Datary until late in the sixteenth century.[33]

The circumstances of the decision leading to the separation of the Irish Dominicans from the jurisdiction of the English provincial raise a number of unresolved questions. Precisely in what capacity was David Brown acting, and on whose behalf, when he undertook his mission to Rome, culminating in his appointment as provincial of Ireland? Why did the Farnese Pope, Paul III, noted for his tact and diplomatic skills, play the major part in re-establishing what must have seemed a remote and insignificant province of Dominican friars as far as papal policy was concerned? One of the principal aims of Pope Paul III was to stem the spread and influence of Protestantism. Yet at this time he still hoped for a reconciliation with England and would not have wished to further provoke the excommunicated English king by a unilateral decision which seemed likely to run counter to the trend of Henry VIII's religious policy in Ireland.

One is still left to ponder what precise turn of events led David Brown away from his career as a courtier of the English crown, and instead to devote his energies to removing the province of Ireland from English control. Certainly with the beginning of the Henrician policy of reformation and suppression in England, he would have quickly deduced the fate that would soon befall the religious houses in Ireland. He sought, therefore, to save the Irish communities and houses by distancing them from state interference or at least to delay such action for as long as possible. Quite naturally his strategy led him to Rome. David Brown, as will be shown in Chapter 2, had become a champion of the Observant reform ideals and perceived that the Irish province could be reinvigorated

32 Reichert, *MOPH*, x, 10–11.

33 The secret registers (*libri secretorum*) of Pope Paul III in which sensitive politico-religious decisions were recorded do not survive. See B. Katterbach, *Inventario dei Registri delle Suppliche*, Vatican City 1932, 113 note 1.

and kept alive by the Observant brethren. In pursuing his mission he had long since come to terms with his Anglo-Irish background and his years of loyal service to the Tudor monarch. His achievement, however, was overshadowed by the corpus of legislation of the first Reformation parliament held in Dublin in 1536. The Act of Supremacy declared Henry VIII 'the only Supreme Head on earth of the whole Church of Ireland called *Hibernica Ecclesia*'. This led to the creation of a state church, as by law established, which was virtually unopposed by the Irish parliament.[34] This act granted the king, explicitly, supreme spiritual jurisdiction over Irish religious communities, thus paving the way for their dissolution and the wholesale expropriation of their properties.

34 G. A. Hayes-McCoy, 'The Royal Supremacy and Ecclesiastical Revolution, 1534–47' in *NHI*, iii, Oxford 1976, 60–61; B. Bradshaw, *The Dissolution of the Religious Orders in Ireland under Henry VIII*, Cambridge 1974, 461, 49–51; N. Canny, *From Reformation to Restoration: Ireland, 1534–1600*, Dublin 1987, 24.

ONE

The Henrician Reformation and the First Suppressions, 1536–47[1]

The suppression of monastic and religious houses in Ireland was at once an episode of Irish politico-ecclesiastical history and of the English Reformation. The genesis of Henry VIII's policy of suppression and reformation in Ireland lay within the broader framework of sixteenth-century Tudor expansionism and absolutism. Henry's extension of his ecclesiastical revolution to Ireland derived first and foremost from his assertion of unqualified royal jurisdiction and sovereignty over the entire island.

The Henrician ecclesiastical revolution was essentially concerned with the rejection of papal jurisdiction, the nationalisation and reorganisation of the Church. This was implemented by the provisions of the Act of Supremacy and a series of laws which severed financial, juridical and administrative bonds between Rome and Henry VIII's dominions. Nonetheless, contrary to the will of the Tudor monarchs, there was no real Reformation in Ireland in the sixteenth century in the sense in which there was one in Germany, Switzerland, Scotland and England. Only after the foundation of the University of Dublin (1592) and the advent of Archbishop James Ussher, the prime founding father and ideologue of Irish Protestantism, did the new church establish itself as a distinct visible reality with several religious and cultural expressions.

The initial general reaction in Ireland to the king's Reformation was characterised by confusion and uncertainty, rather than by bitter religious controversy as in England. Such dissent as there was to the king's policies was somewhat reserved and muted. From within the Dominican community and the Irish episcopate, however, one voice was immediately raised in loud and forthright condemnation of the new reforms; and this denunciation was followed by an active and personal intervention both in Ireland and at Rome. The career of this vigorous defender of papal jurisdiction in ecclesiastical affairs is worth tracing in some detail.

1 See Bradshaw, *The Dissolution of the Religious Orders in Ireland*, *passim*; R. D. Edwards, *Church and State in Tudor Ireland*, Dublin 1935, *passim*.

QUENTIN COGLY, BISHOP OF DROMORE: AN EARLY OPPONENT OF ANGLICAN REFORMATION, 1536–9

Master David Brown was not alone on his mission to Rome in that momentous year of 1536. On his departure from Rome in 1536, he was accompanied by three other Dominicans, who had the Master General's permission to seek alms on the homeward journey.[2] Quentin Cogly,[3] who was nominated Bishop of Dromore by a Roman consistory on 29 May 1536,[4] was almost certainly one of Brown's companions. He may have studied at the Sorbonne when a student in Paris in the early 1520s. He was described as a Dominican of Mullingar in 1528 when the Master of the Order absolved him from the canonical censures incurred by apostasy about 1526. Matthew Orius, a Paris Dominican, was designated at the time to receive him to the religious habit once more. The nature of his apostasy, whether from the Church or the Order, was not mentioned; at that time one could become an 'apostate' simply by not wearing the religious habit, even in the face of harassment or inconvenience of long-distance travel. On that same day, 1 February 1528, he was assigned to the University of Oxford as a student of theology.[5] In April 1536 the register of the Master General noted that he was a bachelor of canon law and holder of the licentiate in theology.[6] One might also hazard a guess that he was a pupil in Paris of the Scottish Robert Wauchope, the future reform-minded Archbishop of Armagh and noted theologian and canonist.[7] In fact Quentin Cogly may have owed his promotion to the see of Dromore to Wauchope's recommendation.

The bull of his episcopal appointment (29 May 1536) followed the stereotype of such documents, yet with pronounced emphasis on his pastoral responsibilities.[8] The diocese had been vacant for the previous

2 Fenning, *Irish material*, 270.

3 The Irish form of this surname is Ó Coigligh (anglicised as Cogly, Quigley or Kegley). The name was that of a branch of the Uí Fiachrach who were anciently settled in the barony of Carra, Co. Mayo. In the sixteenth century the sept was dispersed to Sligo, Donegal, Ulster and elsewhere in Ireland. Woulfe, *Sloinnte Gaedhal is Gall*, 470.

4 ASV, Archivum Concistoriale, Acta Miscellanea, vol. 8, f. 51v; Acta Camerarii, vol. 2, f. 54v; ibid., vol. 3, f. 119v; Acta Vicecancellarii, vol. 4, f. 13.

5 Fenning, *Irish material*, 269.

6 Ibid., 270. Almost certainly indentical with the 'Malachi Cogley' who was admitted to the degree of bachelor of canon law at Oxford on 2 December 1529. A. B. Emden (ed.), *A Biographical Register of the University of Oxford, A.D. 1501 to 1540*, Oxford 1974, 126; J. Foster (ed.), *Alumni Oxonienses, 1500–1714*, i, Oxford 1891, 298.

7 B. Millett, 'The Pastoral Zeal of Robert Wauchope' in *Seanchas Ardmhaca*, 2 (1956), 32–60.

8 ASV, Registra Vaticana, 1473, ff 29–32rv.

ten years since the death of Thaddeus O'Reilly in 1526.[9] On 7 June he was granted '*motu proprio*' a dispensation to be consecrated a bishop outside Rome by bishops of his own choice, in communion with the Apostolic See, without any further formalities.[10] As a newly appointed bishop, Quentin Cogly offered fifty gold florins (reckoned as one-third of a year's revenue from the diocese of Dromore) by way of tax to the office of the Camera on 12 September through his agent or procurator at the Roman curia. It was noted that the bulls of his appointment had been expedited *gratis*.[11]

In 1537 two papal briefs were addressed to him by Paul III which shed much light on the rapidly changing pattern of church affairs in Ireland. These documents afford a glimpse of Bishop Cogly's sharp reaction to the introduction of Anglicanism and his unswerving loyalty to the Apostolic See. In the first brief (8 April 1537)[12] it was noted that Cogly had reported to the Pope that several Irish dioceses were vacant either *de jure* or *de facto*. But there were also problems with the sees that were occupied. Some of their bishops had been tinged with Anglicanism, while others, although truly Catholic bishops, were English by birth and spent their time as absentees in England.

As a consequence, much scandal was given, the bishops failed to take pastoral charge of their flocks, and religion was said to be in decline. Concerned for the good of the faithful, the Bishop of Dromore made a remarkable proposal to the Pope: he suggested that he might personally intervene to exercise his episcopal office in those dioceses where such responsibilities and duties had long been neglected. The Pope agreed with this proposal and granted Bishop Cogly special faculties which permitted him to carry out episcopal functions anywhere in Ireland should he find that the bishop was non-resident or that the bishop occupying the diocese was heretical or that the diocese was vacant, provided the consent of the diocesan chapters was obtained. He was authorised to exercise extended jurisdiction as long as he lived and as often as he wished, freely and licitly, notwithstanding any published conciliar or synodal decrees, constitutions, church law or even decisions to the contrary.

The second brief (20 June 1537)[13] was concerned primarily with the Archbishop of Armagh, the Englishman George Cromer, formerly a priest of the Chichester diocese and royal chaplain. From entries in Primate Cromer's register it appears, in fact, that Cromer was spiritual administrator (*custos spiritualitatis*) of the diocese of Dromore from the second half

9 Brady, *Ep Succ.*, i, 299.
10 ASV, Reg. Suppl., 2213, f. 14v.
11 Brady, *Ep. Succ.*, i, 299.
12 ASV, Brevia Lateranensia, 24, f. 419rv; reproduced in Appendix 4 (p. 321 below).
13 Ibid., f. 427rv; reproduced in Appendix 4 (p. 322 below).

of 1526 to the autumn of 1534[14] at least. The indications are that Cromer did not welcome the papal nomination of Quentin Cogly to the suffragan see of Dromore and subsequently clashed with him on theological and jurisdictional issues. This brief revealed that the Pope had been informed that Cromer was in agreement with the King of England's rebellious views, had resolutely rejected the authority of the Roman Church and Apostolic See, and was obedient only to his English sovereign.

This incisive judgement of Primate Cromer may well have been too harsh. Cromer, like many other high-ranking ecclesiastics of his time, had found himself inextricably caught up in the politico-religious web of Henry VIII's manoeuvrings. In October 1521 he had been appointed to Armagh by Pope Leo X and within a year had been nominated Henry's Lord Chancellor of Ireland. After the excommunication of Henry VIII in July 1533 Cromer was confronted by the dilemma of trying to remain loyal to the papacy while at the same time representing the authority of the excommunicated English king in his lordship of Ireland.[15]

The brief of June 1537 also addressed a particular difficulty faced by the Bishop of Dromore, his clergy and his people. By canonical prescription, in certain instances, Dromore was normally expected to have recourse to the metropolitan see of Armagh. However, Bishop Cogly claimed that this procedure could no longer be observed without danger of contagion as long as Henry VIII remained 'perfidious and obdurate'. In response to the bishop's predicament, the Pope decided to remove the see of Dromore from the control or metropolitan jurisdiction of the incumbent Archbishop of Armagh. Should the faithful of Dromore find themselves in litigation with outsiders, they were to present themselves to their bishop or vicar general and not to the archbishop's ecclesiastical court. Should Bishop Cogly become involved in lawsuits, he was instructed to have recourse to the Apostolic See. Any steps taken in the future by Armagh against Dromore would be considered null and void.[16]

By 1539, having been 'publicly defamed as a heretic by good and grave men', Cromer was deprived by Rome of all canonical jurisdiction and of the administration of the see of Armagh. The archbishop outlived Quentin Cogly, his suffragan, and largely ignored Rome's decisions.

14 See L. P. Murray and A. Gwynn, 'Archbishop Cromer's Register' in *Louth Archaeological Journal* (1932–8, 1942–3); A. Gwynn, *The Medieval Province of Armagh*, Dundalk 1946, 148.

15 See W. P. O'Brien, 'Two Sixteenth-Century Munster Primates: Donnchadh Ó Taidhg (1560–62) and Richard Creagh (1564–85)' in *Seanchas Ardmhaca*, 14 (1990), 36.

16 The existence and content of these two briefs, unknown to Gwynn, disprove his assertions that Quentin Cogly resigned his claims to Dromore soon after papal provision and that the new bishop never returned to his diocese from Rome. See Gwynn, *The Medieval Province of Armagh*, 149, 148.

During his final years, burdened by ill-health and distrusted both by Rome and his own king, he spent his time in voluntary obscurity at the archiepiscopal manor of Termonfeckin until his death in 1543. Meanwhile the administration of his see had been delegated to his official, George Dowdall, the last prior of the Crutched Friars in Ardee and a future Archbishop of Armagh.[17]

But what of Cogly himself? His name no longer appears explicitly in official papers of any sort. However, the Irish State Papers of 1538 contain several references to an outspoken bishop imprisoned in Dublin Castle who was put on trial at Trim for his criticism of Henry VIII in his sermons. The Anglican Archbishop Browne of Dublin wrote on 20 May 1538 to Thomas Cromwell, Henry VIII's chief minister, who had been placed in charge of church affairs:

> I have committed now of late in toward the Bishop of Meath's suffragan, which, in his sermon, prayed first for the Bishop of Rome, then for the Emperor, and at last for the King's Majesty, saying; 'I pray God he never depart this world, until that he hath made amends.'[18]

On 28 October of the same year a Dublin official, Thomas Alen, complained of

> a Bishop and a Friar put in the castle of Dublin for their high and notorious offences against the King's Majesty; and at the last sessions were brought to Trim, to have been indicted, arraigned, and suffered accordingly: yet our masters of the law, and all other . . . have been such papists, hypocrites, and worshippers of idols, that they were not indicted.[19]

This is the first record of an attempted indictment under the royal ecclesiastical supremacy acts. It would appear that the unnamed bishop and his friar companion came to the attention of Henry VIII himself, as may be judged from another allusion in Archbishop Browne's correspondence, dated 6 November 1538:

> As touching the Bishop, that the King's Highness wrote of to the Council, and the Friar of Mullingar, they have been both at Trim, and there arraigned, being indicted upon *Praemunire*, which shall not be worth the King's Highness one groat. How that matter was

17 O'Brien, 'Two Sixteenth-Century Munster Primates', 36.
18 *Cal. S.P. Ire., Hen. VIII*, iii, pt 3, p. 9.
19 Ibid., 103.

> canvassed, I know not; but well I am assured they be good clerks, and may do the King good service, if their fidelity would be good, which were hard to trust unto.[20]

The identity of the bishop and the Mullingar friar still remain elusive, although it is relevant that the Dominicans were the only friars in Mullingar. After 1538 they are no longer heard of in the State Papers. The bishop may very well have been Quentin Cogly, Bishop of Dromore, once a Dominican of Mullingar, whose brief episcopate came to a close before 16 June 1539.[21] Quentin Cogly's tenure of episcopal office in Dromore (1536–9) was short but was characterised throughout by manifest personal integrity. In a world where Irish ecclesiastical loyalties were bought and sold under crown auspices Cogly acted as a lone bulwark against the introduction of the Anglican Reformation into the Ulster dioceses as promoted by the Lord Deputy, Lord Leonard Grey, Archbishop George Cromer of Armagh and Bishop Edward Staples of Meath. His thorough rejection of the Reformation is reflected in the briefs of 1537 discussed above. He did not surrender the papal bulls of his appointment or take the Oath of Supremacy, as most of the northern bishops did by 1543.[22] And though Henry VIII did not recognise Cogly's provision to Dromore by the Pope, he made no nomination of his own to the see. The bishop's strong complaints to Rome concerning the heterodoxy and pro-Anglican policy of Archbishop Cromer in 1537 must surely have contributed to the removal from office of that English prelate by the Pope in July 1539. Quentin Cogly's untimely death removed perhaps the sole Catholic bishop in the province of Armagh to remain wholeheartedly loyal to Rome. Cogly withstood both crown coercion and judicial process and remained untainted by political expediency or religious compromise when such trends had become the accepted order of the day.

THE REFORMATION CAMPAIGN AND THE FRIARS, 1538–9

The first moves against the religious houses in England (1524–9) predated the Reformation period and were devised by Cardinal Thomas Wolsey, with papal approbation. In Ireland, however, there was an intrinsic connection between the Henrician reformation of religion and the dismantling of the network of religious foundations. The process of dissolution was put in train by virtue of the Act of Supremacy without prior consultation

20 Ibid., 104–5; see also Edwards, *Church and State in Tudor Ireland*, 62–3.
21 Eubel, *Hier. Cath.*, iii, 188.
22 J. J. Silke, 'Some Aspects of the Reformation in Armagh Province' in *Clogher Record*, 11 (1984), 349–50 and *passim*.

with Rome. As in England, this resulted in the sequestration of monastic and religious property and its transfer from ecclesiastical to secular ownership. While the plan for the dissolution of the religious corporations came from England, the exact proposals were formulated in Ireland and were a response to political and social needs; the pre- and early medieval patterns of landholding were fast disintegrating and were in urgent need of restructuring.

Developments in England and Ireland finally coalesced in the year 1536 with the announcement in both parliaments of a systematic, though at first limited, plan of monastic suppressions to be launched by royal authority. A bill presented for the suppression of eight monasteries was rejected outright by the Irish parliament. Initially the bill was viewed as predatory in intent; it was perceived as a direct threat to the political position of the landed gentry and the professional lawyers of the Pale as much as to their vested interests in monastic property. Once it was discovered that the proposals could swiftly lead to lay expropriation of the landed wealth of the religious orders, the bill had a swift passage in October 1537. The purpose of the act was to confirm the crown's title to the possessions of all dissolved religious houses. By the summer of 1538 a royal commission had carried out the first series of suppressions in the Pale and border areas.

Late in 1537 the first campaign to execute Henry's reformation policy was put into operation in Dublin by Archbishop George Browne, formerly provincial of the English Augustinians. Surviving evidence suggests that the popular and intellectual response was a mixture of scandal, scorn and open hostility. This contrasted markedly with the lesser sensitivity of public opinion, especially within the Pale, towards the closure of some religious houses. While the campaign did not constitute a direct challenge to the existence of the religious, its emphasis on Henry VIII's spiritual supremacy and its tone of hostility to the Catholic faith could not but heighten the general insecurity of religious communities. The life of the friars in the crown-controlled territories in the years immediately preceding the suppression was, like that of the monks, unruffled by the kind of official government visitations experienced in England.

As early as 1538 harassment of the Irish friars began with the launching of the Reformation campaign by Archbishop Browne and English agents of the crown. Travelling through the Pale and crown-controlled regions, they denounced 'the usurped authority of Clement VII and proclaimed Henry VIII as Head of the Church'. A number of friars publicly refuted the monarch's claims to spiritual supremacy and his anti-papal declarations. For this they were vilified and suffered execution or imprisonment. At Waterford in January 1539 five men were hanged for daring to oppose the royal claims: 'four felons', to use the words of the king's agents, 'accompanied with another thief, a friar', whom they hanged in his habit and left hanging as a warning to all who challenged the supremacy of the king in matters of Church or State.[23] The State Papers also record that in March of the same year a Waterford Franciscan, Dr Sall, preached against the Reformation and the dissolution of church property. This Franciscan was arrested by the Mayor of Waterford, who sent him to the Lord Deputy and Council, who in turn imprisoned him in Dublin Castle.[24]

Generally the friars reacted to the designs of the English reformers by a campaign of passive resistance. They did not provide propagandists for the cause of the Anglican Reformation as in England, with the notable exception of Richard Nangle, former provincial of the Augustinians, who undertook to spread Reformation propaganda in Irish-speaking areas. Archbishop Browne's attempt to mitigate the vigorous opposition of the Observant communities to the Reformation by amalgamating them with unreformed brethren was an unqualified failure. His visitations to administer the Oath of Supremacy were considered legally dubious, since the regular clergy were canonically exempt and their status was unchanged by the Reformation legislation of 1536–7. Direct action by other members of the crown administration did little to enable Browne to cope with the resistance of the Observants.[25] Nevertheless, his aggressive policy did aggravate the strain of life and feelings of insecurity among the friars in the corporate towns and crown-controlled territories. The regular life of the friaries was increasingly disturbed by ominous rumours as to their future, so that they began to dispose of property and take other precautions.

In the middle of the winter of 1538–9 an official commission, including Archbishop Browne, set out from Dublin to visitate part of the south of the country. Its declared purpose was to announce the royal supremacy and to destroy saints' shrines and images. This enterprise, while distinct from the suppression campaign, was the prelude to total destruction of

23 *Cal. S.P. Ire., Hen. VIII*, iii, pt 3, p. 114.

24 Ibid., ii, pt 3, p. 562. Active opposition on the part of individual friars or Observant communities to the introduction of an Anglican state church and destruction of the religious houses, to which there are scattered references in the State Papers, still remains to be researched and studied. The Roman archives, particularly that of the Holy Office (now the Congregation for the Doctrine of the Faith), have yet to yield up a hoard of documentation which should throw a flood of light on the sixteenth-century Reformation era in Ireland.

25 One of Thomas Cromwell's spies complained bitterly of the opposition of the Observants to the introduction of the English Reformation: 'Here as yet the blood of Christ is clean blotted out of all men's hearts, what with that monster, the Bishop of Rome, and his adherents, in especial the false and crafty blood-suckers, the Observants, as they will be called most holiest, so that there remains more virtue in one of their coats and knotted girdles, than ever was in Christ and his passion.' *Cal. S.P. Ire., Hen. VIII*, ii, pt 3, p. 570.

the religious orders in areas loyal to the crown. In January 1539 the commission despoiled the shrines of the Crutched Friars and Dominicans in the city of Limerick. In the Dominican church the statue of St Dominic was divested of silver and precious stones:

> shows [reliquaries] of silver weighing ten ounces, with divers stones the value whereof we cannot tell, and four stones of crystal bound with silver weighing in our estimation two ounces, and four score pound wax, as we do think, rather more than less . . . and iron being in the said chapel to the sum of twenty stone and above.

This action was perpetrated by the ecclesiastical commissioners, accompanied by a military escort under Robert St Leger, who was alleged to have seized on 22 January 'both the great bell and the small bell of the same place'.[26] Proceeds from the spoliation of the shrines were made available for urgent payments to the army.

SUPPRESSION OF THE ORDERS OF FRIARS, 1539–41

On 7 April 1539 a fresh commission to deal with Irish religious houses was issued from London. The core of this rarely cited text of the royal commission to the Dublin administration was virulently anti-papal; it indiscriminately anathematised Irish religious of both sexes and ordered the systematic confiscation of religious houses and the extirpation of religious life itself.[27] The tenor of the document displayed a distinctively

26 Bradshaw, *The Dissolution of the Religious Orders in Ireland*, 102; see also B. Bradshaw, 'The Reformation in the Cities: Cork, Limerick and Galway, 1534–1603' in J. Bradley (ed.), *Settlement and Society in Medieval Ireland*, Kilkenny 1988, 453.

27 'From information of trustworthy persons, it being manifestly apparent that the monasteries, abbeys, priories, and other places of religious or regulars in Ireland, are at present in such a state that in them the praise of God and the welfare of men are next to nothing regarded; the regulars and nuns dwelling there being so addicted, partly to their own superstitious ceremonies, partly to the pernicious worship of idols, and to the pestiferous doctrines of the Romish pontiff, that, unless an effectual remedy be promptly provided, not only the weak lower order, but the whole Irish people, may be speedily infected, to their total destruction, by the example of these persons; to prevent, therefore the longer continuance of such religious men and nuns in so damnable a state, the King, having resolved to resume into his hands all the monasteries and religious houses, for their better reformation, to remove from them the religious men and women, and to cause them to return to some honest mode of living, and to the true religion, directs the commissioners to signify this his intention to the heads of the religious houses; to receive their resignations and surrenders willingly tendered; to grant to those tendering it liberty of exchanging their habit and of accepting benefices under the King's authority; to apprehend and

English mode of thought which ran counter to the outlook of the Irish people whose religious sensitivities had been nurtured by highly esteemed monastic influence since the sixth century. Both Anglo-Irish and Gaelic Irish reverenced the papacy and perceived it positively as a force in halting the English crown's ecclesiastical encroachments. So often, in fact, did they make direct appeal to Rome that they were, on occasion, bitterly castigated as Rome-runners.[28]

After some delays occasioned by legal formalities the crown's campaign got under way in mid-July 1539, which marked the starting-point for the destruction of the monasteries and religious houses. Within three years the medieval edifice of the Irish religious foundations in the loyal territories had, with a few exceptions, been dismantled as a result of the ruthless zeal of the royal commissioners. The monastic communities of the Pale and of Ormond capitulated without any form of coercion being exerted, and in practically all cases voluntary surrenders were recorded. The main objective of the campaign was political, to gain some acceptance of the principle of crown jurisdiction, even if not acknowledged in practice.

Evidence for the concerted drive against the friars lacks the substantial documentation available for the suppressed monastic houses, namely the formal legal records of surrender and grants of pensions. The crown officials refused to grant compensation or pensions to friars when the latter were dispossessed of their houses; the meagre profits of their dissolved properties were financially insufficient for the purpose. To obviate the possibility of claims by the friars in connection with voluntary surrender of their houses and churches, the crown surveyors resorted to vague legal formulae as devised in England: 'the withdrawal of the late prior and convent on their voluntary abandonment of their priory'. Thus the crown appropriated the houses and churches of the mendicant friars, regardless of the validity or invalidity of the legal technicalities. Visitation of the friars' houses in 1539–41 for the purpose of obtaining formal surrender may be plotted from the account books of confiscated chattels. The inquisitions or surveys (technically known as 'extents') undertaken between 1540 and 1543 often provide dates of surrender and the names of the priors or superiors.

On the eve of the suppression there were thirty-eight Dominican convents or priories in Ireland, excluding the three minor or vicarial

punish such as adhere to the usurped authority of the Romish pontiff, and contumaciously refuse to surrender their houses; to take charge, for the King's use, of the possessions of those houses, and assign competent pensions to those persons who willingly surrender.' *Cal. Pat. Rolls Ire., Hen. VIII–Eliz.*, i, 55. A separate commission for the leasing of dissolved properties and houses was appointed at the end of May. Ibid., 54–5.

28 See *Cal. S.P. Ire., Hen. VIII*, iii, pt 3, p. 104.

houses of Kilcorban (Co. Galway), Ballinegaul and Rochestown (Co. Limerick).[29] By 1543 the Order had lost twenty of its houses: all twelve houses in Leinster, six in Munster, and two in Ulster (see Table 1).

TABLE 1: SUPPRESSED DOMINICAN HOUSES, 1539–42

House	Date of suppression	Date of extent	Name of prior
Athy	30 Apr. 1539	27 Nov. 1540	Robert Woulff*
Rosbercon	20 Jun. 1539	Jan. 1541	Matthew Fleming
Dublin	8 Jul. 1539	12 Mar. 1541	Patrick Hay
Longford	Nov. 1539	1540	
Arklow	1539	27 Jan. 1541	Edmund Kenny†
Carlingford	1540	4 Oct. 1540	
Trim	1540	10 Oct. 1540	
Kilkenny	1540	4 Jan. 1541	Peter Cantwell
Aghaboe	1540	11 Jan. 1541	
Kilmallock	1540	18 Jan. 1541	
Drogheda	20 Mar. 1540	10 Oct. 1540	Peter Lewis
Naas	30 Mar. 1540	22 Nov. 1540	Nicholas Walshe
Waterford	2 Apr. 1540	18 Jan. 1541	William Martin
Cashel	8 Apr. 1540	13 Jan. 1541	Edward Brown
Mullingar	24 Apr. 1540	10 Oct. 1540	John Skeney, subprior
Coleraine	1 Feb. 1541	1 Feb. 1543	Shane O'Boyle
Cork	*c.* Feb. 1541	Feb. 1541	
Glanworth	*c.* Feb. 1541	Feb. 1541	
Newtownards	*c.* Feb. 1541		Patrick O'Doran
Limerick	*c.* 20 Feb. 1542	31 Jan. 1541	Edmund (?)

* N. B. White, *Extents of Irish Monastic Possessions, 1540–41*, Dublin 1943, 23.
† E. Curtis (ed.), *Calendar of Ormond Deeds*, v, Dublin 1941, 52.

29 For a résumé of their medieval antecedents see A. Coleman, 'De Conventibus Provinciae Hiberniae' in *Analecta Sacri Ordinis Fratrum Praedicatorum, 3* (1897), 16–25; A. Gwynn and R. N. Hadcock, *Medieval Religious Houses: Ireland*, London 1970, 218–34.

Athenry in east Galway, the only Dominican house in Connacht threatened with dissolution, was spared in July 1541. At the request of Bermingham of Athenry, the Lord Deputy allowed Adam de Coppynger, described as '*custos*', and his brethren to remain undissolved in their house by agreeing 'to change the habit and weeds of a friar into a secular habit, as they lay among the Irishry . . . amongst disobeisance'. The community also undertook to maintain divine service and to offer their customary hospitality to the king's deputies.[30] A similar arrangement was reached with the Limerick Dominicans, according to which it was agreed that their house, St Saviour's, should be erected into the collegiate church of Jesus.[31] This arrangement was probably facilitated by the Bishop of Limerick, John Quin, O.P. One or both of these communities, therefore, became legally collegiate foundations, with the Dominicans installed as secular canons.

The priories of Derry, Lorrha, Youghal and Tralee escaped the general wave of suppression. Derry,[32] unlike Newtownards[33] and Coleraine,[34] then situated in the Donegal territory of the O'Dohertys, and outside the ambit of royal control, remained untouched. Lorrha, in north Tipperary and within the area of effective crown jurisdiction traversed by the commissioners in 1539–40, seems to have been overlooked until 1552.[35] Of far greater significance were the non-dissolved houses of Youghal, Tralee and Ballinegaul.[36] Together with Limerick, Kilmallock and Cork, these were located in the lands of the Earls of Desmond, staunch supporters of the Dominican and Franciscan Observants.

30 Gwynn and Hadcock, *Medieval Religious Houses: Ireland*, 221.
31 *Cal. S.P. Ire., Hen. VIII*, iii, pt 3, p. 465.
32 For grant of lands see Appendix 3.
33 For grant of lands see Appendix 3.
34 For grants of lands see Appendix 3.
35 For grant of lands see Appendix 3.
36 Ballinegaul *alias* Ballinegaule, Ballinegaulle, Ballinegall (Y. M. Goblet, *A Topographical Index of the Parishes and Townlands of Ireland*, Dublin 1932, 87) is situated in the modern parish of Effin (diocese of Limerick) about seven miles south-east of Kilmallock. In its medieval origins the Dominican house is said to have been founded by the family of Roche in the fourteenth century and to have been a cell or dependency of Kilmallock. J. Ware, *De Hibernia et Antiquitatibus eius* . . . London 1654, 203; O'Heyne, *Epil. Chron.*, 102; J. Ferrar, *The History of Limerick*, Limerick 1787, 437. In the 1540s its fortunes changed for the better when it became autonomous and acquired conventual status as one of the flourishing houses of observance under the patronage of the Earls of Desmond. Some modern authors (A. Coleman, *The Ancient Dominican Foundations in Ireland*, Dundalk 1902, 62; Gwynn and Hadcock, *Medieval Religious Houses: Ireland*, 191) have confused or justaposed the Dominican house of Ballinegaul with the Carmelite foundation of Milltown (*Villa Molendine*), which lies in Knockaney parish (diocese of Emly) several miles away, because the latter adjoined a townland variously rendered Balliegalah, Ballinegalliah or Balline-

Ambiguity surrounds the history of the dissolution of the Dominican community in Limerick. The house was surveyed, but not suppressed, in 1541 during Lord Deputy St Leger's visitation of the religious houses in the city. To avoid confrontation between central and local authority, St Leger was prepared to procrastinate and temporise in such decisions, for the sake of his policy of gradual extension of royal jurisdiction over the whole island by conciliatory and diplomatic means. A recent historian has described how an ingenious plan of double protection for the preservation of Limerick was devised by its two principal patrons, 'the two most powerful political figures in the south, Desmond, whose family had endowed it, and O'Brien of Thomond, who held it in esteem as a family burial place. According to an exchequer inquisition conducted at the beginning of March 1542, the houses of the Dominicans and Franciscans at Limerick were declared suppressed following the passing of the act of suppression in parliament there in mid-February, and the resultant abandonment of their houses by the friars as and from 20 February. But obviously O'Brien raised the question of the future of the Dominican house with the Lord Deputy in the course of negotiations at the parliamentary session. It was not included in the survey of crown possessions in the city undertaken towards the end of March, and when O'Brien went to court the following year he sued for a patent of confirmation for the house as a secular college, explaining that it was lately granted that status by the Lord Deputy and Council. However, a month previously Desmond had obtained a patent for the purchase of the property. The object of this move on Desmond's part was to rescue the lands of the priory, which were largely an endowment of his forebears, from the clutches of the crown, even at the cost of a £96 ransom. His intentions towards the community were, undoubtedly, of the best. He explained to Queen Mary, and the claim is borne out by other evidence, that he regarded himself merely as a custodian of the mendicant houses he acquired in the reigns of Henry and Edward, preserving them in good condition, and restoring them to the friars on Mary's accession. The Dominicans at Limerick thus enjoyed a double indemnity, under the charter of secularisation obtained

galliagh (Goblet, op. cit., 77) and because of the mention of Whitefriars or Carmelites of Ballinegaul in sixteenth-century surveys and inquisitions. In the aftermath of the dissolution of the religious houses it was not uncommon for Dominican and Carmelite foundations to be confused in such legal documents on account of similar robes worn by the two orders. Moreover, white vesture was almost invariably adopted by late medieval monks or friars as the outward sign of reform or strict observance. Hence there arose a fundamental confusion in the popular mind as well as in the mind of government officials. Once a mistaken identification was made in the original 'extent' or inquisition it was repeated in all subsequent legal documentation. For grants of the lands of Ballinegaul in and after the 1550s see Appendix 3.

by O'Brien from the Lord Deputy and Council, and through the benignity of Desmond who purchased their property.'[37]

The Dominicans of Limerick certainly survived into the reign of Edward VI. At Kilmallock the church, house and belongings of the Dominicans were leased to James, Earl of Desmond on 29 June 1541 for three years at a rent of 26s 8d sterling.[38] Thus the Dominicans of Kilmallock also came under the legal protection of their powerful patron. The swift dissolution of the three mendicant houses, Dominican, Franciscan and Augustinian, at Cork must have been due to failure to elicit support from the Desmond family or local magnates, which might have kept them alive in some form. When the crown commissioners surveyed the friars' possessions at Cork in the spring of 1541 they allowed them to be leased almost immediately. When precisely the Dominican house ceased to function cannot be ascertained as the enrolment of the lease is undated. In 1543 the Dominican and Franciscan houses were sold to local merchants.[39] The city of Cork, which enjoyed a charter, jealously guarded its independence and was ruled by its rich merchant class. This, however, can scarcely explain why the Earl of Desmond did not intervene as he had done in Limerick.

In January 1541 William Cavendish, a crown surveyor, in the company of Lord Deputy St Leger, was allowed to survey the Dominican priory of Kilmallock, implying recognition, at least in principle, of the royal jurisdiction over the religious houses. Seven months later a commission was nominated for the dissolution of the religious houses of Desmond (Counties Limerick, Cork and Kerry) in August 1541.[40] This commission proved to be far from successful in its appointed task. Some twenty-five mendicant houses and seventeen monastic ones remained intact. Although Youghal came within the scope of the survey made at Cork in February 1541, no mention whatsoever was made of the Dominican house there, 'the chief centre in Munster of the Dominican Observant movement, which enjoyed the special favour of James of Desmond'.[41] Likewise the Dominican priory and church of Tralee, the burial place of the Earls of Desmond, and Ballinegaul in Co. Limerick were deliberately omitted from official surveys, although the crown was perfectly aware of their existence. It is clear, therefore, that no serious disruption in the rhythm of Dominican conventual life resulted from the suppression campaign in the extensive territory of the Earls of Desmond. Before very long the Dominican houses

37 Bradshaw, *The Dissolution of the Religious Houses in Ireland*, 150–51; see also Bradshaw, 'The Reformation in the Cities', 454–5.
38 *Fiants Ire., Hen. VIII*, 52, no. 210.
39 For grants of lands see Appendix 3.
40 Bradshaw, *The Dissolution of the Religious Houses in Ireland*, 164–5.
41 Ibid., 155.

of Desmond were to re-emerge, however briefly, under the leadership of Master David Brown, himself a *filius* of the priory of Tralee.

EXTENTS OF DOMINICAN HOUSES, 1540–43: AN ANALYSIS

The original Latin texts of the 'extents', i.e. the surveys detailing the nature and valuation of material possessions and resources of the dissolved houses, have survived for sixteen of the twenty Dominican houses under review.[42] This source of information is frequently corroborated and amplified—though occasionally serious discrepancies occur—by the Chief Remembrancer's inquisitions and by those of the Auditor General and of the Auditor's Office. For Rosbercon, only the sworn inquisition of the Chief Remembrancer is available.

The purpose of the extents was to furnish accurate summaries and valuations of the confiscated goods and wealth of the dispersed religious, now at the disposition of the crown. The extents were carried out by several small teams of commissioners, mostly from England, and by jurors drawn from the particular locality or county area being surveyed. When the property of the Dublin Dominicans was surveyed, all the jurors named were already its actual tenants or leaseholders.[43] Two Dominicans at least are recorded as having acted as civil jurors: John Skeney, subprior of Mullingar, for his own house,[44] and Robert Woulff, prior of Athy, for the rectories of Arerystell, Templemory and Rathtouthe in Co. Carlow, and for the extent of the rectory of Fassagh Rheban near Athy, which was leased jointly to the Earl of Ormond and himself 'the late prior of Athae for 100s'.[45] The Dominican houses of Limerick and Kilmallock were incorrectly designated 'of Friars Minor' by the crown surveyors, but the extents are not otherwise confused.

While the extents may at first sight appear to be impersonal and of purely legal significance, on close examination they shed invaluable light on the social and economic situation of the Dominicans in the mid-sixteenth century. The names of the priors who held office at the dissolution are supplied by the extents, the inquisitions of the Chief Remembrancer and other legal documents. The extents were concerned first and foremost with the total valuation of churches, priories, lands, properties, chattels, resources and entitlements. Valuations ranged upwards from Glanworth (10s), Rosbercon (£1 2s 2d), Arklow (£1 9s 10d) to Cork (£6 14s 2d), Kilkenny (£7 9s 0d), and Dublin (£64 5s 7d) the

42 White, *Extents of Irish Monastic Possessions* provides an abbreviated English translation of the Latin originals.

43 Ibid., 53–4.

44 Ibid., 291.

45 Ibid., 23, 61.

highest. What is clear from this simple list is the greater affluence of city houses over those in small towns or in the countryside. Whenever there was a genuine doubt about valuation (e.g. in the case of wastelands belonging to Mullingar, Rosbercon, Athy, Cork and Kilkenny; cottages in ruinous condition belonging to Arklow; uncertain tenant customs and obligations relating to food, as at Aghaboe and Arklow) no valuation was entered in the extent.

The size of the site or ground enclosed by the conventual precinct varied greatly from house to house: Trim (4 acres); Dublin (3 acres); Arklow, Cashel, Kilkenny and Kilmallock (2 acres); Carlingford, Drogheda and Limerick (1½ acres); Aghaboe, Glanworth and Rosbercon (1 acre); Cork, Athy, Naas and Waterford (a mere half acre). The size of the sites at Coleraine, Mullingar and Newtownards was not recorded. The site was normally occupied by a church, cloister or a small close, priory, cemetery, gardens and plots of land.

The first item to be considered was the church and priory buildings, whose general state was reported on. In the case of Drogheda, surprisingly, 'the church and a greater part of the dormitory had fallen down from age before the dissolution'.[46] At Mullingar 'the roof of the church, which is thatched with straw, is very ruinous. . . . Within the precinct, a stone tower and other buildings lately inhabited by the friars; these are now in decay and unoccupied.'[47] These comments indicated not merely dilapidation of conventual buildings and fabric, but also a decline of religious spirit and numbers, if not outright apathy. In June 1540, between the suppression and the taking of the survey, all the priory buildings at Athy were burnt by Donal McCare Kavanagh,[48] indicating the serious instability of the Pale border areas. At Dublin and Cork it was noted that the church and adjacent buildings, probably on account of their poor quality and the high market value of the sites, could be demolished. The building materials—timber, glass, iron and stones—remained unvalued at Dublin, whereas in Cork their value was fixed at £6. From Carlingford it was reported: 'The house is a strong mansion needing no expenditure on repairs, but on every side strongly fortified, and will be a very sure defence for the town in case of attack through rebellion of those living close by.'[49]

In several instances the sale or lease of buildings by the suppression commissioners took place at the time of formal dissolution: Mullingar (house and land leased for twenty-one years at £2 per annum); Trim (church, cloister, chancel and other buildings sold to the Bishop of Meath);

46 Ibid., 244.
47 Ibid., 291.
48 Ibid., 272.
49 Ibid., 245.

Naas (church and chancel sold for £4); Cashel (church, chancel and cloister sold for £4); Waterford (church sold to the mayor for £10).

The commissioners for the extents regularly refer to 'superfluous buildings', namely other minor buildings of little value or practical use. There were none at Carlingford, Kilkenny, Aghaboe, Arklow, Limerick or Glanworth; those at Naas were sold, while superfluous buildings remained unsold at Drogheda and Athy. Frequently some of the priory buildings were described as 'worth nothing above repairs'. All the indications point to very modest structures, for the most part neglected, in urgent need of repair, and certainly of little economic value to anybody when surveyed. From the physical description alone of the complex of buildings at Waterford it is clear that the Dominicans catered for the comings and goings of important visitors. A hall there called 'le Baron' with its three upper rooms, the doctor's chamber (conventual lector's apartment), the little hall with its kitchen and upper room, the great hall with its upper rooms, and several other apartments enumerated in the extent are strikingly suggestive of elaborate arrangements for the hospitable entertainment of guests.

Practically all houses were in possession of messuages, cottages, tenements, tofts, gardens and land of varying quality, in proportion to the size and importance of the house in question. Dominican constitutional law forbidding the acquisition of property outside the convent precincts had been abrogated on papal authority long before the crisis of suppression. Subsequently the Dominicans in Ireland had acquired property in houses, lands and other resources, yet these were unpretentious indeed, in value or size, compared with the landed wealth and possessions of the monks.

Dublin stands at one end of the scale, with its two messuages and twenty-one tenements spread through a number of city parishes, a meadow (located at the east end of the present Phoenix Park), and approximately ninety acres of arable land in Londreston, Co. Meath.[50] If one accepts as reliable the list of possessions of the Black Abbey, Kilkenny, contained in the Chief Remembrancer's inquisition taken in the year of its suppression, 1540,[51] Kilkenny was even wealthier. The inquiry stated that Peter Cantwell, prior of Kilkenny at the suppression, was found seised of, in the precincts, a church and belfry, a small castle near the church, a dormitory above the chapter house, the king's chamber with a small turret, a granary with two cellars, a toft, the prior's chamber, Will Dowlaghe's chamber, etc., with about thirty messuages, over 180 acres of land, an unroofed castle at Tullaghpissane, and the site of a mill on the

50 For grants of lands see Appendix 3.

51 M. Archdall, *Monasticon Hibernicum*, London 1786, 372–3; Gwynn and Hadcock, *Medieval Religious Houses: Ireland*, 226.

River Nore, valued at £12 4s. Much of this land was lost by 4 January 1541, when the values given by the extent jurors, excluding land then laid waste by rebellion, amounted only to £7 9s, derived from eighteen messuages, ten gardens, four plots, and an indeterminate amount of land, some of which was unlawfully detained or intruded upon.[52] By way of contrast, Glanworth owned no moveable property and only ten acres of arable land. Carlingford held seven messuages and only one and a half acres of land. There are other examples of notable discrepancies. In the case of Athy, Dominican property included two fishing weirs subsequently granted to Martin Pelles in 1554.[53] Limerick, whose property included fishing rights on a salmon weir, St Thomas's Island, and land called Monabrahir near Parteen.[54] There was a notable discrepancy in the land acreage of Naas: eighteen acres were noted by the Chief Remembrancer, as cited by Archdall, while eleven acres were recorded in the extent.[55] Finally, according to the Chief Remembrancer, the Waterford Dominicans held fifteen acres of land, of which a four-acre portion known as 'the king's meadow' was excluded from valuation in the extent.[56]

These differences in the records, particularly noticeable in the case of Kilkenny, suggest that there was deliberate concealment or illegal alienation of Dominican property in the space between formal suppression and compilation of the extent. Did the friars connive at these practices in the hope of an early recovery of their houses and possessions? Did they surrender on the day of suppression the title deeds and other legal instruments to their properties and rights, voluntarily or under compulsion? To these questions there are as yet no definite answers. However, in a few instances land and property were leased out quite some time before the day of dissolution. Trim leased thirty-three of its seventy-two acres—most of which was in 'the common field'—to one John Fyan; the deed was indentured on 27 May 1537, and the land was leased for thirteen years. In 1535–6 the prior of Cashel, Edward Brown, leased out a considerable portion of property within the precincts of the house: nine tenements or cottages with six gardens to Peter Kelley and others for £1 19s 8d. Outside, two messuages with four gardens, valued at 12s 8d, were leased to Walter Fleming[57] and others. The questions naturally

52 For grant of lands see Appendix 3.

53 Archdall, *Monasticon Hibernicum*, 309; Gwynn and Hadcock, *Medieval Religious Houses: Ireland*, 222.

54 Archdall, *Monasticon Hibernicum*, 428; Gwynn and Hadcock, *Medieval Religious Houses: Ireland*, 227.

55 Archdall, *Monasticon Hibernicum*, 336; Gwynn and Hadcock, *Medieval Religious Houses: Ireland*, 228. For grant of lands in 1558 see Appendix 3.

56 Archdall, *Monasticon Hibernicum*, 703–4; Gwynn and Hadcock, *Medieval Religious Houses: Ireland*, 231.

57 For grant of lands see Appendix 3.

arise as to what use the Dominicans made of their land before the era of suppression, and to what extent they depended on it for their support.

A chancery inquisition of Waterford's possessions in 1539–40 serves only to stimulate such a line of inquiry. William Martin, who was prior at the dissolution, held the same office in 1522 and 1524. On 17 October 1522 he leased by deed the meadow called 'the king's meadow' near Lysdogan (Lisduggan) to one Thomas Lumbart for twenty-four years at 10s per year. On 24 October he leased to Robert Lumbart and William Lyncoll, members of the chapter of Christ Church Cathedral, a stream popularly known as the 'water of Kilbarry' for a term of sixty-one years. And at Easter 1524 he issued a deed to Robert Gibb granting him accommodation within Waterford Blackfriars at 20d a year for a term of sixty-nine years.[58] The true significance of the granting of these particular leases is still a matter for conjecture: was it a case of economic difficulties, spiritual malaise or increasing lay and clerical encroachment on the property of religious orders ?

Table 2 shows the total acreage of each house, the quality of the land and the aggregate land acreage for sixteen of the twenty-one suppressed Dominican houses (over 633 acres). Kilkenny and Dublin represented the highest acreage, while Cashel, Carlingford and Arklow had the lowest. With the exception of the cities of Kilkenny and Dublin and the towns of Mullingar and Trim, the other Dominican houses owned very little land. These figures show no obvious difference of attitude towards poverty or landownership between Observant and Conventual Dominicans. Basically both groups maintained their mendicant status up to the time of suppression and were never regarded as wealthy religious corporations.

The extents of four Leinster houses—Aghaboe, Arklow, Athy and Trim—record tenant obligations and customs. These involved annual personal services and the offerings of livestock and foodstuffs to the Dominicans. At Aghaboe the customs for each tenant and cottier included three boondays (days of unpaid service) and two weeding days. Each individual owner of seven sheep or more gave one sheep in autumn and one gallon of butter. This last custom was declared uncertain. At Arklow a messuage holder was bound to pay 12d, and for victuals a quarter of beef (12d), six cakes (12d) and three gallons of butter (2s). Each tenant of a messuage likewise gave the friars for their sustenance from every brewing of beer for sale three and a half gallons of beer (13s 4d). This last duty at Arklow was no longer paid, but each tenant also gave the community a hen (8d). Athy had similar customs. Two tenants paid at Christmas forty-eight gallons of beer (2d each), forty-eight loaves (1d each), and a quarter of beef (2s). The tenants of six

58 'Waterford Inquisitions' in *Waterford Arch. Soc. Jn.*, 11 (Jan.–Mar. 1908), 37. For subsequent government grants of lands see Appendix 3.

TABLE 2: COMPOSITION OF DOMINICAN LANDHOLDINGS

House	Total acreage	arable	pasture	meadow	wood	moor	other	townland
Kilkenny	181 approx.	134¼	26	5	6	8	2 ac. (scrub) 2 orchards 15 gardens	
Dublin	90	80	6	–	–	4	1 garden	
Trim	72	66	3	–	–	3	1 orchard 2 gardens	
Mullingar	63½	60	2	–	–	1½	1 orchard 1 garden	
Cork	54	30	20	½ stang (= ⅛ ac.)	–	–	3 ac. + 1 orchard 3 small gardens	
Rosbercon	39	29	6	2	2	–	1 garden	
Limerick	34	30	–	–	–	–	4 ac. garden	
Aghaboe	18	14	2	–	–	2		
Athy	16	16	–	–	–	–	1 orchard 1 garden	
Waterford	15	–	–	15	–	–	2 gardens	
Kilmallock	12	12	–	–	–	–		
Naas	11 +	11	–	–	–	–	8 gardens	
Drogheda	10 +	–	3	–	–	5	2 ac. + 1 orchard 2 gardens	
Glanworth	10	10	–	–	–	–		
Arklow	6	–	–	–	–	–	1 garden	
Carlingford	1½	–	–	–	–	–		
Cashel	?						1 orchard 13 gardens	
Coleraine	?							several named townlands
Longford	?	(no returns; no receipts)						
Lorrha	?							Freres Rathe*
Newtownards	?							townlands of Newtown, Kilcowman & Barnes†
Total acreage	633 approx.	492¼	68	22⅛	9½	22	11+	

* *Fiants Ire., Edw. VI*, 134.

† Chief Remembrancer's inquisition.

cottages rendered six boondays and six hens. Finally, one tenant of Trim supplied a quarter of beef for the feast of St Dominic.

The legal language of the extents reveals that lands and property were leased before the suppression on various terms: '*ad voluntatem*' (at will), '*pro termino annorum*' (for a fixed term of years), '*per indenturam*' (by indenture), etc. The survey carried out by the commissioners also implied that by 1540–41 some of the feudal customs mentioned had already fallen into disuse or abeyance. The Observant Dominican reform, following the primitive Dominican constitutions, prescribed strict adherence to perpetual abstinence from meat. The references to beef, sheep and hens in the extents of Aghaboe, Arklow, Athy and Trim appear to show that observance of the law of abstinence had fallen off and that these houses remained unreformed before the dissolution.

Besides land and property holdings, the Dominicans enjoyed the benefits deriving from resources such as water mills, fishing weirs, watercourses, orchards and woodlands. Water mills were to be found at Carlingford, Cork, Kilkenny, Kilmallock, Athy (where it was in ruins) and Mullingar (where ownership was disputed). The extents provide numerous details of weirs and fishing rights held by Dominican houses situated close to rivers or the sea. Athy had two fishing weirs on the Barrow; Coleraine had extremely valuable fishing rights on the Bann;[59] Cork had control of half a salmon weir and half a fishing pool; Limerick had its salmon fishery (locally known as the Lax weir)[60] on the Shannon, and Rosbercon's was situated at the confluence of the Nore and the Barrow. Ownership of weirs and fishing rights was considered highly advantageous for an Order whose medieval constitutions and Observant tradition insisted on a meatless diet. Hence it is not to be wondered at that many houses were so situated and that plentiful supplies of fish, a substantial item in the daily diet, were readily available. Watercourses aided land cultivation at Naas and Waterford. Orchards provided a valuable fruit supply at Athy, Cashel, Cork, Drogheda, Kilkenny, Mullingar and Trim. A small acreage of woodland served the practical needs of the Dominicans of Kilkenny, Rosbercon and Mullingar: 'two small closes contain one and a half acres, full of ash trees reserved for the repair of buildings and for burning as firewood', according to the extent of Mullingar.

While the suppression commissioners were engaged principally in securing the official surrender of the monastic houses, they also availed of the opportunity to take formal possession of the houses and properties

59 T. M. Healy, *Stolen Waters: A Page in the Conquest of Ulster*, London 1913, 66, 75, 100 and *passim*.

60 R. Herbert, 'The Lax Weir and Fishers' Stent of Limerick' in *N. Munster Antiq. Jn.*, 5 (1946–9), 49–50; M. Lenihan, *Limerick: History and Antiquities*, repr., Cork 1991, 650.

of the mendicant orders. Though prevented by time and circumstances from disposing of all Dominican buildings and immoveable goods, the commissioners compiled exact returns of whatever chattels were seized on the day of dissolution.[61] Forewarned by the English pattern of suppression, the Dominicans, in common with the orders of monks, Canons Regular and other friars, very often entrusted their valuables such as sacred vessels, liturgical paraphernalia, church ornaments, household goods and furniture to benefactors and supporters for the time being. Exceptions, seemingly, were Kilkenny, whose chattels were valued at £57 17s 15d; Dublin, £37 8s 6d; and Waterford, £24 13s 8d. Sometimes leases had been granted, as already seen, well in advance of suppression and dispossession. Drogheda was still in receipt of an annual alms worth £6 13s 4d voted by an act of the parliament held in that town in 1468. Church bells generally remained in place on account of their weight and inconvenience. Unsold bells turn up repeatedly in the extents: Carlingford, Mullingar, Trim, Naas, Athy, Kilkenny, Cashel and Dublin. The bells of Drogheda, Waterford and Rosbercon were in the possession of laymen, who were deemed accountable for them.

Table 3 illustrates roughly the confiscation of chattels in chronological order, as well as the total property valuations for most of the houses. In all, chattel returns were made for ten priories, dating from 30 April 1539 (Athy) to 8 April 1540 (Cashel). Drogheda yielded a mere £2 5s and Athy only £2 15s 11d. Several priories, including Rosbercon, Longford, Arklow, Aghaboe, Mullingar, Cork, Glanworth and Limerick, yielded nothing in the line of saleable moveable goods in the accounts of the crown surveyors. The Dominicans in these places were obviously well prepared for the coming of the king's officials and had implemented their own contingency arrangements. Inexplicably the Dominicans of Kilkenny, Dublin and Waterford failed or perhaps were stopped from selling or otherwise disposing of valuables which realised very substantial sums of money for the royal treasury. It might be thought that the reason for this was that these houses and their assets, located in 'royal cities', were subject to stricter surveillance on the part of the civic authorities; but this can hardly have been so, as the other friaries at Kilkenny were caught with next to nothing of market value.

61 C. McNeil, 'Accounts of Sums realised by Sales of Chattels of some Suppressed Irish Monasteries' in *RSAI Jn.*, 52 (1922), 11–37.

TABLE 3: TABLE OF CHATTELS AND TOTAL PROPERTY VALUATIONS

House	Date of suppression	Chattels valuation	Total property valuation
Athy	30 Apr. 1539	£21 5s 11d	£1 12s 0d
Rosbercon	20 Jun. 1539	–	£1 2s 2d*
Dublin	8 Jul. 1539	£37 8s 6d	£64 5s 7d
Longford	Nov. 1539	–	–
Arklow	1539	–	£1 9s 10d
Carlingford	1540	(£3 12s 0d later entry)	£4 6s 8d
Trim	1540	£14 13s, 4d	£4 17s 0d
Kilkenny	1540	£57 17s 5d	£7 9s 0d †
			£12 4s 0d*
Aghaboe	1540	-	£2 10s 2d
Kilmallock	1540	£4 2s 0d	£4 2s 0d
Drogheda	20 Mar. 1540	£2 5s 0d	£2 7s 0d
Naas	30 Mar. 1540	£4 0s 12d	£5 13s 6½d
Waterford	2 Apr. 1540	£24 13s 8d	£3 19s 4d [*recte* £4 0s 4d]
Cashel	8 Apr. 1540	£7 11s 1d	£2 15s 8d
Mullingar	24 Apr. 1540	–	[£4 5s 0d approx.]
Coleraine	1 Feb. 1541	–	£2 0s 0d*
Cork	*c.* Feb. 1541	–	£6 14s 2½d
Glanworth	*c.* Feb. 1541	–	10s 0d
Newtownards	*c.* Feb. 1541	–	13s 3d
Limerick	*c.* 20 Feb. 1542	–	£5 2s 0d

* Chief Remembrancer's inquisition.

† White, *Extents of Irish Monastic Possessions,* 198–9. This extent did not include 'parcels of land now waste' or 'lands detained from the king'.

EFFECTS OF SUPPRESSION: DISLOCATION AND SECULARISATION

It is almost impossible to penetrate the thick veil that descends upon Irish Dominican affairs for the last five years of Henry VIII's reign. How the dispossessed Dominicans of the Pale and Ormond territories and elsewhere reacted to the seizure of their churches, priories and belongings, the abrupt overthrow of normal conventual life, and, above all, how they coped with discouragement and uncertainty, is not known. Nor are there any clues as to what became of Dominican communities and individual members after the blow of suppression and formal surrender. Some may have found refuge with their families or with communities west of the Shannon; a small number may have sought refuge in the Order's continental houses; others may have remained close to their former houses supported by the hospitality and sympathy of benefactors; others still may have survived by the tactic of temporary withdrawal, especially in the countryside, with the tacit agreement of the new owners. In the case of Longford, supposedly dissolved in 1540–41 and concerning which the jurors belatedly reported no receipts and no goods, it may be assumed that the community remained intact and retained their buildings well into the Elizabethan era. This was a dangerous territory for the royal commissioners, and they doubtless never went near it, being content to survey it from afar. While there is no evidence of defections from the Order, regular community life became a rarity in Leinster. There was a break in continuity for practically all the suppressed houses until the 1620s. On the other hand, there is reliable evidence that the Dominicans of Tralee, Youghal, Limerick and Kilmallock suffered no serious disruption in their way of life and for some years were left in peaceful possession of their houses, not least because of the Earl of Desmond's protection of and goodwill towards the Observant friars.

There are some indications that a minor wave of emigration of Dominicans and others took place to the continent. In 1558 the general chapter transferred Friar Edward of Ireland from 'the English province' to the convent of Santo Domingo, Sanlúcar de Barrameda, in the south of Spain.[62] A far more striking commentary on the times comes from an entry in the register of Francisco Romeo, vicar general of the Order, in 1545. An Irish Dominican, Terence of Ireland, had made his way to Rome, fearful of returning to his province on account of fierce persecution from Lutherans ('*metuens sibi redire ad provinciam suam propter saevam persecutionem Lutheranorum*'). On leaving Rome (10 February 1545) he was given letters of commendation to Dominican houses and superiors. Besides requesting fraternal hospitality the letters recommended that he

62 Reichert, *MOPH*, x, 17.

should be allowed to remain wheresoever he might be made welcome and be inserted into that community and province.[63] This is the earliest reference to religious persecution of Dominicans in Ireland. Obviously the friars, especially after their eviction, were open to harassment and persecution by the English administration in Dublin. The menacing tones of the instruction to the royal commissioners in 1539 'to apprehend and punish such as adhere to the Bishop of Rome' were still loud in the ears of the mendicant friars who persisted in their religious views and in their loyalty to the papacy. They cannot have been unaware of the fate of the London Carthusians and the Franciscan Observants of Greenwich who were martyred in the 1530s for their firm allegiance to the Holy See.[64]

Indeed, an Irish Dominican named Ulick de Burgh was reported as having been hanged by Richard (perhaps an error for Thomas) Cromwell for celebrating Mass for seventy-four participants in the Pilgrimage of Grace, all of whom had been hanged and quartered in Westmorland and Cumbria in 1537. The Dominican priest had been judged 'an incendiary offering prayers for rebels who died without benefit of clergy'.[65]

As an immediate consequence of the 1539–40 suppression, secularisation of mendicant property commenced and proceeded steadily for the remainder of Henry VIII's reign and beyond. The buildings of the friars were more prone to be demolished or converted to government use than those of the greater and lesser monasteries situated in quiet rural settings. The Dominican church at Carlingford, looking across the fiord of Carlingford Lough to the mountains of Mourne, was assigned for the accommodation of fishermen, especially during the herring season.[66] The Irish parliament of 1541 directed that the conventual buildings of Mullingar be used as a jail.[67] Petitions from the Dublin government administration (29 August 1541 and 6 May 1542) requested permission to transform the Blackfriars building into the King's Inns of Court.[68] Eventually, in about 1582, the existing buildings were demolished and the new Inns of Court established on the site.[69] A number of houses were granted to large towns and cities and were subsequently adapted for

63 Fenning, *Irish material*, 271.

64 A. G. Dickens, *The English Reformation*, London 1964, 56–7.

65 S. H. Burke, *Historical Portraits of the Tudor Dynasty*, i, London 1879, 500–1, citing Woodville's *Anecdotes of the Pilgrims of Grace*. The Pilgrimage of Grace was a formidable popular uprising in the north of England in defence of the suppressed religious houses and against the autocratic religious policy of Henry VIII's officials.

66 White, *Extents of Irish Monastic Possessions*, 246. For grant of lands see Appendix 3.

67 Coleman, *Ancient Dominican Foundations*, 34. For grants of lands see Appendix 3.

68 *Cal. S.P. Ire., Hen. VIII*, iii, pt 3, pp 322, 375.

69 Burke, *Hib. Dom.*, 195. The walls of the Dublin Blackfriars priory were still intact on 22 November 1581. *Calendar of Exchequer Inquisitions*, 253.

municipal use. The Dominican and Franciscan properties at Kilkenny were granted to the sovereign and commonalty of the city in 1543.[70] The Dominican churches of Kilkenny and Waterford were converted for use as courthouses. Several houses, such as Trim,[71] Drogheda,[72] Arklow,[73] Naas[74] and Cork, were acquired by merchants and speculators. The buildings of rural houses were taken over by farmers for agricultural use and as convenient shelter for livestock. In such circumstances conventual buildings were altered and often torn down, as happened at Aghaboe[75] and Rosbercon.[76] The fact that Dominican properties were to be found mainly in towns and did not have demesne or extensive lands attached to them led to their speedy conversion as secular buildings.

As secularisation progressed, the Dominicans, in common with other friars, were left with little hope of regaining their former properties. To the extent that the new proprietors entrenched themselves in friaries, the friars were prevented from returning and thus the success of the crown's expropriation policy was ensured. However, there is reason to suspect that this policy met with some objections. In several instances the earliest purchasers or leaseholders changed rapidly, indicating either speculation or local opposition and trouble for the new owners. Nevertheless, leases or grants, temporary or in perpetuity, were confirmed or newly given to countless lay occupants by Edward VI and Mary Tudor, clearly indicative of the fact that such houses were dead and beyond hope of revival.

The suppression campaign of 1539–40 set in motion a relentless process of disintegration by the confiscation and reallocation of religious foundations to secular use. Still, beneath the turmoil and the new thinking, which swept away most mendicant communities in Leinster, some in Munster and four out of five in Ulster, there ran a current of continuity, strong enough to carry a small number of mendicant houses into the reign of Mary. The era of late medieval Dominican life in the Pale and Ormond territories had come to a close. The suppression within Desmond was only partially successful. The Lord Deputy, Sir Anthony St Leger, consistently subordinated the suppression programme to his political aspirations for Ireland as a whole. It is almost certain that no viable Dominican communities except Cork were dispersed in the

70 Gwynn and Hadcock, *Medieval Religious Houses: Ireland*, 226.
71 For grants of lands see Appendix 3.
72 For grants of lands see Appendix 3.
73 For grants of lands see Appendix 3.
74 For grants of lands see Appendix 3.
75 See T. S. Flynn, *The Dominicans of Aghaboe: c.1382–c.1782*, Dublin 1975, 16–18, 24.
76 See T. S. Flynn, *The Dominicans of Rosbercon: 1267–c.1800*, Dublin 1981, 18–20, 28.

regions under Desmond's control. However, the campaign inaugurated the formal process of secularisation, even if the change from ecclesiastical to secular ownership was merely a theoretical one. Survival of Dominican communities in Desmond was merely by exception. Expropriation of the ecclesiastical estate had successfully taken place by royal authority. Ultimately the fortunes of the Dominicans were to collapse with those of the Geraldines, their devoted protectors.

According to Fr Bradshaw's study of the process of dissolution, the Henrician confiscations touched no more than 40 per cent of some two hundred mendicant communities. While he claims that some of the principal towns—Dublin, Drogheda, Waterford and Cork—were cleared of such communities under Henry VIII, the concealed and informal presence of the friars cannot be ruled out. Likewise the basis for his assertions about the friars of Cork ('communities dispersed altogether') and Limerick ('they were barely able to hold on') is open to question.[77] Certainly the Dominicans of Limerick and Kilmallock, though nominally suppressed, came under Desmond's protective wing. Why the same protection was not extended to the Dominicans of Cork in February 1541 is something of an enigma; the Earl of Desmond's brother, Sir Maurice FitzGerald, escorted the crown surveyors to the city of Cork.

In Connacht suppressions took place in a very limited and haphazard way. This was due to the failure of the crown to interest the Irish lords in a systematic scheme of suppression and personal profit. The web of Dominican houses in Connacht remained untouched and undisturbed. The entire situation reflected the weakness of crown jurisdiction in Connacht, even within the English enclaves of Galway and Athenry, as well as the complexity of political structures in the province, and the deep attachment of all classes to the religious houses. The situation was aptly summed up in 1545 by John Alen, Lord Chancellor of Ireland, when he forthrightly blamed the policy of Lord Deputy St Leger for the total failure of the suppression campaign outside English areas: 'In Munster, Connacht and Ulster the friars maintained their own popish sort with impunity and the king did not have so much as the revenues of the religious houses in these areas.'[78]

Even before any Irish religious house had been dissolved, Henry's leading officials were deeply hostile towards the friars, the Observants in particular, whom they regarded as stubborn upholders of papal claims. One may reasonably assume that the spirited response of the friars helped to stem the spread of Henry VIII's Reformation doctrines in Ireland and determined in large measure the reaction and psychological response to

77 Bradshaw, *The Dissolution of the Religious Orders in Ireland*, 161.
78 Ibid., 179.

the Protestant Reformation as a whole. The Augustinians, Dominicans and Franciscans had long been alerted to the implications of the English Reformation and thus were prepared to resist it under Henry and Edward VI. There is ample evidence too that the papacy quickly turned to the friars, through episcopal appointments, to resist and counter Henry's designs on the Irish Church. This was precisely the context in which the Dominican Quentin Cogly was made Bishop of Dromore in 1536—the same year in which David Brown was appointed prior provincial of the Dominicans by Pope Paul III.

TWO

Survival: Munster and Connacht, 1548–1600

FIRST ATTEMPTS AT RECONSTRUCTION: CONTACTS WITH ROME, 1548–9

By the end of the 1540s much of the Irish Dominican province had been made desolate and lay in ruins. The Order's houses west of the Shannon had escaped the Henrician wave of suppressions, if not the tensions between the *avant-garde* Observant Dominicans and their more medievally-minded Conventual brethren. The death of Henry VIII in January 1547 set in train a review of the Order's position in Connacht and elsewhere. This in turn led to a number of visits to Rome, especially by Dominicans from Sligo and other Dominican houses in the diocese of Elphin.[1] The Irishmen renewed contact with the Master General and the central administration of the Order. Several individuals sought reconciliation with the Apostolic See and absolution from canonical irregularities such as illegitimacy and apostasy. The latter was incurred by long and unauthorised absence from one's own house or simply by not wearing the religious habit. The 'apostates' here, whether from the Order or from the Church, were partly victims of the implementation of the suppression policy and of disturbed times. Others, acting on behalf of their houses, petitioned the Pope for ecclesiastical exemptions, indulgences and special faculties.

One party of Dominicans set out from Sligo to Rome some time in 1547. They had reached the north Italian city of Bologna by 5 December. There the Master General granted the requisite permission to Brothers Patrick, Donagh and Thomas (two friars of this name) and to a layman to continue on to Rome, where they might meet the Pope and present their petitions. By the same letters patent they were permitted to visit other places on their way and were commended to the priors of Dominican houses in order that they might be charitably received.[2] Of this group was Donagh O'Healy (Donatus Ohallay), a priest of the diocese of Elphin, the son of a priest and an unmarried woman, who petitioned the Pope on 7 February 1548 to absolve him from canonical penalties

1 Sligo, Roscommon, Cloonshanville, Tulsk and Ballindoon.
2 Fenning, *Irish material*, 271.

incurred by apostasy.[3] Another was Patrick MacGillarind *alias* O'Suadat, also resident in Elphin diocese, the son of a priest and a married woman named Usuadat, who tendered a similar petition on the same day.[4] Yet another petitioner was John Oberyard from the same diocese. Originally he had taken the Dominican habit and vows, but he too had become an 'apostate' when he left the Order without due permission and had taken charge of the parochial vicarage of Anaghdun in the diocese of Elphin. His association with Canons Regular led him to consider joining the same order of canons. In the meantime he was gravely worried by doubts concerning the validity of Masses and other divine offices celebrated during his apostasy. The lifting of the censures imposed for apostasy was required for his eventual acceptance by the Canons Regular. He stated that he was of noble but illegitimate birth and therefore requested papal absolution for all his faults. His two petitions or supplications on this matter were dated 3 January and 16 March 1548.[5]

Almost simultaneously a set of three documents, in the form of papal briefs, was issued by Paul III for the Dominicans of Sligo and Elphin on 3 March 1548.[6] The first document was a commission to the Bishop of Elphin asking him to exempt the Dominicans of Sligo from the payment of tithes to laymen. The Dominicans had been accustomed to pay tithes to the Cistercian abbot of Boyle and to the parochial rector of St John the Baptist, Sligo. Ever since these offices had become vacant their entitlements had been usurped by laymen. The Sligo Dominicans were to be freed from their obligations for as long as the monastery and parish lacked an abbot and rector.

The second document was issued in response to a report received from the priors and Dominican communities of Sligo and Roscommon, in which they reminded the Pope that they had enjoyed certain exemptions, immunities, faculties, privileges and indults conferred and repeatedly approved by Popes in the past. However, the petitioners now complained that certain laymen were covetous of their possessions and had attempted to compel the Dominicans to appear before ecclesiastical and secular judges and tribunals, to pay tithes and other monetary contributions, and to hand over funeral offerings, all of which was prejudicial to their privileges and rights. As a result, Paul III issued a commission to the Bishop of Elphin and two of his cathedral canons to take appropriate measures, even canonical ones, to safeguard and guarantee the legitimate rights, freedom and privileges of the Sligo and Roscommon Dominicans and to prevent laymen intruding on their property.

3 ASV, Reg. Suppl., 2625, f. 181rv.
4 Ibid., ff 181v–182r.
5 Ibid., 2624, ff 281v–282r; 2629, f. 139rv.
6 ASV, Arm. XLI: Brevium Minutae, vol. 41, ff 181rv, 182r–183r, 186rv.

The third document sheds light on contemporary devotional practices. It contained a grant of indulgences to all the faithful who would venerate an image of the triumph of the Holy Cross in the Dominican church of Sligo. Indulgences might also be gained, under prescribed conditions, in the same church on the feasts of St Patrick, Corpus Christi and the Assumption of the Blessed Virgin Mary. When these Irish Dominicans completed their business in Rome, their return to Ireland was approved by the Master of the Order on 9 March 1548. By letters patent he commended them to the prelates of the Order and other ecclesiastical and civil personages who might offer them alms.[7]

By far the most important Irish Dominican who visited Rome in 1548 was Quentin O'Higgins, vicar of the province. The following account of his life, though uncritical in some respects, is taken from Archdeacon John Lynch's *De Praesulibus Hiberniae*.[8] Conn or Quentin O'Higgins was born at Termonhiggin in Co. Sligo.[9] As a young man he devoted himself to the study of ancient Irish learning, probably under the direction of the Dominicans of Sligo. Later he entered the Dominican Order at Sligo, became a bachelor of theology and a celebrated preacher, and was successively prior of Sligo and vicar provincial, though unfortunately Lynch does not indicate the precise dates at which he held these offices. By admonition and personal example he urged those of his own brethren who were hostile to him, to remain firmly committed to the way of virtue. His reputation for sanctity was such that once, while visiting the convent of Killybegs (Franciscan Third Order Regular?) in Donegal, he was associated with a 'miraculous' increase of fish in the bay. In his preaching he took a resolute stand against Catholics who temporised by attendance at Protestant services or admitted the royal supremacy over the Church. As spiritual adviser of Hugh Dubh O'Donnell, he obliged that chieftain to go to Rome to seek papal absolution from the censures he had incurred by taking the Oath of Supremacy in England. While at Rome, O'Donnell was said to have obtained the nomination of Quentin O'Higgins to the see of Raphoe.[10] Shortly after his 'appointment' to

7 Fenning, *Irish material*, 271.

8 Lynch, *De Praesulibus Hib.*, i, 246–7. Valuable information on the Irish Dominicans was supplied to Lynch by John O'Hart, O.P., provincial (1659–68) and diligent student of the history of the province.

9 Ó hUige, Ó hUigín, Ó hUiginn (signifying knowledge, skill, ingenuity) was the name of a branch of the southern Uí Néill and one of the most distingiushed literary families in Ireland. The Four Masters mention no fewer than eleven poets and professors of poetry of the name. One branch of the O'Higgins family settled in the county of Sligo, with large estates in the districts of Achonry and Kilmacteige which they retained until the Cromwellian plantation. Woulfe, *Sloinnte Gaedhael is Gall*, 576.

10 Eubel, *Hier. Cath.*, iii, 282 does not list O'Higgins as Bishop-elect of Raphoe. This dubious assertion rests with Lynch, who does not give the exact date of his nomination.

Raphoe, O'Higgins earned the extreme displeasure of O'Donnell and some of his noblemen by fearlessly denouncing their scandalous way of life.[11] In consequence, O'Donnell prevented the impending consecration of O'Higgins as Bishop of Raphoe, and the latter voluntarily withdrew.

Quentin O'Higgins's principal business at Rome in the spring of 1548 was with the Master of the Order.[12] His first request was for the retention of Sligo as a convent of strict observance. Because of their poverty, that community was given dispensations to eat meat three times a week and to wear linen clothes. On the same day (9 March) O'Higgins was appointed vicar, with power to introduce observance with the authority of a provincial. The Master excused the Irish Dominicans from paying their tax contribution to the curia of the Order;[13] they might use it rather for the upkeep of poorer houses. Three days later O'Higgins's status and authority were officially clarified: he became vicar provincial and coadjutor of the Irish provincial, with competence over both Observants and non-reformed brethren. This detail reveals that despite the emergence of a single unified province, the wounds of old divisions had not been fully healed. On 5 May the register of the Master recorded that O'Higgins had obtained orally from the Pope the faculties required by David Brown, provincial of Ireland, to reconcile apostate Dominicans to the Church, provided they first abjured all traces of heresy and accepted a prescribed penance; afterwards they might again receive the habit and be restored to their rights and place in the Order. According to Lynch, Quentin O'Higgins served two terms as provincial of Ireland. It was during his priorship of Sligo that Andrew O'Crean and Eugene O'Hart, future Bishops of Elphin and Achonry respectively, entered the Order there. No other significant particulars of his life and activities are known except the circumstances of his death. This occurred late one evening in 1565 while he was travelling with ten companions to a provincial chapter meeting. As he was crossing the River Maigue (*Mangum fluvium*) in east Limerick, O'Higgins was drowned.[14]

A mysterious figure, Gabriel Martinez, was appointed commissary for the reform of all Dominicans in Ireland on 8 March 1549. The Master General gave him plenipotentiary powers for his mission, extending to

11 See B. Bradshaw, 'Manus "the Magnificent": O'Donnell as Renaissance Prince' in A. Cosgrove and D. McCartney (eds), *Studies in Irish History presented to R. Dudley Edwards*, Dublin 1979, 20, 18–19.

12 Fenning, *Irish material*, 271–2.

13 Non-payment of annual contributions for the support of the Master General and upkeep of his curia was recorded for the years 1525–31, 1542–7 with the comment '*Provincia Hiberniae debet omni anno ducatos sex, et a multo tempore non solvit*'. In the volume of contributions from 1625 to 1643, Ireland is not even mentioned in the index of provinces and congregations. Fenning, *Irish material*, 331–2.

14 Lynch, *De Praesulibus Hib.*, i, 247.

all Dominicans, in matters spiritual and temporal alike. In the work of reform he was to adhere to the advice of the Archbishop of Armagh, Robert Wauchope. Martinez, apparently a Spaniard, was at Paris when he received this commission, which ordered him to accompany the archbishop to Ireland and to place himself at his service during his own mission there. On completion of his task he was to return to his studies at Paris.[15] There is no information whatsoever on the outcome of this extraordinary mandate. What is fairly certain is that it was bound up with the ambitious Tridentine plan of reform for Ireland as conceived by Archbishop Wauchope of Armagh.[16]

DAVID BROWN AND THE REVIVAL OF THE PROVINCE, 1553–*C.*1559

Master David Brown was provincial of the Irish Dominicans from 1536 and seems to have held this office for most, if not all, of his active life. A most valuable source of information, a book published in 1607 by an Italian Dominican historian, Michele Piò, which casts fresh light on this provincial and especially his efforts to re-establish a reformed province in the Marian period, has only recently been noted.[17] The information contained in this work was largely drawn from letters and in particular from a lengthy report submitted by David Brown to Master General Usodimare and the definitors of the general chapter held at Rome in 1558.

The digest of David Brown's report spoke of religious persecution in Ireland under Henry VIII and some of its consequences. Brown went on to list twenty-seven ruined or despoiled houses: Dublin, Kilkenny, Waterford, Cashel, Limerick, Cork, Rosbercon, Mullingar, Naas, Athy, Sligo, Arklow, Newtownards, Coleraine, Drogheda, Athenry, Strade, Derry, Rathfran, Carlingford, Tuigse (Tulsk?), Rochildese (Roscommon?), Romachelese

15 Fenning, *Irish material*, 272–3.

16 Robert Wauchope, Archbishop of Armagh (1545–51), was a notable figure at Trent (1545–7), having earned a sound reputation as a theologian and canonist at the University of Paris in the 1530s and 1540s. Previously he had been employed by the Holy See on several missions, including attendance at the German diets of Worms, Ratisbon and Spires. In 1550 he visited the north of Ireland secretly, but not his own diocese of Armagh. By 1551 he had returned to Paris, where he was reappointed papal legate to Ireland. In that year he made plans for his return to Ireland, with the intention of launching a full-scale Catholic revival in the spirit of Trent. He died unexpectedly at Paris on 10 November 1551. F. X. Martin, 'The Council of Trent' in *IER*, 5th ser., 100 (1963), 272–8; B. Millett, 'The Pastoral Zeal of Robert Wauchope' in *Seanchas Ardmhaca*, 2 (1956), 32–60; J. Durkan, 'Robert Wauchope, Archbishop of Armagh' in *Innes Review*, 1 (1950), 48–66.

17 M. Piò, *Delle Vite degli Huomini Illustri di S. Domenico*, pt 1, i, Bologna 1607, 383–4; noted by Fenning, *Irish material*, 270.

(Burrishoole?), Youghal, Kilmallock, Ailingese (Ballinegaul?)[18] and an unidentified house styled 'Monte del Signore'.[19] All these houses had suffered from the ravages of time and men; some had been burnt down, some had been occupied by heretics and others demolished. Vestments, bells and books had been sold, and furniture and fittings converted to profane use. Tralee alone had survived the storm and was unique as a house of full regular observance. Sadly, however, owing to lack of brethren and the indifference of the people, this house too fell into disuse. The year in which this happened was not mentioned.

The most startling revelation in this report was that in addition to naming eighteen of the twenty officially suppressed houses (Aghaboe and Longford were omitted) it mentioned nine houses in Connacht, Munster and Ulster, among them Sligo, Rathfran, Strade, Athenry, Derry and Youghal, which suffered decline before the close of Edward VI's reign. Even the favoured houses of the Desmond family—Limerick, Youghal, Kilmallock and Tralee—had been subject to depredation. There is no evidence that any of these despoiled houses was in fact suppressed, nor were the western houses dissolved; at least no extents dating from the provincialate of David Brown have survived. Their problems stemmed from declining numbers, uncertainty, social and political instability, a lessening of lay support and increasing intrusions on their houses and landholdings by local lords. The real reasons for these developments, so unexpected in Connacht at least, were not explained in the text as it now stands.

With the accession of Mary Tudor in 1553, a qualified Catholic restoration, subject to political considerations, took place in England and Ireland. But while the revival of the religious orders was permitted, their confiscated churches, houses and properties were not restored unless these were in crown possession or titles of ownership were found to be defective. As a result of the intervention of James FitzJohn FitzGerald, Earl of Desmond (1540–58) and royal treasurer in Ireland, all sources of annual income or revenue due to their houses were restored to the Dominicans by royal consent. With the added generous financial support of the earl, the Dominicans began to recover and repair some houses which had been sold or leased to laymen. The houses in question, Tralee,

18 In all probability the Latinised *Ailingese* is to be identified with Ballinegaul. For government grants of land see Appendix 3.

19 In a later work entitled *Delle Nobile e Generosa Progenie del P.S. Domenico in Italia*, ii, Bologna 1615, 439–40, Michele Piò printed a list of 'thirty houses then extinct in the province of Ireland'. This list has much in common with David Brown's, but regrettably it is undated and the author did not indicate the source of this amplified list in this lesser-known work. See J. Quétif and J. Echard, *Scriptores Ordinis Praedicatorum*, ii, Paris 1721, 540 for a biographical notice on Piò and a list of his works.

Limerick, Youghal,[20] Kilmallock and Ailingese (Ballinegaul?), were all within the Desmond sphere of influence. The attempted recovery of Cork had failed.

In these revived houses the carefully planned nucleus of a restored province, strict observance of the Dominican rule and constitutions and a lifestyle not dissimilar to that of the ancient Fathers of the Church was initiated. However, there were too few Dominicans, and these could scarcely minister to the pastoral needs of the newly reconciled faithful. Although David Brown gave the habit to many young people who advanced spiritually under his guidance and training, death soon claimed them all.

The Earl of Desmond regarded Master David Brown as the sole Catholic doctor, the guide and consoler of the Irish. According to Piò, Brown had served as provincial of England, but this assertion has not so far been supported by other evidence. He travelled to Rome about 1549 in connection with the troubles of his country and returned to his people with the jubilee bull (presumably for the Holy Year 1550) granted by Pope Paul III. By his preaching in Ireland and his work as inquisitor he reconciled innumerable people. In view of the dire poverty of his Dominican confrères and the unlikelihood of their ability to survive indefinitely, he had written to the authorities of the Order deploring the desolation of his province, relating his own activities, and begging the general chapter of 1558 to render every possible assistance. His declared objective was to further the growth of the province now once more canonically established in the five houses patronised by the Earl of Desmond.

What is inexplicable is David Brown's almost total silence concerning the Dominican houses of Connacht, some of which continued to function, in one form or another, certainly within the sprawling diocese of Elphin. There, as noted earlier, Brown's able vicar, Quentin O'Higgins, continued to act as overseer of the Connacht Dominicans, reformed and unreformed alike. Brown's strange omission may simply indicate that their houses and survival were not threatened as in Desmond, or it may suggest the strength of Irish provincialism, verifying the remark of a seventeenth-century Italian Franciscan, once visitator of the Irish friars, that the provincial, outside his civil province of origin, was like a foreigner in another country: '*un provinciale forestiero di lontan paese*'.[21]

Another Dominican active in the recovery of Munster was Robert Gogan,[22] prior of Youghal. In 1557, as head of the reformed Observant

20 For government grant of lands see Appendix 3.

21 P. Conlan, *Franciscan Ireland*, Cork 1978, 33.

22 Probably identical with the Robert Gogan described as a preacher under the heading 'learned men and authors of Ireland' in *Holinshed's Irish Chronicle, 1577*, ed. L. Miller and E. Power, Dublin 1979, 102.

house of Youghal, he addressed a petition to the English court for the recovery of St Mary's of the Isle in Cork.[23] At the outset he mentioned that Youghal had been newly rebuilt and returned to strict observance. He asked that legal measures be taken to persuade two Cork merchants occupying the Order's house to vacate and hand it over for rededication to its original purpose. St Mary's of the Isle, he said, was then partly demolished and profaned, and held by the merchants on the pretended plea that they had bought it. It soon becomes apparent that the appeal was partly motivated by the local need for a consecrated burial ground. The point at issue here was that many of the old churches and cemeteries, although secularised, had not always been replaced by the new state church. As a result, the poor and wealthy alike were often obliged to bury their dead in unconsecrated ground. 'This bearer [Robert Gogan] may do much good among your Grace's poor savage people in these parts, that knoweth not decently where to be buried.' The Earl of Desmond stated that neither the church nor house had as 'yet been defaced nor plucked down' and that 'a great part of the gentlemen hereabouts have had their monuments there'.[24] His description of Robert Gogan as 'governor of his Order' suggests that this Dominican was vicar of the houses of the reform.

From the phrase 'pretended plea' in Robert Gogan's petition, the approach decided upon seems clear, namely to prove defective legal ownership. This would warrant the return of St Mary's of the Isle to the Dominicans if the defect could be established in law. Somewhat later two Franciscans of Trim travelled to London, with a view to recovering some of their former houses and brought back a letter of instructions for the Lord Deputy to the same effect.[25] The outcome of Robert Gogan's petition is not known. In 1571 Edmund Goule, merchant of Cork, was pardoned for having intruded on the site of the monastery of the Friars Preachers, which would imply that his ownership had been successfully upheld.[26]

Problems concerning cemeteries and funerals also arose in Galway city. A charter of Edward VI, dated 29 April 1551,[27] reveals that the mayor, bailiffs and burgesses of Galway had informed the king that their Irish enemies, the O'Flahertys and others, lived close to the city

23 Original Latin text of petition in Moran, *Spicil. Ossor.*, iii, 7; *Cal. S.P. Ire., 1509–73*, 140.
24 *Cal. S.P. Ire., 1509–73*, 139.
25 Moran, *Spicil. Ossor.*, iii, 7–8.
26 *Fiants Ire., Eliz.*, 50, no. 1837.
27 Authenticated copy of extract from charter in APF, SOCG, 929 (1823), f. 581rv; not in J. T. Gilbert, 'Archives of the Town of Galway' in *HMC Report 10*, appx, pt v, London 1885.

and for a long time had been accustomed to bury their dead in the collegiate church of St Nicholas. When these people entered the city for funerals, they disturbed the citizens and inflicted damage. The king decided, as requested, that the churches and cemeteries of the three mendicant orders, Dominicans, Franciscans and Augustinians, situated in the suburbs and outside the city walls should be incorporated perpetually in the church of St Nicholas. The warden, vicars and their successors should regulate these cemeteries and allow them to be used by the Gaelic Irish. The grant of this royal charter was intended in the first place to put an end to the incursions of the Irish on the pretext of funerals. It also reflected the growth of the Galway city population, and probably also the desire of the leading Anglo-Irish families to be buried in the churches and cemeteries of the regulars chosen by their ancestors. What is beyond doubt is that the charter effectively gave the warden of St Nicholas's control of all consecrated cemeteries in Galway. The question naturally arises as to whether the Dominicans and other friars were in agreement with the terms of the charter. At any rate, there is ample documentary evidence that quarrels concerning funeral offerings flared on several occasions between the regulars of Galway, the warden of the collegiate church of St Nicholas and the diocesan clergy right down to the nineteenth century.[28]

Not until the general chapter of 1558 did the Dominican Order acknowledge the decision of Paul III and give public recognition to the existence of an independent Irish province. The province had been unrepresented in six general chapters between 1536 and 1553: Lyons (1536), Rome (1539), Rome (1542), Rome (1546), Salamanca (1551) and Rome (1553), at all of which Ireland was omitted from the list of provinces, though England and Scotland were included. Following David Brown's submission of his detailed report to the general chapter of 1558, the acts of that chapter declared: 'We recall that the province of Ireland was constituted as such in the year 1536 by Pope Paul III, was accepted by the Master of the Order, and we grant it a place among the other [provinces].'[29] The year 1558, therefore, marked a high point in the career of the indefatigable Master David Brown; but the accession of Elizabeth in that same year would cast long and deep shadows over his achievements. Within a decade of his death, which occurred about 1559, the chain of Observant Dominican houses in Munster was broken forever.

In the supplement to a Portuguese hagiographical work published in the eighteenth century, David Brown's life is summarised and eulogised:

28 Documentation in APF, SOCG, 929 (1823). Reference supplied by Revd H. Fenning.

29 Reichert, *MOPH*, ix, 255, 266–7, 291–2, 302–3, 311–12, 338–9, 346–7; x, 10.

> As befitted a true religious and son of St Dominic, he was renowned for his virtue and the untiring zeal with which he strenuously opposed the spread of the diabolical doctrines of Luther when they appeared in England and Ireland. He ruled the Order in these two kingdoms as visitator general for both provinces; with the sword of his eloquence and true zeal for the Order and the faith, he benefited not alone the Order, in which regular observance flourished under his rule, but also the Church, by his determined opposition to the detestable teachings of Luther. His tongue uncovered their errors and his eloquence refuted their horrible falsehood. . . . The intrepid zeal of Father David became a refuge and a consolation for all sufferers. He comforted them in their distress, restored their courage, and administered the sacraments until death put an end to his labours.[30]

MUNSTER AND CONNACHT, 1558–1570S

Between the death of Queen Mary and the year 1570 Dominican life in Leinster and Ulster was simply eclipsed. As for Munster and Connacht, there is some scattered evidence of its precarious survival. An act of the English parliament, the final Act of Suppression of 1559, unambiguously declared religious life to be 'a thing repugnant to the usage of the holy, Catholic, apostolic Church of Christ'. Mirroring the Elizabethan administration's bitter anti-Romanism and hostile attitude towards religious life, this act did not augur well for the as yet unsuppressed religious houses of Desmond and Connacht.

The closure of the Dominican houses of Desmond took place amidst the increasing political turmoil, which engulfed the principal Munster centres of population, sparked off by the Desmond rebellion of the 1570s. The fine site, conventual buildings and gardens of the Limerick Dominicans, restored to them in Mary Tudor's reign, were forfeited to the crown in 1569–72.[31] At Kilmallock the Dominican church and house

30 This entry occurs under the date 2 February—possibly the day and month of his death—in the year 1529, which is patently wrong, probably owing to a typographical error. Perhaps it should have read 1559. The author did not indicate his sources. So far there is no real evidence of Brown's appointment as a Dominican superior in England. J. da Natividade, *Additamento ao Agiologío Dominico*, v, Lisbon 1743, 305.

31 *Cal. Carew MSS, 1515–74*, 392, 415; Gwynn and Hadcock, *Medieval Religious Houses: Ireland*, 227. About 1558 Richard Creagh, the future Archbishop of Armagh, opened a school on popular lines in Limerick. From 1561 or perhaps from its inception he conducted the school in the former Dominican priory. The school continued under the care of the Jesuits from 1565 to 1568, when it was closed as a result of the attempts to enforce the state religion. J. Begley, *The Diocese of Limerick*, ii, Dublin 1927, 161, 175.

passed to the sovereign and commonalty of the town in 1569–70.[32] At Cork the Dominicans never regained their buildings from the merchants Brown and Gould who held them. In 1578 St Dominic's statue was publicly burnt in Cork by the Protestant bishop, to the great sorrow of the people.[33] The town of Youghal too was invaded and sacked by the Earl of Desmond on 15 November 1579, but was recaptured by English soldiers under Ormond *c.* 1581, whereupon the Dominican 'monastery' and its six gardens were disposed of by grant to William Walshe.[34] The fine buildings and property of Tralee were occupied by English forces in 1580. An inquisition of its belongings was carried out in 1584 and again in 1586.[35] In Peyton's Survey of 1586 Ballinegaul was unambiguously named as 'Braher Duffe' (Blackfriars) and was then in ruins: 'The town and lands of Ballinegaul and the said house of friars do all lie waste.' These catastrophic events spelt final disaster for David Brown's Observant Dominican communities.[36]

Turning now to Connacht, one finds that the Lord Deputy Sir Henry Sidney, on his visit to Sligo on 22 October 1566 noticed the large monastery of 'White Friars'. Sligo abbey was still intact, inhabited and its buildings admired by Sidney, who did not interfere with the Dominicans.[37] However, by 20 January 1568 a perceptible change in attitudes had occurred when O'Connor Sligo, on account of his voluntary submission to Elizabeth, was allowed to preserve the Dominican church and house of Sligo, in which his ancestors were buried, on condition that secular canons be substituted in place of the Dominican friars. Under

32 Coleman, *Ancient Dominican Foundations*, 61. An inquisition of 11 August 1587 found that there had been an abbey or religious house in Kilmallock, known as Flacispaghe. Archdall, *Monasticon Hibernicum*, 810. On 12 February 1589 the superior and burgesses of Kilmallock were declared to have forfeited their interest in the monastery of Kilmallock (53s 3d p.a.) for non-payment of rent. Likewise Lord Maurice Roche, Viscount Fermoy, was declared by the same inquisition to be deprived of the Dominican house of Glanworth (15s p.a.) for the same reason. *Calendar of Exchequer Inquisitions*, 279. In 1594 the priory, with some land and a water mill, was again granted to the sovereign and commonalty of the town at an annual rent of 53s 8d., *Cal. Pat. Rolls Ire., Eliz.*, ii, 275.

33 Gwynn and Hadcock, *Medieval Religious Houses: Ireland*, 224.

34 Ibid., 231.

35 Ibid., 230.

36 Besides the various ruined buildings, the survey noted that there were certain gardens which all together amounted to half an acre. Its other possessions in the vicinity amounted to a half quarter and two acres of land. J. Begley, *The Diocese of Limerick*, i, Dublin 1906, 355. The originals of Peyton's Survey, otherwise known as *The Book of the Survey of the Attainted and Escheated Lands in the Countye of Lymerick (1586)*, perished in the Custom House fire in 1921. A Latin transcript in Trinity College, Dublin (MS 2988), with the same title does not, however, mention Ballinegaul.

37 M. V. Ronan, *The Reformation in Ireland under Elizabeth*, London 1930, 191–2.

these arrangements, the house might continue to serve as a fitting burial place for his family, as also for prayer and the service of God.[38] Almost contemporaneously the Earl of Clanrickard was granted a concession of much the same kind with respect to Athenry.[39] In both cases one may well surmise that the friars and their protecting lords were acting in unison concerning the survival of the religious establishments of Connacht, to forestall the implications of certain discernible trends.

A diocesan register of the temporalities of Achonry, probably compiled for the use of Bishop Eugene O'Hart, O.P. (1562–1603) and his successors, in the context of imminent or actual confiscations, lists the lands and parochial rights of the three Dominican houses in the diocese: Strade (Co. Mayo), Urlar (Co. Mayo) and Clooneymeaghan (Co. Sligo). The contents of the register conform to the style and technical language of a canonical treatise; the recital of items is terse and precise, yet containing a wealth of social detail concerning the land assets of the diocese. Internal and external evidence of an authentic Latin transcript would suggest that this diocesan inventory was drawn up in the late sixteenth century.[40]

The monastery of Strade, once said to have been a daughter house of Sligo, is listed as possessing four divisions of land (*quarteriae*) in its vicinity and one at Ballinamore. The four divisions, it was explained, had formerly consisted of two lots, but owing to the malice of lay occupiers the land had been redivided. The Dominicans of Urlar likewise held four *quarteriae* of land adjacent to their house. The smaller house of Cloonivihane, *alias* Runnirogue or Clooneymeaghan, held only one *quarteria* of land in the vicinity. Apparently the Dominicans of these three houses had the surrounding parishes in their gift and regularly exercised parochial patronage: Strade in respect of the parish of St Nechah (St Nathy) of Templemore, Urlar in respect in Kilmovee, and Cloonivihane (Clooneymeaghan) in respect of the parish of Cloonoghill. In each case an appointed parish priest had responsibility for the spiritual needs of the people, while the parish revenues pertained to the Dominicans. Similar rights were held by the Augustinians of Banada in connection

38 Ibid., 236.

39 'Whereas the said Earl requireth to have the house of the friary of Anry, in Connacht, reserved for the burial of his house and other Lords of that province, we are pleased that the said house shall be preserved to the said uses as the said Earl can devise, and that licence of mortmain may be granted for land to be annexed thereunto, for the maintenance thereof, to the value of 100 marks.' Cited in Ronan, *The Reformation in Ireland*, 236.

40 P. Grady, *The Radical Anti-Veto*, Dublin 1814, appx, vi–vii (NLI, Joly Pamphlets, no. 528; St Patrick's College, Maynooth, Pamphlet Collection, vol. 713, 3). The original MS disappeared in the nineteenth century; its transcript still awaits critical study.

with the parish of Kilmacteige. Information about the landholdings of the Franciscans (Court and Ballymote), the Carmelites (Coolavin), Augustinians (Banada), the Canons Regular of Ballysadare and the Cistercians of Boyle in the diocese of Achonry is also supplied by this fascinating register.

That Dominicans should have had the right of presentation to parochial livings was highly unusual. One finds an earlier example at Newtownards (Co. Down), where the rectory of Newtown was impropriate to the Dominicans until the suppression (1541).[41] Intractable situations and serious conflict of interests would inevitably arise between the diocesan priest administrators and the regular clergy. To cling to parish clerical rights—inherited from founders and wealthy patrons—such as the enjoyment of tithes was an unwarranted intrusion into the parochial system and alien to the Dominican spirit and constitutions. In the future such rights on the part of Dominicans and other religious orders in the west of Ireland would be successfully challenged as at variance with the spirit and letter of the Tridentine decrees setting out the duties, rights and responsibilities of parish clergy.

Renewed political pressure under Elizabeth to accept the nascent state church as a test of loyalty to the crown, combined with a more ruthless policy in Ireland, caused the surviving Dominicans of Connacht and Munster to intensify their contacts with Rome. In 1567 their most notable spokesman at Rome, described as a professor of the Order and perhaps vicar provincial, was William MacAneaney.[42] He presented a petition to Pius v on behalf of the priors and brethren of all the houses in Ireland seeking the confirmation of a number of privileges, rights and indults as exempt mendicant religious. Among the privileges previously granted by several Popes to the Irish Dominicans and their houses was the right of the founders and other persons to choose their burial places within the precincts of the houses and to be granted immunity from the payment of funeral dues (*tertia partis canonica*), offerings of candles etc. to episcopal administrators or parochial rectors. MacAneaney complained of diocesan clergy and officials who had carried away family tombstones and other monuments from Dominican churches by force and set them up in parish churches. Moreover, the parochial clergy claimed the offerings of the mourners at funerals in Dominican burial grounds and attempted to levy diocesan dues on the friars and their dependants

41 Gwynn and Hadcock, *Medieval Religious Houses: Ireland*, 228.

42 Though obviously a prominent Irish Dominican in the 1560s, no personal or family details of MacAneaney (Mac Conaonaigh) have survived. He may very well have belonged to the Roscommon branch of the family, which gave its name to the townland Kilmacenanny, or Kilmacananneny, parish of Lissonuffy. Woulfe, *Sloinnte Gaedhael is Gall*, 336.

(*familiares*). He also appealed for the rights of the friars to collect and use the tithes donated to their houses by founders and benefactors, as approved and fully set out in apostolic letters. MacAneaney was successful in obtaining a papal bull (dated 16 February 1567) in response to the petition.[43] It upheld the Dominicans' rights and privileges in detail and at very considerable length, threatening with all kinds of canonical penalties and deterrents those who should dare to infringe the provisions of the bull. The journey of William MacAneaney to Rome and the distressing complaints he made reflected the very strained relations and disedifying episodes involving diocesan and regular clergy in several unnamed dioceses. Perhaps what really motivated the Irish Dominicans to have their rights and privileges papally approved was their sense of shock and insecurity in the face of Tridentine legislation curbing the scope of exempt religious and subjecting them more and more to episcopal control.

CORMAC O'FERGUS, PRIOR PROVINCIAL AND CONTINENTAL ENVOY, *C.* 1569–72

Cormac O'Fergus,[44] prior provincial of the Irish Dominicans, was captured with his companion, Richard Roche, by Miler Magrath, Elizabeth's Archbishop of Cashel, in the summer of 1571. O'Fergus was summarily charged with 'preaching against the queen's proceedings'.[45] On 14 July 1571 the archbishop interrogated the provincial on the purpose and range of his recent continental travels and forwarded a report to the Lord Deputy and Council at Dublin. The extant Latin statement made and signed by O'Fergus (*Confessio fratris Cormaci O'Fergusa*)[46] provides valuable information on the career of this otherwise unknown Dominican personality.

When asked why he had sailed from Ireland in 1567 and from what port he had embarked, O'Fergus replied that he had sailed from Galway in order to study and had landed at Lisbon in Portugal. From there he had set out for Rome with Redmond O'Gallagher, formerly the papal

43 Text of bull in *Bullarium Ord. Praed.*, v, 149–51; *Bullarium Romanum*, ed. G. Tomasetti, vii, Turin 1862, 546–50; Burke, *Hib. Dom.*, 102–4.

44 The Irish forms of the name are Ó Fearghuis, Ó Fearghusa and Ó Fergusa, anglicised principally as O'Farris, O'Ferris, Fergus and Farrissy. It was the name of an ecclesiastical family in Co. Leitrim who were coarbs of St Mogue, or erenaghs of Rossinver, and also the name of a medical family in west Connacht who were hereditary physicians to the O'Malleys. Woulfe, *Sloinnte Gaedhael is Gall*, 524.

45 L. Marron, 'Documents from the State Papers concerning Miler McGrath' in *Archiv. Hib.*, 21 (1958), 80–81.

46 Bodl., Carte MSS, LVII, f. 57a. This is the only known document bearing the signature of a sixteenth-century Irish Dominican provincial.

Bishop of Killala and now of Derry, and remained in Rome for nine months. He had petitioned for a rescript confirming the privileges of his Order and was chosen by his Master General as provincial of Ireland. He had petitioned for nothing else apart from certain faculties for dispensation of degrees of kindred forbidden by law. These petitions he had left in the care of Nicholas Kirwan, a merchant of Galway living in Lisbon, whom he had heard had been lost by shipwreck. He had brought no letters with him except one confirming the privileges of the rosary of the Blessed Virgin Mary and the bull proclaiming the coming jubilee year (1575?). All these he had left at Ballyntemple near Glenbalycoillynan in the county of Tipperary. He added that he had also brought some books and altar furnishings in two cases which he had left at a town called Templemichael near Youghal. He had dispatched his servant, John Viwere, together with a servant of the archbishop, to collect these items and bring them to Cashel.

Cormac O'Fergus's assertion that he had gone abroad four years before to study may be interpreted as a smokescreen for his real mission as the province's latest messenger to the continent. His Dominican brethren would not have entrusted Roman business to an inexperienced priest, nor would the Master General have appointed an untried member to govern the Order in Ireland. The confirmation of the Order's rights and privileges which he had obtained implied that some bishops would not admit the Order's role or status within their dioceses—an attitude then general throughout Europe in consequence of the recently promulgated decrees of Trent. That council had so stressed the power of bishops that in September 1567 the Dominican Pope, Pius V, was constrained to issue a bull safeguarding the exempt status of his own Order. The bull of jubilee was probably that announcing the indulgences to be gained by pilgrims to Rome in 1575. In the context of Irish devotional history and practice, by far the most interesting document carried by O'Fergus was that concerning the rosary, since it may well be the earliest evidence for the preaching of this devotion in Ireland. The rosary document was probably the bull *Inter desiderabilia* of 29 June 1569, by which the spiritual privileges of the Holy Rosary Confraternity and the exclusive right of the Dominican Order to establish it were decreed. Cormac O'Fergus may have been responsible for obtaining permission for the setting up of the Holy Rosary Confraternity in the dioceses of Killaloe and Raphoe on behalf of their respective bishops (21 December 1569).[47]

When asked what he had heard about the stirring of war in France and Spain against the queen, he said that he had been informed that some ships in both kingdoms were ready to set sail for Ireland, and that

47 Fenning, *Irish material*, 273.

he had believed that this fleet would have arrived before him. Questioned as to what had set this movement on foot, he answered that one Maurice Reogh (MacGibbon), the papal Archbishop of Cashel, had done and still did all he could to promote this discord, and the citizens of Racellie (La Rochelle?) were intended to be the chief movers in one part of the enterprise. Here O'Fergus clearly implicated the Catholic Archbishop of Cashel, the personal representative of James FitzMaurice FitzGerald to Philip II of Spain, as well as the people of La Rochelle in promoting preparations for the dispatch of ships to Ireland. This plan was to lead to the ill-fated landing of FitzMaurice at Dingle with limited Spanish aid in 1579. How deeply Cormac O'Fergus was involved in these schemes one cannot accurately say. It has been claimed that he was employed by King Philip to urge harbour-keepers in France and Spain to facilitate the arrival and passage of Irish refugees.[48] This might help to explain why the provincial took almost four years to complete his mission. It might also explain why he visited Cork, Youghal and Waterford and later travelled to Sligo via Limerick and Galway, Irish ports which, apart from having Dominican communities, always had strong shipping ties with continental Europe. Surely O'Fergus is the same friar mentioned in the report made by Walter French, merchant of Galway, at Kinsale on 30 March 1571:

> The said Rory [O'Rourke] returned to Spain, and was entertained by the king . . . as a friar of Ireland, who called himself provincial of Ireland told him. . . . The friar showed letters he had from the king of Spain to the Bishop of Cales [Cadiz?], commanding him to stay [arrest] and punish any that should be coming into Ireland that would refuse to bring him over. Whereupon the Frenchman said they were bound to Flanders, not Ireland, upon which the friar turned to a Portingale [Portuguese] of a ship bound for Waterford wherein was a merchant of that city called James Fagan, and by means of the Bishop [of Cales] which threatened the Portingale, with whom James Fagan bargained, the loss of his ship and goods, he [the friar] was conveyed towards Waterford.[49]

The remainder of Cormac O'Fergus's statement was taken up with more personal details. When asked whether he had any possessions, he insisted that he had only forty silver testoons (shillings, but by then worth only three pence), which he had given to another friar, his companion, to buy a habit. Asked when he had landed in Ireland, he replied

48 R. Bagwell, *Ireland under the Tudors*, ii, London 1885, 226.

49 Cited in Ronan, *The Reformation in Ireland*, 405. This author mistakenly identified 'the provincial of Ireland' with Donagh O'Gallagher, Bishop of Killala.

on Easter Sunday in the city of Cork. On that same day he preached and said Mass, and since then he had lived at the house of his Order at Youghal. He went once to Waterford, but did not preach there, and moved thence to Clonmel, where he preached twice and said Mass in secret. Afterwards he turned towards Fethard, where he preached but did not celebrate Mass. When asked for his opinion on the authority of the Pope in England and Ireland, he said he would answer in eight days' time. O'Fergus disclosed too that he had as a companion on his travels another friar, Richard Roche, who had kept him company at least from Youghal, but he knew nothing of his doings apart from what he had learned during the interrogation.

At first sight the reader may be taken aback by how freely O'Fergus spoke about the plans for the Desmond invasion, but he may have been simply retailing information already well known to the English authorities through their highly organised intelligence network. On the sixth day of the friars' captivity Miler Magrath received a letter from James FitzMaurice, then based in the Glen of Aherlow. It was an undisguised threat to hang the archbishop and burn his property unless he freed his prisoners:

> As I am informed that you have taken prisoner the poor friars for preaching the word of God to the poor people who are blinded with ignorance these many years for lack of good pastors that would show them their duty; wherefore I do require you to enlarge at free liberty the said friars that we may receive good fruit and illuminate our hearts receiving from their mouths the just way of salvation, which we need very much by reason of our long continuance in obscurity.[50]

On the eighth day, while the archbishop was conveniently absent from his house, Edward Butler released the friars on the pretext 'that they were poor men which do nothing against their prince'.[51]

By the autumn of 1572 Cormac O'Fergus had reached his native Connacht and reappeared at Sligo, where he was reported to have published indulgences from Rome.[52] On All Saints' Day of that year friars preached publicly at Galway before the former mayor and other leading citizens. Some concluded that the friars wished to subvert the English government and 'set up their own wickedness'. Hostile observers reported that the mendicants of Galway bore themselves like princes, behaving as though the Pope were King of England and Ireland. Clanrickard himself dared not say a word, and Limerick threatened to be

50 L. Marron, 'Documents . . . concerning Miler McGrath', 81–2.
51 Bodl., Carte MSS, LVII, f. 60a.
52 Ronan, *The Reformation in Ireland*, 421; Bagwell, *Tudors*, ii, 227.

soon as bad as Galway.[53] News of Pius V's bull excommunicating Elizabeth had filtered through to Ireland, and the friars naïvely took for granted its successful implementation. After 1572 silence descended on the activities of the intrepid Cormac O'Fergus,[54] so deeply attached to the preaching of the Word of God even at considerable peril to his own life.

No Irish representatives were listed at the general chapters of the Order held at Rome in 1569 and 1571. At the chapter of 1571 all provincials and conventual priors were exhorted to receive suitable young men into the Order, most of all in 'desolate provinces'. Smaller non-reformed houses had already been forbidden by Pius IV to accept novices at all. It was urged that the greatest care should be taken in the religious formation of novices in the larger convents of the observance.[55] Precisely these problems confronted Cormac O'Fergus and his Irish brethren. They could not look for much assistance from the European provinces, however, since by that time those of France, Belgium, Holland, Germany, Hungary and others were being torn apart by the consequences of religious wars.

EUGENE O'HART, BISHOP OF ACHONRY (1562–1603): AGENT OF TRIDENTINE REFORM

Between 1550 and 1600 five Dominicans presided over Irish dioceses: Cormac O'Coyne, Bishop of Achonry (1556–61),[56] was an uncle of his successor Eugene O'Hart; Peter Wall, Bishop of Clonmacnoise (1556–68),[57] of whose personality or episcopate nothing is known beyond the

53 Bagwell, *Tudors*, ii, 226.

54 Writing from Waterford on 24 March 1578, Sir William Drury reported to the Privy Council, Dublin, that about four hundred persons, including a friar and a brehon, had been executed in Munster under martial law over a period of nineteen months. A friar had also been arrested and hanged in his habit at Limerick for possessing letters and blanks and seals of several abbeys and friaries of Munster, with letters of commendation 'to the provincial of Portugal . . . importing seditious practices to be intended and he [the friar] as a trusty messenger sent to negotiate'. The friar had been arrested as he was about to depart from the Shannon river estuary for Portugal 'for whose life also a good sum would have been given'. W. M. Brady (ed.), *State Papers concerning the Irish Church in the Time of Queen Elizabeth*, London 1868, 24–5. While conclusive evidence is lacking, it is not beyond the bounds of possibility that this friar was none other than Cormac O'Fergus.

55 Reichert, *MOPH*, x, 125, 129.

56 P. F. Moran, *History of the Catholic Archbishops of Dublin*, Dublin 1864, 419; Lynch, *De Praesulibus Hib.*, ii, 314; Brady, *Ep. Succ.*, ii, 187. David Wolfe inaccurately described him as a Franciscan in a letter to the Cardinal Protector of Ireland.

57 C. Giblin (ed.), 'Vatican Library: MSS Barberini Latini' in *Archiv. Hib.*, 18 (1955), 80; *Bullarium Ord. Praed.*, v, 56; Brady, *Ep. Succ.*, i, 246; Lynch, *De Praesulibus Hib.*, i, 276; Eubel, *Hier. Cath.*, iii, 170: *Cluanen.* note 5. Brief of

dates of his appointment and death; Eugene O'Hart, Bishop of Achonry (1562–1603),[58] and Andrew O'Crean, Bishop of Elphin (1562–94),[59] both of whom vigorously promoted the reforms of Trent in Connacht and further afield; finally there was Thaddeus O'Farrell, Bishop of Clonfert (1587–1602), who for the most part was a shadowy figure, a non-resident bishop who spent many years at the court of Spain as an Irish diplomat. Chronological details of all these episcopates are given in Appendix 2.

By far the most remarkable of these five bishops was Eugene O'Hart, who attended the final sessions of the Council of Trent, was thoroughly imbued by the spirit and reforms of the council, and afterwards sought to implement its decrees in Connacht and Ulster. Eugene O'Hart is said to have been a member of the O'Hart family of Carbury, Co. Sligo,[60] the most distinguished family of that district after the O'Connors. He entered the Dominicans at Holy Cross, Sligo, where he received his religious formation and made profession. He also studied letters (Classical Greek and Latin and possibly other elements of Renaissance learning) and showed marked ability. On account of his intellectual gifts he was sent for higher studies to Salamanca and Paris, two of the most distinguished universities of the day. During a lengthy stay at Paris he would have become familiar with Protestantism in its several forms, especially in its French Calvinist expression, and with other contemporary intellectual trends. Returning to Ireland, he shared his learning, devoted himself to preaching, and was elected prior of Sligo. Later he was chosen by the clergy of Connacht to represent them as their procurator at the Council of Trent.

In the autumn of 1561 he set out for Italy accompanied by his confrère, Andrew O'Crean, Bishop-elect of Elphin. He was entrusted with letters by David Wolfe, S.J.,[61] papal commissary, recommending him as 'a great

appointment described him as a bachelor of theology and fifty years of age; granted absolution from apostasy and any other canonical irregularities. Erroneously referred to as Bishop of Cloyne (*Episcopus Clonensis*) instead of Clonmacnoise (*Cluanensis*) by Burke, *Hib. Dom.*, 486.

58 Giblin, 'Vatican Library: MSS Barberini Latini', 80, 82; Brady, *Ep. Succ.*, ii, 187; Eubel, *Hier. Cath.*, iii, 94; J. Hagan (ed.), 'Miscellanea Vaticano-Hibernica: Ireland in 1580' in *Archiv. Hib.*, 5 (1916), 169.

59 Giblin, 'Vatican Library: MSS Barberini Latini', 80, 82; Brady, *Ep. Succ.*, ii, 200–1; Eubel, *Hier. Cath.*, iii, 191; Hagan, 'Miscellanea Vaticano-Hibernica: Ireland in 1580', 169.

60 T. O'Rorke, *The History of Sligo*, ii, Dublin 1889, 105. Ó hAirt (O'Hart, Harte) was the name of a Meath family originally seated near Tara, but dispossessed soon after the Anglo-Norman invasion when they settled in Co. Sligo. Woulfe, *Sloinnte Gaedhael is Gall*, 552. The primary biographical source for Eugene O'Hart is still that of Archdeacon John Lynch's *De Praesulibus Hib.*, ii, 339–42, to which the following account is partly indebted.

61 See Moran, *Archbishops of Dublin*, 418–19, 87.

preacher of exemplary life, and full of zeal for the glory of God'. Wolfe noted that O'Hart had lived in Paris[62] for about eight years and would be well suited for a bishopric. Should anything befall Andrew O'Crean, he would recommend O'Hart to fill his place. If O'Crean should be consecrated Bishop of Elphin, then he would recommend O'Hart for the vacant see of Achonry. Wolfe reported that the cathedral church of Achonry was then used as a fortress by the gentry of the neighbourhood and did not retain one vestige of its religious character. He expressed the conviction that O'Hart with the aid of his friends would recover the church and take charge of it as Dr Christopher Bodkin had done with the cathedral of Tuam. Wolfe had earlier received instructions from Rome to select the most worthy candidates for promotion to bishoprics. This was part of his task of reorganising the Irish church and ensured Ireland's representation at the Council of Trent. His episcopal nominees, Andrew O'Crean, Eugene O'Hart and Thomas O'Herlihy, future Bishop of Ross, significantly were of Gaelic Irish stock.

O'Hart was formally appointed to Achonry at a papal consistory on 28 January 1562, and was ordained bishop in Rome shortly afterwards. On 25 May 1562 O'Hart, together with Bishops O'Herlihy of Ross and MacGongail of Raphoe, reached Trent in the Italian Alps. He immediately took his place at the council and contributed regularly to the theological debates.[63] His votes and arguments were officially recorded in the acts of the council. He spoke on a host of theological questions: ecclesiastical jurisdiction and episcopal obligation of residence, the expiatory character of the sacrifice of Christ, the significance of the Last Supper, communion under both kinds, and the sacrament of holy orders. He was of the view that all ecclesiastical power was regulated by the Bishop of Rome. He spoke against clandestine marriages and upheld the traditional doctrine on purgatory, the veneration of the saints and reverence for holy images. The straitened circumstances of O'Hart and the other two Irish bishops at the council were commented on by an observer: 'The three Irish bishops that are here with nothing to live on, but the trifling allowance of twenty crowns a month apiece, granted by His Holiness, make great complaint, that living being so dear, they cannot subsist.' The Pope responded by raising their monthly allowance to twenty-five crowns.[64] The council ended on 4 December 1563.

62 Mentioned in a letter written in 1555 by the provincial of Scotland to an unnamed Dominican in Paris; the provincial was to write soon to O'Hart, perhaps then also living and studying at Paris. Piò, *Delle Vite degli Huomini Illustri di S. Domenico*, pt 1, i, 383.

63 A. M. Walz, *I Domenicani al Concilio di Trento*, Rome 1961, 327, 329–30, 336, 350, 355, 390, 394.

64 *Cal. S.P. Rome, 1558–71*, 11.

While the council failed to satisfy Protestants of all shades and opinions and its reforms were less comprehensive than many Catholics had hoped for, it established a solid basis for the renewal of discipline, the administration of the sacraments and the emergence of more modern forms of spirituality. Trent's precisely formulated doctrinal system, combined with an enhanced religious resurgence, prepared the Catholic Church for the subsequent struggle with Protestantism as much in Ireland as in continental Europe.

In 1566, together with O'Crean, Bishop of Elphin, and O'Gallagher, Bishop of Killala, Eugene O'Hart convened a provincial synod for Connacht in which the decrees of Trent, dogmatic and disciplinary, were promulgated. One decree of the synod was particularly stressed: all matrimonial cases in Connacht dioceses were henceforth to be considered in accordance with the stricter legislation of the council. O'Hart was reputed to be particularly active for the rest of his episcopate in encouraging the implementation of the decrees and discipline of Trent within his own and neighbouring jurisdictions.[65] In 1568 Archbishop Creagh of Armagh, writing from captivity to Rome about the vacant see of Clogher, advised consultation with O'Hart. In that year too Cardinal Morone, Protector of Ireland, suggested Bishop O'Hart as administrator of Armagh during the imprisonment of its archbishop. The cardinal also advised that in each ecclesiastical province one bishop should be designated to give testimonials to clergy travelling to Rome. He named O'Hart for the province of Tuam, and also for Armagh during the detention of its metropolitan.[66]

On 4 May 1575 O'Hart was given special faculties for Achonry and the ecclesiastical province of Tuam, to absolve from censures reserved to Rome those who had lapsed into heresy or who had secured possession of confiscated church property.[67] In the same year, when writing to Cardinal Como, Secretary of State, O'Hart grimly reported that the personal safety of his priests was in danger from dissidents who had attached themselves to the Anglican religion; even the safe

65 Lynch, *De Praesulibus Hib.*, ii, 232, 340; D. Rothe, *Analecta Sacra Nova et Mira* (Cologne 1617), ed. P. F. Moran, Dublin 1884, 438; P. F. Moran, 'The See of Achonry in the Sixteenth Century' in *IER*, 1st ser., 1 (1865), 214.

66 Moran, 'The See of Achonry', 214. A commendatory letter of O'Hart in favour of Miler O'Higgin, priest of Achonry, seeking admission to the Teutonic College at Rome, dated 23 July 1575, is printed in A. Bellesheim, *Geschichte der Katholischen Kirche in Irland von der Einführung des Christenthums bis auf die Gegenwart*, ii, Mainz 1890, 715.

67 ASV, Secret. Brevium, vol. 35, f. 258v. At least twelve Irish bishops obtained similar faculties drawn up in almost identical terms in 1575. Latin text of typical original document in F. M. Jones, 'Canonical Faculties on the Irish Mission in the Reign of Queen Elizabeth, 1558–1603' in *Ir. Theol. Quart.*, 20 (1953), 164–5.

departure of ecclesiastics from the country could not be assured as the ports were under close observation. Should anyone attempt to depart contrary to the edict of the queen, he would be apprehended and executed or by special concession be committed to perpetual incarceration. Older ecclesiastics were terrified by such dire measures and did not dare to appear in seaports or in public, while young men had disappeared from the choirs of religious orders.[68]

In 1585 Bishop O'Hart was arrested by Sir Richard Bingham, Lord President of Connacht, and brought to Dublin Castle. The Lord Deputy, Sir John Perrot, asked the Anglican Archbishop of Armagh, John Long, to visit him. The archbishop optimistically reported (4 June 1585) that O'Hart had admitted his spiritual blindness, wished to prostrate himself before the queen, renounced his bishopric, and was thoroughly persuaded that 'the man of sin sat in Rome'.[69] How was such a report to be interpreted? To the Dublin government, political and not religious considerations were paramount in Connacht at that time. For O'Hart it was the reverse. Hence his alleged willingness to resign his see which for him, at most, meant relinquishing the temporalities and perhaps certain civil functions such as competence in some matters of law and justice, but not his essential spiritual office as a bishop. His clear-cut stance was in sharp contrast with the political agility and more worldly outlook of his temporising colleagues, Christopher Bodkin, Archbishop of Tuam, and Roland Burke, Bishop of Clonfert. Both these bishops had taken the Oath of Supremacy to the Tudor monarchs Henry VIII, Edward VI and Elizabeth I, but in spite of their outward submission as nominal Anglicans they lived and died as Catholic prelates.[70] What the government sought from Bishop O'Hart, therefore, was minimal recognition at the temporal level. This represented its calculated strategy of levering its way through the stout fabric of Gaelic society and was very soon to be verified in Connacht. On 3 September 1585 Bishop O'Hart, having regained his freedom, became a party to a treaty between Elizabeth and the Gaelic lords of Sligo which confirmed him in the temporalities of his diocese.[71] The significance of the treaty lay precisely in the policy of forwarding the royal writ in areas of the province of Connacht where hitherto it had not been recognised or proved ineffectual. The submission of the Gaelic nobility and gentry of Connacht was such a

68 Bellesheim, *Geschichte*, ii, 715.

69 Brady (ed.), *State Papers concerning the Irish Church*, 97; W. M. Brady, *The Irish Reformation, or the Alleged Conversion of the Irish Bishops*, London 1867, 159.

70 F. X. Martin, 'Confusion Abounding: Bernard O'Higgin, Bishop of Elphin, 1542–1561' in A. Cosgrove and D. McCartney (eds), *Studies in Irish History presented to R. Dudley Edwards*, Dublin 1979, 68–9.

71 *Cal. Pat. Rolls Ire., Eliz., 146; The Compossicion Booke of.Conought*, ed. A. M. Freeman, Dublin 1936, 125, 132, 136, 177.

momentous event that the Dublin administration did not insist on the Oath of Supremacy. In 1587 O'Hart joined the Bishops of Derry, Raphoe, Down and Connor, Ardagh, Kilmore and Clogher to promulgate the decrees of Trent for Ulster.[72] His presence at this synod showed how groundless were the hopes and expectations of the Anglican primate, who had been deluded as regards O'Hart's real intentions and beliefs. The indenture of composition which Perrot made with the Gaelic magnates of Mayo and Sligo included members of O'Hart's wider family and those allied with the O'Harts socially and politically, on whom the bishop could count for strong support.

Not until 1591 were there signs of a shift in the policy of conciliation of the western Catholic aristocracy. On 1 December of that year Elizabeth appointed by letters patent the Anglican Bishop of Killala to be administrator of Achonry. The bishop in question was Eugene O'Connor, a court favourite, who earlier had been the friend of O'Hart. O'Connor was easily persuaded not to interfere in the administration of the diocese or to exercise his episcopal orders. In return for allowing him quiet possession of his see, O'Hart undertook to pay him annually 180 marks, the entire yearly diocesan revenue.[73]

That Bishop O'Hart's role in the leadership of the Catholic Church in Ireland was not restricted to Connacht and Ulster is most strikingly revealed by his presence in Munster in the summer of 1593. William Lyon, the zealous Reformation-minded Bishop of Cork, Cloyne and Ross (1583–1617), dolefully reported to Lord Deputy William Fitzwilliam that O'Hart was conducting confirmation services throughout the country and that people were flocking to him from all parts to have their children confirmed. While at Mallow on 23 July, O'Hart was interrogated by Thomas Norris, Vice-President of Munster, and the Chief Justice. He displayed a licence granted to him by Sir John Perrot, the former Lord Deputy, which indicated that he had taken an oath of loyalty to Queen Elizabeth as already seen. He denied, however, that he had ever taken the Oath of Supremacy. Bishop Eugene O'Hart was of a similar mind to Bishop Quentin Cogly, therefore, in wishing to exercise his episcopal ministry, when necessary for the wider Catholic community, in parts of Ireland very distant indeed from his own western diocese of Achonry.[74]

In 1597 the Franciscan provincial, Donagh Mooney, while visitating the houses of his order in Connacht, met Bishop O'Hart and accurately described him as a man of great age and yet robust in constitution.[75] On

72 L. F. Renehan, *Collections on Irish Church History*, i, Dublin 1861, 435.
73 Lynch, *De Praesulibus Hib.*, ii, 340.
74 PRO, SP 63/183/161.
75 B. Jennings (ed.), 'Brussels MS 3947: Donatus Moneyus, de Provincia Hiberniae S. Francisci' in *Anal. Hib.*, 6 (1934), 25.

19 April 1603 he was admitted to pardon by James I, still as Bishop of Achonry, with other prominent citizens of Sligo.[76] Later that year he died, being one hundred years old, having been Bishop of Achonry for forty-one years. He was buried in his cathedral of Achonry near the high altar on the Gospel side.[77]

Eugene O'Hart's long episcopate marked the transition period of Irish Catholicism from medieval to modern spirit and practice. He was by far the most energetic and outstanding bishop of his epoch, intensely committed to the adaptation of the Tridentine reform movement to the peculiar circumstances of the Irish Church. In the 1560s an anonymous Italian writer aptly summed him up as 'a vigorous advocate and defender of the Catholic faith'.[78] This Italian testimonial was endorsed by Philip O'Sullivan Beare, who said of him that 'he endured many adversities for the sake of his faith in Christ'.[79]

ANDREW O'CREAN, BISHOP OF ELPHIN (1562–94), AND THE CONFLICT OF ECCLESIASTICAL JURISDICTIONS

That Andrew O'Crean owed his promotion to Elphin in 1562 to the pragmatic judgement of David Wolfe is clear from one of Wolfe's letters to Rome, dated 12 October 1561:

> Bernard O'Higgin, Bishop of Elphin, had resigned his see in favour of a Dominican, Andrew Crean, the prior of Sligo, a man of piety and sanctity, who is moreover held in great esteem by the laity, not so much for his learning as for his amiability and holiness. The said Bernard was a good and religious man in himself, but he was not acceptable to the people. Seeing that he was losing the temporalities of the see through this dislike which the people had for him, he chose Father Andrew, who is beloved by everyone, that thus all that was lost might be regained. Father Andrew now goes to Rome, with the permission of his provincial, to obtain that see,

76 *Cal. Pat. Rolls Ire., Jas. I*, pp vii, 5.

77 Lynch, *De Praesulibus Hib.*, ii, 342.

78 ASV, Archiv. Arcis, XIV, 11, vol. 41, f. 68r: '*Acaden. eps. ord. praed. strenuus catholicae fidei propugnator.*' The details of O'Hart's career set out above disprove the inaccurate assertion made by S. Ellis that the bishop 'managed to remain acceptable to both sides', namely pope and queen. See S. Ellis, *Tudor Ireland, 1470–1603*, London 1985, 197.

79 P. O'Sullivan Beare, *Selections from the Zoilomastix*, ed. and trans. T. J. O'Donnell, Dublin 1960, 21. Similar tributes in A. Fernandes, *Concertatio Praedicatoria pro Ecclesia Catholica*, Salamanca 1618, 282; A. De Altamura, *Bibliothecae Dominicanae*, Rome 1677, 434, 538; G. M. Cavalieri, *Galleria de'Sommi Pontefici*, i, Benevento 1696, 407.

> bearing with him the resignation of the said Bernard. Father Andrew asked me for testimonials, and though I personally know little about him, I can attest to the reputation for virtue which he enjoys throughout the country.[80]

Andrew O'Crean's Augustinian predecessor, Bernard O'Higgin, quitted Ireland definitively for continental exile in about 1554. This had caused a serious void in the diocese of Elphin. Bishop Roland Burke, who had been papally appointed to Clonfert in May 1534, had subsequently surrendered his bull of appointment in order to receive the temporalities of the see from Henry VIII. During O'Higgin's absence from his diocese Burke was nominated Anglican Bishop of Elphin on 23 November 1551. From this point it became imperative for Rome to install an effective Catholic bishop to counter Burke's influence, exceptionally strong in the southern part of this important diocese.

A recent study has shown that a vital factor in O'Crean's nomination was the local socio-political support which his predecessor had lacked. O'Crean was evidently very acceptable 'to the people', most of all to the ruling Irish lords and the leading merchant families of Sligo. 'O'Crean was a member of the well-known Gaelic merchant family at the port of Sligo, where the fish trade was the lucrative industry.'[81] The O'Creans were second only to the O'Connors Sligo, and with them had learned to survive and thrive between the two powerful lay lords contending for control of the area, the O'Donnells of Tyrconnell or north-west Ulster and the MacWilliam Burkes of Lower Connacht.[82] As prior of Sligo abbey, Andrew O'Crean belonged to the most important of five Dominican houses in the extended diocese of Elphin, stretching from Sligo to Athlone.

In the late autumn of 1561 O'Crean set out for Rome with Eugene O'Hart to obtain the letters of his appointment to Elphin. While passing through France he fell ill, and being unable or unwilling to travel further he remained in France until the bull of his appointment reached him.[83] Made bishop by papal provision (28 January 1562) in the same consistory

80 Cited by Moran, *Archbishops of Dublin*, 417–19 (trans. 85–7) at 85. For a summary of his episcopate see P. F. Moran, 'The See of Elphin in the Sixteenth Century' in *IER*, 1st ser., 2 (1866), 152–4.

81 Martin, 'Confusion Abounding', 70–76. Ó Croidheáin (O'Crean) was the name of a family of Cinél Eoghain who in the sixteenth century settled at Sligo, where they prospered as merchants, and afterwards acquired a considerable amount of landed property in the area. Woulfe, *Sloinnte Gaedhael is Gall*, 484; see also *Annála Uladh, Annals of Ulster*, ed. W. M. Hennessy and B. MacCarthy, iii, Dublin 1895, 482, 572–4; *Annals of Loch Cé*, ed. W. M. Hennessy, ii, Dublin 1939, 512; *Cal Pat. Rolls Ire., Jas I*, 20, cited in *NHI.*, iii, 15.

82 Martin, 'Confusion Abounding', 81–2.

83 Lynch, *De Praesulibus Hib.*, ii, 291.

that named O'Hart to Achonry, O'Crean returned to Ireland without participating in the last sessions of Trent (1562–3). Later, in common with his fellow bishops of Achonry and Killala, O'Crean accepted the decrees and legislation of the council as normative for Catholic life and practice in Connacht. This decision was given concrete effect in marriage procedures, where all three dioceses decided on a uniform policy concerning the conditions for the validity of sacramental marriages and the banning of clandestine ones.[84]

It has been suggested that O'Crean's active government did not extend outside the northern portion of his diocese, where he would have had the open assistance of his own kinsmen and that of the O'Connors, and that Roland Burke, the Anglican nominee, exercised more than a nominal control over the rest of the see, with the weight of his Clanwilliam supporters behind him.[85] This is simply surmise, perhaps accurate or quite inaccurate. The truth is that there is no firm evidence one way or the other on which to base a reliable judgement. Andrew O'Crean lived mostly in Sligo abbey, whose fine church he designated the cathedral church of Elphin.[86] For the most part he was left undisturbed by the reformers or by sporadic attempts to introduce Anglicanism on the part of officialdom.

Bishop Roland Burke's death in 1580 may have prompted O'Crean to assert full jurisdiction over the whole diocese, especially in the matter of the temporalities, a significant portion of which may have been retained by Burke. The issue may have become more pressing with the appointment of John Harvey, an Englishman, as administrator, who was granted the diocese '*in custodium*' by royal letters patent in 1582.[87] An entry under this same year in the Annals of Loch Cé suggests that O'Crean sought some form of recognition from the Dublin government: 'The bishopric of Elphin (Olifinn) was given to Andrew O'Craidhen by the Council of Eirinn at Ath-Cliath.'[88] What O'Crean in fact was seeking was confirmation for the totality of the diocesan revenues, thereby accepting them as the gift of the crown. There was no hint of temporising or of external compliance with Elizabethan religious policy on the part of O'Crean, otherwise this would have been dolefully chronicled by the Annals of Loch Cé or mentioned in the contemporary State Papers. It is on record that he consistently and strenuously refused to take the Oath of Supremacy.[89] The mentalities and the complexities surrounding

84 Ibid.
85 Martin, 'Confusion Abounding', 71.
86 ASV, Reg. Suppl., 3401, f. 61v.
87 J. Ware, *The Whole Works of Sir James Ware concerning Ireland*, ed. W. Harris, i, Dublin 1739, 634.
88 *Annals of Loch Cé*, ii, 455.
89 Lynch, *De Praesulibus Hib.*, ii, 291.

so many issues of the age may not be perfectly definable or capable of proof, but the appointment of another Englishman, Thomas Chester, as Anglican Bishop of Elphin, who died shortly afterwards in June 1584,[90] speaks for itself. Had O'Crean really temporised, Chester would not have been named Bishop of Elphin. When Lord Deputy Sidney and his retinue had encamped in O'Connor Sligo's country on 21 October 1566, 'O'Connor Sligo came unto us with the Bishop of Elphin, most humbly offering service and fealty to your majesty and all courtesy to us.'[91] His conduct on that occasion illustrated his diplomatic and conciliatory character, but this could hardly be described as displaying evidence of compromise or vacillation.

Thomas Burke, author of *Hibernia Dominicana*, referred to O'Crean as 'Andrea Xerea',[92] which may indicate that O'Crean once studied at Jerez de la Frontera in the south of Spain. Beyond this designation, Burke had nothing further to say of O'Crean's episcopate. He was at some stage of his career awarded the degree of master of theology, which in that era would indicate that he was a trained theologian. He was responsible for the erection of a marble cross (Leacht an Easpaig) in the town of Sligo.[93] Towards the end of his life he retired from the active administration of his see and lived quietly with his Dominican brethren, having earned for himself a reputation for sanctity. He died at Sligo in 1594, in the midst of his fellow Dominicans, who, through the influence of Domhnall Mór O'Connor, enjoyed comparative tranquillity and security. Almost certainly Andrew O'Crean was buried in the Dominican church, his 'cathedral'. It was this same prominent O'Connor who was regarded with such favour by Elizabeth that when he refused the title of earl she gave him the right to be styled The O'Connor of Sligo. It was through his intervention that an order was issued prohibiting the destruction of Sligo abbey. This was typical of the policy of compromise and concession made by English officialdom in Elizabethan Connacht. Lynch concluded his biographical notice on O'Crean by adding a most valuable and telling comment on current Elizabethan religious policy in Sligo: it was the custom that those who had received holy orders during Mary's reign were not compelled 'to change their habit' or go into exile; and hence it was that Andrew O'Crean was not in the least molested once he stayed within the walls of his Dominican monastery of Sligo.[94] Andrew O'Crean's episcopate differed notably in style and expression from that of his fellow Dominican bishop, Eugene O'Hart of Achonry.

90 Ware, *Works*, i, 634.
91 Ronan, *The Reformation in Ireland*, 191.
92 Burke, *Hib. Dom.*, 486.
93 Lynch, *De Praesulibus Hib.*, ii, 291.
94 Ibid.

While he was not moulded in the Tridentine spirit to the same extent as O'Hart, he nonetheless favoured its spread and implementation because of his loyalty to the Holy See, with which he had regular correspondence.[95]

95 Ibid. Lynch was aware of (and may have had in his possession) two papal briefs addressed to O'Crean, dated 5 June 1575 and 13 August 1579, but did not comment on their content.

THREE

Resistance to Suppression: Connacht, 1570–1600

HOUSES IN THE 1570S: CONTEMPORARY RECORDS

The only substantial list to be considered was compiled anonymously for Seraphinus Cavalli, Master of the Order (1571–8).[1] From one point of view it is of purely antiquarian interest; many of the houses included had been destroyed or lost to the Order for almost thirty years. Yet it retains its value as a pointer to the compiler's 'Dominican memory' and his hope for future recovery.

Hyberniae Conventus

Dubliniensis [Dublin]	Pons [Drogheda]	Carling [Carlingford]
Baleatruim [Trim]	Molindinus Curtus [Mullingar]	Asleain [Athy ?]
Waterfordia [Waterford]	Rylconii [Kilkenny]	Fiard [Fethard]
Casselensis [Cashel]	Enverinor [Arklow]	Lotoria [Lorrha]
Portus Dominici [Portumna]	Athnarii [Athenry]	Roscomayn [Roscommon]
Athlean [Strade]	Seligia [Sligo]	Tulay [Tulsk]
Bealach [Toombeola]	Baleindnayn [Ballindoon]	Inturlar [Urlar]
Rafranna [Rathfran]	Derensis [Derry]	Banna [Coleraine]
Novavilla [Newtownards]	Galnia [Galway]	Loncordia i.e. Loucord [Longford]
Burries [Burrishoole]	Lumbriensis [Limerick]	Praliensis [Tralee]
Gorcagnensis [Cork]	Joorliensis [Youghal]	Ryllimcealoin [Kilmallock]
Gleannuir [Glanworth]	Rylcarbayn [Kilcorban]	

1 Fenning, *Irish material*, 274.

The register in which this list occurs contains similar incomplete lists of English and Scottish convents and houses. The Irish list is relatively complete, but clearly a faulty transcript. It is not known how it came into Cavalli's hands. He may have received the correct original from an Irish Dominican visiting Rome in the early 1570s, or it may have been given to him during his sojourn at Paris in the autumn of 1573 or somewhat later in the Low Countries while on visitation in those parts.

Thirty-five houses are listed. Houses not mentioned are mostly minor ones: Aghaboe, Rosbercon, Naas (Leinster); Clooneymeaghan and Cloonshanville (Connacht). Included in the list are Kilcorban, a filial house of Athenry, and Fethard, where the Order is not known to have had a medieval foundation but where a Dominican presence may have been briefly established, as witness Cormac O'Fergus's visit and preaching there in 1571. In May 1574 the King of Spain's envoy, Diego Ortiz, reported that at Dungarvan Franciscans and Dominicans had to flee to the mountains or seek refuge in caves and cellars every time English troops appeared; but they returned as soon as the way was clear and continued with their ministry.[2] The Dominicans never had a house at Dungarvan, but may have been from Youghal or Waterford on a temporary preaching mission in Dungarvan and west Waterford.

Internal evidence points to the copying of the list by a secretary unfamiliar with Irish place-names. The spelling of three place-names begins with *Ryl* instead of *Kyl*, and *Praliensis* is clearly a mistake for *Traliensis*. While many of the names are Latinised, others are given in purely Irish forms (e.g. *Baleatruim*, not Trim; *Gleannuir*, not Glanworth; *Enverinor* (*recte* Invermor), not Arklow; *Athnarii*, not Athenry), indicating an Irish-speaking Dominican as their source. The identification of some place-names remains problematical. The list represents the houses that existed on the eve of the Reformation. No distinction is drawn between suppressed and non-suppressed houses, nor is any indication given as to the houses that were actually functioning at the time of compilation. The impression given is that the authorities of the Order hoped for the retrieval of the medieval foundations, even after the religious policy of Mary Tudor had demonstrated that there could be no return to the pre-suppression state of affairs.

The earliest Elizabethan government-sponsored surveys of monastic and other religious houses in Thomond and Connacht provide a hint as to the *status actualis* of the Dominican houses in Connacht. The first extant survey was that carried out in April 1569 by Michael Fitzwilliam, 'treasurer of all the queen's majesty's inheritance in Ireland'.[3] Of the

2 Ronan, *The Reformation in Ireland*, 500.

3 This survey by inquisition of the possessions and rights of most of the religious houses of Counties Clare, Galway, Roscommon and Mayo survives in two

fourteen friaries surveyed, only two were Dominican: Roscommon and Galway. Both houses, designated 'the late freerhowse', had already been suppressed. The latter had passed into the hands of the mayor, bailiffs and burgesses of the city of Galway. The next survey, carried out *c.* 1574,[4] continues to show the pattern of further suppressions, undoubtedly with a view to future expropriation and implementation of political strategy. The Dominican entries are as follows.

Co. Galway	Portumna and Kilcorban: possessed by the Earl of Clanrickard. Athenry: held by the commons of the town. St Mary's by west Galway: held by the town.
Co. Mayo	Abbeys and religious houses 'possessed either by friars or rebels, so as her Majesty hath no commodity by the same'. Dominican houses listed: Burrishoole, Strade and Urlar.
Co. Sligo	Sligo: occupied by the friars. Mohill:[5] Black Abbey occupied by Dominicans (?).
Co. Roscommon	Tulsk: by the baron of Devlin (*recte* Delvin), but now occupied by friars. Roscommon: by Mr Strange. Lands also pertaining to it. Lysonvhy: a cell of Roscommon, held by friars. No lands.

From this report several Dominican houses were omitted: Toombeola (Co. Galway), Rathfran (Co. Mayo), Ballindoon and Clooneymeaghan (Co. Sligo) and Cloonshanville (Co. Roscommon), largely small, isolated and poor houses which had been overlooked or unsurveyed.

Far more comprehensive and informative was the survey entitled 'A Rentall of Mounster and Connaugh', made by Lancelot Alforde, surveyor general of Ireland, and dated 4 February 1576 (o.s.).[6] This systematic

defective versions: the more reliable and comprehensive one in the State Papers (PRO, SP 63/29/87, ff 189v–199rv), and the other extremely abbreviated version in TCD, MS 656, ff 165v–167r, which lists no Dominican houses. The State Papers version does not include Strade, Co. Mayo, and Tulsk, Co. Roscommon.

4 *Cal. Carew MSS, 1515–74*, 473–5.

5 The medieval foundation of Mohill belonged to the Canons Regular of St Augustine until its dissolution. Its link in this survey with the Dominicans was not necessarily a mistake on the part of the surveyors; it may possibly be evidence of dislocation. Leitrim was then still considered part of Sligo territory, and this abandoned house may have become a cell or house of refuge for Sligo Dominicans.

6 K. W. Nicholls, 'A List of the Monasteries in Connacht, 1577' in *Galway Arch. Soc. Jn.*, 33 (1972–3), 28–43.

survey reveals that a large number of Connacht friaries were still in the free possession of the friars; it also furnishes property valuations and, most valuable of all, the names of many friars.

The friars preachers of Ahinrie [Athenry]	In the tenure of William McKennye and other friars.	p.a. 40s
The friary of Boreswell [Burrishoole]	In the tenure of William O'Molane and other friars.	p.a. 20s
The friary of Urlare	In the tenure of Teig Og O'Mara.	p.a. 20s
The friary of Clonshanballie otherwise named Clonshanwell [Cloonshanville]	Bryan McDermode of the Carick in the Countie of Roscoman enjoyeth the same by what title I know not.	p.a. 6s 8d
The monastery of Rossecomyne [Roscommon]	In the tenure of Sir Dermode O'Connor, priest.[7]	p.a. £20
The frierie of Portomna [Portumna]	In the Earl of Clanricarde's hands.	p.a. 20s
The chapel of Kilcorbaine [Kilcorban]	Waste and yet valued at	p.a. 10s
The friary of Sligaghe [Sligo]	In the occupation of Dermod O'Bolane and other friars and valued at	p.a. 6s 8d

This survey made no mention of Galway, Strade, Rathfran, Ballindoon, Tulsk, Clooneymeaghan and Toombeola. The explanation, in some instances, was that dissolution or secularisation had already occurred. What is worthy of note is that the friars in many cases succeeded in obtaining leases of their former houses and possessions from friendly lords and gentry.

ELIZABETHAN SUPPRESSIONS, 1570–1590S

So far the suppression of the Irish religious houses in the reign of Elizabeth has not been the subject of systematic study or investigation. From the very start of her rule government antipathy manifested itself towards the institution of religious life as such. Prejudice and deep suspicions were compounded by the consistent refusal of the Irish religious, particularly the friars, to accept the Oath of Supremacy, the Anglican state church, its vernacular liturgy and anti-papal parliamentary measures.

7 Ibid., 33, note 41, identifies this Dominican priest as a member of the house of O'Connor Roe, vicar of Temple-enan and prior of the Roscommon Dominicans, whose death was recorded in 1590 (*Annals of Loch Cé*, ii, 510–11).

In the long-term interests of a conciliatory policy, Elizabeth appears to have exerted influence on the side of leniency in respect of anti-Catholic legislation, dissuading vigorous application of the laws in the earlier years of her reign. Before 1570 the queen was content to overlook 'the wilful obstinate separation' of the Irish from the state church in order to lessen civil resistance and the spirit of rebellion.[8] However, the publication of the bull *Regnans in excelsis* (25 February 1570) by Pius V proved to be a watershed in religious diplomacy and government policy, in Ireland no less than in England. This disastrous document went much further than simply declaring her to be heretical and excommunicated. Elizabeth was declared to be deprived of her royal title and throne and the loyalty of her subjects. All were to be forever absolved from their oaths of allegiance and expressly commanded not to obey her as their ruler. Such dire provisions, though inapplicable, had repercussions in the political thinking of the Gaelic lords, the Irish people generally, and on relations with England. Moreover, the highly successful policy of Philip II of Spain in the early 1580s transformed these years into a period of deep crisis on account of the growing fear of Spanish invasion of Ireland and England. The ideological struggle between Catholics and Protestants was intensified by the simple equation wherein Protestants were considered loyal to the queen and government, while Catholics were suspected of disloyalty because of their continuing religious allegiance to Rome.

Hardened attitudes were reflected in Ireland not by attempts to strengthen and buttress a largely phantom state church, but by intimidation and persecution of the Catholic leadership: bishops, seminary priests, Jesuits, friars and their lay protectors. The willing involvement of Irish friars in political communications between Irish lords and Spain, France and the papacy was well noted and became a thorn in the side of the Dublin administration. As is shown by the extant State Papers, long before 1570 the friars collectively were viewed as emissaries of papal propaganda, challengers of state church arrangements, and increasingly as political agents of Spain. In short, the friars, some of whom were truly cosmopolitan in outlook and temperament, became identified as dangerous undesirables. They were thus categorised on account of their unwavering allegiance to the external jurisdiction of Rome.

Another issue was the influential status of the friars among the Gaelic lords of Ulster and Connacht, which was judged to be of no little importance. This position, however, was undermined when the interlocking socio-politico-religious structures of Gaelic Ireland were undone by means of the deliberate and persistently prosecuted policy of the English government. When the cherry of monastic and religious property holdings

8 G.A. Hayes-McCoy, 'The Completion of the Tudor Conquest and the Advance of the Counter-Reformation, 1571–1603' in *NHI*, iii, 113.

was finally tasted by the smaller no less than the greater political leaders, the friars suddenly found themselves without their traditional local support.

The suppression and reassignment of the remaining Dominican houses in Ulster, Munster and Connacht took place gradually but inexorably, often concomitantly with military campaigns. This was especially true of Ulster and Munster. In 1571 Queen Elizabeth granted the Dominican house of Newtownards, with other religious houses, to Sir Thomas Smith and his natural son Thomas. In the following year Brian MacPhelim O'Neill of Clandeboye invaded the Ards peninsula and burnt down these buildings in order to prevent them from being used by English expeditionary forces as forts against the Irish.[9] The Dominican house of Derry, situated in the O'Donnell territory, had escaped the Henrician wave of suppressions. The community continued in occupation until 1566 or later, when an English garrison was placed near the city, remaining in the area for several years.[10] According to an Ulster tradition, first recorded in 1622 and later in 1706 by Michael MacQuillan, O.P., of Coleraine, the Derry Dominicans were slain together at some unspecified time during Elizabeth's reign.[11] About the year 1600 a few Dominicans had returned to Derry, John Ó Luinín being their prior. He was given 'a quarter of land' to live on when Sir Henry Docwra and his expeditionary force came to Derry. Imprisoned for celebrating Mass, he was set free by Sir Arthur Chichester, who had hopes of his conformity to Anglicanism.[12] He was executed in 1607, together with his brother William, also a Dominican, while in 1608 another Derry friar, John O'Mannin, was crippled for life by torture.[13] The commissioners who held an inquisition in Derry in 1609 found that the ruins of the priory of the begging friars of St Francis (*recte* St Dominic) had a churchyard of three acres 'on the north side of the bog near the city of Derry'.[14] Again according to Michael MacQuillan, O.P., the whole community of Coleraine, 'the Abbey of the Bann', was

9 Gwynn and Hadcock, *Medieval Religious Houses: Ireland*, 228; G. Morton, *Elizabethan Ireland*, London 1971, 36.

10 Bagwell, *Tudors*, ii, 109.

11 See *Brevis Relatio de Statu Provinciae Sanctae Crucis Hyberniae* (Appendix 5, p. 323 below). In 1706 Michael MacQuillan, an Irish member of the Dominican province of Paris and then subprior of Rouen, compiled *Catalogus Conventuum quos olim habuerunt Fratres Praedicatores in provincia Ultoniae*. In this historical work he unambiguously asserted the martyrdom of the entire communities of Derry and Coleraine in the Elizabethan era. AGOP, IV E, 655–8. See H. Fenning, 'The Irish Dominican Province under Appointed Superiors' in *AFP*, 38 (1968), 291.

12 *Cal. S.P. Ire., 1606–8*, 126; Coleman, *Ancient Dominican Foundations*, 8.

13 P. O'Sullivan Beare, *Historiae Iberniae Catholicae Compendium* (Lisbon 1621), Dublin 1903, 78, testified to the martyrdom of John Ó Luinín. Coleman, *Ancient Dominican Foundations*, 8. For John O'Mannin see general chapter acts of 1656 in Reichert, *MOPH*, xii, 475–6.

14 Coleman, *Ancient Dominican Foundations*, 6 cites Ordnance Survey of Derry, 26.

martyred under Elizabeth, but the exact details of the event have not been preserved.[15] Miscellaneous materials collected by Sir James Ware also asserted the mysterious demise of the reassembled Dominicans of Coleraine, which according to his sources took place in 1559.[16] A much more likely date, however, for the final disappearance of the Coleraine Dominicans would be sometime after 1593, as a community was still in existence there in August of that year.[17] Not surprisingly, the Irish State Papers and other hostile contemporary English sources are silent about such alleged executions at a time when the excesses of martial law prevailed in Ireland. David Kearney, Archbishop of Cashel (1603–24), writing to Cardinal Barberini in Rome a short time after these events, stated that troops of horse and foot were sent in pursuit of priests, with power to hang them from the nearest tree without formality of trial.[18] In conclusion, though an arguable fundament exists, a definitive judgement cannot yet be made concerning the reported mass martyrdom of the Dominicans of Derry and Coleraine in Elizabethan times.

A memorandum of the queen's revenue in Ireland (30 September 1578) noted that thirty-four abbeys and religious houses, with good lands attached to them, had come to light and had not been surveyed before 1569. Altogether seventy-two houses had been concealed from the queen's officials.[19] It may safely be presumed that these religious houses were in Connacht and Ulster, in remote or sparsely populated areas. The memorandum clearly implied that there was a deliberate policy to conceal the existence of religious houses by friendly local lords and gentry and that unsuppressed religious houses were unashamedly viewed as a potential source of income for the royal coffers. In summary, by the end of the century, the tempo of suppressions and expulsions of religious in Connacht and Ulster reached a climax in the wake of consolidation of English influence in these provinces.

In Munster the collapse of organised Dominican conventual life coincided with the destruction of the Desmond lordship. When Tralee was occupied by English forces in 1580, the Lord Justice, Sir William Pelham, wrote to the lords and council in England: 'All the country between the earl's house and Tralee was burnt by the rebels, and all the houses in Tralee burnt and the castles razed, saving the [Dominican] abbey . . . a very convenient place for a garrison.'[20] A comprehensive

15 Fenning, 'The Irish Dominican Province under Appointed Superiors', 291.

16 TCD, MS 579: *Collectanea de Rebus Monasticis Hiberniae et Registris Domuum Religiosarum*.

17 Fenning, *Irish material*, 334.

18 Coleman, *Ancient Dominican Foundations*, 8.

19 *Cal. Carew MSS, 1575–88*, 137.

20 Ibid., 235.

survey of the Desmond estates was carried out in 1586,[21] with a view to expropriation and plantation. This survey contains the extent of 'the late House of Friars of the Order of St Dominic, *alias* White Friars, within the Borough of Tralee, in the said County of Kerry', which supplies valuable particulars of the material resources of this well-endowed foundation.

The house was situated on the estuary of the River Lee, near the port of Tralee in a plain of fertile land. The river, navigable at spring tide, enabled boats of five tons' capacity to come to the walls of the house. John FitzThomas FitzGerald, the original patron and several of the Earls of Desmond, including Thomas FitzGerald, founder of the houses of Kildare and Desmond, were buried in the adjoining church, but all these buildings were then ruinous and in decay. The precinct of the house, enclosed by a stone wall and covering five acres[22] valued at £2 13s 4d, must have been the largest of any Dominican house in Ireland.

Outside the precinct lay several parcels of land, gardens and tenements, the latter for the most part thrown down, yet worth 8s annually. The community owned thirteen excellent acres of meadow and pasture land on the west side of Tralee at Ballyvoylan, *alias* Ballylevalaen, valuation 32s 6d; fishing rights in a river running through its lands which were part of the demesne lands of the manor of Tralee, and worth 20d per annum; a corn mill, then in ruins, valued at 6s 8d. A house in disrepair with two acres of land in the eastern part of the parish of Dingle, *alias* Dingleiushe, valued at 2s 6d, also belonged to the friars.

The survey also enumerated the towns, villages and lands over a large geographical area which yielded tithes,[23] consisting of the twentieth part of corn. These non-parochial tithes, 'renewing annually, to the late Earl of Desmond', were collected at Easter and Michaelmas. The above technical phrase may indicate previous attempts at crown expropriation and how the Earls of Desmond devised a legal formula to safeguard the rights of the Tralee Dominicans. The annual income from tithes and property alone amounted to £15 4s 8d. By May 1587 the Tralee

21 The Latin originals of the Desmond Survey Papers perished in the destruction of the Public Record Office of Ireland in 1922. S. M. Hussey (ed.), *The Desmond Survey of County Kerry*, Tralee 1923 (privately printed); reprinted in *The Kerryman*, Aug.–Oct. 1927, and available on microfilm in NLI; copies of English version also in Tralee and Limerick city libraries.

22 The church, house, cloisters and churchyard were sited on grounds later known as Abbey Street and Mary Street, and closes and gardens occupied much of the present area of Staughton Row, Godfrey Place, Ivy Terrace and the Square of Tralee.

23 The town of Tralee (£1 16s); the town of Island (£1 4s); the town called Coggrekerry (£1 16s); the countess's lands in or near Tralee (1s); the town of Tullough (12s); the New Manor (12s); the town of Barrow (6s); the town of Ballyhe, parish of Dingle (4s); the town of Kilballylahiff near Glanegalt (2s); the Park of Dingle (3s); the town of Monenery, parish of Dingle (8s).

Dominicans had been dispersed and their conventual buildings passed, with a large grant of lands, to Sir Francis Walsingham, Edward Denny and their associates.[24]

In common with Tralee, Youghal had been saved from dissolution by the influence of its Geraldine protectors. On 15 November 1579 Youghal was sacked and occupied by the Earl of Desmond himself. By 1581 the town was recaptured by English soldiers under Ormond. In that year the Dominican house with six gardens (tithes excepted) were granted forever to William Walshe *in capite*, the rent being 22d. Perhaps this grantee belonged to the same family as the William Walshe who was responsible for the rent of the house in 1548 when the Earl of Desmond's brother acted as custodian of the Dominican property. If the Dominicans were still in occupation in 1581, they were probably driven out of Youghal at the same time as the Franciscans in 1583, when the Geraldines finally forfeited the town. The Dominican property was granted to a soldier in 1584 and to Sir Walter Raleigh in 1587, at which time the buildings of the 'North Abbey' were destroyed.[25]

The fact that the presidency of Connacht was first held, and held for so long, by the same determined person, Sir Edward Fitton (December 1569 – September 1575), facilitated continuity of policy and widening control of southern Connacht and Thomond. Fitton on his first tour of Counties Galway and Roscommon had by 1570 succeeded in antagonising and estranging the lords, people, secular clergy and regulars by his depredations in places of worship and his militant opposition to Catholic devotional practices. He went to work with more zeal than discretion in seeking to introduce the reformed Anglican church services, burning 'idols' and driving the friars into hiding. According to his own account, he visited 'sundry and many of the idols and images in their churches and committed them to the fire, and expulsed and discharged sundry of the friars of Athenry [Dominicans] and Kylconnel [Franciscans]'.[26]

This type of policy characterised Fitton's early rule of Connacht, and had he not desisted, it would have galvanised the opposition of the province against him. Later Sir Nicholas Malby subdued southern and other districts of Connacht by 1578, by burning houses and corn and by executing all who opposed him. His policy amounted to legalised use of violence to combat 'Irish lawlessness'. In the words of the annalists (1584), he 'placed all Connacht under bondage'.[27] Malby's successor, the notorious Sir Richard Bingham, employed even more drastic and

24 *Cal. Carew MSS, 1575–88*, 450–51.
25 Gwynn and Hadcock, *Medieval Religious Houses: Ireland*, 231–2.
26 N. P. Canny, *The Elizabethan Conquest of Ireland*, Hassocks, Sussex 1976, 109, 111.
27 *Annals of Loch Cé*, ii, 459.

questionable methods in coming to terms with Gaelic Connacht. He encouraged the seizure of property, thus making more lands available for settlement, and above all sought to enforce and justify the abridgement of due legal processes in the province.[28] Such was the extremely disturbed scenario of the late Elizabethan wave of suppressions of the religious houses of Connacht as a renewed policy of conquest by force of arms was implemented. Dominican houses hitherto intact were caught up in the general destruction.

The minor house of Toombeola (parish of Moyrus in the heart of Connemara), dedicated to St Patrick, was taken early in Elizabeth's reign (*c.* 1570) by Protestants who used its stones and rubble to build a castle nearby.[29]

Roscommon was surveyed in 1569, at which time it would seem, from the use of the words 'the late house', to have been dissolved. The site contained a church, a cloister, a dortery (dormitory), a hall, two chambers covered with shingles, a churchyard, an outhouse, three cottages, seventeen acres of pasture, and eleven acres of arable land. Moreover, the house owned a parcel of land named Ardenenagh consisting of twelve acres of arable land, and a house for the poor named St Bride's Garden, *alias* Garry Bride, which had two acres of pasture. Among the spiritualities of Roscommon were the tithes of its lands and the rectories and chapels of Drometample and Cloncorinsland in the MacDavis country.[30] The site of the house was leased in 1573 to Thomas le Strange, and on 1 November 1577 to Sir Nicholas Malby, with one quarter of land and its tithes in Roscommon and other landholdings.[31]

Athenry, with thirty acres in the vicinity of the town and twelve acres in Ballidana, was granted to the commonalty of the town in 1574. In the same year Athenry and its priory were sacked by Clanrickard's sons. Afterwards the Dominicans reoccupied the conventual buildings, which were spared when Red Hugh O'Donnell took Athenry in 1595.

According to one source, the Dominicans of Athenry possessed 1,500 acres of land and abundant tithes. Their property included a good mill and several houses in the town of Athenry; land at Killokelly; a chapel built on land north of the river called Carrowardahrah in Toulabane; the district of Glaimhe an Blain, which had formerly belonged to the Benedictines; land to the south called Friars' Wood, and to the north land called David's Village (Baile Dhaibhidh), where the friars had a chapel; a farm called Beann Dheara, a mile to the north-east; another farm with a chapel called Coill Craobhanta; the chapel of Kilcorban

28 Canny, *The Elizabethan Conquest of Ireland*, 158.
29 Gwynn and Hadcock, *Medieval Religious Houses: Ireland*, 230.
30 PRO, SP 63/29/87, f. 193r.
31 Gwynn and Hadcock, *Medieval Religious Houses: Ireland*, 229.

(situated in the parish of Tynagh on the River Kilcrow, over twenty miles from Athenry), with a good farm belonged to the Athenry Dominicans, according to Ware; and there was a large fertile district, with a farm and a chapel, known as *Rathghalaig tuadh lubain an Teampaill.* The town and Dominican convent suffered severely in the wars at the end of the sixteenth century. The whole town was burnt in 1597.[32]

The Dominicans of Galway remained in undisturbed possession of their church and convent in the reigns of Henry VIII, Edward VI and Mary Tudor. About 1569 the houses and churches of the Dominicans, Franciscans and Augustinians were dissolved and passed officially to the Mayor and Corporation of Galway. According to Michael Fitzwilliam's survey, the Dominicans had a garden of eleven acres adjacent to their house, and in the fields near the town eleven acres of arable land called 'Quarter Jordane', with its tithes. The Dominicans had the right to take one salmon every Friday from 'Ryse's place near the bridge of Galway'.[33] Nicholas Blake, burgess of Galway, made his will on 28 September 1568 and seemingly foresaw the possibility of the expulsion of the Dominicans and other friars from Galway city, for he made special provision for the return of bequests made to the friars:

> The testator bequeathed 3s 4d yearly for ever to the friars of Our Lady's Hill, by the west of Galway [Dominicans] . . . and directed that his anniversary should be held in the said abbeys as long as the friars were there . . . and in case that the friars should be put out of the abbeys about Galway, then that the legacies made to them should return to the heirs of the testator, to be divided by them amongst such of the poorest and neediest persons.[34]

The three mendicant houses of Galway were regranted to the mayor and corporation in 1578.[35]

32 Ibid., 222. Athenry was reputedly the wealthiest of Irish Dominican houses. O'Heyne in *Epil. Chron.*, 168–9 stated that it once held 1,500 acres of land. He claimed that he found it so recorded in original deeds preserved in Athenry in his time. However, the extant register of the Athenry Dominicans (BL, Add. MS 4784; edited by A. Coleman, 'Regestum Monasterii Fratrum Praedicatorum de Athenry' in *Archiv. Hib.*, l (1912), 201–21) gives in great detail particulars of benefactions and land donations received by the Athenry community from its foundation in 1221 to 1565. It is extremely difficult to reconcile information from this source concerning land acreage with O'Heyne's assertion. Gwynn and Hadcock accept uncritically O'Heyne's account. It would appear that the maximum figure representing its landed possessions might stand at about five hundred acres, no reliable estimate being yet available. See Coleman, *Ancient Dominican Foundations*, 79–86 *passim.*

33 PRO, SP 63/29/87, f. 197v.

34 M. J. Blake (ed.), *Blake Family Records, 1300–1600,* London 1902, 113.

35 Gwynn and Hadcock, *Medieval Religious Houses: Ireland*, 225.

Cloonshanville was leased to Hugh Boy O'Donnell in 1577, its lands to the Mayor of Galway in 1578, and the priory and appurtenances to Bryan MacDermot in 1580. Cloonshanville was leased to William Taaffe of Sligo in 1596, and its lands to William Brouncker in 1608.[36]

Portumna, located at the head of Lough Derg on the Shannon, was appropriated by the Earls of Clanrickard by 1577,[37] and ever afterwards remained a family possession. No details are available as to what land or property it once held, but they were presumably incorporated into the Clanrickard estates.

Rathfran, sited on the long inlet of Killala Bay had at the moment of its dissolution two quarters of land valued at 26s 8d which were leased to Thomas Dexter. There was also a small house adjoining the site and a mill in ruins. With the Franciscan friaries of Moyne and Rosserk, Rathfran was burned by Sir Richard Bingham's army in 1590. The conventual buildings were granted to William Taaffe in 1596.[38]

Strade was leased to James Garvey in 1578 for twenty-one years, to Patrick Barnewall in 1588 for forty years, and some of its land was granted to Edmond Barrett in 1595. The precise land acreage was not disclosed.[39]

During the Desmond war Sir Nicholas Malby ravaged the neighbourhood of Burrishoole in 1580. It may have been then that Honoria Burke, a young tertiary sister (martyred in 1653) who lived with other sisters in a house near the Dominican convent, hid in the vaults of the church for about a week without food. The Dominican house and church, which commanded a majestic view of Croagh Patrick from the shores of Clew Bay, were granted later to Nicholas Weston and assigned to Theobald, Viscount Costello of Gallen. In 1606 the property passed to John King of Dublin. An inquisition of 1615 found that half a quarter of land in Rosnabracher belonged to the Dominicans of Burrishoole. In another Jacobean inquisition it was found that the royalty (equivalent to feudal rights exercised by the lord of a manor) of the Burrishoole river where it becomes tidal just west of Newport was owned by Burrishoole abbey. This fishery, besides serving community needs, must have been an extremely valuable economic asset in such an isolated place.[40]

Ballindoon, situated on a limestone cliff overlooking Lough Arrow, was dissolved about 1585, when its prior was found to be in possession of a church, cemetery and half a quarter of land, valued at 6s 8d. After the death of Melaghlin Oge MacDonagh in 1588 the lands of Ballindoon

36 Ibid., 223.

37 Nicholls, 'A List of the Monasteries in Connacht, 1577', 36; Gwynn and Hadcock, *Medieval Religious Houses: Ireland*, 228.

38 Gwynn and Hadcock, *Medieval Religious Houses: Ireland*, 228.

39 Ibid., 230.

40 Ibid., 222; A. E. J. Went, 'Irish Monastic Fisheries' in *Cork Hist. Soc. Jn.*, 63 (1955), 50.

priory were granted to his wife. Ballindoon, with its land and tithes, was leased again in 1591.[41]

An inquisition of the possessions of Clooneymeaghan in 1585 disclosed a quarter of land of every kind, called Ronyroge, with tithes, which was found to be worth 13s 4d per annum. This land had been concealed from the surveyors for a long time 'owing to the wars and incivility of those parts'. On 12 March 1588 the house and site were first granted to Richard Kindlemarsh, later to the Taaffes, and later still to the Earl of Shelbourne, except for two acres in and around the ruins, which belonged to the Dodwell family.[42] This remote house was in the ecclesiastical parish of Cloonoghill, Co. Sligo.

An inquisition of 1591 found that two quarters of land which had formerly belonged to the Dominican house of Tulsk, valued at 8s, were held or occupied by the mayor and bailiffs of Galway, who had concealed this fact from the queen. This land was given to Terence O'Byrne in 1594, and the house was included in the grant of Inchmacnerin to William Taaffe in 1596. The house was repaired by Bingham in 1595, and thirty-four acres, both arable and bog, belonging to the priory were granted to William Brouncker in 1608.[43]

An inquisition taken at Sligo in 1584–5 found that the Dominican abbey contained a church with a steeple, cemetery, and two other stone buildings of no value; properties belonging to the abbey comprised a quarter of land of every kind, with its tithes when under tillage, called the 'Fynut' quarter, and a fishing weir besides reprises, all valued at 16s 8d. The house and property were held by certain priests who had formerly been friars there. It seems that the Dominicans were left in quiet possession of their abbey until the coming of George Bingham, brother of the President of Connacht, in 1595. He took up his quarters in the abbey when he was besieging O'Donnell's forces in a nearby castle, and ordered an 'engine' to be constructed for demolishing it. This he did by using the rood-screen of the church, the dormitory, and other materials found in the abbey. The Dominicans were finally driven out by these events, but remained in the vicinity of Sligo. The abbey was granted to William Taaffe by James I.[44]

A cursory examination of the Irish State Papers of the period reveals that the Elizabethan destruction of religious houses was motivated by a mixture of political and anti-Catholic considerations. The struggling houses of Ulster (Derry and Coleraine) and Munster (Youghal, Limerick, Kilmallock and Glanworth) all received a *coup de grace*, while the Order's

41 Gwynn and Hadcock, *Medieval Religious Houses: Ireland*, 222.
42 Ibid., 223.
43 Ibid., 230–31.
44 Ibid., 229–30; Coleman, *Ancient Dominican Foundations*, 98–9.

houses in Connacht, hitherto the backbone of the province, were eliminated one by one. In the space of thirty years the vital infrastructure of Dominican conventual life was mercilessly wiped out. The sole exception to this pattern of desolation was Urlar (Co. Mayo). Though mentioned in the survey of 1574 and actually surveyed in 1576, it escaped destruction because of its isolation and survived as a place of refuge until 1608.[45]

Unrelenting persecution and the disappearance of normal Dominican life very seriously curtailed the acceptance of fresh vocations and inexorably led to the breakdown of whatever faltering attempt at formation was offered locally by the Connacht Dominicans. The utterly changed and inimical circumstances did not, however, prevent the reception of young men into the Order, though they did impel the declining Dominicans to adopt a drastic strategy for their future survival. Accordingly it became accepted policy to send young men abroad for their training and education, to the flourishing continental convents of Spain, Portugal, Italy, France and the Low Countries. What was at first perceived as a great risk would later be acknowledged as a divine blessing when the first-fruits of the changed strategy would make themselves felt in Ireland in the opening decades of the seventeenth century.

DOMINICAN PROPERTY AND ECONOMY IN CONNACHT

Even less information is forthcoming about the dissolutions in the post-1579 period than that which emerged from the Henrician series of suppressions. Elizabethan extents or inquisitions, often incomplete, are available for some twelve of nineteen Dominican houses in Connacht, with no returns for the remaining houses, of which at least Portumna and Strade were prosperous. This unsatisfactory situation rules out a systematic economic analysis and review of the material goods and landholdings of the Connacht houses such as was possible with the Leinster and Munster foundations dissolved by Henry VIII. Except in the survey of 1576, the names of individual Dominicans are not given. Nor is there any indication as to the number of friars in each house. The larger communities such as Athenry, Sligo and Roscommon might have had ten to twelve members, while some of the minor houses such as Ballindoon, Cloonshanville and Tulsk might have numbered four to six brethren. Medium-sized foundations such as Portumna, Galway, Strade and Burrishoole probably had six to nine members.

With one notable exception, Athenry, Dominican landholdings in Connacht were quite modest. There is no doubt that Athenry was the wealthiest of the Irish houses.[46] It was the oldest and most prestigious

45 Gwynn and Hadcock, *Medieval Religious Houses: Ireland*, 231.
46 See note 32 above.

house west of the Shannon in medieval times, and had enjoyed the patronage of the Gaelic and Anglo-Irish noble families for more than three hundred years. By the sixteenth century, however, its influence had waned and it had been overtaken by Sligo as a religious centre, while its status in Connacht had been eclipsed by the growing mercantile importance of the town. Roscommon and Sligo enjoyed the patronage of the related branches of the O'Connor families, and the latter was also actively supported by the Sligo merchant and middle class. As for the minor houses, they relied for the most part on the support of the local patrons or the descendants of the founding families, together with questing rights and occasional testamentary bequests.

An interesting feature in the economic life of several houses was the possession or right to tithes.[47] These are mentioned explicitly in the inquisitions of Athenry, Roscommon, Sligo, Rathfran, Tulsk, Clooneymeaghan, Galway and Urlar. A custom, peculiar to Ireland, was the setting aside by a benefactor of a fixed portion of corn or some other crop grown on his land to be given to friars during the annual autumn quest for alms. This type of grant was improperly referred to as a 'tithe'. Many examples of such 'tithes' are recorded in the register of Athenry. These 'tithes' should not be confused with the standard parochial tithes. It is not always possible to decide on the nature of Dominican tithes. With the gradual collapse of the medieval parochial system and the consequent state of confusion into which the church in Ireland was plunged in the second half of the sixteenth century, Dominican houses administered, wholly or in part, some of the parishes in their neighbourhood, as already exemplified in Strade, Urlar and Clooneymeaghan, and were therefore entitled to draw the parochial revenues. Perhaps more common was the situation of customary donated 'tithes', as in Athenry, Roscommon and Sligo. Such 'tithes' were intended as an inbuilt form of stable economic support for a particular house and altogether distinct from parochial 'tithes', which sometimes were in the gift of founders. Longstanding possession of tithes helps to explain concern about conservation of their ownership by communities in the west of Ireland in the wake of Trent, as may be seen, for example, in the papal bull obtained by the Dominicans in 1567.

In Sligo the tithes had to do with land cultivation, more precisely when certain land was under tillage, perhaps for barley and other grain crops. Sligo, Galway and Burrishoole had rights on fishing weirs and rivers, and most other houses had fishing rights of some sort.[48] In the

47 B. O'Sullivan, 'Medieval Irish Dominican Studies' in *Irish Rosary* (Jan.–Feb. 1952), 46–7.

48 Went, 'Irish Monastic Fisheries', 47–56 *passim* provides key references to Dominican weir and fishery possessions at Athy, Burrishoole, Coleraine, Cork, Galway, Kilkenny, Rosbercon, Sligo and Tralee.

inquisitions the term 'quarter of land' frequently occurs. In Connacht it signified a fairly large territorial division, often of mixed quality and indeterminate acreage. It was roughly equivalent to the Norman or English 'cantred'. Sligo's holding of one quarter of land seems particularly low, for such relatively obscure foundations as Clooneymeaghan possessed as much, and others, for example Rathfran and Tulsk, held two quarters of land. However, it is not improbable that Sligo, witnessing the wholesale confiscation of the lands of its sister houses, disposed of most of its holdings long before the day of inquisition. Additional details of land held by some houses emerged in the early Jacobean era. What is perfectly clear, from a necessarily incomplete overall picture, is that all Connacht houses held some land, to a greater or lesser extent, and that land was of far greater significance as a means of establishing independent economic existence in the west of Ireland than it was for Dominican houses in the towns of the provinces of Leinster and Munster.

SURVIVORS: THADDEUS MacDUANE AND OTHERS, 1577–1602

It is extremely difficult to sustain a historical narrative about the Irish Dominican experience during several long 'valley periods' of Elizabeth's reign. However, once more a key figure, another Dominican of great moral stature, towering above the growing desolation of the province, emerged in the person of Thaddeus MacDuane.[49] His Dominican career antedated Elizabeth's accession, spanned her entire reign, and extended into the early years of James I. He twice visited Rome on behalf of his Order, and was thus one of the small number of distinguished sixteenth-century Dominicans (including his predecessors David Brown, Quentin Cogly, Quentin O'Higgins, Eugene O'Hart, William MacAneaney and Cormac O'Fergus) to have undertaken the arduous journey.

The acts of the general chapter held at Rome in 1656,[50] almost fifty years after his death, provide the only early account of MacDuane's life. In the pages of the acts he is portrayed as a patriarchal figure whose life's work linked the sharply contrasting medieval and early modern worlds. This brief account of his life did not have its origins in a documentary source, but was rather the product of the well-founded if scattered oral tradition of his province. He is described as a person of outstanding zeal

49 Variously Dubhnaeus, Mhaca Dubganayus, Macaduanay, Duanus in contemporary documents, all deriving from the Irish form Ó Dubháin, a Connacht name. Ó Dubháin should not be confused with the Donegal name Ó Duibheannaigh, anglicised O'Devany, O'Devenney, Devaney or Devany, a renowned Ulster clerical name. Woulfe, *Sloinnte Gaedhael is Gall*, 509, 515.

50 Reichert, *MOPH*, xii, 474–5.

for the Church and for the Order; one who served his province twice as provincial, who received many young men into the Order in the most perilous times lest the Dominican tradition should die out. There follows a recital of a number of alleged edifying incidents from his life, extolling his holiness and virtues.

In the summer of 1577, as prior of Sligo, MacDuane showed himself to be a man of initiative and energy in Rome when he submitted three petitions (*supplicationes, suppliche*) to the office of the Apostolic Datary on behalf of his community. Each petition is valuable because of its direct commentary on contemporary Irish Dominican affairs supplied as *obiter dicta* or contextual material in the petition's formulation.

The first petition[51] was by far the most important and informative, if somewhat illegible owing to the hurried and careless hand of the scribe. It was presented in the name and on behalf of the prior and convent of Sligo in the diocese of Elphin. In the first place the Sligo Dominicans sought confirmation of the privileges and graces granted repeatedly to the Order by several Popes. The petition explained that their status and privileges were opposed and contested by parochial rectors, vicars and other clerics, regular and secular, whose churches were dirty and not conducive to the celebration of divine services. In fact some of these buildings were unroofed and resembled filthy caves. The prior and brethren of the convent of the Blessed Virgin Mary complained of the vexations they had to endure from the laity, nobles and peasants alike. The Dominican church in Sligo had become, in effect, the cathedral church, since the Bishop of Elphin (Andrew O'Crean, O.P.) actually resided in the convent. There was no other church worthy for use as a cathedral where he could remain in peaceful possession.

MacDuane also pointed out that the Dominicans were denied their rights to the canonical stipend (*quarta funeralium*) or the offerings of candles, monetary contributions and other alms or benefactions graciously offered by the faithful on the occasion of funerals in their own church. Furthermore, the Sligo Dominicans were in dire need of resources to repair and refurnish their dormitory, cloisters, rooms, undercroft, external walls and outbuildings. There were problems too concerning the collection of tithes and income from possessions willed or granted to them by the founders and other benefactors, and guaranteed to them by the tenor of apostolic privileges and canon law. So injuriously were their rights interfered with and prejudiced that their current sources of income were scarcely adequate for the sustenance of the brethren and the upkeep and repair of the fabric already being carried out. Here once more there is accumulating evidence of the pressing problem of lay and clerical intrusion on Dominican property and rights.

51 ASV, Reg. Suppl., 3401, ff 61v–62r.

The Pope was requested, therefore, to restrain rectors and other clerics, seculars as well as regulars, also laymen, from interfering with their rights, especially with respect to ministerial stipends and the like offerings made at funerals; to threaten the imposition of ecclesiastical penalties such as excommunication, suspension, interdict, etc., and also pecuniary penalties on the disobedient and rebellious; to invoke the authority and decrees of church councils, including citation of the Council of Trent justifying their rights as mendicant friars, the decisions of Boniface VIII, and even the assistance of the secular arm and whatever else might be judged necessary to secure their lawful rights. Papal approval of the petition was gained, and its expedition in due form was referred to Cardinal Sforza. The petition was granted on 6 May 1577 by Pope Gregory XIII.

In the second petition[52] Thaddeus MacDuane, impelled by religious devotion, requested permission to take relics of certain saints from the monastery of Tre Fontane, reputedly the place of St Paul's martyrdom outside the walls of Rome, to the Dominican house of Sligo, which would be very fitting, since in those parts there were no relics of the saints whatever. He wished to transfer them to Ireland and to place them with all due reverence and honour in the Dominican church of Sligo. He asserted that this would contribute to the spiritual uplifting of the faithful, would be in harmony with their devotional spirit, and would result in spiritual graces and favours redounding to the benefit of the faithful. In this connection he sought letters and faculties whereby he would be authorised freely and licitly to install and display the holy relics. Moreover, he asked for an indulgence under the usual conditions for those who would venerate the said relics. His petition was granted on 13 May 1577.

The third petition[53] was concerned with a crucifix kept in his church at Sligo, famous for miracles as was piously believed. Whether the crucifix was a sculpture, a carving or a painting was not made clear. MacDuane stated that great devotion and honour was paid to it by the people of Sligo and the surrounding area. On both feasts of the Holy Cross the people flocked to the Dominican church, with the lively hope of obtaining the salvation of their souls and of increasing their faith. He went on to stress the importance of promoting devotion to the Holy Cross in what he termed 'these calamitous times', marked by the deep shadows and spread of so many and diverse heresies and errors. He requested a plenary indulgence to be made applicable universally and individually to benefactors and to the faithful who would visit the church on the feasts of the Finding and Exaltation of the Holy Cross. The indulgence was made conditional on the offering of prayers in the church for the Pope and his

52 Ibid., 243v.
53 Ibid., 3403, f. 198rv.

successors, for the fruitfulness and conservation of the Holy Roman Church, for the exaltation of the Catholic faith, the extirpation of heresy, the return of heretics, the conversion of infidels, for mutual peace, concord and union among Christian princes, etc. The indulgences granted were to be valid for ten years, notwithstanding the provisions of apostolic constitutions or anything else to the contrary. This grant was accorded on 13 June 1577.

Friars, including some Dominicans, were very much to the fore and conspicuous in the public eye from the early 1570s. On 27 April 1571 Sir Henry Cobham wrote to Lord Burghley, Elizabeth's chief minister, that 'The Archbishop of Cashel [Maurice MacGibbon] is a bastard of the Geraldines . . . [for whom] a Dominican friar, going to Rome, procured this bishopric of the Pope.'[54] Two undated reports in the Vatican *Nunziatura d'Inghilterra* series, despite the title of their source, have to do solely with Ireland.[55] Their compilation has often been attributed to Dermot O'Hurley, the future Archbishop of Cashel (1581–4). The first, entitled *De moribus et studiis Hibernorum maxime in comitatu Desmoniae*, is surprisingly silent concerning the Dominicans. The second, headed *Qui sunt in Hybernia*,[56] is a mine of information on diocesan seminarians studying in France, Belgium, Spain and Portugal. Four Dominicans, all from Connacht, are mentioned: Eugene O'Hart, Bishop of Achonry; William O'Kenny, a celebrated preacher; Thaddeus O'Farrell *alias* Tergallus or Fergallus, a schoolmaster; and Matthew Machuard (Mac an Bhaird), also a teacher. All four were distinguished for their preaching. It was noted that O'Farrell and Machuard could speak only in Irish. That there were no young Dominicans studying abroad at this time contrasts with the abundance of diocesan students in continental colleges.

Marmaduke Middleton, Anglican Bishop of Waterford and Lismore, sent an account of his diocese and of religious practice in Waterford to Sir Francis Walsingham on 29 June 1580. He complained that Rome-runners and friars were maintained by the people of Waterford city, and that certain houses ostensibly built as hospitals were in fact places for the entertainment of friars.[57] In 1583, as the crisis of the impending Spanish invasion deepened, an anonymous *Discourse for the Reformation of Ireland* was printed and proposed that friars, monks, nuns, Jesuits and suchlike should be executed by martial law.[58]

54 *Cal. S.P. For., 1569–71*, 435; cited in D. A. Binchy, 'An Irish Ambassador at the Spanish Court, 1569–74' in *Studies*, 10 (1921), 358.
55 J. Hagan (ed.), 'Miscellanea Vaticano-Hibernica: Ireland in 1580' in *Archiv. Hib.*, 5 (1916), 157–63.
56 Ibid., 163.
57 Ronan, *The Reformation in Ireland*, 655–6. The Franciscan house in Waterford had in fact been put to use as a hospital.
58 *Cal. Carew MSS, 1515–74*, 369.

A most unusual occurrence, contrary to the prevailing trend of the age, took place about 1580 in the territory of Breffni when the O'Reillys founded a house for Dominicans at Clonfad near Cavan. A genealogical history of the O'Reillys, written in the seventeenth century, relates that 'Friars of St Dominic were in the monastery of Cavan when Eoghan Ruadh, son of Cathal, was the Ó Raghallaigh, and it was the offspring of Seán, son of Cathal, who expelled them.'[59] The reason for the quarrel between Seán and the Dominicans, resulting in their expulsion, is unknown. In spite of this reverse, oral tradition had it that the friars returned to 'Cluain Fada on the border of the parish of Ath'. However, the Dominican presence at Clonfad was of short duration, and no attempt was ever made to revive it until 1734.[60]

Sometime between 1583 and April 1585 Thaddeus MacDuane went to Rome for a second time, to consult with the Order's authorities concerning his province. He may have been then provincial or vicar of the province, and it was perhaps during this period of authority that he presented the Dominican habit to Honoria Burke who, in the next century, was to die a martyr at Burrishoole. On 10 June 1586 special faculties were given by the Master of the Order to the Archbishop of Tuam, Miler O'Higgin, to readmit 'apostates' to the Dominican habit, even those who had apostatised from the Order several times, provided they were willing to return and amend their lives.[61]

In 1587 Richard Burke, a diocesan priest, while transacting business in the Roman curia, made a petition on behalf of the Galway Dominicans.[62] Their house, described as being situated in the diocese of Annaghdown, and dedicated to the Blessed Virgin Mary, had a much-venerated image of their patroness. Galway was formerly renowned for its full observance of the monastic life, in which a considerable number of religious were accustomed to celebrate the canonical hours and other offices with the highest degree of devotion. The Dominicans petitioned through their agent, Richard Burke, for a plenary indulgence for all who would venerate the said image on certain feasts (the Visitation, Annunciation, Purification and Nativity of the Blessed Virgin Mary), provided the faithful confessed their sins, received the Holy Eucharist, visited the church and there

59 E. Ó Raghailligh, *A Genealogical History of the O'Reillys*, ed. J. Carney, Dublin 1959, 48–9, 95.

60 H. Fenning (ed.) *The Fottrell Papers*, Belfast 1980, 76–7.

61 Fenning, *Irish material*, 275.

62 ASV, Reg. Suppl., 3638, f. 54r. The union of the diocese of Annaghdown with Tuam had been formally decreed in 1580 (*NHI*, ix, 382) but might not yet have taken full effect. A similar indulgence, applicable on the solemnities of SS Peter and Paul, St Patrick and the Exaltation of the Holy Cross, was obtained by Richard Burke representing the parish church of Athenry on the same day (20 Oct. 1587) as the Dominican concession. ASV, Reg. Suppl., 3638, ff 53v–54r.

offered prayers for the Pope, the prosperity and happiness of all faithful Catholics, for the defeat of the Church's enemies, the conversion of the infidel, etc. The indulgence was granted for twenty years under the date of 20 October 1587. In 1570 Queen Elizabeth had confirmed the grant of the Dominican convent to the corporation of Galway, and it is remarkable to find the house and church still flourishing in 1587, if in more reduced circumstances, obviously with the connivance and agreement of the Catholic corporation of the town.

On 8 April 1588 Diego Callahorrano, prior of Santo Domingo, Sanlúcar de Barrameda in Andalucía, accompanying the Spanish Armada to Britain, was given authority by the Master General over all Dominicans in countries occupied by heretics; not only England, therefore, but also Ireland and Scotland were implicitly included. As vicar general he could oblige Dominicans to return to their convents, appoint temporary superiors, re-establish houses, recover their property, and take steps to restore the pristine dignity of the Order. Callahorrano actually sailed with the Armada and survived the disastrous outcome of the expedition,[63] but he was never in a position to implement the special commission he had received.

The most illuminating document from late sixteenth-century *Hibernia Dominicana* was a letter of Thaddeus MacDuane to the Master of the Order, Hippolytus Maria Beccaria, dated 1 August 1593, from the convent of Coleraine[64]—proving that this house survived into the 1590s. The letter was conveyed to Rome by MacDuane's trusted friend and protector, James O'Healy, Archbishop of Tuam. His immediate purpose in writing to the Master General was to legalise his position as vicar of the Irish province. He had been appointed to this office by the dying provincial Eugene MacHugan[65] on account of very disturbed times and the continuing decline of the province. In more peaceful circumstances his appointment would have been deemed irregular. Some of the points he made touched on the increasing ferocity of religious persecution: the

63 Latin text in AGOP, IV, f. 103 bis rv (since repair f. 103Av); A. Quiros, *Apuntes y Documentos*, Seville 1915, 520–33 supplies a faithful Spanish translation and other biographical details. About 180 religious accompanied the fleet, including more than twenty Dominicans of the province of Andalucía. AGS, Estado, leg. 431.

64 Latin version in Fenning, *Irish material*, 333–4. Earlier defective readings of the text in D. A. Mortier, *Histoire des Maîtres Généraux de l'Ordre des Frères Prêcheurs*, vii, Paris 1914, 115; Pochin Mould, *The Irish Dominicans*, 247–9.

65 Virtually nothing is known of this provincial's term of office or family background. His surname, Mac Aodhagáin, anglicised as MacKeagan, MacEgan, McHegan, MacHugan, was that of a distinguished brehon family. It belonged originally to the district of the Uí Maine in Connacht. Besides being brehons to local chieftains, they also kept schools of law, and many of their eminent number are mentioned in the Irish annals. Woulfe, *Sloinnte Gaedhael is Gall*, 319.

Order was threatened with extinction because of deaths; so few brethren remained that they would scarcely be sufficient to ensure the viability of four priories; for many years the brethren had been unable to assemble to elect a common superior, owing to the vigilance of their persecutors backed by the authority of the English queen, the lack of a safe meeting-place, and their distance from each other. MacDuane had been unable personally or by delegate to report their miseries and deplorable plight. Having taken on responsibility for the scattered flock of the province, he had encountered many problems that had arisen in the wake of persecution: priests living outside their houses tended to evade the supervision of their superiors; those who had laid aside the religious habit, even through fear, had been automatically excommunicated under the canonical legislation of the times. For all these brethren MacDuane sought absolution from their apostasy. His own authority did not derive from free election and would soon expire. He therefore pressed for the appointment of a new provincial with authority to deal with the problems outlined. He referred to houses of reformed and unreformed brethren and requested the Master General to prohibit unreformed Dominicans from electing their own vicar. There were problems too with the bishops of the northern province, especially those of Derry and Down and Connor. These bishops, observing the dispersal of the brethren, sought to infringe on and deny the right of exemption which protected their liberty, so as to subject Dominicans and their houses to episcopal control. MacDuane asked the Master General to intercede with the Pope on their behalf in this matter.

The overall picture sketched in this letter was that of a besieged group of Dominicans faced with extinction. The impression given is that persecution had become a constant menace. Violent death could occur as the result of their accidental presence at skirmishes in their own localities between Irish lords and English soldiers, while there was always a danger of the haphazard slaughter of individuals. MacDuane's claim that religious had been persecuted and killed raises a problem in that no individual Dominican is known to have been martyred under Elizabeth. The probability is that there were Dominican martyrs, though they had no contempory chronicler to record their deaths. Far more disastrous was the heavy falling off in numbers due to death by natural causes.

MacDuane's remarks on the strength of the province deserve comment. Exactly how many Dominicans would be considered necessary for four houses? Did he have in mind the minimum number or the larger complement of brethren that Master General Beccaria would take for granted in a sixteenth-century Italian convent? The constitutional requirement of the times envisaged twelve brethren as the legal minimum for the status of a convent or priory. Hence it would seem that the minimum strength of the Irish Dominicans ranged between forty and fifty men. These men would have been scattered across the north and west of Ireland, for the most part cut off by rough roadless country from regular contact with their houses of assignation. Nonetheless, they could have been engaged in the itinerant ministry of preaching and administration of the sacraments as well as acting as chaplains to the Gaelic lords. The unfriendliness of the Bishops of Derry (Redmond O'Gallagher) and Down and Connor (Conor O'Devany) towards the Dominicans living in their respective dioceses gave Thaddeus MacDuane reason to appeal to Rome. In 1593 as in 1567 the Irish regular and diocesan clergy were quarrelling among themselves, seemingly oblivious to the destructive nature of their conflicts in the face of so many perils. The problem of relations between diocesan and regular, involving lack of mutual comprehension, would continue to rise like a spectre from practically every page of Irish church history after the sixteenth century.

The Observants, who had been a minority grouping at the time of the great dissolution of the Dominican houses in 1539–41, had by 1593 emerged as the dominant group, stronger than their unreformed or Conventual brethren. Yet the latter had remained an autonomous body with the right to elect their own vicar provincial and thus enjoyed a separate jurisdiction. MacDuane now sought to have this jurisdiction abolished and to have the unreformed placed under the jurisdiction of the provincial of a single province. Thirty years later the distinction between the Conventual and the Observant Dominicans would disappear for ever, when the Observant tradition alone prevailed.

An undated draft of a document based on MacDuane's plea for the upholding of the exemption of his Order is still extant.[66] It mentions the determined efforts of the Bishops of Derry and Down and Connor to curb Dominican rights and to bring their houses under episcopal supervision. The draft, addressed to some unnamed Roman curial official, was begun in the hand of a secretary and corrected and finished in the hand of John Vincent of Asturia, procurator general and vicar of the Order. The outcome of this letter is not known.

Master General Hippolytus Beccaria replied to Thaddeus MacDuane on 13 April 1594.[67] He reappointed him vicar of the Irish Dominicans, with the same authority given him by Eugene MacHugan, and his competence was to be that of similar vicars in line with the Order's constitutions. At a general chapter in Valencia in 1596 an ordination was approved ordering that houses or places with less than four clerical brethren were to be given up and vacated, unless in 'desolate provinces'.[68]

66 Fenning, *Irish material*, 332–3.
67 Ibid., 275.
68 Reichert, *MOPH*, x, 367.

Hence the Irish situation remained untouched by this legislation. On 28 March 1597 MacDuane was again confirmed as vicar of the Irish province.[69] This confirmation was issued at Seville and was entrusted by the Master General to Bishop Thaddeus O'Farrell of Clonfert, then resident in the city.

THADDEUS O'FARRELL, BISHOP OF CLONFERT (1587–1602): AN IRISH DIPLOMAT IN SPAIN

In November 1572 Edward White, clerk to the Earl of Clanrickard, reported to the Lord Deputy that a priest whom he named as Theg O'Farrelly had lately arrived in Galway by ship from France.[70] This was the Dominican Thaddeus O'Farrell, the same Thaddeus *alias* Tergallus or Fergallus, whose name appeared in the *Nunziatura d'Inghilterra* reports in the mid-1570s as a schoolmaster (*ludi magister*) in Connacht. On 1 May 1582 his name was entered as a priest student of theology among the '*extravagantes*' or latecomers in the matriculation lists of the University of Salamanca.[71]

Five years later (11 May 1587) Thaddeus O'Farrell obtained the Master General's consent to accept the bishopric of Clonfert.[72] At a papal consistory on 8 June 1587[73] he was formally named bishop of the see and received episcopal consecration at Rome on 30 August.[74]

Thereafter Thaddeus O'Farrell lived in Spain and spent much of his time at the Spanish royal court as spokesman and trusted counsellor on Irish Catholic and political affairs. In 1595, on the orders of Philip II, together with the king's confessor and Bishop Cornelius O'Mulrian (O'Moloney) of Killaloe, he was given the task of sending a competent person to Ireland to give encouragement to the Catholic lords O'Neill and O'Donnell, who at that time were beginning to make war against 'the English Lutherans'. Their choice fell on Bernard O'Donnell, an Irish priest who had taken his university degree, and he duly set out on his mission to the two Irish leaders.[75] On 26 December 1595 the Mayor of Waterford warned the Lord Deputy that the Bishop of Clonfert was active as the Earl of Tyrone's agent with the Spaniards.[76] And indeed,

69 Fenning, *Irish material*, 276.
70 Ronan, *The Reformation in Ireland*, 421.
71 AUS, Libros de Matriculas, 296, f. 20r.
72 Fenning, *Irish material*, 275.
73 Hagan, 'Miscellanea Vaticano-Hibernica: Ireland in 1580', 177; C. Giblin, 'Vatican Library: MSS Barberini Latini' in *Archiv. Hib.*, 18 (1955), 84, 92; Brady, *Ep. Succ.*, ii, 214.
74 ASV, Schedario Garampi 42, Vescovi 12 (Indice 486), f. 97v.
75 AGS, Estado, leg. 1799; M. Kerney Walsh, *'Destruction by Peace': Hugh O'Neill after Kinsale*, Monaghan 1986, 163.
76 *Cal. S.P. Ire., 1592–6*, 446.

O'Neill and O'Donnell in a letter (16 May 1596) to the King of Spain explicitly referred to Bishop Thaddeus O'Farrell, their representative in Spain, as one on whom they relied very much.[77] A Spanish document, also of May 1596, stated that 'All that the Bishop of Clonfert has told his Majesty concerning Irish affairs is true.'[78] A letter written from Lifford to the King of Spain at the same time referred Philip II to the Bishop of Clonfert, then resident at Burgos, for further information.[79]

In the spring of 1597 Thaddeus O'Farrell had reached Seville and was given permission to take Didacus de Savariego of the Dominican convent of Queen of the Holy Angels to Ireland as his confessor. The bishop might also bring with him Dominicans suitable for the preaching of the Gospel, with the consent of their provincials. He was commissioned to recover the property of abandoned Dominican houses and to inform the Master General about this without delay. Should he find on arrival in Ireland a provincial or vicar general, the same should be subject to him, so that the bishop might not be impeded in his service of the Master General. He was granted faculties to establish the societies of the Holy Name of God and of the Holy Rosary by himself or through Dominican agents. He was authorised also to nominate a vicar for whatever friars of the Spanish provinces he might choose to accompany him.[80] Here one glimpses the careful proximate preparations undertaken by the Bishop of Clonfert in expectation of joining the projected Spanish expeditionary force to Ireland.

While the Master General was at Lisbon in March 1598 he was made aware of requests by the faithful in Ireland for the establishment of the Confraternity of the Most Holy Rosary. Priests were given permission to start the confraternity in secret chapels where churches were no longer open or had been destroyed. Where there were churches and brethren of the Order, the confraternity might be set up by the Dominicans only and in their churches.[81]

A Roman document, circulating *c.* 1597–1600 among the cardinals deputed '*pro negotiis Hiberniae*', mentioned Thaddeus O'Farrell, Bishop

77 AGS, Estado, leg. 839. The bearer of this letter was the Spanish ensign, Alonso Cobos, who in the spring of 1596 passed through Burgos. There he met 'the Irish bishop' and the Archbishop of Burgos and delivered a letter from Philip II. The contents of the letter were discussed, and the bishops decided who should accompany Cobos on his business to Ireland. On 22 April Cobos took ship at Santander. Later he wrote a report on the outcome of his Irish mission, detailing his impressions and travels, and the Irish chieftains and ecclesiastical personalities, including the Dominican provincial, that he met in the north-west. Ibid.

78 Ibid.

79 *Cal. S.P. Spain, 1587–1603*, 619–20.

80 Fenning, *Irish material*, 276.

81 Ibid.

of Clonfert.[82] It stated that he had been consecrated a long time ago and had since remained in Spain, where he promoted the interests of Ireland. So advanced in age was he that it was thought that he might not survive much longer. The document mistakenly asserted that all the episcopal sees of Connacht were then vacant except Clonfert. At any rate, in 1601 Thaddeus O'Farrell sailed with the Spanish expedition to Ireland from Lisbon, aboard the flagship *San Andres* of Don Juan del Águila.[83] At least one other Irish Dominican, Cormac O'Kerin, accompanied the Spanish fleet from Lisbon.[84] The latter had been assigned to the *studium generale* of Bologna on 14 June 1595.[85] Having been designated an honours student in February 1596, he was conferred with the lectorate in theology degree on 7 April 1600.[86]

Bishop Thaddeus O'Farrell was captured in the aftermath of the defeat of Kinsale and died there in 1602.[87] Cormac O'Kerin weathered the disaster of Kinsale and managed to return to Spain, where he received a subsistence pension from the Spanish crown.[88] He died at the Dominican house of La Coruña in Galicia in the early 1620s.[89]

82 Pistoia, Biblioteca Fabroniana, vol. 52 (unfoliated).
83 J. J. Silke, *Kinsale*, Liverpool 1970, 106, 98. AGS, Estado, leg. 840 states that Bishop O'Farrell took an active part in discussions concerning the fleet prior to sailing, together with Oviedo, Archbishop of Dublin.
84 O'Sullivan Beare, *Selections from the Zoilomastix*, ed. O'Donnell, 26.
85 Fenning, *Irish material*, 276.
86 R. Creytens, 'Il Registro dei Maestri degli Studenti di Bologna (1576–1604)' in *AFP*, 46 (1976), 58–79.
87 B. Jennings (ed.), 'Brussels MS 3947: Donatus Moneyus, de Provincia Hiberniae S. Francisci' in *Anal. Hib.*, 6 (1934), 25; Lynch, *De Praesulibus Hib.*, ii, 314.
88 AGS, Guerra Antigua, leg. 593; ibid., Estado, leg. 225.
89 AHN, sección de libros, 15436: Acta cap. prov. Hispaniae, 1623, 18.

FOUR

Irish Dominican Revival in Seventeenth-Century Europe

THE IRISH BACKGROUND

From the late fifteenth century a steady flow of Irish Dominicans studied at English and continental universities as well as Dominican *studia generalia*. General chapters made explicit provision for Irish students to obtain places in major European centres of learning. These arrangements were disrupted, with disastrous consequences for the intellectual life of the province, by the suppression of convents in Ireland. English crown officials also hoped that the spread of the Protestant Reformation in Ireland would isolate the country from the fresh spiritual renaissance of various Catholic reform movements in Europe. Yet there is evidence that, in spite of diminishing numbers, Irish Dominicans, notably from the west of Ireland, continued to study abroad during the sixteenth and seventeenth centuries. Notable personalities such as Bishop Eugene O'Hart studied at Salamanca and Paris, John Chrysologus Burke at Rome or in Italy, and Cormac O'Kerin at Bologna. Long before the enactment of the reforming measures of the Council of Trent on priestly formation and education there was a well-founded tradition of Irishmen, diocesan and religious, studying in European universities and colleges.[1] The late sixteenth-century flow of Dominican students to the continent was influenced by a combination of circumstances: the lack of a fully organised Dominican *studium generale* in Ireland; intensified hostility and persecution on the part of government officials, which threatened the extinction of surviving religious; the impact of the Tridentine decrees; and, perhaps not least, the ongoing reform legislation of the general chapters of the Order and reform initiatives of the Masters General.

The activities of priests trained abroad, particularly of the regulars, caused much concern to the Irish government in the last quarter of the

1 H. Hammerstein, 'Aspects of the Continental Education of Irish Students in the Reign of Queen Elizabeth I' in *Hist. Studies*, 8 (1971), 137–53; J. Brady, 'The Irish Colleges in Europe and the Counter-Reformation' in *Ir. Cath. Hist. Comm. Proc.*, Dublin 1957, 1–8; T. J. Walsh, *The Irish Continental College Movement*, Dublin/Cork 1973, 9–20; R. Walsh, 'Glimpses of the Penal Times' in *IER*, 4th ser., 28 (1910), 379–91.

sixteenth century and again in the early decades of the seventeenth century; the fears of the government stemmed from political as well as religious considerations. Between 1590 and 1615 well over five hundred Irish diocesan and regular priests were trained in seminaries and religious houses overseas.[2] The number of ordained religious returning to Ireland increased significantly between 1600 and 1650. In the latter part of Elizabeth's reign, as in that of James I, it was considered illegal to leave Ireland to study in mainland Europe, and *a fortiori* to be trained for the priesthood.[3] Those who returned as priests or religious, with the intention of ministering to the Catholic community, were gravely menaced by martial law, prerogative acts, and proclamations which could put into effect measures far more stringent than those permitted under statute law. However, such measures stopped short of the English statute of 1585 which made priests guilty of high treason by the very fact of their presence on English soil.[4]

THE EUROPEAN DOMINICAN BACKGROUND[5]

From the early sixteenth century Dominican Masters General were frequently drawn from the Observant congregation, whose tradition aimed at suppression of all private ownership, restoration of conventual fraternal life, solemn celebration of the Dominican rite liturgy, more careful training of novices and students, and the improvement of philosophical and theological studies. Success came with the reform programme of Master General Thomas de Vio Cajetano or Cajetan (1508–18), together with his procurator general, Nikolas von Schönberg, and his successor, Garcia de Loayasa (1518–24). In his first encyclical letter to the Order in 1508 Cajetan stressed the role of study and commitment to the intellectual life in carrying out the Order's fundamental preaching and doctrinal mission.

2 J. J. Silke, 'The Irish Abroad, 1534–1691' in *NHI*, iii, 624.

3 N. Robbins (ed.), *An Exact Abridgement of all the Irish Statutes*, Dublin 1736, 185–6.

4 P. J. Corish, 'Two Seventeenth-Century Proclamations against the Catholic Clergy' in *Archiv. Hib.*, 39 (1984), 53.

5 This section relies on material to be found in H. Jedin (ed.), *History of the Church*, v, London 1980, 437–8, 445, 537–8; D. A. Mortier, *Histoire des Maîtres Généraux de l'Ordre des Frères Prêcheurs*, v–vi, Paris 1911–13, *passim*; W. A. Hinnebusch, *The History of the Dominican Order*, ii, New York 1973, for a comprehensive study of the intellectual and cultural life of the Order to the eve of the Reformation; W. A. Hinnebusch, *The Dominicans: A Short History*, New York 1975, 111–36; Reichert, *MOPH*, v, 91–2; ibid., vi, 146, 245; M. H. Vicaire, 'Frères Prêcheurs' in *Dictionnaire d'Histoire et de Géographie Ecclésiastique*, xviii, Paris 1977, 1399–402; A. M. Walz, *Compendium Historiae Ordinis Praedicatorum*, Rome 1930, 257–70, 320–43 *passim*; B. Montagnes, 'Sebastien Michaelis, Frère Prêcheur, 1543–1618' in *Dictionnaire de Spiritualité*, x, Paris 1980, 1165–71.

In the first decades of the sixteenth century Francisco de Vitoria, O.P., principal initiator of Thomistic renaissance in Spain, was at the height of his career and pursued it to 1546. He inspired a distinguished line of Dominican Thomists at Salamanca University, including Peter de Soto, Dominic de Soto, Melchior Cano (whose *De Locis Theologicis* elaborated a scientific theological methodology), Dominic Bañez (who contributed significantly to the development of the theology of grace) and many others. Vitoria used the *Summa Theologiae* of St Thomas Aquinas as the basis of his enthusiastically received lectures. His specialist treatment of pressing questions of moral theology, colonial ethics, political theory and international law, reform of the Church and general councils was inspired in part by the extensive corpus of Aquinas's works.

The Order's schools of theology claimed the constant attention of the general chapters. Throughout the sixteenth century further graduate colleges for Thomistic studies were established in addition to Luchente and Salamanca, both founded late in the previous century. Among the new colleges were Valladolid (1501), Seville (1515), Orihuela (1560s) and Rome (1577). By 1551 the Order's *studia generalia* numbered twenty-seven. Those at Oxford and Cambridge and several in the German-speaking world disappeared with the advance of Protestantism. Paris and Toulouse had long since lost their medieval pre-eminence and were overshadowed by Salamanca and Coimbra.

The Dominican Order adapted its curriculum of studies to the demands of the Renaissance and Protestantism rather slowly, though individual members were thoroughly *au courant* with the literature, new cultural expression and intellectual climate of their day. In the Reformation era Hermann Rab, provincial of Saxony, pointed the way to a fundamental change in outlook when he exhorted young Dominicans not simply to study but to 'love the science of Holy Writ'. In obedience to the decrees of Trent, the Order introduced systematic courses in biblical exegesis. In 1564 the general chapter of Bologna ordered the study and observance of the canons and decrees of Trent, particularly those concerning regulars. Conventual lectors of theology were encouraged to specialise in cases of conscience, to contribute by their studies to the renaissance of moral theology and sacred scripture and instruct their communities accordingly. The 1569 chapter, however, followed papal example by banning the works of Erasmus and writers of his kind who satirised both religious orders and the institutional Church. The chapter also forbade students to study Greek or Hebrew without permission. The 1585 chapter reversed this negative trend, ordering novices and newly professed Dominicans to begin the study of biblical languages before philosophy and theology and to continue studying these languages for four years. Late in the century a theological controversy arose concerning the manner in which divine grace operated (technically known as '*de auxiliis*') and the precise relationship of grace and free will. Theologians of the Thomist (mostly Dominicans) and Molinist (largely Jesuit) schools debated the question with such acrimony that Paul V imposed silence on both parties in 1607, though allowing each school to hold its own views.

The Order was strong and vigorous when it entered the seventeenth century. It played its part in the restoration of Catholic life after Trent. The Dominican reform movement soon came to substantial completion; a series of first-rate theologians had brought about a genuine revival of Thomistic studies, and the core provinces of Italy, Spain and France progressed from strength to strength. In the south of France a remarkable if painful reform of some leading Dominican houses—such as Toulouse and St Maximin in Provence—was carried out by the controversial reformer Sebastian Michaelis. However, this vigour was offset by the weakness of the Order elsewhere in Europe; the provinces of northern and eastern Europe were but shells. The provinces of Central and South America were strong internally, but too distant and too greatly absorbed by local pastoral and political problems posed by Spanish and Portuguese *conquistadores* to exert their influence on more central issues. By 1650 the intellectual renaissance of the Order had spent much of its strength; irrelevant controversies preoccupied many theologians, while the burning issues of royal absolutism, Gallicanism and Jansenism increasingly damaged the fabric of the church and went unchallenged by the Order's thinkers, except those of the Roman theological schools. Absolutism crept into the papacy and into the Dominican Order, which in turn found its freedom of action curtailed by papal and royal interventions. In vain did the Order seek to break free of its entanglements with the politics of both parties in the unholy union of throne and altar, which would seriously compromise its mission and integrity.

Nevertheless, the Order continued to shape its plan of basic studies in accordance with the exigencies of the times and at the insistence of the papacy. Courses in practical moral theology were introduced into the syllabus of studies (*ratio studiorum*) and implemented. This growing emphasis on moral theology, as distinct from the more speculative tradition of theology, was intended to renew pastoral competence, which in turn was a stimulus to developments in the Order's spirituality. General chapters punctuated the first decades of the century with directives providing for increased study of the Bible in all its aspects in all major houses, as well as the appointment of professors of scripture and daily biblical lectures to accompany the four-year course in theology. The 1608 chapter required provinces to establish a Greek and Hebrew language school wherever possible, and an ordination of 1622 commended the serious study of Latin and Arabic as aids for biblical studies.

These gains were overshadowed by an ominous prohibition contained in the Paris chapter acts of 1611 concerning the sending of students to schools, colleges and universities which did not have direct links with the Order. Henceforth studies were to be pursued in the Order's colleges and *studia generalia* only. The prohibition marked the emergence of a definite bias against the study of philosophy and theology at the universities in the post-Reformation era, and the beginning of intellectual withdrawal from the 'secular university world' fostered by the Tridentine spirit. This trend within the Order began, ironically, when Cajetan, one of the most brilliant intellectuals of his time, was Master General (1508–18). It was not simply by way of reaction to the disappearance of the authentic Catholic tradition in German and English universities, and the distressing defections of many well-known Dominican men and women (for example, Martin Bucer) to the Protestant cause. The judgemental attitude of Cajetan and his successors towards the secular universities was conditioned above all by the grim realisation that their dissemination of decadent philosophy (Nominalism) and theology (Augustinianism) had sown the seeds which sprouted in the intellectual revolt of Protestantism against the Church. A substantial body of opinion within the Order decided that only the proclamation of the Word of God and the exposition of sound Catholic doctrine as imbibed in Dominican theological, biblical and apologetical schools would form an adequate response to the reformers, something that could no longer be guaranteed by the universities. And in this, Cajetan's theological and biblical commentaries set a formidable headline.

Pope Pius V in his *motu proprio* of 1572 entitled *Cum sacer Ordo Praedicatorum* granted powers and rights to the Masters General and to those Dominican *studia generalia* where the humanities, philosophy, theology, sacred scripture and ecclesiastical subjects were systematically taught to exacting standards, to confer degrees hitherto the prerogative of the universities, thus elevating the status of such houses of studies. The ordination was repeated at the general chapter of Bologna in 1615. Wherever students were not sent to the *studia* of the Order, their provincials and priors were to be dismissed from office. Obviously there was dissension on this vital issue. Fortunately for the Irish Dominicans, universities such as Salamanca and Louvain, though pontifical universities by charter and origin, did not come under papal censure. Several Masters General promoted the Order's reform in the first half of the seventeenth century: Beccaria, Xavierre, Galamini and Secchi—the latter an exemplary religious who conducted frequent visitations in person or employed visitators. The progress of the Order was not greatly impeded by the Thirty Years' War (1618–48), though the already weakened provinces of Germany, Hungary and Bohemia were beaten down by the destruction of this war and so badly hurt by Protestantism that several centuries would pass before these provinces could be reorganised. Portugal, Spain and Italy, on the other hand, unlike France and Flanders, lay outside the principal theatres of war. This would help to explain why the majority of Irish Dominican students were sent to the nations of the Iberian and Italian peninsulas in this troubled period, to the Latin provinces which dominated the Order until the present century.

THE IRISH CONTINENTAL COLLEGES

The beginning of the continental-based revival of the Irish Dominicans may be dated from about 1580. The process took place almost simultaneously though not in logical or co-ordinated sequence in several countries: Spain, Portugal, France, Italy and Flanders. Two distinct streams of young people entering the Order in this epoch are discernible. In the first place there were the Dominicans sent from Ireland for ecclesiastical formation and studies. The earliest known of these, John Chrysologus Burke, was educated in Rome or elsewhere in Italy before his nomination to the prestigious post of penitentiary at the Roman basilica of St Mary Major's in the jubilee year of 1600.[6] Cormac O'Kerin completed his studies as a priest, graduated in theology and lectured briefly at Bologna in the 1590s.[7] Thaddeus O'Farrell, also a priest and a schoolmaster of many years' standing, studied in Andalucía and at the University of Salamanca in the 1580s.[8] Patrick MacTeig (Mac Taidhg), an Ulsterman, Roland Burke from Connacht and Thomas de Sancta Maria were students at Salamanca in 1601. On 30 November of that year they addressed a letter to Pope Clement VIII suggesting the nomination of a legate for Ireland. For the post they recommended a Roman Dominican, Gabriel Naro, then living in Salamanca.[9] All these Dominicans were representatives of the lesser stream of recruits to the Order until about 1620 and were predominantly of Gaelic stock.

A far more significant stream of students, from continental Irish colleges originally founded for the service of the diocesan priesthood, entered the Dominicans and other religious orders between roughly 1593 and 1620 in spite of official discouragement from the colleges concerned. It was certainly the policy of Salamanca, and of most other Irish colleges

6 A. Zucchi, *La S. Penitenzeria Apostolica e l'Ordine di S. Domenico*, Florence 1942, 92–3.
7 Fenning, *Irish material*, 276; Creytens, 'Il Registro degli Maestri degli Studenti di Bologna', 58; O'Sullivan Beare, *Selections from the Zoilomastix*, ed. O'Donnell, 26.
8 AUS, Libros de Matriculas, 296, f. 20r.
9 J. Hagan (ed.), 'Miscellanea Vaticano-Hibernica: 1420–1631' in *Archiv Hib.*, 4 (1915), 230.

under the control of the Jesuits, to dissuade their students from joining religious orders, though this regularly occurred in Spain and Portugal. Nonetheless, the Jesuits themselves accepted a constant flow of talented Irishmen from these colleges to the Society, much to the chagrin of Irish diocesan administrators and priests, who were not slow to voice their complaints and criticise Jesuit administration of the foreign colleges.

Students were normally obliged, shortly after registering at their college, to take the 'missionary oath', sometimes repeated, to return to Ireland as priests on completion of their studies. What motivated Irish students, therefore, to pass from their colleges to the religious orders? At that time lively theological debates in Spain and Portugal, highlighting and contrasting the merits and values of the diocesan priesthood and religious orders, influenced many young students to respond to what they considered the more perfect evangelical calling of the religious life. Besides the theological climate, the religious orders throughout Spain and Portugal and in some parts of France and Italy showed a renewed vigour born of genuine reform. There was also the attraction, cultural and intellectual, of belonging to the European fraternities of the international religious orders. The smaller number of bishops in Ireland from 1590 to 1620 probably also contributed to this loss of potential diocesan clergy. Ties with individual bishops or vicars apostolic, themselves on the run from the authorities and virtually incommunicado, were necessarily weak. Where dioceses lacked episcopal supervision, the seminarian's position was even more unsatisfactory and insecure. There was also the uncertainty of getting a benefice in Ireland after ordination due to lay impropriations and to expropriations made by clergy of the Established Church. Moreover, membership of a religious order offered the average student freedom from ever-recurrent financial worries.

As far as one can ascertain, the following continental colleges provided candidates for the Dominicans. Owing to the mobility of the student body, the same individuals tend to appear in different lists as they progressed from college to college. From the Irish College, Lisbon, sixteen students entered the Order between 1593 and 1615: Simon O'Hallahgan (Youghal), John White (Waterford?), Anthony Lynch (Galway), William Talbot (Navan), another John White (Waterford), Ross MacGeoghegan (Westmeath), Thomas Bathe (Dublin), Michael Brown (Thurles), William Harold (Limerick), Nicholas Lynch (Galway), Stephen Lynch (Galway), Barnabas Murphy, Peter Martin (Galway), Thaddeus Murphy (Kilkenny), Thomas Brandan (Dublin) and James Nelan (Waterford). The first seven had already returned as priests to Ireland before 1615; the rest were still in that year students inscribed at Salamanca University.[10]

10 ARSI, Lusitania, 44, f. 347; Dublin, Irish Jesuit provincial archive, MacErlean transcript of same; M. Gonçalves da Costa, *Fontes Inéditas para a Historia de*

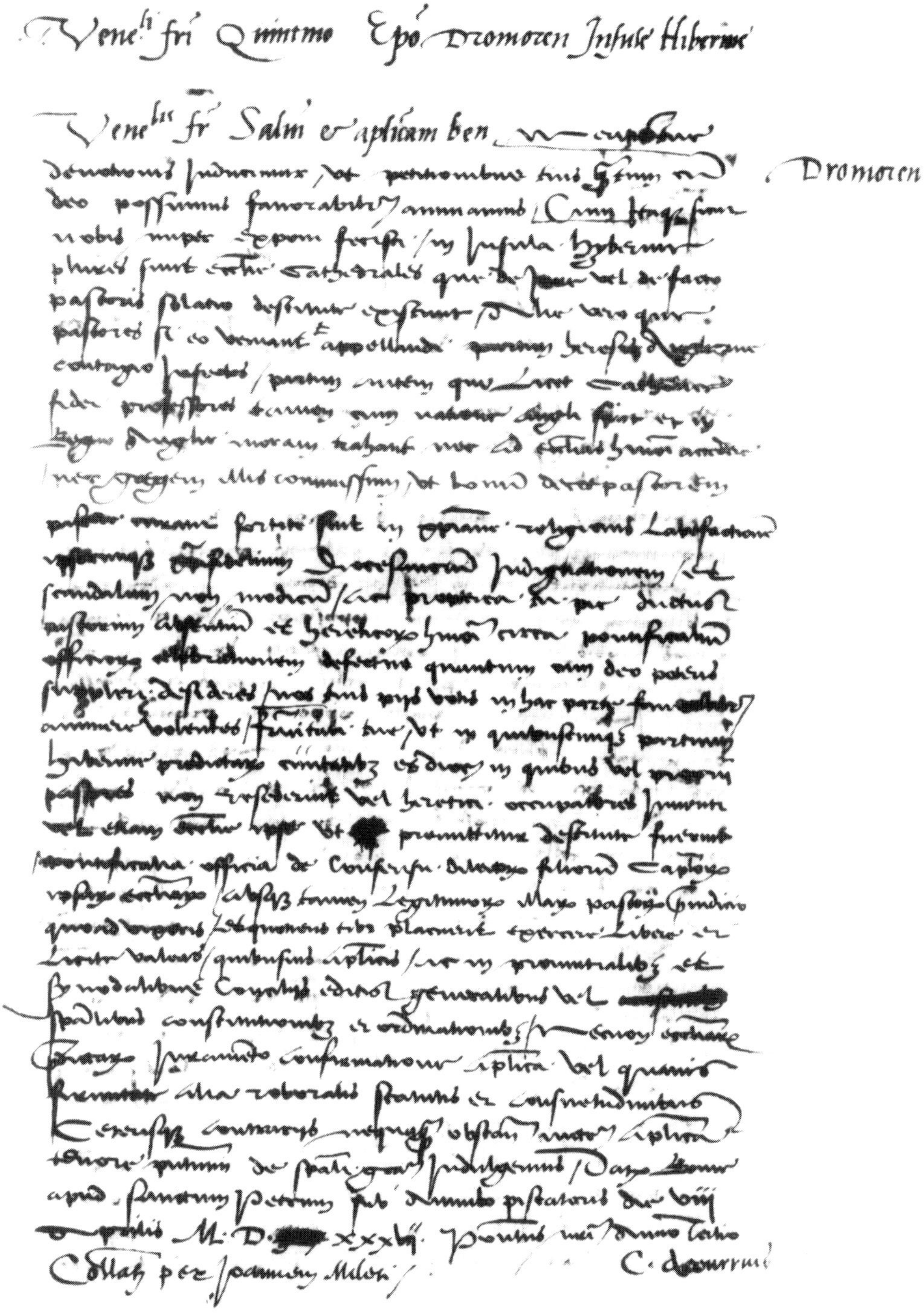

1 Papal brief addressed to Quentin Cogly, O.P., Bishop of Dromore, 8 April 1537
(see page 14)

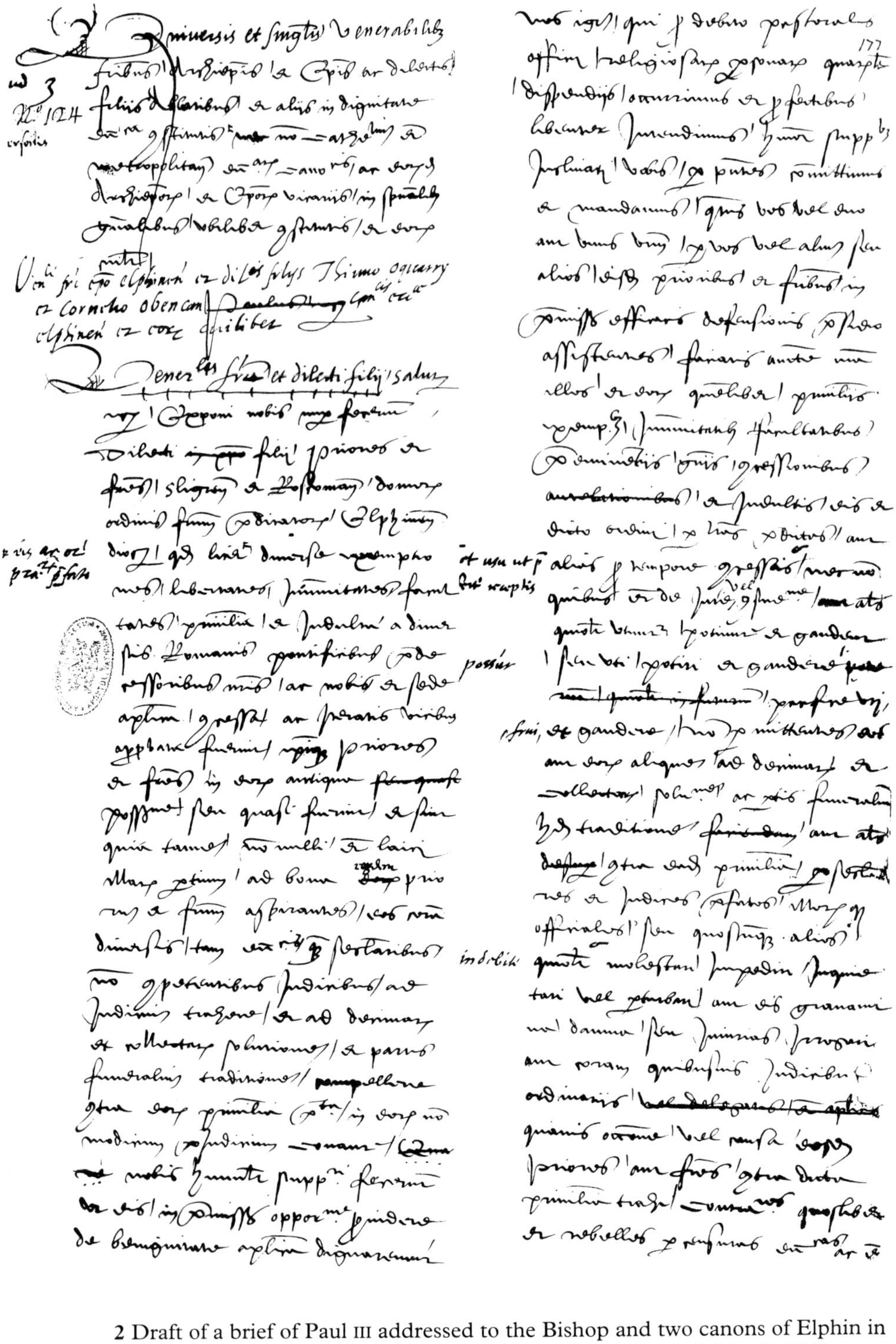

2 Draft of a brief of Paul III addressed to the Bishop and two canons of Elphin in favour of the Sligo and Roscommon Dominicans, 3 March 1548 (see page 41)

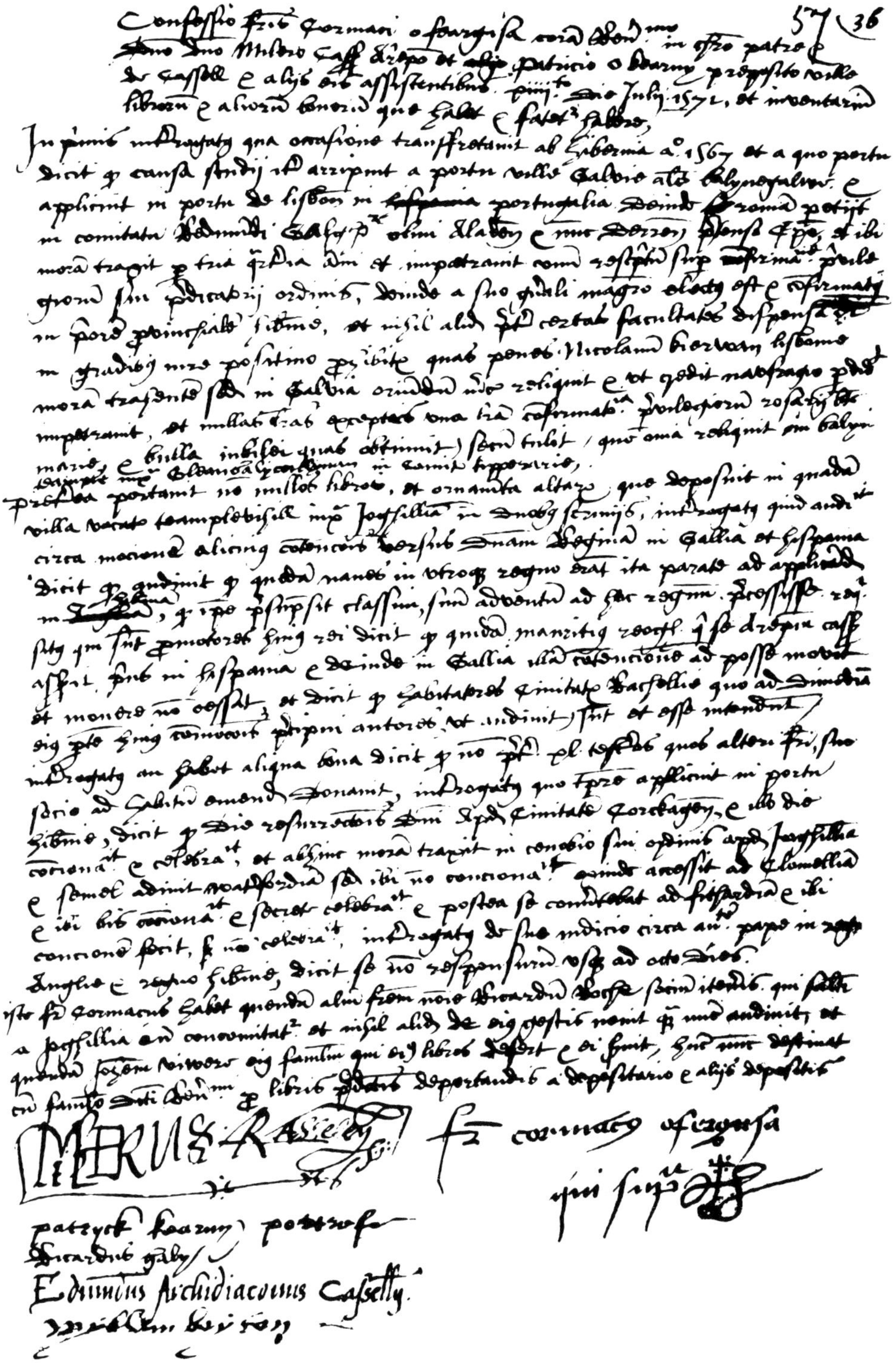

3 Examination of Cormac O'Fergus, O.P., provincial, 14 July 1572 (see pages 53–6)

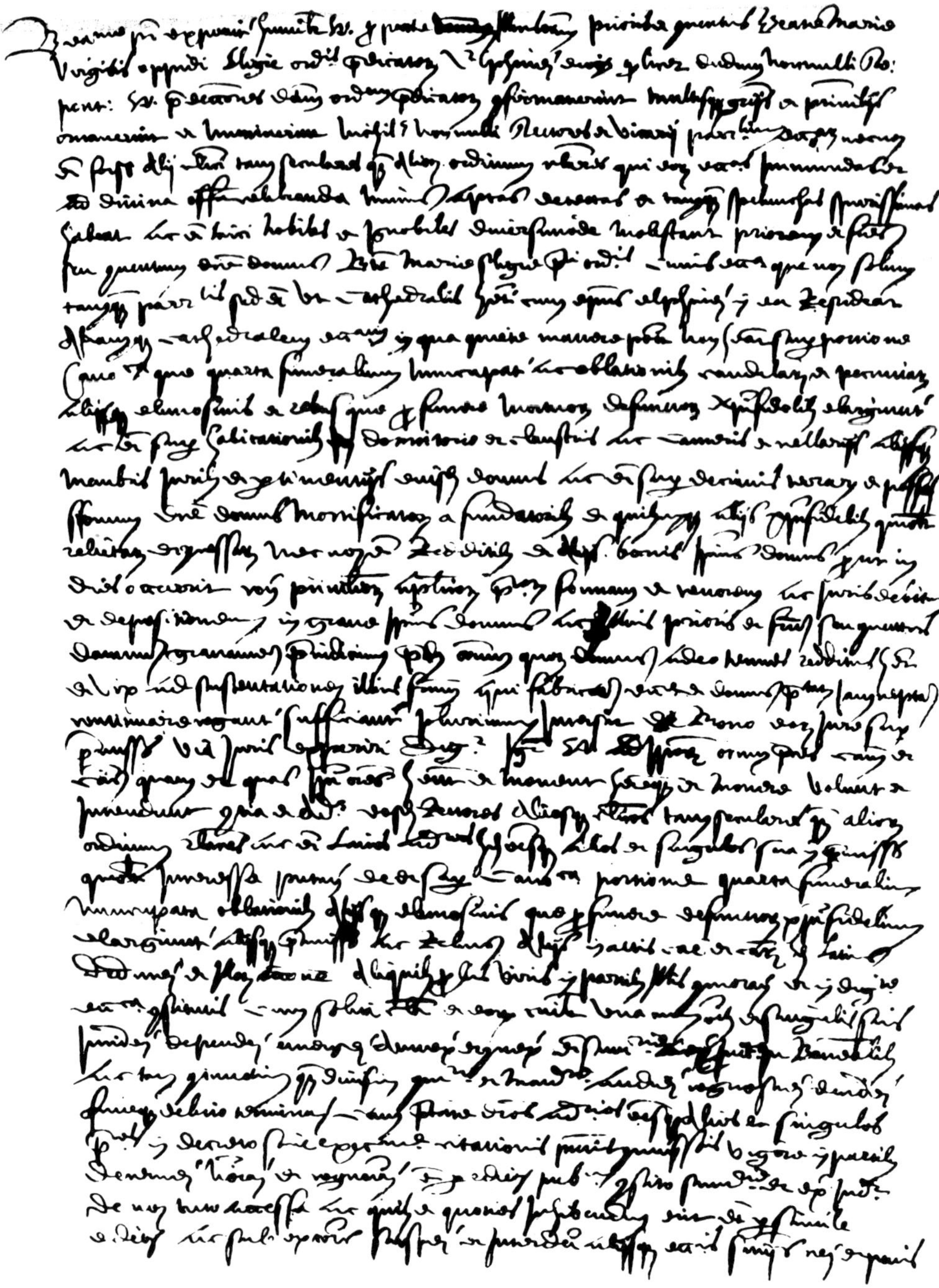

4 Extract from a petition of Thaddeus MacDuane, O.P., provincial, to Pope Gregory XIII on behalf of Sligo Dominicans, 6 May 1577 (see pages 84–5)

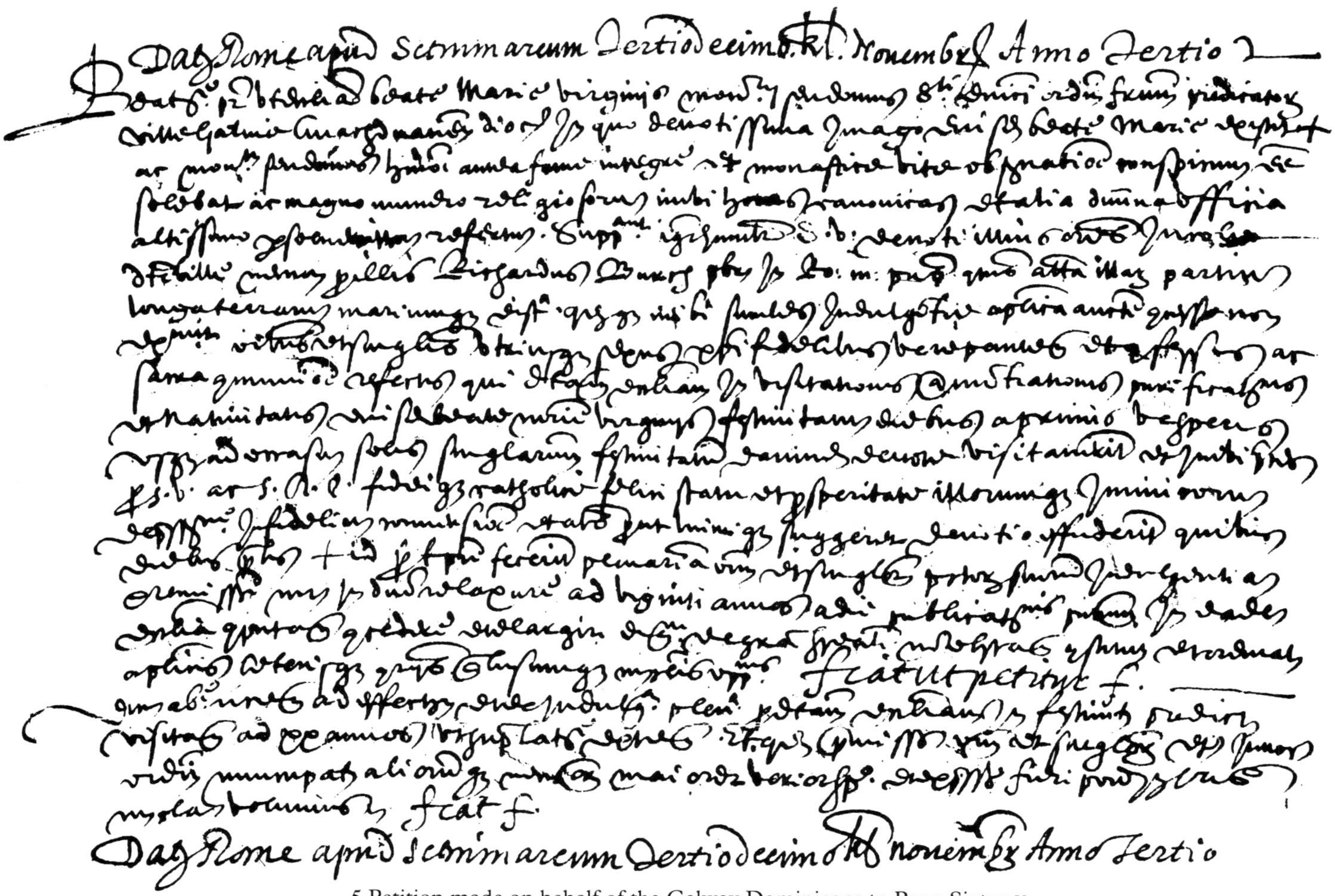

Dat. Romae apud Sanctum Marcum Tertiodecimo Kl. Novembris Anno Tertio

Fiat ut petitur

Fiat

Dat. Romae apud Sanctum Marcum Tertiodecimo Kl. Novembris Anno Tertio

5 Petition made on behalf of the Galway Dominicans to Pope Sixtus v, 20 October 1587 (see page 87)

6 Athenry Abbey (f. 1241), Co. Galway

7 Kilmallock Abbey (f. 1291), Co. Limerick

9 Roscommon Abbey (f. 1253), Co. Roscommon

8 (opposite page) Lorrha Abbey (f. 1269), Co. Tipperary

11 Portumna Abbey (f. 1414), Co. Galway

10 (opposite page) Ballindoon Abbey (f. 1507), Co. Roscommon: the night stairs from dormitory to choir

13 Sligo Abbey (f. 1252): complex of conventual buildings

12 (opposite page) Rathfran Abbey (f. 1274), Co. Mayo

15 Burrishoole Abbey (f. before 1486), Co. Mayo

14 (opposite page) Urlar Abbey (f. 1434), Co. Mayo: restored west gable front

16 Cashel Abbey (f. 1243), Co. Tipperary

From the Irish College, Salamanca, at least seven students (five formerly of Lisbon) joined the Dominicans in the early 1600s: Richard Caron, Ross MacGeoghegan, Anthony Lynch, John White, James Arthur, Thomas Bathe and Michael Brown.[11]

From the Irish College, Bordeaux, four students entered the Order between 1602 and 1616: John Archer (Kilkenny), John Fox (Limerick), Thomas Ly or Lyehe (Ardfert) and William Harold (Limerick). All were described as 'reformed Jacobins'.[12] By 1610 the following had made solemn profession at the convent of St Thomas Aquinas, Toulouse: Thomas Quirke (21 May 1603), John Archer (15 June 1607), Vincent Hogan (6 June 1609), Thomas Bathe (6 May 1610) and Raymund Lycaeus (16 June 1610).[13] Those whose profession records have not survived may have made their profession at the important reformed convent of St Maximin near Toulouse. It is noteworthy that most of these Irishmen opted to enter the Order through the reformed convents of the congregation of Aquitaine (Occitanie) in the south-west of France.

From the Irish College, Douai, at least three alumni became Dominicans before 1620: John (Fitz)David, Dominic Meade and John Archer.[14]

From the Irish College, Seville, yet another Munsterman, Nicholas Moloney of Limerick or its environs, came to the Order in 1615. He made his profession the following year at San Pablo, Seville, and later ministered with the Cork Dominicans. Long before his death he was renowned for holiness of life.[15]

This influx of students included representatives from the Old Irish families, but rather more were from an Anglo-Irish or Old English background. This surprising phenomenon of Irish diocesan students coming to the Order from the newly founded continental colleges, together with the trickle of Dominican students sent from Ireland, would in time provide a seed-bed for the next generation of Irish Dominicans and result in a

Irlanda, Braga 1981, 408: the list of students is inaccurately presented here. Besides the sixteen Salamanca University students who became Irish Dominicans, twenty-one went to the Franciscans, twenty-eight to the Jesuits, seven to the Augustinians, four to the Discalced Carmelites, and three to the Cistercians. ARSI, Lusitania, 44, ff 347–8.

11 D. J. O'Doherty, 'Students of the Irish College, Salamanca (1595–1619)' in *Archiv. Hib.*, 2 (1913), 11–25

12 *Cal. S.P. Ire., 1615–25*, 319; D. O'Donoghue, 'The Congregation of Irish Priests in Bordeaux (1602–1617)' in *IER*, 4th ser., 5 (1899), 516.

13 Toulouse, Archives départmentales, Haute-Garonne, Clérgé Régulier: Fonds des Jacobins, Registre de Vêtures et de Professions (1521–1753), ff 22–4.

14 J. Brady, 'The Irish Colleges in the Low Countries' in *Archiv. Hib.*, 14 (1949), 80; *Cal. Carew MSS, 1603–24*, 285–6.

15 Seville, Archivo de la Provincia Dominicana de Andalucía, F. Ramirez de Solorzano, *Historia del santo y real Convento de S. Pablo de Sevilla, 1625*, libro iii, cap. 17, ff 112v–113r.

revitalised province. Over the next several generations these men, products of diverse and excellent traditions of European education in one of its finest ages of learning, would transform the life, activities and mental outlook of the Irish province beyond all expectations. A total of twenty-seven students left the five colleges under review. These are the only Irish colleges whose surviving records show a transfer of their alumni to religious orders. The true total may well have been considerably higher, since details are lacking for the Irish colleges of Spain, apart from Salamanca and Seville.

As regards the question of ordination to the priesthood before or after the requisite studies, it would appear that there was no fixed policy in Ireland. At the close of the sixteenth century almost all Irish dioceses were without bishops, and ordinations were rare. Some candidates were ordained on the understanding that they would pursue appropriate studies when the opportunity arose. This procedure enabled priest-students to support themselves by offerings received when they exercised their ministry. It safeguarded them too from being penalised by imprisonment or torture under an English statute of 1585 against supporting seminaries and seminarians overseas, or under a proclamation of 1605, repeated in 1611, expelling Jesuits—then a comprehensive term covering all regular clergy—and seminary priests from Irish soil. Finally, their status helped them to avoid the temptation of entering one of the professions abroad. Thaddeus O'Farrell was already well known as a priest, preacher and schoolmaster in Connacht before travelling to Spain to continue his studies about 1590. Cormac O'Kerin had also been ordained a priest before he was sent to complete his studies at Bologna in 1595. In the first decades of the seventeenth century very few Irish students had been ordained before setting out for the continent. Those who entered the Dominican Order, with few exceptions, had not been priests before completion of studies. The most significant evidence of all is that of the hundred students who took the missionary oath on entry to the Irish College of Salamanca in the same years 1595–1619, only five were already priests.[16] On all sides greater cognisance was being taken of the stricter conditions stipulated by Trent for the ordination of priests.

After the destruction of the provinces of England, Ireland, Scotland, Denmark, Saxony, Hungary, Holland and Poland, the general chapters of the Order made spirited appeals on behalf of these 'desolate provinces' to the provinces of southern Europe, to accept responsibility for the education and maintenance of their students. Echoes of the responses to these appeals may be discerned in the provincial chapter acts of Castille, sometimes in a negative vein owing to the problems caused by foreign

16 O'Doherty, 'Students of the Irish College, Salamanca', 1–36.

students. The chapters of 1613, 1617 and 1621 refer to students arriving in Spain invariably badly dressed and probably without Dominican habits and other essential clothing, and the task and expense of fitting them out with decent clothes on their departure to other convents or their home provinces. Nevertheless, it must be emphasised that extraordinary magnanimity and generosity was shown to exiled Irish Dominicans, both students and priests, by Dominican houses throughout Spain, Portugal, France, Italy, Flanders and Lower Germany. A formidable task confronts the historian in keeping track of the innumerable assignations of Irish students of religious orders to religious houses all over mainland Europe; for only very exceptionally did they complete all their studies in one place.

The first recorded postings of Irish students to continental houses by the Masters General began in 1595.[17] Frequently the assignations were made directly to individual houses of studies. Assignation simply to a province left the destination to the discretion of a provincial, who had the right to choose houses of assignation within his jurisdiction. Some students came under the direct scrutiny of the Masters General, possibly because they turned up in Rome. Many others did not, but would have carried letters of identification and recommendation to the provincials of the countries in which they hoped to study.

The masters and vicars of the Order assigned twenty-four students to houses of the Spanish provinces between 1611 and 1640: Luchente, Salamanca, Pamplona, Zaragoza, Valladolid, Valencia, Cordoba, Seville, Burgos, Calatayud, Barcelona, Jerez de la Frontera, Lérida and Madrid. In the period 1595–1640 nineteen students were sent to the Italian provinces: Bologna, Rome, Naples, Milan and Alessandria. Eleven students were assigned to French Dominican houses in the slightly later period 1622–40: Paris, Avignon, Rennes and Toulouse. Together with three students sent to Cologne and two to the Louvain house of the Belgian Dominicans, the figures come to a total of fifty-nine students studying at European *studia generalia*.[18] While it is true that the Masters General played a preponderant role in finding houses for the education of Irish students, it is perfectly clear from the entries in various registers that a much higher number had been accepted in these houses and in many others not named, such as Lisbon and Benfica.

IRISH DOMINICANS IN SPAIN

In the year 1615 the Dominican province of Castille had eighty-seven convents, seventeen of which were houses of studies, specialising in arts and theology: Segovia, Toledo, Burgos (theology only, but with great

17 Fenning, *Irish material*, 276–305.
18 Ibid.

distinction), Salamanca (three courses of arts and two chairs of theology '*de Prima y Visperas*' in the university), Pamplona, León, Valladolid (San Pablo and the elitist graduate college of San Gregorio), Toro, Plasencia, Trujillo, Avila, Carboneras, Trianos, Madrid (Nuestra Señora de Atocha), Tabara and Alcalá de Henares (two chairs of theology '*de Prima y Visperas*' in the university).[19]

In the same year the Dominican province of Aragón had seventy-three convents, including twenty-three houses dedicated to studies in which arts and theology were the principal courses: Barcelona, Zaragoza (*studium generale*, with a graduate theology college), Lérida, Valencia, Mallorca, Perpignan (then part of Spain), Tarragona, Gerona, Calatayud, Huesca, Puigcerdan, Xátiva, Tortosa, Alcaniz, Luchente, and Orihuela in the civil province of Murcia, which had a college and pontifical university (arts, theology and several other faculties).[20]

In the Dominican province of Andalucía there were seventy-four convents, twelve of which had the status of formal houses of studies (*studia generalia*): Seville (four foundations: San Pablo; Queen of Angels; college and university of Santo Tomás; college of Mount Sion), Córdoba, Murcia, Jerez de la Frontera, Granada, Málaga, Osuna (theology and the chair of theology '*de Prima*' in the university), Almagro (college and university) and Ecija.[21]

The houses of the province of Castille were already severely under pressure to accommodate their own large numbers. The provincial chapter of 1607 urged caution in receptions to the habit and profession, especially in regard to persons who might prove to be a burden to the Order in the future and unsuitable for the exercise of the sacred ministry. The chapter quoted from the prophet Isaiah (9:3) the splendid line: '*Multiplicasti gentem, sed non magnificasti laetitiam*' ('Thou hast multiplied the nation, but not magnified the joy'). The influx of not merely Irish but other foreign students from northern Europe must have greatly aggravated a strained internal situation. The chapters of 1615 and 1619 repeated the warnings concerning the quality of candidates, and this must have applied to all candidates. However, the problems were not limited to overcrowding and standards, but also involved down-to-earth economics as well. In 1619 the Master of the Order, Seraphinus Secchi, recommended strongly that the houses of Castille should calculate exactly how many brethren each could support out of their particular resources and take care not to exceed these numbers.[22]

19 I. Lopez, *La Historia General de Santo Domingo y de su Orden de Predicadores*, iv, Valladolid 1615, 987–8.

20 Ibid., 989.

21 Ibid., 990.

22 Salamanca, San Esteban provincial archives, chapter acts of the province of Spain (Castille).

In 1611 and 1615 two Spanish Dominican historians stated that in recent years about a dozen English students from the colleges of Valladolid and Seville had entered the Order at Valladolid, Seville and Jerez de la Frontera and taken up their studies with a view to preaching the faith on their return to England.[23] From another contemporary source it is clear that the attraction of some students of the English College at Valladolid to the Dominicans caused some disturbance in the Jesuit-administered college there.[24] Almost certainly the designation 'English', as used by the Spanish authors, covered Irish students too, quite a number of whom joined the Bética or Andalusian province and spent all their lives in Spain. The Irish Jesuits made a request between 1614 and 1620 that one of the Irish colleges in Spain be designated for the training of young Jesuits for Ireland. In passing it was noted that the Irish Dominicans were being trained in convents of their Order in Andalucía.[25] Only one name, however, that of Nicholas Moloney, has come to light from a search of the Seville ordination registers before 1640. He received all sacred orders in Seville, in the years 1617–18.[26]

A number of prime archival holdings have been examined and analysed for Irish Dominican material. In so many cases what would have proved to be invaluable sources have been lost or destroyed. The Salamanca ordination registers were taken or destroyed by the French during the Napoleonic campaigns in the Iberian peninsula. The standard conventual registers of all Spanish religious houses, if not already confiscated by the French, were lost or expropriated at the time of the great *exclaustración*, 1834–6. Dominican records that somehow survived the disasters of the nineteenth century, such as the profession book of San Esteban, Salamanca (from 1595 onwards to the last century) and an important archival deposit in the ancient convent of Santo Tomás d'Aquino, popularly known as El Olivar, in Madrid, were destroyed by fire in 1936 in the course of the Spanish Civil War.

By far the most important archive in Spain, with invaluable, indispensable documentation on practically every aspect of Irish history from the sixteenth to the eighteenth centuries, is that of Simancas near Valladolid. Extensive use has been made in this study of its Irish Dominican records (1602–40) such as reports, memorials and requests.

The Salamanca University matriculation lists (*libros de matriculas*) teem with Irish names for the entire seventeenth century. From the 1580s

23 Alonso Fernandez, *Historia Ecclesiastica de Nuestros Tiempos*, Toledo 1611, 449; Lopez, *La Historia General de Santo Domingo y de su Orden*, iv, 1101.

24 E. Henson (ed.), *Registers of the English College at Valladolid, 1589–1862*, London 1930, xxii.

25 W. McDonnell, 'Irish Ecclesiastical Colleges since the Reformation: Salamanca' in *IER*, 2nd ser., 10 (1873–4), 527.

26 J. J. Silke, 'The Irish College, Seville' in *Archiv. Hib.*, 24 (1961), 140.

to 1640 about thirty Irish Dominican names appear in their pages and can be identified with certainty. Conjectural cases would raise the number somewhat. This problem arises on account of the use of religious names and hispanified versions of Irish surnames. Irish Dominican students were not in any way distinguished from Spanish collegial students, except by the use of Spanish and Latinised forms of names and surnames: Juan Vitus (John White); Diego Arturo (James Arthur); Guillermo de Spiritu Santo (William Talbot); Ricardo de la Peña (Richard Caron); Dominic Linze (Dominic Lynch). Thus Irish names, which understandably the Spanish were unable to handle, were camouflaged to accommodate their hosts. Therefore great caution is called for in making identifications. Nevertheless, one can safely conclude that a regular flow of Irish Dominicans, those with Old English and Anglo-Irish names predominating, passed through the Dominican *studium* of San Esteban, one of the glories of the Spanish Gothic and Renaissance styles, and through the University of Salamanca for the complete range of humanistic and ecclesiastical studies in the period under review.

Eight Irish Dominicans are mentioned in the pages of the only surviving house council register (1630–60) of the convent of San Pablo of Seville, for the period 1630–46.[27] The first of these was Robert of Ireland, a student, who was examined and approved for entry to the Order. He had come from Ireland with a strong desire to join the Order, and his knowledge of Latin was judged to be sufficient. The house council of San Pablo decided, however, that other candidates should not be admitted to the Order at San Pablo, but rather at the convent of Alcalá de los Gazules, as that convent had been designated for the reception of English and Irish candidates. The other Irish names in the register are those of Raymund of Jesus, Gregory French, Andrew of the Visitation Brown, Anthony of Ireland, Timothy of St Antoninus (?), Dominic Lynch and Stephen Lynch, some of whom were from Connacht. One of the original registers of the Irish College of Seville, a volume bound in vellum, and entitled *Historia de el Collegio Irlandes, de Sevilla*, covering the years 1619–1770, has found a home in Dublin.[28] It pays scant attention to the names and details of its students and personnel and supplies no information about students who left the college to become Dominicans.

How the Irish Dominican students reacted to the new world of their continental surroundings—the extremes of the Castillian and Andalusian climates, food, languages, varying ethnic groups, studies and Mediterranean culture—is simply not known. In a memorial to the King of Spain and his council, dated 17 June 1606, Florence Conry, O.F.M., reported

27 Seville, Archivo de la Provincia Dominicana de Andalucía, Consultas, 1630–35 (Convento de San Pablo, Sevilla).

28 NLI, MS 16, f. 236. Revd H. Fenning kindly drew my attention to this register.

that some of the Irish Franciscans sent to Spain had found the climate insupportable and had died.[29] There are also obits of Irish Dominican students and priests recorded in the acts of the Spanish provincial chapters (Castille, Bética or Andalucía and Aragón). At least six Irish students died at Salamanca alone between 1615 and 1635.[30] No enlightening memoirs, diaries or autobiographical accounts are extant.

IRISH DOMINICANS IN PORTUGAL

Although Portugal was under Spanish rule from 1580 to 1640, the Portuguese Dominicans retained their autonomy. In the year 1615 there were twenty-five houses in the province of Portugal, and five of these were houses of studies: Lisbon, Coimbra (a college specialising in theology), Evora, Santarem and Batalha.[31] Coimbra (founded 1290) was one of the oldest and most renowned of European universities. Evora (founded 1559) was the second university of Portugal.

From perhaps as early as 1614 Ross MacGeoghegan, partly Portuguese educated, was superior of the Irish Dominicans in Ireland, Spain and Portugal.[32] In consultation with the Portuguese provincial, he may have been permitted to send students and priests wherever they would be accepted, as, for example, at the houses of São Domingos of Lisbon, Benfica, Evora and Coimbra. They were certainly living at Lisbon and Benfica from the opening years of the seventeenth century.[33] Before the actual establishment of the Irish Dominican college in Lisbon—though formally erected in 1615, it was not a viable entity until the 1630s nor truly established until 1659—the Irish pursued their studies in Portuguese *studia*.

Eighteen Irish Dominican names appear in the incomplete series of the Lisbon ordination registers (*livros de matriculas, ordens gerais*), still

29 AGS, Estado, leg. 2768.

30 *Nomina defunctorum* in provincial chapter acts of the province of Castille (Spain).

31 Lopez, *La Historia General de Santo Domingo y de su Orden*, iv, 989–90.

32 AGS, Estado, leg. 2750.

33 Don Raymundo de Burgo (Burke), Baron of Leitrim, submitted a memorial to the Spanish council of state on 21 February 1617. He expressed the desire to serve God in the Dominican Order by joining the Irish Dominicans in the convent of Benfica who lived according to the strict rule of observance. He asked for the continuation of his pension of 80 crowns which he had been receiving at Lisbon for his upkeep. The council decided that he would continue to receive it even though he should become a religious. AGS, Estado, leg. 2749. He was also listed in a report (dated 3 July 1610) of prominent Irishmen resident at the Spanish court. Ibid., leg. 2513. For further details of his career in Spain see M. Kerney Walsh, *'Destruction by Peace': Hugh O'Neill after Kinsale*, Monaghan 1986, 13, 15, 143, 154, 157.

preserved in the archives of the diocese, most of which can be corroborated by other contemporary documents. A major gap occurs in the extant series of registers between 1624 and 1642. In contradistinction to general ordinations (*ordens gerais*), the series of particular ordinations (*ordens particulares*), 1623–31, records no Dominican, Irish, English or even religious candidates. Particular ordinations seem to have been reserved to diocesan candidates who could claim benefices, mostly clerics of the city and environs of Lisbon. There probably were registers for general ordinations, including those of religious, from the 1620s to the early 1640s, but they are no longer available. In the extant registers the names of Irish candidates are listed indiscriminately with those of Portuguese Dominicans. For the most part only the religious name was employed, which makes the business of identifying Irishmen even more difficult. The missing registers were lost, misplaced after confiscation, or destroyed in the political upheavals of 1910 and thereafter. A few Irish names occur in the profession books of São Domingos, Lisbon (1517–1777) and São Domingos, Benfica (1551–1707).[34] However few, these entries help one to control information from the registers of ordinations, while at the same time providing valuable detail concerning names of parents and places of origin in Ireland. The Lisbon profession book contains the professions of Simon of the Holy Spirit O'Hallaghan (18 June 1592); Anthony of St Mary Lynch (1 September 1606) and Stephen of the Rosary Lynch (25 February 1611). The profession book of Benfica—then situated seven miles from the heart of Lisbon and a convent of strict observance—records the professions of Jordan of the Holy Spirit O'Morahan (3 June 1614); Michael of the Rosary *alias* Miler Magrath or MacCraith (3 October 1629); Patrick of St Dominic Aspol (14 December 1631); and Michael Clarus (Cleere or Cleary) (22 July 1640). From the paucity of Irish names in these books one might be tempted to conclude that the majority of young Irish Dominicans coming to Lisbon had already completed their novitiate in Ireland or elsewhere.

IRISH DOMINICANS IN FLANDERS

A list of Spanish royal alms to foreign religious resident in the Low Countries in 1613 included 'the religious of St Dominic, Louvain'.[35] They were almost certainly Irish living in the city's Flemish convent. In

34 Oporto, Archivo Histórico Dominicano Português, where the original Lisbon profession book of São Domingos is preserved, and also a photographic copy of the Benfica profession book. The original of the latter is now MS Port. 4789 in Harvard College Library.

35 B. Jennings (ed.), 'Miscellaneous Documents, I: 1588–1634' in *Archiv. Hib.*, 12 (1946), 76–8.

that same year Peter Lombard, Archbishop of Armagh, petitioned the King of Spain to found a college for the Irish Dominicans within his dominions, either in Spain or in Belgium.[36] The Irish Dominican college was founded in Louvain in 1624, while the Thirty Years' War was being waged on the borders of the country. When the community deserted its college and fled the country in 1794, the French invaders suppressed the college. In the event the Dominicans lost their library, academic records and indeed the archives of the province; no trace of any of this material has ever been found.

The ordination registers of the archdiocese of Malines represent the most important source of information about the first Dominican students of Louvain. Irish Dominican names first appear in the registers of the archbishops under the year 1623. Sixteen Irish candidates received orders within the diocese, either at Malines or Brussels in the period 1623–40. Only three of these Louvain-based Dominicans received all sacred orders in the diocese (unlike Lisbon, where many candidates did), a clear indication of their surprising mobility. The list is as follows: John (Fitz)David, Dominic de Caena, James Barry, James Hannon, Dominic MacCarroll, Laurence Ailward, Stephen Harold, Bernard Neill, Walter Archbold, Henry Bietagh, Dominic Wale (Wall), Augustine Nugent, Eugene Gallagher, Thomas Magner, James Butler and Humbert Prendergast.[37] It would appear that some did their philosophy at Louvain, whereas others finished their theology there, but very few indeed did all their studies in Louvain. The fact that the college was still in its infancy and beset with many problems, especially financial, would partly explain this situation. John (Fitz)David was a former alumnus of the Irish College, Douai, and received all orders at Malines between 1623 and 1625.[38] Dominic de Caena was conferred with minor orders while at Louvain in 1624,[39] but was ordained deacon and priest elsewhere before going as a collegial student to San Domenico, Naples, in 1629.[40] Mobility, therefore, explains why some students, recipients of minor orders, disappear from the Malines registers, while others make their first appearance only on reception of diaconate and priesthood.

36 Rome, Archive of St Isidore's (Irish Franciscans), MS W 2, no. l, f. 1r; AGS, Estado, leg. 2643. For a detailed account of the Irish Dominican college at Louvain see pp 212–30 below.

37 A. M. Bogaerts, *De Dominikanen in de Wijdingsregisters van het Aartsbisdom Mechelen*, Brussels 1965, *passim*.

38 Ibid., 30, 33.

39 Ibid., 32.

40 Fenning, *Irish material*, 285.

In 1615 the principal houses of studies in the Italian provinces were as follows: *province of Lombardy*: Bologna, Bosco Marengo (Alessandria), Genoa, Milan and Venice; *Roman province*: Rome (college of St Thomas Aquinas at Santa Maria sopra Minerva), Florence (Santa Maria Novella), Viterbo (Santa Maria della Quercia) and Perugia; *province of Naples*: Naples (San Domenico Maggiore; San Tommaso d'Aquino) and Santa Maria dell'Arco near Naples.[41]

The newly ordained Cormac O'Kerin was assigned in 1595 for his theological studies to the *studium generale* of Bologna, one of the very few Irishmen educated in Italy before 1600. As from 1614, the Giustiniani benefaction to the college of St Thomas Aquinas at Rome favoured students from 'desolate' Dominican provinces such as Ireland, England, Scotland, Poland, Dalmatia, Lithuania and Hungary.[42] From this date a line of Irish Dominican students extended through the first half of the seventeenth century. The names of collegial students—those chosen to take the Dominican Order's degree of lector of theology—included Oliver Burke (1627), Dominic Burke (1629) and Theodore de Pietate O'Connell (1633).[43] A fresh search of the official Roman ordination registers has failed to yield the name of a single Irish Dominican before the foundation of the province's college of San Clemente at Rome in 1677.[44]

41 Lopez, *La Historia General de Santo Domingo y de su Orden*, iv, 994–8.

42 G. Moroni (ed.), *Dizionario di Erudizione Storico-Ecclesiastico*, xiv, Venice 1842, 215; I. Taurisano, 'Note Storiche sul Collegium Divi Thomae de Urbe e gli Studi Domenicani in Roma' in *Analecta Sacri Ordinis Praedicatorum*, 17 (1925–6), 162–77; H. Garrastachu, *Historia Synopsis Instituti Pontificii Internationalis Angelici*, Rome 1929, 4–15; A. Walz, *L'Università San Tommaso in Roma*, Rome 1966, 12–15. These works deal with the history of the Giustiniani bequest and the Minerva College of St Thomas Aquinas; see also I. P. Grossi, 'Dal Collegium D. Thomae de Urbe al Pontificio Ateneo Angelicum' in *Memorie Domenicane*, 35 (1959), 5–33.

43 Rome, Archivio di S. Maria della Minerva, Libro dell'uscita del Collegio di S. Thomas Aquino, ff 3r, 4v, 5r, 6r, 181r. These Irish Dominicans are also in a list of students compiled on a loose sheet inserted in the above register. See B. Carderi, 'I Registri del Collegio S. Tommaso d'Aquino in Roma conservati nell' Archivo del Convento di S. Maria sopra Minerva' in *Memorie Domenicane*, nuova ser., 7 (1976), 346–58. The vital register entitled 'Liber Collegii Sancti Thomae de Aquino Ordinis Praedicatorum, 1603–1646 ca.', which detailed the entry and duration of stay of Irish Dominican students, disappeared *c.*1980.

44 See also incomplete lists in B. Egan, C. Giblin and C. McGrath (eds), 'Irish Students Ordained in Rome (1625–1710)' in *IER*, 5th ser., 61 (1943), 116–24.

In the French provinces the most important houses of studies in 1615 were at Paris (St Jacques and that of the convent of the Annunciation), Rennes in Brittany, Avignon[45] and Bordeaux (1617). Five Irish Dominicans were solemnly professed in the reformed convent of Toulouse between 1603 and 1610. The Irish province continued to have a connection with the reformed province of Aquitaine (Occitanie), at least during the first half of the century. Irish students thereafter were assigned to the other French provinces, but the widespread destruction of ecclesiastical archives during the French Revolution precludes a more complete picture of Irish Dominicans in seventeenth-century France.

DOMINICAN STUDIES IN THE PROVINCE OF CASTILLE

The academic year in Spain, as in other continental Dominican houses of study, commenced on 14 September, the feast of the Exaltation of the Holy Cross. Regents of studies, lectors, masters of students and other officials were ordered to be present in their houses for the solemn opening of the year. Lectures and literary exercises were to begin punctually, and 'cases of conscience' were to be discussed regularly, especially in the seasons of Quadragesima and Advent, until 24 June (feast of St Mary Magdalene, patroness of the Order). The form and content of studies were regulated by general statutes contained in a *ratio studiorum* and by the ordinations of successive provincial chapters. The summary provided here is gleaned from the provincial chapter ordinations (1595–1629) for the province of Castille or Spain, then one of the most flourishing in the Order.

It was presumed that every student was well grounded in the study of the humanities and specifically grammar, in other words the basic rudiments of Latin and Greek. This was made mandatory for admission to religious profession. Students were forbidden to discontinue or interrupt their studies until they had completed three years of arts (largely philosophy) and three of theology, otherwise they would be judged unfit for preaching or hearing confessions. Likewise students were not allowed to transfer from one house of studies to another during the academic year except on the grounds of health or other exceptional circumstances. Nobody was to be promoted to the priesthood unless he had finished the prescribed arts course and had read the full course of theological studies.

The first division of studies was the arts course. This consisted mainly of a course of Aristotelian philosophy accompanied by the commentaries of Thomas Aquinas extending over three or four years. Though not

45 Lopez, *La Historia General de Santo Domingo y de su Orden*, iv, 999–1000.

explicitly stated, it generally included the study of literature, the art of composition and intensive study of languages, above all Latin and Greek. The first year was devoted to the study of works on logic, including the *Summulae Logicales* of Peter of Spain. (At Bologna this year served as an introduction to a three-year philosophy course.) The second year was spent reading the first books of Aristotle's *Physics* and his *De Generatione et Corruptione*. The third year was taken up with reading Aquinas's commentaries on Aristotle's *De Anima* and *Metaphysics*, and other classical philosophical texts such as Aquinas's *De Ente et Essentia*. Philosophy debates and disputations (*conclusiones*) were to be held diligently every week in the *studia generalia* of the province and monthly in the *studia minora*.

The second and major division of studies was theology. Again, though not the subject of an ordination, the course included sacred scripture, the Councils of the Church, canon law and apologetics or controversial theology (*controversia*).[46] Students read speculative as well as practical moral theology. Great stress was laid on study of the theological works of Thomas Aquinas, above all the *Summa Theologiae*, which was systematically treated from beginning to end. Sacred doctrine was to be taught and interpreted according to the mind of Aquinas, and exposition was to follow the tradition of the Dominican schools and commentators. All theological students were obliged to have a copy of the *Summa Theologiae*; those lacking copies were to be deprived of holidays. Annual holidays were from mid-July to mid-September. Lectures on dogmatic theology alternated with lectures on speculative and practical moral theology, to ensure that students would be adequately prepared for preaching, confessions and pastoral counselling. In all *studia generalia* public theological disputations were held every month, and with particular solemnity on six occasions during the year. Lectors were strictly forbidden to suspend lecturing or to grant holidays on any pretext except on major festivals and the feasts of Dominican saints. Priors and lectors, under pain of dismissal, were to examine all students twice a year. Negligent students were to be reprimanded and punished. The second examination was to be held at the end of the academic year, when a mature judgement was to be made by the lectors about the intellectual and moral calibre of the students. If individual students were found to be insufficiently instructed, they had to repeat their courses in philosophy or theology.

46 That Irish Dominicans were trained in apologetics or controversy is indicated by surviving fragmentary evidence. In J. Wadsworth, *Further Observations of the English Spanish Pilgrim*, London 1630, 24, there is reference to an Englishman thought to have been sent to the inquisition of Toledo, 'in that he had disputed with an Irish Dominican friar, Fr Thomas, in matters of religion'. The Irish Dominican theologian, John Baptist Hackett (b. Fethard, *c.*1604), published a theological work entitled *Controversorium Theologicum* at Rome in 1654 (see p. 119 below).

Essentially the same scholastic regime, inspired by a tested *ratio communis studiorum*, obtained in the *studia generalia* of France, Portugal, Italy, Lower Germany and Flanders. Happily the late medieval curriculum of Salamanca University proved itself singularly flexible and adaptable. Salamanca's 'humanist teaching became a natural part of the rhetoric and philosophy course, and what was particularly valuable to the community's Irish students, the best traditions of scholasticism were combined with modern mysticism in theological studies'.[47] Dominican students were, moreover, steeped in the Order's distinctive liturgy, sung several times a day in choir, its own devotional practices and its accumulated spiritual heritage. Early rising, semi-monastic silence, readings from the Bible, the constitutions of the Order and spiritual classics, austere conventual observances such as fasting, allied to strict discipline, all served the single purpose of an intense life of prayer and assiduous study. The reform-minded Master General, Sixtus Fabri, took a particular interest in the leading Italian *studium generale* of Bologna and issued special ordinations for its government in 1585. Likewise the Masters General Jerome Xavierre and Thomas Turco made similar and fresh ordinations to the same end in 1604 and 1645. It was to this classical Dominican scheme of education that young aspirants were introduced on their arrival from Ireland. While it would be interesting and instructive to know the average age of Dominican students, the necessary evidence is lacking. However, it is possible to offer an accurate estimate of the average age of almost one hundred Irish students on their enrolment at Salamanca during the period 1595–1619. Almost seventy of their number ranged in age from fifteen to twenty-five.

And so it came about that a new generation of Dominicans, who hitherto had known only the disturbed and unstable Ireland of the seventeenth century, came into contact with and were moulded by a revivified European civilisation enjoying unparalleled intellectual, religious and social vitality. They received from European universities and Dominican intellectual centres a formation that made them clearly aware of the issues raised by the Protestant Reformation and a thorough grounding in Catholic apologetics that was vigorously Tridentine in spirit. All this was achieved in an intellectual context wider and more objective than would have been possible in Ireland. Religiously, intellectually and culturally these Dominicans were well fitted to face, on return 'to the North' (a recurrent phrase in the Spanish State Papers at Simancas), the challenges awaiting them on the Irish mission.

47 Hammerstein, 'Aspects of the Continental Education of Irish Students in the Reign of Queen Elizabeth I', 147. For a valuable survey of Salamanca University arts, philosophy and theology curricula see A. M. Rodriguez Cruz, *Historia de las Universidades Hispanoamericanas*, i, Bogota 1973, 47–51.

From the late sixteenth century Spanish university and ecclesiastical authorities often contributed to the expenses of Irish priests returning to Ireland on completion of their studies.[48] From the second decade of the seventeenth century it became customary for the King of Spain to approve of grants ranging from 50 to 200 ducats from the state treasury. The standard payment was 100 ducats, which was a generous donation. The royal contribution was called '*ayuda de costa*' or more precisely '*viatico*' (viaticum or travelling allowance). The viaticum was intended to cover the costs of suitable secular dress, the passage home by ship, vestments, sacred vessels, liturgical and theological books and general travel expenses. To obtain it the applicant had to present a certificate that showed that he had finished his studies and to give a firm promise that he was returning to Ireland, Scotland or England to work as a priest. Such requests were at first referred to the king's confessor and later consistently to the royal almoner, who was normally the court prelate with the honorific title 'Patriarch of the Indies'. He in turn personally interviewed the applicants and made a decision on their requests which was afterwards endorsed by the council of state and initialled by the king. In order to prevent petitioners obtaining the viaticum and then remaining on in Spain or applying for it again, the royal treasury often ordered that the viaticum be paid only once, or almost at the last moment at a designated port of departure.

In the case of the Irish Dominicans, this aid was applied for and granted from 1614, at first erratically, but from the mid-1620s in a gradually more regular way by the Spanish kings Philip III (the Pious), Philip IV, and their successors until the end of the eighteenth century. One of the first to receive a viaticum was Ross MacGeoghegan in 1614, when he was granted 200 ducats.[49] None was granted in 1615–16, and only one in 1617. However, in 1618 eight named Dominicans obtained the viaticum at the request of Ross MacGeoghegan.[50] From the 1620s the viaticum was normally given to three Dominicans a year. Owing to severe financial restraints on the royal finances, the payment of the viaticum during 1630–36 fell constantly into arrears.[51] This effectively hindered the flow of Dominicans to Ireland for a short time. The Irish Franciscans and Augustinians also availed of the viaticum to dispatch an average of three priests to Ireland yearly from roughly the same date. Altogether about seventy Irish Dominicans availed of the viaticum between 1614 and 1640.

48 A. Huarte, 'Petitions of Irish Students in the University of Salamanca, 1574–91' in *Archiv. Hib.*, 4 (1915), 96–130.

49 AGS, Estado, leg. 2748.

50 Ibid., leg. 2750.

51 Ibid., leg. 2759, 2797, 2798, 2799.

The principal ports of embarkation were Bilbao and the smaller fishing ports in the north-west Basque country, and also La Coruña, Lisbon, Seville, Bayona, Sanlúcar de Barrameda, Cádiz and Málaga. Spanish ships went direct to Irish ports such as Galway, Limerick, Cork and Waterford, or sometimes only as far as the Flemish ports, necessitating further and dangerous crossings to Ireland. Personal tragedy and perils at sea were not uncommon.[52] Piracy resulting in the loss of goods and money or capture by north African corsairs and subsequent sale into slavery happened from time to time. One victim of such an experience was Anthony Lynch of Galway. A former merchant in the city of Lisbon, he studied as a late vocation at the Irish College there and at Salamanca before entering the Order at São Domingos, Lisbon, in 1605. While travelling from Spain to Ireland about 1615, his ship was captured by Turkish pirates and he was soon sold to the King of Morocco. He remained in captivity for eight years. In 1621 his kinsman Nicholas Lynch, a future Dominican provincial, was granted permission by the Master of the Order to go to Spain with the ransom money to redeem him.[53] He regained his freedom in the year 1623, when he also submitted two memorials describing his captivity and giving information about Morocco and its strategic defences to the King of Spain.[54] Another Dominican, Raymund or Edmund O'Hehir, *en route* to Ireland from Spain where he had studied, was also captured by Barbary pirates in the late 1620s or early 1630s. He was tortured for refusing to renounce his Christian faith and suffered greatly during a long captivity. Yet he managed to preach and administer the sacraments to Christian prisoners. When he was freed, he returned to Ireland, where he devoted himself to the ministry until his death in 1642.[55]

SOME DOMINICANS WHO DID NOT RETURN

Not all Irish Dominicans applied immediately for the viaticum. Either by personal wish or force of circumstances many prolonged their stay in Spain or Portugal. Still others never set foot in their native land again, perhaps preferring more civilised European life to the rigours and uncertainties of the Irish situation. Inevitably there were those who

52 J. J. Silke, 'The Irish Abroad, 1534–1691' in *NHI*, iii, 625. The author mistakenly identifies an Irish student priest, John de la Roche, as a Dominican. The priest set out four times from Cadiz for Ireland, but each time was forced back by storms. The Spanish abbreviation for ducats was misread as 'Order of Preachers' in AGS, Estado, leg. 2752.

53 Fenning, *Irish material*, 281.

54 AGS, Estado, leg. 2752.

55 Acts of general chapter, Rome 1644, in Reichert, *MOPH*, xii, 207; Frei Manoel de Lima, *Agiologio Dominico*, i, Lisbon 1709, 250; Burke, *Hib. Dom.*, 563.

became tutors in wealthy families, chaplains to the Irish regiments in Flanders in the Spanish service, those who excelled in the academic field or were chosen by the Masters General to assist them in the government of the Order, and finally those who became secret agents and negotiators for the Kings of Spain and Portugal because of their knowledge of English politics, language and social customs.

In February 1605 Dominic Burke petitioned Philip III for permission to go to Flanders, where he wished to preach and minister to the Irish regiment. He had heard how the heretics had killed his brother in Ireland, exiled another brother and would persecute him also if he should return there. It was proposed that he should be given letters of recommendation to the Archduke Albert in Flanders and 1,000 reals for the journey.[56]

There is an abundance of evidence from the Spanish State Papers at Simancas to show that the Anglo-Irish William of the Holy Spirit Talbot was employed during the 1620s as a secret agent of the Spanish crown in relation to political affairs in England and Ireland.[57] On closer inspection the documentation reveals that he may have been a double agent working for the King of England and his officials, notably John Bathe and the Duke of Buckingham. English instructions and misinformation were passed on to him chiefly by his cousin, John Bathe, a member of the English court, also a spy, who feigned to be the loyal agent of the King of Spain. It was this same John Bathe who assassinated Donal O'Sullivan Beare close to the royal convent and church of Santo Domingo in Madrid on 16 July 1618.[58] In September 1627 Spanish state officials carried out a secret investigation into the activities of William Talbot, in the course of which they consulted John Falvey, a prominent Irish exile at the Spanish court, and Florence Conry, O.F.M., Archbishop of Tuam, for their opinion of this Dominican friar. Both warned that Talbot was, beyond all shadow of doubt, an English spy. Falvey alleged that Talbot was in regular communication with the ambassadors of England, that he professed to know what went on at the meetings of the Spanish council of state and passed on vital information to his English contacts, that he was in hiding for some time because he was sought by the Inquisitor General, that he took advantage of Count Gondomar's journey to Flanders to go there with him, and that he was friendly with all the spies of England in Spain. In conclusion, Falvey referred his correspondent, the Marques de Montes Claros, to speak of the matter with Archbishop Conry of Tuam and his companion Fr Hugh Burke, O.F.M., with Richard de la Peña, O.P., Fr Richard Gould of the Trinitarian Order, and other Irish gentlemen, ecclesiastic and lay, who were resident in Madrid.

56 AGS, Estado, leg. 2767.
57 Ibid., leg. 2041, 2785, 2787, 2758.
58 Walsh, *'Destruction by Peace': Hugh O'Neill after Kinsale*, 109–11.

Archbishop Conry did not mince his words when he wrote his estimation of William Talbot. At the outset he described him as an absurd person (*persona absurdissima*), who was not Irish at heart, but an Englishman. Talbot, he continued, had been born in the anglicised part of Ireland and was most hostile towards those of his nation who served the King of Spain in Ireland and who were exiled as a result. When the Prince of Wales was in Spain, Talbot sought to ingratiate himself with him by presenting a memorial in which he reviled all the Irish gentlemen who served the King of Spain and in this connection threatened to denounce the Baron of Louth to the Privy Council in England for having had traitorous dealings with Irish exiles in Spain. Conry alleged that Talbot had communicated to John Bathe confidential information presented at the court, touching on matters of importance against England. Bathe had then presented this document to the King of England, who was very grateful for it. For this and for other similar reasons Talbot had been exiled from the court several times and was badly thought of among those of his Order. The archbishop intimated that Irish exiles were saddened to see William Talbot and his likes admitted and favoured at court. He hoped that the king's ministers did not trust them and only used them in the interests of Spain—which was exactly what the Spanish authorities did.

While admittedly the testimony of the Gaelic Irish John Falvey and the Archbishop of Tuam against Talbot might be biased or open to question, the Spanish were extremely adept in checking and counter-checking the credentials and real intentions of their agents, Gaelic Irish and Anglo-Irish alike. Their declared policy with reference to William Talbot was that he should be shown approval, given some travelling expenses for his countless journeys, and asked to continue supplying information. Other prominent contemporary personages mentioned in this fascinating bundle of Simancas documents of September and October 1627 were the Earl of Dorset, James Talbot (proposed for the archbishopric of Armagh), the Anglo-Irish in Flanders, the Earl of Tyrconnell and Thomas Preston, brother of Viscount Gormanston. Earlier, before he was caught up in the web of Spanish and English espionage, William Talbot, procurator of the Irish congregation in 1613, had been charged with the task of obtaining a college exclusively for his province from the King of Spain.[59]

Michael of the Holy Spirit (O'Donnell or O'Connor) was assigned to Prague in the province of Bohemia as a lector of philosophy in September 1627.[60] He had previously lectured in Louvain until late in 1626, when

59 Fenning, *Irish material*, 278.
60 Ibid., 282–3.

Ross MacGeoghegan sent him as procurator to Rome.[61] By November 1630 he had already served as prior of the convent of St Aegidius in Prague. At the end of his term of office he was allowed to return to Ireland by the Master General,[62] but was never heard of again.

Easily the most renowned Irish Dominican theologians in this epoch were James Arthur and John Baptist Hackett. The former, a member of the leading merchant family of Limerick, was educated at the University of Salamanca (1610–16).[63] In rapid succession he filled a series of teaching posts: lector of theology at León (*c.* 1626)[64] and elsewhere in Spain in the 1620s,[65] regent of Collegio di San Tommaso, Naples, in 1630,[66] and regent of the *studium generale* of Avila in the 1630s.[67] He had temporarily (1627 or 1628) occupied one of the chairs of theology at Salamanca University,[68] was afterwards regent of studies at the premier theological graduate college of San Gregorio, Valladolid,[69] and was nominated to the principal chair of theology at Coimbra University by Philip IV in 1640.[70] He died in Lisbon on 1 February 1644. A devoted Thomist, James Arthur wrote a series of commentaries on virtually the entire *Summa Theologiae* which survived in manuscript form in Spain and Portugal entitled *Commentaria in totam fere S. Thomae de Aquino Summam*.[71]

Even more influential was the brilliant Thomist philosopher and theologian John Baptist Hackett, of the prominent Fethard Anglo-Norman family, who entered the Order at Cashel[72] *c.* 1622. He studied in Spain and was ordained deacon and priest at Barcelona in 1630.[73] Later he lectured with distinction in the Order's *studia generalia* of Milan, Naples and Rome. He was eagerly sought as theological adviser by several Roman cardinals, including Cardinal Altieri, who, as Pope Clement X, appointed him his

61 APF, SOCG, 129, f. 313r; B. Millett, 'Catalogue of Irish Material in Vols 129–131 of SOCG in Propaganda Archives' in *Collect. Hib.*, 11 (1968), 12.
62 Fenning, *Irish material*, 286.
63 AUS, Libros de Matriculas, 315, f. 13r; 318, f. 15r; 319, f. 15r; 320, f. 13v.
64 *Wadding Papers*, 175.
65 APF, SOCG, 294, f. 104r; Moran, *Spicil. Ossor.*, i, 160.
66 Fenning, *Irish Material*, 286.
67 Salamanca, San Esteban provincial archives, provincial chapter acts, 1637, p. 3.
68 APF, SOCG, 294, f. 28; *Wadding Papers*, 209, 226; B. Millett, 'Catalogue of Vol. 294 of SOCG in Propaganda Archives' in *Collect. Hib.*, 8 (1965), 10 (name Archer *recte* Arthur).
69 J. Barrio, 'Historia del Convento de S. Esteban' in J. Cuervo (ed.), *Historiadores del Convento de San Esteban de Salamanca*, ii, Salamanca 1914, 927.
70 Fenning, *Irish material*, 304.
71 Quétif and Echard, *Scriptores Ordinis Praedicatorum*, ii, 536; Burke, *Hib. Dom.*, 541–2.
72 Burke, *Hib. Dom.*, 542.
73 Barcelona, Archivo Archidiocesano, Register of Ordinations (1621-41) (unfoliated).

personal theologian.[74] While regent of studies at St Eustorgius, Milan, Hackett became celebrated for his role in strengthening the resolve of Philip Thomas (later Cardinal) Howard, son of the Protestant Duke of Norfolk, in his dramatic decision to join the Dominican Order in 1645. He died at Rome on 26 August 1676.[75] His published works included: *Controversorium Theologicum complectens omnes Tractatus totius Primae Secundae Doctoris Angelici D. Thomae Aquinatis* (Rome 1654); *Synopsis Theologica in Tractatum de Fide, Spe, & Charitate* (Rome 1659); *Synopsis Summulistica* (Rome 1659); *Synopsis Physica* (Rome 1659); *Synopsis Metheorica* (Rome 1659); *Synopsis Philosophica* (Rome 1662); *Synopsis Universa Theologiae Scholasticae et Moralis in quinque tomos distributa iuxta mentem Doctoris Angelici D. Thomae Aquinatis* (Rome 1663).[76]

Arthur MacGeoghegan, an alumnus of Mullingar, was born in Westmeath. As chaplain to the Spanish navy and port chaplain at Lisbon in the early 1630s,[77] his duties included the censorship of books and inspection of suspect English and Dutch ships, Spain being then at war with Holland. Partly because of his proficiency in several languages, the Spanish viceroy had employed him in this work. In pursuing his duties, he detained an Englishman, Captain Bust, whose ship had been confiscated on suspicion that it was Dutch. In the spring of 1633 he set out for Ireland via London to select students for the new college of the Irish Dominicans at Lisbon and also to transact some business for the viceroy of Portugal. While in London, MacGeoghegan encountered Bust, who had him imprisoned. Bust charged that MacGeoghegan had said at Lisbon that if he ever returned to England, he would kill the king as a heretic. MacGeoghegan, under questioning, admitted some slight foundation for the charge, but insisted that his words had been misconstrued. He explained that what he had hypothetically said in his dispute with the English sea captain was that without free will fanaticism would find its excuse, even if a man were to assassinate the King of England. Few believed his account, and all defence proved useless. King Charles, hearing the case, expressed the hope that the friar would be acquitted. His minister Windebank and Queen Henrietta Maria also tried to save him from false conviction before the King's Bench on 25 November for speaking treasonable words. On 27 November 1633 Arthur MacGeoghegan was executed at Tyburn out of hatred for the Catholic faith. His body underwent the mutilation prescribed for treason, but, contrary to custom, his members were not displayed upon the four gates of the

74 Burke, *Hib. Dom.*, 542.
75 Ibid., 542–4.
76 Ibid., 544; Quetif and Echard, *Scriptores Ordinis Praedicatorum*, ii, 579.
77 AGS, Guerra Antigua, leg. 1044. For MacGeoghegan's connection with Lisbon see also p. 204 below.

city. He was either buried beneath the scaffold or carried off by friends to be interred respectfully elsewhere. His execution gratified that portion of the London populace that believed Catholics to be regicides.[78] According to another testimony, the death of the Irish Dominican had done more good than injury to the Catholic cause, as almost everybody judged that he died innocent of the crime of which he had been accused.[79]

Daniel Dominic O'Daly (1595–1662) was a most distinguished and versatile Irish Dominican, the quintessential Irish European of the seventeenth century. The brilliance of his diplomatic, political and ecclesiastical career is reflected in the diversity of his appointments and interests. He was agent of Philip IV of Spain in diplomatic business with Charles I and Charles II of England, unofficial representative of Queen Henrietta Maria and her son Charles II to Pope Innocent X, envoy of John IV of Portugal to Charles I, and finally ambassador of Portugal to Louis XIV of France in the years 1656–7.[80] Towards the end of his career the Portuguese government authorities nominated him to the archbishopric of the primatial see of Braga, and later to the archbishopric of Goa in the East Indies (both of which he declined), and finally to the bishopric of Coimbra, which he accepted.

Born at Kilsarkan in the modern parish of Killeentierna (Cillín Tiarna) near Castleisland, Co. Kerry, in 1595, he was almost certainly a member of the Kerry branch of the famous bardic family of Ó Dálaigh.[81] He entered the Dominican Order at Lugo[82] in Galicia, Spain, and studied at Bordeaux, Burgos and Salamanca (1622–3).[83] After a short stay in

78 The original minutes of the arraignment of Arthur MacGeoghegan on the charge of high treason, 25 Nov. 1633, are preserved among the muniments of the Duke of Westminster, Heaton House, Cheshire; see also Reichert, *MOPH*, xii, 206; A. Carvalho da Costa, *Corografia Portuguesa*, iii, Lisbon 1712, 488; J. da Natividade, *Additamento ao Agiologio Dominico*, v, Lisbon 1743, 470–1; Burke, *Hib. Dom.*, 419, 559–60; R. Walsh, 'Some of Our Martyrs' in *IER*, 3rd ser., 15 (1894), 885–916; R. Devas, *Dominican Martyrs of Great Britain*, London 1912, 75–6; M. J. Havran, *The Catholics in Caroline England*, London 1962, 114. (This last item contains the most concise modern account of his life.)

79 BAV, Barberini Latini MSS, no. 8105, f. 61.

80 Burke, *Hib. Dom.*, 492.

81 See M. B. Curtin [MacCurtain], 'Daniel O'Daly, 1595–1662: A Study of Irish-European Relationships in the Seventeenth Century' (MA thesis, University College, Dublin, 1958); B. MacCurtain, 'An Irish Agent of the Counter-Reformation: Dominic O'Daly' in *Irish Historical Studies*, 60 (1967). A summary of his career appears in M. MacCurtain, 'Dominic O'Daly' in A. M. Brady and B. Cleeve (eds), *A Biographical Dictionary of Irish Writers*, Mullingar 1985, 340–1.

82 Frei Lucas de Santa Catarina, *Historia de S. Domingos*, iv, Lisbon 1711, 733; Burke, *Hib. Dom.*, 418.

83 Frei Lucas, *Historia de S. Domingos*, iv, 733, for studies at Burgos; Burke, *Hib. Dom.*, 419, for studies at Burgos and Bordeaux; AUS, Libros de Matriculas, 327, f. 10v, for studies at Salamanca.

Ireland he was deeply associated with the fledgling Irish Dominican college of Louvain and subsequently was the driving force behind the foundation of the Lisbon college of his province in the face of unyielding local Portuguese administrative opposition and other daunting obstacles. The definitive establishment of this college, with which he was involved from 1634, became the great passion of his life. He was chiefly responsible for the founding of a convent of Irish Dominican contemplative nuns in the suburbs of Lisbon in 1639.[84] Two or three years before this date he visited Ireland at least once, because part of the agreement with Philip IV respecting the establishment of the nuns' convent of Bom Sucesso was that O'Daly should raise Irish troops in Limerick to serve with the Spanish forces in France and Catalonia.[85] However, when Portugal recovered its independence in 1640 and set up the Braganza monarchy, O'Daly became adviser to the Queen of Portugal.

Sometime after 1642 he was sent by the King of Portugal on a mission to Charles I of England, who urged him to visit Ireland and help form a coalition of royalist factions against the parliamentarians.[86] In turn, O'Daly urged the English king to grant civil and religious liberties to his Irish Catholic subjects, but failed to obtain guarantees; this left him with no option but to withdraw from the royal proposal to intervene diplomatically in Ireland.[87] This O'Daly might very well have succeeded in achieving, as there is evidence that he was a harbinger of what crystallised as the Confederation of Kilkenny, and that his diplomatic skills and experience might have succeeded in reconciling the disparate points of view of its several parties. Already at the Spanish court in April 1633 O'Daly represented himself as the person chiefly responsible for the foundations of Louvain and Lisbon, and indeed for the Irish Dominican mission itself. In a memorial to Philip IV[88] he disclosed his commitment to a project of much greater importance to Ireland than any continental college foundation. What he envisaged was the creation of a league or union of Catholics whose objectives would extend beyond their spiritual welfare and stimulate the hope of freeing or ransoming their country. To facilitate this scheme he asked the King of Spain for letters of recommendation to the Pope and the Spanish ambassador in Rome. Regretfully, details of these politico-religious aspirations and plans were not spelt out in this petition to the king, perhaps on account

84 A detailed account of O'Daly's role in the Irish continental college movement, and in particular his close association with the foundation of the two Irish Dominican establishments at Lisbon, is given in Chapter 7.

85 Frei Agostinho de Santa Maria, *O Santuario Mariano*, ii, Lisbon 1707, 12–13.

86 M. MacCurtain, 'Dominic O'Daly' (1985), 341.

87 Ibid.

88 AGS, Estado, leg. 2796.

of diplomatic reticence or sheer shrewdness. Nowhere was the enigma of O'Daly more sharply highlighted than in his political aspirations for Ireland. The convinced royalist and consistent upholder of Stuart monarchist claims abandoned his customary diplomatic persona and declared his bold vision of a free and independent kingdom of Ireland in a letter to the beleaguered Earl of Ormond, which provoked a horrified comment.[89] The explanation may lie in O'Daly's unremitting devotion to the Catholic cause which runs as a strong thread through the complexities of all his Irish and European endeavours and ultimately determined his politics and allegiances. In 1656 he became Portuguese ambassador to Louis XIV of France. In the previous year 1655 he published in Latin at Lisbon his *History of the Geraldines and an Account of the Persecution in Ireland*, a work which disappointingly says little about the lives of his confrères, especially those martyred for their faith and religious vocation. He died at Lisbon on 30 June 1662 as Bishop-elect of Coimbra and president of the state council of Portugal.

John Nolan, originally of Kilkenny, distinguished himself as an academic and as an administrator in the Order. In the 1620s he had been received into the Order at Zamora, and studied and taught at Pamplona.[90] In the 1630s he was conventual lector of theology at Rennes.[91] In 1639 he was made rector of the Irish Dominican college at Louvain.[92] He was appointed vicar general of the congregation of Lithuania in 1644, and in the same year companion to the commissary of the province of Poland, and was also charged with the reorganisation of the Order in Hungary.[93] As representative of the Master General he helped settle disputes in the French convent of Besançon.[94] About 1650 he was deputed to deal with a Mexican dispute.[95] When regent of studies in the college of St Thomas Aquinas at the Minerva, Rome, he unsuccessfully applied to the Holy See to have Rinuccini's censures revoked in 1656.[96] While at Rome he became deeply involved in the controversy concerning the efficacy of divine grace and predestination. So strongly did he oppose those who impugned the doctrine of St Thomas Aquinas that it was ordered that he should be imprisoned.[97] In

89 Bodl., Carte MSS, XXIX, p. 506, addition 642 (new pagination): O'Daly to Ormond, received 28 Aug. 1650, cited in M. B. Curtin, 'Daniel O'Daly' (1958), 201.
90 O'Heyne, *Epil. Chron.*, 36.
91 Fenning, *Irish material*, 293, 298.
92 Ibid., 298.
93 Ibid., 313, 314.
94 ASV, Fondo Domenicani, pergameno 266; Fenning, *Irish material*, 317.
95 AGOP, XIV, Liber I, ff 795–851.
96 Moran, *Spicil. Ossor.*, iii, 195.
97 O'Heyne, *Epil. Chron.*, 36.

the late 1650s he retired to Rennes in Brittany, where he promoted studies until his death.[98]

Three other Irish Dominican authors are worthy of mention. The first is Brother Maurice of the Presentation Roche, a native of Kinsale. On 22 November 1613 he made profession as a simple brother of the Order at the convent of Santo Tomás, Madrid. He wrote a book entitled *Arte de la Memoria* (*The Art of Memory*), for which he was justly celebrated. He died in 1632.[99]

Henry O'Rian (Ryan), who lived at Rome in the 1630s, was an accomplished Latin poet. To celebrate the visit of Charles de Crequi, envoy of the French king, to Pope Urban VIII in 1633, he was commissioned to compose a laudatory poem. It has been described as most elegant, consisting of 250 verses in high-flown language.[100] It was certainly monumental and in keeping with baroque style.

Pádraigín Haicéad (*c.*1604–54) was one of the finest Irish poets of the seventeenth century. He was born in Tipperary of a prominent Old English family, the second son of James Haicéad FitzPiers and Margaret Kearney of Baltarsna, three miles north of Cashel.[101] He entered the Order before 1627 at Limerick, where he was joined by two cousins: Patrick Kearney and John Baptist Hackett of Fethard,[102] the future theological writer. Thereafter he spent much of his life in exile mostly at Morlaix, Rennes, Paris and Louvain.[103] In 1638 he returned to Ireland, where he was soon involved in peace-making efforts between the Old English and Old Irish (with whom he allied himself) in the aftermath of the 1641 rising. He was mentioned in the political correspondence of the nuncio Rinuccini. When prior of the Cashel Dominicans he was obliged to flee the country in 1651 and go again as an exile to Louvain. There he

98 Ibid. John Nolan is the subject of a long notice by J. Toravel, *Nomenclature des Religieux de la Congregation de Bretagne au XVIIème et XVIIIème siècles*, Angers 1964, 121.

99 Seville, Archivo de la Provincia Dominicana de Andalucía, J. de Muñana, *Ilustres Fundaciones y yarones de España*, 1720, f. 10; A. M. Escudero, *Historia del Convento de Santo Tomás de Madrid del Orden de Predicadores*, ed. D. F. Viñals, i, Madrid 1900, 84.

100 The poem was entitled: *Poema Encomiasticon de Adventu Excellentissimi Ducis Caroli de Crequi Marescalli, Ducis & Paris Franciae, Christianissimi Regis ad SS. Patrem Urbanum VIII Oratoris Extraordinarii*, published by Ludovico Grignani, Rome 1633. See Quétif and Echard, *Scriptores Ordinis Praedicatorum*, ii, 476.

101 H. D. Gallwey (ed.), 'A Kearney Funeral Entry of 1641' in *Irish Genealogist*, 5 (1975), 265.

102 APF, SOCG, 294, ff 103v–104r.

103 *Filíocht Phádraigín Haicéad*, ed. M. Ní Cheallacháin, Dublin 1962, x: Louvain (1630), Morlaix (1632); archival notes of Père Toravel, Convent des Dominicains de Rennes: Rennes (Sept. 1634 – Sept. 1635); Fenning, *Irish material*, 295: assigned to St Jacques, Paris (19 Dec. 1635).

became embroiled in controversy with his provincial and the domestic squabbles of his confrères. He died in Louvain in November 1654.[104]

This Dominican poet was a most passionate, sensitive person; and though frequently contentious and troubled in spirit, his verse spoke straight from the heart. At times the ferocity and sheer brilliance of his poetry is breathtaking, reflecting the complexities of religious and political divisions of his age. In exile his love for Ireland intensified, and devastating loneliness pervades much of his continental poetry. Some fifty poems attributed to Haicéad consist of rousing patriotic verse, love poems, elegies and occasional poems. In collaboration with Baothghalach Óg Mac Aodhagáin, O.F.M., he compiled a Latin *Annals of the Kingdom of Ireland*, a work later lost.[105] Pádraigín Haicéad was a contemporary of another Munster priest-poet and celebrated writer, Seathrún Céitinn (Geoffrey Keating). He too was of Old English descent and had been educated likewise for the priesthood on the continent, where he wrote Irish verse, afterwards ministering in the ancient parishes of Knockgraffon and Tubrid (New Inn/Cahir area). Their poetry is so alike in style and outlook that their authorship has often been confused.[106]

Finally, in a totally different category were Raymund of St Catherine and Peter French, both of whom sailed to the New World. Having spent some years wandering about in the prosperous province of Peru, collecting funds for the Irish colleges of Spain, Raymund of St Catherine was peremptorily ordered to return to Ireland in September 1640.[107]

Peter French was a native of Galway. On completion of his studies in Andalucía in the 1640s, he was permitted to sail for Spanish America. For thirty years he worked zealously among the Indian peoples of Mexico. His command of one of the Indian languages was so accurate that he compiled a catechism for the people to whom he ministered in their own language. In Latin it was entitled *Catechismus seu Expositio Fidei Christianae.* The Dominican province of Mexico honoured him by making him a preacher general. He subsequently returned to Ireland and was a member of the Galway community from before 1683 until his death in 1693.[108]

The exceptional individuals whose overseas careers are outlined above were not typical of the Dominican Order in general. It was expected

104 A. Valkenburg, 'Pádraigín an Doiminiceach as Caiseal Mumhan' in *Feasta*, 36 (1983), 15–19; *Filíocht Phádraigín Haicéad*, ed. Ní Cheallacháin, ix–xx.

105 Ó Raghailligh, *A Genealogical History of the O'Reillys*, 9, 11.

106 B. Ó Cuív, 'The Irish Language in the Early Modern Period' in *NHI*, iii, 539–40. Editions of his collected poems: T. Ó Donnchadha, *An t-Athair Pádraigín Haicéad*, Dublin 1916; *Filíocht Phádraigín Haicéad*, ed. Ní Cheallacháin.

107 Fenning, *Irish material*, 305.

108 Quétif and Echard, *Scriptores Ordinis Praedicatorum*, ii, 735; TA, *Liber Provinciae* or *Registrum Provinciae* [1680–1717], ff 1, 7, 8, 12, 19, 22, 28, 34; O'Heyne, *Epil. Chron.*, 136–9; Burke, *Hib. Dom.*, 545.

that the students who received their education on the continent would, on completion of their studies, return to minister in their native lands, and in the case of the vast majority of Irish Dominicans this expectation was fulfilled. They lost neither their courage, their vocation nor their idealism; and when the appointed time came, they freely returned to Ireland despite the obvious dangers and hardships ahead of them.

DOMESTIC AND INTERNATIONAL DIVISIONS

In the seventeenth century a person's civil province of origin, as well as his ethnic and cultural background, was important and consequential. As far as members of international religious orders were concerned, the problem of provincialism in this era was mitigated by the deep experience of life in continental Europe. Although provincialism must have been a live issue for the Irish Dominicans, it did not become the severe problem it did for their more numerous Franciscan brethren. Each of the four Franciscan colleges of Louvain, Prague, Rome and Paris was tinged unapologetically by provincial rivalries paralleling those among the diocesan clergy. Indeed, about 1623 an effort was made to split the Irish Franciscan province into two on a purely racial or ethnic basis: Leinster and Munster for the Anglo-Irish and Ulster and Connacht for the Old Irish.[109]

At the provincial chapters of the various orders of friars each civil province was represented formally by its own definitor (leading official and influential legislator), and the office of provincial rotated—in what was technically known as the *alternativa* system—between representatives of the civil provinces. Dominicans selected by provincial chapters for honorary theological degrees were carefully chosen from each of the four provinces, as was patently demonstrated by the petition of the 1635[110] and subsequent chapters. The question of rotation of the provincial's office was referred to Master General Nicholas Ridolfi for his advice after the 1638 chapter of Youghal, as will appear later.

Just as serious for religious life in the Irish setting were the fissures and problems caused by a racialist spirit between Old Irish and Anglo-Irish. However, the experience of religious life in an international context forced people to come to terms with their differences of outlook and to adopt a realistic *modus vivendi*. The friars tended to unify those disparate Irish groups and their interests. The English agent in Brussels reported to James I in 1615: 'The perfidious Machiavellian friars [Irish Franciscans] at Louvain . . . seek by all means to reconcile their countrymen in their affections and to combine those that are descended of the English

109 Conlan, *Franciscan Ireland*, 32–3.
110 Fenning, *Irish material*, 295. For evidence of the use of the *alternativa* system in the appointment of provincials see pp 297–8 below.

race and those that are mere Irish, in a league of friendship and concurrence against your Majesty and the true religion now professed in your kingdom.'[111]

Less serious but highly revealing was the rivalry that flared up from time to time between Dominicans educated in diverse continental schools. The French traveller and intellectual Boullaye Le Gouz who was invited to dine with the Cashel Dominicans in 1644 has left a delightful vignette of the members of that community.[112] The prior and host, Fabian Mulryan, was French-educated. Two unnamed members of the community were proud Salamanca men who did not conceal their prejudice and hostility towards Frenchmen and all things French as the guest endeavoured to swallow his '*soupe a l'Iroise*'. Falling in with the prior's rather malicious suggestion and causing him much delight, Boullaye Le Gouz silenced and vanquished the Irish representatives of Salamanca by his erudition and knowledge of physics, philosophy, theology and biblical problems.

111 Cited in full by C. P. Meehan, *The Fate and Fortunes of the Earls of Tyrone and Tyrconnell*, Dublin 1870, 492–3.

112 F. de la Boullaye Le Gouz, *Les Voyages et Observations du Sieur de la Boullaye Le Gouz*, Paris 1653, 442–9; T. Crofton Croker (ed. and trans.), *The Tour of the French Traveller Boullaye Le Gouz in Ireland, 1644*, London 1837, 17–23.

FIVE

Revival in Ireland, 1600–1627

RESTORATION ATTEMPTED: THE WORK OF SIMON O'HALLAGHAN, 1600–*c.*1607

In 1600 the Dominican vicar provincial, Thaddeus MacDuane, was succeeded by Daniel O'Crean of Sligo, while a younger confrère of almost equal consequence, Simon of the Holy Spirit O'Hallaghan, finally returned to Ireland after twenty years in Portugal. MacDuane was still provincial when he signed a petition (with the Franciscan and Carmelite provincials) to Rome on 13 June at Donegal, pressing for the appointment of proctors for the diocesan chapter of Raphoe;[1] shortly afterwards he was succeeded by O'Crean as vicar of the reduced Irish congregation from 1600 to 1604.[2] By 1603, it is claimed, not one Dominican house in Ireland remained unprofaned. Many religious had either been driven from the country or swept away by death. The survivors were forced to conceal themselves in the most remote places.[3]

News of the death of Queen Elizabeth on 24 March 1603, though somewhat delayed in reaching Ireland, signalled the start of a minor revolt by the corporations and citizens of the towns of Munster and south-east Leinster. The movement was popular, spontaneous and overtly Catholic in its expression. It manifested itself by large enthusiastic religious processions, the public celebration of Mass with great solemnity according to the Roman rite, the reappearance of friars in their habits, and the reconciliation or reconsecration of churches and cathedrals in Waterford, Cork, Limerick, Cashel, Kilkenny, Wexford, New Ross and other principal towns.[4] What was outwardly a religious insurrection mirroring intense Catholic feelings and aspirations had much deeper and more complex roots.

1 J. Hagan (ed.), 'Some Papers relating to the Nine Years' War' in *Archiv. Hib.*, 2 (1913), 293.

2 Burke, *Hib. Dom.*, 521 asserts that O'Crean was prior provincial (1600–4), but went to Spain in 1603, leaving MacDuane as his vicar who succeeded him in the office in 1604.

3 O'Heyne, *Epil. Chron.*, 274–5; B. de Jonghe, *Belgium Dominicanum sive Historiae Germaniae Inferioris Sacri Ordinis FF Praedicatorum*, Brussels 1719, 417–18.

4 Hagan, 'Some Papers relating to the Nine Years' War', 316–17.

By the spring of 1603 a combination of circumstances precipitated open protest and defiance on the part of the towns, traditional centres of English influence and culture. The Nine Years' War (1594–1603) had brought about general disruption of trade and an influx of fleeing English colonists into the hard-pressed towns. Widespread poverty and distress had been caused in the same towns by the currency debasement of 1601–3. Deep anger spilled over into formal protests against the Munster presidency concerning the blatant violations of urban charters and liberties which had been a common occurrence under Carew, President of Munster until 1603. On his departure for England, the relaxation of his stern rule and control of the towns encouraged the resistance and independence of the corporations. Catholic religious feeling and the desire for greater tolerance in religious practice in the towns became more outspoken throughout the war. To the Dublin government this represented potential civil rebellion and the remote possibility of the loyalist towns joining forces with Hugh O'Neill and the Gaelic Irish. Political and socio-economic as well as religious considerations, therefore, sparked off the disturbances in the corporate towns of the southern Irish counties in April and May 1603.[5]

The laws which had constrained Catholicism in the towns were openly defied and disregarded by citizens and clergy alike. With the proclamation of James VI of Scotland as King of England, it was universally believed for a time that the son of Mary Stuart would reign as a Catholic monarch or would speedily grant full civil and religious liberties to Catholics. An Englishman, William Farmer, sourly observed: 'Now came abroad in open show the Jesuits, seminary priests, and friars out of every corner, and walked up and down in every city and corporation. Now they began to alter the churches and religion, bringing forth old rotten stocks and stones of images, setting them up in their churches.'[6] The Dominicans re-emerged in some towns, notably Kilkenny, Waterford and Limerick, where they participated in the short-lived public restoration of Catholic life and worship. In Kilkenny, which had a large Catholic population, two Dominicans, Edmund Barry and Edward Raughter, with the aid of some townspeople broke open the doors of the Black Abbey, which for some sixty years had been in use as a courthouse. A contemporary report graphically described what ensued:

> A seditious friar carrying the name of Edmund Barry forcibly entered the building . . . a part whereof was converted to a sessions house for the whole county, being accordingly furnished with bars and

5 A. J. Sheehan, 'The Recusancy Revolt of 1603: A Reinterpretation' in *Archiv. Hib.*, 38 (1983), 10, 3–13 *passim*.

6 Cited ibid., 9.

> benches for that use, which he pulled down and therein erected [an altar for] the Mass, and dispossessed him that dwelt in the rest; which friar, being attended by two priests of the like profession, was daily guarded by the commons and attended by the Sovereign of that town and his brethren in his processions in and about the same, affronted the Earl of Ormond, disobeyed his voice and commandments; and some also of the higher calling carried a canopy over his head.[7]

Thus the Kilkenny Dominicans took possession once more of their desecrated church, where, according to an Elizabethan chronicler, even the tombs and funerary monuments of the Marshalls, the family of the founder, and those of eighteen other knights had been defaced and turned into swine-troughs.[8] Within a month the Lord Deputy, Mountjoy, gave orders that the churches should once more revert to Protestant worship. At the same time he commanded the citizens of Kilkenny 'to pull down certain relics of popery which they had put up [in the Black Abbey] and to reduce the place to the use of a sessions house'.[9] The city officials refused to comply. Mountjoy, in a letter of 2 July 1603, bitterly complained that despite his orders, 'they have made new additions of idolatrous images and many other idle toys; and they maintain openly there a friar of great note among the Papists'.[10] This 'friar of great note', hitherto unidentified, was almost certainly Simon of the Holy Spirit O'Hallaghan, O.P., who, as will be shortly seen, was a leading figure in an attempt to revive the Dominicans in Ireland. At length a mandate was issued to Sir Walter Archer, Sovereign of Kilkenny, to put to secular use the church of the Dominicans so recently reconsecrated for Catholic worship. This he absolutely refused to do. As a consequence, he was incarcerated for a considerable time. On his liberation or escape, he left for the continent, where he died shortly afterwards on 24 August 1604.[11]

Events in Kilkenny had been inspired by the audacious example of the city of Waterford. Already in 1597 Thomas Comerford, a merchant of the city, on arrival in Lisbon, asserted 'that in Waterford all are Catholics, hear Mass and receive the sacraments, though clandestinely from the English'.[12] The leader of the Catholic revival in Waterford was

7 W. Carrigan, *The History and Antiquities of the Diocese of Ossory*, i, Dublin 1905, 78; Coleman, *Ancient Dominican Foundations*, 28.
8 M. Hanmer, *The Chronicle of Ireland* (Dublin 1633), Dublin 1809, 346.
9 *Cal. Pat. Rolls Ire., Jas. I*, cited by Carrigan, *The History and Antiquities of the Diocese of Ossory*, i, 78.
10 Ibid.
11 Rothe, *Analecta*, 392; Carrigan, *The History and Antiquities of the Diocese of Ossory*, iii, 180.
12 AGS, Estado, leg. 434, f. 68.

James White, vicar apostolic of the diocese, who had authorised the purification of 'the monastery of St Dominic in the diocese of Ossory', namely Kilkenny. With the arrival of Mountjoy at Gracedieu near the city at the end of April and his threat to reduce Waterford to ashes, a delegation of Catholic clergy, secular and religious, headed by James White, was sent by the Mayor of Waterford to speak to him. Sir Richard Cox in his *Hibernia Anglicana* describes how the talks developed into a theological debate and mentions 'a young pert Dominican friar, to discourse with his lordship in matters of religion . . . and the friars had the confidence to come in their habits, with the crucifix exalted before them, and to tell the deputy, that the citizens of Waterford could not in conscience obey any prince that persecuted the Catholic faith'.[13] A contemporary writer identified the Dominican who spoke to Mountjoy as Edmund O'Callaghan, 'renowned for his holiness and learning', who flourished in the time of Elizabeth and the first years of James I.[14] Despite the friar's courageous action in openly confronting the Lord Deputy, the latter's military superiority exposed the deep insecurity of the townspeople of Kilkenny, Waterford and the rest of Munster. For the moment, however, Mountjoy was content to overlook the implications of the revivalist spirit of the Catholics.

The most important Dominican personality involved in the events of 1603, a man previously unheard of, was Simon of the Holy Spirit O'Hallaghan. In this writer's view, he is one and the same as the 'Edmund O'Callaghan' who made a brief appearance at Waterford. The names O'Callaghan and O'Hallaghan scarcely differ when pronounced in Irish; moreover, what little is known of these 'two' distinguished Dominicans does not in the least prevent one from identifying them as a single individual—particularly since there were hardly any distinguished Dominicans in Munster in 1603. In 1584 O'Hallaghan had set out for Portugal and entered the Irish College at Lisbon.[15] Before completing his studies for the diocesan priesthood he joined the Portuguese Dominicans in 1591. Simon of the Holy Spirit was the name he was given in the Order. The record of his solemn profession at the convent of São Domingos, Lisbon, on 18 June 1592, stated that he was the son of John O'Hallaghan (*Joannis Halychanis*) and Elinora Cunt, residents of the

13 R. Cox, *Hibernia Anglicana*, pt 2, London 1690, 6.

14 O'Sullivan Beare, *Historiae Iberniae Catholicae Compendium*, 179; O'Sullivan Beare, *Selections from the Zoilomastix*, ed. O'Donnell, 20.

15 AGS, Estado, leg. 2766. See also M. Gonçalves da Costa, *Fontes Inéditas Portuguesas para a Historía de Irlanda*, Braga 1981, 408. The Irish form of this family name in Munster is Ó hAllachacháin, a variant of hAilleacháin. The name, anglicised as O'Hallaghan, Hallaghan and Hallihan, was that of an old family in Co. Cork. See Woulfe, *Sloinnte Gaedheal is Gall*, 553, 549.

parish of St Mary's in Youghal.[16] What motivated him to transfer to the Dominicans was not disclosed. He received minor orders up to the fourth grade on 19 December 1587 in Lisbon cathedral[17] while still a student of the Irish College. As a Dominican he was made a subdeacon on 19 December 1592 at Lisbon cathedral and was ordained deacon at the city monastery of São Filipe on 18 December 1593. On all three occasions the orders were conferred by the exiled Irish Franciscan bishop, Cornelius O'Mulrian or Ryan of Killaloe.[18] His ordination as a priest probably took place in 1594.

Simon O'Hallaghan's first attempt to return to his native land proved abortive. It would appear that he sailed with the ill-fated Spanish fleet from Lisbon to Ireland late in October 1596. The senior admiral of Castille, commanding the armada, and the Bishop of Killaloe had requested his release from the Portuguese Dominican province in order to act as adviser and serve Philip II's interests in Ireland. About thirty ships were lost in a series of disastrous storms off Cape Finisterre, the remaining seventy were forced back to Spanish ports, and the expedition was cancelled. In this situation, O'Hallaghan felt it necessary to appeal to Philip II for letters of recommendation to the Portuguese provincial so that he might be reinstated in his own convent of Lisbon where he would continue his studies until such time as a fresh opportunity of serving the king should arise. His petition, presented at Madrid on 14 April 1597, was soon granted, the necessary document being endorsed by Philip II's initials.[19]

In the course of his sixteen years' stay in Lisbon, Simon O'Hallaghan had received financial help through the good offices of the Archduke Albert. He claimed to have rendered many services to God and the King of Spain in Lisbon, especially in the time of plague. He had been in charge of more than ten thousand sick people and heard confessions in five different languages. In the year 1600 he returned to Ireland to preach the Catholic faith. According to his vividly expressed personal testimony, he travelled almost the entire kingdom, principally where heresy was strongest and flourishing, combating it by the sword of the divine Word. He claimed to have inscribed forty thousand people in the Confraternity of the Holy Rosary and received back to the faith 152 heretics. He had reconciled one of the principal monasteries of his Order, that of the city of Kilkenny, which had been in the hands of heretics, and had it repaired

16 Oporto, Arquivo Histórico Dominicano Português, Profession Book, 1517–1777, Convento de São Domingos, Lisbon, f. 91r.

17 Lisbon, Arquivo Patriarcado, Livros de Matriculas/Ordenaçoes 1587, vol. 237 (unfoliated).

18 Ibid., 1592, vol. 240; ibid., 1593, vol. 535 (unfoliated).

19 AGS, Guerra Antigua, leg. 508. For a photocopy of this document I am indebted to Dr Micheline Kerney Walsh.

at a cost of 300 pounds of silver. For taking this initiative he had been summoned before the Lord Deputy and Council of Ireland. He presented his case so well that he persuaded these officials to allow the monastery to remain standing.[20]

Inspired by the hope of these fresh beginnings, he presented himself at the Spanish court as 'vicar general of the Order of St Dominic in Ireland', with twelve companions, two of whom were religious of his own Order, in October 1604. Having outlined his career in a memorial to Philip III, he put before the king some of his pressing current needs. He had incurred heavy expenses in supporting his companions, for which he asked to be recompensed. He went on to petition on behalf of the Irish Dominicans for breviaries, missals, books, liturgical vestments and vessels. He asked for his requests to be expedited, having already spent much time at the court. Moreover, he was preoccupied by the ill-health of some of his companions. The king's council approved his requests and ordered a grant of 2,000 ducats for all his liturgical needs, naming an agent to acquire what he needed. The king endorsed the decision of his council provided that it could be executed in such a way as not to cause envy or injury to the Catholics in Ireland.[21]

On 15 December 1604 the memorial of Simon of the Holy Spirit was once again reviewed and approved by the Spanish state council. The petitioner was noted as prudent, highly respected in Ireland and one who would know how to distribute the requested goods discreetly and without causing dissension. He could also be relied upon to be of service to the king. Philip III again endorsed the council's decision, ordering the Duke of Lerma to sign the petition, and thereby released the very considerable sum of 2,000 ducats for his needs. Simon O'Hallaghan may have had a highly esteemed friend at court in the person of a Dominican confrère, James MacDonnell (Diego Magdonel), who was confessor to Philip III in 1605–6 when the court was in residence at Valladolid. MacDonnell held a mastership in theology, was reputed to be a man of great learning, virtue and other excellent qualities, and was the recipient of 600 ducats annually for his own services.[22]

A letter dated 14 May 1603 reveals that the people of Limerick had already expelled the Protestant ministers and recalled the Catholic clergy. Amid much rejoicing public processions were held and altars were rededicated to their original use.[23] Sir John Burke, one of the prime

20 AGS, Estado, leg. 2766.
21 Ibid.
22 Madrid, Archivo del Palacio Real, sección de personal, 518/43. For this reference I am indebted to Dr Micheline Kerney Walsh.
23 J. Hagan (ed.), 'Miscellanea Vaticano-Hibernica: 1420–1631' in *Archiv. Hib.*, 4 (1915), 232.

instigators of the Catholic restoration and a future martyr, probably took forcible possession of Old St Saviour's Dominican church in the city, though without the active support of whatever Dominicans were in the area (in contrast to the situation in Kilkenny). For this activity he was apprehended by the viceroy Mountjoy and imprisoned in Dublin Castle in 1604–5.[24]

Simon of the Holy Spirit O'Hallaghan can probably be identified with the priest called Edmund Halligan (otherwise Halaghan or Hallican) who headed the Dominican presence in the Limerick area by 1606. At that time there was no established Dominican community within the city, but a handful of Dominicans were employed as chaplains to private families. In 1606 Sir John Burke, who resided at Brittas castle, about eight miles from Limerick, was received by Edmund Halligan into the Confraternity of the Holy Rosary. The large banqueting hall of Brittas castle, of which the ruins may still be seen, became the meeting place of the confraternity, especially on the first Sundays of the month, until October of that year, when the castle was besieged by English soldiers and the faithful who had assembled for the celebration of Mass were dispersed. Burke was taken prisoner and condemned to death. Shortly before his execution he sent a letter from prison to Edmund Halligan, director of the confraternity, who had managed to escape, beseeching him to instruct his wife in the Catholic faith.[25]

Simon O'Hallaghan's clear aim was to restore and revitalise the Irish province by undertaking new and daring initiatives in decidedly unstable times. To judge by his competence, unwavering resolution and the high regard in which he was held by the Catholics of Limerick and Kilkenny as well as by the Spanish authorities, one can scarcely doubt that he was the dominant and dynamic force in Dominican affairs at the dawn of a new age. Towards the end of the first decade of the seventeenth century he made his exit prematurely from the Irish scene just as abruptly as he had entered it. He may have fled the country in consequence of a proclamation by the Lord President and Council of Munster, issued at Cork on 14 August 1604, for the apprehension and banishment 'of Jesuits, seminary priests and others'.[26] This proclamation was reinforced by a

24 Rothe, *Analecta*, 495–6.

25 Ibid., 493–504.

26 Bodl., Carte MSS, LXI, f. 180. This historic proclamation was the first decree attempting to banish priests from Ireland. It was fundamentally flawed in its legality for two reasons. Firstly, the laws of Ireland did not give any authority to the Lord President of Munster, or indeed to the English sovereign, to banish Irish Catholic priests by arbitrary decree. This fact had been openly admitted in contemporary state papers by Sir John Davies, Attorney-General (1606–19), and by other lawyers administering English justice in Ireland. Secondly, the issue of a proclamation, unsupported by law, depriving subjects of their rights

general edict of James I (29 September 1605) ordering all bishops, priests and religious into exile before 10 December of that year under pain of imprisonment, torture and trial, unless they conformed and attended the Protestant church.[27] Was Simon of the Holy Spirit O'Hallaghan the 'senior father, Simon of the Holy Spirit' whose death at San Esteban, Salamanca, was recorded in the provincial chapter obits of the Castillian province in 1607?[28]

THE BACKGROUND TO SUCCESSFUL REVIVAL, 1607–17

Father Simon of the Holy Spirit O'Hallaghan's activities took place against the wider canvas of a general and sustained Catholic recovery from the opening years of the century. We have seen how the passing of the Elizabethan age signalled public manifestations of Catholicism and the willingness of a professionally trained Catholic clergy to assume religious leadership, especially in the largely Catholic corporate towns. All these signs thoroughly alarmed the Dublin government. Foremost in its mind was the ever-increasing influx of Irish priests from the continent into the country since the 1570s, and this anxiety found renewed expression in reports to the Privy Council in London. Lord Deputy Chichester wrote on 27 October 1607:

> They [priests] land here secretly in every port and creek of the realm (a dozen together sometimes as they are informed), and afterwards disperse themselves into several quarters in such sort that every town and country is full of them and most mens' minds are infected with their doctrine and seditious persuasions. They have so gained the women that they are in a manner all of them absolute recusants. Children and servants are wholly taught and catechised by them, esteeming the same a sound and safe foundation of their synagogue. They withdraw many from the Church that formerly had conformed themselves; and others of them, of whom good hopes had been conceived, they have made altogether obstinate, disobedient and contemptuous. Most of the mayors and principal officers of the cities and corporate towns, and justices of the peace of this country refuse to take the Oath of Supremacy, as is requisite by the statute. . . . The people in many places resort to Mass now in greater multitudes,

and liberties was a serious breach of constitutional law which protected people from acts of tyranny by the crown or its officials as guaranteed by Magna Carta, whose provisions had been extended to Ireland and subsequently incorporated in Irish law by act of the Irish parliament.

27 J. Hagan (ed.), 'Miscellanea Vaticano-Hibernica: 1580–1631' in *Archiv. Hib.*, 3 (1914), 256–60.

28 Salamanca, San Esteban provincial archives, provincial chapter acts, 1607, p. 63.

> both in town and country than for many years past, and if by chance that any priest, known to be factious and working, be apprehended, men and women will not stick to rescue the party. . . . Such as are conformed and go to church are everywhere derided, scorned, and oppressed by the multitude.[29]

A slightly earlier report from the same Lord Deputy declared that 'The people of Ireland will never be cured of their disease so long as they drink of the poison of Rome.' Most infected, in his opinion, were the cities of Waterford, Cork, Limerick and Galway. He urged the building of strong citadels in these cities.[30] In the following year, 1608, the Protestant Bishop of Limerick complained bitterly of the 'noisome puddle of priests who have newly run out from the great sink of treason and rebellion to infest this miserable nation; who are so thick everywhere that they are ready to bemire them'.[31]

While the evidence from Catholic as well as hostile sources clearly suggests a great deal of enthusiastic priestly activity in these years, it was unevenly distributed and haphazard, lacking episcopal supervision and direction. For the most part secular and regular clergy were content to go their own separate ways.[32] This lack of co-ordination inevitably gave rise to confusion, rivalries and disedifying conflicts. Clearly the reappearance of priests, diocesan and religious, unimpeded and in such increased numbers, was synonymous in official eyes with the 'deadly threat of treason and rebellion'.

By 1611 government apprehension concerning the visible increase of religious in and around their former houses in town and country reached such a point that the title-head of a proposed act for their banishment was framed:

> An act that all friars and monks and nuns shall be expelled out of their dissolved houses where, for the most part, they still keep and hover, and if those persons to whom the king has given or let those houses or lands, with intent they should convert them to better uses, by planting and peopling the same, shall, by negligence or otherwise, suffer them to continue there contrary to this law, or shall participate in their abominable lures of supposed offerings or oblations as many do, they shall forfeit their estate therein to the king, and endure fine and imprisonment.[33]

29 *Cal. S.P. Ire., 1606–8*, 310.
30 Ibid., 140.
31 Ibid., 570.
32 A. Clarke, 'Colonial Identity in Early Seventeenth-Century Ireland' in T. W. Moody (ed.), *Nationality and the Pursuit of National Independence*, Belfast 1978, 63.
33 *Cal. Carew MSS, 1603–24*, 155–6.

A parliamentary act was also envisaged against receivers and harbourers of Jesuits (the term included all regular priests), seminary priests and other popish priests and schoolmasters and a prohibition against sending children for their education 'beyond the seas'. Only the latter proposed act became part of the legislative programme in September 1612, which initially had aroused Catholic fears.[34] The body of statute law directed against Catholic clergy in Ireland in the sixteenth and seventeenth centuries was limited in scope because of the parliamentary strength of the Irish recusants, especially in 1585 and again in 1613–14, though it could on occasion be exceeded through the imposition of martial law.[35]

Thaddeus MacDuane had once more been appointed vicar of the Irish Dominican congregation on 20 October 1608 by Agostino Galamini, Master of the Order,[36] but in that same year he had died and had been laid to rest in the Dominican church of Sligo.[37] As a result of his death, the greatly depleted body of Dominicans was deprived of effective leadership. And even though provision was made for a successor to MacDuane in the person of Patrick MacTeig (or Mac Taidhg),[38] there is no real evidence that the latter ever became superior or vicar of the Irish Dominicans. MacDuane's successor was reputedly Roland Burke, a member of the Clanrickard family, who had received his education at Salamanca at the turn of the century. Nothing is known of his term as vicar of the Irish congregation (1608–*c.* 1612), apart from an impressive account of his personal character and zeal. He died in 1615 and was buried in his own convent of Athenry.[39] A document presented at Rome in 1627 stated that Thomas Quirke had been 'provincial of Ireland for four years'.[40] This can only have been between 1611 or 1612, the date of Quirke's arrival from France, and 1617, when Ross MacGeoghegan assumed responsibility as vicar of the Irish congregation. With the disintegration of Dominican community life, the survivors had scattered among the laity, their relatives, and the gentry or nobility to whom they acted as chaplains, and so remained living privately until their younger predominantly Spanish-educated confrères, already arriving in a steady trickle from 1600, gathered them into two or three remote houses of

34 A. Clarke with R. D. Edwards, 'Pacification, Plantation and the Catholic Question, 1603–23' in *NHI*, iii, 225.
35 P. J. Corish, 'Two Seventeenth-Century Proclamations against the Catholic Clergy' in *Archiv. Hib.*, 39 (1984), 53.
36 Fenning, *Irish material*, 277. Formal letter of appointment in AGOP, XIV, Liber K, p. 5.
37 Burke, *Hib. Dom.*, 521.
38 AGOP, XIV, Liber K, p. 5.
39 Reichert, *MOPH*, xii, 475.
40 *Wadding Papers*, 209.

refuge. From these country houses they spread out gradually over the whole of Ireland, thereby effectively reconstituting the Irish province.[41]

One of the prime initiators of this fresh strategy of resurgence was the Westmeath Dominican, Ross MacGeoghegan, who during the intervening years, 1617–27, was to become the principal architect of the province's restoration. On 13 March 1614 he requested and received from Philip III of Spain a viaticum of 200 ducats for his journey to Ireland where he was to dedicate himself to the preaching of the Catholic faith as he had vowed as a seminarian. In passing he mentioned another Irish confrère, Paul of St Thomas, who had died at the court of Madrid in 1611 while awaiting payment of his viaticum.[42] The latter had once lived in the convent of San Pablo, Seville, and had earned for himself a reputation for sanctity.[43] From a list of Irish exiles at the royal court in 1610, he may possibly be identified as Thomas Stronge.[44]

According to a short historical account of the convent of Athenry during the seventeenth century, Ross MacGeoghegan met and consulted with three surviving Dominicans at a place called Brosk near Athenry, probably in 1614, as to what ought to be done to bring about the restoration of the Order in Ireland. The friars decided to approach Ulick Burke, Earl of Clanrickard, who was deeply attached to the Order, to obtain both his support and a place of refuge where young people might be received discreetly into the Order. The earl was a kinsman of the former provincial Roland Burke, and the Dominican church of Athenry was the burial place of the Clanrickard family. The earl willingly gave them a place on his estate, a wood between two lakes near Loughrea, remote and difficult of access. A graphic physical description of the location (then called Coillascail, now known as Esker) is supplied by the author. There the Dominicans built a small house and began to take in aspirants and novices, including young men from the leading local families, who afterwards went to Spain for their studies. In due course lectures on the classics, philosophy and theology were organised, and the community lived in accordance with the standards of strict regular observance.

Edmund Burke, O.P., the compiler of this account,[45] made his solemn profession there in 1683. For several of his statements he quoted the oral testimony of Dominic Burke, Dominican Bishop of Elphin (1671–1704),

41 APF, SOCG, 294, f. 102v.
42 AGS, Estado, leg. 2748.
43 I. Lopez, *De la Historia General de Santo Domingo y de su Orden de Praedicadores*, iv, Valladolid 1615, 1101–2
44 AGS, Estado, leg. 2513.
45 *Brevis Notitia Provinciae Hiberniae Ordinis Praedicatorum ab anno 1600 ad 1736 inclusive*: incomplete transcript in AGOP, XIII, 157; full transcript in TA: Ryan series, vol. 2, pp 34–87; summarised in Coleman, *Ancient Dominican Foundations*, 84.

who was received into the Order in the same place in 1641. The only serious inaccuracy in this account is the statement that there were only four Dominicans in Ireland at the end of Elizabeth's reign. More reliable sources, as outlined below, indicate a somewhat greater number, though there were undoubtedly very few and there was an almost total lack of communication among them outside Connacht. This is corroborated by the report of Bentivoglio, the Brussels nuncio, dated 31 January 1609, but this report is also subject to reservations. It stated that in Ireland there were 800 diocesan clergy, 130 Franciscans, 20 Jesuits, and 'a few Cistercians and Dominicans'.[46] This last rather vague comment clearly reflects an underestimate of the Order's numerical strength in Ireland; unfortunately the precise number of Dominicans remains problematical.

In the second decade of the century the Dominican churches in Dublin, Mullingar, Sligo, Waterford and Kilkenny were used as law courts. Former Franciscan churches in Trim, Leitrim, Cavan, Ennis, Enniscorthy, Wicklow and in Co. Galway were used for the same purpose.[47] Dominicans, however drastically reduced in numbers, were still active and maintained themselves quietly in several localities. In 1611 or thereabouts John McDavid Cormack, a Munster Dominican, was chaplain to Lord Barry, as was reported to the authorities:

> My lord Barry brought with him in his company a chaplain of his, being a Dominican friar named John McDavid Cormack, to Dublin in the time of the parliament, to be ruled and advised by him what to say and how to answer, and so have all the Lords done who went to parliament. Every one of them brought his priest with him.[48]

About 1615 a government spy named FitzGerald supplied scattered information on priests in the south and west. Dominicans were resident in Co. Kerry (Thomas Quirke, doctor of divinity); in Co. Limerick (Dominic White and John (Fitz)David); and in Co. Galway (Anthony Lynch, Manus Ward and Roland Burke, incorrectly described as provincial of the Order).[49] In Cork tentative repairs on the church and convent of St Mary's of the Isle had to be abandoned, and in 1616 James I granted the entire property to one John King at a crown rent of 9s.[50]

Didacus Sarmiento de Acuña, Count Gondomar, the Spanish ambassador in London, reporting (30 December 1617) to Philip III on the state

46 C. McNeill (ed.), *The Tanner Letters*, Dublin 1943, 509.
47 Moran, *Archbishops of Dublin*, 240; T. Gimlette, *The Dominican Priory of 'St Saviour', Waterford*, Waterford c.1888, 6–7.
48 *Cal. Carew MSS, 1603–24*, 199.
49 TCD, MS 567, ff 32rv, 33v, 34v. By 1615 Roland Burke was probably a local or area superior.
50 E. Bolster, *A History of the Diocese of Cork*, ii, Cork 1982, 153.

of Catholicism in England, Ireland and Scotland, stated that he had been informed that in Ireland there were more than two thousand priests, religious of different orders and clerics, but that he had been unable to discover the true numbers.[51] The Spanish Dominican author Fernandez in 1618 referred to more than thirty Dominicans in England and Ireland. Some, he said, were in prison, some were suffering from fatigue and privations, but all were dedicated to the return of Protestants to the faith and the growth of the Church.[52]

CONSOLIDATION UNDER ROSS MACGEOGHEGAN, 1617–22

By the summer of 1617 Ross MacGeoghegan, the new force among Dominicans in Ireland and the diaspora, had taken charge of the Irish congregation.[53] Surprisingly, his appointment as vicar of the congregation was not entered in the registers of Master General Secchi until 1618.[54] Between 1614 and 1618 Ross MacGeoghegan worked tirelessly in reorganising the Irish province, personally supervising the introduction onto the Irish scene of Dominicans arriving from Spain and Portugal.

Obviously hampered by the lack of formal missionary faculties, MacGeoghegan applied for these to the Roman Congregation of the Holy Office. On 8 June 1617 he was given one set of faculties, unspecified by the notary, 'customarily granted to the other regulars of those parts'.[55] A further set of papal faculties, dated 16 August 1617, 'normally granted to other priests of Ireland',[56] provide a telling commentary on the exigencies of the Irish pastoral situation. These faculties were spelt out in full:

(1) faculties for the reconciliation of heretics and the absolution from censures and other canonical irregularities mentioned in the bull *In Coena Domini* of all Catholics, even secular and regular clergy;

(2) power to dispense clerics from all irregularities except homicide voluntarily committed;

51 A. Ballestros y Baretta (ed.), *Correspondencia oficial de Don Diego de Sarmiento*, i, Madrid 1936, 182.

52 A. Fernandez, *Concertatio Praedicatoria pro Ecclesia Catholica*, Salamanca 1618, 316. An anonymous Irish writer whose apologetical work against the Scot, Thomas Dempster, was published in 1621, simply affirmed that there were some Dominicans active in their ministry in Ireland at that time. G.F., *Hiberniae sive antiquioris Scotiae vindiciae adversus . . . Thomae Dempsteri moderni Scoti nuper editam*, Antwerp 1621, 19.

53 TA, provincial's file 'Miscellaneous: 1897–1930'. For a full account of the career of Ross MacGeoghegan see pp 166–80 below.

54 Fenning, *Irish material*, 27.

55 TA, provincial's file 'Miscellaneous: 1897–1930'.

56 Fenning, *Irish material*, 335–6.

(3) to own and read prohibited books for the purpose of refuting them and the right to give this permission to others, provided such books would not be widely disseminated;

(4) to administer the sacraments, omitting ceremonies and non-essentials;

(5) to substitute the rosary, other prayers or the psalms known by heart in those circumstances where it would not be possible to carry the breviary or perilous to recite the divine office;

(6) to bless vestments and everything necessary for divine worship not involving consecration by holy oils;

(7) to celebrate Mass in whatever decent place, in the open air or underground, three hours before daylight, in winter up to one hour after midday, twice in the day if judged necessary, even in the presence of heretics and excommunicated persons;

(8) to reserve the holy Eucharist without lights and the other ceremonies customary in churches;

(9) to dispense with vows in respect of pilgrimages to the Holy Land, Rome and Compostella, and to absolve from binding oaths (i.e. to go on pilgrimage);

(10) to grant matrimonial dispensations in cases of urgency;

(11) to grant plenary indulgences on the occasion of first confession, yearly for the principal feasts, at the hour of death and for annual general confession;

(12) to print and read books of Catholic authors lacking the name of the author or printer and other books besides, notwithstanding the regulations of Trent;

(13) to absolve converts to the Catholic faith who had wrongly benefited from the revenues of ecclesiastical property;

(14) to use these faculties in Ireland, England, Scotland and other dominions of the King of Great Britain, with the right to communicate the same to secular priests or prelates, theologians, clerics, and to suitable regulars of his own Order.

On 7 June 1616 at the request of Dermot MacCarthy, president of the Irish College, Bordeaux, and Vicar Apostolic of Waterford and Lismore, the Master General permitted three Irish Dominicans to return to Ireland. All three were Munstermen and former alumni of the Irish College, Bordeaux: Vincent Hogan and John Fox (then at Pamplona) and Thomas Lyehe (of the convent of Toulouse). MacCarthy testified that they were well known to him, that they had read arts and part of their theology course at Bordeaux and had completed their studies in the Order's houses. The Master General forwarded faculties as well as his permission for them to go to Ireland, but made his decision conditional on the advice and judgement of their respective Dominican superiors.[57] In May 1617 permission was likewise granted by the Master General to Peter Martin and Richard de la Peña Caron to set out from Spain to Ireland, in the company of Vincent Hogan and John Fox, who had apparently remained in Spain throughout 1616.[58] In January 1617, anticipating the Master General's decision, Richard Caron and two unnamed Dominican companions had been granted a viaticum of 100 ducats each to cover the expenses of the journey, books, vestments and secular dress.[59] Two months later (14 March 1617) Caron mentioned this grant already made to himself and to two others whose aim was to preach in Ireland and Scotland, and he asked for an additional viaticum for John Fox, who was to accompany them.[60] In the same year a proclamation was issued in Dublin, ordering the banishment of priests educated abroad. The view that no serious effort was made to enforce it[61] is not quite accurate. Richard Caron and one of his companions, Aeneas O'Callanan, were promptly arrested on arrival at Galway in the summer of 1617 and incarcerated in Dublin Castle for one and a half years.[62]

It was at the general chapter of Lisbon held in June 1618 that the eighteen assembled provincials considered the case of the Irish congregation. Ross MacGeoghegan had set out from Ireland to Spain in the early spring of that year and was at Valladolid on 10 March, when he received the Master General's approval to go to Madrid and afterwards to attend the general chapter at Lisbon. He also obtained letters whereby the Master General assigned the young friars accompanying him to whatever Dominican houses would be willing to receive them.[63] The Irish congregation could not be officially represented at the chapter because of its lesser status. Nonetheless, the assembly, having listened to Ross MacGeoghegan as vicar of his congregation, made the following decisions: Irish Dominicans on completion of their studies abroad must return to Ireland; the regulations for religious observance drawn up by

57 Ibid., 278. It might be argued that Dermot MacCarthy thus helped re-establish the Dominicans in Waterford, where Thomas Power was already active in the city in 1616, and in the wider province of Munster.
58 Ibid., 279.
59 AGS, Estado, leg. 2749.
60 Ibid.
61 Clarke with Edwards, 'Pacification, Plantation and the Catholic Question', 225.
62 O'Sullivan Beare, *Selections from the Zoilomastix*, ed. O'Donnell, 29.
63 Fenning, *Irish material*, 279.

MacGeoghegan for his brethren were approved; as vicar he was authorised to invite four Dominicans from any nation he might choose, with their provincial's permission, to go to Ireland, to teach and promote the intellectual life of students; and he might recall all brethren then living abroad who had completed their studies.[64] In other words, the Lisbon chapter unreservedly endorsed the policy decisions and plans of Ross MacGeoghegan for the revival of the Irish province. His standing and authority were further enhanced when the Master General awarded him the theological degree of *praesentatus*, after the requisite examination, for his devotion to preaching in Ireland.[65]

With the increasing intake of members, the problem was where to educate them. The traditional hospitality of Spain and Portugal could hardly be expected to bear the extra burden of the burgeoning Irish congregation. Hence the possibility of educating students in Ireland was to be explored, though the political situation did not give much hope of further religious amelioration or toleration. The other logical possibility was the foundation of colleges on the continent specifically for the Irish Dominicans. Already tentative moves had been taken to establish a college at Lisbon (for which a papal brief had been obtained on 13 November 1615);[66] and there is some evidence that a small nucleus of Irish Dominicans had settled in Louvain by 1613[67] with a similar aim.

Leaving Lisbon, MacGeoghegan reached Madrid by 13 December 1618 on the business of the congregation. In a petition to Philip III he recalled his attendance at the Lisbon chapter, and how he had brought six young friars with him from Ireland and had placed them in several convents of the Castillian province. On the instructions of the Master General he was to send four lectors of theology to Ireland once they had finished their studies. Five such Dominicans were then available, for whom he requested a travel allowance. The king and his council approved 100 ducats for each religious.[68] In another petition (3 February 1619) he stated that nine friars were then ready to set out for Ireland, including himself, as attested by the provincial of the province of Spain. The request for a viaticum to cover the expenses of the additional three friars was approved on 9 February.[69] The testimonial of the provincial of Spain supplied the names of the eight Dominicans and their former houses: Master Jacinto de Luna (province of Sicily), Dominic Nugent (San

64 Reichert, *MOPH*, xi, 317.
65 Fenning, *Irish material*, 279.
66 Burke, *Hib. Dom.*, 416–18; see also pp 195–7 below.
67 B. Jennings (ed.), 'Miscellaneous Documents, I: 1588–1634' in *Archiv. Hib.*, 12 (1946), 76–8; see also p. 213 below.
68 AGS, Estado, leg. 2750; Fenning, *Irish material*, 279.
69 AGS, Estado, leg. 1774.

Esteban, Salamanca), Stephen of the Holy Spirit (São Domingos, Evora), Thomas of the Ascension (São Domingos, Benfica), Joseph Langton (San Pablo, Valladolid), John of the Cross (São Domingos, Lisbon) and Paul of St Dominic (Santo Tomás, Avila).[70] Later this party of Dominicans made its way southwards to Seville, where the cathedral chapter on 7 June 1619 authorised payment of 50 ducats in alms to Ross MacGeoghegan, 'commissary general of Ireland', for the expenses of some religious travelling 'to those islands'.[71]

William of the Holy Spirit Talbot obtained permission to go to Ireland from Spain on 30 November 1619. The permission was valid from the date of issue for eight months, within which time he was expected to reach his destination. It was stipulated that during his stay in Ireland he was to live in a religious house and be subject to the vicar of the Irish congregation.[72] The terms of the permission were intended to offset the temptation of freelance living by travelling religious. However, William Talbot did not depart from Spain within the appointed period, and he was still submitting petitions at the court of Madrid in connection with his journey in the spring and summer of 1621.[73]

Priests from Spain, France and Italy continued to return to Ireland in 1620. Priest theologian Nicholas Lynch (later provincial, 1627–34), who had read philosophy and theology at the University of Paris, was permitted (8 April 1620) to graduate in the University of Caen[74] and was soon to return to Ireland. Permission was also given to Peter Martin to return home (15 May 1620). He had studied for two and a half years at Bologna and had been approved as a lector of theology.[75]

On 20 April 1620 the Master of the Order commissioned Richard Caron to lead home those Irish Dominicans who had recently finished their studies in the three Spanish provinces. He was at the same time appointed superior for the duration of the journey, but on arrival in Ireland they were to come under the obedience of the vicar of the Irish congregation.[76] As procurator general he applied on 3 September for the Spanish king's viaticum for ten confrères. He asserted that religious persecution had been stepped up and that there was a shortage of preachers for Catholics and for the reconversion of those who had strayed into error. His petition was approved, with the stipulation that arrangements for the gradual giving of the viaticum to two friars at a time were

70 Ibid., leg. 2750.
71 J. J. Silke, 'The Irish College, Seville' in *Archiv. Hib.*, 24 (1961), 119.
72 Fenning, *Irish material*, 280.
73 AGS, Estado, leg. 2783.
74 Fenning, *Irish material*, 280.
75 Ibid., 280–81.
76 Ibid., 280. For a full account of the career of Richard Caron see pp 180–88 below.

to be supervised by the king's ambassador.[77] Dissatisfied with this cumbersome proviso, Caron submitted a new petition (14 November)[78] on behalf of the ten Dominicans he had found suitable for the mission in Ireland, Scotland and England, remarking that the faith was in danger of extinction if it were not kept alive by preachers. He went on to refer to the king's order that financial aid be given first to two religious and that, when news of their arrival in Ireland was received, two more should be sent in the same way, and so on until all ten had actually gone, so as to avoid the attention a large group might attract. He pointed out that, even by taking one priest aboard his ship, a trader risked his life and his property—as indeed had happened to the trader who took Caron himself to Ireland in 1617. In any case, priests never travelled more than two at a time.

Caron objected also to the idea that members of his Order should be required to pass through England or to present themselves to the ambassador in London in order to have their arrival verified. This would only put them at greater risk, and he proposed that they should be allowed to go directly to Ireland instead. He protested that no religious of his Order and nation who received financial aid for his journey had ever remained in Spain, or was permitted to do so, any longer than necessary. He concluded by asking that he be given the usual financial assistance for the ten religious already mentioned, and that he and his Order be trusted as they had been in the past. The king read the petition, but did not indicate his decision.

William Semple, a Scotsman, a member of the royal court, professional soldier and military adviser to Philip III, presented a memorial to the king, dated 29 December 1622, on religious affairs in Ireland, Scotland and England.[79] In passing, he commented somewhat unsympathetically on the 'great numbers' of Irish and English students emerging from the colleges of the religious orders founded on their behalf in Spain and the Spanish dominions. He alleged that their numbers had multiplied to such an extent that many of them had become vagabonds, making pretentious claims as ecclesiastics, requesting increased stipends for their services in the war, and failing to assume their proper responsibilities. Semple's complaint would not be the last.

77 AGS, Estado, leg. 2750; AGS, Contaduria Mayor de Cuentas, 3a época, leg. 1161.
78 AGS, Estado, leg. 1175.
79 AHN, Estado, libro 739, f. 110.

On 15 May 1622 the general chapter of Milan acted decisively and advantageously in the interests of the Irish Dominicans. It formally restored Ireland to the status of a province and appointed Ross MacGeoghegan as its provincial. Transfer of the French convent of Beauvoir-sur-Mer (La Vendée) to the Irish Dominicans was agreed on. The new province was commended to the good offices of the provincial of Lower Germany, who was asked to promote its interests with the Flemish magnates. The chapter asked the *studia generalia* to provide places for one or two Irish students whenever vacancies occurred. Irish Dominicans might petition the Pope for the right to confer the Order's degrees by title of preaching in view of their emphasis on the dircct preaching ministry and the task of converting heretics. On the death of Irish Dominicans formerly affiliated to other provinces, there would be no obligation to share part of the deceased's moveable goods with that province. The chapter reiterated a number of measures of the Lisbon chapter of 1618, notably its admonition that the provincial might recall all students to Ireland at his discretion, and its stipulation that none might leave the Irish province without the written permission of the provincial under pain of conventual incarceration.[80]

The earliest known report on the Irish province was presented to this chapter. Entitled *Brevis Relatio de Statu Provinciae Sanctae Crucis Hyberniae, de eiusdem antiquitate, de numero Conventuum, et Fratrum in ea laborantium,*[81] it is difficult to date with precision. Some of the students named in it received assignations from the Master General in May 1622, presumably at the request of John Fox,[82] who had been appointed procurator for Ireland at the general chapter then in progress at Milan. The fourteen students so assigned on 28 May 1622 did not include the ten students 'sent to Spain' in the year the report was compiled. Internal and external evidence would suggest that it was drafted in the spring of 1622. The desire strongly evident in the report was to stress the 'antiquity and sanctity' of the Irish province: this is seen in the care with which the number of convents and friars was set down, and in the presence of a paper entitled '*In causa Hiberniae*' (proving the former existence of the province by extracts from the Master General's registers) inset between the pages of the report, all combining to suggest that the report was presented to the Milan chapter in May 1622 with the purpose of achieving

80 Reichert, *MOPH*, xi, 342.

81 AGOP, XIV, Liber K, pp 1, 29, 10, 12, 13; reproduced as Appendix 5 (pp 323–5 below).

82 Fenning, *Irish material*, 281. John Fox was allowed to return to his province on 29 May, having handled the business of his province at the general chapter of Milan.

the re-establishment of the Irish province. The report commenced by recalling that the medieval Irish province had thirty-eight priories besides many dependencies and chapels. Several of these had already been founded in the time of St Dominic, as was apparent from the saint's letter to the Prince of Tyrconnell sent in favour of two brethren dispatched to Ireland by St Dominic himself. The letter, it was claimed, had been preserved with great devotion by the friars of the convent of Derry until its loss during the devastation of the convent by heretics. This information came from a very ancient manuscript of the convent of Limerick and from many other old documents and fragments which had escaped the hands of the heretics. Seven houses had been reoccupied by 1622, and the names of the superiors were given: Dublin (residence of the provincial and eight friars); Galway (ten friars); Limerick (seven friars); Cork (eight friars); Kilkenny (seven friars); Waterford (seven friars); Urlar (two friars and novices). All of these houses were situated in cities and towns, with the exception of Urlar in the remote Mayo countryside, which was designated for the reception and education of novices.

Were this report to be taken as complete, it would reflect extraordinary weakness of the Dominicans in Connacht in 1622. Roscommon and even Athenry were not mentioned, although the latter was already very important. Inexplicably Sligo, Tralee and Drogheda were also omitted. The compiler of this information was probably John Fox, a Munster man, which presumably explains the weakness of the report concerning Dominicans in Leinster, Connacht and Ulster. In all, it was stated that there were fifty-seven brethren in Ireland (not counting novices), twenty-four students abroad, and ten to be sent to Spain that year for studies.

Each revived community was given responsibility for the remaining thirty-one foundations. At fixed times the areas of these desolate houses were to be visited, and the people in these places were to be supplied with preachers and confessors. In the absence of Dominicans, diocesan priests of exemplary life might be appointed as heads of the rosary confraternities. Properties and immoveable goods once pertaining to Dominican houses could not be precisely established because the heretics had carried off the relevant inventories and documents; these could still be found in the royal archives. When the suppression of the monasteries took place under Henry VIII, inventories of all immoveable ecclesiastical goods had been drawn up and recorded in the royal registers. In the meantime it had become evident to the brethren both from property which by acknowledged fact belonged to each convent and by the accounts of the older friars that there was not one of the thirty-eight houses which could not have supported a minimum of thirty or forty friars—indeed in some cases as many as eighty, or even more. This last assertion was, of course, a gross exaggeration.

The report mentioned two very ancient images of the Blessed Virgin Mary venerated at Youghal and Tralee.[83] Though the heretics had made innumerable attempts to seize them, having been accurately informed of where the images were kept, by divine providence they could never find or succeed in confiscating them. So great was the daily veneration of these sacred images by the faithful that the Youghal image was commonly known as 'Mary of Graces and Miracles'.

Next the report gave a rather amusing account of what befell the Protestant occupiers of former Dominican properties. According to the author, it was singular and worthy of note that in the houses made over by the king (Henry VIII) to the heretics for dwellings (or rather profanation) the new owners were not allowed to rest one single night without nocturnal disturbances and noises. They had visions of white-robed friars who angrily expelled them from their domiciles with cudgels and sticks. The result was that sometimes the inhabitants on the morning after a distressing night were found beaten and bruised with broken limbs and left half-dead. Thus, willingly or unwillingly, the new occupiers were forced to give up the hallowed places which they had seized. When, however, Catholics with the permission of the brethren lived in these houses, they never experienced such vexations. This situation was attributed to the sanctity of these places which was admitted by the heretics themselves as well as by Catholics. Such details and many other things worthy of note, which had to be omitted for the sake of brevity, witnessed to the antiquity and holiness of the Irish province.

Three lists of Dominicans are given at the end of the report. The first list is of twenty-five priests active as preachers. The second list is of fourteen priests described as 'confessors and men of exemplary and laudable life'. All these priests were resident 'in the kingdom of Ireland'. The third list is of non-ordained brethren and contains eighteen names, most of whom are immediately recognisable as students from the registers of the Master General and other student lists. Besides these there were

83 The image known as 'Our Lady of Graces' belonged to this house and is now preserved in the Dominican church of St Mary's, Cork. It is an ivory carving about three inches in length, much worn and discoloured by the passage of time. The silver case which encloses it bears the following inscription: '*Orate pro anima Onoriae filiae Jacobi de Geraldinis quae me fieri fecit. Anno Domini, 1617*'. Nothing is known of the Tralee image of the Blessed Virgin Mary which has disappeared. The famous statue of Our Lady of Coleraine was destroyed somewhat earlier. In September 1611 Brutus Babington, Anglican Bishop of Derry, had ordered that the statue, which belonged to the Dominicans, should be burnt, but all attempts to do so were in vain. The bishop was reported to have died suddenly in the midst of his alarm at the failure of this first attack on the statue. Moran, *Spicil. Ossor.*, i, 119; Coleman, *Ancient Dominican Foundations*, 51, 10; U. Flanagan, 'Our Lady of Graces of Youghal' in *Cork Hist. Soc. Jn.*, 55 (1950), 1–13; 56 (1951), 1–10; Pochin Mould, *The Irish Dominicans*, 97–8.

many mere novices (whose names were not listed), the ten students sent to Spain that year, and twenty-four students in Spain. The lists are endorsed: 'Names of the friars of the Order of Preachers in the kingdom of Ireland, who number fifty-seven'. It is possible that this total includes the ten students who had as yet to leave for Spain. Altogether the total figure for the entire Irish Dominican province was about eighty-two, excluding some priests resident abroad (such as Richard Caron, William Talbot, James Arthur and Nicholas Lynch) and novices in Ireland.

While the report is less comprehensive than one might wish, it does supply essential information about the rapid recovery of the Irish Dominicans, particularly in urban centres. It was drawn up simply for the needs of a chapter intervention and for an audience for whom Ireland was but a name, a remote island on the edge of northern Europe. Regrettably it supplied no vivid details of everyday life in Ireland in the early 1620s, still less of the particular problems of adaptation and confrontation, socially, culturally, religiously and politically faced by the continentally formed young Dominicans. The general impression conveyed is of vigour, optimism and continuing progress implanting themselves in the mainstream of Catholic life. The report achieved its aim when the Milan chapter raised the status of the Irish congregation to that of a fully-fledged province and moreover expressed considerable benevolence towards it in the chapter ordinances.

DOMINICAN RELATIONS WITH CHURCH AND STATE IN THE 1620S

Throughout the reign of James I a basic disagreement existed between the London and Dublin governments concerning the treatment of Irish Catholics, with the result that public policy and its implementation vacillated disturbingly and erratically. In the end Dublin resentfully followed the more moderate course dictated by London. Action, however, was to be taken against priests, especially continentally trained regulars, where there was grave suspicion of treason which often enough gave rise to paranoia on the part of officialdom. The rapid increase of priests of all types and their manifest influence among the people continued to preoccupy the administration at Dublin Castle.

On 1 October 1622 Lord Deputy Falkland and the Council of Ireland reported to London: 'Priests do everywhere swarm and grow much more insolent than before, infusing into the people hope of alteration and toleration of the religion so generally professed here.'[84] A list of Catholic clergy, diocesan and regular, known to the council in 1623 to

84 Bodl., Carte MSS, XXX, ff 131–2.

be resident and succoured in Dublin, named no recognisable Irish Dominicans, but included James Hamilton, a Scottish Dominican, later active in Munster.[85] Towards the end of January 1624 Falkland received permission to publish a proclamation against priests and instructions to enforce recusancy laws. A month later, however, he was ordered to suspend the operation of some of these laws, and a year later was forbidden to enforce the proclamation of 1624. The formulation of religious policy in Ireland had come to depend upon international rather than local considerations.[86] Despite the more pacific outlook which this implied, it was probably the proclamation of 1624 that led to a scaling down of the Dominican communities in Dublin, Galway, Limerick, Cork and Kilkenny before 1627.

With the general non-enforcement of Falkland's proclamation, it was anxiously noted that Jesuits and other regular priests 'flocked up to Dublin very thick'. The same observer has left a vivid account, worthy of citation, illustrating this new-found confidence and contemporary funeral customs: 'On 29 January 1626 their great friend Thomas Plunket, alderman of that city (and the richest alderman that ever was in Dublin), was buried. The several Romish Orders, then being in Dublin, clothed this alderman sometime in the Franciscan weed [habit], so in the Dominican, and other of the Orders' habits to sanctify him, that he might not tarry long in Purgatory: and truly these Orders had reason so to do, for the alderman left to them a thousand pound to be distributed.'[87]

Already in 1623 the Archbishop of Dublin, Eugene MacMahon, reported to Propaganda Fide that there were 800 diocesan priests in

85 R. Ware, *The Hunting of the Romish Fox*, Dublin 1683, 189, 216.

86 Clarke with Edwards, 'Pacification, Plantation, and the Catholic Question', 233.

87 Ware, *The Hunting of the Romish Fox*, 193. Ware did not disclose the sequel to the Plunkett bequest and how it was frustrated by Lord Deputy Wentworth, acting on the advice of William Laud, Archbishop of Canterbury. Moreover, the Dublin friars were not the sole beneficiaries of Thomas Plunkett's charity as asserted above nor 'the priests of Douai' (TCD, MS 6404, f. 65v). From a legal deposition (10 Jan. 1634) it is clear that in the early 1620s Thomas and his brother, Luke Plunkett, decided that half their property in Meath and Dublin, which was worth about £2,000 should be devoted to pious purposes in Ireland (£400) and to the support of Catholic students in the colleges of the Low Countries (£600). By 1634 Wentworth had confiscated the money 'lent in mortgage' in Ireland and had brought considerable psychological and legal pressure to bear on the executors, Luke and Robert Plunkett, with a view to recovering the remainder of the money invested in the Brussels stock exchange for his own disposition. See Sheffield City Library, Fitzwilliam Papers, Strafford Letter-Books, vol. 8, 1633–6, under 31 Oct. 1633 (NLI, microfilm pos. no. 2853); PRO, SP 63/254/89 (NLI, microfilm pos. no. 2697). Summary in *Cal. S.P. Ire., 1633–47*, 37; *The Earl of Strafforde's Letters and Dispatches*, ed. W. Knowler, i, Dublin 1740, 172, 189, 213. For the above references I am indebted to Professor Aidan Clarke.

Ireland, about 200 Observant Franciscans who merited special praise for their qualities of perseverance and fidelity to the people, forty Jesuits, more than twenty Dominicans, four or five Capuchins, and unspecified numbers of Augustinians and Cistercian monks.[88] The archbishop did not say how he came by these oft-quoted statistics, and their reliability is certainly open to question. There were in fact about sixty Dominicans active in the country in 1623. At Kilkenny on 4 September 1624 the bishops and vicars general of Munster, with Bishop David Rothe of Ossory, held a synod. One of its aims was to formulate resolutions to restore peace and harmony between the secular and regular clergy. Not only the government, but the diocesan priests were annoyed by the growth of friars and their independent activities. The Kilkenny discussions dealt with specific issues:

> Any doubtful or contentious privileges which might be claimed by the religious are to be jealously watched over by their respective superiors; their assemblies, too, and chapters, are to be held with secrecy, and in some retired place, not to alarm the government. The number of novices is to be limited in accordance with the decrees of Pope Urban VIII, nor are they to be sent to the Irish missions until they have completed their studies and prepared themselves for the particular needs of our suffering Church. On the other hand, religious are to be cherished by the parochial clergy, and invited to assist in the discharge of the sacred ministry. . . . The Sacred Congregation of Propaganda will be petitioned by us not to allow the bond of union between the bishop and his flock to be lessened by the exemption or exceptional faculties of the religious orders.[89]

Already the spectre of suspicion, dissension and misunderstanding which would plague relations between seculars and regulars, and indeed among the regulars themselves, had appeared. A memorandum of 1626 addressed to Propaganda Fide by the Capuchin Francis Lavalin Nugent concerned the multitude of regulars in Ireland and detailed the abuses of which they were said to be guilty: vagrancy, inordinate questing, imprudent reception, and inadequate training of novices.[90] The congregation issued a decree (13 August 1626) ordering the superiors of the religious orders in Ireland—Dominicans, Franciscans and Augustinians—to reform themselves. In particular the orders were to receive novices only where they could be properly trained and wear the religious habit, emergency circumstances excepted. At the same time Rome asked the

88 APF, SOCG, 294, f. 20r; Moran, *Archbishops of Dublin*, 290.
89 Moran, *Archbishops of Dublin*, 391–2.
90 APF, SOCG, 294, ff 34r–35v.

archbishops of Ireland to do everything possible to remove the causes of friction between diocesan clergy and religious.[91] In so far as the Dominicans were affected by disputes in the 1620s and 1630s, these will be dealt with in a later chapter.

A DOMINICAN SCHOOL IN GALWAY, 1625–30

As early as the spring of 1625 the Dominicans founded a public school in Galway and thus became involved in the education of youth from the city and further afield. In the sixteenth century Galway had been renowned for its schools and educational initiatives ever since Dominic Lynch FitzJohn, after many delays, opened a school near the Spanish Arch when he became Mayor of Galway in 1580. This school, organised somewhat along the lines of an English grammar school, specialised in the study of the classics and Renaissance learning, with Irish and Latin as the languages of instruction. Its success was immediate and enormous to the point that Galway city almost provided the genesis of a university. The future Jesuit Archbishop of Tuam, Nicholas Skerrett, was probably one of its first masters. Alexander Lynch, his successor as headmaster (*c.* 1609) and a former Jesuit student, was educated there too.[92]

It is no exaggeration to claim that the unqualified success of Galway as an educational centre in the Catholic tradition may have prompted the English government to found the College of the Most Holy and Undivided Trinity at Dublin in 1592 as a counter-measure. After all, it was not without significance that Queen Elizabeth's original intention was to site her new Irish university at Clonfert in the Co. Galway countryside.[93] The Galway schools were suppressed in 1615 by order of Thomas Jones, Protestant Archbishop of Dublin and Lord Chancellor of Ireland—an eloquent indication that the Galway schools still provided an alternative to the government challenge of Trinity College.

The tradition of Catholic education in Galway was then secretly continued by James Lynch. He had previously assisted Alexander Lynch and the Jesuit-educated John Lynch (1600–*c.* 1673), supposedly the son of Alexander Lynch, and future Archdeacon of Tuam, writer and historian.

91 APF, Acta, 4 (1626–7), ff 105v–106r; B. Jennings (ed.), 'Acta Sacrae Congregationis de Propaganda Fide, 1622–1650' in *Archiv. Hib.*, 22 (1959), 40.

92 F. Grannell, 'Galway' in *Dictionnaire d'Histoire et de Géographie Ecclésiastiques*, xix, Paris 1981, 939–42, provides a good summary of the history of education in Galway (1536–1660) and of the religious orders in the city.

93 G. A. Hayes-McCoy, 'The Completion of the Tudor Conquest and the Advance of the Counter-Reformation, 1571–1603' in *NHI*, iii, 139. In the sixteenth century there had been serious proposals for the establishment of universities at Armagh, Clonfert and Limerick. See T. Corcoran, *State Policy in Irish Education*, Dublin 1916, 49, 50.

This clandestine school, like its predecessors, enjoyed very considerable renown. Student numbers increased dramatically; and disquiet over the number of poor students attracted to Galway led to the corporation promulgating regulations in 1628 with a view to investigating the growing presence and the identity of students.

It was in this setting that the Dominicans made their entry in the 1620s, perhaps not for the first time, into the field of education in Galway. On 20 September 1626 a convention was drawn up between Thomas Lynch, Mayor of Galway, and the Dominicans whose house lay just outside the city walls, ratifying the establishment and special status of Dominican schools in Galway.[94] These public schools were intended to serve the needs of the young people of Galway and others from outside by providing courses in the humanities, liberal arts and theology, all without fees. The consent and blessing of the Dominican provincial had been obtained. The staff consisted of the prior, Nicholas Lynch, *sacrae theologiae praesentatus*, Peter Martin, *lector primarius* and moderator of studies, Stephen Lynch, second lector, Dominic Lynch, third lector, and Richard Bermingham, fourth lector. In all likelihood there were some lay masters as well. The schools were described in the document as having been functioning for sixteen months (i.e. since March 1625), and their continuity by the named Dominicans and their successors was envisaged. The Dominicans now sought official approval for their enterprise lest others should dare to take over their teaching responsibilities or interfere with the schools. The schools were highly esteemed by citizens and students alike and had been conducted free of charge, which had never been the case in Galway in the past.

The mayor duly granted formal approbation to the operation of these free schools, entrusted exclusively to the Dominicans of Galway and their successors forever, as far as possession, teaching and administration were concerned. The teachers were recognised as masters, with all rights, privileges, exemptions, liberties and immunities as enjoyed by teachers of similar schools in virtue of law or custom. The foundation of other schools was forbidden under penalty by any other persons no matter what their qualifications, status, or institute they might belong to, thus guaranteeing the unique position of the Dominican schools in Galway. Binding arrangements for the eventuality of persecution or changed circumstances followed in the agreement. Should evil times prevent the Dominicans from teaching, this fact would not derogate in the least from their rights. Further, with the return of peace they should be able to take up their interrupted work as often as that might be necessary or judged opportune. Should any others wish to teach in time of persecution, it should only be with the permission

94 APF, SOCG, 391, ff 116rv, 117v.

of the friars. In the event of others neglecting to seek licence and approval, besides punishment being meted out by the mayors or Dominicans, everything they attempted contrary to this agreement should be reckoned as void, nor should they be able to gain recognition for anything that would prejudice the rights of the Dominicans.

The legal tenor of the document was formidable, especially in granting what amounted to almost a monopoly to Dominican priests in the sphere of education at Galway. But what of the famous school of James Lynch—the school associated from 1622 with the future archdeacon John Lynch, whose reputation was to draw many pupils to its doors? There is certainly no evidence that it went into decline or out of existence. On the contrary, the Galway corporation in recognition of the services of James Lynch voted him an annual contribution of £10 in 1632, and he remained in charge of this school until his retirement in 1638. In this epoch Jesuit influence in Galway was very considerable. From the information available it may be inferred that they conducted a private school of their own for young men. Were the Dominicans, in virtue of the terms of this convention with the city authorities, seeking to restrict the Jesuits and other religious in running public schools—or indeed even to exclude them from the entire domain of education in Galway? It is more likely that the Dominicans and Jesuits of Galway were simultaneously catering for students of different social classes, and were therefore not in direct conflict. The Dominicans had in effect a 'poor-school' where no fees were charged, open to all whatever their social background. The Jesuits perhaps tended to concentrate on educating the sons of the Galway magnates and members of the city patrician families. Unfortunately, owing to paucity of documentation, it is not possible to answer these questions satisfactorily.

The Dominicans first sought Roman approval for their schools about 1627, after the corporation's convention.[95] The matter was again reviewed on 12 April 1631, when Propaganda Fide raised objections to certain clauses as being contrary to canon law precisely on the point of the unique status of the schools which excluded other religious from having the same type of establishment.[96] However, a later decision (no date given) favoured the Galway Dominicans, and the congregation sent a confirmatory rescript to the Archbishop of Tuam, with the instruction that it was to be implemented '*in forma commissoria*', namely by means of an intermediary or executor.[97]

In December 1630 the Galway Dominicans felt so secure and so pleased with their educational venture that they planned to set up a house

95 Ibid., 391, f. 117v.
96 APF, Acta, 7 (1630–31), f. 309v, cong. 139, no. 37.
97 APF, SOCG, 391, 117v.

of studies for the benefit of the clergy generally, both regular and secular, with the aid of the endowments of the former monasteries of the Augustinian Canons Regular of Annaghdown and Cong. To this end they addressed a petition to the cardinals of the Congregation of Religious.[98] The Canons Regular, it was stated, had disappeared from the area after the suppression of their monasteries and had never returned. Meanwhile lay people, both Catholics and Protestants, occupied the former monastic properties and enjoyed their revenues. The Dominicans asked that these monasteries should be canonically united to their convent of Galway. Then they would seek out a way of obtaining peaceful possession of them by agreement and would commit themselves to the erection of a *studium* for the education of clergy. The petition of the Dominicans to the Congregation of Religious was certainly given a hearing by the Roman authorities, but the outcome is unknown. At roughly the same time the Drogheda Franciscans were engaged in educating not only their own novices and students, but also in teaching philosophy to the youth of the town and instructing the *ordinandi* of the district in their future parochial duties.[99] After 1630 no more was heard of the Dominican ventures in education in Galway.

EARLY CONTACT WITH PROPAGANDA FIDE, 1626–7: THE QUESTION OF EPISCOPAL APPOINTMENTS

With the establishment of the Sacred Congregation for the Propagation of the Faith (Propaganda Fide) in 1622, the affairs of the Irish Church were supervised almost exclusively by a single Roman body whose competence extended to all countries considered 'missionary'. From its inception it undertook special responsibility for the search and nomination of candidates for Irish bishoprics. This new congregation became the final arbiter in all matters affecting the well-being of Irish Catholics, such as episcopal appointments, clerical discipline and the frequently tortuous relations between diocesan and regular clergy. Throughout the seventeenth and eighteenth centuries Propaganda Fide maintained a subtle but effective balance between rival interest groups: Gaelic Irish and Anglo-Irish, regular and secular clerical factions, including their influential lay supporters. It may be fairly asserted that the congregation's remarkable objectivity and impartiality more than once averted the threat of splits or even schism in Ireland. When it came to the nomination of bishops, the congregation insisted on taking into account political factors and social and family standing as well as Spanish, French, Italian, Portuguese and Low Countries college background. As a consequence of this

98 *Wadding Papers*, 453.
99 Ibid., xiv.

independent policy, the various strands of Irish Catholic life were given representation in the episcopate, with salutary benefits pastorally, theologically and ecclesiologically. Most importantly, the decisions of Propaganda Fide mediated the Tridentine spirit and the concepts of the new church order and extended the revised canon law (*jus novissimum*) on a practical basis to Ireland.

By the year 1626 there was an Irish Dominican procurator, Michael of the Holy Spirit, resident at the Minerva Convent in Rome. In that year he placed before Propaganda Fide three memoranda in Latin.[100] The first document was addressed to Francesco Ingoli, secretary of Propaganda. It stressed the desirability of promoting at least one Dominican to a bishopric in Ireland and suggested for Armagh either the provincial, Ross MacGeoghegan of Meath, or Patrick MacTeig of Derry. It was noted that the former had held office in the province by the authority of the Masters General for twelve years and had greatly edified clergy and laity alike, while the latter for two whole years had been subjected to much suffering for bearing witness to the faith in England as well as in Ireland. The motivation of the procurator's request would seem to have been a form of Dominican self-defence. Serious dissensions had arisen between the Dominicans, Franciscans and Jesuits on the one hand, and, on the other, with bishops who wanted to appropriate rights over Dominican houses. Recourse in disputes was limited to bishops who were not so well disposed towards Dominicans. It was pointed out that two archbishops and one bishop had already been chosen from among the Franciscans. The second document was simply a list of Irish dioceses. The third was a list of Irish Dominicans considered worthy of holding episcopal office, with some biographical details on each of them: Ross of the Cross MacGeoghegan, Patrick MacTeig, Richard de la Peña Caron, Anthony of St Mary Lynch, Dominic Nugent, Thomas Quirke, James Arthur, Dominic of the Rosary O'Daly, John of the Cross Murphy, Daniel of the Cross O'Crean and Nicholas Lynch.[101]

From a letter of Ross MacGeoghegan written in Spanish at Louvain (6 August 1627) to Michael of the Holy Spirit in Rome,[102] it is clear that the candidature of Armagh and that of other vacant bishoprics was still

100 APF, SOCG, 294, ff 26r–29v; *Wadding Papers*, 203–10, 225–6; B. Millett (ed.), 'Catalogue of Vol. 294 of the SOCG in Propaganda Fide Archives' in *Collect. Hib.*, 8 (1965), 9; AGOP, XIV, Liber K, pp 20–22.

101 Several versions of the third document are extant. The Propaganda Fide version lists nine names. Eleven Dominicans appear in Jenning's version in *Wadding Papers*, ten in the AGOP version, and nine in the Millett edition in 'Catalogue of Vol. 294 . . . in Propaganda Fide Archives'. The *Wadding Papers* edition is a revised text addressed to Cardinal Monti of the Office of the Inquisition, 1627.

102 *Wadding Papers*, 211–13; see H. F. Kearney, 'Ecclesiastical Politics and the Counter-Reformation, 1618–1648' in *Jn. Ecc. Hist.*, 11 (1960), 202–12.

a very live issue. Several Dominicans were spoken of as potential candidates. The declared motive of Ross MacGeoghegan for seeking episcopal nomination for his brethren was to strengthen the Dominicans and protect them from the vexations and interference of the Irish Franciscans. Mention was made too of the ecclesiastical intrigue involved in such appointments at Rome. Current Franciscan conduct was intimidating both to the other religious orders and to diocesan clergy, and was narrowly designed to forward Franciscan interests. Candid commentary on the diverse politico-ecclesiastical combinations and factions, with Old English and pro-Spanish Gaelic Irish pitted against each other, is immensely revealing. During Primate Lombard's exile at Rome (*c.*1598–1625) the balance of power in the Roman curia favoured the Old English ecclesiastical party, but after his death the balance was tilted in favour of the Ulster and pro-Spanish party. Ross MacGeoghegan as an episcopal candidate was supported by the Spanish court; as a bishop he could be relied on to be sympathetic to Spain because in his early training and as provincial he was more accustomed to look to Madrid and Flanders rather than to London or Rome for the realisation of his religious vision. His thinking is revealed in his letter of August 1627:

> If by any chance your reverence cannot obtain the bishopric of Armagh, it would please me if you were to get that of Clogher for Father Dominic Nugent, seeing that his county of Meath adjoins that diocese, and I think some of his kinsmen are either living or have their properties there. If the Bishop of Meath should be promoted to the primacy through Jesuit influence, your reverence could ask Meath for Father Dominic. In case Sir John Roche be elected you will ask the bishopric of Ferns for Father John of the Cross [Murphy]; for the Archbishop of Dublin and all the clergy and people of that diocese have already postulated John Roche. In case they are determined there [Rome] not to choose any Anglo-Irish priest as primate—on account of the favour of the Infanta and of the King of Spain—through the intervention of Tyrone and of the Archbishop of Tuam, they might elect Bishop Reilly or the Bishop of Down. I would be pleased if Father Patrick [MacTeig] could get the vacant bishopric, that we might have some prelate with authority to defend us against our brothers, who, to judge by appearances, wish to destroy us everywhere. Certainly, if any of them were primate now, I am afraid that they would accomplish it; for their quarrels, for the most part, are always directed against our Order, although they oppose all the bishops and archbishops of the kingdom, except those who are of their own Order or were appointed through their influence. The clergy and parish priests of the kingdom,

seeing them prosper so much and doing whatever they like, are afraid of them and do not dare to oppose them. And so they have almost the whole country under their power, doing many injuries to our Order and to some others, without being prepared to make any satisfaction. If they acted so when they had in the kingdom only the Archbishops of Dublin and Tuam, what will they do now that they have three or four?

So I would prefer one of the present bishops to be chosen as primate rather than any of them; and since they have Father Luke [Wadding] with so much favour in Rome, the Archbishop of Tuam in Madrid, and the Earl of Tyrone in Brussels, it seems impossible to gain any advantage over them on any point. Each one of those I have named has more influence and credit in those respective courts than all the others of his country. Because Tyrconnell has lost much of his former standing since his sister came here, Tyrone alone enjoys all favour, and it will be difficult for your reverence to gain anything from these, unless you join yourself with some strong adversary of theirs and try to deprive Father Luke of the favour of Spain. If those in Rome were open to argument, we could prove with evidence that what Tyrone and the Archbishop of Tuam put forward as suitable for the service of the Spanish king—from whom they derive their influence—is not best suited for the above-mentioned post nor for the common good of the kingdom. They ask this favour, not out of zeal for the common good, nor for this particular position, but from concern for their own flesh and blood, and for their own Order. May God correct them, and may God preserve your reverence as I desire.

A SECOND REPORT ON THE PROVINCE, 1626–7

Throughout 1627 Michael of the Holy Spirit presented several memorials to Propaganda Fide about the Dominicans in Ireland and the needs of the new college established at Louvain. By far the most significant was a report on the state of the province,[103] compiled jointly, it would appear, by Ross MacGeoghegan and his Roman procurator. The first portion was composed by the provincial at Louvain early in 1626, while a very different hand completed it in 1626–7, supplying the names of the brethren on the continent. This is clearly indicated as much by differences in handwriting as by the use of paper of different texture and watermarks.

The report was entitled *Nomina Conventuum ordinis Praedicatorum in Hybernia ac fratrum ibi degentium* and was endorsed by an official of

103 APF, SOCG, 294, ff 102r–105v; reproduced as Appendix 6 (pp 326–9 below); edited in Moran, *Spicil. Ossor.*, i, 151–61, but unreliable.

Propaganda Fide on 10 September 1627.[104] It had already been delivered to the Master General by 10 April 1627 and represented Ross MacGeoghegan's final account of his fourteen-year stewardship of the Irish province. A provincial chapter to elect his successor was held at Sligo, where the vicar provincial, Daniel of the Cross O'Crean, resided, probably in the summer of 1627.

The report on the province opened with a tabulation of the medieval priories, with the surprising inclusion of Inchaquire (near Athy?). In all, thirty-eight houses were listed, distributed over all the civil provinces. It continued with an incomplete résumé, touching on the vicissitudes of the Irish Dominicans from 1539 to 1613. That the province was never entirely destroyed was stressed. Though turned out of their houses, the Dominicans 'did not flee the kingdom', but lived concealed by lay Catholics. From time to time they met in one of their country foundations (then in Catholic possession), where they held chapters as best they could and made ordinances in keeping with those calamitous times. With the passing of Thaddeus MacDuane (which is dated in the report as having occurred in 1612, almost certainly in error for 1608) the remaining brethren dispersed among their lay benefactors and friends.

A fresh beginning in the history of the province was made with the arrival of young Spanish-trained Dominicans from about 1613. After this year the account is more authoritative and supplies detailed information about the strategy and progress of revival. The essentials of conventual living were restored in two or three remote houses in the countryside, and this reform was gradually extended throughout the province. By 1626 twelve houses had been organised, eight of which were in the towns and cities. The city houses differed from those in the country in that it was not possible to reoccupy former Dominican properties. Instead the brethren lived in rented houses or where they could obtain a lease; these houses were to all appearances secular but were arranged to suit conventual life. Provision was made for a separate oratory, dormitory, refectory and other apartments necessary for a religious community shut off from contact with outsiders. This accommodation was paid for by an annual rent derived from offerings. All food and clothing was supplied as alms by their Catholic supporters. In addition, the brethren had been able to reoccupy four of the Order's own houses in the countryside, in which they might live more at ease, though liable to nocturnal disturbance.

The report then went on to outline a number of features of everyday life in the Dominican houses. The brethren were recorded as leaving houses only to preach, to quest or to perform some work of charity. In

104 Fenning, *Irish material*, 282.

some houses regular observance was such that abstinence from meat was observed (an exception was made for the infirm); moreover, Matins and all the canonical hours were recited (though without song) by the whole community. Eight of the houses had priors elected by their own communities; the other four were ruled by vicars. Novices were instructed in seven houses, and these, on finishing their novitiate, were sent to Spain or to some other province where there were flourishing houses of study for classical studies. Having become proficient in both arts and theology, they returned to Ireland as preachers of the faith. There were then fifty Irish brethren in Spain, and many others had died there. The procurator in Spain had written recently to say that in the preceding year (1625) he had sent five Dominicans to Ireland. When Ross MacGeoghegan left Ireland (1625 or 1626), there were in excess of one hundred friars divided between twelve houses.

The report closed with an account of the various houses and the names of the priors. Curiously, it was not finished, for it broke off abruptly while treating of the eleventh house, Lorrha. The twelfth house was not mentioned. The city houses were those of Dublin, Sligo, Galway, Limerick, Cork, Waterford and Kilkenny. The remaining four—Mullingar, Urlar, Athenry and Lorrha—must be classified as being in the country. Once more the omission of Roscommon and Drogheda is baffling, since it is on record that Ross MacGeoghegan visited and preached in the Roscommon area, at which time it must surely have had a community. As will later be seen, the Drogheda Dominicans had been re-established before 1622. Every province except Ulster was well represented, and in the following decade many more houses were opened, including one or two in Ulster, where there had been medieval Dominican churches. The list is extremely valuable in showing the deployment of priests and the strength of the listed houses, Mullingar (situated in MacGeoghegan country) being the largest with a community of about twenty-two. Seven priests were described as old or centenarians—a fact which convincingly proves that (unless these men had returned from exile) the province could not have been reduced to four individuals in 1603, as stated by Edmund Burke, O.P., in his eighteenth-century historical account of the province.

There followed in a different hand lists of Irish Dominicans, priests and students, living in Spain and Portugal (twenty-four priests and more than twenty-two students), Flanders, France and Italy (eight priests and eleven students), totalling sixty-five brethren plus others abroad. The report therefore shows a strong and growing nucleus of Dominicans being trained in Europe.

The accompanying tables illustrate the situation in Ireland in 1626–7 and provide a contrast with the province as it stood in 1622. Since that date four defunct houses (Sligo, Mullingar, Athenry and Lorrha) had been revived and new communities established in them. A noticeable decrease in the number of priests in Dublin, Galway, Limerick, Kilkenny, Waterford and Cork had taken place, while numbers had increased at Urlar, and dramatically so at Mullingar, and there were sizeable communities in Sligo and Athenry.

TABLE 4: NUMBERS OF DOMINICANS IN IRELAND RECORDED IN 1626–7

Convent	*Priests*	*Students*	*Novices*	*Lay brothers*	*Total*	
Athenry	5	–	2	1	8	
Cork	4	4	some	–	11	approx.
Dublin	4	–	3	1	8	
Galway	4	5	some	–	12	approx.
Kilkenny	3	–	some	–	6	approx.
Limerick	3	5	some	2	12	approx.
Lorrha	2	–	–	1	3	
Mullingar	8	4	6–8	2	20–22	
Sligo	8	3–4	some	–	14	approx.
Urlar	5	–	4–5	–	9–10	
Waterford	5	–	–	–	5	
					110	approx.

TABLE 5: COMPARATIVE DATA IN LISTS OF 1622 AND 1626–7

Athenry	1622	Unmentioned.
	1626	Peter Martin, prior, with four priests, two students (novices) and one lay brother.
Cork	1622	John of St Mary, prior, and seven friars.
	1626	Thomas Lynch, prior, with three priests, four students and some novices.
Dublin	1622	Ross MacGeoghegan, prior provincial, and eight friars.
	1626	Thomas of the Ascension, prior, with three priests, three students (novices) and one lay brother.

Galway	1622	Daniel of the Cross, prior, and nine friars.
	1626	Nicholas Lynch, prior, with three priests, five students and some novices.
Kilkenny	1622	Thomas Quirke, prior, and six priests.
	1626	John of the Cross, prior, with two priests and some novices.
Limerick	1622	Bernard O'Brien, prior, and six friars.
	1626	Thomas Quirke, prior, with two priests, five students, some novices and two lay brothers.
Lorrha	1622	Unmentioned.
	1626	Anthony Madden, prior, and one priest.
Mullingar	1622	Unmentioned.
	1626	Thomas of St Dominic, prior, with seven priests, four students, six to eight novices and two lay brothers.
Sligo	1622	Unmentioned.
	1626	Daniel of the Cross, vicar provincial, with seven priests, three or four students and some novices.
Urlar	1622	Stephen Lynch, prior, with one priest for education of many novices.
	1626	Dominic Kerin, prior, with four priests and four or five students (novices).
Waterford	1622	Thomas Power, prior, and six friars.
	1626	John Fox, prior, with four priests.
Summary:	1622	49 friars recorded in convents in Ireland; seven names only. Supplementary lists give names of 57 friars resident in Ireland. Estimated total for Irish province: approximately 82.
	1626	About 110 friars recorded as resident in convents in Ireland, of whom 51 (all but two of whom are named) were priests. Supplementary lists give names of 64 priests and students in Europe. Estimated total for Irish province: over 175.

That such a vast programme of recovery and reform should have been carried through within twelve years of its initial undertaking in 1614 speaks admirably for the ability, dedication and stamina of the provincial, Ross MacGeoghegan. A man of vision, courage and perseverance, he was at all stages ably and devotedly assisted by the intrepid and ever-active Richard de la Peña Caron, his procurator at the court of Madrid. He it was who co-ordinated the inward and outward flow of Irish Dominican students and priests. The generosity of Philip III and Philip IV of Spain, coupled with the perennial hospitality and friendship of the Spanish, Portuguese, Italian, French and Flemish Dominicans, cannot be exaggerated. It was European backing that guaranteed the transition of a revived and rejuvenated province from the continent to Ireland. In addition, with the accession of Charles I of England in 1625, a more tolerant attitude was reluctantly adopted by the Irish administration, and the Dominicans, like other religious, took advantage of the temporarily improved politico-religious climate to re-establish themselves intelligently. Another factor that played a decisive role, if in a more subtle way, was the quality and character of the new generation of Dominicans. These were of a more resilient stock than their late medieval predecessors and knew how to meet the challenge of a transformed Ireland undismayed, being the products of the Tridentine world and its distinctive militant perspective. In short, Ross MacGeoghegan's report signified that the restoration of the Dominicans in Ireland was substantially achieved.

SIX

Architects of the New Province: Ross MacGeoghegan and Richard Caron

Ross MacGeoghegan and Richard Caron may be justly singled out as the principal architects and pillars of the revived and reformed Irish Dominican province from 1614 to the late 1620s. Both were natives of the midlands county of Westmeath and belonged to Old Irish families. Ross MacGeoghegan's distinguished family had deep roots in the Gaelic aristocracy, but had close connections through his mother with the Dempseys of Clanmalier, a family recently ennobled by the English crown and thus inserted in the official peerage of the country. Ross MacGeoghegan and Richard Caron, by coincidence, received their primary education in the same school; both went to Spain in 1600, and the two studied together for the diocesan priesthood at the Irish College, Salamanca. Within a short time both were irresistibly attracted to the Dominican Order as they found it in Spain and Portugal. Simultaneously they entered the Order at La Peña de Francia, in the civil province of Salamanca in 1601, and made their solemn commitment to the Order on 8 November 1602.

Afterwards they worked harmoniously in furthering the building up of the Irish province, MacGeoghegan being concerned primarily with the implementation of a renewed and reformed vision of Dominican life in Ireland and overseas, Caron with its complex material needs and practical organisation as it developed embryonically in Spain, Portugal and Flanders. And though geographically separated while promoting their common endeavours, they remained ever deeply united by strong bonds of fraternity and friendship, dating from their first days of shared idealism in the Iberian peninsula. For both MacGeoghegan and Caron a restored and spiritually vibrant Irish Dominican province, stemming from the rich experience of the Irish Dominican continental colleges, became the paramount objective of their life's work. Throughout the eleven years (1617–27) that Ross MacGeoghegan was head of the province their intensive collaboration never slackened.

TABLE 6: THE MacGEOGHEGANS OF MOYCASHEL AND KINELAGH, 1540s–1640s

(a) *First and second marriages of Connla MacGeoghegan*

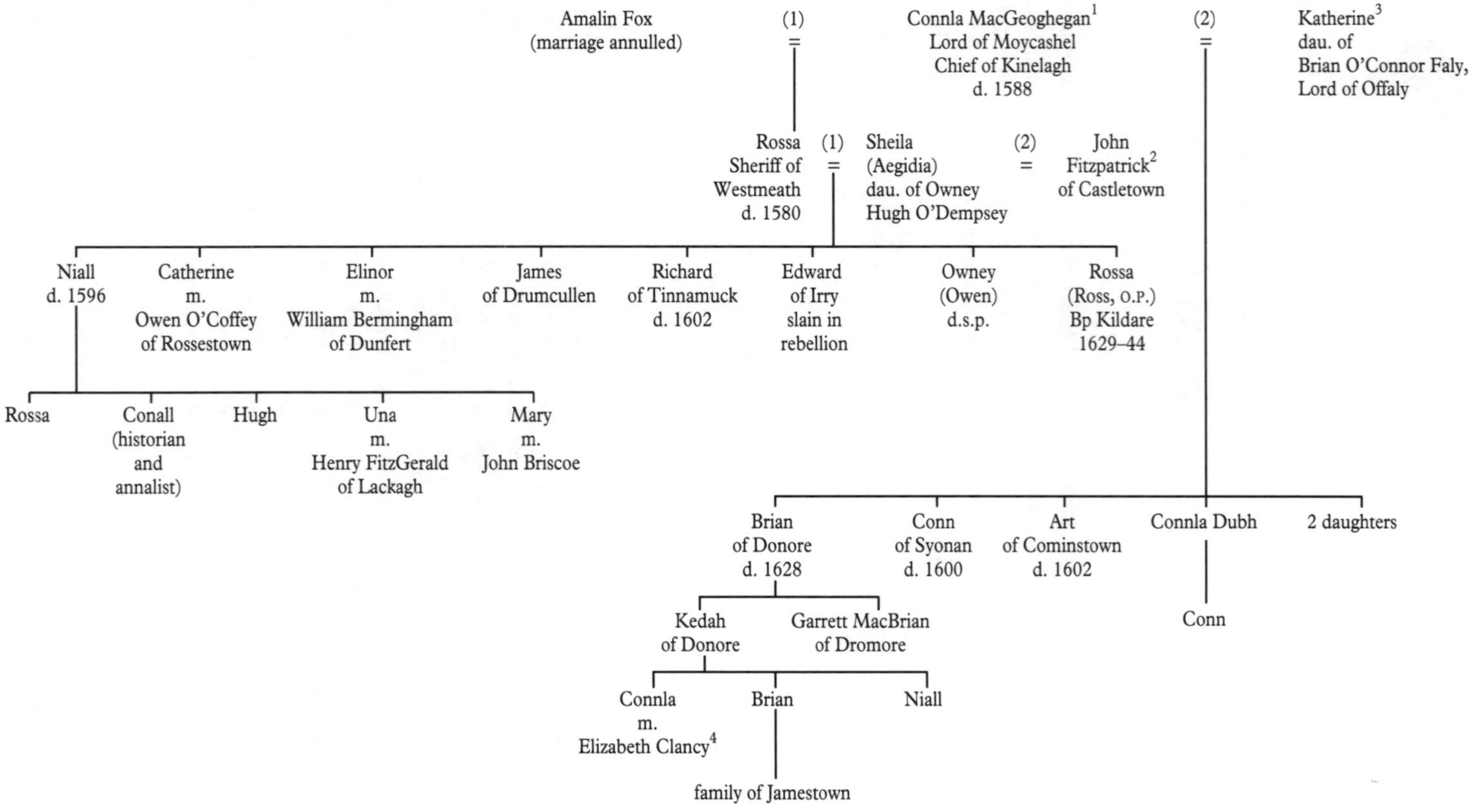

(b) *Third and fourth marriages of Connla MacGeoghegan*

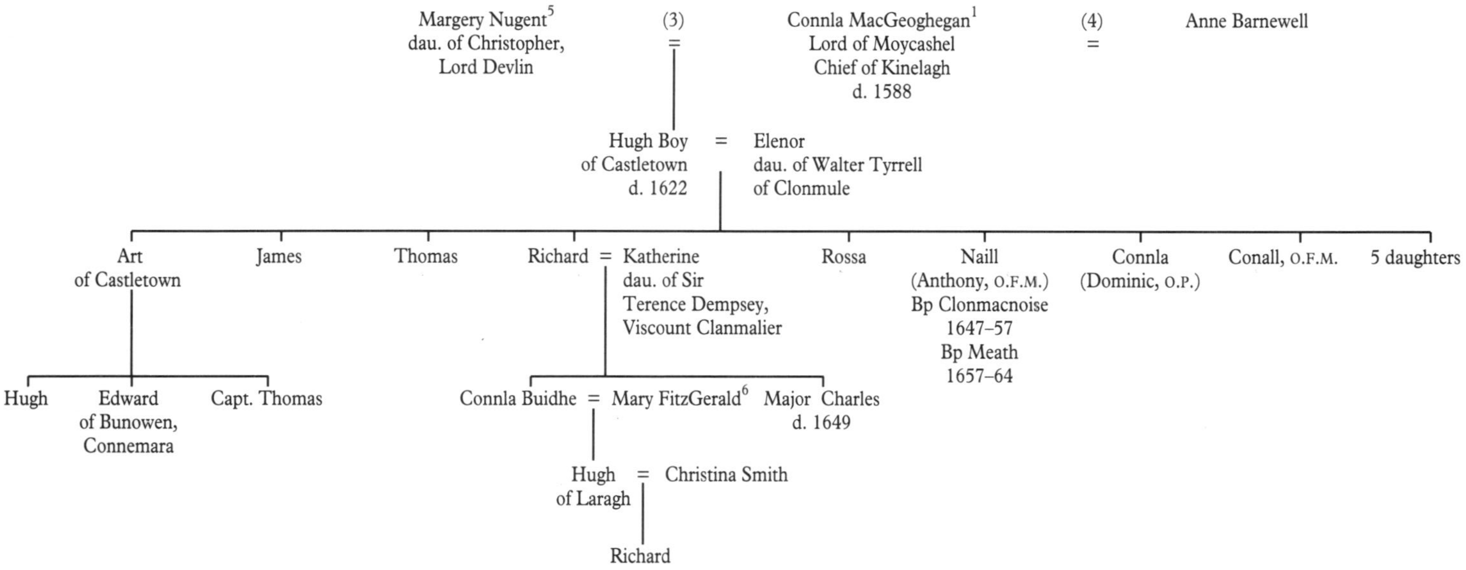

1 For his four marriages see Dublin, Genealogical Office, MS 85, ff 176–89 (part out of order).

2 See PROI , salved chancery pleadings, B. 224, 227.

3 Connla and Katherine were married in church by dispensation from Cardinal Pole, papal legate to England in the reign of Mary, being related in the second and third degrees, i.e. first cousins once removed.

4 See note 37 below.

5 Connla and Margery were husband and wife in August 1564 and September 1569. PRONI, Kildare Deeds, D. 3078. She was also married to Philip O'Reilly 'the Prior', who survived until 1576, so this third marriage must have been dissolved too.

6 See *Irish Genealogist*, 4, no. 1 (1968), 5, 8.

ROSS MACGEOGHEGAN (C. 1577–1644)

Ross MacGeoghegan was born at Moycashel, Co. Westmeath, about 1577.[1] He was the sixth son of Ross MacGeoghegan, lord of Moycashel (one of the five flourishing houses of the MacGeoghegan princely sept). His mother was Sheila Dempsey, sister of the first Lord Clanmalier of Clonygowan castle, Co. Offaly, where, according to another tradition, Ross MacGeoghegan was born.[2] The family background of Ross MacGeoghegan, future Dominican provincial and Bishop of Kildare, and of his cousin Anthony MacGeoghegan, O.F.M., future Bishop of Clonmacnoise and later of Meath, placed them centrally within the MacGeoghegan clan,[3] since both were grandsons of Connla, lord of Moycashel and 'captain of the nation' of Kinelagh. Two younger cousins also became Dominicans: Dominic MacGeoghegan and the London martyr Arthur MacGeoghegan. It was Connla's eldest son, Rossa, the Dominican provincial's father, who was given a grant by Queen Elizabeth of all the lands of Kinelagh or 'MacGeoghegan's country', then named the barony of Moycashel, with the title of seneschal and sheriff of Co. Westmeath. The family landholding is estimated to have been somewhere between five and ten thousand acres.[4]

Ross MacGeoghegan was a Gaelic aristocrat, a descendant of the MacGeoghegans of Cinél Fhiachach,[5] a branch of the southern Uí Néill, whose genealogy has been traced from the thirteenth century.[6] In his early childhood his father was murdered at Newtown, Co. Westmeath, on 7 September 1580. The deed was allegedly perpetrated by his father's brother, Brian, with the assistance of other relations as part of a dynastic

1 D. J. O'Doherty (ed.), 'Students of the Irish College, Salamanca' in *Archiv. Hib.*, 2 (1913), 11.

2 Lynch, *De Praesulibus Hib.*, i, 335. For general information on the history of the MacGeoghegan family see E. MacLysaght, *Irish Families*, Dublin 1957, 132–3.

3 There may have been a MacGeoghegan (Mag Eochagáin) clan connection with the family of the former provincial Eugene MacHugan (a version of the original Mac Aodhagáin). One gains the distinct impression that many of the leading sixteenth- and seventeenth-century Dominicans, particularly in the midlands and the west, were drawn from extended family connections.

4 D. F. Cregan, 'The Social and Cultural Background of a Counter-Reformation Episcopate, 1618–1660' in A. Cosgrove and D. McCartney (eds), *Studies in Irish History presented to R. Dudley Edwards*, Dublin 1979, 94, 101.

5 The patrimony of Cinél Fhiachach, in the sixteenth century, comprised essentially the barony of Moycashel, but was anciently much more extensive. The MacGeoghegans retained their rank as lords of Moycashel down to the Cromwellian confiscations, when they lost their estates. Woulfe, *Sloinnte Gaedhael is Gall*, 418–19.

6 P. Walsh, *The MacGeoghegans*, Mullingar 1938, genealogy inserted between pp 30 and 31. For the detailed genealogical table of Ross MacGeoghegan's immediate family reproduced in this chapter I am extremely grateful to Dr Kenneth Nicholls, University College, Cork.

struggle prompted by political intrigue and the grant of all the traditional family lands to one brother.[7] Ross MacGeoghegan's elder brother was Captain Richard MacGeoghegan of Tinnamuck, who was slain in 1602 during the heroic defence of the castle of Dunboy, Co. Cork, one of the last great exploits of the Nine Years' War. One of his nephews was Conall or Connla, celebrated translator of the so-called Annals of Clonmacnoise, who also left a description of the various branches of the MacGeoghegan family and their whereabouts in 1627.[8] Several of the MacGeoghegans combined the family characteristics of priesthood, love of Gaelic learning and historical scholarship. It was Ross MacGeoghegan's letters of approbation (8 January 1637) as Bishop of Kildare that were prefixed to the first editions of *Annála Ríoghachta Éireann* (Annals of the Kingdom of Ireland, commonly known as the Annals of the Four Masters) and to the Martyrology of Donegal (*Calendarium Sanctorum Hiberniae*) produced by the Franciscans of Louvain.[9] In 1638 he forwarded a valuable account in Latin of Kildare place-names with religious connections to John Colgan, the eminent Franciscan scholar, also resident at Louvain.[10]

The early environment of Ross MacGeoghegan was Gaelic, but his home life was almost certainly bilingual. His peregrinations in search of a grammar school type of education are succinctly documented. He started his education in the humanities (Latin and Greek literature) under Master Humphrey Powell Walsh at Fertullagh in his native county and continued to study under Master Thomas 'a Gargia' at Clonmel, Co. Tipperary, both laymen and Catholics. He also spent six months with Master Brok, a Protestant, perhaps in a state-sponsored school. Later he was taught for about two years by John Power, a priest and bachelor of theology. He completed his study of *litterae humaniores* by a five-month course at the Irish College, Lisbon, early in 1600. Almost immediately afterwards he was admitted to the Irish College at Salamanca (1 June 1600) on the recommendation of the rector of Lisbon. On Pentecost Sunday, 10 June 1601, he took two oaths to abide by the constitution of the college and confirmed what he had promised by a third oath on 13 June.[11] In common with the

7 Ibid., 31; Cregan, 'The Social and Cultural Background of a Counter-Reformation Episcopate', 95.

8 R. Flower (ed.), *Catalogue of Irish Manuscripts in the British Museum*, ii, London, 1926, 473; A. Cogan, *The Ecclesiastical History of the Diocese of Meath*, ii, Dublin 1867, 417.

9 FLK, MS A 13, f. xxxii; MS A 16, f. vi verso; M. Dillon, C. Mooney and P. de Brún (eds),*Catalogue of Irish Manuscripts in the Franciscan Library, Killiney*, Dublin 1969, 24–7, 32–5.

10 FLK, MS A 31, no. 6; Dillon *et al.*, *Catalogue of the Irish Manuscripts in the Franciscan Library, Killiney*, 66; text edited by D. de hÓir, 'Blúire Cillsheanchais faoi Fhairche Chill Dara' in *Dinnseanchas*, 2 (1966), 29–39.

11 O'Doherty, 'Students of the Irish College, Salamanca', 11–12.

majority of those who would constitute the new resident Irish episcopate (1618–60), the humanistic stage of his education as well as his professional studies were completed abroad. Thus Ross MacGeoghegan and his future colleagues in the episcopate all gained some experience of post-Tridentine seminary formation, and nearly all acquired university degrees.[12]

It would appear that while in Portugal he visited the University of Coimbra. It was there that he met the Dominicans, who were then well represented in the philosophy and theology faculties of the university, and attended theological disputations held in the Dominican college (*studium generale*). So impressed was he by the standards of doctrine, preaching and the Dominican way of life that he decided to join the Order of Preachers.[13] In November 1601 he began his novitiate at the Spanish convent of Peña de Francia, which marks the highest point of the Sierra de Peña de Francia, about forty-five miles south-west of Salamanca. This convent incorporated an ancient Marian sanctuary and place of pilgrimage for the entire Iberian peninsula, sited 5,653 feet above sea level. On account of extreme climatic conditions, the community transferred from its medieval upper house on the mountain summit to a lower house just above the plain for the winter season, returning to the summit once again with the advent of spring.[14] Here he was given the name of Ross of the Cross (Roque de la Cruz), and made his solemn profession on the same day, 8 November 1602,[15] as his fellow countryman, Richard de la Peña Caron. Both were affiliated to this Spanish house, though some later writers would describe Ross MacGeoghegan as an 'alumnus' of Mullingar.[16] When asked to make a statement about MacGeoghegan in January 1629, his confrère and contemporary, Patrick MacTeig, said that they had studied together at Salamanca and indicated that Ross MacGeoghegan had been ordained a priest before 1609.[17] As a student he delighted in attending sermons and scholastic disputations and was an assiduous learner.[18] On completion of his studies, he took the lectorate

12 Cregan, 'The Social and Cultural Background of a Counter-Reformation Episcopate', 107.

13 Lynch, *De Praesulibus Hib.*, i, 335.

14 F. Soria Heredia, *El Santuario de Nuestra Señora de la Peña de Francia*, Salamanca 1982, 17–19, 31–2 and *passim*; M. de Los Hoyos, 'Real Monasterio de Peña de Francia' in *Registro Documental*, i, Madrid 1961, 175–85.

15 AHN, sección de clero, libro 10585, f. 26r for original record first brought to light by Dr M. MacCurtain; Los Hoyos, *Registro Documental*, i, 218–19, where the month of profession is omitted.

16 Burke, *Hib. Dom.*, 522.

17 C. Giblin, 'The *Processus Datariae* and the Appointment of Catholic Bishops in the Seventeenth Century' in *Father Luke Wadding: Commemorative Volume*, ed. Franciscan Fathers, Dublin 1957, 550.

18 Lynch, *De Praesulibus Hib.*, i, 335.

in theology and lectured publicly for a long time.[19] By his religious and intellectual training during a sojourn of fourteen years in Spain, he assimilated the Tridentine tradition in the Castillian mode. Though imbued with the doctrinal and spiritual heritage of the Dominican Order, he would have been perfectly familiar with the spirituality of Ignatius of Loyola, Teresa of Avila and John of the Cross, as well as with the Spain of Cervantes and other outstanding sixteenth-century poets, prose writers and literary figures. His delight in scholarship and the university world of Salamanca would be an abiding influence in his life, while the great missionary impulse of the Spanish Dominicans consequent on the discovery of the Americas and the Far East must have sharpened his own missionary vision.

In 1617, or possibly as early as 1614, Ross MacGeoghegan was appointed vicar of the Irish Dominicans in Ireland and on the continent, with a commission to reorganise and reconstitute the province, then extremely weak and in a state of disarray.[20] After an absence of fourteen years he returned to Ireland in 1614, to fulfil, as he declared himself, the missionary oaths he had taken at Salamanca as a student.[21] Surveying the sad condition of his province, he took pains to consult with its dispersed members, in particular the Dominicans of Athenry, as to what could be done to ensure the revival of the Order. With the co-operation of these friars and of the Earl of Clanrickard, he obtained an obscure place on the earl's estate outside Athenry, and a simple house was built there for the reception of novices.[22]

Early in 1618 he returned to Spain accompanied by six young Dominicans who had been prepared to commence their studies for the priesthood.[23] In recognition of his valiant efforts to promote fresh beginnings for the Order in Ireland and for his sustained dedication to preaching there for five years, he was nominated for the Order's *praesentatus* degree in the course of the Lisbon chapter held in May and June 1618.[24] The chapter, moreover, gave unqualified approval to his proposals for the continuing reorganisation of his province.[25] In the winter months of 1618 and spring of 1619 he was immersed in preparations for setting out for Ireland once more. This time he was accompanied by eight Dominicans who were trained to teach philosophy and theology.[26] In 1622,

19 Giblin, 'The *Processus Datariae*', 549.
20 Strongly implied in Fenning, *Irish material*, 335–6.
21 AGS, Estado, leg. 2748.
22 TA, MS: Burke, *Notitia Brevis Provinciae Hiberniae*; Coleman, *Ancient Dominican Foundations*, 84.
23 AGS, Estado, leg. 2750.
24 Fenning, *Irish material*, 279.
25 Reichert, *MOPH*, xi, 317.
26 AGS, Estado, leg. 2750; ibid., leg. 1774; Fenning, *Irish material*, 281.

at his instigation, John Fox ably represented Irish Dominican interests at the general chapter of Milan, which gave full provincial status to the congregation and made Ross MacGeoghegan, hitherto vicar, its prior provincial.[27]

Most likely it was during his protracted stay in Ireland in the years 1619–26 that he established a novitiate at Urlar, situated on the shores of Urlar Lough, Co. Mayo. Of the Dominican houses, Urlar uniquely had escaped total spoliation on account of its solitary location.[28] Sometime shortly after March 1612 it had been granted to Lord Dillon; and probably owing to the fact that his family remained Catholic, the Dominicans seem to have been able to retain possession of their house.[29] There he spent two years accepting and instructing novices, who later joined veteran Dominicans in small houses which he had restored in the other civil provinces. Other Dominicans trained at Urlar became curates in parishes and chaplains to the nobility in their houses, while yet others were obliged to live conventually according to the traditions of the Order in different parts of the country. MacGeoghegan was particularly successful in bringing about a restoration of the Order in Leinster, re-establishing a Dominican nucleus in Mullingar, Dublin, Drogheda and Athy.[30]

Ross MacGeoghegan's policies, however, met with opposition among some of his own brethren. Archdeacon John Lynch, on whom we are dependent for much of our information concerning this phase of MacGeoghegan's career, relates that one false brother, a fugitive from religious life who refused to give up his licentious lifestyle, denounced his superior to the government authorities for introducing 'Roman customs' into Ireland. As a result, MacGeoghegan's likeness was put on display at the port of Dublin, and an officer called Lyons and his adjutant named Archison (Acheson?) were ordered to hunt him down and bring him a prisoner to Dublin. MacGeoghegan evaded his enemies by means of a disguise.[31] About 1622 an informer reported to the government that 'Father Ross mc Geogheyan, a Dominican friar, keepeth at Ballybark [Co. Meath] with one Christofer Terrell'.[32]

At this stage the recurring problem of Lynch's evidential reliability arises yet again. In dealing with Ross MacGeoghegan, he provides highly interesting and detailed information which cannot now be substantiated, concerning MacGeoghegan's conversion to Catholicism of some prominent officials of the Anglo-Irish establishment with a midlands family

27 Reichert, *MOPH*, xi, 342.
28 Lynch, *De Praesulibus Hib.*, i, 336.
29 Coleman, *Ancient Dominican Foundations*, 96.
30 Lynch, *De Praesulibus Hib.*, i, 336.
31 Ibid.
32 R. J. Hunter, 'Catholicism in Meath, *c.*1622' in *Collect. Hib.*, 14 (1971), 8.

background. It would seem that Lynch confused the identities of some of these personalities, inflated the status of individuals and perpetuated inaccuracies as a result of an uncritical treatment of his sources. Bearing this caution in mind, the following anecdotes related by Lynch[33] are given here in the hope that some historian may be able to disentangle truth from error and set the whole material in correct historical perspective. In the 1620s MacGeoghegan is said to have persuaded Edward Herbert, 'baronet and Privy Councillor',[34] and his entire family to become Catholics. It is also asserted that he converted another public official named Blundell[35] when he was close to death. Despite danger to his life, MacGeoghegan hastened to Dublin and administered the sacraments to the dying man. Later, when the government heard of his audacity, an edict was issued for his capture which compelled MacGeoghegan to quit Leinster and to seek refuge in Galway. When this storm had passed, he preached on one occasion to a vast congregation gathered at the well of St Brigid in Co. Roscommon. His sermon on miracles so touched the resident judge, a Protestant whose name is given by Lynch as 'Eospert', that he resigned his office worth £40 per annum and became a Catholic. In the counties of Longford and Kildare he was credited with recalling more than twelve elderly priests to resume their ministry as Catholic priests. The fear of being deprived of their ministry from which they derived considerable annual revenues had struck at their faith, and their avarice to retain them had put it into their minds to conform to Protestantism and become Protestant clergymen. When MacGeoghegan pointed out their waywardness and errors, they came to their senses and returned to their priestly duties. MacGeoghegan was also said to have brought about the conversion of a noted Anglican theologian, Richard Ó Duinn (Dunne, O'Doyne), son of the Baron of Iregan, whose ancestral territory lay in Leix. As a young man he had been sent to England, where he had been educated as a Protestant. After a brilliant student career at the University of Cambridge he took his doctorate of divinity when he was twenty-five years old, became a high official of his college, and soon held a teaching post in theology in that university. At the same time his proficiency in the arts of magic was such that he had no equal in England. His reputation for learning was so great that he was offered several bishoprics, all of which he declined. After lecturing in theology for

33 Lynch, *De Praesulibus Hib.*, i, 336–7.

34 There is no evidence that Herbert ever held these offices; his name does not appear in the lists of office-holders.

35 This may be a reference to Sir Francis Blundell, surveyor general and member of the Court of Exchequer in 1609–10 and vice-treasurer of Ireland before 12 April 1625. See J. L. J. Hughes (ed.), *Patentee Officers in Ireland, 1173–1876*, Dublin 1960, 13.

forty years in England he returned to Ireland, became an official of Trinity College, Dublin, and resumed teaching theology. MacGeoghegan, at that time resident in Dublin, frequently held friendly discussions on religious matters with Richard Ó Duinn, who was his blood relation. As a result, the latter finally embraced Catholicism, whereupon he gave up his university office and lectureship. When he died at the family estate (in the present barony of Tinnahinch) in north-west Leix, Ross MacGeoghegan preached the panegyric at his funeral. Historical research as yet has found no member of the Ó Duinn family to accommodate these facts. One member of the family was indeed a Richard Duinn, described as a Catholic priest and vicar general of Kildare. The tantalising question remains as to who was the mysterious midlands personality behind Lynch's narrative.

Ross MacGeoghegan was also said to have led to the Catholic faith Thaddeus O'Donnellan,[36] vicar general of the Anglican Bishop of Kildare, and Elizabeth Clancy,[37] heiress of the barony of Rosclogher in Co. Leitrim, along with very many others. Learning of his unbounded zeal, the exasperated authorities forbade anybody to receive him into their homes. To harbour him would be considered a felony and therefore a crime punishable by death. A reward of £200 sterling was promised to whomsoever would deliver him alive to the Dublin authorities.

Considering the serious consequences which this edict might have, not for himself but rather for his loyal friends, Ross MacGeoghegan is said to have quickly convened a chapter of the Dominicans in Connacht.[38] Regrettably Lynch did not indicate the place or date of this chapter which met in the 1620s and at which MacGeoghegan freely yielded up the office of provincial which he had held for nine years. He had decided that Stephen Lynch should succeed him, a man so pious that he had always been entrusted by superiors with the formation of novices. However, since Stephen Lynch evaded the burden of office, MacGeoghegan, according to Lynch, with the consent of the chapter, conferred it on

36 Teig O'Donnellan was the fourth son of Nehemiah (Fearganainm) Donnellan, Anglican Archbishop of Tuam (1595–1609). This family went different ways religiously. See N. P. Canny, 'Why the Reformation failed in Ireland: *une question mal posée*' in *Jn. Ecc. Hist.*, 30 (1979), 442.

37 See genealogical table, p. 164. Elizabeth Clancy was the daughter and heiress of Cahir or Charles MacClancy of Dartry. PROI, Lodge MSS, Records of the Rolls, v, 47; vi, 239. (The name of the barony appears in this source as 'Rosenoles'.) She was married (?) first to the son of a John O'Carroll, but was carried off and married to Connla MacGeoghegan. He was the son of Kedagh of Donore, whose father killed Bishop Ross MacGeoghegan's own father. Sheffield Public Library, MS WWM, 24/411. For this information supplied by letter I must thank Dr Kenneth Nicholls, University College, Cork.

38 Lynch, *De Praesulibus Hib.*, i, 338.

Daniel O'Crean, who had saved the province from extinction before the advent of MacGeoghegan himself by placing some novices within the house of Martin Font at Galway. It is far more likely that O'Crean was elected vicar provincial rather than prior provincial at this chapter and that MacGeoghegan continued to hold the latter office until the elective chapter of Sligo in 1627, when Nicholas Lynch of Galway was chosen as his successor.

According to Lynch, the brethren at the mid-1620s chapter (probably held in 1626, when MacGeoghegan was forced to flee the country) authorised their provincial to seek the King of Spain's permission to found a house at Louvain in which young aspirants might make their novitiate and pursue their studies. Having approached Philip IV, MacGeoghegan obtained in Belgium favourable letters from the king, thanks to which the archduke in Flanders gave him funds as requested, plus a yearly allowance for the upkeep of the convent.[39] His initiatives in favour of the struggling, newly founded college of Louvain may be dated from 1626,[40] the year of his departure from Ireland. After he had ceased to be prior provincial he was made vicar provincial (29 December 1627), with special responsibility for the college at Louvain as the war situation engulfing Flanders made it impossible for the Irish prior provincial to supervise the affairs of Louvain. On 2 September 1628 his jurisdiction was extended to cover all Irish Dominicans resident outside Ireland.[41]

Ross MacGeoghegan's name appeared in a list of twenty-three former alumni of the Irish College, Lisbon, considered worthy of promotion to bishoprics, compiled on 30 August 1625 by the papal collector in Portugal.[42] He was proposed for the vacant see of Armagh in 1627 by various parties, including the King of Spain, the Spanish ambassador at Rome, the Master General, the procurator general of the Order, the Irish Dominican procurators at Rome and Madrid and his own brethren; however, his candidacy proved to be unsuccessful.[43] The official summary of papers concerning the vacancy at Armagh rejected him as a candidate on the following grounds: the deep hostility between Meath, his diocese of origin, and the other dioceses of Ulster; and the implacable opposition of the Earl of Tyrone and the O'Donnells, who regarded him as a Palesman from 'the little province of Meath' and demanded his exclusion and that of any other member of his Order because there were then no Dominicans in the province of Ulster. The nuncio at Brussels, who held

39 Ibid.
40 Burke, *Hib. Dom.*, 431–3, 435.
41 Fenning, *Irish material*, 283, 284.
42 APF, SOCG, 294, ff 174r–175rv; B. Millett (ed.), 'Catalogue of Vol. 294 of SOCG in Propaganda Archives' in *Collect. Hib.*, 8 (1965), 20.
43 *Wadding Papers*, 162, 163–4, 204–7, 210, 225.

a brief for Irish ecclesiastical affairs, opposed his nomination too, but did not give his reasons. Against the choice of a Dominican candidate it was added that the Dominicans did not possess in the eyes of the Irish people the aura or standing of the far more numerous Franciscans.[44]

Lynch asserts that, in response to the urgency of the Dominican postulations, the Pope agreed to name as bishop one of their own Order and choice, and that the choice fell on Ross MacGeoghegan.[45] At any rate, MacGeoghegan was named Bishop of Kildare by Urban VIII on 4 January 1629.[46] His appointment was formally announced in consistory on 12 February, when he was granted a dispensation for two years to accept the office of vicar general in another diocese.[47] On 5 January the vicar general of the Order, Nicholas Ridolfi, had given his assent for Ross MacGeoghegan to accept Kildare.[48] Oliver Burke, O.P., and Patrick MacTeig, O.P., made sworn statements on 16 January concerning the life and good morals of Ross MacGeoghegan to an inquiry set up by the Datary. Attestations were also supplied by the vicar general of the Order, by John O'Cullenan, once his fellow student at Salamanca and now Bishop of Raphoe, and by Florence Conry, the Franciscan Archbishop of Tuam,[49] who had also been educated at Salamanca. Oliver Burke, who had been at Rome since 1628, forwarded the pontifical brief of MacGeoghegan's appointment to Kildare even before MacGeoghegan was aware that he was being considered for the see.[50] On 26 April 1629 MacGeoghegan wrote to Cardinal Barberini protesting his unworthiness to fill the see of Kildare, but accepted his nomination and added his thanks to the cardinal.[51]

He was still at Louvain, unconsecrated and simply Bishop-elect of Kildare, on 9 September 1629 when he arranged at the Dominican

44 Ibid., 225–6, 165; Lynch, *De Praesulibus Hib.*, i, 338; H. F. Kearney, 'Ecclesiastical Politics and the Counter-Reformation, 1618–1648' in *Jn. Ecc. Hist.*, 11 (1960), 202–12, for excellent treatment of social, political and religious factors governing Irish episcopal nominations.

45 Lynch, *De Praesulibus Hib.*, i, 339.

46 Brady, *Ep Succ.*, i, 352–3; Giblin, 'The *Processus Dataria*', 550–51, where the official record shows that MacGeoghegan was chosen by Urban VIII on 4 January 1629 to fill the see of Kildare at a meeting of the Holy Roman Inquisition; Eubel, *Hier. Cath.*, iv, 212.

47 C. Giblin, 'Vatican Library: MSS Barberini Latini' in *Archiv. Hib.*, 18 (1955), 79, 85; M. Comerford, *Collections relating to the Dioceses of Kildare and Leighlin*, i, Dublin 1883, 4, 30, where the Barberini source is cited in full; Eubel, *Hier. Cath.*, iv, 212.

48 Fenning, *Irish material*, 284.

49 Giblin, 'The *Processus Dataria*', 549–51.

50 Lynch, *De Praesulibus Hib.*, i, 339.

51 Giblin, 'Vatican Library: MSS Barberini Latini', 124; printed in B. Jennings (ed.), 'Miscellaneous Documents, I: 1588–1634' in *Archiv. Hib.*, 12 (1946), 146–7.

convent of Antwerp for a loan of £24 from an Irish priest, James Conall. In one clause of the legal agreement MacGeoghegan pledged, in the event of his death preventing repayment of the loan, that the entire debt should be met by the sale of his books in Ireland or of any other property which he might have under the supervision of the Irish provincial or his vicar.[52] The money was probably borrowed to purchase the costly episcopal insignia, vestments and liturgical books and to defray the expenses of his consecration and his journey to Ireland. Writing from Louvain on 10 October, he described himself as Bishop of Kildare when he recommended Dr John Burke for the vacant diocese of Clonfert.[53] The episcopal consecration of Ross MacGeoghegan took place therefore between 9 September and 10 October 1629. The rite was performed at Brussels by the Archbishop of Malines assisted by other bishops,[54] and more than likely took place in secrecy in the archbishop's private chapel. Shortly afterwards MacGeoghegan set out for his diocese. On 17 November 1629 Cardinal Antonio Barberini wrote to James Talbot, Vicar Apostolic of Kildare, to inform him that his office had been terminated by the appointment of the new bishop of the diocese.[55]

At his first diocesan synod Bishop Ross MacGeoghegan found that there were only three of his own priests born in the diocese of Kildare, the remainder being outsiders from Connacht and Ulster. He found that the nobility were more given to the pursuit of worldly pleasures than concerned with the Christian education of their sons. By means of admonition and correction many eventually returned to lives of righteousness. He took pains to introduce schoolmasters into his diocese in order to promote the study of literature and the classics. As a result, young men who had been refined by courses in the humanities were sent abroad for higher studies and returned as priests to cultivate the vineyard of the Lord. After twelve years as bishop he succeeded in forming a body of native diocesan priests whose learning outshone that of the clergy of all other dioceses in the province of Dublin. He was so zealous in spreading the Word of God that every year he preached to the people in each of the twenty-eight parishes of the diocese, stimulating parish priests and parishioners alike to carry out their duties more faithfully. Monthly meetings of the clergy took place, to discuss 'cases of conscience' and other religious matters, and by examination he ensured that all his priests were well informed to deal with the pastoral problems of the laity.[56] Regular

52 B. Jennings (ed.), 'Miscellaneous Documents, III: 1602–1715' in *Archiv. Hib.*, 15 (1950), 3.
53 *Wadding Papers*, 316–17.
54 Lynch, *De Praesulibus Hib.*, i, 339.
55 *Wadding Papers*, 318–19.
56 Lynch, *De Praesulibus Hib.*, i, 339.

episcopal visitations and clergy conferences were typical of the activities prescribed for bishops by the canons of Trent.

The unhappy affair of the 'Irish propositions' condemned by the University of Paris preoccupied the Irish clergy throughout 1631. In a calculated effort to malign the Irish regulars and sow deadly seeds of discord, Patrick Cahill, a Dublin priest supported by other diocesan clergy, submitted a series of propositions to the Sorbonne, attributing them to the Irish regular clergy. Bishop Ross MacGeoghegan was a member of an episcopal commission set up by Rome to investigate the propositions and the consequent charges against the regulars. After his investigation he exonerated the regular clergy and duly sent his report to the nuncio at Brussels.[57]

By letters patent dated 14 February 1634 he appointed Oliver Burke, O.P., and his cousin Anthony MacGeoghegan, O.F.M., his procurators to act on his behalf in judicial cases and all other business involving him at the Roman curia.[58] He signed a letter of commendation with the Archbishops of Armagh and Tuam on 4 September 1631, postulating Thaddeus Clery, vicar general of Derry, for the vacant see of Derry. On 14 February 1637 he recommended his relative, Edmund Dempsey, provincial of the Dominicans and son of Viscount Clanmalier, for the bishopric of Leighlin.[59]

In 1637 he sent a report, dated 15 November, on the state of his diocese to Rome.[60] He explained that he was not in a position to visit Rome in person, because of danger to his life or the risk of incarceration, which would most certainly be the case should he be captured either going to or coming from Rome, and on account of the expense involved in such a journey. For these reasons he had delegated a priest called Anthony Jacob or FitzJames as his procurator *in curia*. This Irish priest took care of the formalities connected with the *ad limina* visit and presented MacGeoghegan's report to the Roman Congregation of the Council in the spring or early summer of 1638. This particular congregation was charged with the examination of the *relatio status* submitted periodically by all dioceses. Bishop MacGeoghegan referred to an earlier and more comprehensive report he had submitted to Rome in 1633. In the report of 1637 he simply updated information about the number of priests in his diocese, about chapels, religious houses, charitable bodies and consecrated cemeteries.

57 *Wadding Papers*, 574–6, 579, 581, 586; HMC, *Report on the Franciscan Manuscripts*, Dublin 1906, 45, 46.

58 APF, SOCG, 398, f. 390r.

59 B. Jennings (ed.), 'Miscellaneous Documents, II: 1625–1640' in *Archiv. Hib.*, 14 (1949), 26.

60 J. Hagan (ed.), 'Miscellanea Vaticano-Hibernica: Ireland in 1580', in *Archiv. Hib.*, 5 (1916), 101–4.

Half the report concerned his troubles with Bartholomew Moore, whom he had removed as parish priest of Naas on account of very serious faults. Moore went to Wentworth, the viceroy, and denounced his bishop for exercising episcopal jurisdiction deriving from Rome. Wentworth encouraged Moore to institute criminal proceedings against MacGeoghegan for exercising foreign jurisdiction contrary to the law of the land.[61] This was in line with Wentworth's policy to weaken the influence of Irish Catholics by exacerbating dissensions between laymen and clergy.[62] It would seem that pressures intensified in Bishop MacGeoghegan's life so that he felt compelled to write on another occasion to the Cardinal Prefect of Propaganda Fide about the grave harassment he was subjected to as a consequence of deposing Moore. He begged the cardinal to write to George Conn, papal agent to Queen Henrietta Maria, to use his influence with the queen and the English court to bring to an end the relentless hounding carried out by the Irish administration, leaving him free to carry out his responsibilities as a bishop.[63]

On another occasion he was said to have been denounced to the state authorities by the Franciscan friar, Peter Walsh, later author of the 'Remonstrance'. The perpetrator of this incident was thus apostrophised:

> Your persecuting brave prelates is innate in you, as from your cradle, when but a slip of a friar, you informed the Protestant state of Dublin, in a time of persecution, against an apostolic prelate, a true child of Dominic's Order, Ross MacGeoghegan, Bishop of Kildare, saying that he was not Kildare's but Tyrone's bishop, to exasperate the state against the holy prelate, which cost him many a night's wail.[64]

In 1640 a provincial synod under the presidency of Archbishop Thomas Fleming, O.F.M., of Dublin was held at Tyrchogir, near the town of Portarlington, in the diocese of Kildare. Bishop Ross MacGeoghegan signed the decrees of the synod on 29 July 1640.[65] In 1641 he regained full freedom of movement and was said to have asserted his authority over the cathedral of Kildare. In sworn testimony recorded on 24 March 1642, Golburne, the Anglican Archdeacon of Kildare, and the parish clerk, William Lightbonde, stated that during the rebellion of 1641

61 R. D. Edwards, 'Church and State in the Ireland of Michél Ó Cléirigh' in S. O'Brien (ed.), *Measgra i gCuimhne Mhicíl Uí Chléirigh*, Dublin 1944, 16.

62 Ibid.

63 Jennings, 'Miscellaneous Documents, II: 1625–1640', 31 and note 26.

64 TCD, MS 846: *An Aphorismical Discovery of Treasonable Faction*, whose accuracy must be treated with caution. Printed in J. T. Gilbert (ed.), *A Contemporary History of Affairs in Ireland from A.D. 1641 to 1652*, i, Dublin 1879, 276.

65 Comerford, *Dioceses of Kildare and Leighlin*, i, 32–5.

> the ornaments of the cathedral of Kildare and the books belonging to the same, value ten pounds, also the cathedral chest, containing all the evidences and rescripts of the chapter, was in December last taken away by Ross MacGeoghegan the popish or titular bishop of Kildare, Dempsey his vicar general, William Berry, priest, by two friars of the Grey Abbey and Henry Dempsey and one Cosby his companion . . . and the church and tithes and rents belonging to the said chapter were seized by the said bishop, friars and priest, to the yearly loss of the said Dean and chapter of more than £130.[66]

Another Protestant, Thomas Hewettson, an Englishman settled in Kildare, complained of the desecration of graves within the cathedral, allegedly carried out 'by command of Ross MacGeoghegan, titular Bishop of Kildare, James Dempsey, the popish vicar general there, William Berry, priest, Dominic Dempsey, guardian of the friars who lived in Kildare' and other friars, some of whose names he could not remember. To justify their action, the Catholic party said 'they could not sanctify or hallow their church of Kildare until the heretics' bones were removed out of it'.[67]

While staying with the Franciscans of Multyfarnham in May 1644 Bishop MacGeoghegan was seized by paralysis while actually preaching. It was decided that he should travel on horseback to Westmeath, to obtain the medical services of Dr Eoghan O'Shiel, a celebrated physician. He died at Kilbeggan before he could be treated, in the company of some of his priests and Dominicans summoned from Mullingar, on the feast of Corpus Christi, 26 May 1644 (n.s.), in his sixty-eighth year.[68] In his will he left the library he had as a religious to the brethren of his Order; the library he had built up as a bishop, together with his episcopal insignia, he donated to the diocese of Kildare.[69] According to Lynch, he was given a solemn public funeral in the cathedral church of Kildare, in which no Catholic bishop before him had been buried since the practice of the Catholic religion had been proscribed.[70] However, his obituary notice, published in the general chapter acts of 1656, said that he was buried in the tomb of his ancestors in the Franciscan friary of

66 TCD, MS 813: Depositions, Co. Kildare, f. 264. Reading of MS unreliable in Comerford, *Dioceses of Kildare and Leighlin*, i, 35.

67 TCD, MS 813, f. 260rv.

68 Lynch, *De Praesulibus Hib.*, i, 340. The correct year of his death was 1644, not 1641 or 1642, as stated by this author. According to Luke Wadding, Bishop Ross MacGeoghegan died in 1644: 'moritur anno 1644, ante mensem Junium'. See Comerford, *Dioceses of Kildare and Leighlin*, i, 32.

69 Lynch, *De Praesulibus Hib.*, i, 340.

70 Ibid., 341.

Multyfarnham.[71] No reliable record has survived which might clarify the question of the bishop's burial place.[72]

Ross MacGeoghegan's career can be divided into three phases of almost equal length. The first phase of his adult life (1600–14) was spent very briefly in Lisbon and then in Spain as a Dominican student, priest, and lecturer in theology. There he was much influenced by Castillian *gravitas* of manner, religious devotion, love of learning and a strong sense of religious discipline apparent in his life ever afterwards. His profound grasp of theology and apologetics and his lifelong habit of study enabled him to be very effective and persuasive in preaching the Catholic faith.

The second phase (1614–29) was devoted to the restoration of the Irish Dominican province; he was the prime architect of this continental-based plan of revival. His reputation was consistently that of a most zealous priest and preacher, lover of the Catholic faith and of his Order, and highly gifted as a practical organiser and administrator even in adverse circumstances. In the short space of fifteen years he directed the re-establishment of Dominican communities and preaching all over Ireland and in many places, especially in Leinster, where there had been no Dominican presence for almost a century.

The third phase of his life, as Bishop of Kildare (1629–44), was distinguished by an unshakable commitment to his diocese at a time of sharp, intermittent persecution, instability and bewildering uncertainty. Despite problems of every sort, betrayal by people and even by priests whom he had censured, and the hostility of the civil authorities, he devoted himself to the pastoral care of his discouraged clergy and laity. Throughout an episcopate of fifteen years he showed immense concern for the poor and disadvantaged, even to the point of pledging and sacrificing much of his personal library. Several times he willingly sold off his best horses and distributed whatever food and money he could command. His kindness and concern for others were matched by almost excessive severity in his personal life. He did not wear linen as was the custom of people of rank, but preferred the woollen habit of his Order unless by necessity he had to appear in the company of Protestants. He was accustomed to spend several hours daily in solitary meditation, to fast, to wear hair-shirts and chains, to sleep on the bare ground on the coldest nights, and to eat only the plainest food. When he ate in company, he invariably made a spiritual discourse at table.[73]

71 Reichert, *MOPH*, xii, 476; Burke, *Hib. Dom.*, 48. Burke, however, accepted uncritically 1641 as the date of Bishop MacGeoghegan's death as erroneously given in the 1656 general chapter obituary.

72 The matter is fully discussed in T. O'Donnell, *Franciscan Abbey of Multyfarnham*, Multyfarnham 1951, 142–5.

73 These details of his generosity and personal life come from Lynch, *De Praesulibus Hib.*, i, 339–40.

Philip O'Sullivan Beare described him in about 1625 as '*insulae nostrae stella clarissima*'. He encouraged many exiled Irish women in Galicia, including the writer's sister, Leonora O'Sullivan, to become contemplative Dominican nuns. He was outstanding for his knowledge of the sciences, sacred and secular, as much as for his radiant holiness of life. He was ever a most eloquent preacher of the divine Word.[74] Such was the character and achievement of Ross MacGeoghegan, Bishop of Kildare, who is rightly regarded as the second founder of the Irish Dominican province.

RICHARD CARON (1579–C.1630)

Richard Caron, born in the barony of Kilkenny West in 1579, belonged to an ancient and distinguished Westmeath Gaelic family claiming descent from the southern Uí Néill.[75] His parents were Henry Caron and Evelyn Nicholas, both natives of the same place. He received the first rudiments of education from a local schoolmaster, Humphrey Powell Walsh, who was also Ross MacGeoghegan's first teacher. He studied grammar under William MacGillaboy and Bernard Quirke, rhetoric and the other branches of the humanities under a master surnamed Hussey, all of whom were Catholics.[76]

In the spring of 1600 he went to Spain with the intention of becoming a priest. On 29 February 1600 he presented himself at the Irish College of Salamanca. He carried testimonial letters from James Archer, the cosmopolitan and influential Jesuit from Kilkenny and first rector of Salamanca. After he was examined by the college rector, James White, S.J., he took the normal college and missionary oath and renewed the same on 10 and 13 June 1601. He was then aged twenty-two years.[77]

In the late autumn of 1601 Richard Caron joined the Dominican province of Castille. What made him decide to leave the Irish College at Salamanca is not known. He made his novitiate and subsequently his religious profession on 8 November 1602 at the convent of Nuestra Señora de Peña de Francia together with Ross MacGeoghegan.[78] Ever afterwards

74 O'Sullivan Beare, *Selections from the Zoilomastix*, ed. O'Donnell, 25, 33.

75 Mac Carrghamhna is the Irish form of the name; the principal English forms are MacCarroon, MacCaron, Caron, O'Growney, Gaffney and, surprisingly, Caulfield. The Caron or MacCaron clan name was Muinntear Mhaoilsionna. The clan lands, which embraced the district of Cuircne near the River Shannon, passed into the possession of the Dillons and were incorporated into the barony of Kilkenny West after the Anglo-Norman invasion. The MacCarons, nonetheless, maintained a measure of independence as a clan until late in the sixteenth century, as is demonstrated in the fiants of Elizabeth. Woulfe, *Sloinnte Gaedhael is Gall*, 326–7.

76 O'Doherty, 'Students of the Irish College, Salamanca', 11.

77 Ibid.

78 AHN, sección de clero, libro 10585, f. 26r.

he was known as and invariably signed his name as Richard de la Peña, omitting his surname. Until recently he was consistently confused by all writers (misled by Burke's *Hibernia Dominicana*) with his contemporary Richard Bermingham, O.P., one of the founders of the Irish Dominican college at Louvain. At the conclusion of his studies somewhere in Castille, he graduated in theology and spent some years teaching,[79] possibly in Galicia. There is then almost total silence about his activities until 8 October 1613, when the Master General appointed him deputy to William Talbot, O.P., procurator of the Irish province at Madrid.[80] From this date until his death in 1629 or 1630 he was indefatigable in rebuilding the Irish province. Through his diplomacy and considerable organisational skills, he played an indispensable role as Ross MacGeoghegan's representative at the Spanish court in negotiations which led to the foundation of the colleges of Lisbon and Louvain. The world of the royal court of Madrid did not limit his apostolic outreach, but rather stimulated it. He was always prompt in promoting the interests of his exiled countrymen and in converting Protestants. According to Philip O'Sullivan Beare, he was expert in both English and Irish. At La Coruña in Galicia, he converted three English pirates captured by the Spanish, and at Madrid an Anglo-Scottish gentleman named MacGrannell.[81]

Perhaps Richard Caron's first missionary journey dates from about 1615 or even earlier. An undated letter[82] addressed by him to the Conde de Águila from the convent of San Pablo, Seville, has all the marks of the young inexperienced missionary in his first fervour. He described himself as a poor Dominican friar being sent under obedience to preach the faith in England because of his knowledge of the language, but without money to cover expenses or to buy secular attire. He pleaded earnestly with the Spanish nobleman for alms so that he could fittingly carry out his mission in London. Though he signed himself '*irlandes de nación*', he made no reference to his later status as procurator, to companions, or to going to Ireland. A postscript stressed the urgency of his request: he had to take ship without delay. What the outcome of his attempt to be a missionary in England was is nowhere related.

In 1617 while still at Madrid Richard Caron acted as sponsor for Donal O'Sullivan Beare to be admitted to the knighthood of the Order of Santiago, a military distinction.[83] In January he and two other Dominicans

79 AGS, Estado, leg. 2754.

80 Fenning, *Irish material*, 278.

81 O'Sullivan Beare, *Selections from the Zoilomastix*, ed. O'Donnell, 29.

82 Archivo Municipal de Sevilla, Libros de Conde de Águila, tomo 7 (*sección de memoriales sin fecha al final*), no. 16.

83 M. Walsh, *Spanish Knights of Irish Origin*, i, Dublin 1960, 6. Founded in the twelfth century, the three Spanish military orders of chivalry of Santiago, Calatrava

applied for travelling expenses to return to Ireland.[84] When he crossed to Ireland that summer, he was already the appointed vicar of the Dominicans in Ireland and superior of the Dublin community.[85] Soon after his return, however, he was taken prisoner at Galway together with a young Dominican, Aeneas O'Callanan, not as yet ordained, and both were dispatched as prisoners to Dublin Castle by English officials.[86] There they lay in darkness under rigorous conditions for about eighteen months. During their captivity they were subjected to various threats and alternatively were offered enticing rewards should they renounce their faith. O'Callanan was confirmed in his faith and vocation by the frequent exhortations of Caron.[87] Catholics secretly sent alms for their support and bribed their jailer. In return for a clean cell, the jailer received payment of 1½ rials per day from Caron's friends.[88] Such may have been the totally unforeseen circumstances which caused Ross MacGeoghegan to be made vicar of the Irish congregation in 1617.

After much suffering and tribulation they were released in July 1618 through the personal intervention of Count Gondomar, the Spanish ambassador in London.[89] Released at the same time were about one hundred other ecclesiastics and regulars of various orders imprisoned in different parts of the country.[90] Banished from the kingdoms of Ireland, England and Scotland, Richard Caron and Aeneas O'Callanan were first transported to England under armed escort and thence to France. During the time of their captivity and during the sea crossing and journey through England they were reputed to have zealously attempted to preach controverted and difficult teachings of the Gospel, arousing so much admiration and interest that many people flocked to listen to them and to observe the spectacle of their public witness.[91] Eventually they disembarked at

and Alcantara carried enormous prestige. Membership was restricted to those of noble birth.

84 AGS, Estado, leg. 2749.

85 O'Sullivan Beare, *Selections from the Zoilomastix*, ed. O'Donnell, 29.

86 Ibid.; R. Walsh (ed.), 'A Memorial presented to the King of Spain on behalf of the Irish Catholics, 1619' in *Archiv. Hib.*, 6 (1917), 30.

87 O'Sullivan Beare, *Selections from the Zoilomastix*, ed. O'Donnell, 29.

88 AGS, Estado, leg. 2750.

89 Ibid., leg. 2598: Gondomar reported to Philip III his petition (15 July 1618) to James I for the release of all priests, secular and regular, imprisoned for life or sentenced to death, in the prisons of England and Ireland. More than a hundred priests were then incarcerated. Leg. 2597 has two documents dealing with negotiations between the Duke of Buckingham and Diego de la Fuente, Gondomar's chaplain, about priests imprisoned and under sentence of death (12 Oct. 1618) and the king's decision to suspend the death sentences on two unnamed priests (17 Oct. 1618).

90 Walsh, 'A Memorial presented to the King of Spain', 30.

91 O'Sullivan Beare, *Selections from the Zoilomastix*, ed. O'Donnell, 29.

Bordeaux, whence Richard Caron made his way to the convent of Peña de Francia. When he had recovered from his ordeals, he returned once more to Madrid and went to the court as ordered by Gondomar, to give an account of the spiritual and temporal state of Ireland. He remained at court for approximately one and a half years and placed himself at the service of Gondomar for secret business.[92]

Early in 1619 he presented to Philip III a memorial on behalf of the Irish Catholics.[93] This report represents the only detailed commentary on the sufferings of Catholics written in the early seventeenth century. From this it derives its unique historical value. In the introductory section Caron gave a résumé of his ill-fated visit to Ireland in 1617, to which he had returned as a missionary after an absence of twenty years in Spain. He remarked how this in itself was reckoned a crime and led to his imprisonment in Dublin Castle; when he was freed he was punished by perpetual exile and forbidden to return under pain of death. After the introductory section the memorial or report was divided into two parts. The first dealt with the condition of Irish Catholics in matters spiritual, the second with their temporal concerns. It was accompanied by a list of the principal laws enacted against Catholics and the practice of Catholicism. Caron implored the Spanish king to intervene on behalf of Irish Catholics, who lay under such serious disabilities, were threatened with permanent oppression as a people, and whose faith was in danger of extinction. The country, he alleged, was full of English and Scots Protestants, and persecution had become more severe than ever. He concluded by asking that his report be referred to Count Gondomar for verification. Philip III endorsed the report on 17 February 1619 and referred it to his council for their study and observations. The king also directed that Gondomar's opinion should be sought.

With other leading Irish personalities in Spain, Richard Caron signed a recommendation on 9 January 1620 in favour of the impoverished Leonora O'Sullivan, who sought some financial entitlement in Flanders, Italy or Spain from Philip III.[94] Undeterred by his experiences of 1617–18,

92 AGS, Estado, leg. 2750.

93 AHN, Estado, libro 741, ff 23r–41rv. Spanish text with incomplete summary in English printed by Walsh, 'A Memorial presented to the King of Spain', 27–54.

94 AGS, Estado, leg. 1775. Surprisingly Philip III refused this request although it was supported by the testimonials of Philip O'Sullivan Beare her brother, count of Bearehaven, Dermot O'Sullivan Mór, Thaddeus O'Driscoll and other notables, including Ross MacGeoghegan, 'vicar general'. One of her brothers and cousins, she said, had died in Philip III's service in the war in Ireland. In the 1630s she addressed several piteous appeals to Philip IV for alms on account of her abject poverty and that of her companions consecrated to God. She then described herself as a solemnly professed nun (*beata professa*) of the Dominican Order of the Irish nation and asserted that she was the sole survivor and heiress

he requested travelling expenses to return to Ireland in the spring of 1620 to preach the Catholic faith. A grant of 100 ducats was approved for his needs.[95] In another memorial, dated 23 June 1620, he again recited his experiences of 1617 in Ireland. He estimated that the loss of his books, with liturgical and devotional requisites, amounted to the sum of 1,000 ducats. His penury and losses obliged him to seek the king's assistance and recompense for his services. His suggestion that he should receive 100 ducats by way of ordinary alms for his material support was approved.[96] Meanwhile he had been given leave by the Master General (30 April 1620) to lead to Ireland a party of Dominicans who had completed their studies in Spanish provinces and was appointed their superior for the duration of the journey.[97]

There is evidence of his religious influence amongst Irishmen resident in Madrid, in a petition presented on 9 July 1620 by Thomas Bradagan and Daniel Flanagan, former servants of the English ambassador, who sought the royal favour and a grant to clothe and arm themselves. They had become Catholics against the wishes of the ambassador, who had turned them out of his house and service. They wished both to serve in one of the king's armies and to preserve the faith in which they had been instructed by Richard Caron. They were of good birth and of Catholic parentage, and their families harboured priests in Ireland. They were prepared to authenticate their case by documentary proof.[98]

Richard Caron was still in Madrid on 3 September 1620 when he successfully requested the viaticum for ten Dominicans going to Ireland.[99] On the same day he received payment of 100 ducats from the Spanish treasury in response to his request of 23 June.[100] It would appear that he went to Ireland in the autumn of 1620 and this time escaped detection. For two years no memorials or documents in his name were laid before the Spanish council of state.

By 1622 Richard Caron had returned to Madrid, for in that year he acted as sponsor for Simon French of Galway, who sought to be admitted

of Dermot O'Sullivan Beare and Lady Joanna Sweeney. In Galicia she was joined by other Irish women such as Ellen O'Mahony and Ellen O'Driscoll, who submitted similar desperate pleas for help. Ibid., leg. 2759, 2797, 2798, 2800 etc. See O'Sullivan Beare, *Selections from the Zoilomastix*, ed. O'Donnell, 33, where he refers to his sister as '*virgo valde miranda*' and lists some of the prominent founding sisters of the contemplative tradition of the Irish Dominican nuns initiated in the first decades of the seventeenth century in Spain and Portugal.

95 AGS, Estado, leg. 2750.

96 Ibid.

97 Fenning, *Irish material*, 280.

98 AGS, Estado, leg. 2750.

99 Ibid.

100 AGS, Contaduria Mayor de Cuentas (3a epoca), leg. 1161.

as a knight of the military Order of Santiago.[101] On 19 August he made a request for financial aid on behalf of the two servants of the English ambassador, converted to the Catholic faith about two years earlier through his mediation, who had been destined to join the Irish brigade in Flanders. He testified to their honour and integrity. The request was approved, and 100 ducats was assigned to cover the expenses of their journey to Flanders.[102] Once more, on 10 September, he requested the king's assistance for two other former servants of the English ambassador, Matthew Quinlan and William Dun, who had also converted to Catholicism. It had previously been decided that they should be accommodated and supported, one by the Bishop of Coria, and the other by the Bishop of Pamplona, to ascertain the sincerity of their conversion. However, owing to the absence of any ecclesiastic of their nation in those regions, to whom they might talk about their faith or make their private confession, it was suggested that they might be accommodated with the Bishop of Salamanca or one of the Archbishops of Burgos, Seville or Valladolid. Finally it was agreed that they should be entrusted to the supervision of the Archbishops of Seville and Burgos.[103] This conversion work in which Richard Caron specialised was carried out in virtue of a commission from the Roman Holy Office of the Inquisition.[104]

During the visit of the Prince of Wales (later Charles I) to the court of Madrid in 1623 Richard Caron had brought about yet another conversion, that of Daniel Riordan, an Irishman, who had been brought up a Protestant and had been a member of the prince's retinue. When Riordan returned to England, he was unable to practise his faith freely, was harassed and suffered privations. He was dismissed from his post on resisting reconversion to his master's faith. The prince forbade him to be received by anybody in England, and thereafter he was persecuted by Protestants. An Irish Dominican resident in London advised him to seek the protection of the King of Spain, and Riordan accordingly declared himself prepared to serve the king in Flanders or elsewhere. Richard Caron petitioned for an allowance for clothes and travel expenses, and it was agreed that Riordan should be sent to Flanders.[105]

In 1625 Caron's name appeared in the list of sponsors for Albert Hugh O'Donnell, who wished to be accepted as a knight of the military Order of Alcántara,[106] and for Gerald Geraldine (FitzGerald), who sought admission to the Order of Santiago.[107] From 1626 Richard Caron was

101 Walsh, *Spanish Knights of Irish Origin*, i, 7.
102 AGS, Estado, leg. 2751.
103 Ibid.
104 Ibid., leg. 2754.
105 Ibid., leg. 2788.
106 Walsh, *Spanish Knights of Irish Origin*, iv, 2.
107 Ibid., i, 11.

busy collecting money in Madrid for the new college at Louvain,[108] while continuing his principal work of facilitating the return of his young confrères to Ireland and other business. On 18 April 1626 he asked for the viaticum for three friars: Vincent of St Mary (San Pablo, Valladolid), Thomas Burke (Atocha, Madrid) and Thomas O'Brien (San Pablo, Burgos); and he also noted that eight priests were ready to go to Ireland at that time.[109]

On 16 December he petitioned the King of Spain to write to the Pope concerning the nomination of a Dominican to the see of Armagh or to one of the other vacant Irish sees. The council of state advised the king to write to his ambassador at Rome to propose a suitable Dominican for Armagh, an appointment which would have the effect of consolidating the Order's position in Ireland.[110] So a concerted effort got under way on the part of the central administration of the Order[111] and on the part of the Irish Dominican procurators at Rome and Madrid to secure a Dominican nomination for the diocese of Armagh, vacant by the unexpected death of Primate Hugh MacCaughwell, O.F.M., on 22 September 1626. Francis Lavalin Nugent, superior of the Irish Capuchins, when consulted by the Pope in 1626 or 1627, warmly recommended Ross MacGeoghegan for the office, but his promotion was opposed successfully by the O'Neill and O'Donnell factions.[112]

On 30 March 1627 Richard Caron gave his views about the administration and allocation of the 1,000 ducats deriving yearly from the bishopric of Cádiz for the support of the Irish and Scottish missions. He indicated that by his exertions as procurator of the Irish Dominicans at the Spanish court he had incurred heavy expenses which could not be met by his province; hence his request for a grant from some endowment. The king ordered the Cádiz money to be applied in equal parts to Scotland and Ireland and sought the council's advice about the distribution of the Irish portion.[113] In April Caron requested the crown authorities for increased financial support for Dominicans setting out for Ireland. He wished to send more than the customary three friars that year, but the council of state decided that it was not desirable to increase the fixed number eligible for the viaticum.[114] There were pressing reasons for this decision. From January there was internal monetary chaos coupled with economic crisis in

108 Fenning, *Irish material*, 284.
109 AGS, Estado, leg. 2753.
110 Ibid., leg. 2788; *Wadding Papers*, 197–8, 225.
111 *Wadding Papers*, 225.
112 Lynch, *De Praesulibus Hib.*, i, 338; *Wadding Papers*, 225; F. X. Martin, *Friar Nugent*, London/Rome, 1962, 258.
113 AGS, Estado, leg. 2754.
114 Ibid.: another document.

Spain.[115] The capture of the Spanish treasure fleet on the high seas from the Americas made 1627 a most infelicitous year, a year of national bankruptcy. Such misfortunes, however, did not deter Richard Caron's work. When requesting the annual grant of 300 ducats on 10 February 1628, he renewed his plea for an increase in the royal concession. He pointed out that every year five, six or seven Dominicans had left for Ireland among whom he had divided the annual grant. As a consequence, there was not sufficient money for the purchase of books and other liturgical requirements. In that year eight Dominicans were prepared to go to Ireland, and the provincial of Castille, by whose licence preachers left Castille for Ireland, would verify his assertions. Moreover, the Dominicans were sending more friars home every year than any other order, as could be shown from the papers of the secretariat of state. The king and his council considered the plea to be reasonable and endorsed it.[116]

In 1627 Richard Caron was listed among Irish Dominicans worthy of promotion to an Irish bishopric. He was described as belonging originally to the diocese of Clonmacnoise and fifty years old.[117] In the following year he was proposed for Armagh. It was urged in his favour that he belonged to an Old Irish family and that his diocese of origin belonged to the province of Armagh.[118] However, nothing came of these attempts to have him made a bishop. He continued to work devotedly as procurator of his province in Spain until the spring of 1629. Most regrettably his personal papers and correspondence which would have demonstrated the full scope of his work and apostolic concerns are not known to have survived.

In October 1627 the Master General had informed him that he must leave Madrid before Dominic O'Daly could go there on the business of the province.[119] With the end of his post as procurator in sight, he wrote twice to the king and his council (10 December 1627[120] and 21 February 1629),[121] with a view to making some material provision for his future. First he recalled how throughout his time of service at the court he had received generous alms from the king, not having had any other means of support. On account of his labours and sufferings for the Catholic cause and his enforced exile he asked for an annual ecclesiastical pension of 100 ducats. This would enable him to continue more conveniently to be of service to the king. Since it would not be appropriate for him to reside in Spain, he asked that the pension might be made available to him from a

115 H. Kamen, *Spain: 1469–1714*, London 1983, 216.
116 AGS, Estado, leg. 2755.
117 *Wadding Papers*, 208.
118 Ibid., 225.
119 Fenning, *Irish material*, 283.
120 AGS, Estado, leg. 2754.
121 Ibid., leg. 2791.

Flemish bishopric or from the general finances or granted by means of an incremental allowance. The council of state, having noted his lengthy stay at court and how he had competently promoted the affairs of the Irish nation, considered it very just that he should be given a pension from some bishopric or abbey in Flanders. This decision was approved and endorsed by Philip IV. From his final petition to the council of state, dated 3 April 1629, it is clear that arrangements had been made for his pension to be made payable in Galicia since September 1628. He was then receiving 10 escudos per month in La Coruña, where he had once been active as a priest, serving the numerous Irish exiles who had settled in that region. He stated that in obedience to his Order he was preparing to set out for Louvain to take charge of the Irish Dominican college. He therefore petitioned for his stipend to be transferred to the states of Flanders without obligation of residence in a particular town or place because of his religious obedience. The council of state approved his request, noting that the transfer of his pension to Flanders would not inconvenience anybody.[122] Soon afterwards he was ordered (28 April 1629) by the vicar of the Order to submit an account of the money he had raised over the past three years for the use of the Irish Dominican college of Louvain, and was also asked to settle accounts with a friar, Antoninus of St Nicholas, O.P., of Belgium, by paying him 20 ducats.[123] On 18 August, at the general chapter of 1629, the Master of the Order, Nicholas Ridolfi, promoted him to the theological degree of *praesentatus* at the request of Nicholas Lynch, the Irish prior provincial.[124]

Whether or not Richard Caron ever reached Louvain to take charge of the Irish Dominican college, he was dead by 11 May 1630. On that date his confrère and head of the college at Louvain, Patrick MacTeig, petitioned the Spanish state council for the annual pension 'which had become available by reason of the death of Richard de la Peña'.[125] Thus Richard Caron passed quietly from the Irish Dominican scene about the year 1630. Not even his burial place is known. His hitherto unrecognised contribution towards the re-establishment of the Irish province entitles him to be counted as one of its founding fathers in the second phase of its existence.

122 Ibid.
123 Fenning, *Irish material*, 284.
124 Ibid.
125 AGS, Estado, leg. 2793.

SEVEN

The Continental College Movement: The Dominican Contribution, 1615–40

From as early as 1590 colleges for Irish diocesan and religious students were established on a formal basis in continental Europe. Among the first colleges for the diocesan clergy, most of which were under Jesuit supervision, were Alcalá de Henares (1590), Salamanca (1592), Lisbon (1593), Douai (1594), Bordeaux (1603), Paris (1578/1605), Santiago de Compostella (1605) and Seville (1611). The Franciscans spearheaded the college movement among religious orders by establishing colleges at Louvain (1606), Rome (1625) and Prague (1629). The Dominicans made foundations at Lisbon (1615), Louvain (1624) and, much later, Rome (1677). Irish Cistercians attempted to set up a college at Bonlieu near Bordeaux about 1615. These colleges were opened largely through the efforts of individual priests, religious and occasionally lay people. The first foundations were located in Spain or Spanish-ruled territories. Spain under Philip II had assumed leadership of the Counter-Reformation as it moved towards standards of rigid religious orthodoxy. During the seventeenth century France vied with the Spanish dominions as the main supporter of the Irish colleges on the continent.[1]

However, there were always grave financial problems for these foundations. In particular there were never sufficient endowments or money available for their regular maintenance. Many individuals and corporate bodies intermittently received a Spanish or royal subsidy. By the first decades of the seventeenth century the burden on state finances was particularly heavy in Flanders (the Spanish Netherlands). Constant wars with the Dutch Calvinists, France and England, especially during the reign of Philip IV (1621–65), gradually drained the resources of the once flourishing Spanish Low Countries. Laws had long since been enacted strictly prohibiting any new religious foundation without the express licence of the Spanish monarch. Such a licence was granted, and even then very reluctantly, only when it could be proved that the proposed house or college would have an adequate regular income or stable endowments to render it independent of local support. Other stringent conditions

1 J. J. Silke, 'The Irish Abroad, 1534–1691' in *NHI*, iii, 616–29; T. J. Walsh, *The Irish Continental College Movement*, Dublin/Cork 1973, 1–87 *passim.*

often accompanied the formal permission, besides the specific conditions laid down by founders and benefactors. This was the context in which the Irish Dominicans made their first unsuccessful efforts to establish continental colleges of their own.

The increasing number of aspirants in Ireland and of students in European houses gave rise to the problem of where they should be educated in the future, a problem which became more acute after 1610. The disadvantages of dispersing Irish Dominicans in continental houses were soon perceived. Moreover, the generous hospitality of Spain and Portugal in particular could not be expected to bear indefinitely the extra burden of an entire new province. Nor could Spanish, Portuguese, Italian and French convents provide a training specifically orientated to the harsh realities confronting Irish Catholicism—a training at once robustly missionary for the conditions of northern Europe, theologically apologetical, and imbued with Irish spirituality and culture. The obvious solution to the problem was the opening of colleges (*studia generalia*) in continental Europe, in line with the requirements of the Council of Trent. This train of thought had already been adopted towards the close of the sixteenth century by Thaddeus MacDuane, who clearly perceived the need for a solid continental base to ensure the survival of the Order and its future work in Ireland. With the aid of other like-minded Dominicans he devoted himself to finding a house of refuge in Flanders, and is said to have been successful in his search, though Irish Dominicans did not go to Louvain during his provincialate.[2]

The precedent of independent Irish colleges for the diocesan clergy since the late sixteenth century, with such beneficial results for the Irish Church, probably encouraged the Roman Dominican authorities to adopt the same strategy. The scheme to establish autonomous Irish Dominican spiritual and intellectual centres abroad received fresh impetus in Rome in 1613. In the autumn of that year the Master of the Order and Peter Lombard, Archbishop of Armagh, took steps independently to promote the establishment of a college within the King of Spain's dominions. It is likely that these related initiatives were prompted by Ross MacGeoghegan with his vision of a restored and reformed Irish Dominican province.

In September 1613 Archbishop Lombard addressed a petition from Rome to Philip III of Spain favouring the foundation of a college for the Irish Dominicans either in Spain or Flanders, where the petitioner had himself been educated at the University of Louvain. He asserted that many young Irishmen had become members of the Dominican Order in Spain, while others intended to join the Order. In such a Dominican

2 O'Heyne, *Epil. Chron.*, 274–7; B. de Jonghe, *Belgium Dominicanum sive Historia Provinciae Germaniae Inferioris Sacri Ordinis FF. Praedicatorum*, Brussels 1719, 418.

college or seminary, students selected for their exceptional qualities and intelligence might be trained to preserve, revive and spread the Catholic faith in Ireland. The archbishop stressed the benefits and achievements of the Irish seminaries of Spain and Flanders under royal patronage, proved by their success in sustaining the Catholic faith of Ireland. He then made an explicit plea that a seminary for the Irish Dominicans should be supported by the king.[3]

The king and his council of state considered the archbishop's memorial on 16 November 1613. It was noted by an official that the king had been petitioned already by Irish Dominicans to the same effect, as also by the English Dominican, Paul of London, who sought a college for the English Dominicans in Spain. This latter venture would be supported by Alonso Velasquez, a native of Seville, who had offered 300 escudos towards its foundation and would continue his support for nine years, at a total expense of 3,000 ducats. Permission had been sought to found this college or seminary in Seville. Individual views expressed by members of the royal council of state were for the most part negative. It was pointed out that there was an excessive number of such foreign colleges in Spain: there were English colleges at Alcalá, Lisbon, Seville and Valladolid, with Irish colleges at Salamanca, Lisbon and Santiago in Galicia. One councillor suggested that the number of such colleges be reduced rather than increased, as the new foundations caused problems for the older ones, which had much to be said in their favour. Another suggested that the existing colleges for the secular clergy might also be used for the training of religious. Finally the council made it clear that while some colleges thrived without royal patronage, the endowments required for others had put a serious strain on the exchequer.[4] Following the council's consideration of the petition of Archbishop Lombard and those of the Irish and English Dominicans, no decision was taken or recommended. In effect the petitions were shelved.

The draft versions of several incomplete letters of Archbishop Lombard indicate his awareness of the predicament facing Irish religious in search of a continental base for the education of their new recruits.[5] One letter mentioned how Irish clerical students in Spain and Portugal had entered religious orders such as the Augustinians and Dominicans and were later sent from Portugal to the East Indies. In a letter addressed to L.W. (Luke Wadding?), dated 29 January 1614, the Archbishop of Armagh spoke of his hopes that the King of Spain would found and endow seminaries or colleges in Spain as well as in the Spanish Low Countries

3 Rome, Archives of St Isidore's, MS W 2, no. 1, f. lr; Moran, *Spicil. Ossor.*, i, 126–7.

4 AGS, Estado, leg. 2643.

5 FLK, MS D III, ff 63–4 (105–6), 65–7 (109–11).

for the education of Irish Catholic youth, and referred to the letters he had written on behalf of the Irish Dominicans on learning that there were many professed young Irishmen of the Order in Spain. There are marked similarities in the wording of this letter to his petition or memorial to the King of Spain.

On 8 October 1613 the Master General gave instructions to William Talbot (*alias* William of the Holy Spirit), procurator of the Irish Dominicans at the court of Madrid, to do all in his power to obtain a college for the Irish members of the Order from the King of Spain. At the same time the Master General ordered the convent of Santo Tomás to receive William Talbot and made arrangements with its prior for his contribution to the convent, namely the celebration of a daily Mass. Should Talbot find himself unable to carry out this new task, Richard Caron was to take his place.[6] Obviously the Master of the Order attached great importance to the accomplishment of this objective. In a letter (dated 27 January 1615)[7] from the convent of Santo Tomás, Madrid, to Ross MacGeoghegan, described as his provincial, Talbot reported that he had been in Seville for three months in pursuit of his objective. He went on to outline his personal views and the difficulties he was encountering. At the same time he provided valuable information on the other religious groups abroad, and how they fared in obtaining a continental base for training their students. According to Talbot, Ross MacGeoghegan himself had been in correspondence for some time with the Master of the Order concerning the proposed college, and this had resulted in letters of commendation to Aloysius Aliaga, the King of Spain's Dominican confessor. Talbot stressed the importance of Aliaga's continued support for the venture. He complained that certain brethren of his own Order (probably Spanish) were strongly opposed to the Irish foundation; the enterprise had been criticised by men of serious reputation for frivolous and stupid reasons, but with such determination that he felt he was no match for those who opposed his plans. Talbot asked MacGeoghegan to inform Aliaga, if he should think it pertinent, that the Irish Franciscans had a convent of their own at Louvain which for the past six years had received a royal monthly allowance of 100 ducats. More than eighty Franciscans had been sent to Ireland in that time, many of whom were learned and well versed in languages. In his view, the Irish Dominicans were deprived of similar highly trained personnel because they did not

6 Fenning, *Irish material*, 278.

7 Madrid, Bibl. Nac., Gayangos MS 18420, ff 186rv–187rv. The letter is written in Spanish, perhaps for the sake of confidentiality and to avoid postal censorship. It is simply endorsed (f. 177v): 'Mi Pe [Padre] Provincial', but does not give the address of Ross MacGeoghegan. This is the only extant letter written by an Irish Dominican procurator in Madrid from the first half of the seventeenth century.

have their own college where languages would be taught, where controversial theology would be studied, and where religious formation would conform to the strict rule and primitive observances of the Order. He judged that the Order with such a college would be able to produce in Ireland the spiritual good which could not otherwise be achieved or expected from the free though very religious way of life prevailing in many Spanish convents. Commenting on other religious orders, he noted that the Cistercians were establishing a house in France for the same purpose, supported by the principal monasteries of their order. A letter from Salamanca informed him that Father Master Antolinez wished to start a college there for the Irish Augustinians, to whom he had entrusted his library and the income from his university chair during his lifetime. As was well known, the Jesuits dispatched many learned men to Ireland who had read their courses of studies in the Irish seminaries, all of which were under their control. In Talbot's opinion, the Irish Dominicans alone lacked men of distinction, and this would continue to be the case unless a foundation could be made. Talbot concluded by repeating his plea to have the plan for the establishment of an Irish Dominican house placed before Aliaga or a certain unnamed duke.

Eight days later, on 3 February 1615, Talbot added a most revealing postscript to his letter, forecasting his vision of political and religious developments in Ireland. He had learned that there were serious negotiations under way for a royal marriage between England and Spain, from which it was hoped liberty of conscience would follow. Such hopes, however, should not lead MacGeoghegan to give up the idea of founding a college in Spain. In the event of the marriage taking place, the Irish Dominican foundation would be more necessary than ever; for with ease of entry into the kingdoms of Britain and Ireland the religious orders, with colleges and convents established abroad, would be able to send many to those kingdoms. The religious orders would flourish in the number and quality of their members. Talbot considered that it would be for the benefit of Spain and the Dominican Order that they should be able to take advantage of the situation so that, when the English came to regret their decision and revoked liberty of conscience, Spain would have many friends and sympathisers. It would then prove to be an easy matter to remove Ireland from English control. He added that the Master General wished the Irish Dominicans to have at least the form of a congregation. For this reason the Master General wanted to establish a formal convent which would have the support of that congregation, and since this could not be done in Ireland, he wanted such a convent in Spain. In this connection the Master General had written two or three times to the Spanish king's confessor, almost certainly as a direct result of the letters Ross MacGeoghegan had sent to the Master General from the court of Madrid.

The intense dedication with which William Talbot worked at his project is impressive. In his eyes, the foundation of an Irish Dominican college was doubly important, partly for the political interests of Spain, and partly for the recovery of the Order in Ireland. It is interesting, given the Meath-born William Talbot's Anglo-Irish cultural and political background, that he should have wished to see Ireland ruled by Spain rather than by England, though admittedly he might have seen things differently had the English monarch been a Catholic.

There is some evidence to suggest that a few Irish Dominicans had formed a discreet presence in Louvain by 1613. The list of royal alms to foreign religious communities resident in the Spanish Low Countries in 1613–14 included a seminary of the Dominicans at Louvain.[8] Almost at the same time a site for a convent or college at Loures, near the city of Lisbon, was donated to the Irish Dominicans then living in the convent of Benfica, also near Lisbon. This house was formally established by a papal brief of Paul v (13 November 1615).[9] Simultaneously English Dominican hopes for houses in Spain (notably in the province of Andalucía) and Portugal (Lisbon) were heightened and became the subject of intense correspondence between the English Dominicans Nicholas of St Vincent (*alias* Hildinge), William of St Thomas, and Paul of London and Diego de la Fuente,[10] chaplain to Count Gondomar, Spanish ambassador in London.

In July 1619 Richard Caron submitted a memorial to the Spanish king proposing the foundation of a college for Irish Dominican students at Trianos in north-western Spain where he had received the gift of a house from the Dominicans of Trianos, and the moral support of the Dominican province of Castille.[11] Later there were plans for an Irish Dominican foundation at Beauvoir-sur-Mer (situated in the Vendée, western France). The general chapter of 1622 at Milan entrusted the French convent at Beauvoir-sur-Mer to the Irish friars provided that the Dominicans of the Paris province agreed.[12]

Of all these initiatives, only Lisbon and Louvain came to fruition—proof of the intensity and perseverance of all the efforts made to establish more than one continental base for the future supply of well-trained and forward-looking Irish Dominicans. The successful establishment of these colleges was, furthermore, achieved in spite of bureaucratic, financial and personality problems that at times seemed insurmountable. Undoubtedly

8 B. Jennings (ed.), 'Miscellaneous Documents, I: 1588–1634' in *Archiv. Hib.*, 12 (1946), 78.

9 *Bullarium Ord. Praed.*, v, 704–5; Burke, *Hib. Dom.*, 416–18.

10 G. Anstruther, *A Hundred Homeless Years: English Dominicans, 1558–1658*, London 1958, 94, 119, 120–22.

11 AGS, Estado, leg. 1175.

12 Burke, *Hib. Dom.*, 450.

the impressive achievements of the Irish Franciscans in securing three foundations at Louvain (1606), Rome (1625) and Prague (1629) set a headline for the Dominicans and inspired them along the rough roads of negotiation, disappointment, temporary reversals and fresh approaches.

LISBON (FOUNDED 1615)

In 1615, or perhaps even a year or two earlier, a Portuguese nobleman, Garcias 'Horunca' (*recte* Norohna),[13] presented a site for a Dominican convent of regular life at Loures, not far outside the city and suburbs of Lisbon, to John of Portugal, prior of São Domingos, Benfica, and his twin brother, Dominic of the Rosary, formerly Count of Vimiozo. These two Dominicans, with the consent of their community of Benfica and the approval of the Master General, donated the site to the Irish Dominicans who were preparing themselves at that time in various Portuguese convents (Benfica, Lisbon, Evora and elsewhere) for their priestly ministry in Ireland. The motive of the donation was to enable the founding of an Irish Dominican house or college in Portugal where novices might be received and students study the liberal arts and theology. The donors later enlarged the site by the addition of an adjoining field.[14]

In the summer of 1615 a high-level diplomatic campaign on behalf of this proposed Irish Dominican foundation was continued by no less a person than Cardinal Scipio Borghese, papal Secretary of State and cardinal protector of the Dominican Order. On 17 August 1615 he wrote to Antonio Caetano, Archbishop of Capua and nuncio in Spain, informing him that the Earl of Tyrone had petitioned the King of Spain to obtain a papal brief for the opening of a convent for Irish reformed Dominicans near Lisbon, and for the customary help to enable them to return to Ireland. A member of the Portuguese Dominican province, Dominic of the Rosary, proposed to build this convent out of his private resources.[15] That the Earl of Tyrone actively sponsored this project may have been due to the fact that a member of his entourage and one of his chaplains at Rome was the Ulster Dominican, Thaddeus MacTeig, who reached Rome in 1613 after suffering much for the Catholic faith in Dublin and

13 The correct form of this Portuguese surname is Norohna. The reading in the original supplication or *supplica* of 4 November 1615 is 'Nirona' (ASV, Reg. Suppl., 4193, f. 41rv), 'Horonca' in *Bullarium Ord. Praed.*, and 'Horunca' in Burke, *Hib. Dom.*, 417.

14 Burke, *Hib. Dom.*, 416–17.

15 ASV, Fondo Borghese, I, vol. 939, ff 434–5r; D. Conway (ed.), 'Guide to Documents of Irish and British Interest in Fondo Borghese, Series I' in *Archiv. Hib.* 23 (1960), 135; ASV, Nunz. di Spagna, vol. 339, f. 288r; J. de Olarra Garmendia and M. L. de Larramendi (Olarra) (eds), *Correspondencia entre la Nunciatura en España y la Santa Sede*, vi (1615–17), Rome 1966, 64, no. 331.

London, as he personally testified.[16] Whether MacTeig played any part in encouraging the Master General to launch the movement for an Irish Dominican house in Spain, as the latter did in the very same year, is not known. The nuncio Caetano, replying to the cardinal from Burgos on 28 September 1615, approved of the Earl of Tyrone's proposal. He expressed himself willing to do all in his power to help bring this 'consolation' to the Irish friars. He promised to take up the matter at the first opportunity with the Archbishop of Braga, one of the leading members of the state council of Portugal. He asked to be kept informed of the progress of negotiations and to be allowed to promote it personally.[17] In October 1615 Cardinal Borghese recommended the project to various prominent figures in Spain and Portugal. On 14 October he wrote to the influential Duke of Lerma, informing him that the Earl of Tyrone desired the King of Spain to permit the construction of a convent in Lisbon for 'Irish reformed Dominicans' and requested the duke's support.[18] At the same time the cardinal wrote to Ottavio Accoramboni, Bishop of Fossombrone, papal collector in Portugal, commending the plan to him.[19] And on the same day the cardinal wrote also to the confessor of the Spanish king, asking him to favour the foundation.[20]

The campaign for the establishment of a college at Lisbon came to a climax on 13 November 1615 when Paul v issued a brief *In apostolicae dignitatis culmine*, addressed to the papal collector of Portugal, granting papal approval to the new foundation.[21] It is clear from the text of the brief that it had been solicited in separate petitions by the vicar general of the Dominican Order and by the Portuguese Dominicans, John of Portugal, prior of Benfica, and his brother Dominic of the Rosary, recently Count of Vimiozo. The petition of the latter had been approved by Pope Paul v on 1 November, being duly entered in the register of supplications on 4 November by the Datary.[22] The text of the supplication, drawn up in curial style, was incorporated almost verbatim in the brief from the papal Chancery.

The brief recalled the benefaction of Garcias Norohna to his friends, John of Portugal and Dominic of the Rosary, to whom he gave absolute

16 AGS, Estado, leg. 2793.

17 ASV, Nunz. di Spagna, vol. 60c, f. 394; Ollara Garmendia, *Correspondencia*, vi, 75, no. 391.

18 ASV, Fondo Borghese, I, vol. 943, f. 418v; S. L. Forte, 'I Domenicani nel Carteggio del Card. Scipione Borghese, Protettore dell'Ordine (1606–1633)' in *AFP*, 30 (1960), 377.

19 ASV, Fondo Borghese, I, vol. 942, f. 361r; Conway, 'Guide to Documents . . . in Fondo Borghese', 136.

20 ASV, Fondo Borghese, I, vol. 943, f. 421; Forte, 'I Domenicani nel Carteggio del Card. Borghese', 377.

21 *Bullarium Ord. Praed.*, v, 704–5; Burke, *Hib. Dom.*, 416–18.

22 ASV, Reg. Suppl., 4193, f. 41rv.

discretion over the property, provided they honoured the benefactor's intention, namely that a Dominican house of regular observance be erected on the site. The grantees decided that the property, to which they added an adjacent field, should be given to the Irish Dominicans for the construction of a college or house of studies to serve the missionary needs of the Dominicans in Ireland. Having obtained the approval of the Benfica community and that of the Master of the Order, they then sought papal permission for the execution of their plans. This was duly granted. The canonical permission allowed the building of a house of strict Dominican observance, with a church or chapel under a title to be decided by the prior and Irish brethren, with a modest bell-tower, cloister, dormitory, refectory, cells, gardens, and all other necessary offices and buildings for a community consisting of a prior and ten Dominicans, who would live in conformity with their rule of regular observance and come under the supervision of the Dominican province of Portugal. In the church the members of the community would attend Mass and other divine services, including the canonical hours by day and night, with rights of possession and habitation in perpetuity. The college was to have a lector, who would instruct its members, whether novices or professed, in the liberal arts, theology and sacred letters.

The foundation of the Lisbon college, thus provided for with even papal approval, was nevertheless to remain on paper and in abeyance for fifteen years, largely because of opposition from the Portuguese civil service and for lack of the royal consent. On 4 February 1617 Dominic of the Rosary wrote to Cardinal Borghese and asked him to solicit the active support of the Master General of the Order for the proposed Irish Dominican house in Lisbon.[23] From this date nothing further is heard of Garcias Norohna or the other Portuguese patrons of the Irish friars. It must have seemed to all concerned in Portugal that their efforts had been in vain.

Meanwhile the English Dominicans too had moved closer towards their objective of founding a college in Spain. As early as 5 July 1613 the Master General empowered the Dominican confessor of the King of Spain, Aloysius Aliaga, to order the provincial of the Portuguese province to designate a convent in his province for the reception of Dominicans destined to work in England.[24] From a letter of Nicholas of St Vincent Hildinge, O.P., at Benfica, dated 9 July 1616, to Diego de la Fuente, Dominican chaplain at the Spanish embassy in London, it is evident

23 ASV, Fondo Borghese, III, vol. 50 A2, f. 110; Forte, 'I Domenicani nel Carteggio del Card. Borghese', 401, mistakenly identifies the Portuguese Domenico del Rosario with his younger Irish contemporary, Dominic (Daniel) of the Rosary O'Daly .

24 AGOP, IV, 58, f. 41.

that Antonio de Mascarenhas, a nobleman, priest and dean of the chapel royal of Portugal, had virtually promised to give a house to the English Dominicans in Lisbon.[25] An English Jesuit priest, John Blackfan,[26] in a letter dated 21 August 1621, angrily accused a secular priest (once educated by the Jesuits), William Newman, who had been appointed about 1612 to board all English ships arriving at the port of Lisbon, of attempting to put a residence in Lisbon, intended for a seminary, into the hands of diocesan priests or Dominican friars. In his reply, on 28 August 1621, Newman vehemently denied Blackfan's charge. Indeed, he claimed that he had dissuaded the patron from making such a grant, and, further, that had he not intervened, the Dominicans would long since have come into the possession of the house.[27] It is not absolutely clear from this correspondence whether the episode concerned an attempted Irish or English Dominican foundation. Since at Benfica both Irish and English Dominicans lived in a single community, they may have separately approached Mascarenhas on learning that he wished to establish a seminary or college in Lisbon.

The next step in favour of the Irish Dominicans was taken with persistent diplomacy by the redoubtable Richard Caron, procurator of the Irish province in Madrid. In response to his representations, Philip IV of Spain wrote to his officials at Lisbon on 23 March 1623, stating that Richard de la Peña (Caron), procurator of the Irish province of the Holy Cross, had petitioned for the royal licence to open a college in the city of Lisbon which would be aided by Antonio de Mascarenhas. Before granting his consent the king requested, without delay, the written opinion of the Desembargo do Paço (the Portuguese administrative council of state) on the matter and the reasons upholding its point of view.[28] On 29 September 1623 the king reminded the Desembargo do Paço of the matter and again asked its members to forward their views to the Spanish council of state.[29] After a very long delay the officials of the Desembargo do Paço replied negatively (13 July 1624) to the royal request. Their reasons are revealed in a further letter (31 July) from the king to his Portuguese administration. They thought it would be preferable to enlarge the college of St Patrick, already established at Lisbon for the Irish diocesan clergy, to meet the needs of the Irish Dominicans rather than permit a second foundation or college so slenderly endowed. Such

25 Madrid, Bibl. Nac., Gayangos MS 18420, ff 168–9rv.

26 John Blackfan was procurator of the English College, Valladolid, at various times between 1608 and 1616. E. Henson (ed.), *Registers of the English College at Valladolid*, London 1930, xxii–xxiv.

27 Westminster Cathedral Archives, B. 25, no. 26; *Dodd's Church History of England*, ed. M. A. Tierney, v, London 1843, cclv–cclvi.

28 ANTT, Correspondencia do Desembargo do Paço, 1623, f. 39.

29 Ibid., f. 193rv.

a foundation, it was felt, would not serve the best interests of their citizens.[30] Undaunted by the negative and uncooperative attitude of the Portuguese authorities, Richard Caron, obviously enjoying the goodwill of Philip IV, requested a review of the situation in 1625. The king wrote once more to the Portuguese Desembargo do Paço on 27 May 1625 asking to find a solution to the problems preventing the foundation of a college in Lisbon 'for the religious of St Dominic of the English [*sic*] nation' as petitioned by Richard de la Peña.[31] The Portuguese council of state showed its disapproval of the reopening of the subject by saying nothing. And there the matter rested for a number of years until a new and more spirited approach was adopted on the arrival in Lisbon of a young Irish Dominican who would devote much of his brilliant career and talents to bringing about the building of a splendid college and church for his province in Lisbon.

In June 1629 Daniel O'Daly, known among his brethren as Dominic of the Rosary O'Daly or simply Dominic O'Daly, arrived in Lisbon from Madrid, in the company of two Irish confrères, Matthew of the Holy Cross and Peter Martyr Piercy. O'Daly brought with him letters of commendation from King Philip IV to the governors of Portugal, favouring the establishment of an Irish house or hospice in the city. At the convent of São Domingos in Lisbon, O'Daly won the support and admiration of several religious of high standing: Emmanuel Telles, the Portuguese provincial, Master Alvaro de Castro, and Master John de Vasconçellos, inquisitor of Lisbon, who belonged to one of the most important families in Lisbon. In due course Dominic O'Daly presented himself to the patriarch Rodrigo da Cunha.[32]

On 24 September 1629 the Master General commissioned Emmanuel Telles to draw up statutes for the Irish Dominican college to be founded in Lisbon. At the same time he appointed Antonius Olivares to oversee the material construction of the college.[33] Also in 1629 Oliver Burke, procurator for the Irish province at Rome, presented a memorial on the subject on behalf of his provincial to the Congregation of Propaganda Fide. He asserted that a certain devout gentleman, a native of Lisbon, wished to establish it at his own expense, in order to spread the Catholic faith in northern Europe where heresy was rampant. This devout person also promised to endow the college with appropriate revenues in perpetuity, so that the college would never become a burden on the citizens of Lisbon. However, as new religious foundations and the collection of alms were stringently forbidden by royal decree, the procurator asked

30 Ibid.,1624, f. 263rv.
31 Ibid., 1625, f. 141.
32 Lisbon, Bibl. Nac., MSS Reservados, 145, ff 300–01r ; Burke, *Hib. Dom.*, 419.
33 Fenning, *Irish material*, 285.

the congregation to draw up a special exhortatory brief in favour of the proposed foundation.[34] At a plenary meeting on 6 November the congregation gave its permission for the Irish Dominicans to found a house in Lisbon, having listened to their case as presented by Cardinal Borgia. The congregation ordered that the nuncio at the court of Madrid was to be given specific instructions on the handling of the case. In his dealings with the Spanish king and his ministers the nuncio was to voice Rome's disapproval of the royal prohibition against new religious houses in Portugal, for it encroached on the liberty of the Church.[35] While supporting the projected Irish Dominican college in Lisbon, even to the extent of employing the good offices of the nuncio, Propaganda Fide also sought to profit from the occasion by showing its opposition to the royal decree banning new religious houses in the dominions of Spain. The question of an Irish house in Portugal therefore became linked to a point of principle being strenuously upheld by the Roman curia; it was to become a test case in diplomatic relations between Rome and Madrid.

Meanwhile Dominic O'Daly had presented the royal letters of introduction to the Portuguese authorities and asked their permission to open a 'hospice'. This house would serve the needs of Irish Dominicans who had finished their studies in Spain or Portugal and would provide a point of assembly for their embarkation, as there were frequent sailings from Lisbon to Ireland. On presentation of the permission already given by Propaganda Fide to the apostolic collector of Portugal, Laurence Tramaglio, Bishop of Gerace, he in turn gave them a licence in the form of a brief to open such a hospice (*hospitium*) for Irish Dominican students arriving from Spain. The licence was subject to certain conditions: the students' stay in Lisbon was to be strictly temporary, no longer than was necessary before taking ship for Ireland, where they were expected to devote themselves to the preaching of the faith; and only one friar might stay in the hospice to see to its proper upkeep and to ensure that it was situated in a 'good neighbourhood' (*in loco honesto*), but nobody might reside there for more than three years. The collector forwarded to the nuncio at Madrid copies of the licences granted by himself and by Propaganda Fide.[36]

Late in 1629, on receiving the apostolic collector's licence and possibly some form of *nihil obstat* from the municipal authorities, O'Daly and his

34 Ibid.; APF, SOCG, 389, ff 341, 344r–345v, 347v.

35 APF, Acta, VI, ff 346v–347r.

36 Lisbon, Bibl. Nac., MSS Reservados, 429, f. 60v; ibid., 145, f. 301rv; A. Carvalho da Costa, *Corografia Portuguesa*, 3rd ed., Braga 1869, 484–5; Frei Lucas de Santa Catarina, *História de S. Domingos*, vi, Lisbon 1711, 356ff; E. Freire de Oliveira, *Elementos para a História do Município de Lisboa*, Lisbon 1882–1911, ii, 517; vi, 227, note 2; xiv, 240–42, note 4; M. Gonçalves da Costa, *Fontes Inéditas Portuguesas para a História de Irlanda*, Braga 1981, 72 and note 115.

companions immediately set up a hospice (the term used in the collector's licence) rather than a formal convent or college. By this strategem O'Daly would seem to have deftly circumvented the strictures of the Desembargo do Paço, which had repeatedly thwarted what the King of Spain actually favoured by citing an edict of one of his predecessors forbidding the opening of new religious houses in the formal sense. It was clear to O'Daly that the original papal brief of 13 November 1615, however impressive canonically, was inoperative as far as the Portuguese civil authorities were concerned. A house or houses were first rented from an estate (the *quinta de Legacia*) in the Cotovia district (*bairro*) at some distance from the city of Lisbon. Here O'Daly, his two companions and another Irish Dominican, Edward Nagle, who had been living in the convent of Benfica, resided for about a year. The house, however, was considered distant from the city, too far away from those to whom they might preach and from the noble families for whom they acted as confessors. They were also badly positioned for the reception of alms, the conduct of business, and the specific purpose of the house itself, namely the dispatch of missionaries to Ireland. After less than a year they transferred their residence or hospice to the Calçado do Combro area within the city, where they remained for almost two years (from about November 1630 to about November 1632). The hospice was then transferred again to a better location near the Italian church and convent of Our Lady of Loreto, where the little community stayed until September 1633. While accommodation was cramped, the opportunity of celebrating Mass in the adjacent church saved the friars from having to go daily to the private chapels of the Portuguese nobility.[37]

In the meantime Propaganda Fide on 15 June 1630 decided to write to the principal bishops of Portugal commending the establishment of a college for the Irish Dominicans, following representations to this effect from the Irish Dominican procurator at Rome and the assessor of the powerful Congregation of the Holy Office. The procurator's petition had asked for letters to be sent to the nuncio in Madrid to obtain the king's formal approval for the entire project. Letters were subsequently dispatched to the apostolic nuncio and collector of Portugal, to the Archbishops of Braga, Lisbon and Evora, and to the Bishop of Coimbra.[38] Rome was persistent in its diplomatic efforts to aid the Irish Dominicans. In the Master General's register (16 October 1631) Antonius Olivares,

37 Lisbon, Bibl. Nac., MSS Reservados, 429, ff 60v–61r; ibid., 145, f. 301v; Carvalho da Costa, *Corografia*, 485.

38 APF, SOCG, 390, ff 219r, 226v; APF, Acta, VII, f. 84, no. 49; B. Jennings (ed.), 'Acta Sacrae Congregationis de Propaganda Fide, 1622–1650' in *Archiv. Hib.*, 22 (1959), 52; *Wadding Papers*, 436, for positive reply of Lisbon nuncio to Cardinal Ludovisi, dated 13 Nov. 1630.

O.P., was somewhat inaccurately described as '*auctor et benefactor insignis*' of the Irish Dominican college in Lisbon, exactly as he had represented himself.[39] At most he had been deputed to take charge of the actual building of the college which at that date was still a matter of discussion. In the autumn of that year the Master General forbade any Irish Dominicans, except those recently arrived from Ireland, to come to the 'college or hospice' at Lisbon unless they had first told the superior about their business and obtained his written permission to remain. Those staying at the hospice were not to quest, nor even to accept offerings, without the express permission of the superior on each occasion. They were to leave Lisbon as soon as they had wound up their affairs.[40]

On 18 January 1632 Nicholas Lynch, the Irish provincial, was given permission by the Master General to set up a college or seminary at Lisbon for the members of his province. He was permitted to gather a number of friars in some decent place or house and to form a regular community. A formal precept was imposed on all involved not to oppose the provincial, directly or indirectly. On the following day the Master General decided that the first 300 ducats which the King of Spain would grant to those leaving Spain or Portugal for Ireland were to be set aside for the establishment of the Lisbon college. Those thus deprived of a travel allowance were to remain for another year in whatever convents or provinces they were actually in. Those who had completed their studies should return to Ireland in the following year, dividing the royal alms between them for the journey. This permission, slightly more amplified, was reissued by the Master General's curia on 20 January: the hospice at Lisbon might serve the brethren coming from or going to Ireland; the provincial, who was not to be opposed or contradicted, was given the right to assign a vicar and some friars to the hospice, and was told to see to its decent maintenance and upkeep.[41]

In a sense Nicholas Lynch was seeking belatedly, with the Master General's authority, to secure the transfer to himself as provincial of the rights which had been conferred by the apostolic collector's brief on the superior of the hospice. At the same time the Master General ordered the procurators or their deputies of the Irish province at Madrid, or those who had been charged with the administration of the Lisbon hospice, under precept and threat of excommunication, to give an accurate account to the provincial of all goods and business in hand; they were to surrender all money, books, ornaments, furnishings and any other property which belonged or pertained either to the province or to the hospice. All other Irish friars and Dominicans of the other provinces who held goods

39 Fenning, *Irish material*, 287.
40 Ibid., 289.
41 Ibid., 291.

belonging to the hospice or province or to Irish brethren, or who knew the whereabouts of such goods, were to hand them over or reveal where they were to the Irish provincial.[42] On 18 February 1632 Walter Archbolde, O.P., was ordered not to ratify his father's will unless he received compensation from the heirs. He was to devote that sum to the founding of the Lisbon college as ordered by his provincial, who might, however, grant part of the legacy to Archbolde for his personal needs. Archbolde was given permission to go to Ireland and return later to Portugal to continue his studies.[43]

In 1633 the Irish Dominicans were befriended by the nobleman Luis de Castro do Rio, lord of Barbacena, Grand Alcayde of Covilhã, and his wife Catarina Telles de Meneses. Much impressed by these friars, and in particular by Dominic O'Daly, they sympathised with them in having had to move house so often. This nobleman, who was of Jewish extraction and reputedly the wealthiest merchant in Lisbon,[44] donated to the Dominicans a property on the Patio das Comédias beside his own residence. These pious donors wanted to found a college worthy of the name, but both death and the refusal of official permission prevented them giving the Dominicans anything more than a new and better house.

The Irish Dominicans installed themselves in their new home at the Patio das Comédias in the Fángas da Farinha adjacent to Calcetaria only on 13 September 1633, the eve of the feast of the Exaltation of the Holy Cross, the feast-day of the Irish province. Now they could enjoy at last that cloistered life by which the community set great store, though for some time performances in an adjacent theatre were an inconvenience. Soon a chapel of Madeira pinewood was constructed, painted on the inside and hung with pictures, especially that of Our Lady of the Rosary, to whom the chapel was dedicated. The first Mass, celebrated on 21 November, to the accompaniment of an organ, was attended by many of the nobility. Since the new hospice and chapel were in the heart of the city, close to the Rua Nova de Almada, the Irish friars came to be well known and appreciated. When the Master of the Order, Nicholas Ridolfi, appointed Dominic O'Daly as the first rector of the 'new college' in 1634, alms were regularly offered by certain wealthy citizens for the support of the twelve friars in community.[45] Previously O'Daly's title had been that of 'vicar of the hospice'. Formal recognition of its collegial status on the part of the Order marked yet another step in O'Daly's diplomatic strategy to win full recognition for the college from the local

42 Ibid.
43 Ibid., 292.
44 Gonçalves da Costa, *Fontes Inéditas Portuguesas*, 72 and note 115.
45 Lisbon, Bibl. Nac., MSS Reservados, 429, f. 61r; ibid., 145, ff 301v–302r; Carvalho da Costa, *Corografia*, 486.

authorities, civil and ecclesiastical. One dark shadow that fell across these favourable developments in Lisbon was the arrest on a false charge of treason and the execution in London, on 27 November 1633, of Arthur MacGeoghegan, O.P., despite the personal intervention of Queen Henrietta Maria.[46] Arthur MacGeoghegan had been port chaplain and censor of books passing through the port of Lisbon and had joined Dominic O'Daly and his companions in the hospice at Fangas da Farinha in 1631.[47] In the spring of 1633 he had left Lisbon for Ireland via London, principally to find Irish students to increase the Lisbon community as it rapidly assumed a collegial character.[48]

From about 1633, while setting up the chapel and house in Fanghas da Farinha, the Irish Dominicans attracted several devoted benefactors for the foundation of the college they had in mind. Cristóvão de Almeida donated all his goods to them, Antonio de Mascarenhas granted them revenue from his Brazilian sugar plantation, and Andreza de Vargas remembered them in his will.[49] The latter bequest, as will be seen, was bitterly contested by the Vargas family. On 28 May 1633, at Dominic O'Daly's request, the viceroy, the ministers of Desembargo do Paço and the provincial of the Portuguese Dominicans were ordered by the Spanish king to discuss the project for the Lisbon college of the Irish Dominicans.[50] Before receiving a reply to this command from the crown procurator, Tomé Pinheiro de Veiga, the Dominicans had erected their chapel and set up their conventual quarters.

A reply to the king's demand was drawn up and signed only on 23 October 1634 and did not receive consideration at the court of Madrid until 10 October 1635.[51] Tomé Pinheiro de Veiga, the celebrated jurist and crown procurator, strongly opposed the foundation of the college on three counts. Firstly, there were already too many monasteries and religious houses in Lisbon whose upkeep alone would finally lead to the ruin of the nation. Secondly, the religious motives for such a foundation were not uniquely Irish. (These two arguments could be advanced against all expatriate groups: English, Scots, Muscovites, Saxons, Dutch, Armenians,

46 For details see pp 119–20 above. This sad occurrence was summed up in one contemporary report as follows: 'The death of the Irish Dominican has done more good than harm to the Catholic cause, seeing that almost everybody judged that he died innocent of the crime of which he was accused.' BAV, Barberini Latini, MS 8105, f. 61; Reichert, *MOPH*, xii, 206; Burke, *Hib. Dom.*, 419, 559–60; R. Walsh, 'Some of Our Martyrs' in *IER*, 3rd ser., xv (1894), 885–916; M. J. Havran, *The Catholics in Caroline England*, London 1962, 114.

47 D. O'Daly, *History of the Geraldines*, ed. C. P. Meehan, Dublin 1878, 364.

48 Burke, *Hib. Dom.*, 419.

49 Gonçalves da Costa, *Fontes Inéditas Portuguesas*, 73.

50 ANTT, Correspondencia do Desembargo do Paço, 1633, f. 122rv.

51 Gonçalves da Costa, *Fontes Inéditas Portuguesas*, 73.

Egyptians, and so on.) Thirdly, there was already a convent of English nuns under Jesuit direction in which the Irish Dominicans might study. Better still, they might enlist in the king's navy to fight the Dutch. Whether he envisaged their role as that of marines or chaplains he failed to say. In his opinion, all foreign soldiers resident in Portugal wanted to found a monastery. Basically he stressed that new religious foundations constituted an intolerable burden for the nation in that they tended to accumulate wealth while the ordinary people remained poor.[52]

Peter O'Heyne, *sacrae theologiae praesentatus*, was made rector of the 'new college' on 24 January 1636 for a period of three years in succession to Dominic O'Daly. This appointment was made by the Master General and not by the provincial of Ireland.[53] Henceforth the college and its affairs came under the immediate jurisdiction of the Master of the Order. On 26 June 1636 the Patriarch of Lisbon permitted the community to reserve the Blessed Sacrament in their chapel.[54] Yet another letter from the King of Spain, dated 12 November 1636, came before the Desembargo do Paço seeking information concerning the setting up of a college for the Irish Dominicans, the property they held, the bequest that had been made to them by Andreza de Vargas, and by whose authority and backing the college or seminary was to be built.[55] This was to be the last time that the question of the Lisbon college would be reviewed by Philip IV. Clearly the king was well disposed towards the college project, but chose nonetheless not to overrule the views of his Portuguese administrators because of increasingly strained relations between Spain and Portugal.

The endeavours of the Irish Dominicans to secure adequate financial resources for the building of a better college involved them in at least one dramatic and distressing incident. Three sealed copies of a document written at Lisbon on 5 December 1637 by Bishop Alexander Castracani, apostolic collector (with the authority of a papal nuncio), were addressed to all abbots, priors, rectors, etc., in Lisbon, declaring that the Irish rector and Dominican Fathers of Our Lady of the Rosary of Lisbon were to be left in peaceful possession of their goods. They had been violently dispossessed of their property by Andreza de Vargas de Saraina of Lisbon, who was thereby declared excommunicated. The collector referred to a papal *motu proprio* of 11 July 1636. A copy of the collector's document

52 ANTT, Miscelaneas da Graça, Peculios, caixa 18, vol. 3, ff 307–13; Gonçalves da Costa, *Fontes Inéditas Portuguesas*, 73. Pinheiro actually referred to Irish nuns, but there was no such convent in Lisbon before the establishment of the Irish Dominican nuns at Bom Sucesso in 1639. The nuns the crown procurator had in mind were the English Brigittines (founded at Lisbon, 1594) who in due course accepted Irish members.

53 Fenning, *Irish material*, 295.

54 Carvalho da Costa, *Corografia*, 486.

55 ANTT, Correspondencia do Desembargo do Paço, 1636, f. 271rv.

expedited on 17 December 1637 bore a dorsal note (signed on 5 January 1638) by the vicar of the parish of São Paulo in Lisbon to the effect that he had put up the decree of excommunication on the door of his church.[56] The then Irish Dominican hospice, on the Rua Nova de Almada, was within the parish boundaries of São Paulo. Obviously the heirs of Andreza de Vargas had not only hotly contested the bequest to the Irish Dominicans but had taken drastic unilateral action. The matter was brought to the attention of the King of Spain himself, but after this no more was heard of this unseemly episode, and it is not known whether or not the Dominicans ever received their legacy.

By 1636 or even earlier community life was well established in conformity with the Dominican constitutions. The canonical hours of the divine office and other devotions were fully and punctually observed. The rosary too was recited every day in public. In fact, as a result of the example of the Irish Dominicans, devotion to the rosary spread to many Portuguese Dominican houses.[57] Their way of life earned them very considerable respect throughout the city and particularly among the upper classes of Lisbon. Princess Margaret of Savoy, Duchess of Mantua and viceroy of Portugal, became one of their most devoted supporters. Every first Sunday of the month it was her custom to assist at the solemn recitation of the rosary in their chapel and to walk in the rosary procession. She proved herself an extremely generous benefactor and wished to further the plans for the new college building.[58] On 16 April 1639 Dominic O'Daly was granted an annuity of 5,000 cruzados, the first of a long series of annuities, settled in real estate and bonds.[59] The reasons for the annuity were set forth in the first licence: the great poverty of the Irish Dominicans and their inability to support themselves. Over a period of twenty years the Irish friars would continue to receive increases of this annuity, which frequently coincided with the founder's absence from the college on matters of state business. However, the enforced departure of the Duchess of Mantua from Portugal early in 1641, after the tumultuous events of December 1640, prevented the realisation of her good intentions. At that point John IV of the house of Braganza succeeded by popular acclaim to the Portuguese throne, and Portugal once more became an independent kingdom.

It was on the eve of the Portuguese revolution and abrupt change of government that Dominic O'Daly brought to fruition his plans for a

56 ASV, Arch. Nunz. di Lisbona, vol. 23, sezione 2, no. III.
57 Carvalho da Costa, *Corografia*, 486.
58 Ibid., 486–7.
59 ANTT, Livro de Consultas e Repostas do Gov. de Castello (1639), f. 97v. See M. B. Curtin, 'Daniel O'Daly, 1595–1662: A Study of Irish–European Relationships in the Seventeenth Century' (M.A. thesis, U.C.D., 1958), 57.

convent of Irish Dominican contemplative nuns, called Nossa Senhora do Bom Sucesso, in the suburbs of Lisbon. The King of Spain, Philip IV, had given his assent to the foundation on 21 March 1639, and the community took possession of their cloistered convent on 12 November.[60] The ever-perspicacious Dominic O'Daly, aware of the fast-changing political currents in Portugal, applied for and was given permission to transfiliate to the Portuguese province on 24 June 1639.[61] However, he never availed of this option and remained a member of the Irish province, while astutely changing his political allegiance in 1640 from Spain to the Portuguese dynasty of the house of Braganza. O'Daly quickly ingratiated himself with the new government and particularly the royal court, concentrating all his energies on making his new college a reality. Shortly after the restoration of the Portuguese monarchy O'Daly became confessor to the queen, Luisa de Gusmão, who proved to be the most generous benefactor of the Irish Dominicans in Lisbon.[62]

The college formed few students before the outbreak of revolution in late 1640. There is no reliable list of its early alumni, nor any indication that they were numerous,[63] yet among these were representatives of a tradition which merited the college the title of 'seminary of martyrs'.[64] Among the notable priests associated with the college in the 1630s were Arthur MacGeoghegan (d. London, 1633), Michael of the Rosary McGrath (d. Clonmel, 1651), Ambrose Aeneas O'Cahill (d. near Cork, 1651), Vincent Gerald Dillon (d. York, 1651) and Thaddeus (Tadhg) Moriarty (d. Killarney, 1653), all of whom were put to death for their religious convictions.[65] It appears that about forty Dominicans, including perhaps as many as thirty priests educated in the college, left Lisbon for Ireland by 1663.[66]

For thirty years the actual implementation of the plans for an autonomous Irish Dominican college in Lisbon was obstructed both by Spanish and Portuguese civil authorities in the face of the most persistent diplomatic initiatives of its original Portuguese patrons, papal representatives, Richard Caron, and Dominic O'Daly, its eventual founder and protector. The college and church were definitively established on a new site, commanding a magnificent view of the River Tagus and facing the then royal palace. All this was done under the auspices of the

60 Frei Agostinho de Santa Maria, *O Santuario Mariano*, ii, Lisbon 1707, 11–13. The original royal charter authorising the foundation is extant in the archives of Bom Sucesso convent.
61 Fenning, *Irish material*, 297.
62 Burke, *Hib. Dom.*, 420; H. Raposa, *Dona Luisa de Gusmão*, Lisbon 1946, 343.
63 The Lisbon ordination registers for the years 1624–42 are missing.
64 Burke, *Hib. Dom.*, 419.
65 Ibid., 559–60, 566–7, 569–70, 573.
66 Carvalho da Costa, *Corografia*, 488–9.

Queen Regent of Portugal, Dona Luisa de Gusmão, whose name was inscribed on the foundation stone laid on 4 May 1659.[67]

TRIANOS (ATTEMPTED FOUNDATION, 1619–20)

A second but unsuccessful attempt was made to establish an Irish Dominican house in the Iberian peninsula in the years 1619–20. The initiative was launched by the intrepid Richard de la Peña Caron, then deputy procurator of the Irish province in Madrid. His first memorandum to Philip III[68] was received at the Spanish court on 13 April 1619, shortly before the king and his court set out for Portugal, where they were to remain from the end of April to September 1619. It was at Lisbon that the matter was referred to Juan de Ziriça, the powerful secretary of the council of state.

In his memorandum Richard Caron stated that he had been greatly helped by the Dominican province of Castille and especially by the convent of Santa Maria de Trianos (civil province of León) in his efforts to start a college for the education of the members of his province in Spain. At Trianos he had accepted the gift of a house which could accommodate up to twenty-four students. There was, he said, urgent need for preachers in Ireland because of increased religious persecution. He admitted that the Irish Dominicans lacked learned men for their ministry. He then mentioned that the royal patronage extended to several colleges and seminaries of religious and secular clergy in Flanders, in Spain and elsewhere, all of which were under Jesuit direction. The Irish Dominicans were thus at a disadvantage and low in numbers precisely because they did not have a college within the King of Spain's dominions in which they might be trained and educated with a view to increasing their presence and impact in Ireland. He requested the king's patronage and financial aid for the proposed college of Irish Dominicans to be erected at Trianos with the same support as was enjoyed by other seminaries in Spain, so that in time it might benefit the afflicted Catholics of Ireland. It was suggested that the king should draw on a particular section of the royal treasury known as *las Arcas*, sometimes called *las Arcas de Tres Llaves*, for the money required to maintain this college. Evidently Richard Caron was by this time well versed in the workings of the royal council and treasury, for when the king granted pensions, alms or allowances it was important that he should designate precisely the exact funds or that part of the treasury from which the money was to come.

The council of state discussed the memorial at Lisbon on 13 July 1619 and decided to ask for the views of the king's confessor and inquisitor

67 Ibid., 488; Burke, *Hib. Dom.*, 420.
68 AGS, Estado, leg. 1775.

general. On 16 July the latter gave his opinion that, since the royal treasury (specifically the *las Arcas* section) had not the means of acceding to this request, Caron and his companions should suggest in what manner and from what other funds they might be helped. The final paragraph in the list of comments made by state council officials on his original proposal records Caron's most unexpected answer to this difficulty. He requested permission to ship 2,000 black slaves to Buenos Aires over a period of two to three years, without disclosing what country the slaves were to be transported from. The venture would be registered with the *casa de la contratación* of Seville, observing the correct legalities and paying royal taxes at the port of Potosí in Bolivia. The last two lines, dated 27 August 1619, demanded more information so that Richard Caron's proposal would not contravene existing contracts. It should be noted that in the sixteenth and seventeenth centuries the export of black African slaves to the New World—to work the mines, estates and plantations of European conquistadors and settlers—was treated in the same way as the export and transport of commercial goods.[69] Humanitarian or moral considerations did not enter much into the thinking of the colonising nations, although at first sight it might seem strange to find an Irish Dominican involved in such a scheme for providing the initial funds for the proposed Dominican college at Trianos.

On 15 February 1620 Richard Caron renewed his petition for appropriate assistance from the king in setting up a house to accommodate twenty Irish Dominicans at Trianos in conjunction with his proposal of shipping slaves to Buenos Aires. It appears that certain quotas of slaves were agreed upon over specified periods of time. This second memorial[70] showed that, from each quota, the Spanish king reserved for himself, to dispose of as he wished, the revenue from the sale of 2,000 or 3,000 slaves. It seems that Richard Caron hoped that the king would pass this revenue over to him. But the king had already disposed of it, the sale having been carried out by his department of finance, and the money used. In the light of this document, it is possible to suggest that Caron simply wanted part of the king's normal share of the trade and had no intention of becoming a slave-trader himself. In those very years the

69 Bartholomé de las Casas, O.P. (1474–1566), Bishop of Chiapas in Mexico, devoted most of his long life to upholding the rights of the indigenous peoples in Spanish America in the face of cruel colonial exploitation. He nonetheless favoured the importation of negro slaves into America, a practice which had long existed and was not considered contrary to Christian ethics. See *The Oxford Dictionary of the Christian Church*, ed. F. L. Cross and E. A. Livingstone, Oxford 1974, 800.

70 AGS, Estado, leg. 1775. I am grateful to Dr Micheline Kerney Walsh for helping me to make sense of a complicated series of secretarial notes on these two memorials.

economy of Spain was in a critical condition. The king, in turning down the petition, endorsed it with his own hand to the effect that it was out of the question.

Richard Caron took no further steps to pursue his plans for a college at Trianos. The project was untimely, the means proposed to finance it were immoral, and the economic circumstances of Spain unpropitious.

BEAUVOIR-SUR-MER (ATTEMPTED FOUNDATION, 1622 AND 1631)

In May 1622 the general chapter of the Order at Milan entrusted an obscure convent called Beauvoir-sur-Mer in the west of France to the Irish province, provided that the brethren of the province of France in whose territory it lay agreed to the transfer.[71] The chapter acts do not reveal who was responsible for the idea or refer to the negotiations which led to the short-lived establishment of an Irish Dominican community in the Vendée, an acknowledged Protestant stronghold. Beauvoir-sur-Mer, lying on the Bay of Biscay, to the south-west of Nantes, had the advantage of direct, safer and shorter accessibility from Irish seaports.

Did the initiative come from the Italian Master of the Order, Serafino Secchi? He was already in office in 1613 when the Irish Dominicans organised a campaign to obtain a continental house or college for the education of novices and students, though their aims then focused on a foundation in Spain or some other country under Spanish rule. He was undoubtedly well informed of the situation of the Dominicans in Ireland and had willingly approved the proposal of a college in Lisbon. It is more than likely that it was from among the Irish Dominicans educated in France that the first approach was made to the French Dominicans. Had the province of France abandoned this house, deep in Huguenot territory, or did they intend shortly to do so? Was it hoped that the Irish Dominicans might be more capable of confronting and challenging French Calvinism? For the moment these questions must remain unanswered. At all events, though matters hung fire for nine years, it is surely significant that the French-educated Nicholas Lynch was provincial in 1631 when a formal legal instrument was composed concerning the conditions of tenure of Beauvoir-sur-Mer by the Irish Dominicans.

In the spring of 1631 a memorial, couched in atrocious Italian, on the subject of Beauvoir-sur-Mer was presented to Propaganda Fide. It declared that the French Dominicans were offering this convent to their Irish brethren in order to enable young Irish friars to be educated in France, something which was then impossible in Ireland, while providing

71 Reichert, *MOPH*, xi, 342.

a refuge for Nicholas Lynch, their provincial. The petitioner (possibly Lynch himself) asked Propaganda Fide to write to the nuncio at Paris, who might obtain the consent of the French king (Louis XIII) and the blessing of the Bishop of Luçon in whose diocese the convent was situated, as also that of Cardinal Richelieu, while at the same time the nuncio should recommend Nicholas Lynch to all three.[72] At the request of Cardinal Pamphili, Propaganda Fide agreed on 27 March 1631 to write to the nuncio in Paris in favour of the Irish Dominicans, asking him to obtain the royal consent, with the blessings of Cardinal Richelieu and the Bishop of Luçon, so that they would be in a position to accept the convent offered to them at Beauvoir-sur-Mer.[73]

Several entries in the registers of Master General, Nicholas Ridolfi throw light on this short-lived Irish house in France. In *Hibernia Dominicana* Thomas Burke wrongly alleged that the French Dominicans did not consent to the transfer, adding drily that the Irish Dominicans never actually obtained possession of the convent.[74] The truth is that the Irish province abandoned it for undisclosed reasons shortly after taking possession. On 19 December 1631 William du Douit, O.P., the French provincial, made over Beauvoir-sur-Mer to the Irish Dominicans under well-defined and rather inhibiting conditions.[75] It would appear that after consultation with both parties the Master General and his curial officials drew up the legal instrument of transfer.

The Irish brethren were granted rights over the convent, its buildings, vineyard, orchard, garden and all other goods and income, as well as furniture pertaining to the church or conventual buildings, for the duration of the heresy or schism in Ireland. The convent as such would still belong to the province of France, and its provincial would have the right to visitate and inspect it personally or through a representative. The divine office should be recited there as regularly as in any convent. The provincial of the province of France would be entitled to confirm as prior the person presented to this office by the Irish provincial. The Irish Dominicans would be responsible for the preservation of the conventual buildings. They were not to dispose of the land, revenues or goods of the convent, but rather seek to improve them. An inventory of all its property was to be compiled, including not only all goods, moveable and immoveable, but also all titles, documents and legal papers. Copies were to be given to the provincial of France and to the Irish Dominicans. Should it happen that the Irish Dominicans left Beauvoir-sur-Mer and returned to their own country, then whatsoever moveable or immoveable goods

72 APF, SOCG, 391, ff 67r, 70v.
73 Jennings, 'Acta Propaganda Fide', 57–8.
74 Burke, *Hib. Dom.*, 450.
75 Fenning, *Irish material*, 289–90.

they might have acquired or added to the existing ones should remain on the spot and no compensation be offered for them. Finally, the Irish brethren should allow a paralysed French Dominican to remain in the convent. And should a *studium* be established, the Irish Dominicans would be obliged to educate and offer hospitality to those affiliated to Beauvoir-sur-Mer.

The Master General confirmed all these conditions and ordered the convent to be transferred to the Irish province. The French provincial and the superior and friars resident at Beauvoir-sur-Mer were instructed to permit the Irish Dominicans to take peaceful possession of the convent and all its property. On 20 December 1631 Thomas Lynch was appointed prior of Beauvoir-sur-Mer by the French provincial, having been nominated to the office by the Irish provincial, and this too was confirmed by the Master General. The friars belonging to the convent were ordered to accept him as their legitimate superior. Hyacinth Charpentier, O.P., was commissioned by the Master General on 21 December to inspect the account books of the prior of Beauvoir-sur-Mer and to hand over the convent to the Irish friars. On the following day the Master of the Order assigned four non-ordained Irish Dominicans to Beauvoir: Dominic of Jesus, Raymund Stephens, Dominic of the Passion and John Geraldine (FitzGerald). The final entry in the Master General's register (7 January 1632) concerns Thomas Lynch, the first and perhaps the last Irish prior of Beauvoir-sur-Mer. He had been given 100 florins from the college funds of Louvain by Nicholas Lynch when setting out to take over the French convent on the latter's behalf. The Master General obliged him to repay this sum of money to Louvain if it could be drawn from the assets of Beauvoir-sur-Mer, otherwise repayment was to be made by the Irish province, for whose common good the money had been spent.[76] After this, complete silence descends on the affairs of Beauvoir-sur-Mer and its link with the Irish Dominican province. It seems to have been a foundation only on paper, and presumably the abortive outcome was a bitter disappointment to those Irish Dominicans who had patiently negotiated for a house on French soil.

LOUVAIN (FOUNDED 1624)

In the opening years of the seventeenth century the Irish province was ruled by Daniel O'Crean (*alias* O'Credigan) (1600–4) and Thaddeus MacDuane (1604–8). Despite the appalling difficulties facing their subjects, who grew fewer every year, both vicars provincial were men of hope and vision. MacDuane in particular saw the need of a continental

76 Ibid., 290–91.

house of refuge which might become a house of studies for young Dominicans. He explored the possibilities of establishing a convent in the Spanish Low Countries. According to John O'Heyne, author of *Epilogus Chronologicus* (1706), MacDuane succeeded in finding a refuge for his brethren in Flanders, though no Irish Dominicans settled there while he was in office.[77]

The first veiled reference to an Irish Dominican presence in Louvain occurs in 1613. On 24 October of that year Philip III wrote to the Archduke Albert, governor of the Low Countries, concerning alms to be granted to seminaries and convents of English, Scots and Irish as recommended in a memorial submitted by the papal nuncio in Flanders. It is in this document that Dominicans are first named among the 'foreign religious' who had seminaries at Louvain. They were to receive a monthly allowance of 40 escudos.[78] Since at that time there were no English, Scots or other foreign Dominicans with seminaries in Flanders, the reference can only be to the Irish. In May 1622 the general chapter of Milan commended the Irish Dominicans to John de Loix, O.P., provincial of Lower Germany, that he might gain for them the favour of Flemish magnates.[79] A formal commission in broader terms was issued to the same provincial by the Master General on 1 January 1623, empowering him to procure alms and other forms of support among magnates and prelates, with a view to building a house or houses for English, Scots and Irish Dominicans in Belgium or in some other convenient territory.[80] Some months later John (Fitz)David became the first Irish Dominican to receive holy orders at Brussels and Louvain (between March and June 1623) in the archdiocese of Malines.[81] This too may indicate that the Irish Dominicans already had a house of some kind at Louvain by 1623. However, it must be admitted that John (Fitz)David could have lived in a Flemish Dominican house.

The first known house of the Irish Dominicans in Louvain was opened in 1624[82] during the provincialate of Ross MacGeoghegan. In that year too the Irish Pastoral College of Louvain for diocesan clergy was established

77 O'Heyne, *Epil. Chron.*, 274–7. Followed by de Jonghe, *Belgium Dominicanum* (1719), 418; Burke, *Hib. Dom.* (1762), 430–31; E. Reusens and V. Barbier, *Analectes pour servir à l'Histoire Ecclésiastique de la Belgique*, 2e sér., vii, Louvain 1892, 149.

78 Jennings, 'Miscellaneous Documents, I: 1588–1634', 78.

79 Reichert, *MOPH*, xi, 342.

80 Fenning, *Irish material*, 282.

81 A. M. Bogaerts, *De Dominikanen in de Wijdingsregisters van het Aartsbisdom Mechelen*, Brussels 1965, 30, 33. David (Davidis) was an alumnus of the Irish college of Douai. J. Brady (ed.), 'The Irish Colleges in the Low Countries' in *Archiv Hib.*, 14 (1949), 80.

82 The year of the foundation was not later than 1624. Burke, *Hib. Dom.*, 431. O'Heyne and de Jonghe mistakenly give the year as 1626.

by Archbishop MacMahon of Dublin.[83] The University of Louvain, founded in 1425, was one of the foremost centres of learning in Europe, and it had strong Irish connections. Richard Bermingham, O.P. (*alias* Richard of St Dominic) of Athenry, procurator general of the Irish province, rented the church of St John the Baptist and an adjoining house called the Niklaashof on Mont César from James de Martinet, knight of the Order of St John of Jerusalem (Knights of Malta) on a six-year lease. This historic property, once owned by the Knights Templar, had been vacated by English members of the Society of Jesus. Here the Irish Dominicans lived for two years within the parish of St James.[84] They were then compelled to move to another house, near the chapel of St George, which would shelter the community for forty years until finally they established their own college in Louvain.[85]

The years 1626–7 were marked by intense activity, most notably on the part of Ross MacGeoghegan, but also by Richard Caron, Propaganda Fide and the community itself, to obtain recognition and royal financial support. Two lists compiled at this period provide valuable evidence on the personnel of the Irish Dominican community at Louvain. The first list, drawn up in the spring of 1626,[86] records twelve Irish Dominicans as resident in the Louvain house: Ross MacGeoghegan, prior provincial of Ireland; Dominic of the Rosary O'Daly, superior; Michael of the Holy Spirit, lector of philosophy; James of St Mary, priest; Dominic de Caena, priest; Edmund of the Rosary Barry, priest; Antoninus of the Holy Spirit, student; Dominic of St Thomas, student; Michael of St Mary, student; Dominic Creagh, novice; Thaddeus of the Ascension, laybrother; and Richard Power, laybrother. The second list, entitled 'The Names of the Irish Brethren of the Order of Preachers resident in the College of the same Order and Nation at Louvain',[87] was compiled in the autumn of 1626 for the Archduchess Isabella and the Spanish authorities. It contains seventeen names: in addition to those appearing in the earlier list, it includes John Fox, lector of philosophy; Richard Barry, bursar; and three students, James Barry, John Turry and Patrick Herbert. While this list indicates a slight increase in staff and students since the spring of 1626, it should be noted that neither list gives the names of the simple (non-professed) novices, which accounts for the inflated figures given for community membership in correspondence with the Flemish and Spanish administration.

83 Walsh, *The Irish Continental College Movement*, 64–5.
84 Burke, *Hib. Dom.*, 431; Reusens and Barbier, *Analectes*, 149–50, 152.
85 Coleman, *Ancient Dominican Foundations*, 112.
86 APF, SOCG, 294, f. 105r; Moran, *Spicil. Ossor.*, i, 161; reproduced in Appendix 6 (p. 329 below).
87 AGS, Secretarias Provinciales, Flandes, leg. 2434.

As early as 15 July 1626 King Philip IV wrote to his aunt the Archduchess Isabella Clara Eugenia, governor of the Spanish Low Countries, in reply to a memorial submitted to him by Richard Caron at Madrid (12 May 1626) concerning the foundation of an Irish Dominican college 'within the University of Louvain'. The king had been told that the Irish Dominicans wished to attend the theological schools of Louvain in order that they might later preach the Gospel, extirpate heresy and build up the Catholic faith in Ireland. It was proposed that a house be established in Louvain for twelve Dominicans with formal recognition as an academic community. Since these religious lacked the necessary means to accomplish the foundation and had appealed to him for aid, he requested the archduchess to inform him of the entire situation, and to favour these Dominicans in whatever way she thought best. This decision was based on the advice the king had received from the president of the council of Flanders, Inigo de Brizuela, a Dominican and formerly Bishop of Segovia.[88]

On 20 September 1626 Ross MacGeoghegan reminded the archduchess of a letter written by the King of Spain commending the Irish Dominicans of Louvain which he had presented to her 'a few days ago', together with a fresh memorial on the problems and situation of his confrères. In due course this memorial was handed over to the Flemish council of finances, but no action resulted. He subsequently brought the matter to the attention of the archduchess once again, because he had been informed that she was about to distribute a number of pensions deriving from abbeys on her personal estates. He delicately expressed the view that the alms which might be granted to the Irish Dominican college would be the more gracious were they to come directly from her royal hands; he added that they would remedy pressing needs and be a fitting reply to the king's letter. He therefore asked the archduchess to grant a pension to the college for the purpose of paying the annual rent and supporting some of its members.[89]

The archduchess thereupon consulted the university, the city of Louvain and the Archbishop of Malines on the advisability of formally recognising the Irish Dominicans as a collegial body or community. The reply of the rector and University of Louvain (8 November 1626) is extant.[90] The university confirmed that some Irish Dominicans had

88 AGRB, Conseil Privé, régime espagnol, carton 1168; original Spanish text of letter and Latin translation in Burke, *Hib. Dom.*, 434. This list contains a number of inaccuracies and inconsistencies in comparison with the earlier list; for example, Michael of St Mary is erroneously entered as Michael of the Assumption, and Thaddeus of the Ascension as Thaddeus of the Assumption.

89 AGRB, Papiers d'État et de l'Audience, carton 1168.

90 Latin text of letter in B. de Jonghe, *Belgium Dominicanum*, 418–19, and Burke, *Hib. Dom.*, 432.

been living in a rented house of the Order of St John of Malta on the hill opposite the royal castle for about two years, and stated that they were in possession of a papal bull granting them the right to have a privileged altar in their house. The university authorities highly commended their spirit of study and piety, which in time would enable them 'to resist the enemies of the church with the arms of erudition and virtue and fight manfully against them on their return to their country'. The testimonial concluded by commending the Irish Dominicans not simply because they would study in the theological schools of Louvain, but also on account of Belgium's debt to the Irish nation which had sent the first heralds of the Gospel and Catholic faith to their country.

The Flemish council of state reported on 28 November 1626 that the provincial of the Irish Dominicans had petitioned that their residence in Louvain be given legal recognition as a 'community within the city of Louvain'. When consulted, the Archbishop of Malines and the University of Louvain were both of the view that such recognition could only be granted by the king. The civic authorities of Louvain were, however, staunchly opposed to formal recognition. Their suggestion was that the Irish Dominicans should reside in another city or place where the people would be better able to receive and support them. Louvain, they pointed out, was already greatly burdened by houses of religious orders which it could scarcely support. The Irish Dominicans, already in Louvain for about two years, had found themselves without means and were almost destitute. In view of the position expressed by the municipal authorities, the council of state decided that it could not grant the Dominican request. It was admitted that while the Irish Dominicans did not wish to be a burden on the city, nonetheless it was felt that finding themselves in great need, they would then take steps which would interfere with the citizens and the interests of the other mendicant houses of Louvain.[91] There is strong evidence, therefore, that in their first years at Louvain the Irish Dominicans lived in extreme poverty, without royal patronage or that of the Archduchess Isabella Clara Eugenia. On 16 December 1626 the council of state informed the archduchess that it had consulted the Archbishop of Malines about the inconvenience alleged by the municipality of Louvain should a formal right of residence be accorded to the Irish Dominicans. The archbishop had replied that such objections were not his business, and while acknowledging that Louvain was burdened with religious houses, he believed that the Dominican provincial and his brethren would not obtain much assistance from the city anyhow.[92] Meanwhile the petitioner Ross MacGeoghegan had presented another

91 AGRB, Conseil Privé, régime espagnol, carton 15. There are three versions of this document, showing purely verbal and minor differences.

92 Ibid.

memorial which he hoped the archduchess might take into consideration before reaching a final decision. A note in Spanish was added by an official to the effect that the licence sought could be granted under conditions to be determined by the council.[93]

Finally, on 18 December 1626, the Archduchess Isabella granted the long-sought legal recognition required by the Irish Dominicans of Louvain, formally announcing that their house was 'an established community within the University of Louvain'. The document of approbation noted that Ross MacGeoghegan had obtained earlier in that year permission for a privileged altar in their chapel, but that the archbishop objected to their using this faculty until the community received official recognition within the university. More importantly, the document contained a clause forbidding them to beg for alms.[94] The question of their material support was not raised. However, the course of political events soon compelled Ross MacGeoghegan to raise the matter urgently.

Dominic O'Daly was superior of the house from at least 1626 to 1628, a time of great economic crisis and uncertainty about the college's survival. He surely played a key role with Ross MacGeoghegan in helping to surmount the obstacles endangering its stability, though curiously he is not mentioned in the extant Flemish State Papers. In October 1627 the Master General gave him leave to go to Madrid for one year on the business of the province and to procure help for the college of Louvain. The permission was renewed on 30 April 1628,[95] and in that year he left for Madrid and ceased to be a member of the Louvain community.

When writing to her nephew King Philip IV on 3 February 1627,[96] the archduchess asserted that up to that date the Irish Dominicans had maintained themselves by the continual aid they received from relatives and friends in Ireland. As a result of the estrangement in relations between Spain and England, this means of support had been cut off. As they had no other source of income, the Irish provincial had appealed for help to the king, to compensate them for the losses they had suffered. The archduchess, in turn, had promised commendatory letters to the king in which they would be declared worthy of the royal alms. Undeterred by financial problems, Ross MacGeoghegan worked to enhance the status of the fledgling Louvain community and to extend its scope by having it designated a novitiate of the Irish province. The letters patent setting up the novitiate, granted by Master General Serafino Secchi,

93 Complete Latin version of text in O'Heyne, *Epil. Chron.*, 276–9. Incomplete Latin versions of original document in French in de Jonghe, *Belgium Dominicanum*, 419–20, and copied by Burke, *Hib. Dom.*, 433.

94 AGRB, Papiers d'État et de l'Audience, carton 2017. French text (undated) in Burke, *Hib. Dom.*, 435.

95 Fenning, *Irish material*, 283.

96 AGRB, Conseil Privé, régime espagnol, carton 1168.

were addressed to Ross MacGeoghegan on 9 February 1627. It was noted that the Louvain community, 'the cloistered house of St John', then numbered fourteen and was devoted to religious life and study. The reception of young Irishmen as novices who would later study in Louvain, it was claimed, would contribute significantly to the restoration of the Irish province. The vicar or superior of the house was authorised to take in novices, at least four at a time, provided that in each single case they were expressly approved by the provincial and met the requirements of Dominican and canon law. The house should be so ordered spiritually and materially that it might accommodate the novices and ensure their education under strict discipline.[97] This development indicated an increase of novices who could not be catered for in Ireland owing to political pressures; it may also have been perceived as an advantageous arrangement whereby professed novices could study in the same house or go elsewhere.

By the spring of 1627 the financial situation of the Louvain community had become alarming. On 14 April 1627 the cardinals of Propaganda Fide instructed the nuncio at Brussels to do all in his power to assist the poverty-stricken Irish Dominicans of Louvain.[98] This letter revealed that Ross MacGeoghegan, the provincial, had taken up residence in Louvain owing to intensified religious persecution in Ireland. He was living with sixteen of his brethren who were engaged in 'the study of the sacred sciences', for the purpose of eventually returning to Ireland to convert heretics. The Dominicans having been deprived of their annual financial contributions and all other help from Ireland on account of hostilities between England and Spain, the nuncio was asked to intervene with the archduchess on their behalf. Financial assistance was imperative if the Dominicans were not to be forced to give up their convent to the great detriment of the faith in Ireland. Evidently the archduchess and her council had not helped the Irish Dominicans with alms either from state funds or from her privy purse, nor had the ban on their right to quest for offerings been lifted.

97 Latin text in Burke, *Hib. Dom.* (Supplement, 1772), 858; Fenning, *Irish material*, 282.

98 AGRB, Conseil Privé, régime espagnol, carton 1168. On 24 April 1627 Propaganda Fide wrote to the Archbishop of Malines soliciting his support for the Irish Dominicans in Louvain. APF, Lettere Latini, I, f. 140. On 28 May Fabio de Lagonissa, nuncio at Brussels, informed Cardinal Bandini of Propaganda that as instructed he had recommended the Irish Dominicans of Louvain to His Highness (prince unnamed), who was well disposed to help them. APF, SOCG, 129, f. 278r. The same cardinal wrote (24 Aug. 1626) to the Archbishop of Malines requesting him to extend his favour to the Irish Dominicans studying at Louvain. Mechelen (Malines), Archives of Archbishopric of Mechelen–Brussels, Dominikanen, doos 36. On 3 August the nuncio at Madrid wrote to Cardinal Ludovisi saying that he would do his best to help Ross MacGeoghegan and his fellow Irish Dominicans in Louvain. APF, SOCG, 129, f. 173r.

Towards the end of April the archduchess informed her nephew Philip IV that before granting legal recognition to the Irish Dominicans of Louvain as a collegiate body she had consulted the Archbishop of Malines and the University of Louvain. She had conceded to the Dominicans what they had asked for, and not finding any other way in which she could be of service to them, she left the outstanding issues to the king's discretion.[99] To this bland, non-commital letter the king replied on 18 May that he had been unable to make a decision whether or not to help them. The matter could not be resolved until Madrid had received a direct and formal reply to the king's letter of 15 July 1626 requesting full information concerning the actual needs of the Irish Dominicans and the archduchess's personal assessment of them. Before making his decision, therefore, the king asked his aunt to state unequivocally whether these Dominicans should be helped, and, if so, in what precise way, so that he might make the necessary arrangements.[100]

Probably as a result of more inquiries by the secretariat of the archduchess, the Irish Dominicans submitted yet another memorandum of their affairs dated 9 July 1627.[101] At last they understood that negotiations were in train to extend assistance. The polite but tiresome decision-shuffling between Brussels and Madrid was drawing to a close. The memorandum showed that the Irish Dominican community paid an annual rent of 300 florins for their house, without having any legal title to it. They lacked house furnishings, a library, altar requisites and a (public) church. Even when taking into account the enormous drain on the royal finances caused by wars against heretics in so many places, the Irish Dominicans considered their request modest and stated that it was not sought in perpetuity. What they wanted was adequate support for twenty-four friars, to cover the cost of maintaining the two courses of arts and theology which would be obligatory until such time as God would grant them a place to conduct their studies in Ireland. While awaiting a more satisfactory financial arrangement they would be content with a decent allowance from the budgets of the garrisons of Antwerp or Ghent or provision similar to that made for their brothers, the Irish Franciscans of Louvain. (They did not elaborate on the precise nature of this provision.) They therefore begged the archduchess to inform the king of their abject poverty in the hope that he would speedily remedy it.

In August the archduchess replied to Philip IV clarifying the needs of the Irish Dominicans and the help she thought they required. While fully aware of the great number of religious houses at Louvain and the impossibility of helping all of them, she reminded the king that the Irish

99 AGRB, Conseil Privé, régime espagnol, carton 1168.
100 Ibid.
101 Ibid.

Dominicans had settled at Louvain without endowments of any sort and therefore gave it as her opinion that the twenty-four members of the community should be given financial assistance, and that this assistance should be at the rate of at least 100 florins each per annum. The archduchess left it to the king's judgement whether this provision would be sufficient for the support and education of the Dominicans at Louvain or elsewhere. The current group of students would in turn be replaced by others, and thus the community would become a seminary which would play an essential role in promoting the growth of the Catholic religion in countries subject to the King of England. These aims could not be achieved by the meagre alms of individual benefactors. She therefore recommended that the king should assign 100 florins yearly to each Dominican either from the army funds, from those of Antwerp or Ghent, or from those set aside to maintain the Irish Franciscans. Considering the moderation of the Irish Dominican request at a time when the cost of living was very high in the Low Countries, the archduchess also recommended payment of 1,000 *philippas* yearly, with the obligation of continuing to maintain twenty-four students in the seminary, in accordance with its declared aims.[102] The archduchess's earlier unexplained reservations about the Irish Dominicans had quite disappeared.

In early September 1627 the Irish friars sent a memorandum to Philip IV in reply to his request for information about their numbers, the way in which he might support them, and the purpose of their house at Louvain.[103] The principal aim of this house, they said, was to prepare Dominicans to preach the faith competently in Ireland by studying arts and theology. With this in view, four lectors and a master of students were employed, and in each course of studies there were seven or eight students. Three officials governed the house: the prior, subprior, and bursar. Two or three laybrothers looked after the sacristy, the door, the kitchen and refectory. To achieve its purpose the house needed a community of twenty-four, and the minimum support for each one, not counting clothes, books and other expenses, would be 100 florins yearly. Such assistance was not being sought in perpetuity, but only for such a time as the king would be pleased to help them and until they would be able to train their students in Ireland. They asked for alms by way of an ecclesiastical pension or from the funds of the armed forces (as was the arrangement for the English Carthusians and Irish Franciscans of Louvain) or in any other way, so that the alms requested by the cardinals of Propaganda Fide, the papal nuncios of Spain and Flanders and by the Infanta Isabella might be made available to them.

102 Ibid. Original minute of letter (dated 12 Aug. 1627) in Jennings, 'Miscellaneous Documents, I: 1588–1634', 136.

103 AGRB, Conseil Privé, régime espagnol, carton 1168.

In the autumn of 1627, when the grave financial crisis at Louvain still remained unresolved, Michael of the Holy Spirit, O.P., formerly a member of the community and then procurator at the Roman curia, presented a memorial to the Pope outlining their difficulties and asking him to write on their behalf to the King of Spain, the Infanta Isabella of Flanders, the Archbishop of Malines and the University of Louvain. This memorial was handed over to Propaganda Fide and was endorsed on 7 October 1627, with the comment that letters had been dispatched to the papal representatives and replies to them had already been received.[104] In November Michael of the Holy Spirit informed Ingoli, secretary of the congregation, that the commendatory letters had already brought relief to his brethren at Louvain. He asked that similar letters be written to Prince Leopold Ferdinand, the Elector of Cologne, to the University of Louvain and to the archbishop in charge of the Roman curial office which controlled appointments to benefices. His petition was endorsed on 23 November 1627, when a meeting of the congregation approved of it.[105] The drafts of four letters from Propagande Fide to the archbishop of the Camera, the Archbishop-Elector of Cologne, the University of Louvain and to Benedictine abbots of Belgium are basically the same in content.[106] Grave economic difficulties had arisen for the Irish Dominicans of Louvain, principally on account of the wars involving England, Spain, France and Holland, which had cut off their normal income from Ireland. The Dominicans had been reduced to penury, while the very existence of their college which had already produced most commendable 'fruits' was now threatened. Propaganda stressed that there was a shortage in Ireland of priests specially trained for the mission, and that Ireland itself was in serious danger of becoming Protestant. Financial aid for the Irish Dominican college of Louvain was urgently needed.

On 26 November 1627 a memorandum from Ross MacGeoghegan was considered by the King of Spain and the president of the council of Flanders, Bishop Inigo de Brizuela, O.P.[107] The memorandum recalled the many appeals of the Irish Dominicans for royal assistance in the form of some revenue available in Flanders, and referred to the correspondence exchanged between the Infanta Isabella and the king on the subject over the past year. The support required for twenty-four Dominicans was calculated as being not less than 2,400 florins per annum. The bishop-president was of the view that since these Dominicans had managed to live without the king's alms in the past, half the amount requested might be sanctioned from the funds of some Flemish garrison

104 APF, SOCG, 387, ff 313r, 318v.
105 Ibid., ff 403r, 408v.
106 APF, Lettere Latine, I, ff 158rv–160rv, 170v.
107 AGS, Secretarias Provinciales, Flandes, leg. 2434.

or from those of the Flemish army. With this less than generous opinion the king concurred. It appears that this annuity was first paid some time late in 1627, but only intermittently thereafter for as long as Flanders was ruled by Spain (the Spanish Low Countries became part of the Austrian empire in the eighteenth century). At the end of 1627 or early in 1628 Oliver Burke, Dominican procurator representing the interests of the Irish province at Rome, asked Propaganda Fide to thank the University of Louvain for its singular kindness to the Irish Dominicans; not only had they been admitted to the university for their studies, but the university had been most liberal in providing for their material needs.[108] His silence about the response of the other high ecclesiastics in the Low Countries and elsewhere may indicate that the appeals of Propaganda Fide for the Louvain college had been futile. On 29 December 1627 Ross MacGeoghegan, whose extended provincialate had come to an end, was appointed vicar provincial with full authority over the college at Louvain on the grounds that the war situation impeded the new provincial from exercising his authority in the college. The appointment was to last until normal conditions prevailed and alternative arrangements were made by the provincial.[109]

That the Irish Dominicans of Louvain had close links with other groups of Irishmen in the Low Countries is shown from a petition to the archduchess in February 1628.[110] Some captains of the Irish brigade at Santuliet, aware that the Dominicans were forbidden to eat meat, had given them two barrels of fish. Two further barrels of fish donated to the Irish Franciscans of Louvain had been placed under embargo at Antwerp, though permission was later obtained to retrieve them. The Dominicans, apprehensive of finding themselves in a similar situation, obtained a licence from the archduchess to transport their two barrels of salted fish to Louvain, free of tax. From the late 1620s there is impressive evidence that Irish Dominicans based at Louvain ministered to English-speakers, Irish soldiers especially, in Flanders.[111] The Franciscans, and Irish diocesan priests too, were much involved in this ministry.[112]

108 APF, SOCG, 388, ff 3r, 4rv, 6v.
109 Fenning, *Irish material*, 283.
110 AGRB, Papiers d'État et de l'Audience, carton 2023.
111 The following Irish Dominicans received faculties for preaching and hearing confessions within the jurisdiction of the archdiocese of Malines, 1628–44: John Baptist David (23 Dec. 1628), Patrick MacTeig (7 Sept. 1629, 1 July 1633), John Walter (20 Feb. 1633, 1 Feb. 1634), Thaddeus Haurke (22 Aug. 1636), Patrick Carny (7 Nov. 1644). A. M. Bogaerts, *De Dominikanen in de Jurisdictiebrieven van het Aartsbisdom Mechelen*, Brussels 1966, 17–23. Not listed in B. Jennings (ed.), 'Irish Preachers and Confessors in the Archdiocese of Malines, 1607– 1794' in *Archiv. Hib.* 23 (1960).
112 Jennings, 'Irish Preachers and Confessors', 148–66.

The Master General appointed John of St Raymund vicar of Louvain on 24 March 1629.[113] This is the first recorded instance of direct intervention by the Master of the Order in the affairs of the college—an interference which would increasingly cause strain and eventually become the subject of appeals to the Spanish crown. On 24 April 1629 Richard Caron, then winding up his affairs as Irish Dominican procurator in Spain, was peremptorily ordered by the Master General to give an exact account of the money he had gathered for Louvain since 1626 and to pay 20 silver ducats to the otherwise unknown Antoninus of St Nicholas, O.P.[114] The general chapter of Rome in June 1629, at which the provincial, Nicholas Lynch, represented the province, made a strongly worded admonition about Louvain. The brethren of the college were strictly forbidden to interfere with the curriculum of studies. This was to be the business only of the rector or the superior of the college, and of the moderators and students chosen by the provincial or the diffinitory of the provincial chapter. The college itself was to be totally subject to the provincial in every way.[115] On 25 August 1629 the Flemish Dominican Philip de Wannemaeckere was made procurator of the college, with responsibility for the collection of alms throughout Belgium.[116] In the course of that year the community petitioned Propaganda Fide that in the papal brief permitting them to have a privileged altar the clause stipulating that ten Masses be celebrated daily in their church should be modified. It was pointed out that though they had a church or chapel of their own, their main occupation was study. Only the superior and three lectors were priests, the rest of the community consisting of young students. They therefore asked for a reduction in the number of Masses to be celebrated from ten to four.[117]

In September or October 1629 Ross MacGeoghegan, now Bishop-elect of Kildare, secretly received episcopal consecration at Brussels[118] and left Louvain for Ireland. He was undoubtedly responsible for the efforts leading to the establishment of the college in 1624, for obtaining the permanent right of residence of a collegiate body of Irish Dominicans in the university and city of Louvain, for channelling benefactions and aid for the new college from Ireland and Spain, for rescuing the community from financial disaster and providing for their everyday needs in the first critical years of the college's existence, and finally for obtaining their annual subsidy from the royal treasury. He also had the college designated

113 Fenning, *Irish material*, 284.
114 Ibid.
115 Reichert, *MOPH*, xii, 2, 52.
116 Fenning, *Irish material*, 285.
117 APF, SOCG, 389, ff 430r, 435v.
118 Lynch, *De Praesulibus Hib.*, i, 339.

a novitiate and obtained for his students the entrée to the arts and theology schools of Louvain. To him, therefore, more than to anybody else belongs the distinction and honour due to the founder of the college at Louvain.

In the meantime relations between the community and the Master General had deteriorated to such an extent that the Irish Dominicans felt constrained to make an appeal about their grievance to the King of Spain. On 20 December 1629 Philip IV ordered his council of state to consider a memorial submitted to him by the Irish provincial and by the prior and community of 'Holy Cross College' concerning the interference of the Master General in their affairs.[119] The Dominicans claimed that from the start the college had been placed under the jurisdiction of the Irish Dominican provincial, and was therefore not immediately under that of the Masters General, and that this accorded with the rule and constitutions of the Order. What is clear is that the then Master General, Nicholas Ridolfi, exercised immediate jurisdiction over the college, overriding that of the Irish provincial, notwithstanding the declaration of the June 1629 chapter to the contrary. This situation had created difficulties for the college. The memorial gave no hint as to why the Master General took such a keen interest in Louvain's affairs, or of what the consequent difficulties for the community were. The Louvain Dominicans asked that the Spanish ambassador at Rome be instructed to confer with the Pope about the much-resented novelty of the Master General's interference. The Spanish state council advised that the matter should be referred to the state council of Flanders and its opinion sought on the dispute.

There is little to say about the internal life and development of the college during the 1630s; sources of information rarely go beyond routine personal appointments in the registers of the Masters General. In May 1630 Patrick MacTeig recalled how he had been lately sent to Louvain, though he was sixty years of age, to govern the college, which he described as poor, unable to support its resident members, and even deprived of the revenues destined by the King of Spain for its annual upkeep.[120] Nicholas Lynch, the Irish provincial, visiting the college in September 1630, was permitted to forward his correspondence to Rome by courtesy of the Flemish administration.[121] On 9 October 1631 Peter Malpe,[122] of the province of Lower Germany, was nominated lector of Hebrew at the

119 AGS, Estado, leg. 3888.

120 Ibid., leg. 2793.

121 AGRB, Papiers d'État et de l'Audience, carton 2045.

122 Petrus Malpeus, Flemish Dominican author of *Palma Fidei Ordinis Praedicatorum*, Antwerp 1635, and several other works on the Dominican Order. Quétif and Echard, *Scriptores Ordinis Praedicatorum*, ii, 547.

college by the Master General. It was noted that he might not be dismissed from his post by anybody less than the Master of the Order himself.[123] The appointments of Philip de Wannemaeckere and Peter Malpe clearly indicate problems of staffing the newly established Irish Dominican college, as well as the concern of the Master General and the willingness of the Flemish Dominicans to co-operate with their Irish confrères.

Patrick MacTeig's tenure of office as rector of the college was brief. On 17 October 1631 Dominic Nugent, the first effectively to hold the office of rector, having been nominated by Nicholas Lynch himself, was confirmed as 'rector of the college of St John the Baptist, Louvain';[124] he held the appointment until 1634. Regulations for the government of the college were drawn up and forwarded to Louvain by Nicholas Lynch on 23 October,[125] most likely in consequence of a canonical visitation carried out by Lynch himself in the autumn of 1630. In a memorial to the Spanish king, dated 1633, Dominic of the Rosary O'Daly rather brashly described himself as being responsible for two continental Irish Dominican foundations: one in Flanders and one in Lisbon. He saw each college 'as a fortress against the heretics' and blithely asserted that both houses were in a sound state. John Walter was appointed vicar *in capite* of the college on 11 March 1634. It was left to the coming provincial chapter to nominate a new rector, Dominic Nugent having offered his resignation on account of illness to the Master General.[126] Oliver Burke, the former Roman procurator and a *filius* of the convent of Galway, was chosen as rector of Louvain by the Irish provincial chapter of 1634.[127] The Master of the Order apparently accepted his nomination.

In the spring of 1635 Oliver Burke, simultaneously rector of Louvain and Vicar Apostolic of Kilmacduagh in the west of Ireland, petitioned the Pope concerning pastoral ministry among the Catholic regiments of Spain in the Low Countries. He reported that there were several thousand Irish, English and Scots soldiers fighting for Spain against the Dutch. Individual Irish and English Dominicans had been looking after the spiritual welfare of two regiments. As there were opportunities here of strengthening the faith of Catholics and of converting Protestants, he asked for apostolic missionary faculties (such as were normally granted to priests working in the dominions of the King of England) to facilitate his ministry among the Irish, English and Scots. He also asked permission to delegate such faculties in whole or in part to the military

123 Fenning, *Irish material*, 288.
124 Ibid.
125 Ibid., 289.
126 Ibid., 294.
127 APF, SOCG, 396, f. 71r.

chaplains and preachers concerned. Propaganda Fide, to whom the Pope had passed on this request, referred it to the Congregation of the Holy Office on 23 April 1635, noting that attestations to the good character and conduct of the chaplains should be supplied.[128] At a meeting of Propaganda Fide on 14 January 1636 a request from Dominic Burke, Irish Dominican procurator in Rome, was put before the cardinals about an impending change of house on the part of the Louvain community. The Dominicans were under pressure to quit the house they lived in, as the owner wanted to repossess the premises that very year. The community, which had about twenty members, had applied to the Spanish administration for possession of a house recently confiscated from a heretic. Dominic Burke asked the cardinals to recommend his confrères to the Archbishop of Malines, who might intercede with the Spanish officials for them. Propaganda Fide decided to write to the Archbishop of Malines on the matter.[129]

The Master of the Order, Nicholas Ridolfi, wrote to the Pope in January 1636 about Oliver Burke, still concurrently rector of Louvain and vicar apostolic of the small rural diocese of Kilmacduagh. He recalled that Burke had been appointed to the office, with the right of deputing another person in case of necessity, as his diocesan responsibilities did not exempt him from obedience to his Order. He had been made rector of Louvain by his provincial and provincial chapter at a time when the college was close to ruin as a result of fierce warfare in Flanders. His provincial and definitors, whose total confidence he enjoyed, requested permission for Burke to reside outside his Irish diocese in order to concentrate on his work at Louvain; they also asked for a learned and suitable person to be appointed to govern Kilmacduagh as his deputy. It was mentioned that no emolument could be received or expected from this apostolic vicariate. The Pope forwarded the Master General's petition to Propaganda Fide. There Ingoli, secretary of the congregation, added a number of comments. He explained that the Irish Dominican college at Louvain had been deprived of its customary subsidy from the Spanish crown because of the war. He judged that it was not appropriate to grant the indult sought, as there was no shortage of Irish secular clergy to whom the vicariate might be entrusted. Indeed, it would be better not to have religious appointees in such vicariates, as they considered themselves and their vicariates subject to the jurisdiction of their own superiors.[130] The matter came up for discussion at a meeting of a

128 Ibid., 395, ff 48r, 51v. Burke had received the Master General's approbation to hold the office of vicar general of Kilmacduagh on 7 November 1629. Fenning, *Irish material*, 285.

129 APF, SOCG, 396, ff 15r, 22v; Jennings, 'Acta Propaganda Fide', 97.

130 APF, SOCG, 396, ff 71r, 74v.

general congregation on 11 February 1636, where a negative decision was made: Oliver Burke should resign from Kilmacduagh, as his responsibilities there could easily be undertaken by an Irish diocesan priest.[131]

At all events Oliver Burke managed to retain his dual responsibilities as Vicar Apostolic of Kilmacduagh and rector of the Irish Dominican college of Louvain until December 1636. Following Rome's refusal to grant him a dispensation from the obligation of personal residence in his diocese or permission to name a substitute, he was finally forced to choose between his conflicting responsibilities. On 6 December 1636 he was released by the Master of the Order from the rectorship of Louvain and was ordered to proceed to Ireland at the very first opportunity.[132] On the same day letters for the formal appointment of a vicar *in capite*, to be selected from among the members of the college by the Flemish Dominican, Master Thomas Leonard, were sent in blank form, to be filled in with the appointee's name. Master Leonard was to see to it that somebody competent was appointed and that the business was transacted peaceably. The Master General also wrote to the Irish provincial asking him to find a new rector for the college.[133]

The departure of Oliver Burke to assume his diocesan duties may genuinely have caused a serious void at Louvain and made the period of transition to the next rector a very uneasy one, if not a time of indecision and dissension. Whatever the reason, the Master General intervened once more in the business of the college on 1 August 1637, following a set pattern, by naming James Dunn, O.P., as vicar, with full responsibility for the college until such time as the Irish provincial sent a rector to Louvain.[134] Later in the year (3 October) two college appointments were approved: Patrick Kearney, O.P., as lector, and Thomas Burke, O.P., as master of studies. On 9 November both these men were permitted by the Master General to graduate from the university.[135]

131 Jennings, 'Acta Propaganda Fide', 98.

132 Fenning, *Irish material*, 296. First appointed Vicar Apostolic of Kilmacduagh on 28 Nov. 1629, he remained in office until 11 Mar. 1647, when Hugh Burke, O.F.M., his cousin, succeeded as bishop of the diocese. Eubel, *Hier. Cath.*, iv, 177. In the 1640s he governed Kilmacduagh and concurrently acted as vicar general to his brother, John Burke, Bishop of Clonfert. *The Memoirs and Letters of Ulick, Marquis of Clanricarde and Earl of St Alban's*, London 1757, 322; *Letter-Book of the Earl of Clanricarde, 1643–47*, ed. J. Lowe, Dublin 1983, 377.

133 Fenning, *Irish material*, 296.

134 Ibid.

135 Ibid. Richard Pauli-Stravius, papal representative in Flanders, writing to Propaganda Fide about the affairs of the Irish colleges in Louvain on 28 February 1636, referred to a letter of Thomas Fleming, Archbishop of Dublin (1623–51), in which he supported increases in burses for Franciscans and Dominicans studying at Louvain University. W. Brulez, 'Correspondence de Richard Pauli-Stravius (1634–1642)' in *Analecta Vaticano-Belgica: Nonciature de Flandre*, x, Brussels/Rome 1955, 126, note 2.

The rector (unnamed) and college of Louvain sent a petition, dated 17 August 1638, to the King of Spain about their royal subsidy.[136] They recalled the decision of the president of the council of Flanders in 1627, whereby they were to receive a grant of 1,200 florins per month (*recte* per year). Yet when the grant was collected, more than half this amount had to be paid out in unspecified expenses. The king was asked to make a more satisfactory financial arrangement, such as a regular income from an abbey or from the same fund which supported the Irish Franciscan college at Louvain, and with equal punctuality. The Spanish state council recommended that the Infanta Isabella be requested to see to the prompt payment of the amount granted by the king every year. On 18 August 1640 Walter Butler was installed as rector of the 'college of St Margaret's, of the Irish province, at Louvain', replacing Master John Nolan, rector from before April of that year.[137] This third title of the college probably indicated its latest location in the city of Louvain. The yearly grant of 1,200 florins for the upkeep of the college and the wider aim of supporting the Catholic faith in Ireland continued to be paid by the Spanish authorities until about 1640. Thereafter problems arose and payments were postponed because of extreme pressure on the financial resources of Flanders.

In the first two decades of its existence the title of the Irish Dominican college often changed—a symptom, perhaps, of its own instability and lack of security. It was variously referred to in official documents as the college of St John the Baptist, Holy Cross College and the college of St Margaret. Only when the Irish Dominicans succeeded after many vicissitudes in building their own college and church did Holy Cross become its permanent title. Its precarious existence during its first sixteen years was partly due to a succession of financial crises. External political circumstances, particularly the wars waged by Spain against Holland and England, weakened contact with Ireland and hindered the flow of students and money. No information is available on how money passed between Ireland and the Irish Dominicans at Louvain in times of relative calm. Irish Catholic merchants may have helped to arrange matters by supplying letters of credit or exchange to their fellow Irish or Flemish trading partners at the ports of Ostend and Antwerp. Archdeacon John Lynch alludes to the ever-recurrent financial crises at Louvain and mentions a venerable gentleman (but not his nationality) who more than once donated money at the opportune moment to a worried community. Because of the donor's insistence on remaining anonymous, Ross MacGeoghegan too demanded strictest silence and confidentiality from his confrères about these charitable gifts.[138]

136 AGS, Estado, leg. 2801.
137 Fenning, *Irish material*, 304, 301.
138 Lynch, *De Praesulibus Hib.*, i, 338.

Internal dissensions, factions and 'provincialism' and problems of staffing may have been the main reasons why the Masters General insisted on intervening frequently in the college's affairs, in the absence of effective government both by distant Irish provincials and by the Dominicans of Holy Cross as the century advanced. The Irish Dominicans, whether in Ireland or at Louvain, were too weak to offer an effective challenge to any Master General in the age of absolutism. For all the difficulties that marked the foundation of this college at Louvain, it was Ross MacGeoghegan, its real founder and protector, who gave it its essential missionary character. The Irish Dominican college was in fact to play a highly important part in the rebuilding of the province, and it came to constitute a significant portion of the growing Irish presence at Louvain. It helped to form a nucleus around which future Irish-inspired developments would occur, as, for example, in 1655 when three brothers named Joyce, members of a distinguished Galway family, turned a spacious house into a college on Brussels Square and began nearby the construction of a church which was completed in 1666.[139] The college archives and library were confiscated by the French revolutionary armies and disappeared for ever in 1794.

ROLE AND STATUS OF THE COLLEGES

The creation of colleges at Lisbon and Louvain obviously involved an immense struggle on the part of kings, popes, cardinals, bishops, Masters General, nuncios, ambassadors, civil servants and benefactors. The final establishment of the colleges against all odds was an enormous achievement, and an unquestionable blessing for the Irish province. In the first years of their existence the colleges were regarded as temporary, not permanent foundations, since their founders did not know how long they might be needed. The primary supposition was that they would eventually be replaced by *studia generalia* in Ireland when political and religious circumstances changed. An ordination made for the Irish province by the general chapter of 1644 at Rome provided for the erection of five 'universities' or *studia generalia* for the five provinces (*partes*) of the kingdom of Ireland. Such centres of study were to be established at Dublin, Limerick, Cashel, Athenry and Coleraine. Should adverse circumstances prevent the erection of any one of these *studia generalia*, the provincial might temporarily designate another convent in which the *studium* might be established with the academic rights of graduation etc.[140] The house

139 Coleman, *Ancient Dominican Foundations*, 112.

140 Reichert, *MOPH*, xii, 162, 99, 101. The official Irish representatives, Terence Albert O'Brien and John Nolan, would have been chiefly responsible for this proposal and its formulation, possibly acting on instructions from the Kilkenny provincial chapter of 1643.

or college of Lisbon was not strictly speaking considered 'conventual', but simply a 'college'. Its superior was not styled 'prior' but 'rector', and he was not chosen by the free vote of the members of the community, but appointed by the Master General after consultation with the college.[141] Louvain too was technically a 'house' (*domus*) or simply a 'college' until it achieved full conventual status in 1655, from which time it had the right to elect its own prior.[142] Before that date the constitutional status of both Lisbon and Louvain was anomalous—a factor which encouraged the Masters General to assume direct control of their affairs.

141 Burke, *Hib. Dom.*, 423, note a.
142 Ibid., 431, note k.

EIGHT

The Revived Province, 1627–41: Disputes with Regular and Diocesan Clergy

DISSENSIONS BETWEEN THE DOMINICANS AND OTHER RELIGIOUS ORDERS

From the 1620s the revitalised mendicant orders in Ireland held many unwarranted assumptions about their status and rights in the Catholic life of the country; nor did they wish to see them challenged. Their primary assumption was that each order should reoccupy all its medieval foundations, rural as well as urban, even if in reality those former properties were irretrievably lost. Lay friends of the friars frequently rented or secured leases of private houses on their behalf, and these were converted into temporary chapels or oratories and the living accommodation adapted for their way of life. The extent to which conditions of life had changed since the dissolution of the religious houses some fifty or eighty years before, or since the final waning of the middle ages in Ireland, may not have been fully appreciated. Younger religious orders, such as the Jesuits, who came in greater force at the turn of the century, or the Capuchins (*c.*1615) and the Discalced or Teresian Carmelites who followed in the 1620s, were looked upon with suspicion and resentment by the older regular orders: Dominicans, Franciscans, Augustinians and Calced Carmelites. These latter regarded the newcomers as unwelcome intruders and questioned the canonical status of their houses. Inevitably clashes developed between the successors of the medieval friars and the representatives of the new orders, founded or reformed in the spirit of the Council of Trent. Flashpoints developed between the two groups, particularly in the towns and cities where they were forced to live cheek by jowl, and where they found themselves in open competition not only for congregations but more essentially for material support. Nor should one underestimate certain ideological and psychological considerations: the newer orders were the embodiment of the Tridentine spirit, with distinctive modern spiritualities and pastoral methods, representing the 'shock troops' of a reforming Church; whereas the older mendicant orders, while gradually assimilating the legislative provisions of Trent, continued in Ireland to labour under many questionable attitudes which absorbed too much of their time and energy. Hence it was that in the exciting context of restoration and expansion, of obligatory adaptation to the spiritual needs of a small Catholic population, and of a necessarily secretive religious lifestyle in the towns, acrimonious and disedifying dissensions between the various religious orders soon took and held the stage.

The vigorous struggle between the Dominican and Jesuit orders on the continent, particularly on questions of speculative theology and spirituality, was reflected in Ireland in rivalry and disagreement over pastoral concerns. By the late 1620s both Jesuits and Dominicans were to be found in Drogheda, Dublin, Waterford, Cashel, Cork, Galway and Kilkenny—in fact in most of the principal towns and cities in the country—and from as early as 1626 there is a record of dissension between them. In that year the Roman procurator of the Irish Dominicans informed Propaganda Fide that his confrères in Ireland were opposed by the Jesuits and Franciscans.[1] In 1627 the Jesuits of Ireland complained to Rome of having to put up with serious annoyance and even harassment from both the regular and diocesan clergy. They alluded to similar problems which the Capuchins had had to face, and explained that thanks to the mediation of Cardinal Ludovisi, Protector of Ireland, the Capuchins at least had been freed from inconveniences and constraints. Propaganda Fide noted that notwithstanding the provisions of several papal bulls forbidding the foundation of convents without the required canonical number of religious, the Irish Jesuits sought recognition for 'mission hospices', a distinction which Rome accepted, provided certain conditions relating to the jurisdiction of the local bishop or vicar apostolic were fulfilled.[2] In spite of this decision in favour of the Irish Jesuits, it would appear that the concerted campaign of the older religious orders against the Jesuits continued. Once again in 1629 or 1630 the Jesuits protested to Cardinal Ludovisi that the friars were intent on driving them out of Ireland. One of the Jesuit petitions asserted in passing that with the advent of heresy in Ireland the friars had deserted both their monasteries and the people, and that the Apostolic See had subsequently, in 1598, sent the Jesuits to Ireland, to win the people back to the Catholic faith—a task which they had achieved in large measure and in which they were persevering.[3]

Such was the general background to a dispute that exploded in 1629 between the Irish Jesuits and Dominicans on the question of devotional practices in several unnamed towns where both orders worked in uneasy proximity. The dispute specifically concerned the Dominican Confraternity of the Most Holy Rosary and the Jesuit Sodality of the Blessed

1 APF, SOCG, 294, ff 26r, 29v.
2 Ibid., 3875 f. 224rv.
3 Ibid., 390, ff 51r, 58v; another version in f. 90r; a third and more detailed version in ff 251r, 254v, 387r.

Virgin Mary. As a last resort, both parties sought the intervention and arbitration of Rome.

In the summer of 1629 the Dominicans addressed a petition directly to the Pope, who in turn forwarded it to Propaganda Fide on 18 August 1629.[4] The Dominicans insisted that it was they who had established the Holy Rosary Confraternity in Ireland. The Dominican rosary confraternities were accustomed to meet in their own chapels on the first Sunday of the month. The Jesuits held their sodality on the same day. Since the cities and towns of the island were too small for both sodalities to meet conveniently on the same day, the Dominicans requested that the Jesuits be ordered, under threat of censure and ecclesiastical penalties, to hold their sodality meetings at a different and more opportune time in order to avoid confusion and disruption of devotion to the rosary. By stressing that their rosary confraternity considerably predated that of the Jesuits, the Dominicans implicitly claimed privileged status and right of precedence. The earliest reference to the Dominican rosary confraternity in Ireland is dated December 1569, when permission was granted for the erection of the confraternity in the dioceses of Killaloe and Raphoe.[5] The papal bull *Inter desiderabilia* (29 June 1569) had set out the structure, rules and privileges of rosary confraternities and had granted exclusive rights over their establishment to the Dominicans.[6]

The Jesuits and members of their Irish sodalities sent their petition to the cardinals of Propaganda Fide. They pointed out in the first place that the Jesuits had come to Ireland thirty years previously at the behest of the Apostolic See. In virtue of apostolic faculties the Father General of the Jesuits had set up sodalities of the Blessed Virgin Mary in Ireland, and thereafter their pastoral ministry and the promotion of Catholicism was linked to these sodality assemblies. They alleged that the Dominicans, having established their rosary confraternities at a later date, had then begun to challenge the rights of the Jesuits. They noted that on the first Sunday of each month the Dominicans held a procession within their premises and that they were complaining that it was inappropriate of the Jesuits to hold their sodality and other religious exercises on the same day.

The submissions of both parties were discussed by Propaganda Fide on 1 February 1630. It was decided that the causes of dissension between the two parties should be removed by a decree commanding the two sodalities to meet on different Sundays: that of the Dominicans on the first Sunday of the month, and that of the Jesuits on the second Sunday

4 Ibid., 390, ff 95r, 100v.

5 Fenning, *Irish material*, 273.

6 *Bullarium Ord. Praed.*, v, 214. See C. Lennon, 'Civic Life and Religion in Early Seventeenth-Century Dublin' in *Archiv. Hib.*, 38 (1983), 20, re popularity of confraternities of Dominicans, Franciscans and Jesuits.

or else on feast-days occurring between the first and second Sundays of the month, should both parties so agree. A document was formulated on 8 February to resolve the dispute, and the whole matter was referred to Cardinal Ludovisi 'that he might endeavour to reconcile both parties'.[7]

If the Jesuits had not already won Cardinal Ludovisi to their side by reason of his aristocratic family being among the principal patrons of the church of Sant'Ignazio in Rome, they were soon to do so. The Cardinal Protector very ably presented their case, outlining both Dominican objections and Jesuit replies.[8] He began by explaining that the Sodality of the Blessed Virgin Mary directed by the Jesuits, in conformity with its rules as approved by Gregory XIII, was accustomed to assemble on the first Sunday of the month, when its members confessed their sins, received Holy Communion and heard a sermon in the morning, without any procession or further solemnity. The Dominicans of Ireland had objected to this particular day and time for the said spiritual exercises on the following grounds: (1) in small towns the Jesuit meeting interfered with the procession of the Dominican rosary confraternity; (2) the Jesuit devotions diminished alms offered to the Dominicans for their support; (3) devotion to the rosary predated the foundation of the Jesuits; (4) a bull of Leo X forbade other sodalities being held on the Sunday appointed for devotion to the rosary; (5) the arrangement whereby the Dominican rosary confraternity met on the first Sunday of the month had been so approved in an earlier controversy with the Carmelites.

The Jesuits had replied that they had acted with propriety and in accord with the privileges granted to their sodality. They had then replied to the Dominican objections in turn. As to the first objection, they pointed out that the spiritual exercises of the Jesuit sodality took place in the morning, whereas the Dominican procession of the rosary followed the evening prayer of Compline. The centres in which the Jesuits and Dominicans found themselves in competition had populations of at least a thousand; in some cases they lived among a population of forty or fifty thousand. Concerning the second objection, the Jesuits argued that their meetings did not prejudice almsgiving to the Dominicans. No quest was held, nor was a collection box used at their sodality meetings. And were the Fathers of the Company to solicit alms on the same day as the Dominicans, which they roundly denied, their action would still be licit in view of the decree of the Congregation of Regulars, dated 9 January 1628, which laid down that the Discalced Carmelites might beg on the same day as the Carmelites of the Observance (Calced Carmelites). What the Jesuits alluded to here was the 'communication

7 APF, SOCG, 3903, ff 96r, 99rv; B. Jennings (ed.), 'Acta Sacrae Congregationis de Propaganda Fide, 1622–1650' in *Archiv. Hib.*, 22 (1959), 50.

8 APF, SOCG, 390, ff 46rv, 47v, 101v.

of privileges' (*communicatio privilegiorum*). Canonically, privileges granted by law or by the papacy to one mendicant or regular order were in certain instances communicable and communicated *ipso facto* to the other regular orders. Concerning the third objection, the Jesuits asserted that the Sodality of the Blessed Virgin Mary was longer established in Ireland than the rosary confraternity of the Dominicans, which they said was established only after the introduction of heresy. In Jesuit eyes, what mattered was not the date at which a sodality had been established in Ireland, but the date at which it had been introduced in those towns where the antiquity of a particular sodality was a source of controversy. Concerning the fourth objection, the bull of Leo X did not prohibit the meetings of other sodalities on the day the rosary procession took place, as was obvious from a reading of the bull. (This bull, however, was among those which had been suspended by a bull of Gregory XIII.[9] From the Irish Jesuits' observation, typical of the trained Roman canonist, it would seem that they were unaware of the suspension of previous bulls by Gregory XIII, otherwise they would have felt justified in dismissing the fourth objection out of hand.) In addition, it was pointed out that for thirty-two years the Sodality of the Blessed Virgin Mary in Ireland had remained in peaceful possession of its rights with regard to the day and the hour of its spiritual exercises. Concerning the fifth objection, it had been decreed that the Carmelites should not hold their confraternity on the first Sunday, because their processions were not in their own chapel but in the parochial church at precisely the same hour as the Dominicans held theirs. This objection raises the interesting point as to whether the Dominicans too were holding processions in parochial chapels. The Jesuits replied that their sodality meeting took place in their own house in the morning and without a procession.

Furthermore, the Jesuits argued that they could not do what the Dominicans wanted without occasioning disputes with other religious orders, for the Augustinians claimed the second Sunday, the Carmelites the third, and the Franciscans the fourth Sunday for their confraternities. Instead of one dispute, three would arise, and thus the members of the Sodality of the Blessed Virgin Mary would suffer grievously in being deprived of their rights, peaceably held for thirty-two years, in Ireland. Finally, it was argued that it would be harsh to ask for the prohibition in Ireland of the devotions of the Jesuit sodality, which were celebrated in Rome and throughout the world, where Dominicans and Jesuits lived in peace, considering that the contrary reasons were not well founded and that no member of the Sodality of the Blessed Virgin Mary could simultaneously belong to the Confraternity of the Most Holy Rosary.

9 It has not been possible to trace the precise papal bulls mentioned in the Jesuit defence, in the absence of the identifying opening words and dates.

The cardinal concluded his exposition by asking that the Irish Dominicans should be silenced on this question.

The matter was discussed at meetings of the Congregation of Propaganda Fide on 26 February and 19 March 1630.[10] Once more the entire problem was referred to Cardinal Ludovisi, with a view to reconciling the conflicting interests of the Jesuits and Dominicans, though the cardinal could hardly claim at that stage to be perfectly impartial. Ingoli, the secretary of the congregation, noted that a decree for the resolution of the dispute had been drawn up in February and approved by the Pope, but that its publication had been delayed as the Pope had decided that the Dominicans should be consulted in order to ascertain whether they had objections to it. Whether or not the decree was ever published and accepted by both sides to the dispute, or whether the cardinal succeeded in his delicate task of reconciling the Irish Dominicans and Jesuits, is not known. The matter was probably resolved quietly as a result of effective Roman arbitration. At the heart of the matter there were fears and jealousy on both sides compounded by intransigence and financial need.

There is irrefutable evidence that the Discalced Carmelites, Jesuits and Dominicans in Ireland were all made to feel in the 1620s and 1630s the power and the effects of the numerical superiority enjoyed by the Observant Franciscans. At Rome their interests were advanced and protected by the ever-influential Luke Wadding, O.F.M. In this period, nonetheless, an informal alliance existed between the Dominicans and Observant Franciscans against the Carmelites, remembered in satiric verse: 'How the Grey and the Black Friars, who could never agree among themselves, have combined and conspired against the poor White Friars'.[11] Very possibly the issue which led to joint Dominican/Franciscan opposition was the spread and growth of the Carmelite confraternity.

In 1631 a Franciscan Observant reported that his order was suffering from the interference of Augustinians, Carmelites, Dominicans and Jesuits. The controversy between the Franciscans and Dominicans focused on the stigmata of St Francis and St Catherine of Siena, and also on the origins and significance of the various religious habits. The Dominicans, this Franciscan claimed, called their habit that of the Blessed Virgin Mary, and the Carmelites made an equally strong similar claim; all this was done, however, to distract the affection and devotion of the people away from the Franciscan habit, in the knowledge that the people were more devoted to the Blessed Virgin Mary than to any other saint.[12] Franciscan

10 Jennings, 'Acta Propaganda Fide', 50–51.

11 Cited in F. X. Martin, *Friar Nugent*, London/Rome 1962, 258, note 72; mentioned in HMC, *Report on the Franciscan MSS*, Dublin 1906, 35; not edited by Jennings in *Wadding Papers*.

12 *Wadding Papers*, 459–60, 462.

tempers flared too when it became public knowledge in October 1631 that the Bishop of Killaloe had decided to provide a house for the Dominicans in Thomond 'where they never had any residence before, only to affront us and put [pull] us and them by the hairs'.[13] About 1634 the Dominicans asked Propaganda Fide for the requisite dispensation to acquire the property of other religious orders, presumably abandoned, with the consent of the former owners, though no specific houses or orders were mentioned.[14] In spite of temporary alliances and understandings, animosity between the Dominicans and Franciscans continued to fester. Tensions were clearly running very high when Theodore O'Connell, O.P., chaplain at the Spanish embassy in London, wrote to Ingoli of Propaganda Fide on 10 December 1639 that the Church in Ireland was ruled by Luke Wadding, O.F.M., who alone supplied information and recommended candidates for Irish bishoprics. He bluntly alleged that Wadding was partial in his judgements. He was also convinced that the diocesan clergy and the Franciscans were intent on suppressing the Dominicans in Ireland.[15] One can only conclude that the Dominicans and other religious competed unashamedly and sometimes excessively in their efforts to win the affection and financial support of the laity.

A further complaint of the Dominicans to Rome in 1639 concerned the damage allegedly done to them by the Franciscans in the north of Ireland. Dominic Burke, procurator at Rome, submitted two memorials to the cardinals of Propaganda Fide and to Cardinal Antonio Barberini, Protector of Ireland and the Dominican Order. Serious dissensions had arisen among Dominicans and Franciscans over questing rights in the ecclesiastical province of Armagh. The Dominicans claimed that they had become the victims of molestation and had had their questing and preaching rights restricted by the Archbishop of Armagh and the Bishop of Kilmore, while the Franciscans were given full freedom to collect alms in the Ulster dioceses.[16] At this time the Dominicans were intent on a programme of expansion and resettlement especially in the province of Armagh, where their presence had virtually been reduced to Drogheda and Derry. In fairness to the Ulster Franciscans, who had been more closely identified with the province than any other religious order, the

13 HMC, *Franciscan MSS*, 51; *Wadding Papers*, 607.

14 APF, SOCG, 139, ff 283r, 284v. There were precedents for the grant of houses of one order to another with papal approval. In the 1630s the Discalced Carmelites alleged that the Dominicans had taken over a Carmelite house in Munster (supposedly Castlelyons, Co. Cork, where there was confusion as to the ownership of two ruined medieval churches) and the Franciscans' one in Connacht. See S. A. O'Mahony, 'The Irish Discalced Carmelites, 1625–1653' (Ph.D. thesis, TCD ,1976), 80.

15 APF, SOCG, 139, ff 283r, 284v.

16 Ibid., 400, ff 144r, 156v, 127r, 140v.

Dominicans, with their insistence on ancient rights, must have appeared as unwelcome interlopers. In 1639 the Archbishop of Armagh, Hugh O'Reilly, wrote to Propaganda Fide seeking clarification concerning the rights of regulars, the Augustinians in particular, to quest in his diocese.[17] He maintained that the rights of the Augustinians had been opposed by other regulars of the diocese, Dominicans and Franciscans, who had prevailed on him to intervene, partly because the Catholic population was so poor, and partly because it was oppressed by magistrates. The Augustinians were not the only victims of combined ill-feeling on the part of other regulars resident in the archdiocese of Armagh. On 31 July 1639 the Franciscans, Dominicans and one or two Calced Carmelites who appeared on the scene sent a petition to the archbishop to enforce the decrees of Clement VIII (*Quoniam ad institutam*, 1603) and Urban VIII (*Romanus pontifex*, 1624) against permitting new foundations in his archdiocese.[18] The target of their opposition was the attempt by the Discalced Carmelites to establish themselves at Ardee, where there had been a Carmelite house until its suppression in 1539. The archbishop complied, but in the event found himself constrained to excommunicate publicly the Discalced Carmelites, who refused to relinquish their post at Ardee. The distasteful petition resulting in this scandalous episode was signed by two Dominicans: John Genory, prior of Colrahan (Coleraine), and Mark Rochfort, prior of Drogheda.

In 1640, in response to a letter of Cardinal Antonio Barberini (16 April 1639) concerning the Dominicans, the archbishop professed his own personal esteem and affection for the Dominican Order and its members. Nevertheless, he felt bound to say that some Dominicans in the province of Armagh had maltreated diocesan ordinaries and their pastors for several years past and had persisted in this misconduct. There were instances of excess on the part of individual Dominicans who had violated canon law and the customs of the province. Moreover, they were guilty of deeds injurious to the legitimate interests of other religious. Should he take moderate action in defence of other religious, these Dominicans or the Dominican Order as such should not be offended. The archbishop therefore urged the cardinal to admonish the Dominicans resident in the dioceses of Ulster to live in peace and imitate the religious virtues of St Francis. Moreover, they should be persuaded to cultivate good relations with the local ordinaries.[19] At the same time Archbishop O'Reilly asked another Roman cardinal to induce the superiors general of the Dominicans and Discalced Carmelites to tell their Irish subjects to live in peace and quietness with the other regulars.[20]

17 Ibid., 295, ff 37r–38r.
18 O'Mahony, 'The Irish Discalced Carmelites, 1625–1653', 107.
19 APF, SOCG, 295, ff 159rv, 160v; Jennings, 'Acta Propaganda Fide', 119.
20 APF, SOCG, 84, ff 121rv, 124v.

The older mendicant orders such as the Dominicans, Franciscans and Augustinians had earlier in the century decided to multiply their numbers and to reclaim their ancient foundations at all costs. The newer regulars—Jesuits, Capuchins and Discalced Carmelites—were viewed as superfluous, a threat to the very economic resources of the older orders and an obstacle to their expansionist policy. From time to time serious infighting flared among the regulars, with the result that they were frequently and publicly seen to be in conflict. The laity too cannot but have been affected by the scandalous discord among the regulars. Certainly, as the Anglican bishop Thomas Ram of Ferns claimed in 1612, they were burdened in many places with too many priests.[21] For the people had to endure a threefold exaction on the part of the clergy: to support the Established Church, the Catholic secular clergy, and friars of all sorts begging indiscriminately everywhere.

The economic factor loomed large for all the clergy. The older regular orders made no secret of their opposition to the newer orders on the plain grounds that the Catholic population was not in a position to support additional orders. And it was precisely on economic grounds that the Franciscans in 1641 effectively barred the introduction to Ireland of the Mercedarians,[22] in origin a religious military order, founded in Spain in 1218 for the ransom of captives. The Augustinians, Cistercians, Discalced Carmelites and Dominicans had expressed themselves in favour of the coming of this order, which had attracted many Irish members in Spain. The Irish Dominicans would naturally have supported the Mercedarians, who had received their rule from the Spanish Dominican canonist, Raymund of Penafort, declared a saint in 1601. What is most remarkable about incidents of this type is that all the religious orders, who looked upon themselves as purveyors of Catholic reform and the ideals of renewed religious life, should have spent so much time feuding and bickering among themselves to the detriment of their spiritual mission in Ireland.

DISPUTES WITH THE DIOCESAN CLERGY

Still more disastrous for the spiritual renewal of the Irish Church were the disputes that raged between the regular and secular clergy in the 1620s and 1630s. Traces of this acrimony, suspicion and mutual misunderstanding persist even to the present day. In the opening decades of the seventeenth century these disputes sprang from two basic factors:

21 P. J. Corish, *The Catholic Community in the Seventeenth and Eighteenth Centuries*, Dublin 1981, 31–2; Moran, *Archbishops of Dublin*, 326, 330, citing John Roche, Bishop of Ferns, on extortions by Protestant clergy, a fact acknowledged by Protestants themselves.

22 Martin, *Friar Nugent*, 259.

ecclesiastical authority and money. The bishops and vicars apostolic, naturally enough, wished to control the clergy, both secular and regular. The bishops, parish priests and friars all needed the offerings of the faithful. While western Europe had lived with these problems since the thirteenth century, the situation in Ireland after Trent was somewhat different.[23] The nascent religious orders and diocesan priests, both for the most part trained abroad in the spirit of the Counter-Reformation, faced the problems of adjustment—or sometimes maladjustment—in a rapidly changing society where Catholicism was under political pressure and quite uncertain of its future. In order to understand either the misconceptions of seventeenth-century ecclesiastics or the nature of the issues that were to lead to distressing quarrels, disedifying rows and at times downright unchristian behaviour among the Irish clergy, it is first of all necessary to consider the theological-canonical basis of the difference between the two groups of clergy.

From their very origins the orders of friars stood ideologically, ecclesiologically and theologically outside standard diocesan structures, for the most part independent of bishops and parish clergy. What made them so was not merely the vision or inspiration of their founders, their particular charisms and apostolates, but their ecclesial status and source of their jurisdiction which represented a major western canonical innovation and was ultimately papal in origin. While the episcopally exempt religious orders that emerged in the middle ages were used by the papacy to supplement serious deficiencies in the life of the local church—for example, the Dominicans devoted themselves to doctrinal preaching, teaching and study of the sacred and secular sciences—they were in virtue of their fundamental ecclesiological function intended primarily to complement and enrich local and particular expressions of the Church's life. Within the great communion of the western Catholic Church there are subcommunions made up of particular churches, of dioceses, and religious orders. More graphically one could describe this communion as one garden resplendent with distinct and very distinctive flower-beds, all tending towards perfect harmony and unity.

From their inception the orders of mendicant friars and their canonical rights (exemption from episcopal jurisdiction and extensive faculties for preaching and hearing of confessions) aroused bitterness and hostility among bishops, secular clergy and some universities, notably that of Paris, who feared that the new orders would undermine some of the basic structures of the Church. Opposition to the mendicant friars was led by William of St Amour, while the Dominican Thomas Aquinas and the Franciscan Bonaventure wrote in their defence. In 1256 the dispute was

23 J. Bossy, 'The Counter-Reformation and the People of Catholic Ireland, 1596–1641' in *Hist. Studies*, 8 (1971), 155–69.

settled in favour of the friars by Pope Alexander IV. Ireland was touched by the controversy in the fourteenth century when bitter polemics developed between the distinguished theologian and Archbishop of Armagh, Richard FitzRalph, and the regular clergy whom he had once greatly admired. In 1350 at the papal court of Avignon he presented the complaints of the English and Irish secular clergy against the orders of friars, formulating his ideas in the treatise *De Pauperie Salvatoris*. This dealt particularly with evangelical poverty and the connection of worldly dominion and the possession and use of goods with the mystery of grace. In 1357 he reiterated his views more trenchantly and asserted that voluntary begging was against the teaching of Christ. He died at Avignon in 1360 without knowing whether his views had been either approved or condemned.[24]

Within the unity and diversity of the Catholic communion, therefore, a double jurisdiction obtains: ordinary jurisdiction, which is local and episcopal; and universal jurisdiction, which is immediate and papal. Episcopal jurisdiction derives from the apostolic succession, whereas that of the exempt regular and other religious orders derives from a particular form of delegated papal authority. Hence bishops or local ordinaries and general religious superiors enjoy a simultaneous exercise of authority or jurisdiction, the one restricted by diocesan boundaries, the other universal, limited only by the personal authority of a superior general, acting in conformity with the rule and constitutions of his order. Structurally and theologically the dioceses and exempt religious orders represent different yet complementary facets of the full reality of the Catholic Church.

It is undeniable that the Irish Church underwent structural organisation and regeneration during the first four decades of the seventeenth century. From the outset the Council of Trent's legislation and its vision of the Church raised serious problems concerning the precise role of bishop, priest and friar. A new generation of secular clergy, with clear-sighted ideas of a centralised system of parochial ministry and control, found that the traditional ways of Irish Catholicism and opposition from the regular clergy impeded the implementation of the parochial ideals of Trent. The newly arrived regulars, also continentally trained by their orders, faced traumatic problems in adjustment. Their passage from the splendid buildings and settings of continental convents and churches, from a world where Catholicism and religious life flourished and from the comforts of European civilisation, to seclusion in dark, furtively rented back rooms, to a society where they were even less tolerated than their diocesan colleagues, to conditions of enforced poverty and constant uncertainty as far as their personal lives and religious activities were concerned, must

24 K. Walsh, *A Fourteenth-Century Scholar and Primate: Richard FitzRalph in Oxford, Avignon and Armagh*, Oxford 1981, 349–451 and *passim*.

have proved psychologically depressing in the extreme. But at least they had the satisfaction of living and working with their own.

Over and above the question of modification of the religious lifestyle to Irish circumstances, the regulars often inherited practices and situations reflecting the deep-running sociological and distinctive religious traditions of Irish Catholicism which reform-minded clergy regarded as anachronistic. There was the continuing pastoral care of some parishes by religious and reception of the so-called 'parochial sacraments' of baptism, marriage, viaticum and extreme unction at the hands of the regulars; there was also the granting of matrimonial and other dispensations. This medieval Irish arrangement whereby regulars worked as parish priests or religious houses claimed the right of presentation to benefices was in itself an abuse, but was tolerated in virtue of canonical privilege or dispensation. Sometimes the regulars felt that little gratitude was being shown for pastoral services rendered in the past, in the almost total absence or uneven distribution of parish clergy, as they were drawn into different arrangements and obliged to conform to continental concepts of pastoral ministration which did not easily fit the peculiar Irish mould. When inevitably clashes and dissensions arose, the regulars felt themselves at a psychological disadvantage, in that while Trent had very clearly spelt out the details of diocesan and parochial organisation, with the consequent rights and duties of their clergy, the revised canonical status of religious was not so well defined. In this context the friars felt that their basic identity and function within the Irish Church was misunderstood and under attack.

The chief causes of strained relations between the bishops and regulars were the continued use of 'extraordinary' missionary faculties in widespread use since the Elizabethan era; claims of jurisdiction over parishes which in medieval times had been impropriate to some religious houses; matters of precedence between diocesan and regular clergy; the opening of novitiates which the bishops considered canonically inadequate; and, above all, conflicting claims concerning the *jus sepulturae*, or the right of regulars to officiate at burials in the cemeteries of their former ruined churches, and the *quarta funeralium*, or the collection of funeral offerings and their division in three or four portions among the clergy and parish poor. In short, the disagreements concerned ecclesiastical control and finance, issues that recur over and over again and leave one with a very poor impression of the Irish Church. Strenuous efforts were repeatedly made by provincial and diocesan synods at Kilkenny in 1614, 1618, 1624 and 1629, under the firm leadership of Bishop David Rothe of Ossory, to promote harmonious and mutually advantageous relations among seculars and regulars.[25] At an assembly of prelates in Drogheda

25 APF, SOCG, 294, ff 49v–50r; 46rv–48rv; Moran, *Archbishops of Dublin*, 458, 275, 430–31, 391–2, 434–43.

(1626), the diocesan synod of Tuam (1631), the provincial synod of Armagh (1632) and the Dublin provincial synod held at Tirchogir near Portarlington in the diocese of Leighlin (1640) additional efforts were made to regulate these relations and clarify contentious points at issue.[26] It may safely be presumed that the decrees of the provincial synods of Cashel (held at Limerick in 1629), Dublin (1632) and Cashel (held at Fethard in 1632), which have not survived, also contained decrees seeking to heal divisions among diocesan priests and priest members of religious orders.

The first dispute on record in which the Dominicans found themselves embroiled took place at Drogheda in 1622. The principal parties were the Franciscans, the Jesuits and the formidable Balthazar Delahoyd, vicar general of Armagh. A cursory examination of the documents shows that the difficulty was largely caused by an intense clash of personalities between the former Franciscan provincial, Donagh Mooney, then guardian of the Franciscans at Drogheda, and Balthazar Delahoyd.[27] The latter deliberately favoured the Jesuits for his own reasons and fomented ill-feeling among the other regulars by encouraging the Jesuit priests Robert Bathe and James Everard to erect the Sodality of the Blessed Virgin Mary in Drogheda. The Franciscans and Dominicans strongly protested that their rights and privileges were thereby infringed, as the Jesuits had erected the sodality not in their own house, but in Delahoyd's parish chapel where they officiated. The Dominican Confraternity of the Most Holy Rosary had been established in the town 'a long time before', and the Dominicans had a chapel of their own. Matters came to a violent climax in October 1622. Since the Franciscans had no proper oratory, they celebrated solemn Mass and First and Second Vespers for the feast of St Francis on 4 October in the Dominican oratory. A large congregation, drawn from far and near, listened to the sermon of Fr Christopher Plunkett, O.F.M. His words were afterwards misrepresented by the enemies of the Franciscans and the preacher accused of heresy—a charge later dismissed by competent theologians. On 26 October, however, a priest named Christopher Delahoyd, Balthazar Delahoyd's nephew, entered the Dominican oratory of the Holy Rosary Confraternity by night, destroyed the altar, smashed the pulpit, and took away the sacred furnishings. This sacrilegious invasion was probably prompted by spite for the solidarity the Dominicans had expressed with the Franciscans in their dispute with the Jesuits and Balthazar Delahoyd.

Elsewhere in Leinster, most notably in the dioceses of Ossory and Meath, there is further evidence of the hostile attitude shown towards

26 D. Conway, 'The Anglican World: Problems of Coexistence' in J. Metzler (ed.), *Sacrae Congregationis Propaganda Fide Memoria Rerum, 1622–1972*, i, pt 2: *1622–1700*, Rome 1972, 159–60.

27 APF, SOCG, 294, ff 53rv–54rv, 55rv–60rv; *Wadding Papers*, 29–58, 67, 637–41.

the religious orders by the diocesan authorities. In these two dioceses particular ill-feeling arose as a result of a dispute between, on the one hand, the bishops and, on the other, continental canon lawyers who had taken the part of the regular clergy. The origins of this dispute go back to 16 September 1623 when the faculties of theology and canon law of Louvain University made a monumental judgement in favour of the mendicant orders.[28] The verdict upheld the right of regular clergy when expelled by persecution from their religious houses to lease secular buildings or construct new ones licitly and validly, without seeking fresh permission or approbation from bishops or local ordinaries (vicars apostolic, vicars general, etc.). In these houses, under the supervision of superiors, the regulars might celebrate Mass on portable altars by virtue of faculties granted by the Holy See. They might also hold other religious functions in accordance with their ancient privileges as if they were residing in their own proper houses or monasteries. The approbation of the local ordinary, however, was required for the appointment of preachers and confessors. One clause in the statement of the Louvain judgement underlined that should the regulars be Dominicans or Franciscans, canon law (*jus commune* explicitly) upheld their rights no less than those of the bishops to hold sacramental celebrations in appropriate places, without having to ask pardon or permission of local ordinaries. This judgement was almost certainly the outcome of representations to the university faculty boards by the Franciscans and Dominicans of Louvain.

The reaction of some Irish bishops to the considered judgement of the University of Louvain was both negative and aggressive. This would explain the context of the outspoken position taken up by the Bishops of Ossory and Meath on this controverted issue. The core of their objection was that after an absence of almost a century from many of their houses the friars had lost their canonical rights, and members of the newly founded Counter-Reformation mendicant orders such as the Capuchins and Discalced Carmelites were considered by the bishops to have no rights whatsoever.

On 5 April 1631 Fabio de Lagonissa, nuncio at Brussels, informed the Cardinal Prefect of Propaganda Fide that it was true that the Bishops of Meath and Ossory (Thomas Dease and David Rothe, both of Old English stock) had publicly declared that the religious in Ireland had no real claims or right to their monasteries, and therefore without the permission of the ordinaries could not have public oratories because their once consecrated monasteries or houses had been suppressed. The bishops, however, had not asserted that the regular houses had been taken from the friars legally.[29]

28 FLK, MS D. III, ff 291–2.

29 APF, SOCG, 100, ff 130r, 135v; B. Millett, 'Catalogue of Irish Material in

The rumbling discord between seculars and regulars reached a higher pitch at Dublin in 1629 when Patrick Cahill, a secular priest, launched a diatribe in the form of a set of propositions against the entire body of the Irish regular clergy.[30] Cahill, a native of Galtrim and originally of the diocese of Meath, had long been resident in Dublin, had held the city parish of St Michael, and had been responsible for the incarceration of Patrick Brangan, a diocesan priest of Dublin and brother of the Dominican, Thomas of the Ascension Brangan. Cahill, whose main supporters were the Dublin priests Peter Cadwell, Luke Rochfort and Paul Harris, an English priest in the diocese, almost succeeded in introducing into Ireland some ecclesiastical disputes then troubling the diocesan and regular clergy of England.

Cahill had several confrontations with Thomas Fleming, the Franciscan Archbishop of Dublin, who admonished him to return to Meath. Cahill answered the archbishop by publishing hostile verses against him and a treatise highly critical of the Catholic bishops. Cahill had previously displayed a pronounced hostility towards the regular clergy, especially the Franciscans, and threatened 'to trounce them at Rome'. At this stage, with the encouragement of the archbishop, the Dublin regular clergy drew up two declarations on 24 March 1629 and 24 November 1629 expressing their strong disapproval of Cahill and Harris. Cahill was censured explicitly by the regulars for several scandals and for publishing his tract against the hierarchy. Both statements were signed by Dominic Nugent, prior of the Dominicans of Dublin. On his way to Rome about 1630 Cahill presented in Paris a list of eleven propositions which he alleged were held and taught by the regular clergy of Ireland. He also prevailed on the Sorbonne faculty of theology, dominated by the secular clergy, to examine and pass judgement on the propositions:

(1) The ecclesiastical hierarchy consists of the Pope, cardinals, archbishops and regulars.

Fourteen Volumes of the SOCG in Propaganda Archives' in *Collect. Hib.*, 10 (1967), 35; B. Millett, 'Catalogue of Irish Material in Vols 132–139 of the SOCG in Propaganda Archives' in *Collect. Hib.*, 12 (1969), 11. The last point made by the bishops was an allusion to the declaration of Cardinal Reginald Pole to the English parliament on 24 December 1554 when as papal legate he gave formal recognition to the English monastic dissolution. Pope Julius III in the bull *Praeclara* (20 June 1555) sanctioned Pole's decision. By these measures of legate and Pope the religious houses of England became canonically extinct. The validity of this decision was never legally extended to Ireland, but nonetheless became a vexed question in Old English Catholic circles. See D. Knowles, *The Religious Orders in England*, iii, Cambridge 1971, 421–3.

30 This account of the controversy is based principally on documents edited in *Wadding Papers*; W. D. O'Connell, 'The Cahil Propositions, 1629' in *IER*, 5th ser., 62 (1943), 118–23; Moran, *Archbishops of Dublin*, 373–80.

(2) Diocesan priests are merely secular.

(3) Regulars are the only true pastors.

(4) The regular clergy can administer all the sacraments, even against the wish of the parish priest.

(5) Parishioners are not obliged to make their Easter communion in their own parishes.

(6) Only regulars are entitled to be called 'Father'.

(7) The most prudent and best part of the hierarchy is that composed of the regulars.

(8) The superiors of the regulars are more worthy than bishops.

(9) To confess one's sins to regular rather than diocesan confessors is safer and more beneficial.

(10) In countries dominated by heretics, Christians are not obliged to provide material support for the parish clergy, because ecclesiastical property is in the hands of heretics.

(11) The privileges of regulars cannot be revoked by the Pope.

This set of propositions was condemned by the university in January 1631. Patrick Cahill, buoyed up by this triumph, proceeded to Rome, where he sought permission to publish in Dublin both the propositions and the Parisian censure of them. The decision of the Sorbonne sent shock-waves through the ranks of the Irish regulars. Some of the propositions were patently ridiculous, others insidious, but all were calculated to inflame the passions of the clergy on both sides, to deepen the rift between them, and to raise the dispute to the level of bitter feud with grave long-term effects. By the time Cahill reached Rome protestations of innocence had been pouring in from the provincials of the religious orders and some bishops. Mark Rochfort, O.P., a native of Dublin, who had known Patrick Cahill there, wrote an account from Naples (dated 19 April 1631) of the origins of the controversy, which he traced back to 1626. Nicholas Lynch, prior provincial of the Dominicans, wrote from Louvain on 26 April 1631 on the harm the controversy would do. The superiors of the Irish religious orders sent two letters to the Cardinal Protector of Ireland in defence of their orders and addressed a similar letter to the Pope in June 1631. The letters were signed on behalf of the Dominicans by Daniel of the Cross O'Crean, vicar provincial. A solemn attestation dissociating themselves from the propositions was signed by fifteen Dominican superiors at Waterford on 4 July 1631.

Thereafter an avalanche of correspondence flowed to the Roman authorities on all aspects of the Cahill propositions.[31]

In September 1631 two of Cahill's stalwart supporters, James Fallon, Vicar Apostolic of Achonry, and Terence Coghlan, Vicar Apostolic of Clonmacnoise, made depositions concerning the authenticity of the propositions. Those of James Fallon, in particular, implicated several Connacht Dominicans whom he claimed to have heard, personally or indirectly, uphold the substance of most of the condemned propositions. The Dominicans he named in this regard were Peter Martin of Galway, Nicholas Lynch, then prior of Galway but now prior provincial of his Order, Stephen Lynch, prior of Athenry, John Nolan, Hugh O'Grogan, prior of Urlar, Anthony Lynch, then prior of Galway, and Edmund Dempsey when preaching at Athenry. There were also two other Dominicans whose names he could not recollect. The only Dominican denounced by Terence Coghlan bore the surname Bermingham and allegedly held the second proposition, which he was reported to have mentioned in conversation in the district of Ballinahowen, Co. Westmeath, though in whose presence Coghlan could not remember.

A printed reply defending the regulars and refuting Cahill's propositions came from the pen of the guardian of the Irish Franciscans at Louvain, Edmund O'Mahony (*alias* Francis Matthews, *Ursus, Ursulanus*), under the title *Examen Juridicum Censurae Facultatis Theologicae Parisiensis et eiusdem civitatis archiepiscopi latae circa quasdam Propositiones Regularibus Regni Hiberniae impositas*. This forthright rejoinder also attacked the bishops and Irish diocesan clergy, the Sorbonne and the Archbishop of Paris. It would be out of place to elaborate on the full contents of this book and the propositions that provoked it, for they belong to the wider canvas of Irish ecclesiastical history, but suffice it to say that its publication at Cologne in 1631 caused consternation in Ireland, especially among the bishops and prominent ecclesiastics who had refused to reject the Cahill propositions or had maintained a dogged silence on the subject. The Bishops of Ossory, Cork and Ferns, who had refused to sign declarations exonerating the regulars, requested Propaganda Fide to have the *Examen* placed on the *Index Librorum Prohibitorum* and to forbid further debate of the propositions. In the event these three bishops were chosen by Urban VIII to adjudicate between Cahill and Thomas Fleming, O.F.M., Archbishop of Dublin. Once more the regular clergy of

31 Nicholas Lynch to the Cardinal Protector of the Order and Ireland (19 July 1631); Ross MacGeoghegan, Bishop of Kildare, to the same cardinal (20 July 1631); Thomas of the Ascension Brangan, prior of Dublin, signed memoranda from the Dublin regular clergy to the Archbishop of Dublin (July and Oct. 1631); Bishop Ross MacGeoghegan to the nuncio at Brussels (5 Sept. 1631). *Wadding Papers*, 544–7, 558–9, 603–4, 574–6; HMC, *Franciscan MSS*, 45, 46.

Dublin, including Thomas of the Ascension Brangan, O.P., prior of Dublin, wrote to Archbishop Fleming about the Sorbonne censure and the activities of two diocesan priests, Luke Rochfort and Paul Harris, which they judged hostile to their interests.[32] Patrick Cahill was eventually reconciled with the archbishop he had wronged and was reinstated in the archdiocese of Dublin. Harris's venomous thoughts on the religious orders continued to find expression in popular pamphlets such as *Friars, Be Sober*, a play on the biblical text '*Fratres sobrii estote*' (1 Peter, 5: 8) as used in the church's night service of Compline, and in an essay entitled *Arktomastix*, both printed in 1633. The latter was in reply to O'Mahony's *Examen Juridicum* and launched a new and vicious literary onslaught on the Irish regular clergy and on Archbishop Fleming.[33] The favour of Dublin Castle was extended to Harris, who was encouraged by the viceroy Wentworth to remain in Dublin.

As the embers of the controversy died out, except in the diocese of Cork, where the friars suffered much at the hands of Bishop William Tirry, the religious orders in Ireland realised as never before how vulnerable they were to deliberate and unscrupulous misrepresentation. Henceforth they would be far more careful about what they said, publicly or privately, and in their dealings with the parochial clergy and bishops. One grave effect of the furore over the Cahill propositions was that relations between both branches of the Irish clergy were forever soured; reverberations of deep hurt and bitter feelings in Leinster and Munster were prolonged.

Meanwhile another source of friction, again a legacy of the middle ages, surfaced in the 1630s between some diocesan clergy and Dominicans of Connacht. The point at stake was the administration of parishes. On 1 November 1630 Malachy O'Queely, Archbishop of Tuam, wrote to Cardinal Protector Ludovisi that Oliver Burke, the Irish Dominican procurator at Rome, was a thorn in his side because he had obtained the incorporation of parish churches with the monasteries of his Order in the ecclesiastical province of Tuam. Moreover, he alleged that Burke sought the preferment of unworthy or incompetent priests as prelates in western dioceses. This the archbishop could not in conscience accept. He asked that the views of Oliver Burke on the ecclesiastical affairs of Connacht should be ignored.[34] The wider context of his complaint against Burke was the archbishop's plan for the reform and redistribution of

32 *Wadding Papers*, 603–4. Archbishop Fleming in his report on the archdiocese of Dublin (2 Oct. 1632) observed that there were more priests than necessary resident in Dublin. Whereas he could easily deal with the regulars by recourse to their superiors, he found himself powerless in coping with extra-diocesan priests. APF, SOCG, 294, f. 224r.

33 Martin, *Friar Nugent*, 268; B. Millett, 'Irish Literature in Latin, 1550–1700' in *NHI*, iii, 580.

34 *Wadding Papers*, 434.

Connacht parishes,[35] some of which were unwieldy and territorially difficult to administer as they corresponded to ancient civil divisions. Often the faithful lived far from parish churches, which they could reach only by crossing rivers, mountains and woods, so that in bad weather the parish churches were virtually inaccessible.[36] Writing from Galway in the following year (20 May 1631) under the pseudonym David Rice to Luke Wadding, O.F.M., O'Queely mentioned that Burke, Vicar Apostolic of Kilmacduagh (since 28 November 1629), was absent from his diocese and added: 'for Oliver is put in trust to coin bishoprics if otherwise he cannot speed'. Here O'Queely was voicing disapproval of any moves to revive Kilmacduagh and other unviable bishoprics in the west of Ireland. He repeated his complaint that Burke was responsible for the annexation of some unspecified parish churches to Dominican houses. Many inconveniences would result unless Wadding could 'produce a remedy'.[37]

As pointed out earlier,[38] three Connacht parishes were impropriate to the Dominican houses of Strade, Urlar and Clooneymeaghan in the diocese of Achonry. This arrangement already existed in the mid-sixteenth century. In the case of Urlar and Clooneymeaghan, it probably dated from the fifteenth century. Strade, a thirteenth-century foundation, may have enjoyed this right of presentation even earlier.

Haunted by a typical medieval anachronism concerning parochial rights and privileges, some Connacht Dominicans clung tenaciously to their rights of administering parishes even when parish structures and clergy had been restored as part of the gradual implementation of Tridentine reform. The impatience of the Archbishop of Tuam is readily understandable. He feared the perpetuation of parochial anomalies in his own province and resented the alleged efforts of Oliver Burke at Rome to secure the medieval custom. There is no evidence, however, that Burke was personally responsible for the annexation of parishes to Dominican communities. Hugh O'Grogan, prior of Urlar, was said in September 1631 to be assisting at marriages in the diocese of Elphin, although there was a resident bishop in the diocese, and in spite of the fact that the decrees of the Council of Trent had been promulgated there and that the parochial clergy had objected to O'Grogan's ministrations.[39] However, a provincial synod of the dioceses of Connacht, held at Galway on 9 December 1632, made provision for regulars engaged in parishes and in ordinary sacramental administration, provided they

35 Ibid., 454–5; HMC, *Franciscan MSS*, 35.
36 *Wadding Papers*, 445–6.
37 Ibid., 521, 519; HMC, *Franciscan MSS*, 41.
38 See p. 51 above.
39 *Wadding Papers*, 596.

were permitted to do so by their own superiors and presumably by the bishops. The synod also laid down procedures for the ordination of regulars and insisted that religious should have the permission of their superiors to preach in their own churches, and the express permission of bishops to preach in parish churches.[40]

About 24 May 1633 Archbishop O'Queely of Tuam forwarded to Propaganda Fide a copy of a bull granted by Pius v (1566–72) to the Irish Dominicans, in virtue of which, he said, they claimed that the area of their monasteries was exempt, with respect to the care of souls, from all ordinary jurisdiction. The Dominicans in 1633 exercised the care of souls in four quarters of land belonging to the monastery of Urlar, and this had caused a controversy between James Fallon, Vicar Apostolic of Achonry, and Prior Hugh O'Grogan of Urlar. The dispute was settled by mediators who, for the sake of peace, gave the Dominicans the right of presentation until Rome should decide the case. The archbishop's letter concluded by saying that he was sure that the Pope did not approve of this exemption, especially since the decisions of Trent were now in force. James Fallon in his submission said that O'Grogan baptised and assisted at marriages despite opposition from the parish priest and bishop. He claimed too that O'Grogan's vicar provincial, Daniel of the Cross O'Crean, approved of this ministry. Fallon had often spoken to this provincial on the subject, only to receive abuse for his pains.[41]

Finally in 1634 the diocesan clergy of Connacht presented a memorandum to Propaganda Fide on their differences with the Dominicans.[42] The document accused some Dominicans of having disagreements with the secular clergy. They had usurped jurisdiction in the pastoral care of souls, intruded into parishes adjoining their churches, and deputed regulars to act as parish priests, thereby resisting and contradicting the local bishops. The Dominicans sought to justify their position on the basis of a certain bull issued in the time of Pius v, an authentic copy of which was enclosed with the memorandum but which unfortunately has not been preserved. This bull had said nothing of exemption from diocesan ordinaries, nor had it granted regulars concessions *in cura animarum*, as was patent from a reading of it. The memorandum asserted that the bull was no longer valid, for it had been granted seventy years before at a time of schism on the basis of false allegations that the Catholic faith was almost totally extinguished and that there were scarcely any priests in the entire kingdom of Ireland. Nor, in the meantime, had the provisions of the bull been insisted upon in practice or even been brought to the

40 APF, SOCG, 294, ff 201r–204r.
41 Ibid., 14, ff 6r–7v; H. Fenning, 'The Dominicans and Propaganda Fide, 1622–1668' in *AFP*, 41 (1971), 284–5.
42 APF, SOCG, 394, ff 317rv, 318v.

light of day until the year 1633 to defend certain members of the Dominicans. These friars, contrary to the decrees of Trent, continued to administer sacraments reserved by law to the parish clergy in virtue of this papal bull alone.

The Connacht clergy therefore requested Propaganda Fide, in the interests of peace and to prevent scandal, to declare that the bull of Pius V did not confer any special rights on the Dominicans, enabling them to commission other regulars or their own to carry out parochial duties. It should be decreed that such regulars acted unjustly and contrary to ecclesiastical law by intruding into parishes which in living memory were in the actual possession of the parochial clergy. Ingoli of Propaganda Fide endorsed the petition and noted that the papal bull in question, having been revoked by Gregory XIII and Gregory XIV, was no longer applicable to Connacht, where there were now bishops and parish priests. The petition was considered on 18 September 1634 and referred to Cardinal Antonio Barberini for his advice. No more is heard of this dispute, and it would appear that the question was amicably resolved. In Connacht differences between regular and diocesan authorities were generally short-lived, displaying none of the rancour so obvious in the other three provinces. The historical reasons for this peculiarity have yet to be investigated. It is remarkable that six prominent Dominicans of Connacht were among those recommended about 1640 by the priests and bishops of the province to fill the vacant see of Achonry—the very diocese which had been at the centre of the dispute only six years before.[43]

Throughout the 1630s serious discord between secular and regular was more acute in the province of Munster than anywhere else. While there is evidence of disputes between the regulars and the Archbishop of Cashel and the Bishop of Waterford in the papers of Propaganda Fide,[44] by far the most protracted, damaging and acrimonious disputes were those between Bishop William Tirry and the Franciscans and Dominicans in the united dioceses of Cork and Cloyne. From the commencement of his episcopate in 1623 Bishop Tirry showed himself an implacable opponent of the regular clergy, and the same attitude was demonstrated in the firm '*non praevalebunt*' policy of his fellow suffragan, Patrick Comerford, the Augustinian Bishop of Waterford and Lismore, towards religious orders in his diocese.[45] Before his appointment to Cork, Tirry sedulously safeguarded his candidacy for the bishopric by writing in 1619 to prominent regulars such as Hugh MacCaughwell, O.F.M., then guardian of St Anthony's College, Louvain, and future Archbishop of

43 Ibid., 404, f. 412v.
44 Ibid., 294, f. 351r.
45 M. Olden, 'Counter-Reformation Problems: Munster' in *Ir. Cath. Hist. Comm. Proc.*, Dublin 1967, 24–5.

Armagh, to deny any alleged enmity on his part towards the religious orders and the Franciscans in particular—charges which had been levelled against him in reports circulating in ecclesiastical circles. Whether or not he was successful in dispelling the reservations of the Franciscans and other regulars, the friars were hardly prepared for his unrelenting animosity and harsh campaign against them as Bishop of Cork and Cloyne. That he was thoroughly committed to introducing the reforms of Trent and the restoration of order and clerical discipline in his dioceses, after long decades of neglect, must be admitted.[46] However in his vision of a reformed diocese the mendicant orders seemed peripheral: awkward 'leftovers' from another age, serving no good purpose in a well-regulated Tridentine diocese. Not illogically, the bishop looked with favour on the reformed or Discalced Carmelites and granted one of their members, Daniel Donovan (Patrick of St James), a former provincial, wide faculties for the dioceses of Cork and Cloyne on 26 April 1627.[47] Bishop Tirry also encouraged the Jesuits to remain in Cork and to build a college (opposite the Anglican Christ Church), an establishment which was considered detrimental to the local clergy, secular as well as regular.[48]

One of Bishop Tirry's first official acts was to take the regular clergy to task in 1624 on the extremely sensitive issue of the *quarta funeralium* or right to funeral offerings. In the name of the Council of Trent he abrogated the funeral rights which the Franciscans and Dominicans had held with the approval of six Popes and which had been confirmed to them in 1514 by Bishop John FitzEdmund FitzGerald, one of Tirry's predecessors in Cork and Cloyne. Bishop FitzGerald's solemn decree exempted the friars from surrendering any part of funeral offerings to the diocesan clergy. Trent, however, also allowed for this exemption to be continued, in places where the regulars had enjoyed such rights for forty years.[49] Several years after 1624 the wounds and divisions caused by Bishop Tirry's decision were still unhealed. The situation in Cork and other dioceses prompted the Franciscan Bishop of Down and Connor, Bonaventure Magennis, to give his opinion to Rome. He felt that his fellow bishops treated the vexed question of the *quarta funeralium* unfairly. He had seen documents dating from about fifty years before the publication of the decrees of Trent, in virtue of which the Dominicans and Franciscans were judged exempt from payment of funeral oblations by a provincial synod of Armagh, and in Munster by decrees of the Archbishop of Cashel and the Bishop of Cork. He insisted therefore that members of the hierarchy were acting *ultra vires* and strongly recom-

46 E. Bolster, *A History of the Diocese of Cork*, ii, Cork 1982, 158–9, 164.
47 Ibid., 167.
48 Ibid., 169, 172–3.
49 *Wadding Papers*, 106; Bolster, *Diocese of Cork*, ii, 165.

mended that the mendicant religious should not be disturbed.[50] Bishop Tirry maintained, no doubt in all sincerity, that his diocese was plagued by conflicts between diocesan and regular clergy over funeral rights and offerings which made his own intervention imperative. However, Tirry's unbalanced unilateral solution of the problem precipitated a bitter controversy with the regulars of Cork and Cloyne which was to dominate his entire episcopate. The activity of the regulars in Cork and Cloyne was further reduced in 1630 by the statutes of a diocesan synod which rejected the privileges attached to missionary faculties.[51] A typical summary of such faculties then valid for England, Ireland and Scotland granted seculars and regulars the following rights:

(1) to absolve from heresy, apostasy from the faith, and from schism;

(2) to absolve in all reserved cases, even those mentioned in the bull *In Coena Domini*;

(3) to absolve ecclesiastics from canonical suspensions, censures, irregularities and other cases normally reserved to bishops and vicars apostolic;

(4) to grant the apostolic blessing and plenary indulgence to those reconciled to the Catholic Church from heresy;

(5) to grant a plenary indulgence on important feasts and at the hour of death, etc.;

(6) to keep and read prohibited books written by heretics;

(7) to administer the sacraments (except confirmation and holy orders), with permission to omit ceremonies and solemn forms in cases of necessity, subject to episcopal judgement;

(8) to recite the rosary, psalms or other prayers from memory if it be judged dangerous to carry the breviary or impossible to read the divine office;

(9) to bless vestments and to consecrate vessels required for sacred worship;

(10) to celebrate Holy Mass in any decent place and outside the normal hours;

(11) to reserve the Eucharist without customary lights and ceremonies;

(12) to dispense from simple vows and oaths and to commute them for other pious works except the vows of chastity and religion;

50 APF, SOCG, 132, f. 267rv; *Wadding Papers*, 10.
51 Bolster, *Diocese of Cork*, ii, 173.

(13) to grant matrimonial dispensations normally reserved to bishops;

(14) to print and publish books, with name of author, place, printer and publisher, notwithstanding certain stipulations of the Council of Trent;

(15) to authorise permission for those reconciled to the Catholic faith to retain the fruits of ecclesiastical property illegally acquired, provided they make some compensation to the religious order which once owned the property or goods before the schism should that order be still represented in the locality.[52]

In the 1630s the Dominicans lived and ministered in the neighbourhood of St Finbar's Cathedral and in proximity to their once splendid medieval foundation (St Mary's of the Isle) in the southern suburbs of Cork; the Franciscans were within the parish of Shandon on the north side of the city. In the diocese of Cloyne the Dominicans had houses at Youghal and Glanworth, while in the united dioceses of Cork and Cloyne the Franciscans had several communities. The synod of 1630 decided that henceforth the bishop and approved diocesan priests would take care of most pastoral work and the administration of the sacraments. Other priests and religious might function in the diocese only with the consent of the bishop and would be subject to episcopal visitation. Some of the statutes implied that the regulars could exist and move only in virtue of episcopal jurisdiction: they might be ordained only with the bishop's consent; they were to be subject to episcopal supervision in all that pertained to wills; on no account were they to seek alms before or after Mass; and they were to be subject to the episcopal court in cases of clandestine marriages. In future the diocesan clergy would take precedence at all funerals, religious meetings, stations and processions.[53] There was also a reprimand for those Dominicans who insisted on calling themselves members of the Order of the Blessed Virgin Mary, as if the Dominicans were the official custodians of devotion to the Virgin Mary. The diocesan chapter of Cork ordered the Dominicans to revert to their older official title of Order of Preachers.[54] It would appear that it was in identifying themselves as the Order of the Blessed

52 APF, SOCG, 390, ff 380r–382v, 379v. The Irish Dominicans had obtained a similar concession of missionary faculties from the Congregation of the Holy Office, dated 16 August 1617. See pp 139–40 above. About 1634 these faculties were listed for review by a special meeting of Propaganda Fide devoted to the affairs of the Irish Church. See *Wadding Papers*, 630. The Bishop of Ferns suggested that missionary faculties be modified in a report considered by Propaganda Fide on 3 April 1632. APF, SOCG, 294, ff 286rv–287v. The Holy Office did revise and restrict them in 1638.

53 Bolster, *Diocese of Cork*, ii, 173–4.

54 Ibid., 174.

Virgin Mary that the Dominicans gave most offence to the other religious orders. The early Carmelites too took pride in referring to themselves as the Brothers of the Blessed Virgin Mary of Mount Carmel and adopted her as patroness of their Order. The decision of the chapter may have been intended to appease the Augustinians, Franciscans and Jesuits of Cork, as well as the Carmelites of Kinsale. The diocesan chapter itself could hardly have cared less about such an issue. Since the Dominicans were unwilling to obey the chapter's decree, quarrels with the other regulars in Ireland arose, and the matter went to Rome for adjudication. The subject came up for discussion at a meeting on 11 July 1633 devoted exclusively to Irish affairs. It was alleged that the Irish Dominicans described themselves as religious of the Blessed Virgin Mary in order to obtain alms and support more easily. Propaganda Fide was, however, informed that the Dominican Master General intended to settle this particular point.[55]

The fundamental issue between the Bishop of Cork and Cloyne and the religious orders was the question of the funeral rights of the exempt orders. Traditionally, many burial places were attached to the churches of the regulars, and even after the dissolution of the monasteries people continued to be buried within or beside them. Since the loss of their churches, the religious often conducted the office of the dead and other rites in the home of the deceased, which the parish clergy claimed to be a non-exempt place. Consequently the latter logically claimed the exclusive right to conduct funeral services in private houses and to receive the funeral offerings. It was the custom in Ireland that where the regular clergy officiated, the offerings were normally divided into three parts: one to be set aside for the future rebuilding of the religious foundation, the second for the clergy who had officiated at the funeral, and the third for the poor. The situation was aggravated for the diocesan clergy in country districts where they had been deprived of parish churches or where those churches had passed into Protestant hands and some friary churches had been rebuilt.

The new regulations of Bishops Comerford of Waterford and Lismore and Tirry of Cork and Cloyne came in for heavy criticism from religious,

55 APF, SOCG, 294, f. 273r. Among the norms for the spiritual government of the Irish Church drawn up by Rome in the mid-1630s was the following: 'Something else stands in need of correction, namely the friars of St Dominic or of the Order of Preachers in Ireland do not wish to be so called; they perceive that almost the entire kingdom of Ireland, especially the native Catholics, is devoted to the Blessed Virgin Mary. They call themselves and wish to be known by all as the friars of the Order of the Blessed Virgin Mary and not as Dominicans or preachers so that they may gain popular support and attract the esteem of the common people by the title of the Order of the Blessed Virgin Mary.' Ibid., 295, ff 26rv, 27r.

especially with respect to this delicate question of sharing funeral alms. In the new arrangement, the offerings of the faithful were still to be divided into three: the first to go to the bishop, the second to the parish priest or his curates, and the third to any other priests who had taken part, presumably meaning the regular clergy if they had conducted the funeral. No mention was made of the parish poor. This system transferred what was formerly paid towards the rebuilding of the local friary or abbey to the local parish priest. The result was that the churches and cemeteries of the religious decayed still further, as there was no fund for repairs and upkeep or possible restoration. More seriously, wealthy patrons of the friars, whose offerings were considerable, decided not to be buried in the ruined churches and abandoned graveyards of religious orders, but chose the grounds of the parish churches instead.[56]

As far as one can judge, the problems associated with *jus sepulturae* and *quarta funeralium* did not arise at this time to any notable degree in the provinces of Connacht and Ulster, and only sporadically in Leinster, where a smaller number of priests was held firmly in check by Protestant parsons and government officials. For the Dominicans, problems arose chiefly in the dioceses of Munster—Cork and Cloyne, Cashel, Waterford and Lismore, and Limerick—which by the 1630s had a fairly abundant supply of priests, diocesan and regular. The Bishops of Cork and Cloyne, Limerick, Killaloe, Emly and the vicar general of Ross wrote to Propaganda Fide on 30 December 1632 about the *quarta funeralium* question.[57] Their proposals were mainly in line with the anti-regular measures and the rather high-handed tactics of Bishop Tirry. Rome gave them no immediate reply.

In or about 1634 Bishop Tirry composed a series of propositions or questions concerning the rights of the Irish regulars, specifically the Dominicans and Franciscans of his own dioceses, and forwarded them to Rome for arbitration. For the bishop, the disputes focused on four questions which he formulated as follows:

(1) Whether those dying in the religious habit out of devotion had the right to be buried in the monastery corresponding to that religious habit?

(2) When it happened that such people were buried in parish churches, did the regulars have a claim to a portion of the offerings made in the diocesan burial place?

(3) Whether the Dominicans and Franciscans or other regulars should receive a portion of the offerings at burials when the deceased had not been clothed in the religious habit?

56 Olden, 'Counter-Reformation Problems: Munster', 27–8.
57 APF, SOCG, 294, ff 436v–437r.

(4) Whether the bishop or local ordinary could prohibit the said regulars or others from questing at any place or time, especially since, according to local custom, they had fixed times throughout the year in which they did so?[58]

The complicated question of *jus sepulturae* and related issues had been referred many times to Propaganda Fide, which was well aware of the peculiarities of the Irish pastoral situation and was therefore reluctant to formulate definitive guidelines. John Roche, Bishop of Ferns, reporting to Rome early in 1632, had much to say about the abuses of the regular clergy, some of which, if they were true, were crude in the extreme. He stated, very reasonably, that people should be perfectly free to choose their place of burial. Nobody should be unduly influenced to seek burial in the churches of religious orders simply by the promise of excessive indulgences, by being allowed to wear the religious habit in the hour of death, or by the promise of not merely plenary indulgences but also of the soul's immunity in its final agony from temptation and the assaults of the devil, with the assistance and consolation of the Blessed Virgin Mary and all the saints and, after a short experience of purgatory, of certain entry to the heavenly kingdom. Such simplistic thinking represented an exaggerated version of popular beliefs. Regrettably the bishop did not indicate to what extent funeral abuses were local or nationwide. Above all, he was most insistent on the rights of the parochial church and clergy; the canonical portion, whether one-third or one-quarter, due to regulars should not be made if prejudicial to the pastor's rights and needs, particularly when the parish clergy had to live and work in penury.[59]

It was this line of thinking that was to influence Rome finally in its decisions. The complexities of applying the *jus sepulturae* and *quarta funeralium* legislation to the Irish Church were eventually referred by Propaganda Fide to another Roman body, the Congregation of the Council, a body charged with the authoritative interpretation of Tridentine legislation, which decided against the claims of the regulars by a decision on 12 May 1635. In enforcing the applicable decrees of Trent, this

58 Ibid., 321, f. 48r; 295, f. 59r. Bishop Tirry may or may not have been aware that Rome had already handed down a basic decision on the general issue. In 1625 or thereabouts, in reply to an anxious query on the part of the Roman procurators general of the mendicant orders, the Congregation for the Interpretation of the Council of Trent firmly upheld the fundamental questing rights of the regulars. The congregation ruled that the friars could by no means be forbidden by bishops to gather alms in places where they had monasteries. However, in places where they had no houses they were obliged to present to the diocesan ordinary their superiors' authorisation to quest. Salamanca, San Esteban provincial archives, provincial chapter acts, 1625, 2, 3: incorporated Latin texts of inquiry and response of the congregation signed by Cardinal R. Ubaldini.

59 APF, SOCG, 294, ff 286rv–287v.

decision made no allowance for the unique circumstances of the Irish regulars, many of whose houses could not be deemed formal convents by strict canonical criteria and were therefore not entitled to exemption.[60] Several attempts to reform religious houses had been made by Clement VIII, Paul V and Urban VIII, whose decrees forbade convents or houses of less than twelve or six members. In the case of Ireland, the Roman authorities were prepared to tolerate less than perfect fulfilment of the law and in practice turned a blind eye to certain canonical irregularities.[61] This was the policy applied when Bishop Tirry raised the question of the exact status of the technically non-exempt oratories, chapels and dwelling-houses of exempt regulars in his submission entitled *Puncta Controversa inter Episcopum Corcagensem et Regulares* of 1640.[62] Propaganda Fide ruled that the faithful were entitled to frequent the chapels of the regular clergy and there fulfil their religious duties provided that in so doing they did not overlook their obligations to their own parish churches. What this meant in effect was that the obligation of Easter communion as well as the celebration of baptisms, marriages and funerals had to take place in the local parish church except where permission had been granted by the local bishop to the regular clergy. Rome might promulgate solemn decrees and issue precise legal instructions, and Irish bishops might threaten the regulars with censures and other dire canonical penalties for failing to accept the new regulations governing pastoral practice, but the Irish pattern of religious observance was somewhat impervious to sudden change. The Franciscans and Dominicans of Cork would seem to have continued to administer the 'parochial sacraments' (*sacramenta pastoralia seu parochialia*) and insisted on the right of burying (*jus sepulturae*) their faithful followers. The people who frequented their chapels and services would have wished it so, and ecclesiologically their case was sound. Their sentiments, perhaps, found apt expression in the verse of an English poet in the Puritan tradition:

> And they who to be sure of Paradise,
> Dying put on the weeds of Dominick,
> Or in Franciscan think to pass disguised.[63]

Bishop Tirry complained to Propaganda Fide in March 1637 of the influence of the Irish religious in limiting the number of bishops and

60 Olden, 'Counter-Reformation Problems: Munster', 28.

61 In 1630 Master Nicholas Ridolfi ordered the closure or suppression of small Dominican houses in Italy and in the province of Aragón (Spain) where regular life could not be truly observed. S. L. Forte, 'Le Provincie Domenicane in Italia nel 1650' in *AFP*, 39 (1969), 426–7.

62 APF, SOCG, 295, f. 145rv; 401, f. 659rv, 665v; 399, f. 35; 221, f. 48.

63 John Milton (1608–74), *Paradise Lost*, Bk III, vv 478–80.

asked that they should be made obey the decrees relating to the recitation of the office of the dead in private houses.[64] The bishop also referred to Rome in 1638 the dispute between the cathedral chapter and the Dominicans over the latters' persistence in calling themselves the Order of the Blessed Virgin Mary. Propaganda Fide asked him to forward the diocesan documentation on the dispute between the Dean of Cork and the Dominicans. Tirry replied in the following year that the notary employed by him to draw up the *acta* of the dispute had been taken ill and went on to explain that two months' work would be entailed in transcribing almost two hundred pages of testimony in the event of his recovery. The bishop said that he would try to find somebody else to write the report,[65] but after this the matter appears to have been dropped.

Relations between Bishop Tirry and the Dominicans and Franciscans deteriorated so seriously in the course of 1638 that the metropolitan, Archbishop Thomas Walsh of Cashel, felt obliged to come to Cork himself in December of that year. He promptly suspended the friars and strictly forbade them to minister outside their chapels unless in the presence of the parochial clergy.[66] The suspension was probably conditional, because if fully suspended the Dominicans could not even have preached or heard confessions within their own chapels. The regulars defied both bishop and archbishop. Bishop Tirry reiterated his demand that Rome should move against the friars and issue a strong caveat particularly with regard to funerals, anniversary commemorations and confraternity Masses.[67] In 1639 and 1640 Tirry's stand against the Dominicans and Franciscans of his diocese was supported unreservedly by his metropolitan, Archbishop Walsh (with whom he had clashed in the past), and by his fellow suffragans and vicars apostolic of the province of Cashel. They denounced the falsehoods spread by the friars and their supporters and again asked the cardinals of Propaganda Fide to act against them.[68]

A letter to Rome, written on 3 February 1640, spoke of the growing disobedience and rebelliousness of the Franciscans and Dominicans and of their greater bitterness since their suspension. The letter included a detailed account of a debate reputedly held with the bishop and the reduction of the essential points in the dispute to two articles under the signatures of William Connor, prior of the Dominicans of Cork, and Boethius MacEgan, guardian of the Cork friary of the Franciscans, which had been forwarded to Tirry's Roman agent, Donagh O'Connell, in December 1639. The first article postulated one liturgical service (*officium*

64 APF, SOCG, 106, ff 37r–38v.
65 Ibid., 139, f. 315r.
66 Ibid., 295, ff 186r–188r.
67 Ibid., 295, f. 145rv.
68 Ibid., 295, f. 188r.

defunctorum) on the day of burial, to be presided over by the pastor and regular clergy alike. However, should the deceased, his relatives or friends have expressed the wish for a confraternity Mass to be celebrated by the regular clergy, then this should be honoured by the bishop or any other party. The second article dealt with 'the month's mind' (a special Mass said one month after decease) and anniversary celebrations. Again, only one liturgical celebration should be held, attended by diocesan and religious priests, and it should take place in the oratories of the religious if requested. Neither the bishop, his clergy nor anyone else acting on their behalf should by threats, persuasion or any other means bring pressure to bear on the people in this matter; the option should freely remain with the people. Finally it was asserted that the provisions of the articles should remain in force during the time of persecution.[69] Curiously there was no mention here of funeral offerings.

An undated letter (1639 or 1640) from six secular priests of Cork supplied Propaganda Fide with another version of the story. While the Augustinians, Capuchins and Jesuits were, they said, amenable to Bishop Tirry's jurisdiction, the Franciscans and Dominicans persisted in their contumacy. The letter stressed how poor the diocesan clergy were when deprived of their customary funeral offerings. The friars had not only scorned the censures of the Archbishop of Cashel, but had had the temerity to pronounce sentence of excommunication (a canonical impossibility) on the Bishop of Cork and five of the priest petitioners, who had asked for certain points of law to be clarified. (Had the Archbishop of Cashel, as apostolic delegate and investigator into the controversies between the regulars and the bishops of Munster, the right to excommunicate the refractory, especially those who refused his authority? Were the regulars excommunicated or not? If excommunicated, should they be absolved, and if not, should they be so declared?) The desire for peace, shared by many of those concerned, may be detected in this final petition signed by the same secular priests who asked Rome that the bishop or some other acceptable person be given the requisite faculties to reconcile all parties.[70]

In his final letter to Rome on 4 October 1640, concerning the troubles in his diocese,[71] Bishop William Tirry disclosed that he was willing to reach a pragmatic compromise in the short term. To avoid greater scandal he agreed to allow the regulars a share in funeral offerings irrespective of the place of burial. He had given this promise in writing on the assurance that the Franciscan provincial would reprimand one of his friars, William Ferris of Cork. No action was taken by the provincial,

69 Ibid., 295, ff 149rv, 147r.
70 Ibid., 295, ff 150r–152r; Bolster, *Diocese of Cork*, ii, 188.
71 APF, SOCG, 295, ff 176r, 179r.

and the Franciscan example of non-cooperation with the bishop was followed by the Dominicans. However, Tirry acknowledged that the Dominican provincial, James Hurley (in Cork to preside at a chapter) had striven to restore peace between his subjects and the bishop and had even admitted to his secretary that the friars had promoted controversy. Not even the provincial had been able to bring his own subjects to heel. He had to admit defeat and ask the bishop to allow the Dominicans to continue in the united dioceses of Cork and Cloyne 'for the sake of the Order's honour'. The bishop's comment was that the schism of a few unlettered men had aroused many evils in his diocese. Tirry concluded his letter by asking for an apostolic investigation and the application of the law so that he might continue to eradicate abuses and corruption stemming from the privileges and customs of the friars. Only then could he hope to rule his diocese. In his view, an impartial tribunal would defeat the friars and enable justice to prevail. A papal delegate armed with all necessary faculties would provide a legal refutation of all pretensions as to exemptions and privileges granted by various Popes in times past, particularly that of immunity from excommunication enjoyed by regulars, which henceforth should be canonically void unless pronounced by a papal legate.

After 1640 there were no further pronouncements against the regulars of Cork and Cloyne. An uneasy truce prevailed, thanks to the bishop's pragmatic decision on funerals and funeral rights. Henceforth Bishop Tirry's activities extended mostly beyond his diocese as he became directly involved in the politics and proceedings of the Confederation of Kilkenny. Thus the prolonged and very bitter quarrels which had embroiled the seculars, Dominicans and Franciscans of Cork and Cloyne and indeed of greater Munster finally receded.[72] One can only regret that a conflict of such immense proportions should have disturbed the Church in Munster at a time when the regulars as a whole were helping to promote the new Tridentine church order which their own contemporary European education and strict religious formation inclined them to support warmly on every essential point. The prime source of conflict lay in differing attitudes to the practical implementation of the disciplinary decrees of Trent.

Despite serious clashes between regulars and seculars, the Church in Ireland was making unqualified if largely undocumented progress owing to the generous spirit of regulars and seculars alike. The moves to limit

72 Friction between regulars and seculars did not entirely cease in Cork, judging from a letter of the Archbishop of Armagh to Rome in 1641. APF, Lettere di Svizzera, 84, f. 72

the pastoral authority and ministry of the regulars interfered with the catechising of the people of Gaelic-speaking Ireland, then the vast majority of the Catholic community.[73] This was most unfortunate, for the religious and their churches were highly esteemed by the people as inheritors of a tradition rooted in the early history of Christianity in Ireland. Catholic life and practice of the faith still revolved to a marked degree around the houses and chapels of the religious orders. In no way did the unlettered people consider the regulars as superfluous or a merely supplementary clerical body, auxiliaries to the diocesan clergy. The people understood the ecclesiological function of the regulars even though they were unable to articulate it in theological terms.

Rome's role of arbitration, in maintaining concord and the unity of the Irish Church in the seventeenth century amidst a welter of ecclesiastical disputes, was of paramount importance because it saved the Church in Ireland from open schism and worse evils. The deep shadows of dissension and litigation which darkened the first half of the century were caused by the uneven distribution of clergy, clerical poverty and, paradoxically, by the renewal of the Church as it grappled with problems of accommodation to the ideals of Trent and the changing circumstances of early modern Ireland.

73 Corish, *The Catholic Community in the Seventeenth and Eighteenth Centuries*, 36.

NINE

The Revived Province, 1627–41: An Age of Sustained Progress

THE POLITICAL CLIMATE: GOVERNMENT POLICY

A generation of Irish Dominicans, thoroughly new in every sense, was by 1627 solidly established in the cities of Dublin, Sligo, Galway, Limerick, Cork, Waterford and Kilkenny and in the more country settings at Mullingar, Urlar, Athenry, Lorrha and elsewhere in the west of Ireland.[1] In all, there were in April 1627, as Ross MacGeoghegan's term as ruler of the Irish province drew to a close, at least twelve revived Dominican foundations in Ireland (an increase of four communities since 1622) with about 110 brethren, as well as more than sixty-five others in Spain, Portugal, France, Italy and Flanders. Five years later, in November 1632, the number of houses had risen to nineteen. The reason for this sudden and dramatic growth is partly to be found in a general relaxation of the government's attitude towards the Catholic Church in Ireland. For some years before 1627 the provisions of statute law concerning recusancy fines and, more importantly, subscription to the Oath of Supremacy had not been enforced in Dublin nor in corporate towns still under Old English Catholic influence. Since anti-Catholic legislation remained nonetheless a sword of Damocles over the Catholic community, the Old English Catholic leaders sought in 1628 to buy religious concessions as part of the 'Graces' from the cash-conscious Charles I.[2] On the other hand, the Anglican bishops in the spring of 1627 collectively and individually issued forthright statements against toleration or official recognition of Catholicism.[3] Nonetheless, because of the renewed war between England and Spain, the policy of the Irish government, on instructions from London, was sufficiently tolerant and conciliatory to permit the growth of religious communities.[4]

1 APF, SOCG, 294, ff 102r–105v.

2 A. Clarke, *The Old English in Ireland, 1625–42*, London 1966, 44–51; A. Clarke, *The Graces, 1625–41*, Dundalk 1968, *passim*; A. Clarke, 'Selling Royal Favours, 1624–32' in *NHI*, iii, 233–40.

3 Bodl., Carte MSS, I, ff 85v, 86r; Moran, *Archbishops of Dublin*, 311–12; Clarke, *The Graces, 1625–41*, 12–13; Clarke, 'Selling Royal Favours, 1624–32', 236.

4 R. D. Edwards, 'Church and State in the Ireland of Michél Ó Cléirigh' in S. O'Brien (ed.), *Measgra i gCuimhne Mhichíl Uí Chléirigh*, Dublin 1944, 4.

A most informative letter (written in about March 1629)[5] from the superior of the Carmelites in Dublin describes in some detail the security Catholics then enjoyed in the capital as a result of the 'Graces'. Since the summer of 1628 Catholic ecclesiastics had been publicly performing their sacred duties and had been able to set up 'suitable places with open doors' for preaching and celebrating Mass without being molested. The Carmelites, who lived in a rented house, numbered twenty religious, including students and novices. They wore lay clothes outdoors, and the religious habit within their house and church. Their church was sufficiently large for processions, even for that of the Blessed Sacrament. Even Protestants frequented Catholic chapels and listened to sermons. Protestants freely treated with the regular clergy, had them as guests to their houses, and seemed not to object to the religious habit. There were then Carmelites, Dominicans, Franciscans, Capuchins, Augustinians and Jesuits resident in the city, for the most part clustered around Cook Street, Bridge Street and Back Lane.[6]

By the late spring of 1629 this tacit policy of general religious toleration came to an end. In January the Lord Deputy (Falkland) and Privy Council reported to the king and Privy Council of England concerning 'an intolerable increase of Jesuits, seminarists, priests and monastic friars, who have arisen in this kingdom'.[7] In what he termed the interests of security, the viceroy made a sharp and perceptive distinction between those he termed 'loyal' (secular Catholic clergy) and 'seditious priests' (regular clergy), the one to be tolerated within certain limits, the others to be banished from Ireland.[8] His real objection (as it was that of many of his predecessors and would be that of every one of his successors in office) was to the regulars, not simply on account of their continental formation, but because their international organisation made them independent of the local bishops and therefore even less amenable to government control; an additional factor was their known willingness to act as agents of Spain and other foreign powers. Protestant opinion generally had become nervous and apprehensive of the evident vitality of Catholicism and the ever-diminishing restraint on its public practice. Falkland, with the full backing of the London government, issued a proclamation on 1 April 1629[9] in an

5 Moran, *Archbishops of Dublin*, 313–14.

6 J. T. Gilbert, *A History of the City of Dublin*, i, Dublin 1854, 298–9, 327, 240–43. The exact location of the Dominican house and chapel, thought to have been in the vicinity of Bridge Street, has yet to be pinpointed. The residence of the Augustinian friars is reputed to have been situated on the north bank of the Liffey at Arran Quay. T. C. Butler, *John's Lane: A History of the Augustinian Friars in Dublin, 1280–1980*, Dublin 1983, 65.

7 Cited in Moran, *Archbishops of Dublin*, 315.

8 Clarke, 'Selling Royal Favours, 1624–32', 240.

9 Full text in P. J. Corish, 'Two Seventeenth-Century Proclamations against the Catholic Clergy' in *Archiv. Hib.*, 39 (1984), 53–5.

attempt to contain or undo some aspects of the burgeoning Catholic revival. The proclamation explicitly forbade the exercise of Roman ecclesiastical jurisdiction, the public practice of the Catholic religion and the Catholic education of youth. It also decreed the dissolution of religious houses. Members of religious orders were singled out for special treatment; henceforth they were not to preach, teach, celebrate Mass or administer the sacraments in any church, chapel or public oratory. The lay owners of houses occupied by religious were ordered on pain of confiscation of their property 'to expel and thrust forth all and singular such friars, Jesuits and other monastical persons'. The proclamation stopped short of banishing the Catholic clergy outright.

To all outward appearances the proclamation seemed a success as the religious adopted their customary tactic of closing their houses and chapels at the start of a period of harassment and persecution. By 2 May 1629 the viceroy could boast that the regulars were dispersed and their houses abandoned. At that stage he contemplated banishing religious altogether because he considered them a liability to the country. Within a few months, however, most of the regulars were quietly back in their houses, while Falkland himself had been recalled to London.[10] Pending the nomination of Falkland's successor, Viscount Loftus and the Earl of Cork were appointed Lords Justices on 26 October 1629. It would appear that either the Franciscan[11] or the Carmelite chapel[12] in Cook Street, Dublin, was made a test case for Falkland's proclamation. On St Stephen's Day 1629 the Anglican archbishop, mayor and sheriffs of Dublin attempted to interrupt the public celebration of Mass. When the mayor pulled down some pictures, while soldiers smashed a statue of St Francis and Archbishop Bulkeley demolished the pulpit, there was uproar among the congregation. The people resisted, rescued two young friars who had been arrested, and violently drove the archbishop and his entourage through the streets of the city. State papers and other sources assert that all known religious houses in Dublin,[13] Cork, Drogheda and elsewhere were confiscated in the weeks that followed. In Dublin the Cook Street chapel was razed to the ground, to vindicate the honour of the insulted

10 Edwards, 'Church and State in the Ireland of Michél Ó Cléirigh', 6–7.

11 *Wadding Papers*, 330, 333, 341; Edwards, 'Church and State in the Ireland of Michél Ó Cléirigh', 7.

12 Moran, *Archbishops of Dublin*, 317–18, citing Sir James Ware and other contemporary authorities. J. P. Rushe, *Carmel in Ireland, with supplement*, Dublin/ London 1903, 49–51. It is quite possible that the authorities raided both Franciscan and Carmelite establishments on the same day, with the consequence that accounts tended to be confused as if only one chapel had been attacked.

13 'The Houses of Franciscans, Dominicans, Carmelites and Capuchins were seised on to the King's use by the mayor and aldermen and the keys delivered to the Lords Justices.' TCD, MS 6404, f. 108r.

Archbishop Bulkeley, while the Earl of Cork, without legal proceedings of any kind, seized a number of houses on the pretext that they belonged to Jesuits and friars. He disposed of some of these properties, possibly including the Dominican house, to Trinity College, while others were converted to serve as houses of correction.[14] Later the Earl of Cork's action was judged illegal, and the owners succeeded in reclaiming the confiscated property.[15]

Whatever setback the religious experienced seems to have been temporary, though admittedly disruptive of their organisation in cities and towns. As late as November 1631 it was stated that the Franciscans and other religious orders found great difficulty in obtaining leases for houses or properties, because the regulars, being as yet unorganised, could not afford to compensate the owners of forfeited property.[16] The Falkland proclamation was a salutary warning of what lay ahead should the government simultaneously have the will and the power to implement both statute law and proclamations.

The consequences of the proclamation of 1629 came as a grave shock to the Dominicans, but that they were not in any sense disastrous may be seen from a memorandum of 1632. In November of that year Nicholas Lynch, the Irish provincial (1627–34), then in exile in Spain, reported on the affairs of his province to King Philip IV.[17] There were in Ireland, he said, nineteen Dominican convents, all until recently in a satisfactory state and each with an adequate number of religious. Lynch claimed that during his provincialate the viceroy Falkland connived at the religious activities of Catholics to such an extent that religious of all orders dared to build and own houses in the larger towns where they might celebrate the divine office, preach and administer the sacraments, albeit behind closed doors in order not to irritate heretics. However, while he had been outside the country (since 1629) the viceroy's successors (i.e. Loftus, Cork and their agents) had set in motion a persecution hitherto unparalleled. Houses and convents of all orders had been confiscated throughout Ireland. The move was carried out so swiftly and unexpectedly that in many instances the Dominicans had been unable to conceal vestments, chalices or books. Lynch sought royal financial assistance in order to return to Ireland, to restore the fortunes of his ruined province to the best of his ability, and also to buy chalices and other liturgical requisites. The Spanish council of state recommended the rather meagre allowance of 100 ducats, and to this the king consented.

14 Edwards, 'Church and State in the Ireland of Michél Ó Cléirigh', 7–8.
15 *The Lismore Papers*, ed. A. B. Grosart, 2nd ser., iv, London 1887, 183.
16 HMC, *Report on the Franciscan Manuscripts*, Dublin 1906, 54.
17 AGS, Estado, leg. 2795.

While the Dominicans and other regulars continued to expand in Ireland during the late 1620s and 1630s, that period was nonetheless one of great uncertainty and disturbance for communities in town and city where anti-Catholic legislation could be implemented according to the whim of civic office-holders. This uncertain situation severely restricted the regular clergy living in towns and cities, as will later appear, so far as public services, educational initiatives and other apostolic enterprises were concerned. Dominicans attached to country houses, on the other hand, increased and flourished as never before, persevering in their efforts on behalf of the order and of the dioceses to which they belonged. Though personally committed to the eradication of Catholicism, which he detested, and the promotion of the Anglican state church, Lord Deputy Wentworth (1633–40) was obliged to bide his time in religious policy. The government was not sufficiently strong to impose effective measures of repression on the Catholic community, and the Established Church was as yet not a truly viable entity. Above all, Wentworth could not afford to complicate the attainment of urgent political priorities by attempting to deal with the religious question in the short term. In this twilight world of false religious security Catholics were able to practise their religion privately, religious houses became more numerous throughout the country, novitiates were established, and the religious orders involved themselves without restraint in the Catholic life of the country.[18]

PROGRESS IN THE IRISH PROVINCE: A REGIONAL SURVEY

The picture that emerges from the evidence available for Connacht is one of continuing Dominican activity and steady consolidation of the Order's presence west of the Shannon—sometimes achieved in very adverse circumstances. At Galway, as already noted, the flourishing Dominican community had opened schools for the free education of youth in the late 1620s and by December 1630 had ambitious plans to set up a regular *studium* for the education of diocesan and religious clergy alike.[19] During this second springtime two members of one of Galway's patrician families remembered the Dominicans in their wills. John Blake, a city merchant, bequeathed £2 to them in the draft of his will drawn up on 10 October 1622 before setting out for the Canary Islands.[20] The will of Sir Valentine Blake of Galway, while displaying his particular predilection for the Franciscans, also donated 5 marks each to the Dominicans, Augustinians and Jesuits of Galway.[21] Three chalices belonging to the

18 A. Clarke, 'The Government of Wentworth, 1632–40' in *NHI*, iii, 256–8, 264.
19 See pp 151–4 above.
20 M. J. Blake (ed.), *Blake Family Records, 1600–1700*, London 1905, 28–30.
21 Ibid., 250–52.

Galway Dominicans survive from the 1630s, a clear indication of religious toleration in the city and of their fruitful ministry. The first chalice was presented by Joanna French for the use of her son, Gregory French, O.P., in 1634. The second chalice, dating from 1639, was donated by Patrick Bodkin and Mary French. A third, dated 1640, came from Donagh Halorain and his wife Sarah.[22]

Two disparate contemporary references cast unexpected and significant light on the otherwise concealed Dominican presence at Athenry. On 20 May 1623 the town officials leased a parcel of land called Corolesine, once Dominican property, 'to Johnick Bodkin, Andrew Bodkin, Edward Comyen and Gregory Bodkin of Athenry, merchants, in consideration of £55'.[23] The lease contained what at first sight seemed a restrictive clause which made the grant of land subject to 'the free grazing of 20 head of cows for the space of five years, being the proper goods of Sir[24] Manus McWard'. This person is surely identical with the Manus McAward, stated to be an old friar of Athenry who died in 1626, former custodian of the Athenry Dominican annals (*Annales Domus Fratrum Praedicatorum Athenriae*)[25] and mentioned by Sir James Ware in his diary.[26] A herd of twenty grazing cows would have provided a solid economic basis for the support of the Athenry community, whose former legal title to this valuable property was tacitly acknowledged in the arrangement accepted by its current tenants of Catholic and Old English stock. Provision too was made for the lessees to be financially compensated by the corporation of Athenry 'should the lands be recovered or evicted by course of law', possibly suggesting that former Dominican property had been deliberately concealed from the crown surveyors and was perhaps being held in some agreed form of trust by the municipal authorities for its former owners.[27]

22 C. McNeil, 'The Chalices of the West Convent, Galway' in *RSAI Jn.*, 49 (1919), 187; J. J. Buckley, *Some Irish Altar Plate*, Dublin 1943, 60; Pochin Mould, *The Irish Dominicans*, 236–7.

23 Full text of lease in Blake, *Blake Family Records, 1600–1700*, 30–31.

24 The title 'Sir', besides its more common usage, was also used to designate university-educated priests who had taken a degree.

25 These annals, underlying the continuity of the Athenry Dominicans but no longer extant, were probably distinct from the better-known register of the Athenry Dominicans (*Regestum Monasterii Fratrum Praedicatorum de Athenry*) now in the British Library (BL, Add. MS 4784).

26 TCD, MS 6404, f. 85r.

27 While there is abundant evidence that Catholics were as prone as Protestants to intrude on the former landed wealth of the religious orders, Catholic proprietors did in conscience have to face the threat of canonical penalties incurred as a consequence of the alienation of ecclesiastical property. Where the friars succeeded in furnishing evidence as to previous legal title, an informal understanding with Catholic 'occupiers' as to use and fruits of property was frequently arrived at. Athenry may very well have been a case in point.

Reports from Sligo and Roscommon in 1631, compiled by James Fallon, vicar general of Elphin, indicate that the Dominicans of those counties had gone underground, if they were not constantly 'on the run'. The town of Sligo was under the harsh rule of a Protestant minister who had extensive authority from the crown and was unsparing in the use of it. This unidentified clergyman was said to be very severe on the Catholic supporters of priests, as well as on priests themselves, whom he arrested and imprisoned on the charge of usurping ecclesiastical authority. The Dominican convent lay in ruins, and the church had been put to use as a courthouse by Protestants.[28] From this period there survives a beautiful silver pyx still in the possession of the Dominicans of Sligo. It was made in 1629 for Fr Magomus Hugonis (Patrick McHugh), O.P., a native of Collracule or Coolrecuil, a townland in the parish of Kilmacteige, Co. Sligo, who made a gift of it to his own convent of Sligo.[29] However insignificant otherwise, Cloonymeaghan, with its landholding (valuation 17s 9d), was described as a cell of Sligo when it was leased (5 May 1621) to Henry Dodwell of Killian, Co. Galway.[30]

The Dominican monastery in Roscommon had been partly demolished, but part of its buildings served as a courthouse, and the rest had been turned into a dwelling-house for its Protestant owner. James Fallon noted in passing that there were in the diocese of Elphin some old friars acting as parish priests and solemnising marriages without any proper authority.[31] A chalice bearing the date 1636 was presented to the brethren of the convent of Roscommon by Connal Farraile and Rosa Garmley.[32] Two chalices from Portumna and Strade give unmistakable evidence of organised Dominican life in these localities. The Portumna chalice, made on 7 April 1635, asked for prayers for the soul of Dorothea Anslo *alias* Mulloy.[33] The Strade chalice was commissioned in 1641 by John Gillaboy, O.P.,[34] the earliest Dominican associated with the foundation of Gola in Co. Fermanagh, *c.* 1641–3.

On 7 January 1637 Dominic Burke, the Irish Dominican procurator at Rome, compiled a directory of Connacht clergy actively engaged in preaching.[35] All were described as natives of Connacht and resident

28 J. Hagan (ed.), 'Miscellanea Vaticano-Hibernica: 1580–1631' in *Archiv. Hib.*, 3 (1914), 361–2.

29 Full Latin inscription in Pochin Mould, *The Irish Dominicans*, 240

30 TCD, MS 6404, f. 170.

31 Hagan, 'Miscellanea Vaticano-Hibernica: 1580–1631', 362–3.

32 Buckley, *Some Irish Altar Plate*, 66; Pochin Mould, *The Irish Dominicans*, 236.

33 Pochin Mould, *The Irish Dominicans*, 236.

34 Ibid., 237.

35 There are two versions of this document: (1) APF, SOCG, 135, ff 204rv, 209rv; B. Jennings (ed.), 'Miscellaneous Documents, II: 1625–1640' in *Archiv. Hib.*, 14 (1949), 21–2; B. Millett (ed.), 'Catalogue of Irish Material in Vols

there. Burke's document provides valuable biographical details about four secular priests, eighteen Dominicans, seven Franciscans, three Augustinians and two Jesuits. He reported that there were many other priests, diocesan and regular, who had studied overseas and were working in parishes but did not preach. Others too, having completed their studies abroad, were about to return to Ireland. Burke listed twelve Dominican houses and two vicarial houses. The words '*sunt fratres*' or simply '*fratres*' were placed opposite the names of such houses as had a resident community (Athenry, Galway, Portumna, Roscommon, Sligo, Urlar, Strade and Burrishoole), but without any indication of their numbers. The vicarial houses of Kilcorban and Toolooban (which belonged to Athenry) were then unoccupied, as also were the houses of Tulsk, Ballindoon, Cloonshanville and Rathfran.

In 1637 Bishop Boethius Egan, O.F.M., of Elphin reported that there was only one Dominican house (unnamed) functioning in his diocese. He claimed that he himself had restored it, together with a house for the Franciscans, on his promotion to the see. This should be interpreted to mean that there was only one house in the diocese with Dominican regular life and community recitation of the divine office. Formerly there had been five convents of the Order in Elphin: Roscommon, Tulsk, Cloonshanville, Ballindoon and Sligo. The Dominicans of that diocese were then accustomed to live in caves and woods while Protestants occupied their property.[36]

In Munster too the Dominicans had re-established themselves in several strategic towns: Cork, Youghal, Waterford, Limerick and Kilmallock. They had also refounded their country house at Lorrha in north Tipperary.

In January 1631 an unexpected occurrence in Limerick caused consternation among the Dominicans and Catholics of the city. John MacEnery, O.P., presented himself to the Protestant bishop, Francis Gough, as a convert to Anglicanism. MacEnery declared that his conscience would no longer allow him to be a Dominican or of the Roman faith, because 'that Church held damnable, rebellious and uncharitable tenets'. Moreover, he declared that he had been sworn under oath of secrecy to conspire against the Church of England. He wished to recant his faith, take the sacrament (Holy Communion) of the Church of England and to cut himself off definitively from the Catholic Church.

132–139 of the SOCG in Propaganda Archives' in *Collect. Hib.*, 12 (1969), 30. (2) APF, SOCG, 140, ff lv–2rv; B. Millett (ed.), 'Catalogue of Irish Material in Vols 140–143 of the SOCG in Propaganda Archives' in *Collect. Hib.*, 13 (1970), 22.

36 J. Hagan (ed.), 'Miscellanea Vaticano-Hibernica: Ireland in 1580' in *Archiv. Hib.*, 5 (1916), 95–6.

At the bishop's insistence, MacEnery preached a recantation sermon which caused a disturbance in St Mary's Cathedral on 16 January 1631. In the course of his sermon MacEnery was interrupted by a Dominican priest named Gibbon Wall. Wall was arrested by soldiers present at the service, amidst much opposition by other priests and Catholic citizens. MacEnery, however, when pressed to identify his former Dominican brethren and their supporters, refused by reason of his previous oath.

When preaching again at a service on Candlemas Day, MacEnery declared that there were more than 1,600 Catholic regular and diocesan clergy in Ireland. He alleged that 'great conspiracies' were afoot against the realm and its Protestant clergy. He named two Scottish Dominicans, Patrick Gibbs and John Hamilton, alleging that they resorted to aliases and 'deluded the people in the province of Munster, speaking against the church service and manner of their administration of the sacrament of the Church of England'.[37] Nothing further is recorded of John MacEnery, or precisely why his Scottish confrères were preaching in Ireland. On 27 May Gibbon Wall was censured by the Court of Castle Chamber of Dublin Castle, fined £1,000 and imprisoned during pleasure.[38]

Perhaps the dramatic events and revelations in Limerick instigated a raid carried out in the same month of January 1631 on the Cork houses of the Dominicans, Augustinians, Franciscans and Jesuits by Warham St Leger at the command of the Earl of Cork and Viscount Loftus. At each house the religious had been forewarned and escaped with whatever belongings they could carry in haste. It was reported that the Dominican house in Mill Street (in the shadow of their former house, St Mary's of the Isle) was capable of accommodating some twenty friars, 'some of whom had evidently been in bed there the night before my visit, whilst I found malt beer and meal in the house'. St Leger also found a fine pulpit and the frame of an altar in the 'Mass-room', for which he fined the real owner of the house, George Galwey, the enormous sum of £500 and ordered him to stand trial before the Lords Justices.[39] In November 1631 the people of some outlying districts south of the River Lee claimed exemption from the public tax of the city and went to live within the exempted precincts of the former Dominican monastery of St Mary's of the Isle. Orders to remove them were of no avail. In August of the following year force was employed to compel 'the inhabitants of St Finbarr's and some other dissolved abbeys near Cork' to obey the authorities.[40] A

37 R. Ware, *The Hunting of the Romish Fox*, Dublin 1683, 216–18.

38 TCD, MS 6404 (Sir James Ware's notebook and diary of events), ff 113r–114r; transcript in Dublin Corporation Gilbert Library, MS 169, ff 205–6.

39 *Cal. S.P. Ire., 1625–32*, 510; E. Bolster, *A History of the Diocese of Cork*, ii, Cork 1982, 172.

40 *Cal. S.P. Ire., 1625–32*, 584, 374, 620–21; Bolster, *Diocese of Cork*, ii, 181–2.

chalice of 1641, made for the Cork Dominican community, bears the names of Fr William John Connor, O.P., and Brother Gerard Gould, a Franciscan tertiary.[41]

For the other Dominican houses in Munster only the silent testimony of silver chalices indicates their clandestine ministry during the 1630s. The Waterford friars received the gift of a chalice from Anastatia Madan in 1631.[42] The inscription on a Youghal chalice of 1632 simply denotes that it belonged to the convent of Our Lady of Graces, the donor remaining anonymous.[43] Surprisingly, two chalices have survived from the small country house of Lorrha.[44] One, dated 1632, has an inscription asking for prayers for the souls of the donors, Fr Maurice Graven and Charles Hogan. The later chalice, dated 1639, was made for Brother Anthony Kennedy, presumably a scion of the Kennedy family of Upper Ormond, for the use of Lorrha. Three chalices were made for the convent of Kilmallock in 1639, and the inscriptions on all three mention members of the Burgatt family, including Henry Burgatt, prior of Kilmallock about 1639, and his brother, Thomas Burgatt, O.P., who died in 1639.[45] The chalices were presented both by the Burgatt family and by Callaghan O'Callaghan and his wife Juliana Butler. The latter silver chalice was of graceful design, with the figure of the crucifixion. The inscription asks a prayer for Maurice, son of Edward Fitzgibbon, the White Knight, who died in 1608. The donors of the Limerick chalice in 1640 were Patrick Sarsfield and Eleonora White.[46]

The chalices provide a helpful clue to the identity of Dominican lay supporters in the late 1620s and 1630s. The donors were obviously wealthy people, greatly attached to the Dominicans and drawn equally from the ranks of well-established Gaelic Irish and Anglo-Irish Catholic families. Although neither hallmarks nor makers' names are to be found on these pieces of seventeenth-century altar plate, all these silver chalices bear remarkable testimony to the generosity of the donors and the skill of metalworkers in cities such as Dublin, Cork, Galway and Limerick.

Writing to Rome on 6 July 1630, Patrick Comerford, the Augustinian Bishop of Waterford and Lismore, praised the pastoral zeal and moral probity of the thirty regular priests in his diocese, but did not supply

41 Pochin Mould, *The Irish Dominicans*, 237.
42 Buckley, *Some Irish Altar Plate*, 53; Pochin Mould, *The Irish Dominicans*, 236.
43 Buckley, *Some Irish Altar Plate*, 54; Pochin Mould, *The Irish Dominicans*, 236.
44 McNeil, 'The Chalices of the West Convent, Galway', 187; Pochin Mould, *The Irish Dominicans*, 236–7; Buckley, *Some Irish Altar Plate*, 54, 77; T. J. Westropp, 'A Survey of the Ancient Churches in Co. Limerick' in *RIA Proc.*, 25 (1905), sect. C, 463.
45 Buckley, *Some Irish Altar Plate*, 76, 207; Pochin Mould, *The Irish Dominicans*, 237.
46 Pochin Mould, *The Irish Dominicans*, 237.

particulars about their respective orders.[47] The Dominican community at Waterford must have been strong and viable, judging by the fact that it hosted a representative gathering of Dominicans from far and wide in July 1631, attended by the priors of Tralee, Dublin, Kilmallock, Mullingar, Athenry, Waterford, Roscommon, Kilkenny, Galway, Cashel, Limerick, Lorrha and Cork and the vicar of Trim.[48] The Archbishop of Cashel wrote to Rome on 3 May 1632 that his ecclesiastical province had a great number of regular and diocesan clergy. While generous in his comments on both groups, he noted that there were some instances of grave excess among them. The regulars, he said, were disinclined to refrain from indiscriminate administration of the sacraments even since the restriction of missionary faculties.[49] His report supplied no information about the Dominicans of Cashel. In 1633 twelve Dominicans were active as preachers and professors in the united dioceses of Ardfert and Aghadoe.[50] At that time they had only one monastery, probably in or close to Tralee. In 1636 or 1637 thirteen Dominican preachers were named with biographical details in a report to Propaganda Fide on Ardfert.[51] It is clear that there were few obstacles to preaching or pastoral ministry in Kerry. The impression given is that this group of Dominicans traversed the entire diocese from their base at Tralee, but may have used hospices of their own in the countryside. Their medieval hospice at Dingle, confiscated *c.* 1584,[52] may have been re-established.

In Leinster the Dominicans had to contend with various pressures and constant insecurity. Two lists of clergy in Dublin, dated 14 September 1633, were drawn up by the regulars and seculars in a less than fraternal spirit. Both lists were incorporated in a document headed 'The State of the Difference between Seculars and Regulars'.[53] The list compiled by the regulars mentioned only two resident Dominicans: Thomas Brangan and Hugh Duigin, both priests. The list compiled by the secular clergy contained the names of five Dominicans: Thomas Brangan (*malitiosissimus*), Hugh Duigin, Thady Murphy (*astutus*), John Scurlogg (*ignoramus*) and (—) Tigge (*ignoramus*). The secular list of regulars was much the longer. It estimated that there were twenty Franciscans, five Dominicans, six Cistercians, ten Capuchins, fifteen Carmelites, four Augustinians and twenty-one Jesuits. In all there were eighty-one regulars, 'besides their novices, which are thought not to be few, and divers lay brothers

47 APF, SOCG, 294, f. 221r.
48 *Wadding Papers*, 591.
49 APF, SOCG, 294, ff 195rv–196r.
50 Moran, *Spicil. Ossor.*, i, 184.
51 Jennings, 'Miscellaneous Documents II: 1625–1640', 21–2.
52 Gwynn and Hadcock, *Medieval Religious Houses: Ireland*, 230, 233.
53 Sheffield City Library, Strafford MSS, XX (b)/14, 175. I am grateful to Revd Dr Donal F. Cregan for directing me to this source.

unknown'. The regulars remarked of it that it included some people by mistake, while others named in it lived elsewhere in other parts of the kingdom or even abroad. Some of the remarks about the other regulars of Dublin were much worse than those made about the Dominicans. What is really significant is the drop in numbers at Dublin since 1627, when the community numbered four priests, three novices and a lay brother. At all events, the Dublin Dominicans, even if they had a secret novitiate, were maintaining a low profile in numbers and activities.

An order in council dated 20 January 1630 recommended the seizure of two 'Mass-houses' kept by religious orders in Trim.[54] One of these houses belonged to the Dominicans, the other to the Franciscans. There is evidence to suggest that Trim was restored as a very small community between March 1628 and January 1630.[55] Mullingar, a leading house in this period of revival, is not mentioned either in hostile or friendly reports during the 1630s. One of its prominent members at this time was Raymund Moore. Two chalices, made for his own use and that of the community of Mullingar, bear the date 1638.[56]

There is a veiled reference to the Dominicans of Naas in the 1630s: 'Strafford [Wentworth] was exposed to the hatred of the Presbyterians [Puritans] . . . by suffering public Mass-houses at the Naas so near his own house, and by permitting friars to dwell in a house of his own which he had built for other purposes, but notwithstanding all this he was no friend of popery.'[57] It has been suggested that the actual house in which the Dominicans had quietly taken up residence was in Corbanstreet Lane, where Wentworth is known to have owned property. The building occupied by the friars may have been an inn, reputedly named the Rose and Crown, leased by Wentworth to Thomas and Walter Ashe, thought to be Catholics.[58]

In the dioceses of Ossory and Meath, where relations between the diocesan authorities and regular clergy had been soured as a result of a longstanding dispute,[59] episcopal opinion clearly affected whatever concealed presence or ministry the Dominicans may have had at Kilkenny, Aghaboe and Rosbercon (in the diocese of Ossory) or at Trim and Mullingar (in the diocese of Meath). The Bishop of Ossory reported to Rome in 1635 that the Dominican houses of Kilkenny, Rosbercon and Aghaboe, in common with religious houses generally, were either in

54 H. Fenning, 'The Dominicans of Trim, 1263–1682' in *Riocht na Midhe*, 3 (1963), 20.
55 Ibid.
56 Pochin Mould, *The Irish Dominicans*, 237, 239.
57 R. Cox, *Hibernia Anglicana*, i, London 1689, 60.
58 A. Valkenburg, 'The Ven. Peter Higgins, Dominican, 1601?–1642' in *Kildare Arch. Soc. Jn.*, 15 (1973–4), 290.
59 For an account of this dispute see pp 243–4 above.

ruins or put to secular use,[60] but did not comment, perhaps for the sake of their security, on such Dominicans as were actually in his diocese. A chalice of 1640, now in Tallaght priory, bearing the names of Thaddeus Duluhunty and his wife Evelyn Meagher, was probably donated to one of the Ossory Dominican houses.

The former foundations in Ulster were the last to which the Dominicans returned. Ross MacGeoghegan's incomplete report of 1627 lists five houses in Ulster: Derry, Coleraine, Newtownards, Carlingford and Drogheda (then as now in the ecclesiastical province of Armagh); he did not indicate which communities had been revived. The Dominicans had returned to Drogheda and opened a chapel before 1622. There were seven friars, some presumably Dominicans, in Derry city and county in 1631, and they were on such good terms with the Protestant authorities that Sir Thomas Phillips protested to Charles I about the scandal.[61] One of the friars mentioned was 'Prior McKedy, tenant to the Ironmongers', who officiated in the parish of Desert Froghell.[62] The Dominicans were the only friars in the city of Derry. Dominic Connor, prior of the convent, arranged in 1640 for the making of a fine silver chalice, still preserved in Derry.[63]

THE ROMAN AUTHORITIES AND IRISH DOMINICAN AFFAIRS, 1627–30

Contact with Propaganda Fide, which had been established in or before 1626 in the person of the procurator of the Irish Dominican province at Rome, Michael of the Holy Spirit, was maintained and developed during the provincialate of Ross MacGeoghegan's successor, Nicholas D. Lynch. Late in 1627, Father Michael presented two petitions to Propaganda Fide requesting special faculties for members of the Irish province. The first was addressed to the Pope through the congregation and was probably made by order of the provincial chapter recently held at Sligo.[64] The faculties sought were:

(1) permission to put to pious use goods restored by heretics or whose ownership was uncertain;

(2) the right to elect priors and provincials without delay even if strict canonical norms could not be observed;

60 Hagan, 'Miscellanea Vaticano-Hibernica: Ireland in 1580', 86.
61 W. P. Burke, 'The Diocese of Derry' in *Archiv. Hib.*, 5 (1916), 4, 5; *Cal. S.P. Ire., 1625–32*, 643–4.
62 Burke, 'The Diocese of Derry', 3.
63 Buckley, *Some Irish Altar Plate*, 83; Pochin Mould, *The Irish Dominicans*, 237.
64 APF, SOCG, 388, ff 1r, 8v.

(3) permission for holy orders to be conferred outside the customary times because of the need for secrecy and of danger to the religious themselves;

(4) the appointment of four masters of theology (S.T.M.) and six *sacrae theologiae praesentati* (S.T.P.) who would thereby be qualified to teach, in accord with the decisions of the last general chapter of Milan (1622);

(5) the excommunication of those retaining or concealing moveable and immoveable goods of the Order in Ireland;

(6) a grant of these faculties to the provincial *pro tempore*, since only the most theologically suitable and learned friars were ever elected to that office;

(7) permission to the provincial to delegate these faculties to competent subjects.

This petition was discussed at a meeting of Propaganda Fide on 23 November, and it was decided to seek the advice of the Dominican procurator general on the likely outcome of the petition. The latter raised no objection and stated that the Pope might grant the petition if he pleased. What the Pope eventually decided is unknown.

A separate petition concerning the conferring of holy orders was submitted to Propaganda Fide towards the end of 1627.[65] It asked for permission for Irish Dominicans to receive holy orders *extra tempora* on feast-days, with dispensations for interstices. It explained that Irish circumstances made it extremely dangerous for bishops to confer orders except in great secrecy and on rare occasions. This petition was approved by Propaganda Fide and the Pope on 4 February 1628.

At the general chapter of the Order held at Rome in June 1629 the Irish province was represented by the prior provincial, Nicholas Lynch.[66] This chapter incorporated some of the provisions of earlier Irish provincial chapters in fourteen ordinations specially made for the Irish province. One ordination in particular reflected the optimistic mood of the province, for it permitted the provincial to accept land, property or houses for the erection of houses or residences for the brethren. Another approved guidelines for division of the property and personal effects of deceased friars made at the 1627 chapter in Sligo. Yet another empowered the provincial to dispense with many constitutions and conventual observances which could not be implemented in Ireland because of

65 Ibid., 388, ff 56r, 63v; B. Jennings (ed.), 'Acta Sacrae Congregationis de Propaganda Fide, 1622–1650' in *Archiv. Hib.*, 22 (1959), 46.

66 Reichert, *MOPH*, xii, 2.

adverse conditions. The constitutions in question were not explicitly mentioned, but the motive of the chapter was to remove all scruples of conscience, given the needs of the time and the demands of good government. The chapter also committed to the Irish provincial responsibility for the 'province' of Scotland and the mission to the Scottish Isles. Provincials of other provinces were warmly exhorted to receive Irish friars for their studies, something they had in fact been doing for several decades, 'the more especially as the friars of this province do not cease daily to strenuously defend and propagate the faith even unto blood'.[67] Evidently the Irish province was still largely dependent on continental provinces for a continuing supply of well-trained Irish recruits.

An anonymous list of alleged abuses among regulars in Ireland led Propaganda Fide to issue instructions on 11 June 1630 to the heads of religious orders (Dominicans, Observant Franciscans and Augustinians) in Rome, recalling similar measures proposed in 1626. As a result, a spirited refutation of the charges against the regular clergy, especially against the Dominicans, was made in the same year. This was not unlike the reply, basically to the same allegations, made by Hugh McCaughwell, O.F.M., Archbishop of Armagh, in August 1626.[68] Among other things, it had been alleged that owing to the great increase in their numbers the regulars had become vagrants and were of no spiritual benefit to the people; that they recruited many novices whose canonical status after profession was doubtful; that the instruction of novices was inadequate, owing to the presence of women, lay people and even heretics in their houses, as well as to the lack of silence, the wearing of secular dress and the employment of novices on the quest; that the friars exacted alms, especially cattle, out of all proportion for their feasts; that the patronal festivals of their churches and houses were the occasion of over-indulgence in food and drink.[69]

One reply by an unknown Dominican is both lengthy and fascinating.[70] It asserted, perhaps inaccurately, that in 1630 the Order had no more than twelve houses, the maximum number of priests being seven, with a few novices, and in some cases as few as three or four priests. For lack of priests they were frequently obliged to celebrate Mass and preach twice on the same day. The charge that they roamed all over the country was readily admitted, but convincingly clarified. Nobody was allowed to travel without special permission and a definite pastoral objective: works of mercy, teaching Christian doctrine, visitation and consolation of the sick, the hearing of confessions and the administration of the sacraments wherever there was a shortage of parochial clergy. Dominicans therefore

67 Ibid., 52–4.
68 APF, SOCG, 294, ff 119r, 120r–121rv.
69 *Wadding Papers*, 371–2.
70 Ibid., 372–7.

did not travel for leisure or to no purpose; very often they alone attended to the spiritual wants of the people or complemented elsewhere the ministrations of the diocesan clergy. They were particularly devoted to the ministry of preaching, since the bishops did not preach and extremely few of their clergy were equipped to do so. Those who could preach were occupied in other ministries as vicars general, vicars forane or parish priests, so that the office of preaching was for the most part carried out in Ireland by itinerant members of religious orders. Since Irish Catholics were strongly attached to religious, and far more young men came to them seeking the religious habit than could be conveniently received, they had no need to look for or entice postulants. Professed religious had no doubts about their profession either with regard to the legal forms required or the authority of religious superiors to receive candidates to the habit or religious profession. The Irish Dominicans had a papal brief permitting them to receive novices to the habit and profession even in time of persecution, provided they observed the requirements of the Council of Trent and the provisions of canon law. There was no question of dubious profession among Dominicans, save in a single case involving a technicality (concerning the extension of the novitiate year) about which canon lawyers could not agree.

By far the most interesting and revealing part of the reply was that given in defence of the city novitiates of the Order. Since it provides first-hand information and insight into the process of urban adaptation, it deserves to be quoted in full:

> Our novices are instructed daily in the constitutions and rubrics, in prayer (both vocal and mental) and in the other observances of the Order except that they cannot be taught plainchant (for fear of the heretics), and when it is necessary to go abroad neither they nor the professed brothers dare to wear the habit of the Order outwardly. However, they seldom leave the house, and then only from necessity, nor can they do otherwise in these times of persecution. The assertion that women, laymen and heretics may enter the novitiate is false, if their cells or bedrooms are in question, for only the brothers themselves can enter these. But if it refers to the other rooms of the house, the outer and inner courtyard, or the common-room—anyone can enter these as he pleases.
>
> Since religious in these parts live not in cloisters but hidden in secular houses, it is necessary in those towns and cities, in which they fear the attacks of heretics, that some Catholic laymen should live in the outer part of the house facing the street. If these are craftsmen or shopkeepers to whom all sorts of people may resort, then it is a better and more convenient arrangement; for heretics are less likely to

> suspect that religious are living in the back, and those Catholics who come to their Masses and sermons are thought to be conducting business with the shopkeepers or tradespeople. If, then, we speak of those laymen who come to the outer parts of the friars' house, or live in them, it is true that they dwell in the same house as the brothers, but between them and the brothers are certain partitions through which they may not pass without the consent of the religious superior. And when one considers the adverse circumstances of the times, there is nothing unbecoming in this cohabitation.
>
> The allegation that novices are sent on the quest is no longer true. For two or three years this has been specifically forbidden, although formerly they accompanied professed friars assigned to this work. Similarly, it is wrong to say they do not observe silence at certain fixed times, although they cannot always do this because of difficult circumstances. Although the novices wear lay-clothes when they are compelled to go out, in order to escape persecution by the heretics or for other pressing reasons, they still wear the habit of the Order openly at home, and even when they do go out they are accustomed to wear a light habit or small woollen tunic and a short scapular under their lay attire.

The Dominican apologist went on to deny that the number of Dominicans was excessive, since they could neither staff half of their former convents nor provide sufficiently for the spiritual needs of Catholics. Nor were they guilty of importuning the faithful for alms. They thought it reasonable to seek alms on feast-days when Catholics gathered after Mass. That circumstance provided security for the friars who might otherwise be arrested if they were to go separately from house to house. The writer explained that the designated questors sought alms for the wants of the brethren, leaving it to the judgement of each person to give whatever he wished; what was donated was written down so that a servant of the brethren might later gather together what had been given for their use. And although this was the ancient system observed in Ireland for seeking alms, some ecclesiastical innovators now sought to abolish it. The charge of assembling and building up flocks of sheep and cattle beyond their reasonable needs was also strongly denied, as well as the accusation that the money obtained from selling off these flocks was being sent out of the country for the support of their brethren overseas. Again owing to the scarcity of money in the country, the Dominicans and other friars were compelled to accept gifts in kind—particularly cattle, sheep and grain, of which there was an abundance—and then later exchange them for fish and milk products. These were the established customs of the country and gave no rise to scandals whatsoever, though the friars were criticised by the innovators already mentioned who were jealous of the bond of affection between friars and people, and who themselves demanded and accepted only money. Finally, the writer refuted the charge levelled against the friars of drunkenness on the occasion of pattern days and festivals. On such days the friars were so taken up with making provision for the spiritual requests of the people—preaching, hearing confessions, distributing Holy Communion and preparing people for the sacraments—that they themselves scarcely had time to eat. To offer hospitality to their guests on these festival days was not only in line with the ancient tradition of Irish hospitality but also followed the clear example of Christ, who fed those who had left their houses and cities to hear Him preach in the desert.

EPISCOPAL POSTULATIONS

In the late 1620s and 1630s at least fifteen Dominicans were proposed, and some formally postulated, for Irish dioceses: James Arthur (senior) for Cashel and coadjutor to the Bishop of Limerick; James Arthur (junior), declared eligible for a bishopric and particularly Armagh; Richard Caron for Armagh; Edmund Raymund Dempsey for Leighlin; Anthony of St Mary Lynch, declared eligible for the episcopate; Nicholas D. Lynch for Achonry, Clonfert, Killala, Mayo and Armagh; Ross MacGeoghegan for Armagh, Cashel and Kildare; Patrick MacTeig for Armagh; John of the Cross Murphy for Armagh, Ferns and Leighlin; Anthony Nugent, declared eligible for a bishopric; Dominic Nugent for Armagh and Clogher; Dominic O'Daly for Ardfert and Aghadoe; Daniel O'Crean for a bishopric; Gregory O'Farrell, future provincial, for Ardagh; and Thomas Quirke for Armagh.[71]

Of these candidates, only two were successful: Ross MacGeoghegan, Bishop of Kildare (1629–44) and Edmund Raymund Dempsey, Bishop of Leighlin (1642–58).[72] About 1640 Donatus Brouder, priest and formerly a student of the Irish College, Rome, petitioned Cardinal Antonio Barberini, Protector of Ireland, on behalf of the clergy of Connacht concerning nominations to the episcopate in the west of Ireland.[73] He asserted that it was the Irish custom for each province to obtain its bishops from among its own native clergy. Hitherto Connacht had proved an exception to this rule. In future no outsiders should be appointed, as highly suitable candidates were available from the ranks of the diocesan and regular clergy. He then submitted a list of candidates, of whom one

71 *Wadding Papers*: index of persons.
72 Chronological details of these episcopates are given in Appendix 2.
73 APF, SOCG, 404, f. 412v.

should be chosen for the vacant see of Achonry, then a matter of dispute in the Roman curia. Among those proposed were six Dominicans: Hugh Madden, Oliver Burke, Peter Martin, Dominic Burke, Stephen Lynch and Thomas Lynch, all of whom, with the exception of Madden, belonged to leading Anglo-Irish families.

Though the vast majority of postulations to secure the promotion of Dominicans to the episcopate were unavailing, they signalled the growing stature and confidence of the Dominicans in Ireland. Membership of the Irish hierarchy by members of the religious orders was deemed especially important, not so much for honour, title and prestige, but to secure influence in ecclesiastical affairs. In 1626 the three metropolitan sees of Armagh, Dublin and Tuam as well as the diocese of Elphin were all occupied by Franciscans, which naturally aroused apprehension and jealousy among the other regulars. Traditionally, a regular bishop undertook the office of protector of the rights and privileges of his order or of several orders *vis-à-vis* his fellow bishops. The order in question therefore had a sympathetic spokesman and mediator should differences or misunderstandings arise between the bishops or between an individual bishop and the regular clergy. This situation, of course, left the way open for accusations on the part of disgruntled clergy or their factions against regular bishops on the grounds of conflict of interests. The Dominican Master General, Nicholas Ridolfi, privately but actively canvassed leading members of the Roman curia for the nomination of Irish Dominicans to the episcopate to counterbalance Franciscan influence. He twice approached Cardinal Ludovisi, Protector of Ireland, on 11 September and 18 December 1631, reminding the cardinal of a promise to favour the Irish province and to have Nicholas Lynch promoted to an Irish see.[74] Again in the 1630s Propaganda Fide took note of the determination of Ridolfi to obtain a bishopric for an unnamed Irish Dominican, an objective supported by the agent of Queen Henrietta Maria, who was well acquainted with Irish affairs.[75] Rome, however, remained unmoved in the face of this high-powered lobbying.

TRAINING AND INTELLECTUAL FORMATION: THE SPANISH CONNECTION

Successive procurators of the Irish province at the court of Madrid experienced difficulty in obtaining payment of the annual viaticum for Dominicans destined for Ireland between 1630 and 1635. On 31 August 1633 Dominic O'Daly, then engaged in diplomatic negotiations with

74 *Wadding Papers*, 35, 50.
75 APF, SOCG, 397, f. 60r.

the Spanish court,[76] suggested that payments should be made available in Portugal (then under Spanish rule) so that the recipients would be spared the excessive expense of a journey to the Spanish court.[77] When this suggestion was repeated by William FitzGerald, the Dominican procurator, in February 1634, it met with the king's approval.[78] The council of Portugal and the body responsible for Portuguese finances were given instructions in March concerning the precise mode of payment.[79] The difficulty in collecting the royal alms was not simply one of delays and obstacles, heightened by the air of general crisis in Spain, where there was plague in Catalonia, famine throughout the country, and actual war with France in 1635.[80] There were also inescapable human problems. For example, it often happened that students were ordered by their own provincials to return to Ireland before the completion of their studies. In such cases they lacked the royal viaticum to do so promptly.[81] Even when they had finished their academic training, there were serious inconveniences for Irish students in Spanish convents which sometimes were unwilling to accommodate and support them before they left for Ireland. At times there was much personal suffering and misunderstanding, and it was even claimed that there was a high incidence of death among Irish students living in Spanish convents.[82] After 1635 the viaticum was paid regularly and punctually to the procurators at Madrid, and so the orderly flow of Irish Dominican priests from Spain and Portugal to Ireland was assured.

The intellectual life of the Irish Dominicans was energetically promoted from Spain. In a memorandum of William FitzGerald, procurator of the Irish province in Spain, dated 16 September 1636,[83] much information was supplied to Philip IV about the painstaking efforts and diligence of numerous Dominicans who by FitzGerald's order and that of the Irish provincial had assembled a quantity of books for dispatch to Ireland. The muleteer who had transported the books from the convent of Holy Cross, Segovia, for shipment from the port of Bilbao, was confronted by tax demands at the custom house of Vitoria. For every unit of about 25 pounds (*arroba*), a charge of 24 rials in accord with the new customs impositions was demanded, and because he was not carrying letters guaranteeing payment, the officials stopped five loads and one trunk of books. The procurator pointed out that the Irish province did not have

76 For O'Daly's diplomatic activities in Spain and Portugal see pp 120–22 above.
77 AGS, Estado, leg. 2759.
78 Ibid.
79 Ibid., leg. 2797.
80 H. Kamen, *Spain: 1469–1714*, London 1983, 236.
81 AGS, Estado, leg. 2797.
82 Ibid., leg. 2798.
83 Ibid., leg. 2799.

conventual revenues or income, nor did its religious who were completing studies have the means of paying the charges demanded on books obtained by way of gift, nor had they received the 300 ducats already approved by the king to cover their needs and expenses. The king was asked to give orders exempting consignments of books authorised by the Irish procurator from charges at all customs stations and ports. The purpose of the books was stated to be to equip the Irish brethren intellectually for the conversion of heretics. The matter was referred to the council of state, which noted that since the consignments consisted exclusively of books, old and second-hand for the most part, which would be useful to the Catholics of Ireland, they should be declared free from taxes, allowed free transit and not be subject to inspection. With these proposals the king concurred. Earlier documents in the same series, dated July and August 1636, had referred to the difficulties and dangers that often attended the export of goods from the port of Bilbao and therefore requested the right of exemption to extend to all Spanish ports. The four principal ports of embarkation were Lisbon, La Coruña, Bilbao and San Sebastian. By the end of July 1636 some fifty-two loads (1,220 *arrobas*) had arrived at Vitoria, the customs clearance centre for the seaports of the north of Spain, where officials sought payment of 36,600 rials, a very substantial sum of money indeed.

By 1641 John of St Dominic O'Connor had succeeded William Fitz-Gerald as Irish Dominican procurator in Spain and had been for many years past the moving spirit behind the exportation of theological books to Ireland from his base at Segovia. In a memorial to the Spanish king he related how he gathered a great quantity of theological works from the alms contributed 'in these Catholic kingdoms' for the propagation of the faith in Ireland and the rooting out of heresy in England and the neighbouring kingdoms. The books had passed through the customs, the operation being facilitated by the orders of the council of state and the ministry of finance. They were then in the keeping of the Spanish port authorities awaiting embarkation. However, this could not take place because of high transportation costs, and also because the Irishmen who earlier had offered free transportation by way of alms had been killed in the recent wars in the service of the king. The quantity of books was very great, and because the perils attending those who would ensure their conveyance were extremely grave, the petitioner sought 2,000 ducats from state funds to cover transportation fees. It was essential that the carriers should be successful in landing their cargo on the islands of Inishbofin and Burrishoole (Clew Bay), which were controlled by Catholics, so as to prevent the consignment falling into the hands of heretics. The procurator appealed to the king's patronage and clemency, as protector of the Church, to grant the requested alms. The king's council recommended a grant of 200 ducats for the proposed transportation of the books, and the king endorsed this decision on 19 November 1641.[84]

The Dominicans in Ireland too were strikingly made aware of the expenses involved in the scheme for their intellectual improvement. Already on 1 September 1639 Nicholas Ridolfi, the Master General, ordered the provincial to oblige all priests under his jurisdiction to celebrate Masses for the intentions of those who had contributed books or alms for the purchase of books for the Irish province. This work was under the supervision of John of St Dominic O'Connor, who had been appointed for the task by the province, and by the late Nicholas Lynch, provincial.[85] It is therefore certain that several shipments of theological books were landed on the west coast of Ireland between 1636 and the late 1640s. On arrival the books would have been sorted and distributed to Dominican houses and individuals throughout the country. However, on account of the subsequent wars and confiscations, most of these books were destroyed, sold or lost. Some sixteenth- and seventeenth-century books which belonged to the Dominicans and other Irish friars, with inscriptions, names of houses and autograph signatures, are to be found in the library of Trinity College, Dublin,[86] and elsewhere. These volumes may well have been among the books imported from Spain. In the provincial archives at Tallaght there is a copy of a finely printed quarto volume entitled *Sancti Patris Nostri Joannis Chrysostomi Homiliae et Commentarii in Psalmos Davidis etc.*, edited by Fronton du Duc, S.J., and printed in Paris in 1614. The inscription on the back of the flyleaf reads: '*Ad usum fratrum sacri ordinis Praedicatorum provinciae Hiberniae. 29 Julii 1649*', which suggests, if not conclusively, that it came to Ireland under O'Connor's and Lynch's enlightened scheme.[87] Unique among other inscriptions, it ascribes the book, not to any convent or individual, but to the Irish province as such.

Irish Dominican material in the registers of the Masters General for the 1630s, mostly assignations of students and professors to European houses of study, mirrors the growing strength and confidence of the Irish

84 Ibid., leg. 2804.
85 Fenning, *Irish material*, 298.
86 TCD, MSS 5206–8.
87 Irish Jesuits too were beneficiaries of theological books sent from Spain. The Russell Library at St Patrick's College, Maynooth, has a handsomely bound copy of *Divi Thomae Aquinatis Ord. Praed. Ennarationes quas catenam vere auream dicunt in quattuor Evangelia*, edited by Antonius Senensis of Lisbon and published at Paris in 1611. Its title-page bears the inscription, still legible, despite attempts at erasure: '*Collegio Waterfordiensi in Hibernia ex facultate R. Generalis donatum a Paulo Sherlogo, anno 1638*'. Fr Paul Sherlock, the distinguished Waterford Jesuit, biblical scholar and rector of the Irish College of Salamanca, was obviously a patron of the Jesuit college in his native city.

province imbued by the spirit and diverse traditions of continental Dominican life. Some entries from the registers illustrate this point.[88] Michael of the Holy Spirit was procurator in Rome and later a missionary in Bohemia and prior of Prague between the late 1620s and November 1630. James Arthur was instituted regent of the college of St Thomas at Naples on 15 November 1630. John of St Raymund was conventual lector at the convent of St Giles, Prague, until March 1631. Dominic O'Kelly was lector of philosophy at Alessandria in the north of Italy in 1631. John Tirry was appointed lector of philosophy in the French convent of Bourg-en-Bresse (Ain) on 27 March 1632, while his confrère John Nolan was lector of theology at Rennes in the same year. In December 1635 Pádraigín Haicéad, the Gaelic poet, was sent to the convent of St Jacques, Paris, which marked the start of a long sojourn in France. John Baptist Hackett, the noted theologian, was appointed theological instructor at the Parisian novitiate of St Dominic in November 1638 and a year later became conventual lector of theology at Rennes. In 1639 the Master General ordered Dominic O'Daly to devote himself to the business entrusted to him by the King of Spain. Finally, in the same year Dominic Burke was given a commission to go to England to restore peace among the quarrelling Dominicans there, with the right to nominate a provincial superior.

THE DOMINICAN MISSION TO SCOTLAND

The first Irish Dominican mentioned in connection with Scotland was Thomas Bathe, educated at Salamanca, who in 1613 received from the Master General the faculties necessary for a missionary career in England, Ireland and Scotland.[89] In that period such faculties were normally granted for 'the three kingdoms', though in practice options were left open as to their actual use. There is no evidence, however, that Thomas Bathe ever went to Scotland.

In June 1629 the general chapter at Rome temporarily entrusted Scotland and the Isles to the care of the Irish province, with an exhortation to send friars to Scotland as soon as possible 'to restore Catholicism by preaching and example'.[90] Nicholas Lynch, the Irish provincial of the time, was later described, rightly or wrongly, in the Lynch family pedigree as 'Vicar General Apostolic of Scotland',[91] implying that this missionary venture had the highest approval and was indeed taken seriously by the

88 Fenning, *Irish material*, 296–8.
89 Ibid., 277.
90 Reichert, *MOPH*, xii, 54.
91 J. Hardiman (ed.), 'The Pedigree of Doctor Dominick Lynch, Regent of the College of St Thomas of Aquin, in the City of Seville, A.D. 1674, from a coeval MS' in *The Miscellany of the Irish Archaeological Society*, i, Dublin 1846, 57.

Order. In October 1631 Nicholas Lynch was permitted to travel from Ireland to England or Scotland or any other dominion of Great Britain,[92] but he never went as a missionary to Scotland. However, he was probably well informed about the situation of Catholics there and may have been the provincial who informed Ingoli of Propaganda Fide that the Irish Franciscan missionaries, active in Scotland since April 1619, had converted about 5,000 people in the Hebrides alone. This claim was widely believed throughout the Lowlands, and it was corroborated by an unnamed Irish Dominican priest, then a student at the Minerva College in Rome.[93]

Two Dominicans, probably Irish, applied in 1632 to the nuncio at Paris for permission to go as missionaries to Scotland. The nuncio was instructed by Propaganda Fide to report on their fitness for the mission.[94] In 1633 the Master of the Order, Nicholas Ridolfi, wrote to the Pope recommending Dominic Burke, the former Irish Dominican procurator in Rome, and three companions for the mission to Scotland. Burke spoke both Irish and English, had studied theology for five years in Rome, and had faculties to preach and hear confessions. A request for his travelling expenses to Scotland and the customary missionary faculties was made to Propaganda Fide and was approved on 16 September 1633.[95] In the spring of 1634 the Master General appealed to the Irish Dominicans, at the bidding of Propaganda Fide, to select six or at least four suitable missionaries for the Scottish mission at their next provincial chapter.[96] Four Dominicans, perhaps the same four as in 1633, were approved on 25 June 1635 for work in those parts of the Scottish Highlands where Gaelic was spoken and where no Franciscans were at work. They would be supported by Propaganda Fide for three years at the rate of 30 *scudi* a year, and a superior of the mission would be appointed after discussion with the Master General. Missionary faculties would be sought from the Congregation of the Holy Office.[97] At last an Irish Dominican contribution to the Scottish mission seemed to be getting off the ground. On completion of his studies at the Minerva College in Rome, Theodore de

92 Fenning, *Irish material*, 288.

93 C. Giblin (ed.), *Irish Franciscan Mission to Scotland, 1619–1646: Documents from Roman Archives*, Dublin 1964, 152. According to another source, the Franciscan mission claimed in 1627 to have made 10,000 converts and formed ten or twelve parishes in the Hebrides: claims at first seriously doubted through misrepresentation, but afterwards seemingly vindicated. D. Conway, 'The Anglican World: Problems of Coexistence' in J. Metzler (ed.), *Sacrae Congregationis Propaganda Fide Memoriae Rerum, 1622–1972*, i, pt 2: *1622–1700*, Rome 1972, 163, 160.

94 APF, Lettere di Scozia, I, f. 152v; G. Anstruther, *A Hundred Homeless Years: English Dominicans, 1558–1658*, London 1958, 223.

95 APF, SOCG, 393, ff 73r, 88v; Jennings, 'Acta Propaganda Fide', 74.

96 APF, SOCG, 134, f. 264rv.

97 A. Ross, *Scottish Blackfriars in the Seventeenth Century*, Glasgow 1972, 8.

Pietate O'Connell, O.P., sent two petitions to Propaganda Fide in 1637 expressing his desire for faculties to go to Scotland as a missionary and an adequate viaticum. On 14 November Propaganda Fide decided that he should not go alone, whereupon O'Connell requested apostolic faculties for those areas where there was no bishop or ordinary, with authority to communicate them to his companions.[98]

There were many obstacles to the realisation of the Irish Dominican mission to Scotland, as both the authorities of the Order and Propaganda Fide were well aware. When the provincial chapter held at Youghal in October 1638 expressed its intention of sending missionaries to Scotland, it received a discouraging reply from Master General Ridolfi. The Irish Dominicans would scarcely go to Scotland, he wrote, being deterred by the wildness of the terrain, the poverty of the country and other inconveniences which would put them off even more than the prospect of work in their own country, which they sometimes declined. Ridolfi did, however, grant permission for the reception into the Order of any Scots, whether in Ulster or elsewhere in Ireland, who might more readily return to their country.[99] The reference to the mountainous terrain and the poverty of Scotland suggests that the Master General may have had reports, possibly through consultation with the well-informed officials of Propaganda Fide, about the actual conditions of life in the Highlands and western Isles where alone the Catholic population of Scotland survived and where the Irish Franciscans were increasingly active. How, then, did the Franciscans manage in such inhospitable circumstances? The answer, perhaps, may lie in the fact that they were more numerous in Ulster than in any other Irish province. Besides, Ulster families had strong historic kinship and economic ties with the Gaelic-speakers of Scotland and would therefore have been made welcome by the remnants of the Catholic nobility. One Roman observer thought that the 'Scots-Irish' in Scotland were neither Catholics nor heretics: they abhorred the new religion as a heresy, yet they listened to the sermons of the Calvinist preachers out of necessity. As a result, they held erroneous doctrinal views through ignorance of the faith, largely as a consequence of the shortage of priests.[100]

On 10 December 1639 Theodore O'Connell wrote from London to the secretary of Propaganda Fide, Ingoli, informing him that since he was unable to proceed to Scotland he was officiating in the chapel of the Spanish embassy. When reporting on Catholicism in London, he remarked that hardly a day passed but two or three priests travelling from Ireland,

98 APF, SOCG, 397, ff 409r, 410r, 533rv.
99 Fenning, *Irish material*, 301.
100 Cited in C. Giblin, 'The *Acta* of Propaganda Archives and the Scottish Mission, 1623–1670' in *Innes Review*, 5 (1954), 53.

France and Flanders arrived at the Spanish chapel.[101] From another letter of 7 August 1641 to Ingoli it is clear that O'Connell had become one of Propaganda Fide's regular correspondents in London. This time he remarked that he could no longer write regularly to Rome, as such correspondence had become dangerous. Nevertheless, he proceeded to give a brief report on the situation in England. Political affairs were in a desperate state. The king was going to Scotland to hold a parliament, and only God knew what would happen after his departure; the writer feared the destruction of all Catholics.[102] War had already broken out between Charles I and his Scottish subjects in 1640. This had been instigated largely by the imprudent ecclesiastical policy of the king, which sought to subjugate Scottish Presbyterians to an episcopal church system as well as to undermine the independence of Scotland. O'Connell noted that the English Dominican superior was in prison and was in danger of being executed. O'Connell himself was unable to go to Scotland because travel was dangerous and there was great hostility between the two kingdoms. Travel between Scotland and Ireland too was forbidden by royal decree. O'Connell left it to Ingoli to advise what he should do.[103] The secretary replied from Rome on 12 November 1641, allowing O'Connell to remain in England until he could safely proceed to Scotland.[104] In his letter O'Connell had referred to 'my mission', and the reply from Propaganda Fide called him 'a missionary in Scotland'; in spite of this, he continued to bide his time in London, which was rather a long way from western Scotland.

It would appear that the Highlands and Isles of Scotland were not among the top priorities of Propaganda Fide or of the Dominican Order. Their sights were fixed on more extensive missionary enterprises in the Far East, Armenia, the Near and Middle East and South America. Besides, Propaganda Fide did not wish to encourage competition between Franciscans and Dominicans in such a difficult and impoverished area. Hence one can understand why Propaganda Fide on 3 June 1647 refused permission to five Dominicans to go on the Scottish mission: there were four Franciscans there already.[105] The petitioner, Thomas O'Brien (styled Bernardinus in Latin), briefly procurator of the province, had submitted the five names to Propaganda Fide. He asserted that Dominic de Marinis, the vicar general of the Order, had good reports of all concerned and had known the proposed head of the mission, John Baptist FitzGerald, 'a man of great integrity', for a long time. The other members of the

101 APF, SOCG, 139, ff 283r, 284v.
102 Ibid., 84, ff 122rv–123rv.
103 Ibid.
104 Jennings, 'Acta Propaganda Fide', 119.
105 Ibid., 130.

mission band were to be Clement O'Birrin, John Genory, Patrick O'Dwyer and Dominic Pimbrok.[106] Fitzgerald was to be vicar general and to lead the group to Scotland 'for the propagation of the faith, the comfort of Catholics, and the recovery of the convents which our Order had there'—an arrangement already approved by Thomas Turco, the Master General, on 23 March. In the Master General's letter of appointment John Baptist FitzGerald received full authority as vicar general of Scotland over all members of the Order actually in the country, and over their affairs, spiritual and temporal.[107]

Propaganda Fide did not disclose its reasons for discouraging the proposed Irish Dominican mission to the Scottish Highlands and Isles in 1647. The Franciscan mission which began from St Anthony's College, Louvain, with the departure to Scotland of John Ogilvie, O.F.M., in 1612 lasted until 1637, and though Propaganda Fide formally re-established the mission on 22 January 1647, it had by then petered out and did not revive in that century.[108] In the late 1640s political turmoil in Scotland and the civil war between royalists and parliamentarians raging in England must have inclined Propaganda Fide to postpone any fresh missionary venture in those kingdoms.

Notwithstanding the fact that by geography and language Scotland's largely Catholic western Isles often had closer links with Ireland than with the kingdom of Scotland, they were never visited in the first half of the seventeenth century by the Irish Dominicans despite their genuine missionary zeal. The decision of Propaganda Fide in 1647 was a deathblow to their hopes—cherished hopes that would not be fulfilled until the following century. The fault was partly their own, since there must have been some substance in the rather caustic comments of Master Nicholas Ridolfi when the prospect of a Dominican mission to Scotland had been raised in 1638.

DOMINICAN ADMINISTRATION: PROVINCIALS AND PROVINCIAL CHAPTERS, 1627–40

In the period 1627–40 the Irish Dominicans held six or seven provincial chapters, some to elect a new provincial, others half-way through his term of office: Sligo (elective, 1627); Athenry (intermediate, February 1629 n.s.); possibly an intermediate chapter held at Waterford (July 1631); an elective chapter, probably held at Portumna (1634); Trim (intermediate, November 1636); Youghal (elective, October 1638); Cork (intermediate, 1640).

106 APF, SOCG, 414, ff 59r, 68v.
107 Fenning, *Irish material*, 321.
108 Giblin, *Irish Franciscan Mission to Scotland*, xiv–xv.

The acts or proceedings of the chapters have not survived. Fortunately the Master General's comments on the acts of the chapter of 1638 are still in existence, and from his reply one may reconstruct most of its decisions. A number of ordinations or regulations made at the chapters listed above are known from their rehearsal in the acts of chapters held later in the century. And even if the evidence of what took place at these chapters is fragmentary (except in the case of Youghal in 1638), a definite picture of the internal life of the Order and province does emerge. The holding of the chapters was in itself a remarkable feat, given the problem of organisation, the long journeys involved for priors and representatives, and the secrecy required under a hostile government.

The first known chapter of the century assembled at Sligo in the late summer or autumn of 1627 for the purpose of electing a successor to Ross MacGeoghegan. Nicholas D. Lynch, educated in Portugal and France, a member of the Galway community and one of the leading personalities of the province, was elected provincial.[109] This Nicholas Lynch, brother of Sir Henry Lynch, recorder of Galway, had come to the attention of the Lord President of Connacht and the Lord Deputy in May 1624. It was then reported that a Dominican friar named Nicholas Lynch, 'the chief Father of that Order . . . a very learned man and of great estimation among them', had arrived with another Dominican, Callanan, with money from the King of Spain in connection with the expected invasion of Connacht which was to centre on Galway. Aeneas Callanan landed in Munster and came to Galway, crossing the Shannon at Portumna, while Nicholas Lynch reached his native city via Limerick. Callanan apparently was captured and forced to give information to the Lord President of Connacht.[110] Again in August 1628, when rumours of a Spanish landing at Galway were very strong, the Lord Deputy was dismayed to learn that a Catholic and known sympathiser of Spain, Nicholas Lynch FitzStephen FitzArthur, the father of Nicholas Lynch, the Dominican provincial, should have been elected head of Galway corporation. According to the Lord Deputy, both father and son had been brought up in Spain, and though they might be honest men, he distrusted people bred in those parts.[111] Within a year the threat of invasion of Galway and the west coast had passed away.

Less than two years after the Sligo chapter an intermediate chapter was convened at Athenry in February 1629 (1628 o.s.), composed of the provincial and eleven priors. In the course of its business the chapter

109 Burke, *Hib. Dom.*, 522; Reichert, *MOPH*, xii, 53–4. Lynch signed a document as provincial at Galway, 27 Sept. 1627. HMC, *Franciscan MSS*, 106.

110 M. D. O'Sullivan, *Old Galway*, Galway 1983, 206–7.

111 Ibid., 219.

denied that the Dominicans had ever complained to Rome about Thomas Fleming, the Franciscan Archbishop of Dublin, as some malcontents had asserted.[112] The acts of this provincial chapter were printed at Louvain and were probably presented to the Master of the Order, whose prerogative it was to approve provincial chapter acts.

Nicholas Lynch travelled to Rome for a general chapter of the Order in June 1629[113] at which he and Michael of the Holy Spirit became masters of theology, while Richard Caron was awarded the degree of *sacrae theologiae praesentatus*.[114] On 4 December 1630 the Master General, by papal dispensation, prolonged the provincialate of Nicholas Lynch to the third Sunday after Easter of 1632.[115]

Another intermediate, non-elective chapter may have met at Waterford in July 1631. Daniel of the Cross O'Crean, who variously described himself as 'Vicar General' and 'Vicar Apostolic of the Order of Preachers in Ireland', met there with fourteen priors and the vicar of Trim,[116] to transact the business of the province in the absence of Nicholas Lynch, who remained abroad.

In the meantime Nicholas Lynch had gone from Rome to Flanders *en route* to Ireland. At Brussels on 8 March, in virtue of a letter of Philip IV (28 June 1629), he received 100 crowns, as he and his two companions were in great need, after their journey to and from the chapter at Rome.[117] They needed more money still for their fare to Ireland. In fact on 8 December 1629 the Master General had ordered the priors of Ireland to pay the expenses incurred by the provincial and his companion accompanying him to the chapter at Rome,[118] but contributions may not have been forthcoming. In the event, Nicholas Lynch would never see Ireland again. The general chapter of Rome in 1629 had designated the convent of San Pablo in Seville as the venue for a general chapter after Easter 1632, but no chapter was in fact convened. By January 1632 Nicholas Lynch had reached Lisbon, where he learned that the Master of the Order had confirmed him yet again in the office of provincial until the meeting of the next general chapter.[119] Depressing news from Ireland of a sudden burst of persecution and the confiscation of religious houses in 1630–31 almost certainly prompted the provincial to remain in Spain and Portugal from 1632 to 1633. No doubt he felt

112 *Wadding Papers*, 287–8.
113 See pp 276–7 above.
114 Reichert, *MOPH*, xii, 52–4.
115 Fenning, *Irish material*, 287.
116 *Wadding Papers*, 590–92.
117 B. Jennings (ed.), *Wild Geese in Spanish Flanders, 1582–1700*, Dublin 1964, 245, no. 1086.
118 Fenning, *Irish material*, 286.
119 Ibid., 292.

that he could be more useful to the Irish province by continuing his work abroad in this period. Late in the year 1632 he was in Madrid, where he presented an urgent petition to the King of Spain for aid to help restore his province.[120] During his absence from Ireland (1629–34), Daniel O'Crean, later erroneously thought to have been prior provincial,[121] acted as vicar provincial. In June 1633 Lynch was once more at Lisbon, where he presided at an elective chapter of the Portuguese province.[122] From Portugal he went to Rome. On 1 March 1634 he was made prior of the Roman convent of San Sisto. He died in the month of July of that very year and was buried in the church of Santa Maria sopra Minerva in the common vault of the brethren.[123]

An elective provincial chapter assembled in 1634 after Nicholas Lynch's resignation from office and his subsequent death. This meeting probably took place at Portumna, as the proceedings of a chapter held there were confirmed by the general chapter of 1644.[124] The new provincial, Edmund Raymund Dempsey, was the son of Terence Dempsey, Baron of Philipstown and Viscount Clanmalier. As in the case of his uncle, Ross MacGeoghegan, his early cultural experience would have been Gaelic, but growing up as the son of a peer in the planted counties of the midlands, he would soon have been fluent in English as well as Irish. The family lands ran along both sides of the River Barrow in the King's and Queen's Counties and comprised in excess of 22,000 acres.[125] He had read arts and theology at the University of Alcalá de Henares,[126] not far from Madrid. His confirmation in office as provincial on 5 May 1635 appears to indicate that his election had taken place late in 1634.[127]

The Master General, reviewing the acts of the recent elective chapter, decided that there should be two novitiates, wherever persecution was less likely, to offset the heavy death rate within the province. He observed that the number of novices would thus be raised to twelve, drawn from the four civil provinces in equal proportion, so that every year six novices would be received in each novitiate. He also agreed to confer theological degrees on fourteen friars at the request of the capitular fathers; six thus became masters in theology, including Edmund

120 AGS, Estado, leg. 2795.
121 O'Heyne, *Epil. Chron.*, 232–3; Burke, *Hib. Dom.*, 522–3; Pochin Mould, *The Irish Dominicans*, 234.
122 Fenning, *Irish material*, 293.
123 Ibid., 294; L. E. Boyle, *San Clemente Miscellany*, i, Rome 1977, 265.
124 Reichert, *MOPH*, xii, 163.
125 D. F. Cregan, 'The Social and Cultural Background of a Counter-Reformation Episcopate' in A. Cosgrove and D. McCartney (eds), *Studies in Irish History presented to R. Dudley Edwards*, Dublin 1979, 95. For general information on the Dempsey family see E. MacLysaght, *Irish Families*, Dublin 1957, 114.
126 APF, SOCG, 140, ff 114rv, 119rv.
127 Fenning, *Irish material*, 294.

Raymund Dempsey, while eight obtained the necessary preliminary degree of bachelor of theology.[128] Although he served as provincial from 1634 to 1638, no record of Dempsey's administration occurs in the Master General's registers. From 1636 his wealthy family and influential friends proposed him for the see of Leighlin.[129] He was promoted to that see in 1642, but died in exile at the Dominican convent of Pontevedra in Galicia, Spain, in 1658.[130] He was the author of a manuscript treatise entitled *Feed Your Flock*, which was lost on its way to Louvain, whither he had sent it for publication.[131]

Trim was chosen as the meeting-place of the intermediate chapter to be held in November 1636. Once again the acts are not extant, though one of the chapter's ordinations was cited in the provincial chapter acts of 1682: that only rosaries of five or fifteen decades were to be blessed by Dominican priests.[132] Formerly Dominican indulgences were attached to the actual rosary beads of precisely five and fifteen decades, and hence the objection to other rosaries in common use.

After another two-year interval, an elective provincial chapter met at Youghal on 12 October 1638, 'in the convent of Our Lady of Graces'. The Master General confirmed its election of James Hurley, a *filius* of Kilmallock, as prior provincial, on 19 February 1639.[133] Hurley, noted as an exemplary and learned religious, had studied in Spain and had several times been prior since his return to Ireland.[134] On 13 April 1640 the Master General acknowledged from Soriano in Calabria (southern Italy) receipt of a letter from the diffinitory or legislative body of the Youghal chapter, as well as the petitions forming part of its official acts.[135] From his incisive comments on eight petitions and four doubtful matters which the capitular fathers had been unable to resolve, it is clear that the Master General knew his Irish subjects very well indeed. His replies enable us to some extent to reconstruct the actual contents of the chapter proceedings; mainly they shed light on the domestic affairs of the province, problems of reorganisation and adaptation, the quality of Dominican life and legal problems. The frank replies are always to the point, if occasionally lengthy,

128 Ibid., 295.

129 Millett, 'Catalogue of Irish Material in Vols 140–143 of the SOCG', 23, 30, 31, 32, 33, 43; Jennings, 'Miscellaneous Documents, II: 1625–1640', 24, 26.

130 B. Millett and C. J. Woods, 'Roman Catholic Bishops from 1534' in *NHI*, ix, 376; Eubel, *Hier. Cath.*, iv, 218.

131 C. P. Meehan, *The Rise and Fall of the Irish Franciscan Monasteries*, Dublin 1877, 401.

132 G. Mac Niocaill, 'Cáipéisi Doiminiceánacha ón 17ú céad' in *Seanchas Ardmhaca*, 3 (1958), 145; H. Fenning, *Acta Capitulorum Provinciae Hiberniae Sacri Ordinis Praedicatorum, 1669–1688*, Tallaght 1989, 30.

133 Fenning, *Irish material*, 297.

134 O'Heyne, *Epil. Chron.*, 92–3.

135 Fenning, *Irish material*, 298–303.

while sometimes the Master General writes quite bluntly, though without offence. By 1640 Master Nicholas Ridolfi had had twelve long years' experience of the Irish Dominicans and their 'second spring'.

The first three petitions of 1638 concerned provincial chapters. To avoid the expense, danger and inconvenience attending these meetings, it was argued that it should be licit to commit the transaction of all business to the provincial, the diffinitors and four other senior fathers elected by the whole body, thereby allowing the remaining capitulars to return home. The Master of the Order agreed, but only on certain conditions. The authority of the chapter was to last, from its opening day, for three weeks only. If the diffinitory supplemented by the four elected fathers did not complete all business within fifteen of the twenty-one days allotted for the chapter, its authority would cease.

The second petition asked that 'for the duration of [the Protestant] schism' it should not be necessary for priors going to chapters to be accompanied by elected companions (*socii*). It should be sufficient to send the results of the conventual ballot for the *socius*, sealed and closed, with the preacher general of each particular convent or simply with the prior himself for presentation to the chapter.

The third petition requested that the legal requirement of six members to constitute a convent should be considered fulfilled once there were four priests and two others, whether novices or lay brothers. The Master General replied that in his opinion this request contradicted the previous one: for on the one hand they proposed that the companions (*socii*) of priors be exempted from attendance at chapters, while they also wished to multiply the number of eligible priors and preachers general of convents which did not have the normal complement of six priests. The point at issue here for the Irish province was representation for its weaker houses at provincial chapters.

The fourth and fifth petitions concerned the honorific title, office and appointment of preachers general. Each convent had a preacher general of its own, a friar who excelled in preaching and whose ministry extended beyond the confines of his house to a wider area determined by the 'limit' of the house. Whereas the Order's constitutions required that candidates for the preacher generalship should have preached during three Lenten periods, the chapter requested in its fourth petition that it should be enough for the candidate to have preached laudably for five years, even though he might not have preached for three entire Lenten periods within that time. Dispensation was also sought from the legal stipulation that candidates for this degree should be at least thirty-five years of age. The provincials and diffinitors should be empowered to postulate suitable younger candidates whose maturity and preaching ability would compensate for the defect of age.

The Master General objected, since to grant what was asked would open the door to ambition. Were the conferral of the dignity and honour of the preacher generalship to be readily multiplied, the title itself would be worthless and of little esteem. The constitutional provisions were therefore to be observed. In cases of exceptional distinction, where candidates were renowned for the excellence of their lives and preaching, the Master General would willingly consider dispensation from the normal conditions if approached by the diffinitors. That was the common practice of other provinces.

The fifth petition concerned the case of a preacher general appointed for a convent which had the requisite six members and therefore enjoyed the right to vote in an elective chapter. Should the house at a later date have less than six brethren, it was petitioned that the preacher general's rights should in no way be affected by this change of circumstances. The Master expressed himself willing to grant what was asked, provided there was no fraud. As regards representation at provincial chapters, the house should have had a preacher general for a considerable length of time. A house which only recently began supporting six friars was not entitled to be represented by a preacher general.

The question of the reception and number of novices, which was raised by the chapter in its sixth petition, drew from the Master General a long and spirited reply which revealed his intimate knowledge of the Irish Dominicans, their problems and aspirations, and indeed of the Irish character itself. Ridolfi had been informed that many noble youths, of good morals and intellectual ability, when rejected, as they daily were, by the Dominicans, were obliged to join other orders. This was a consequence of the Master's decision limiting their intake to eighteen novices a year. In fact the Master General himself had in 1635 restricted the number of novices to be received annually to twelve: six in each of two novitiates. From the mid-1620s complaints had poured into Propaganda Fide accusing the Irish regulars of indiscriminately accepting many more novices than they actually required. It was also pointed out that the proper conditions for novitiates did not obtain in Ireland and that novices received an unsatisfactory training. Propaganda Fide issued instructions for the reform of this situation in 1626 and 1635, ordering the Roman superiors general to ensure the implementation of reform of the Irish novitiates. This was one of the reasons why Master Nicholas Ridolfi took a strong line on the question of the number of novices to be accepted and their formation in Ireland.

The Dominicans, well aware of the criticism of the secular clergy and Propaganda Fide's proposals for reform, declared themselves dejected as they witnessed the multiplication of other religious orders who imposed no limits on recruitment. These orders, they said, received as many recruits as they liked, when and where they wished. Hence in their sixth petition they requested that they should be allowed to take as many novices as they wanted, subject to the approval of the provincial and his council, and to educate them in those houses that appeared the more suitable, even if particular houses could not simultaneously receive six novices. For it often happened that in certain houses while there were alms enough for the support of two, three or four novices, there were not enough for six. In other provinces, including those of Spain, novices were received from day to day without limitation. Above all, the chapter urgently asked that in Ulster, where there was scarcely one convent, it should be permissible to accept those who applied for admission, so that in the future the vast province of Ulster might have houses of its own whence friars might be sent to Scotland.

The Master General replied that his decision restricting the number of people entering the Order every year to eighteen (in 1635 limited to twelve) was based on his exact knowledge of the state of the Irish province. The province, he said, seemed to have no idea of the inconveniences which arose from the multiplication of religious and their passage to other provinces which received them unwillingly because each province found it hard in those difficult times to look after its own. The Master General himself was obliged to scatter the Irish here and there, so that they wandered the world. What was worse, scarcely one of these religious, having completed his theological studies, wished to return to Ireland. Rather they jeered at the wrinkles of their 'mother' and set up their tents where it pleased them most. The remedy which the Irish provincial considered efficacious, namely to command all who had completed their studies to return to their province and to substitute other young men in their stead, had given rise to an impossible situation. This was because they resisted returning home on a variety of pretexts, and because provincials and priors kept foreign priests who served them better than students yet to be ordained. The fact that the number of novices was unlimited in other provinces of the Order was of little concern to the Irish province, since it was not obliged to support them. In the Italian provinces especially, numbers had been restricted, in line with the decrees of the Council of Trent and the laws of the Order, so that convents were allowed to receive precisely only those whom they could support.

The Master General went on to say that the Dominicans should be far less concerned with what other religious orders did in Ireland; they should aim to excel in virtue rather than in mere numbers. As to the proposal to receive novices in Ulster and later assign them to Scotland, he replied in the memorable words: 'I praise your zeal, but I saw what came of it' ('*laudo zelum, sed novi exitum*'). Irish Dominicans were hardly likely to go to Scotland, where physical conditions were more daunting still than those of their native land where they sometimes refused to work. However, the Master General gave permission for as many Scots as presented themselves to be received into the Order, either in Ulster or elsewhere in Ireland. The provincial had also proposed sending additional students, as many as would be willing, to the overseas colleges, a proposal the Master of the Order did not favour, as the colleges, particularly that at Louvain, were so poor that they could not find a mouthful of bread for the students they already had—so he had been informed by Father Master Nolan, rector at Louvain. The Master General then assured the Irish capitulars that over the past eleven years nothing had received so much of his attention as the growth of the Irish province. He reiterated once more that no fewer than six novices should be educated together; it would be well-nigh impossible effectively to impart the basic rudiments of virtue and religious training where there were only two or three novices. Should what he proposed be thought out of the question, as the Irish petition suggested, then he was prepared to leave the whole matter concerning the number of novices to the judgement of the provincial.

To the seventh petition, which sought confirmation of the postulations of preachers general made by the chapter, the Master consented.

The eighth and final petition took up the question of the day-to-day policy necessarily influenced by the edicts of the hostile secular state and by other changing circumstances. The brethren overseas could not always be kept perfectly up to date by the Master General's decisions for the province. It seemed therefore to the chapter members that, in line with precedent, the provincial and his council should be permitted to formulate and implement their own policy decisions. In reply, the Master gave an assurance that no directives would be made for the Irish province in common with other remote and overseas provinces, unless after deep and prolonged deliberation and on the basis of sound advice. A number of minor legal points about the appointment and rights of preachers general were then put to the Master General for interpretation and adjudication, which he gave in his usual concise and lucid style.

In his own covering letter the Irish provincial, James Hurley, had raised the question of the *alternativa*—the system whereby religious orders elected successive provincials in strict rotation according to their civil province of origin. This, Hurley claimed, the Master General himself had proposed in letters to the Youghal chapter of 1638, when he suggested that the chapter should elect a Dominican of Munster as provincial, as in fact it did. The Master revealed his own mind on the *alternativa* system in his reply. While at first sight the system might seem to serve the interests of peace among civil provinces, that peace was false which was not founded on justice, to which this system was prejudicial. Very frequently it happened that the least worthy candidate was selected. Ridolfi unequivocally stated that he did not wish the *alternativa* to be introduced in the election of Irish provincials. In future such elections should be left free, and he recommended that only the most worthy candidate among all the friars should be elected, without regard to his civil province of origin.

There is evidence, however, to show that the *alternativa* system had been adhered to and preoccupied Irish Dominicans of the sixteenth and first decades of the seventeenth century. So far it has not proved possible to establish an exact succession list of provincials between 1536 and 1643, but the line runs roughly as follows: David Brown (Munster, 1536–*c.*1559); Thaddeus MacDuane (Ulster or Connacht, ?–1563–?); Cormac O'Fergus (Connacht, *c.*1569–*c.*1572); Eugene MacHugan (? Ulster, d. 1590); Thaddeus MacDuane (Ulster or Connacht, 1593–1600); Daniel O'Crean (Connacht, 1600–4); Thaddeus MacDuane (Ulster or Connacht, 1604–8); Roland Burke (Connacht, 1608–*c.*1612); Thomas Quirke (Munster, *c.*1612–17); Ross MacGeoghegan (Leinster, 1617–27); Nicholas Lynch (Connacht, 1627–34); Edmund Raymund Dempsey (Leinster, 1634–8); James Hurley (Munster, 1638–43).

The Master General went on to say that the weaknesses of the province made him blush for shame. While he saw his brethren made strong in the faith among unbelievers and a spectacle on behalf of Christ before the whole world and even prepared to lay down their lives for Him, yet they were caught up in trifles, and though well equipped to foster Christian peace, they refused to leave such bundles of useless baggage behind. That was why they were so little esteemed by lay-people and why the friars could scarcely support themselves from day to day on alms, as their own chapter acts testified. He urged the Irish Dominicans to be earnest in serving God, who would provide abundantly for their needs. In a veiled reference to the problems between regulars and seculars, he advised them to avoid quarrels and to be single-minded in their role as pastors of God's people. Such a spirit would foster peace and shield them far better from the persecution of other orders and the secular clergy than the pontifical decrees for which they wrote to Rome. What purpose could such edicts serve, even if granted, if they could not be put into effect? So much was evident from the content of decrees drawn up by the sacred congregations. What decrees the Master General was alluding to here is not clear from the context. Perhaps they related to the recent controversies surrounding the Cahill propositions and Bishop Tirry of Cork. At all events, the Irish brethren were advised and indeed commanded to write clearly and distinctly about such matters to the procurator general of the Order in Rome, who would do all in his power to obtain redress and consolation for them. It was on this practical note that the Master of the Order rather abruptly brought to a close his reflections on the provincial chapter held at Youghal in 1638.

On 1 January 1642 Master General Ridolfi wrote again to James Hurley and the members of the Irish province.[136] He stated that although he had received no reply to his letter from Soriano, dated 13 April 1640, Master John Nolan had given him satisfactory information especially about the reception of novices, which the Master General had left totally to the provincial's discretion. On the same date Ridolfi forwarded letters patent to the province, designating convents in which novices might be received and trained. Here it should be noted that the Master General was concerned with the education of novices (a term which then covered students of philosophy and theology, as well as simple novices) up to the time of priestly ordination. In this letter to the Irish provincial the Master General laid down norms to be observed in the reception and education of clerical novices, possibly at the instigation of John Nolan, O.P., the Master's confidant, shortly to become his assistant general.

Young men were to be carefully chosen for admission to the Order. Nobody was to be received unless of legitimate birth, honest and pious parentage and irreproachable morals. Information to this effect was to be sent to the provincial by the convent in which the candidate was to be received. The provincial might then consult his council, if he could, and grant his assent, after which the prior might receive the postulant. Only convents of several friars were to accept novices. One particularly grave, discreet and mature friar should be named novice-master, to instruct the novices in the chant and ceremonies of the Order, mental prayer (meditation) and other religious exercises prescribed by the laws of the Order. The area of the novitiate was to be partitioned from the rest of the convent. Should the friars of the house be impoverished, the novices might be sent on the quest. The number of the brethren staffing these houses was to remain constant during the novices' year of probation. At no time was the prior, or in his absence the subprior, to leave the house. During the year of probation the novices were not, under any pretext, permitted to visit their parents or relations, but must remain in those places where they could wear the habit and the tonsure. All the brethren of such convents were ordered to abstain from meat, observe the fasts of the Order, keep the strictest silence, have readings during meals, and say the full grace before and after meals.

Novices therefore were to be received only in the largest houses where there were at least two or three in the novitiate. Why Master General Ridolfi changed his mind since his letter of 13 April 1640 on the minimum number of novices from six to two or three in impoverished Irish novitiates in 1642 he did not say. One suspects that this concession resulted from discussions with Master John Nolan and other trusted Irish

136 Fenning, *Irish material*, 308–10.

Dominican informants who convinced him of the need for greater flexibility on the issue. In any event, the Master General ordered the larger houses to accept novices not only for themselves, but also for the smaller houses, so that little by little the Order might reoccupy all the places in which it was formerly established. The Master General named four leading members of the province, one to represent each civil province, who together with the provincial might designate the novitiates. No convent was to be set aside for novices in which the divine office was not recited daily in common or where mental prayer or meditation were not observed after Matins or early in the morning and again after Compline. In this connection he recommended that there should be readings from the Gospels or from the works of the venerable Louis of Granada, O.P., or from other Dominican authors. Before retiring, the suffrages for the living and the dead were to be recited, together with the hymn *Christe qui lux es et dies*, with the other customary collects and prayers. Having received the prior's blessing and having read the meditation for the following night or daybreak, all should then go to their cells and maintain strict silence until the hour of Prime as the Dominican constitutions directed.

After consultation concerning the behaviour and morals of the novices, the community would decide which novices should be invited freely and willingly to make religious profession, in other words to commit themselves solemnly and for life to the Dominican Order. After solemn profession the novices should devote their time to the study of 'sacred letters', which meant intensive courses in philosophy, theology, scripture and other ecclesiastical subjects. The provincial should see to it that this was done in places where there was no danger to the brethren. Lectures should be held by those who taught best. They should instruct their brethren charitably, uninfluenced by personal vanity or the prevailing intellectual fashions of the day, without commotion, apart from lay-people, and without acrimonious disputations. In this way the excessive number of Irish friars passing to other provinces would be reduced and within a short time the province would have many well-instructed students. When, however, students were sent overseas, they were to be carefully chosen with utter impartiality. They were to be sent only to provinces which had flourishing *studia generalia*. The Master General strictly prohibited anybody who had entered the Order at the advanced age of twenty-five or so from being sent abroad for what he obscurely termed 'exotic studies'; rather such students should be instructed in moral theology and sacred scripture so that they might become competent preachers or at least capable of hearing confessions.

The Master of the Order commanded all these norms to be inviolably observed and ordered the provincial under formal precept and under pain of dismissal from office to see to it that, in his visitation of convents where novices were being instructed, all the foregoing norms were enforced. If not, priors held responsible were to be dismissed from office. And should provincials prove negligent in these matters, permission to receive and educate novices would be revoked.

The Master General also recalled that the incumbent provincial, James Hurley, had been elected at a chapter assembled at an inconvenient time of year. In order that the next full provincial chapter might meet at a more opportune time, he granted permission, at the provincial's own request, to hold the chapter before the usual four years had elapsed, provided the senior fathers of the province agreed. Master Nicholas Ridolfi concluded his letter with a flowery homily, typical of his century, exhorting his Irish brethren to lay quarrels aside and gladly accept responsibility for the harvest of souls in their midst. They would thus ensure the fulfilment of their vocation and win their own redemption.

Curiously, the Master's letter, written in January 1642, made no reference to the Cork intermediate chapter of 1640, though he could hardly have been ignorant of its meetings and decisions, for Master John Nolan, his intimate collaborator and assistant in curia, was undoubtedly his eyes and ears as far as the affairs of the Irish province were concerned. The two long letters written by Master General Nicholas Ridolfi in 1640 and 1642 demonstrate his remarkable understanding of the situation of the Irish Dominican province and his concern for its future welfare and progress.

Meanwhile in 1640 an intermediate chapter had assembled at Cork under the presidency of James Hurley. The general chapter held at Rome in 1644 endorsed one of its ordinations, which declared that since nothing historically authentic concerning the antiquity and 'limits' of the Irish convents survived, priors should adopt the order of precedence dictated by the antiquity of their convents, taking as their guide the information derived from ancient manuscripts in the works of Sir James Ware.[137] The fourth ordination of the general chapter of 1642, whose acts were annulled by another general chapter in 1644, recalled the ordinations which Master Nicholas Ridolfi had drawn up specially for the good government of the Irish province. These included the designation of those convents of strict observance which novices might enter, and the erection in each of the provinces of houses of study which would enjoy the rights and privileges of the Order's *studia generalia*. If anything further needed to be added, clarified or changed in these ordinations, the Master General elect was to effect it without delay.[138]

No provincial chapter met in 1642 as anticipated, possibly as a result of the political commotion of the times. An elective chapter finally met

137 Reichert, *MOPH*, xii, 161.
138 Ibid., 90.

at Kilkenny in 1643 while the Confederation was in session.[139] Some Dominican historians and writers mistakenly close the provincialate of James Hurley in 1640 and state that he was then promoted to the bishopric of Emly.[140] In actual fact, Bishop Maurice O'Hurley filled that see from 1623 until his death in 1646, after which he was succeeded in 1648 by another Dominican provincial, Terence Albert O'Brien,[141] martyred at Limerick on 30 October 1651.[142]

FACING THE FUTURE: IRISH DOMINICANS IN THE EARLY 1640S

In 1640 an immensely complicated and fast-changing political situation developed in Britain and Ireland which led to the Irish rebellion of October 1641. The events surrounding the outbreak of the insurrection have, right from the outset, been the subject of conflicting interpretations and passionate debate extending into our own time. Contemporary English public opinion was heavily influenced by government propaganda which blamed the insurrection on Jesuits, friars and seminary priests whose 'venomous infusion' had taken deep root in the minds of 'blind, ignorant and superstitious people'.[143] What is undeniable is that the rebellion and the ensuing war plunged Ireland into turmoil for over a decade and profoundly changed the course of Irish history. In seeking to adapt to the greatly altered and volatile circumstances of the 1640s, Irish Dominicans achieved a high profile with corresponding vulnerability to hostile forces. While presented with fresh opportunities, they also found themselves confronted with new problems, including proscription and sometimes summary execution. In the years 1641–57 at least thirty-five known Dominicans and many of their devoted, but for the most part unremembered, lay supporters were put to death on account of their courageous witness to the Catholic faith.

139 Burke, *Hib. Dom.*, 524. There was still a copy of the printed provincial chapter acts at Holy Cross College, Louvain, in 1754. Ibid., 329.

140 O'Heyne, *Epil. Chron.*, 92–3 is the source of this false assertion. Copied by de Jonghe, *Belgium Dominicanum* (1719), 423; *Bullarium Ord. Praed.*, vi (1773), 143; Burke, *Hib. Dom.* (1762), 487.

141 Brady, *Ep. Succ.*, ii, 38–9; Millett and Woods, 'Roman Catholic Bishops from 1534', 361.

142 Lynch, *De Praesulibus Hib.*, ii, 67–8, where the author also refers to the lost MS entitled *Rosetum Praedicatorium Hiberniae* of Denis O'Hanrahan, who ministered to Bishop Terence Albert O'Brien at Limerick before his execution by order of Henry Ireton, commander of the Cromwellian forces. The bishop was declared 'blessed' by Pope John Paul II on 27 September 1992.

143 Quoted in J. I. Casway, *Owen Roe O'Neill and the Struggle for Catholic Ireland*, Philadelphia 1984, 53.

Some Irish Dominicans, for example, distinguished themselves in a diplomatic and political capacity by furthering the emergence and aims of the Confederation of Kilkenny from diverse but ultimately converging religious viewpoints. Dominic O'Daly, as early as April 1633, disclosed his intention to devote his energies to the formation of a league or confederation of Irish Catholics and sought the diplomatic support of the King of Spain to realise its objectives.[144] O'Daly may therefore be regarded as one of the earliest harbingers of the Catholic confederate concept.

Two Connacht Dominicans, deeply royalist in sympathy, cousins and kinsmen of the Earl of Clanrickard, played significant roles in the theatre of Irish politics in the 1640s. The first of these, Oliver Burke, sometime rector of Louvain, Vicar Apostolic of Kilmacduagh (1629–47) and vicar general of Clonfert, was the earl's chaplain and personal emissary to the neutral gentry of the Pale in February 1642.[145] He was in fact the bearer and interpreter of the proto-proposals for a form of future government that approximated to the Confederate model. As a result of conversations between the nobility of the Pale and representatives of the Catholic bishops, Oliver Burke, together with Rory O'More, Lord Gormanston and Sir William Hill, was appointed to draft a constitution for Ireland.[146] In April 1642 he was proposed as intermediary between the disaffected citizens of Galway and the Earl of Clanrickard.[147] Soon afterwards, however, the bond of deepest trust between the Burke kinsmen was shattered, and a mixture of complex religious and political motives led Oliver Burke to threaten the earl with censure and excommunication.[148]

In 1642 Dominic Burke, prior of Athenry, became Clanrickard's personal chaplain, political agent and envoy to the Confederation of Kilkenny. Burke dealt directly with the Supreme Council, the nuncio Rinuccini and the leading political personalities of the Confederation as well as with General Thomas Preston and the Earl of Ormond.[149] He remained ever faithful to the Earl of Clanrickard and continued in his service until the latter's departure for England.

Three Dominican bishops, Terence Albert O'Brien of Emly (the third bishop executed under Puritan rule), Edmund Raymund Dempsey of Leighlin, and Oliver Darcy of Dromore, were active members of the

144 AGS, Estado, leg. 2796; see also pp 121–2 above.

145 *The Memoirs and Letters of Ulick, Marquis of Clanricarde and Earl of St Albans*, London 1757, 78.

146 Clarke, *The Old English in Ireland, 1625–42*, 202–4; T. L. Coonan, *The Irish Catholic Confederacy and the Puritan Revolution*, Dublin/London 1954, 139.

147 *Clanricarde Memoirs and Letters*, 116.

148 Ibid., 374–6, 322–5, 350–52; *Letter-Book of the Earl of Clanricarde, 1643–47*, ed. J. Lowe, Dublin 1983, 50, 377.

149 *Clanricarde Memoirs and Letters*, 325–9, 355–6; *Clanricarde Letter-Book*, 292, 295–7, 298, 300, 354, 362–3, 374, 385–91 and *passim*.

Kilkenny General Assembly. The latter, indeed, had twice served as prior of the Black Abbey, Kilkenny, and owed his episcopal nomination to the Confederate General Assembly. In moments of severe crisis Oliver Darcy, a splendid bilingual preacher, was chosen to address the assembly, and undertook diplomatic missions on its behalf. When exiled at Paris he was appointed chaplain to the Irish regiments there. Oliver Darcy continued to be active in royalist politics and to be the subject of bitter controversy long after the Confederation's aspirations had been extinguished. Thomas Quirke, a former prior of Kilkenny (1622) and Limerick (1626–7), held the offices of preacher and chaplain-in-ordinary to the Kilkenny General Assembly.[150]

The respective roles and achievements in public life of these disparate Dominican personalities, amid the perilous quicksands of political and social upheaval, still remain to be assessed dispassionately within a complex Irish, English and Scottish historical context. Certainly the re-entry of the Dominicans into the mainstream of Irish national life gave them a prominence and heightened sense of purpose which they had not enjoyed for centuries. Re-emergence from a proscribed existence in tumultuous circumstances signified the *de facto* but not the *de jure* abrogation of the Tudor and Stuart religious settlement, soon to be reimposed by Commonwealth rule, with barbarous consequences of martyrdom, transportation and exile for the majority of the Dominican fraternity as well as for the wider Catholic Communion.

150 Coonan, *The Irish Catholic Confederacy and the Puritan Revolution*, 143.

TEN

Conclusion

The medieval legacy of division, at once racial, linguistic, cultural and geographical, inevitably engendered decay and disintegration in *Hibernia Dominicana*. In the wider context of ecclesiastical Ireland, the profound transformations in political and social life which marked the end of the middle ages demanded drastic reform and the restructuring of church life, as had happened in the twelfth century when church reform was accelerated by the Anglo-Normans. What was not acceptable to the people of Ireland was an imposed ecclesiastical revolution following the model of Tudor state absolutism, which had resulted in the nationalisation of the Church in England and the establishment by parliamentary statute of the Church of England.

The influence of the Catholic reform movements in mainland Europe had already been received and accepted by high-profile groups of Irish Observant religious: Dominicans, Franciscans, Augustinians and Carmelites. In England, by way of contrast, particularly in the university centres of Cambridge and Oxford, the exhilarating currents of Protestant reform appealed to reform-minded friars and educated laity. Significantly, Ireland was not touched, still less seriously challenged, by the bracing intellectual currents of continental Protestant reform movements in the early sixteenth century.

What seemed to be an irreversible slide towards extinction of an increasingly unstable body of Irish and Anglo-Irish Dominicans was halted by the challenge and dynamism of the Observant movement. Under the leadership of the Anglo-Irish Dominican, David Brown, this movement attempted to transcend the endemic spirit of divisiveness by its fresh vision of Dominican and spiritual renewal. It quickly won strong support among influential laity, Gaelic Irish and Anglo-Irish alike. The irrepressible desire for Irish Dominican autonomy, especially in Gaelic Irish and some Anglo-Irish circles, was realised by papal decision at the instigation of David Brown in 1536. The emergence of an independent Irish province signified a definitive break with tangled medieval antecedents and an undistinguished insular past. Most importantly, it made possible future initiatives to revive the province by encouraging most of the remnant to embrace the reformed model of Dominican life. For the Henrician and

Elizabethan waves of suppression had dismembered and dislocated the tottering late medieval structure. It was west of the Shannon that the impetus for reform survived and where it was to remain a vibrant force in the transmission of a revitalised Catholicism.

Several outstanding Dominican personalities combined to bridge the entire era of suppressions in the sixteenth century and guaranteed continuity, however tenuously, in the midst of disturbing ecclesiastical and secular discontinuity. Their efforts contributed to the well-being of the wider Irish Church as well as that of the Order. Foremost was David Brown, the first true Irish provincial, who succeeded in establishing a nucleus of reformed houses in Munster, with the active support of the Earls of Desmond, only to live to see the collapse of the Observant movement there. Quentin Cogly, Bishop of Dromore (1536–*c.*1539), was the most fearless and outspoken Catholic bishop of his time. Deeply loyal to the papacy, he sought to carry out episcopal responsibilities and oversight far beyond the limits of his own diocese. Quentin O'Higgins, David Brown's close collaborator, served as an effective vicar provincial of Connacht and Ulster and as spiritual adviser to the Gaelic chieftains of the north-west from the 1540s until his death in 1548.

The province continued to be governed by able and dedicated leaders during the troubled years of Elizabeth I's reign. Cormac O'Fergus was an indefatigable provincial, preacher and promoter of Irish Dominican interests at home and overseas in the 1560s and early 1570s. The trace of his achievements resembled that of a meteor, and his life's work remains to be more fully explored in Spanish and Roman archives. Eugene O'Hart and Andrew O'Crean were Bishops of Achonry (1562–1603) and Elphin (1562–94) respectively. Both were staunch upholders of Catholicism and enthusiastic agents of the radical Tridentine programme of church reform in Connacht. By family background both bishops belonged to the core group of the Connacht Gaelic aristocracy which sought to stem Elizabethan cultural infiltration and political subjugation of Gaelic Catholic civilisation. Their contemporary Dominican confrère was Thaddeus O'Farrell, Bishop of Clonfert (1587–1602). His episcopate did not at all mirror the Council of Trent's ideals of a diocesan bishop; he was habitually absent from Clonfert after his consecration, devoting his life to skilled diplomatic work on behalf of the Catholic Irish cause at the Spanish royal court. He died at Kinsale in the disastrous aftermath of the ill-fated Spanish expedition in 1603.

Thaddeus MacDuane was by far the most significant personality who presided over the rapidly declining fortunes of the Irish province from the 1570s to his death in 1608. During his stewardship he displayed remarkable skills as prior of Sligo and as provincial or vicar provincial of his dispersed and demoralised brethren. Even in Connacht and north-west Ulster Dominicans faced extinction, if not by reason of natural causes, then by persecution and sudden violent death, the details of which remain unrecorded. MacDuane corresponded regularly with the authorities of the Order in Rome and indeed journeyed there on at least three occasions. From one of his letters the reader glimpses the problems confronting his 'little flock' (*pusillus grex*): serious internal dissensions at such a late date between reformed and unreformed brethren; the unfriendliness of Ulster bishops towards the Order; sharply increased persecution by secular authorities; and dwindling numbers, with little hope of youthful recruits. Nonetheless, in spite of overwhelming odds and disastrous occurrences, MacDuane's spirit of fortitude and devotion to the Order were never extinguished. And though his heroic efforts could not halt decline and virtual extinction, his vision for the future looked beyond his immediate experience of desolation and catastrophe to the Spanish Low Countries. There he envisaged the foundation of an Irish Dominican college or house of studies for young aspiring Dominicans, from which the future of the Irish Dominican province might be ensured. In all likelihood this radical shift in strategy was influenced by the founding of continental colleges for the training of Irish diocesan priests and by the remarkable impact of these priests on Irish Catholicism. Thaddeus MacDuane's preliminary initiatives in this direction were brought to fruition within twenty years of his passing.

While the suppressions were destructive and demoralising, particularly when they encompassed the reformed Observant houses, they did have a cleansing effect: much of the accumulated dead wood and the ambiguity of an unhappy medieval past were swept away forever. Nonetheless, political, social and religious uncertainty gave rise to painful internal dissensions and fragmentation. Problems arose in Connacht and elsewhere as a result of lay and diocesan intrusion on Dominican property and rights. In the wake of crown secularisation of religious foundations, Catholic as well as Protestant landed proprietors sought impropriation and ownership of religious property. Such lay interference predated the sixteenth-century suppressions, and its full extent and socio-economic consequences will only become clearer with the eventual publication of Vatican and other archival evidence. What happened in Ireland in the Tudor era was not without precedent. When the decayed ancient Irish monastic system collapsed in the twelfth century, local chieftains and powerful ecclesiastical families expropriated monastic lands and incorporated them unchallenged into their own holdings, leaving the monasteries with greatly depleted financial resources.

Far more serious was the ecclesiastical anomaly in Connacht, where the Dominican houses of Urlar, Strade and Cloonymeaghan clung to what were strictly parochial rights of nomination in adjacent parishes inherited from their medieval past. Even after the publication and reception of relevant Tridentine legislation in Connacht, the Dominicans were on occasion largely responsible for long-running acrimony with local secular clergy. Rome finally vindicated the usurped legal rights of the parish clergy in the 1630s, and concord was restored. This particular issue highlighted the phenomenon of 'medieval hangovers' which cast a shadow over the progress of the Dominicans in a new age in which they had been able to recover their true identity and role in the local church. By the opening years of the seventeenth century the surviving Dominicans in Connacht had been drastically affected by the ravages of war, persecution and the confiscation of houses and property which were part of the systematic undermining of the fabric of Gaelic Irish society. With no serious prospects of the Order's survival or regeneration, Dominicans, in common with other friars, were effectively restricted to the remotest areas of the province (except in Sligo), living for the most part privately as chaplains to prominent families.

The training of Irish candidates, religiously and intellectually, within the reformed Dominican framework resulted in a new corps of men equipped for priestly ministry in post-medieval Ireland. This new breed of priests, diocesan as well as religious, were enthusiastic purveyors of a revivified, purified and reform-minded pastoral Catholicism. The Irish Dominican presence was regenerated, at first independently, from two distinct streams of candidates. The earliest stream was composed of a trickle of students of Gaelic Irish and Anglo-Irish background sent abroad to Dominican houses of study, selected by the Masters General and provincials of Spain, France, Portugal, Italy and Flanders, where they immersed themselves in the Order's intellectual and spiritual heritage. The second flow of recruits were those who had experienced the pattern of life in Irish continental colleges or seminaries modelled on Tridentine ideals and legislation for the training of secular clergy. Within this circle of Irish colleges, as indeed within the Order, philosophical and theological formation varied considerably. The *Weltanschauung* of these future Dominicans added much to the richness of diversity in the expression of renewed Irish Catholic faith, as well as to the perception and interpretation of the realities of early seventeenth-century Ireland. Rarely did these men lose sight of the vision and ideals of their European mentors as they returned home to face the hard and daunting challenges of remoulding Irish Catholicism. The massive contribution of the European colleges and the Order's *studia generalia* was decisive in the plan of recovery and uniquely made the first phase of revival a reality in the 1620s.

Reform and reconstruction of the Irish province was speedily and effectively secured by the complementarity and fusion of the two streams of candidates. Moreover, the continental experience of belonging to an international Order in which race and language were uncompromisingly subordinated to the ideals of a common vision provided a model of a realistic *modus vivendi* for Gaelic Irish and Anglo-Irish confrères. The Dominicans, or indeed any of the orders of friars, could never have prospered on an exclusively racial basis. Their living out of a common life, inspired by shared ideals and aspirations, showed seventeenth-century Irishmen that a reconciliation of memories, psychological processes and traditions of life was achievable within a once sharply divided Catholic community. Leadership in the new province stemmed from the talented personalities of a generation of European-educated Dominicans: Simon O'Hallaghan (Lisbon), Roland Burke (Salamanca), Thomas Quirke (Toulouse), Ross MacGeoghegan (Lisbon/Salamanca), Richard Caron (Salamanca), Dominic O'Daly (Lugo/Bordeaux/ Burgos), Nicholas D. Lynch (Lisbon/Paris), Daniel O'Crean, Edmund Raymund Dempsey (Douai?/Louvain?/Alcalá de Henares) and James Hurley.

Of these, the passionate devotion and outstanding achievements of Simon O'Hallaghan, Ross MacGeoghegan, Richard Caron and Dominic O'Daly, the prime founding fathers in the second spring of *Hibernia Dominicana*, shine out with undimmed brilliance. Simon O'Hallaghan's confident personality vigorously heralded an unforeseen, if short-lived, Dominican revival in Leinster and Munster, notably in and around the key cities of Waterford, Kilkenny and Limerick (1600–4). Ross MacGeoghegan's character was moulded after the pattern of the biblical man of God; he was the chosen man of destiny whose depth of spiritual vision revivified, beyond all expectation, a dispirited and dying province and whose policy enabled its new members to experience and assimilate integrated Catholic European civilisation. His contribution as Bishop of Kildare to the renewal of his diocese, especially by the power of example of a life of simplicity, preaching and holiness, impinged on Catholics and Protestants alike.

Richard Caron was pre-eminently the practical idealist, the consummate man of affairs, as clearly emerges in his dealings with the administrative financial secretariats of the Spanish court. Yet his organisational gifts were ever combined with spiritual zeal and practical care for Irish exiles, lapsed Catholics and other Christians who crossed his path in Spain. Heretofore his valuable contribution to the nascent Irish province has not been acknowledged. Also extremely active on the continent was Dominic O'Daly, who sought to draw Irish political and religious developments into the broader context of Catholic European concerns; his deepest aspirations aimed at restoring the legitimacy and public expression of Catholicism and establishing an independent kingdom of Ireland. He excelled as an ecclesiastical diplomat, as an astute political negotiator, and remained an avid participant in the Portuguese political world, as well as in the complex and fast-moving chess-game of European politics. Dominic O'Daly's signal success lay in persuading King Philip IV of Spain to establish the monastery of Bom Sucesso for Irish Dominican contemplative nuns, and Dona Luisa de Gusmão, Queen Regent of Portugal, to build the original college of Corpo Santo, both of which flourished in Lisbon as his memorials until their recent demise.

The royal Spanish assistance to Irish religious and priests returning to Ireland ensured the commencement of their ministry. Most commonly it took the form of a generous travelling allowance which was also intended to cover the expenses of secular clothing and purchase of breviaries and liturgical requisites such as vestments and chalices. Spanish Dominican hospitality and royal generosity created a strong psychological and political bond of loyalty between the Spanish crown and Spanish-educated priests on the ground in Ireland. Because of the sharply perceived Spanish expansionist threat to English sovereignty and commercial interests, Irish government officials became greatly alarmed by the potential influence of the Irish clergy should a Spanish invasion be successfully attempted. Piety and sympathy imbued the motivations of Kings Philip II, Philip III and Philip IV in their political strategy in northern Europe.

The sheer versatility of seventeenth-century Irish ecclesiastics is frequently reflected in the careers of Irish Dominicans, some of whom did not return permanently to Ireland. Among them were chaplains to Irish regiments in Spanish armies (Dominic Burke, senior), administrators (Richard Caron, Michael of the Holy Spirit), honoured philosophers and theologians in universities and houses of higher studies (James Arthur at Naples, Salamanca, Valladolid and Coimbra; John Baptist Hackett at Milan, Naples and Rome), writers (Maurice Roche, Peter French and Bishop Edmund Raymund Dempsey), diplomats (Dominic O'Daly, Oliver Burke, Dominic Burke), secret agents (William Talbot), martyrs (Arthur MacGeoghegan, Terence Albert O'Brien, Bishop of Emly), poets (Padraigín Haicéad, Henry O'Rian or Ryan) and those who distinguished themselves in the international service of the Order (John Nolan) or in their adopted provinces (Peter French in Mexico).

Detailed reports, the first of their kind, dated 1622 and 1626–7, on a new generation of Irish Dominicans offer valuable if strangely incomplete and sometimes confusing data. The general picture is one of vigorous revival in most locations which had a medieval foundation, with the exception of Ulster, where diocesan clergy and Franciscans remained dominant. The vitality of the Dominicans of Galway is highlighted in their establishment of free schools for lay and clerical students alike, which accorded with Galway's long-standing and renowned educational tradition.

Undoubtedly the first major achievement of the era of revival was the reappearance of forward-looking Dominican communities in cities, towns and countryside in the 1620s and 1630s. Far more important and with lasting effects was the establishment against overwhelming odds of two Irish Dominican colleges at Lisbon (1615–1850s) and Louvain (1624–1794). These stable centres of European cultural, religious and intellectual training under Irish auspices, to which later was added the Collegio di San Clemente at Rome (founded in 1677), guaranteed an uninterrupted flow of priests to Ireland. While not considered by their original founders and patrons as permanent establishments, they ensured the continuity of Irish Dominicans over the turbulent centuries that followed.

When the euphoria of re-establishment had passed, the Dominicans and members of other religious orders were severely tested by a whole range of problems relating to adaptation to the Irish scene. Firstly, there was inevitable social and cultural shock. The confidence and self-esteem of Irish Dominicans who had savoured over several years the riches of mainstream European civilisation, were put to the test by the experience of living furtively in the back streets of towns or in rural obscurity. Intolerance and intermittent persecution on the part of government and local magistrates added to their fears, general discomfort and gnawing insecurity

Sharp dissensions among bishops and diocesan clergy and among religious orders pointed to the element of competition for clientèle and economic support. Much more serious, and with disastrous long-term effects, were the clashes of episcopal and religious order jurisdictions which centred on control of personnel and finance. Bishops and secular clergy found it intolerable that regular priests within their dioceses should not be fully subject to episcopal regulation in all matters relating to pastoral ministry and lay economic support. Regulars, for their part, deeply resented attempts to limit the scope or geographical area of their ministry and to deny them the fundamental canonical and jurisdictional autonomy to which they were accustomed. While finance and ecclesiastical control proved to be flashpoints in relations, the real issue was that of disparate jurisdictions apparently misunderstood or misinterpreted. Distressing and disedifying quarrels with diocesan authorities and other religious orders manifested all too clearly Dominican vulnerability and feet of clay. Were it not for the extraordinary generosity and comprehension of human nature on the part of the wider Catholic community, the plight of a squabbling clergy might have been rendered more acute by withdrawal of financial and moral support.

The Master General, Nicholas Ridolfi, showed remarkable perspicacity in his dealings with his Irish brethren. In commenting on their affairs over twelve years, he displayed sharp insight into their native psychology. Directness, shrewdness and objectivity are invariably manifest in his judgements. While praising Irish Dominican missionary aspirations regarding

Scotland, he forthrightly considered them to be unrealistic. He warned them of their weaknesses: internal divisions, a contentious spirit, and preoccupation with trivialities. Such concerns, so much in evidence in points of law arising from the chapter acts of 1638, in his view, soaked up their time and energies to the detriment of their evangelical and preaching ministry.

The passage in St John's Gospel (12: 24), 'Unless the grain of wheat falls into the earth and dies, it remains alone; but if it dies, it bears much fruit' was verified, in the Irish Dominican saga, from 'the abomination of desolation' (Daniel 9: 27; Matthew 24: 15) and near obliteration to fresh beginnings and spiritual regeneration. This momentous dispensation of fortune coincided with the painful transition from late medieval to the first phase of early modern Ireland. It was the remarkable and wholly unexpected second spring of *Hibernia Dominicana* that made possible all subsequent progress and recovery in the face of the devastating reversals of Irish history. At any rate, the years 1640 and 1641 constitute an historical watershed at which this study finds its logical conclusion. The Dominicans continued uninterruptedly to consolidate their position, in a greatly different political setting, but one in which their role would not be inconspicuous.

Appendices

Appendix 1: Provincials and Vicars of the Irish Dominican Province, 1536–1643

David Brown	1536–*c.*1559
Quentin O'Higgins	1548 (coadjutor vicar provincial)
Thaddeus MacDuane	?–1563–?
Cormac O'Fergus	*c.*1569–*c.*1572
Eugene MacHugan	?–1593 (d.)
Thaddeus MacDuane	1593–1600
Daniel O'Crean	1600–4 (vicar of congregation)
Thaddeus MacDuane	1604–8 (vicar of congregation)
Roland Burke	1608–*c.*1612 (vicar of congregation)
Thomas Quirke	*c.*1612–17 (vicar of congregation?)
Richard Caron	1617 (vicar of congregation)
Ross MacGeoghegan	1617–22 (vicar of congregation)
	1622–7 (provincial)
Nicholas D. Lynch	1627–34
Edmund Raymund Dempsey	1634–8
James Hurley	1638–43

Appendix 2: Irish Dominican Bishops, 1536–1650[1]

	diocese	*papal provision*	*death*
John Quin[2]	Limerick	21 Oct. 1524; cons. before 3 Jan. 1525; deprived by Edward VI, 9 Apr. 1551; restored by Mary 1553	1554/5
Quentin Cogly	Dromore	29 May 1536	*c.*1539
Peter Wall[2]	Clonmacnoise	4 May 1556	1568
Cormac O'Coyne[2]	Achonry	1556 (prov. not recorded)	before 12 Oct.1561
Andrew O'Crean	Elphin	28 Jan. 1562	1594
Eugene O'Hart	Achonry	28 Jan. 1562	1603
Thaddeus O'Farrell	Clonfert	29 May/8 June 1587	1602
Ross MacGeoghegan	Kildare	2/12 Feb. 1629 cons. Sept./Oct. 1629	26 May 1644
Edmund Raymund Dempsey	Leighlin	28 Feb./10 Mar. 1642	27 Aug./6 Sept. 1658
Terence Albert O'Brien	Emly	coadjutor with right of succession 1/11 Mar. 1647; cons. 2 Apr. 1648	30 Oct. 1651
Oliver Darcy	Dromore	1/11 Mar. 1647; cons. 7 May 1648	Jan./Feb. 1664

1 See B. Millett and C. J. Woods, 'Roman Catholic Bishops from 1534' in *NHI*, ix, 333-91.

2 These Catholic bishops, together with Denis Moore, O.P. (Bishop of Clonfert, 1509/1510–34) and many others, have been erroneously included in the succession lists of the Anglican or Church of Ireland bishops, simply because they happened to be in possession of their respective sees in 1534 when Henry VIII rejected papal provisions and jurisdiction in Ireland. The ultimate reasons for the split in the lines of episcopal succession were profoundly theological and ecclesiological, pre-eminently the rupture in ecclesiastical communion with the see of Rome and the introduction of Anglicanism. The criteria of episcopal nomination or recognition by a secular ruler as the basis for divergent lines are altogether inadequate. *Pace* B. Bradshaw, J. G. Simms and C. J. Woods, 'Bishops of the Church of Ireland from 1534' in *NHI*, ix, 398, 420, 433ff.

Appendix 3: Disposal of Lands of Dissolved Dominican Houses: Entries in Government Records

Arklow

Edmund Duffe, gentleman, was given a lease on 15 February 1541 'of the site of the priory of Friars Preachers of Arclow, with appurtenances. To hold for twenty-one years at a rent of 20s.'[1] John Travers, Esq., of Dublin was granted the same property on 4 February 1544.[2] An undated twenty-one-year lease (*c.*1547) assigned the Dominican property 'of Arclowe, County Wexford [*sic*]' to Terence McMorho at a rent of 26s 8d.[3] An inquisition (15 Mar. 1595) found that Robert Barnewall, deceased, had granted, *inter alia*, to Theobald Walshe of Carrickmaine [Carrickmines] and others 'the former Dominican house of Arklow, containing about 2 acres, with all its possessions in Arklow and elsewhere'.[4]

Ballinegaul

On 6 February 1551/2 a lease was issued to 'Richard Laules, of Marynerton, gentleman, of the site of the monastery of white friars of Ballynegall, County Limerick, with appurtenances'.[5] This lease may have proved ineffectual, as may be judged from a formal inquisition of 3 January 1557/8 which stated that 'Donough O'Dangane was the last prior of this house . . . and that he was seized of this monastery [Ballinegaul], a church, a water mill and twelve acres of land of the annual value of 10s 4d'.[6] Forty years later its concealed landed wealth was finally disclosed when Ballinegaul (which the patent mistakenly identifies as a Carmelite house), together with half a carucate of land, i.e. about 60 prime east Limerick acres, which had once belonged to it, was granted by Queen Elizabeth I in a charter (28 June 1597) to Trinity College, Dublin.[7]

Carlingford

On 18 July 1541 Martin Soryne, a Dundalk merchant, secured a lease for twenty-one years at a rent of £5 'of the site of the monastery of preachers or black friars of Carlingford'.[8]

1 *Fiants Ire., Hen.* VIII, 48, no. 163.
2 Ibid., 72, no. 404.
3 Ibid., 86, no. 535.
4 *Calendar of Inquisitions formerly in the Office of the Chief Remembrancer of the Exchequer prepared from the MSS of the Irish Recond Commission*, ed. M. C. Griffith, Dublin 1991, 299.
5 *Fiants Ire., Edw.* VI, 130.
6 Ferrar, *The History of Limerick*, 437, cites the Offices of the Chief Remembrancer and the Auditor General; Archdall, *Monasticon Hibernicum*, 809, cites a two-acre site for house and church alone from Chief Remembrancer source.
7 *Cal. Pat. Rolls Ire., Eliz.*, ii, 416, 421.
8 *Fiants Ire., Hen.* VIII, 54, no. 231.

Cashel

Walter Flemynge, a merchant of Cashel, was granted in perpetuity (5 May 1543) the buildings and property of the Cashel Dominicans for the sum of £46, at an annual rent of 2s 6d.[9]

Coleraine

James Hamilton obtained (20 July 1605) the Dominican house of Coleraine and its property and disposed of same (23 Sept. 1605) to Thomas Phillips as follows: 'the site and precinct of the late priory of Coleraine, in the county of Antrim with all barns, edifices, buildings, and curtilages: also, the four and a half townlands of Ballikinsantill, *alias* Mount-Sandall, Ballenefeighe, Atwoare, Ardbeggan, Dunaville, and Balliosally: one and a half townland, called Tollocor: a free fishing in the River Bann, *alias* the Band, for one whole day, viz., the Monday next after the Feast of St John the Baptist, in every year; on which day, all fish taken in the river doth of right belong to the priory: one salmon every day, from time to time, for ever, of all the fishers who shall fish in the river, during fishing time; which salmon likewise belongs to the priory: with all messuages, mills, houses, buildings, lands, tenements, commons, waters, fishings, services, annuities, courts leet, view of frank pledge, franchises, jurisdictions, privileges, and all other commodities to the priory belonging'.[10]

Cork

On 20 December 1543 William Boureman, gentleman, was granted, in consideration of £127 10s sterling to be paid, 'the site of the monastery of Friars Preachers by Cork with appurtenances, the half of Skeaghbegge, land in Rathmyny and Galveiston, County Cork. To hold for ever, by the service of a twentieth part of a knight's fee and a rent of 6s 9d sterling.'[11]Later Edward Galwey of Cork, merchant, obtained an undated lease (*c.*1547) for twenty-one years of the former Dominican house and its lands at an annual rent of £6 14s 2½d sterling.[12] Perhaps the same Galwey family were owners of the property occupied by the Cork Dominicans when it was raided by government officials in 1631.[13]

Derry

Granted by King James I (3 Apr. 1604) to George Carew: 'the site and precinct of the late Dominican friary, and the eighth part of a quarter of land, or there-

9 Ibid., 67, no. 361.
10 *Cal. Pat. Rolls Ire.* [1603–10], n.p., n.d., 221; details of entry omitted in *Cal. Pat. Rolls Ire., Jas I*, Dublin 1966, 71.
11 *Fiants Ire., Hen. VIII*, 70, no. 388; see M. O'Dowd, 'Irish Concealed Lands Papers in the Hastings Manuscripts in the Huntingdon Library, San Marino, California' in *Anal. Hib.*, no. 31 (1984), 108, where the Dominican monastery was located in 'Co. Cork' and leased to Boureman on 20 Dec. 1544.
12 *Fiants Ire., Hen. VIII*, 85–6, no. 533.
13 See p. 271 above.

abouts, situate near the island of Derry, nigh the river Loughfoile, on the north part of said island, in Co. Donnegall'.[14]

Drogheda

On 20 August 1541 a lease was granted to Walter Dowdall of Drogheda and Edward Becke of Merrynerton [Mornington], Co. Meath, merchants, 'of the site of the monastery of Friars Preachers of Drogheda, with appurtenances in Drogheda and Phillippston. To hold for twenty-one years, at a rent of 47s.'[15] Two years later (30 Nov. 1543) this lease was amplified, at a cost of £41 3s 4d, by detailed enumeration of the former concealed properties of the Drogheda Dominicans: 'a messuage in Bowestreet inhabited by Robert Keres, junior, a messuage, &c., in Dwelekestreet, the Cloverhouse park, a garden in the Fayrestreet occupied by Richard Russell, a messuage in Saint Laurence Street and a garden and orchard in Irishstreet occupied by Patrick Russell, land by Philippiston, County Drogheda, and by Bedloweston, County Meath. To hold for ever, by the service of a twentieth part of a knight's fee, and a rent of 2s 2d.'[16] On 31 January 1544 a grant was made to Jenico Preston, knight, Viscount Gormanston, for the sum of £6 13s 4d 'of a messuage and close in Drogheda, held by John Ywe, carter, parcel of the possessions of the Friars Preachers of Drogheda . . . at a rent of 4d'.[17] After his death Edward Becke's estate was seised of half the Dominican priory of Drogheda which he had granted to John Cashel of Drogheda, merchant, who in turn had granted it to Thomas Fitzwilliam, without the royal licence. Walter Dowdall, also a merchant of Drogheda, was seised of the other half of the property.[18]

Dublin

John Alen, chancellor, Gerald Aylmer, knight, chief justice, and others obtained (31 July 1541) a twenty-one-year lease at a rent of £6 'of the site of the monastery of Friars Preachers, beside Dublin, messuages in St Mighan's parish, St Patrick's-street and Newe-street, and a moiety of Helen Hores Meade (meadow) *alias* Gybbetes Meade, County Dublin'.[19] On 24 May 1542 Thomas Cusack, of Coussingeston, knight, obtained a lease of 'the lands of Londreston, County Meath, parcel of the possessions of the late monastery of Friars Preachers by the bridge of Dublin'.[20] After Cusack's death the former lands of the Dublin Dominicans were declared seised by exchequer inquisition (28 Apr. 1572).[21]

14 J. C. Erck (ed.), *A Repertory of the Inrolments of the Patent Rolls of Chancery in Ireland commencing with the reign of James I*, i, Dublin 1846, 133; *Cal. Pat. Rolls Ire., Jas I*, 57: adds detail that annual rent of parcel of land was 8d.
15 *Fiants Ire., Hen. VIII*, 52, no. 210.
16 Ibid., 69, no. 381.
17 Ibid., 72, no. 402.
18 *Calendar of Exchequer Inquisitions*, 138.
19 *Fiants Ire., Hen. VIII*, 54–5, no. 238; *Cal. S.P. Ire., Hen. VIII*, iii, pt 3, 322.
20 *Fiants Ire., Hen. VIII*, 61, no. 309.
21 *Calendar of Exchequer Inquisitions*, 204.

Kilkenny

A grant to Walter Archer, the sovereign, the burgesses and commonalty of Kilkenny, dated 25 August 1543, revealed that besides their conventual property the Dominicans held 'lands in Kilkenny, Irishton by Kilkenny, Aldrenwodde by Keppaghe, Glassanaghe, Ketingeston, Carrickellir, Cowlyshill, Brownistonwaring, Lysnefunchin, Ballynolan, and Ferynbroke, County Kilkenny'.[22]

Kilmallock

See pp 49–50 and note 32.

Lorrha

On 2 June 1552 John O'Hogan, former prior of the Canons Regular priory at Lorrha, was granted leases of his dissolved priory, its lands, the vicarages and rectories once impropriate to the Lorrha canons, together with 'the site of the monastery of friars of S. Dominick's Order in Larrowe [Lorrha] and the land called Freres Rathe, with its tithes in the said town . . . for twenty-one years, in full recompense of his pension, at a rent of £8 during lessee's life, and £13 2s 8d after his death'.[23]

Mullingar

A lease was granted in October 1552 to Thomas Cassie of Athboy, merchant, and Ismay Nugent, his wife, 'of the house, church, and other buildings within the site of the abbey of Molyngar, a small castle and the demesne lands of the abbey, eleven cottages in a street near the abbey', numerous messuages and 'lands of Slewyn, the Graunge, the Annaghe, Tolhan, Raduff, Walteriston, and Rathwogan, and the rectory of Vastina, county Westmeath. To hold for twenty-one years, at a rent of £31 16s 10d.'[24] On 4 March 1590 'the office of gaoler in Mullingar, the courts leet in same and the site of the houses of Friars Preachers of Mullingar' were entrusted to the use of Walter Hoppe.[25]

Naas

On 20 April 1540 Thomas Alen, gentleman of Dublin, was given a lease for twenty-one years 'of the site of the monastery of the Order of Preachers, by the mote of Nase, with its appurtenances' at a rent of £6 9s.[26] The property passed to Robert Eustace and others on 15 June 1542.[27] Sir Thomas Luttrell of Luttrellstown, Co. Dublin, was seised (12 June 1558) 'of the site of the Dominican house of Naas, and of 5 cottages, 12 gardens, a watermill and 11 acres arable' . . . [text defective].[28]

22 *Fiants Ire, Hen. VIII*, 67–8, no. 369.
23 *Fiants Ire., Edw. VI*, 134
24 Ibid., 141.
25 *Calendar of Exchequer Inquisitions*, 379.
26 *Fiants Ire., Hen. VIII*, 44, no. 119.
27 Ibid., 62, no. 313.
28 *Calendar of Exchequer Inquisitions*, 160.

Newtownards

A very extensive grant of lands made by James I to James Hamilton, dated 20 July 1605, included 'the tithes of all the lands and hereditaments to the late priory of Newtown belonging: the site of the late abbey, called the Black Abbey, with all its houses, granaries, edifices, curtilages, and gardens; and the three townlands of Black Abbey, Ballynemanough, and Ballecarrock, with all their tithes . . . the site of the late priory of Newton, with all its granaries, edifices, gardens, curtilages and cemeteries; and the three townlands of Newton, Kilcowman, and Barnes, nigh said priory'.[29] The rectory of Newtown (valued at 14 marks in 1302) was also impropriate to the Dominicans of Newtownards.[30]

Trim

On 26 April 1540 a lease was granted to David Floyde, of Dublin, soldier, 'of the site of the priory of preachers, or black friars of Trym, with appurtenances in Trym, Toullgharde and [?]. To hold for twenty-one years at a rent of 40s.'[31] Two years later (24 May 1542) 'the site of the priory of Friars Preachers of Trym, with appurtenances, County Meath' passed by letters patent to Thomas Cusack of Coussingeston, knight.[32] Cusack's heirs were seised (28 Apr. 1572) of the 'site of the former Dominican priory of Trim, with the church, bell-tower and all other buildings there, 3 messuages, 69 acres and a pasture field and all other lands in Trim'. The same inquisition recited in more precise detail the former possessions of the Trim Dominicans which had been let to Jenetta Sarsfield.[33]

Waterford

Notwithstanding the earlier issue of leases by the prior,[34] James White of Waterford, gentleman, was granted (20 May 1540) a lease for twenty-one years, at a rent of 4 marks, 'of the site of the monastery of preachers, or black friars, of Waterford, with appurtenances in the city, and land by Kylbary, County Waterford'.[35] The same grantee, James White, on payment of the considerable sum of £90 8s, was leased in perpetuity (16 February 1543) the dissolved Dominican possessions.[36] On 20 October 1598 the White family ceded possession of the Waterford Blackfriars' property to the crown, which in turn leased it to various persons for £21 p.a.[37]

29 *Cal. Pat. Rolls, Ire.* [1603–10], n.p., n.d., 225. This edition (ed. anon) not listed in the British Library Catalogue (1991). Entry in *Cal. Pat. Rolls Ire., Jas I*, Dublin 1966, 72 is defective, but records valuation of tithes and property rent as £3 3s 4d.
30 W. Reeves, *Ecclesiastical Antiquities of Down, Connor and Dromore*, Dublin 1847, 13–14, 101.
31 *Fiants Ire., Hen. VIII*, 45, no. 129. See White, *Extents of Irish Monastic Possessions*, 308–9.
32 *Fiants Ire., Hen. VIII*, 61, no. 309.
33 *Calendar of Exchequer Inquisitions*, 204, 206.
34 See p. 30 above.
35 *Fiants Ire., Hen. VIII*, 47, no. 152.
36 Ibid., 66, no. 351.
37 *Calendar of Exchequer Inquisitions*, 310.

Youghal

On 25 November 1550 a lease had been granted to William Walshe, of Youghal, 'of the site of the house of Friars Preachers observant of Yoghill, County Cork, with appurtenances. To hold for twenty-one years at a rent of 59s 6d.'[38]

38 *Fiants Ire., Edw VI*, 93; see Gwynn and Hadcock, *Medieval Religious Houses: Ireland*, 231.

Appendix 4: Papal Briefs of Paul III (8 April and 20 June 1537) Addressed to Quentin Cogly, Bishop of Dromore (1536–9)

[8 April 1537] ASV, Brev. Lat., 24, f. 419rv.

Venerabili fratri Quintino, episcopo Dromorensi Insule Hybernie.

Venerabilis frater. Salutem et apostolicam benedictionem. Meritis tuae devotionis inducimur, ut petitionibus tuis quantum cum Deo possumus favorabiliter annuamus. Cum itaque sicut nobis nuper exponi fecisti in insula Hybernie plures sunt ecclesiae cathedrales que de jure vel de facto pastoris solatio destitute existunt. Alie vero que pastores si eo veniant[1] appelende partim heresis Anglicane contagio infectos, partim autem qui licet Catholice fidei professores tamen cum natione Angli sint et in regno Anglie moram trahant nec ad ecclesias huiusmodi accedere nec gregem commissum, ut bonum decet pastorem // pascere curam fortite sint in christiane religionis labefactionem ipsorumque christifidelium diocesanorum indignationum et scandalum non modicum ac propterea tu, pie ductus, pastorum absentium et hereticorum huiusmodi circa pontificalium officiorum celebrationem defectus quantum cum Deo poteris suppleri desideres, Nos, tuis piis votis in hac parte favorabiliter annuere volentes fraternitati tue, ut in quibuscunque partium Hibernie predictarum civitatibus et diocesibus in quibus vel proprii pastores non resederint vel heretici occupatores inventi vel etiam ecclesie ipse ut[2] premittitur destitute fuerint pontificalia officia de consensu dilectorum filiorum capitulorum nostrarum ecclesiarum absque tamen legitimorum illarum pastorum preiudicio quoad vixeris et quotiens tibi placuerit exercere libere et licite valeas quibusvis apostolicis ac in provincialibus et synodalibus conciliis editis generalibus vel[3] specialibus constitutionibus et ordinationibus necnon ecclesiarum predictarum iuramento, confirmatione apostolica vel quavis firmitate alia roboratis statutis et consuetudinibus ceterisque contrariis nequaquam obstantibus auctoritate apostolica tenore presentium de speciali gratia indulgemus.

Datum Romae apud Sanctum Petrum sub annulo piscatoris die viii aprilis M.D.XXXVII,[4] pontificatus nostri anno tertio.

Collatum per Joannem Mileti. C. Accurruis.

1 In left margin: nomine.
2 Erasure.
3 Adds and cancels: constitutionibus (?).
4 M.D. 37 cancelled; XXXVII in MS.

[20 June 1537] ASV, Brev. Lat., 24, f. 427rv.

Venerabili fratri Quintino, episcopo Dromorensi in Hybernia.
Venerabilis frater. Salutem etc. Supplicare nobis nuper humiliter fecisti ut cum archiepiscopus, primas Ardmachanus, natus Anglus, tuus metropolitanus, Regi Anglie in detestandis eius contra Romanam ecclesiam et sedem apostolicam opinionibus et rebellionibus adhereat et penitus obediat, ac propterea tu tuusque clerus ac populus ad archiepiscopum prefatum rerum metropoliticarum occasione accedere quandiu idem rex // in sua obduraverit perfidia non nisi[1] cum maximo contagionis huiusmodi periculo valeatis, tibi, ut commissum tibi pastorale officium in tuis civitate et diocesi Dromorensi ab execrabilis perversitatis huiusmodi coinquinatione securior exercere possis in premissis opportune consulere de benignitate apostolica dignaremur, Nos, personam tuam nobis et predicte sedi apostolice devotam specialibus favoribus et gratiis prosequi volentes, huiusmodi tuis supplicationibus inclinati, auctoritate apostolica tenore presentium durante huiusmodi, dumtaxat te ac tuos in civitate et diocesi Dromorensi officiales diocesanos subditosque presentes et futuros ac universum tibi commissum gregem ab omni superioritate, iurisdictione, visitatione, correctione, dominio, et potestate moderni et pro tempore existentis archiepiscopi Ardmachani penitus et omnino exhimimus et liberamus ac sub nostra et sedis predicte protectione sucipimus, ita ut dictus archiepiscopus metropolitanus eiusque officiales presentes et futuri nullam superioritatem, auctoritatem, dominium, visitationem aut correctionem in te tuosque officiales, presentes subditos et gregem predictos etiam rationem delicti aut contractus seu rei de qua agetur ubicunque commitatur delictum, initiatur contractus aut res ipsa consistat, exercere possint seu debeant, sed teneantur officiales et subditi tui de se conquerentes coram te vel tuo officiali generali, tu vero [c]oram ipsa sede apostolica vel delegatis eius, duntaxat de iustitia respondere, et processus ac sententias quos et quas contra te tuosque officiales et subditos prefatos per archiepiscopum seu officiales huiusmodi haberi et promulgari, ac quicquid in contrarium scienter vel ignoranter attemptari contigerit irritum et innane decernimus, non obstantibus felicis recordationis Innocentii pape viii predecessoris nostri, que incipit 'volentes', ac aliis apostolicis necnon in provincialibus et synodalibus conciliis editis qualibet vel qualibus constitutionibus et ordinationibus, ceterisque contrariis quibuscumque.

Datum Romae apud Sanctum Marcum sub annulo piscatoris, die xx junii M.D.XXXVII, pontificatus nostri anno tertio.

Collatum per Joannem Mileti. C. Accurruis.

[*In left margin*:] V. Regien.

1 Erasure: ut (?).

Appendix 5: Brevis Relatio de Statu Provinciae Sanctae Crucis Hyberniae, de eiusdem antiquitate, de numero Conventuum, et Fratrum in ea laborantium [Spring 1622]

AGOP, XIV, Liber K, pp 1, 2, 9, 10, 12, 13.

Est haec provincia antiquissima, in qua sunt triginta et octo prioratus, praeter multos vicariatus et capellas, ex quibus quamplures in ipso sanctissimi patris Dominici tempore undati et erecti fuerunt, ut constat ex epistola eiusdem Sancti Dominci ad Illustrissimum Principem de Tyrconnel missa in favorem et commendationem duorum fratrum, quos a se misit in Hyberniam, quae epistola summa cum veneratione et fratrum fideliumque singulari devotione asservabatur in conventu nostro Derrensi, donec incendio et devastatione haereticorum dictum conventum et fratres in eo degentes improvide opprimentium deperdita fuit. Idem constat ex vetustissimo manuscripto conventus nostri Lymericensis, in quo inter alia antiquitatis indicia refertur obitus et sepultura Illustrissimi Principis Donati Brieni, primi fundatoris dicti conventus 1233, et ex aliis multis vetustissimis monumentorum nostrorum fragmentis quae (Deo providente) manus haereticorum evaserunt.

Conventuum autem huius Provinciae nomina sunt quae sequuntur.

Conventus Dublinensis in quo resident Pater Rocus et octo fratres.
Conventus Galviensis in quo praeest fr. Daniel de Cruce decem fratribus.
Conventus Lymericensis in quo praeest fr. Bernardus Brienus septem fratribus.
Conventus Corkeagiensis in quo praeest fr. Ioannes de S. Maria octo fratribus.
Conventus Kilceniensis in quo praeest fr. Thomas Curchaeus septem fratribus.
Conventus Waterfordiensis in quo praeest fr. Thomas Poerus septem fratribus.
Conventus de Urlar in quo praeest fr. Stephanus Lynceus cum alio patre pro instructione et educatione noviciorum qui quotidie recipiuntur. Locus enim ad hoc aptissimus est, et ab haereticorum vicinia separatus.

Reliqui autem triginta et unus conventus in quibus adhuc non resident fratres, divisi sunt inter dictas communitates et praesidentes earum, ut eos frequenter visitent, et statutis temporibus praedicatores et confessores a se mittant, hoc ordine, ut quaelibet dictarum communitatum curam habeat viciniorum sibi conventuum desolatorum, et in absentia fratrum sacerdos aliquis saecularis (pius tamen et exemplaris vitae) in praefectum confraternitatis Rosarii in desolatis conventibus instituitur.

Horum autem conventuum quantitas redituum et bonorum non ita praecise et infallibiliter scitur, propter ablationem inventariorum et scripturarum ad eos pertinentium per haereticos factam. Certum tamen est in archivio regio reperiri posse, quantum immobilium bonorum quemlibet conventum olim pertinebat. Initio siquidem suppressionis monasteriorum, ex mandato Henrici Octavi regis Angliae, coacervata fuerunt inventaria bonorum omnium immobilium ecclesiasticorum et in registrum regium diligenter relata. Interim hoc certo nobis constat, tam ex iis quae in confesso videmus pertinere ad quemlibet conventum, quam ex relatione seniorum fratrum, nullum ex dictis triginta octo conventibus fuisse, in quo ad minus triginta vel quadraginta fratres sustentari sufficienter non posse, in aliis centum et ultra, in aliis octuaginta, et sic de ceteris.

Porro in hac Provincia sunt duae antiquissimae et miraculosissimae imagines Deiparae Virginis, altera pertinens ad conventum Yoghelensem, altera ad Traliensem, quae quotidie prodigiosis et stupendis clarent miraculis, ex quibus unum illudque rarum videri debet, quod licet saepe saepius ab insidiantibus haereticis impetitae fuerint, etiam praemissis exploratoribus, qui certiores eos facerent de loco in quo huiusmodi imagines servabantur, nunquam tamen eas invenire aut deprehendere potuerunt, Deo ita illudente oculis impiorum et excaecante eos propter malitiam ipsorum. Quantus autem fidelium concursus, quantaque vota et preces ad has sacrosanctas imagines quotidie fiant, vix credi potest, indeque communi appellatione priorem ex dictis imaginibus Mariam Gratiarum et Miraculorum vocant.

Hoc etiam in dictis nostris conventibus singulare et notatu dignum animadversum est, quod nunquam haeretici in quibusdam eorum sibi a Rege ad inhabitandum (seu potius profanandum) concessis, ne una quidem nocte sine nocturna vexatione et verberatione (maxime circa gallicinium) conquiescere potuerint fratribus albis (ut eis videbantur) illos e quo domicilio, cum furore et fustibus expellentibus, adeo ut nonnunquam multi illorum post nocturnam inquietudinem sequenti mane contusi, confracti, et semimortui reperirentur: atque ita vel inviti sacra loca deserere cogebantur. Cum tamen Catholici qui de licentia fratrum in iis resident, nunquam talem vexationem persenserint. Hoc autem non solum haerectici, sed et omnes alii, sanctitati locorum attribuebant. Haec et alia multa notatu digna, quae brevitatis gratia lubens omitto, antiquitatem et sanctitatem huius provinciae testantur.

Nomina fratrum praedicatorum ordinis in regno Hyberniae.

fr. Rochus de Cruce
fr. Daniel de Criedgan
fr. Thomas Cuirkaeus
fr. Vincentius Hoganus
fr. Thomas Lycaeus
fr. Gulielmus Talbotus
fr. Stephanus Lyncaeus
fr. Dominicus Nugentius
fr. Bernardus Brienus
fr. Iosephus Langtonus
fr. Thomas Branganus
fr. Gulielmus Seyus
fr. Ioannes Foxius
fr. Hugo Gruoganus
fr. Thomas Poerius
fr. Malachias Mulonus
fr. Thomas Geoghganus
fr. Daniel Dalaeus
fr. Petrus Strongus
fr. Petrus Martinez
fr. Iacobus Olfaeus [Defaeus?]
fr. Aenaeas Calnanas
fr. Ioannes David
fr. Richardus Barraeus
fr. Ioannes de Cruce.

Isti omnes sunt sacerdotes et verbi Dei concionatores. 25 numero.

fr. Manutius Culaeus
fr. Thomas Gneleus
fr. Malachias Brieneus
fr. Ioannes Ruth
fr. Dominicus Miagh
fr. Malachias Cormacus
fr. Edmondus Keganus
fr. David Murillo
fr. Petrus Scotus
fr. Edmondus Suynaeus
fr. Hugo Martinus
fr. Manutius del Rosario
fr. Thadaeus de S. Mario
fr. Raymundus Stapletonus
Isti omnes sunt sacerdotes et confessores, exemplaris et laudabilis conversationis viri.

Nomina fratrum non Sacerdotum

fr. Ioannes Cnavinus
fr. Edmondus Dylonus
fr. Geraldus Dylonus
fr. Thomas Brimigeanus
fr. Thomas Geogganus
fr. Antoninus de S. Dominico
fr. Albertus Brienus
fr. Petrus Lyranus
fr. Ioannes Baptista
fr. Ioannes Geraldinus
fr. Iacobus Barry
fr. Dominicus Medus
fr. Andreas Hurlaeus
fr. Thomas Lyncaeus
fr. Ioannes de Purificatione
fr. Edmondus de Cruce
fr. Ioannes de S. Vincentio
fr. Edmondus de Spiritu Sancto.

Praeter hos sunt multi puri Novicii, et hoc anno missimus ad studendum in Hispania decem fratres, ante quos in ipsa Hispania fuerunt vigintiquatuor actuales studentes. Nomina fratrum ordinis praedicatorum in regno Hiberniae, qui numero sunt quinquaginta septem.

Appendix 6: Nomina Conventuum ordinis Praedicatorum in Hybernia ac fratrum ibi degentium [*c.* 1626–7]

APF, SOCG, 294, ff 102r–105v.

Ultonia

Conventus Derensis [Derry]
Culrathensis [Coleraine]
Novae villae [Newtownards]
Carlinsis [Carlingford]
Pontanae [Drogheda]

Medensis

Conventus de Mullinguear [Mullingar]
de Athrim [Trim]

Lagenia

Conventus Dublinensis [Dublin]
Nassensis seu Decolle [Naas]
de Insecuyr [Inchaquire]
de Athy
Invirmor seu Arcloensis [Arklow]
de Aghabo [Aghaboe]
Kilkenensis [Kilkenny]
Rosensis [Rosbercon]

Momonia

Waterfordensis [Waterford]
Yochuillensis [Youghal]
Corchagensis [Cork]
Gleanuirensis [Glanworth]
Traliensis [Tralee]
Cassellensis [Cashel]
Loracensis [Lorrha]
Killagensis [Kilmallock]
Limbricensis [Limerick]

Conatia

S. Petri Martyris de Portumna
Atthenriensis [Athenry]
S. Mariae Galviensis [Galway]
Urlarensis [Urlar]
de Vico [Strade]
de Rathbrana [Rathfran]
de Maybeoil [Toombeola]
Borecensis [Burrishoole]
de Roscoman [Roscommon]
Tullsque [Tulsk]
Cluansãvil [Cloonshanville]
Villaeduni [Ballindoon]
de Sligo
Longfordensis [Longford]

Omnes vero praedicti conventus habitabantur a fratribus nostris antequam Henricus VIII, Rex Angliae, eiusque familiae Elisabetha sibi supremi capitis Ecclesiae nomen usurpassent, et omnes conventus religiosorum ordinum in Anglia et Hibernia oppressessent, religiosis omnibus ab eis expulsis, eorumque redditus sibi ac suis subditis appropriantes; sed ab Hybernia nunquam poterant fratres nostros penitus exstirpare. Nam quamvis expulsi a monasteriis suis erant, non tamen regnum reliquerunt, sed apud seculares catholicos latitabant, et aliquando etiam ad aliquem conventum suum in desertis locis constitutum, et a catholicis possessum conveniebant, ibique capitula sua, prout poterant, celebrabant, et ordinationes pro temporum calamitate omnibus convenientibus statuebant, remanentes semper sub unius provincialis, aut unius vicarii generalis obedientia, qui fere per totum illud tempus suppressionis usque ad annum circiter 1612 erat Reverendus admodum Pater frater Thaddeus Duanus, eoque tunc per mortem ablato dispersi sunt fratres inter catholicos seculares eorum benefactores, sic remanserunt, donec circiter annum Domini 1613 et deinceps hucusque venerunt in Hyberniam fratres, qui erant educati in Hispania, qui fratres iterum congregaverunt ad duos vel tres conventus solitarios fratres nostros, et ex istis se extenderunt per provinciam ita, ut iam duodecim domos habitatas habeant, ex quibus octo sunt in oppidis et civitatibus, et aliae quattuor in desertis locis, et inter has, ac illas haec intervenit differentia, quod in civitatibus et oppidis non possumus nostris antiquis vivere domibus, sed in domibus deforis saeculari modo fabricatis, et intus ad formam religiosae habitationis ordinatis, ac dispositis. Nam in eis inveniuntur oratorium, dormitorium, refectorium, et aliae necessariae officinae religiosis convenientes a consortio saeculari separatae, quas tamen pretio, seu annuali redditu conducimus, quos redditus et alia omnia nobis pro victu ac vestitu necessaria solum habemus ex eleemosinis catholicorum illarum partium. In conventibus vero illis quattuor, qui extra civitatem sunt, bene possumus vivere in propriis ordinis aedibus et monasteriis, licet aliquando in illis ab haereticis nocturna invasione appetimur. Omnes autem fratres nunc in Hybernia degentes qui sunt numero circa centum, aut supra, in praedictis domibus distributi habitant, nec eis exire licet, nisi ad praedicandum vel ad postulandas eleemosinas, vel aliquod charitatis aut obedientiae opus exercendum, et cum praelati licentia. Et in aliquibus ex praedictis domibus regularis disciplina ita viget, ut in [eis] carnes nunquam (nisi ab infirmis) comedantur, et matutinae et aliae horae canonicae a tota communitate simul (absque tamen cantu) absolvantur. In octo ex illis domibus sunt priores canonice electi per voces conventualium, et in alias quattuor sunt vicarii. In septem vero ex illis novicii educantur, et expleto tempore notitiatus in Hispaniam aut aliam ordinis provinciam, in qua litterarum studia vigent, mittuntur, et postquam cursus tam artium, quam theologiae absolvunt, in patriam iterum ad fidem praedicandum revertunt. Sunt autem nunc in Hispania circa quinquaginta fratres Hyberni, et multi alii obierunt ibidem, et procurator noster ibidem, diebus nuper elapsis, ad me scripsit, quod hoc anno praeterito, postquam ego veni ad has partes, quinque fratres nostros absolutis studiis misit in Hyberniam, et ego cum inde venissem, reliqui in provincia circiter centum fratres per supradictas duodecim domos distributos nam :

In Conventu Dublinensi. Resident quatuor sacerdotes, videlicet R. Pr. fr. Thomas de Ascensione, Prior, R. Pr. fr. Dominicus Nugentius, R. Pr. fr. Petrus Strang, P. fr. Marcus Fearel, et tres juvenes, quorum nominum non recordor, et unus laicus.

In Conventu de Mullinguear. Inhabitabatur ab octo sacerdotibus, quatuor professis juvenibus, duobus laicis, et sex vel octo novitiis. Nomina sacerdotum sunt: R. Pr. fr. Thomas de Sto. Dominico, Prior, R. P. fr. Joannes Hanly sexagenarius, R. P. fr. Hugo Magneill etiam senex, R. Pr. fr. Bernardus O'Brian, R. fr. Petrus Albanagh, Pr. fr. Edmondus O'Hereaghty, Pr. fr. Patritius Breassil, Pr. fr. Guilelmus Ganly. Juvenum autem et novitiorum nomina non occurrunt memoriae.

In Conventu Slignensi. Sunt octo sacerdotes, videlicet R. admodum Pr. fr. Daniel de Cruce, Vicarius Provincialis et Prior Sligenensis, R. Pr. fr. Carolus

Maccuil centenarius, R. Pr. fr. Thomas Magneill sexagenarius, P. fr. Hugo Martin, Pr. fr. Hugo Doncha, Pr. fr. Thimotheus de Nativitate, Pr. fr. Columbanus Higuyn, Pr. fr. Christophorus Beblan, et tres aut quatuor iuvenes et aliqui novicii.

In Conventu Urlarensi. Sunt quinque sacerdotes, nempe R. Pr. fr. Dominicus Kerinus, R. Pr. fr. Donatus Caelan senex, P. fr. Hugo Gruagan, P. fr. David Muril, P. fr. Thomas Casside, et quatuor aut quinque juvenes quorum nomina obliviscor.

In Conventu Galviensi. Sunt quatuor sacerdotes, nempe R. Pr. Praesentatus fr. Nicholas Lynceus, Prior, R. Pr. fr. Antonius de Sta. Maria, R. Pr. fr. Stephanus de Rosario, R. Pr. fr. Petrus Martinez, et quinque juvenes professi, videlicet fr. Richardus Bumeghean, fr. Dominicus Linceus, fr. Edmundus Baret, fr. Stephanus Linceus, fr. Petrus Butler, et aliqui novicii.

In Conventu Athanriensi. Sunt quinque sacerdotes, videlicet R. P. fr. Petrus Martin, Prior, fr. Magomus Baird centenarius, R. P. fr. Malachias Brehun senex, R. Pr. fr. Raymundus de Sto. Michaele, Pr. fr. Thomas de Sta. Maria, et juvenes tres, scilicet fr. Raymundus a Sto. Antonino, fr. Gregorius a Sto. Dominico, et unus laicus.

In Conventu Limricensi. Sunt tres sacerdotes, videlicet R. Pr. fr. Thomas Cuircheus, Prior, R. Pr. fr. Jacobus Vuolf, R. Pr. fr. Dominicus Miagh, et quatuor juvenes, scilicet fr. Stephanus Whet, fr. Patritius Kearni, fr. Patritius Hacket, fr. Joannes Hacket, fr. Moriartus Casseliensis, et duo laici.

In Conventu Corcagensi. Quatuor sunt sacerdotes, videlicet R. Pr. fr. Thomas Liceus, Prior, R. Pr. fr. Dionisius Conensius, Pr. fr. Stephanus Guldeus, et juvenes etiam quatuor quorum nominum non recordor, ac aliqui novitii.

In Conventu Waterfordensi. Sunt quinque sacerdotes, nempe R. Pr. fr. Joannes Foxius, Prior, Pr. fr. Richardus Strang, Pr. fr. Richardus Barry, [*altera manu:*] Pater fr. Gulielmus Shea, Pater fr. Thomas Poverius.

In Conventu Kilkeniensi. Sunt tres sacerdotes, videlicet R. Pr. fr. Johannes de Cruce, Prior, R. P. fr. Josephus Langton, R. Pr. Gaspar Boyton et (ut reor) aliqui novicii.

In Conventu Lorachensi. Sunt duo sacerdotes et unus laicus, nomina sacerdotum sunt R. Pr. fr. Antonius Madden, Predicato [*sic*].

Apud reformatores Galliae sunt tres fratres, videlicet,
Pr. fr. Joannes Gulielmi
fr. Dominicus Miagh
fr. Joannes Geraldinus

In Italia sunt quatuor fratres Hiberni
R. Pr. fr. Patricius Thaddei, Romae
fr. Laurentius Kelleus, Modenae
fr. Guillelmus O'Conor, Neapoli
fr. Patritius Herbert, Papiae

In domo nostra Lovaniensi in Germania inferiori
R. A. Pr. fr. Rochus de Cruce, prior provincialis provinciae Hiberniae
R. Pr. fr. Dominicus de Rossario, praeses
R. Pr. fr. Michael de Spû Sto., philosophiae lector
Pr. fr. Jacobus de Sta. Maria
Pr. fr. Dominicus de Coena
Pr. fr. Edmondus de Rossario
fr. Antoninus de Spû Sto
fr. Dominicus a Sto. Thoma
fr. Michael de Sta. Maria
fr. Dominicus Creagh, novitius
fr. Thaddeus de Ascensione
fr. Richardus Poverius, donatus

[*altera manu:*]

Nomina fratrum ordinis praedicatorum in Hispania nunc commorantium

R. Pr. fr. Ricardus de la Penna, procurator
R. Pr. fr. Didacus Arturo, theologiae lector
R. Pr. fr. Joannes Nollanus, philosophiae lector
Pr. fr. Dionysius Henraghan
Pr. fr. Mauritius de Sto. Petro Martyre
Pr. fr. Philippus Cherinus
Pr. fr. Gibonus Wale
Pr. fr. Mahunus Kenedy
Pr. fr. Edmundus Suiny
Pr. fr. Joannes Gilboy
Pr. fr. Patricius Geoghegan
Pr. fr. Oliverus de Burgo
Pr. fr. Vincentius de Sta. Maria
Pr. fr. Thomas Bernardinus
Pr. fr. Hyacintus de Cruce
Pr. fr. Thomas de Sta. Maria
Pr. fr. Petrus Heggin
Pr. fr. Thimotheus Beollan
Pr. fr. Milerus Ceaghry
Pr. fr. Raimundus Dillonus
Pr. fr. Jacobus de Sta. Maria
Pr. fr. Hiacyntus Arturus
Pr. fr. Thomas Guid
fr. Edmundus Heigher
fr. Thomas Linceus
fr. Robertus Dolfin
fr. Thomas Joise
fr. Edmundus Robuick
fr. Nicholaus Halluran
fr. Gregorius French
fr. Joannes Fahie
fr. Thomas de Victoria
fr. Henricus Burgod
fr. Thomas de Sta. Maria
fr. Thomas Walter
fr. Gregorius Farrel
fr. Arturus Geoghegan
fr. Andreas Hurly
fr. Albertus Brian
fr. Petrus Martyr
fr. Dominicus Geoghegan
fr. Dominicus Brimigam
fr. Guilielmus Gearaldinus
fr. Thadeus Moriarti
fr. Joannes Cuillain et ali quorum nomina modo non occurrunt.

Bibliography

MANUSCRIPT SOURCES

BARCELONA

Archivo Archidiocesano
Register of Ordinations (1621–41)

BRUSSELS

Archives Générales du Royaume de Belgique
Papiers d'État et de l'Audience: cartons 1168, 2017, 2023, 2045
Conseil Privé, régime espagnol: cartons 15, 1168
Transcripts in Irish Dominican Archives, Tallaght

DUBLIN

Trinity College Library
MSS 567, 579, 656, 2988, 5206–8, 6404

Public Record Office of Ireland
Lodge MSS

Genealogical Office
MS 85

National Library of Ireland
MS 16236

Franciscan Library and Archives, Killiney
MSS A 13, A 16, A 31, D III

Dublin Corporation Gilbert Library
Gilbert Collection, MS 169

HARVARD

Harvard College Library
MS Port. 4789

LISBON

Arquivo Nacional da Torre do Tombo
Correspondencia do Desembargo do Paço, 1623, 1624, 1625, 1633, 1636
Miscellanea da Graça, Pecúlios
Livros de Consultas e Respostas do Governo de Castello (1639)

Biblioteca Nacional
MSS Reservados, 145, 429

Arquivo do Patriarcado de Lisboa
Livros de Matriculas/Ordenaçoes, 1585–1624

LONDON

British Library
Cotton MS Vesp. B. XI, f. 137
Add. MS 4784 (Milles Collection)
Add. MS 4793

Public Record Office
SP 63/29/87; 63/183/161; 63/254/89

Westminster Cathedral Archives
MS B. 25/26

MADRID

Archivo del Palacio Real
Sección de personal, 618/43

Archivo Histórico Nacional
Sección de libros, 15436
Estado, libro 739
Sección de clero

Biblioteca Nacional
Gayangos MS 18420

MAYNOOTH

Russell Library, St Patrick's College
C. W. Russell, *Memoranda of Contents of the Several Volumes, especially of Papers not proposed for transcription* . . . [Carte MSS], 5 vols

MECHELEN/MALINES

Archiepiscopal Archives
Dominikanen, doos 36

OPORTO

Arquivo Histórico Dominicano Português, Convento de São Domingos de Lisboa
Profession Book (1517–1777)

Convento de São Domingos de Benfica
Profession Book (1551–1707) (photographic copy; original MS in Harvard College Library)

OXFORD

Bodleian Library
Carte MSS, vols XXIX, LVII, LXI, LXXX

PISTOIA

Biblioteca Fabroniana
MS vol. 52

ROME

Archivum Generale Ordinis Praedicatorum
Series IV E
Series XIII, 26045
Series XIV, Liber K

Archivum Sacrae Congregationis de Propaganda Fide
Scritture Originali riferite nelle Congregazioni Generali (SOCG)
Acta Congregationis de Propaganda Fide

Archivio di S. Maria sopra Minerva
Libro dell'uscita del Collegio di S. Thomas Aquino, 1628–1630s

Archivum Romanum Societatis Iesu
Lusitania 44

Archives of the Irish Franciscans (St Isidore's)
MS W 2, no. 1

SALAMANCA

Archivo Universitario
Libros de Matriculas, MSS 296, 315, 318, 319, 320, 327

Archivo de la Provincia Dominicana de España (Castille) (San Esteban)
Provincial chapter acts (Ghetino transcripts)

SEVILLE

Archivo Municipal
Libros de Conde de Águila, tomo 7

Archivo de la Provincia Dominicana de Andalucía (Convento do San Pablo)
Consultas (1630–65) del Convento de San Pablo
F. Ramirez de Soloranzo, O.P., *Historia del santo y real Convento de San Pablo de Sevilla*, 1625
J. de Muñana, *Illustres Fundaciones y varones de España*, 1720

SHEFFIELD

Sheffield City Library
Fitzwilliam Papers: Strafford MSS, XX (b)/14
Strafford Letter Books, 1633–6, vol. 8

SIMANCAS

Archivo General de Simancas
Estado (State Papers): Sección de Negocios de partes
Guerra Antigua
Secretarias Provinciales: Flandes
Contaduria Mayor de Cuentas, 3a época

TALLAGHT (St Mary's Priory, Co Dublin)

Archives of the Irish Dominican province
Liber Provinciae or *Registrum Provinciae* (1680–1717)
Brevis Notitia Provinciae Hiberniae Ordinis Praedicatorum ab anno 1600 ad 1736 inclusive. Auctore Patre Magistro Edmundo de Burgo, O.P. (transcript in Ryan series, vol. 2, pp 34–87)
Provincial's file marked 'Miscellaneous: 1897–1930'

TOULOUSE

Archives départmentales, Haute-Garonne
Clergé Régulier (Fonds des Jacobins), Registre de Vêtures et de Professions (1521–1753)

VATICAN CITY

Archivio Segreto Vaticano
Archivum Concistoriale: Acta Miscellanea, Acta Camerarii, Acta Vicecancellarii
Archivum Arcis
Registra Vaticana
Registra Supplicationum
Brevia Lateranensia
Brevium Minutae
Archivum Nunziatura di Lisbona
Archivum Nunziatura di Spagna
Fondo Domenicani
Fondo Borghese
Schedario Garampi

Biblioteca Apostolica Vaticana
Barberini Latini MSS

PRINTED AND CALENDARED MATERIAL

T. K. Abbott, *Catalogue of the Manuscripts in the Library of Trinity College Dublin*, Dublin/London 1900

Frei Agostinho de Santa Maria, *O Santuario Mariano*, 10 vols, Lisbon 1707–23

Annála Ríoghachta Éireann: Annals of the Kingdom of Ireland by the Four Masters from the earliest period to the year 1616, ed. and trans. J. O'Donovan, 7 vols, Dublin 1846–51; repr. New York 1966

Annála Uladh, Annals of Ulster; otherwise Annála Senait, Annals of Senat: A Chronicle of Irish Affairs, 431–1131; 1155–1541, ed. W. M. Hennessy and B. MacCarthy, 4 vols, Dublin 1887–1901

The Annals of Loch Cé: A Chronicle of Irish Affairs, 1014–1690, ed. W. H. Hennessy, 2 vols, London 1871; repr. Dublin 1939

'Annals of Multyfarnham (*Annales de Monte Fernandi*)' in *Tracts relating to Ireland*, ed. A. Smith, Dublin 1843

G. Anstruther, *A Hundred Homeless Years: English Dominicans, 1558–1658*, London 1958

M. Archdall, *Monasticon Hibernicum*, London 1786

G. de Arriaga and M. de Los Hoyos, *Historia del Colegio de S. Gregorio de Valladolid*, 3 vols, Valladolid 1928–40

R. Bagwell, *Ireland under the Tudors*, 3 vols, London 1885–90

—*Ireland under the Stuarts*, 3 vols, London 1909–16

A. Ballestros y Baretta (ed.), *Correspondencia oficial de Don Diego de Sarmiento*, 4 vols, Madrid 1936–45

J. Barrio, 'Historia del Convento de S. Esteban' in J. Cuervo (ed.), *Historiadores del Convento de San Esteban de Salamanca*, ii, Salamanca 1914

J. Begley, *The Diocese of Limerick*, 3 vols, Dublin 1906–38

A. Bellesheim, *Geschichte der Katholischen Kirche in Irland von der Einführung des Christenthums bis auf die Gegenwart*, 3 vols, Mainz 1890–91

L. Bertrand, *Histoire des Séminaires*, 3 vols, Bordeaux 1844

D. A. Binchy, 'An Irish Ambassador at the Spanish Court, 1569–74' in *Studies*, 10 (1921)

M. J. Blake (ed.), *Blake Family Records, 1300–1600*, London 1902

—*Blake Family Records, 1600–1700*, London 1905

A. M. Bogaerts, *Archivalia Dominicana: Verzamelde stukken nopens de Dominikanen in het Archief van het Aartsbisdom Mechelen*, Brussels 1953

—*De Dominikanen in de Wijdingsregisters van het Aartsbisdom Mechelen*, Brussels 1965

—*De Dominikanen in de Jurisdiktiebrieven van het Aartsbisdom Mechelen*, Brussels 1966

E. Bolster, *A History of the Diocese of Cork: From Earliest Times to the Reformation*, Dublin 1972

—*A History of the Diocese of Cork: From the Reformation to the Penal Era*, Cork 1982

W. R. Bonniwell, *A History of the Dominican Liturgy, 1215–1945*, New York 1945

J. Bossy, 'The Counter-Reformation and the People of Catholic Europe' in *Past and Present*, 47 (1970)

—'The Counter-Reformation and the People of Catholic Ireland, 1596–1641' in *Historical Studies*, 8 (1971)

—*Christianity in the West, 1400–1700*, Oxford 1985

F. de la Boullaye Le Gouz, *Les Voyages et Observations du Sieur de la Boullaye Le Gouz*, Paris 1653; ed. and trans. T. Crofton Croker as *The Tour of the French Traveller Boullaye Le Gouz in Ireland, 1644*, London 1837

L. E. Boyle, *A Survey of the Vatican Archives and its Medieval Holdings*, Toronto 1972

B. Bradshaw, 'The Opposition to the Ecclesiastical Legislation in the Irish Reformation Parliament' in *Irish Historical Studies*, 16 (Mar. 1969)

—*The Dissolution of the Religious Orders in Ireland under Henry VIII*, Cambridge 1974

—'The Edwardian Reformation in Ireland, 1547–1553' in *Archivium Hibernicum*, 34 (1976–7)

—'Sword, Word and Strategy in the Reformation in Ireland' in *Historical Journal*, 21 (1978)

—'Manus "the Magnificent": O'Donnell as Renaissance Prince' in A. Cosgrove and D. McCartney (eds), *Studies in Irish History presented to R. Dudley Edwards*, Dublin 1979

—'The Reformation in the Cities: Cork, Limerick and Galway, 1534–1603' in J. Bradley (ed.), *Settlement and Society in Medieval Ireland*, Kilkenny 1988

A. M. Brady and B. Cleeve (eds), *A Biographical Dictionary of Irish Writers*, Mullingar 1985

C. Brady and R. Gillespie (eds), *Natives and Newcomers: Essays on the Making of Irish Colonial Society, 1534–1641*, Dublin 1986

C. Brady, R. Gillespie and M. O'Dowd (eds), *Politics, Religion and Society in Ireland, 1515–1641*, Dublin 1993

J. Brady (ed.), 'The Irish Colleges in the Low Countries' in *Archivium Hibernicum*, 14 (1949)

—'The Irish Colleges in Europe and the Counter-Reformation' in *Proceedings of the Irish Catholic Historical Committee*, Dublin 1957

W. M. Brady, *The Irish Reformation, or the Alleged Conversion of the Irish Bishops*, London 1867

—(ed.), *State Papers concerning the Irish Church in the Time of Queen Elizabeth*, London 1868

—(ed.), *The Episcopal Succession in England, Scotland and Ireland, 1400–1875*, 3 vols, Rome 1876–7

L. W. B. Brockliss and P. Ferté, 'Irish Clerics in France in the Seventeenth and Eighteenth Centuries: A Statistical Study' in *Proceedings of the Royal Irish Academy*, 87 (1987), sect. C

—'A Prosopography of Irish Clerics who Studied in France in the Seventeenth and Eighteenth Centuries, in particular at the Universities of Paris and Toulouse' (typescript deposited (1988) in RIA: 12/Y/6)

W. Brulez, 'Correspondence de Richard Pauli-Stravius, 1634–1642' in *Analecta Vaticano-Belgica: Nonciature de Flandres*, x, Brussels/Rome 1955

J. J. Buckley, *Some Irish Altar Plate*, Dublin 1943

S. H. Burke, *Historical Portraits of the Tudor Dynasty*, 4 vols, London 1879–87

T. Burke, *Hibernia Dominicana, sive Historia Provinciae Hiberniae Ordinis Praedicatorum*, Cologne 1762; supplement, Cologne 1772; repr. Farnborough 1970

W. P. Burke (ed.), 'The Diocese of Derry in 1631' in *Archivium Hibernicum*, 5 (1916)

T. C. Butler, *John's Lane: A History of the Augustinian Friars in Dublin, 1280–1980*, Dublin 1983

Bullarium Ordinis FF. Praedicatorum, ed. A. Bremond, 8 vols, Rome 1729–40

Bullarium Romanum, ed. G. Tomasetti, 22 vols, Turin, 1857–72; 5 vols, Naples 1867–85

L. Cacegas, *Historia de S. Domingos*, ed. L. de Sousa and continued by Frei Lucas de Santa Catarina, 6 vols, Lisbon 1707–11; Lisbon 1866

Calendar of the Carew Manuscripts preserved in the Archiepiscopal Library at Lambeth, 1515–1574, 6 vols, London 1867–73

Calendar of the Clarendon State Papers preserved in the Bodleian Library, 1523–1726, ed. O. Ogle, W. H. Bliss *et al.*, 5 vols, Oxford 1872–1970

'Calendar to Fiants of the Reign of Henry VIII—Elizabeth I' in *Reports of the Deputy Keeper of the Public Records in Ireland*, 7–22, Dublin 1875–90

Calendar of Inquisitions formerly in the Office of the Chief Remembrancer of the Exchequer prepared from the MSS of the Irish Record Commission, ed. M. C. Griffith, Dublin 1991

Calendar of Letters, Despatches and State Papers, Spanish, relating to the Negotiations between England and Spain, preserved in the Archives at Simancas and elsewhere, 2 series, 17 vols, London 1862–1954

Calendar of Patent and Close Rolls of Chancery in Ireland, Henry VIII to 18th Elizabeth, ed. J. Morrin, Dublin 1861

Calendar of Patent and Close Rolls of Chancery in Ireland, Elizabeth, 19th year to end of reign, ed. J. Morrin, Dublin 1862

[*Calendar of*] *Irish Patent Rolls of James I: Facsimile of the Irish Record Commissioners' Calendar prepared prior to 1830*, with forward by M. C. Griffith, Dublin 1966

Calendar of the Patent and Close Rolls, Chancery, Ireland [James I, 1603–10], n.p., n.d. This edition (ed. anon) not listed in the British Library Catalogue, 1991.

Calendar of State Papers relating to English Affairs, preserved principally at Rome, in the Vatican Archives and Library, 1558–71, 2 vols, London 1916–26

Calendar of State Papers, Ireland, Henry VIII, 11 vols, London 1830–52

Calendar of the State Papers relating to Ireland, 1509–73 [etc.], 24 vols, London 1860–1911

N. P. Canny, *The Elizabethan Conquest of Ireland: A Pattern Established, 1565–76*, Hassocks 1976

—'Why the Reformation failed in Ireland: *une question mal posée*' in *Journal of Ecclesiastical History*, 30 (1979)

—*From Reformation to Restoration: Ireland, 1534–1660*, Dublin 1987

J. J. Carbery, *A Chronological and Historical Account of the Dominican Convent, Limerick*, Limerick 1867

B. Carderi, 'I Registri del Collegio S. Tommaso d'Aquino in Roma conservati nell'Archivio del Convento di S. Maria sopra Minerva' in *Memorie Domenicane*, nuova ser., 7 (1976)

W. Carrigan, *The History and Antiquities of the Diocese of Ossory*, 4 vols, Dublin 1905

V. D. Carro, *Los Dominicos y al Concilio de Trento*, Salamanca 1948

A. Carvalho da Costa, *Corografia Portuguesa e Descripçam Topografica do Famoso Reyno de Portugal*, 3 vols, Lisbon 1706–12; 3rd ed., Braga 1869

H. de Castillo and I. Lopez, *La Historia General de Santo Domingo y de su Orden de Predicadores*, 5 vols, Valladolid 1584–1621

J. I. Casway, *Owen Roe O'Neill and the Struggle for Catholic Ireland*, Philadelphia 1984

Catalogue of Irish Manuscripts in the Franciscan Library, Killiney, ed. M. Dillon, C. Mooney and P. de Brún, Dublin 1969

Catalogue of Irish Manuscripts in the British Museum, ed. S. H. O'Grady and R. Flower, 3 vols, London 1926–53; repr. Dublin 1992

Catalogue of Early Printed Books, Trinity College Library, Dublin (*Catalogus Librorum Impressorum qui in Bibliotheca Collegii Sacrosanctae et Individuae Trinitatis adservantur*), 8 vols, Dublin 1864; supp. vol., Dublin 1887

G. M. Cavalieri, *Galleria de'Sommi Pontefici . . .*, 2 vols, Benevento 1696

Clanricarde, U. de Burgh, Marquis of, *The Memoirs and Letters of Ulick, Marquis of Clanricarde and Earl of St Alban's . . . printed from an authentic manuscript and now first published by the present Earl of Clanricarde*, London 1757

—*Letter-Book of the Earl of Clanricarde, 1643–47*, ed. J. Lowe, Dublin 1983

[Clarendon, H. Hyde, Earl of], *Calendar of the Clarendon State Papers preserved in the Bodleian Library, 1523–1726*, ed. O. Ogle, W. H. Bliss *et al.*, 5 vols, Oxford 1872–1970

A. Clarke, *The Old English in Ireland, 1625–42*, London 1966

—*The Graces, 1625–41*, Dundalk 1968

—'The Government of Wentworth, 1632–1640' in *A New History of Ireland*, iii, Oxford 1976

—with R. D. Edwards, 'Pacification, Plantation and the Catholic Question, 1603–23' in *A New History of Ireland*, iii, Oxford 1976

—'Selling Royal Favours, 1624–32' in *A New History of Ireland*, iii, Oxford 1976

—'Colonial Identity in Early Seventeenth-Century Ireland' in T. W. Moody (ed.), *Nationality and the Pursuit of National Independence*, Belfast 1978

—'Ireland, 1534–1660' in J. J. Lee (ed.), *Irish Historiography, 1970–79*, Cork 1981

—'Varieties of Conformity: The First Century of the Church of Ireland' in W. J. Sheils and D. Wood (eds), *The Churches, Ireland and the Irish: Studies in Church History*, xxv, Oxford 1989

A. Cogan, *The Ecclesiastical History of the Diocese of Meath*, 3 vols, Dublin 1867–74

A. Coleman, 'De Conventibus Provinciae Hiberniae' in *Analecta Sacri Ordinis Fratrum Praedicatorum*, 3 (1897)

—*The Ancient Dominican Foundations in Ireland*, Dundalk 1902

—(ed.), 'Regestum Monasterii Fratrum Praedicatorum de Athenry' in *Archivium Hibernicum*, 1 (1912)

M. L. Colker, *Trinity College Library, Dublin: Descriptive Catalogue of the Medieval and Renaissance Latin Manuscripts*, 2 vols, Dublin 1991

A. Colunga, *Historia del Santuario de Nuestra Señora de la Peña de Francia*, Salamanca 1968

M. Comerford, *Collections relating to the Dioceses of Kildare and Leighlin*, 3 vols, Dublin 1883–6

The Compossicion Booke of Conought, ed. A. M. Freeman, Dublin 1936

P. Conlan, *Franciscan Ireland*, Mullingar 1988

D. Conway (ed.), 'Guide to Documents of Irish and British Interest in Fondo Borghese, Series I' in *Archivium Hibernicum*, 23 (1960); 'Series II–IV', ibid., 24 (1961)

—'The Anglican World: Problems of Coexistence' in J. Metzler (ed.), *Sacrae Congregationis Propaganda Fide Memoriae Rerum, 1622–1972*, i, pt 2: *1622–1700*, Rome 1972

T. L. Coonan, *The Irish Catholic Confederacy and the Puritan Revolution*, Dublin/London 1954

T. Corcoran, *State Policy in Irish Education*, Dublin 1916

P. J. Corish, 'The Reorganisation of the Irish Church, 1603–41' in *Proceedings of the Irish Catholic Historical Committee*, Dublin 1957

—*The Catholic Community in the Seventeenth and Eighteenth Centuries*, Dublin 1981

—'Irish Ecclesiastical History since 1500' in J. J. Lee (ed.), *Irish Historiography, 1970–79*, Cork 1981

—(ed.), 'Two Seventeenth-Century Proclamations against the Catholic Clergy' in *Archivium Hibernicum*, 39 (1984)

R. Cox, *Hibernia Anglicana*, 2 pts in 2 vols, London 1689–90

D. F. Cregan, 'The Social and Cultural Background of a Counter-Reformation Episcopate, 1618–1660' in A. Cosgrave and D. McCartney (eds), *Studies in Irish History presented to R. Dudley Edwards*, Dublin 1979

R. Creytens, 'Il Registro dei Maestri degli Studenti di Bologna (1576–1604)' in *Archivum Fratrum Praedicatorum*, 46 (1976)

J. Cuervo (ed.), *Historiadores del Convento de San Esteban de Salamanca*, 3 vols, Salamanca 1914–15

B. Cunningham, 'Political and Social Change in the Lordships of Clanricard and Thomond, 1569–1641' (unpublished M.A. thesis, University College, Galway, 1979)

M. B. Curtin [MacCurtain], 'Daniel O'Daly, 1595–1662: A Study of Irish–European Relationships in the Seventeenth Century' (unpublished M.A. thesis, University College, Dublin, 1958)

—'Daniel O'Daly, 1595–1662: An Agent in Seventeenth-Century Diplomacy' (unpublished Ph.D. thesis, University College, Dublin, 1962)

—see also [M.] B. MacCurtain

E. Curtis (ed.), *Calendar of Ormond Deeds, 1172–1603*, 6 vols, Dublin 1932–43

T. D'Arcy McGee, *The Irish Writers of the Seventeenth Century*, Dublin 1857

A. De Altamura, *Bibliothecae Dominicanae*, Rome 1677

D. de hOir, 'Blúire Cillsheanchais faoi Fhairche Chill Dara' in *Dinnseanchas*, 2 (1966)

The Desmond Survey of County Kerry, ed. S. M. Hussey, Tralee 1923; repr. in *The Kerryman*, Aug.–Oct. 1927

R. Devas, *Dominican Martyrs of Great Britain*, London 1912

A. G. Dickens, *The English Reformation*, London 1964

M. Dillon, C. Mooney and P. de Brún (eds), *Catalogue of Irish Manuscripts in the Franciscan Library, Killiney*, Dublin 1969

Dodd's Church History of England, ed. M. A. Tierney, 5 vols, London 1839–43

J. Durkan, 'Robert Wauchope, Archbishop of Armagh' in *Innes Review*, i (1950)

R. D. Edwards, *Church and State in Tudor Ireland*, Dublin 1935

—'Church and State in the Ireland of Michél Ó Cléirigh' in S. O'Brien (ed.), *Measgra i gCuimhne Mhicíl Uí Chléirigh*, Dublin 1944

—'Ireland, Elizabeth and the Counter-Reformation' in S. T. Bindoff (ed.), *Elizabethan Government and Society*, London 1961

—'The Irish Reformation Parliament of Henry VIII, 1536–1537' in *Historical Studies*, 6 (1968)

—*Ireland in the Age of the Tudors*, London 1977

—and D. B. Quinn, 'Sixteenth-Century Ireland, 1485–1603' in *Irish Historical Studies*, 16 (1968)

R. D. Edwards and M. O'Dowd, *Sources for Modern Irish History, 1534–1641*, Cambridge 1985

B. Egan, C. Giblin and C. McGrath (eds), 'Irish Students Ordained in Rome (1625–1710)' in *Irish Ecclesiastical Record*, 5th ser., 61 (1943)

S. G. Ellis, *Tudor Ireland: Crown Colony and the Conflict of Cultures, 1470–1603*, London 1985

A. B. Emden (ed.), *A Survey of Dominicans in England: based on the ordination lists in episcopal registers (1268 to 1538)*, Rome 1967

—*A Biographical Register of the University of Oxford, A.D. 1501 to 1540*, Oxford 1974

J. C. Erck (ed.), *A Reportory of the Inrolments on the Patent Rolls of Chancery in Ireland commencing with the reign of King James I*, i, pts 1–2, Dublin 1846–52

A. M. Escudero, *Historia del Convento de Santo Tomás de Madrid del Orden de Predicadores*, ed. D. F. Viñals, i, Madrid 1900

C. Eubel and P. Gauchat (eds), *Hierarchia Catholica Medii Aevi et Recentioris Aetatis*, Münster 1898–

H. O. Evennett, *The Spirit of the Counter-Reformation*, London 1975

G. F., *Hiberniae sive Antiquioris Scotiae Vindicia adversus . . . Thomae Dempsteri moderni Scoti nuper editam . . .*, Antwerp 1621

H. Fenning, 'The Return to Munster under Desmond and Mary Tudor, 1553–1558' in *Irish Rosary* (Dec. 1961)

—'Cormac O'Fergus, Provincial of the Black Friars, 1571' in *Irish Rosary* (Jan.–Feb. 1962)

—'1593: The Darkest Hour' in *Irish Rosary*, (Jan.–Feb. 1962)

—'Spanish Ale, 1615: Roch MacGeoghegan and a New Beginning' in *Irish Rosary* (May–June 1962)

—'The Dominicans of Trim: 1263–1682' in *Ríocht na Midhe*, 3 (1963)

—'The Irish Dominican Province under Appointed Superiors (1698–1721)' in *Archivum Fratrum Praedicatourm*, 38 (1968)

—(ed.), 'Irish Material in the Registers of the Dominican Masters General (1390–1649)' in *Archivum Fratrum Praedicatourm*, 39 (1969)

—'The Dominicans and Propaganda Fide, 1622–1668' in *Archivum Fratrum Praedicatourm*, 41 (1971)

—(ed.), *The Fottrell Papers*, Belfast 1980

—*Acta Capitulorum Provinciae Hiberniae Sacri Ordinis Praedicatorum, 1669–1688*, Tallaght 1989

A. Fernandez, *Historia Ecclesiastica de Nuestros Tiempos . . .*, Toledo 1611

—*Concertatio Praedicatoria pro Ecclesia Catholica . . .*, Salamanca 1618

J. Ferrar, *The History of Limerick*, Limerick 1787

U. Flanagan, 'The Formative Development of the Dominican and Franciscan Orders in Ireland' (unpublished M.A. thesis, University College, Cork 1947)

—'Our Lady of Graces of Youghal' in *Journal of the Cork Historical and Archaeological Society*, 55 (1950); 56 (1951)

T. S. Flynn, *The Dominicans of Aghaboe: c.1382–c.1782*, Dublin 1975

—*The Dominicans of Rosbercon: 1267–c.1800*, Dublin 1981

V. M. Fontana, *Constitutiones, Declarationes et Ordinationes Capitulorum Generalium Sacri Ordinis Praedicatorum (1220–1651) Emanatae*, 2 vols, Rome 1665–6

—*Sacrum Theatrum Dominicanum*, Rome 1666

—*Monumenta Dominicana*, Rome 1675

A. Ford, *The Protestant Reformation in Ireland, 1590–1641*, Frankfurt 1985

—'The Protestant Reformation in Ireland' in C. Brady and R. Gillespie (eds), *Natives and Newcomers: Essays on the Making of the Irish Colonial Society, 1534–1641*, Dublin 1986

S. L. Forte, 'I Domenicani nel Carteggio del Card. Scipione Borghese, Protettore dell'Ordine (1606–1633)' in *Archivum Fratrum Praedicatorum*, 30 (1960)

—'Le Provincie Domenicane in Italia nel 1650' in *Archivum Fratrum Praedicatorum*, 39 (1969)

J. Foster (ed.), *Alumni Oxonienses, 1500–1714*, 4 vols, Oxford 1891

E. Freire de Oliveira, *Elementos para a Historía do Município de Lisboa*, 16 vols, Lisbon 1882–1911

H. Garrastachu, *Historia Synopsis Instituti Pontificii Internationalis Angelici*, Rome 1929

H. D. Gallwey (ed.), 'A Kearney Funeral Entry of 1641' in *Irish Genealogist*, 5 (1975)

C. Giblin (ed.), *Irish Franciscan Mission to Scotland, 1619–1646: Documents from Roman Archives*, Dublin 1946

—'The Acta of Propaganda Archives and the Scottish Mission, 1623–1670' in *Innes Review*, 5 (1954)

—(ed.), 'Vatican Library: MSS Barberini Latini' in *Archivium Hibernicum*, 18 (1955)

—'The Processus Datariae and the Appointment of Catholic Bishops in the Seventeenth Century' in *Father Luke Wadding: Commemorative Volume*, ed. Franciscan Fathers, Dublin 1957

J. T. Gilbert, *A History of the City of Dublin*, 3 vols, Dublin 1854–9

—(ed.), *A Contemporary History of Affairs in Ireland, 1441–1652 . . .*, 3 vols, Dublin 1879–80

—(ed.), *The History of the Irish Confederation and the War in Ireland (1641–9)*, 7 vols, Dublin 1882–91

E. Gilson, *History of Christian Philosophy in the Middle Ages*, London 1955

T. Gimlette, *The Dominican Priory of 'St Saviour', Waterford*, Waterford *c.*1888

Y. M. Goblet, *A Topographical Index of the Parishes and Townlands of Ireland*, Dublin 1932

M. Gonçalves da Costa, *Fontes Inéditas Portuguesas para a Historía de Irlanda*, Braga 1981

D. I. de Gongora, *Historia del Colegio Mayor de Santo Tomás de Sevilla*, ed. E. de la Cuadra y Gibaja, Seville 1890

P. Grady, *The Radical Anti-Veto*, Dublin 1814, appendix

F. Grannell, 'Galway' in *Dictionnaire d'Histoire et de Géographie Ecclésiastiques*, xix, Paris 1981

I. P. Grossi, 'Dal Collegium D. Thomae de Urbe al Pontificio Ateneo Angelicum' in *Memorie Domenicane*, 35 (1959)

W. Gumbley, *The Cambridge Dominicans*, Oxford 1938

A. Gwynn, *The Medieval Province of Armagh*, Dundalk 1946

—and R. N. Hadcock, *Medieval Religious Houses: Ireland*, London 1970

J. Hagan (ed.), 'Some Papers relating to the Nine Years' War' in *Archivium Hibernicum*, 2 (1913)

—(ed.), 'Miscellanea Vaticano-Hibernica: 1580–1631' in *Archivium Hibernicum*, 3 (1914)

—(ed.), 'Miscellanea Vaticano-Hibernica: 1420–1631' in *Archivium Hibernicum*, 4 (1915)

—(ed.), 'Miscellanea Vaticano-Hibernica: Ireland in 1580' in *Archivium Hibernicum*, 5 (1916)

P. Haicéad [Hackett], *Filíocht Phádraigín Haicéad*, ed. M. Ní Cheallacháin, Dublin 1962

H. Hammerstein, 'Aspects of the Continental Education of Irish Students in the Reign of Queen Elizabeth I' in *Historical Studies*, 8 (1971)

M. Hanmer, *The Chronicle of Ireland*, Dublin 1633; repr. 1809

J. Hardiman (ed.), 'The Pedigree of Doctor Dominick Lynch, Regent of the College of St Thomas of Aquin, in the City of Seville, A.D. 1674, from a Coeval MS' in *Miscellany of the Irish Archaeological Society*, 1 (1846)

M. J. Haren, 'Vatican Archives as a Historical Source to *c.*1530' in *Archivium Hibernicum*, 39 (1984)

—'Papal Secretariate and Datary Correspondence relating to Great Britain and Ireland in the Fifteenth and Early Sixteenth Centuries: Summary, Report of a Survey in the Vatican Archives' in *Analecta Hibernica*, no. 33 (1986)

M. J. Havran, *The Catholics in Caroline England*, London 1962

R. J. Hayes (ed.), *Manuscript Sources for the History of Irish Civilisation*, 11 vols, Boston, Mass. 1965; 3 supp. vols, Boston, Mass. 1979

G. A. Hayes-McCoy, 'The Royal Supremacy and Ecclesiastical Revolution, 1534–47' in *A New History of Ireland*, iii, Oxford 1978

—'The Completion of the Tudor Conquest and the Advance of the Counter-Reformation, 1571–1603' in *A New History of Ireland*, III, Oxford 1978

T. M. Healy, *Stolen Waters: A Page in the Conquest of Ulster*, London 1913

—*The Great Fraud of Ulster*, Dublin 1917

E. Henson (ed.), *Registers of the English College at Valladolid, 1589–1862*, London 1930

R. Herbert, 'The Lax Weir and Fishers' Stent of Limerick' in *North Munster Antiquarian Journal*, 5 (1946–9)

Hierarchia Catholica Medii Aevi et Recentioris Aetatis, ed. C. Eubel and P. Gauchat, Münster 1898–

W. A. Hinnebusch, 'Foreign Dominican Students and Professors at the Oxford Blackfriars' in A. B. Emden *et al.* (eds), *Oxford Studies presented to Daniel Callus* [Oxford Hist. Soc., n.s., vol. 16], Oxford 1964

—*The History of the Dominican Order*, 2 vols, New York 1966–73

—*The Dominicans: A Short History*, New York 1975

Historical Manuscripts Commission, *Report on the Franciscan Manuscripts*, Dublin 1906

Holinshed, R., *Holinshed's Irish Chronicle, 1577*, ed. L. Miller and E. Power, Dublin 1979

A. Huarte, 'Petitions of Irish Students in the University of Salamanca, 1574–91' in *Archivium Hibernicum*, 4 (1915)

J. L. J. Hughes (ed.), *Patentee Officers in Ireland, 1173–1826*, Dublin 1960

R. J. Hunter (ed.), 'Catholicism in Meath, *c.*1622' in *Collectanea Hibernica*, 14 (1971)

S. M. Hussey (ed.), *The Desmond Survey of County Kerry*, Tralee 1923; repr. in *The Kerryman*, Aug.–Oct. 1927

D. Hyde and D. J. O'Donoghue (ed.), *Catalogue of the Books and Manuscripts comprising the Library of the late Sir John T. Gilbert*, Dublin 1918

H. Jedin, 'The Blind "Doctor Scotus"' in *Journal of Ecclesiastical History*, 1 (1950)

—*A History of the Council of Trent*, 2 vols, London 1957–61

—*et al.* (eds), *History of the Church*, 10 vols, London 1965–81

B. Jennings (ed.), 'Brussels MS 3947: Donatus Moneyus, de Provincia Hiberniae S. Francisci' in *Analecta Hibernica*, no. 6 (1934)

—(ed.), 'Miscellaneous Documents, I: 1588–1634' in *Archivium Hibernicum*, 12 (1946)

—(ed.), 'Miscellaneous Documents, II: 1625–1640' in *Archivium Hibernicum*, 14 (1949)

—(ed.), 'Miscellaneous Documents, III: 1602–1715' in *Archivium Hibernicum*, 15 (1950)

—(ed.), 'Irish Names in the Malines Ordination Registers, 1602–1794' in *Irish Ecclesiastical Record*, 75–6 (1951); 77 (1952)

—(ed.), *Wadding Papers, 1614–1638*, Dublin 1953

—(ed.), 'Acta Sacrae Congregationis de Propaganda Fide, 1622–1650' in *Archivium Hibernicum*, 22 (1959)

—'Irish Preachers and Confessors in the Archdiocese of Malines' in *Archivium Hibernicum*, 23 (1960)

—(ed.), *Wild Geese in Spanish Flanders, 1582–1700*, Dublin 1964

F. M. Jones, 'Canonical Faculties on the Irish Mission in the Reign of Queen Elizabeth, 1558–1603' in *Irish Theological Quarterly*, 20 (1953)

—*Mountjoy: The Last Elizabethan Deputy*, Dublin 1958

—'The Counter-Reformation' in P. J. Corish (ed.), *A History of Irish Catholicism*, iii, Dublin 1967

B. de Jonghe, *Belgium Dominicanum sive Historia Provinciae Germaniae Inferioris Sacri Ordinis FF. Praedicatorum*, Brussels 1719

H. Kamen, *Spain: 1469–1714*, London 1983

—*European Society: 1500–1700*, London 1984

B. Katterbach, *Inventario dei Registri della Suppliche*, Vatican City 1932

H. F. Kearney, 'Ecclesiastical Politics and the Counter-Reformation in Ireland' in *Journal of Ecclesiastical History*, 11 (1960)

D. Knowles, *The Religious Orders in England*, 3 vols, Cambridge 1979

N. Kowalsky and J. Metzler, *Inventory of the Historical Archives of the Sacred Congregation for the Evangelisation of Peoples or 'de Propaganda Fide'*, Rome 1983

M. Lenihan, *Limerick: its History and Antiquities, Ecclesiastical, Civil, and Military* . . ., Dublin 1866; repr. 1967, 1991

C. Lennon, 'Civic Life and Religion in Early Seventeenth-Century Dublin' in *Archivium Hibernicum*, 38 (1983)

The Lismore Papers, ed. A. B. Grosart, 2 series, 10 vols, London 1886–8

I. Lopez, *La Historia General de Santo Domingo y de su Orden de Predicadores*: see H. de Castillo

M. de Los Hoyos (ed.), *Registro Documental: Material Inédito Dominicano Español*, 3 vols, Madrid 1961; Valladolid 1962–3

—*Historia del Colegio de S. Gregorio de Valladolid*: see G. de Arriaga

Frei Lucas de Santa Catarina, *História de S. Domingos*: see L. Cacegas

J. Lynch, *De Praesulibus Hiberniae Potissimis Catholicae Religionis in Hibernia, Serendae, Propagandae, et Conservandae Authoribus*, ed J. F. O'Doherty, 2 vols, Dublin 1944

[M.] B. MacCurtain, 'An Irish Agent of the Counter-Reformation, Dominic O'Daly' in *Irish Historical Studies*, 60 (1967)

—*Tudor and Stuart Ireland*, Dublin 1972

—'Dominic O'Daly' in A. M. Brady and B. Cleeve (eds), *A Biographical Dictionary of Irish Writers*, Mullingar 1985

—see also M. B. Curtin

W. McDonnell, 'Irish Ecclesiastical Colleges since the Reformation: Salamanca' in *Irish Ecclesiastical Record*, 10 (1873–4)

E. MacLysaght, *Irish Life in the Seventeenth Century*, Dublin 1979

—*Irish Families*, Dublin 1957

C. McNeil, 'The Chalices of the West Convent, Galway' in *Journal of the Royal Society of Antiquaries of Ireland*, 49 (1919)

—'Accounts of Sums Realised by the Sale of Chattels of Some Suppressed Irish Monasteries' in *Journal of the Royal Society of Antiquaries of Ireland*, 52 (1922)

—(ed.), *Tanner Letters*, Dublin 1943

G. Mac Niocaill, 'Cáipéisi Doiminiceánacha ón 17ú céad' in *Seanchas Ardmhaca*, 3 (1958)

L. McRedmond, *To the Greater Glory: A History of the Irish Jesuits*, Dublin 1991

Frei Manoel de Lima, *Agiologío Dominico: Vidas dos Santos, Beatos, Martyres e outras pessoas veneraveis da Ordem dos Prégadores*, 4 vols, Lisbon 1709–12

R. Mant, *History of the Church of Ireland*, 2 vols, London 1840

L. Marron, 'Documents from the State Papers concerning Miler McGrath' in *Archivium Hibernicum*, 21 (1958)

D. M. Marchese, *Sagro Diario Domenicano*, 6 vols, Naples 1668–81

F. X. Martin, 'The Irish Augustinian Reform Movement in the Fifteenth Century' in J. A. Watt, J. B. Morrall and F. X. Martin (eds), *Medieval Studies presented to Aubrey Gwynn, S.J.*, Dublin 1961

—*Friar Nugent: A Study of Francis Lavalin Nugent (1569–1635), Agent of the Counter-Reformation*, London/Rome 1962

—'The Council of Trent' in *Irish Ecclesiastical Record*, 100 (1963)

—'Confusion Abounding: Bernard O'Higgin, O.S.A., Bishop of Elphin, 1542–1561' in A. Cosgrove and D. McCartney (eds), *Studies in Irish History presented to R. Dudley Edwards*, Dublin 1979

M. J. de Medrano, *Historia de la Provincia de España de la Orden de Predicadores*, 6 vols, Madrid 1725–34

C. P. Meehan, *The Fate and Fortunes of the Earls of Tyrone and Tyrconnell*, Dublin 1870

—*The Rise and Fall of the Irish Franciscan Monasteries and Memoirs of the Hierarchy in the Seventeenth Century*, Dublin 1877

J. Metzler (ed.), *Sacrae Congregationis Propaganda Fide Memoria Rerum, 1622–1972*, 3 vols, Rome/Vienna/Freiburg 1972

B. Millett, 'The Archives of the Congregation de Propaganda Fide' in *Proceedings of the Irish Catholic Historical Committee*, Dublin 1956

—'The Pastoral Zeal of Robert Wauchope' in *Seanchas Ardmhaca*, 2 (1956)

—(ed.), 'Catalogue of Volume 294 of the *Scritture Originali riferite nelle Congregazioni Generali* in Propaganda Archives' in *Collectanea Hibernica*, 8 (1965)

—(ed.), 'Catalogue of Irish Material in Fourteen Volumes of the *Scritture Originali riferite nelle Congregazioni Generali* in Propaganda Archives' in *Collectanea Hibernica*, 10 (1967)

—(ed.), 'Catalogue of Irish Material in Volumes 129–131 of the *Scritture Originali riferite nelle Congregazioni Generali* in Propaganda Archives' in *Collectanea Hibernica*, 11 (1968)

—(ed.), 'Catalogue of Irish Material in Volumes 132–139 of the *Scritture Originali riferite nelle Congregazioni Generali* in Propaganda Archives' in *Collectanea Hibernica*, 12 (1969)

—(ed.), 'Catalogue of Irish Material in Volumes 140–143 of the *Scritture Originali riferite nelle Congregazioni Generali* in Propaganda Archives' in *Collectanea Hibernica*, 13 (1970)

—'Irish Literature in Latin, 1550–1700' in *A New History of Ireland*, iii, Oxford 1978

—and C. J. Woods, 'Roman Catholic Bishops from 1534' in *A New History of Ireland*, ix, Oxford 1984

B. Montagnes, 'Sebastien Michaelis, Frère Prêcheur, 1543–1618' in *Dictionnaire de Spiritualité*, x, Paris 1980

T. W. Moody and F. X. Martin (eds), *The Course of Irish History*, Dublin 1984

—,—and F. J. Byrne (eds), *A New History of Ireland*, iii: *Early Modern Ireland, 1534–1691*, Oxford 1976

—,—,—(eds), *A New History of Ireland*, x: *Maps, Genealogies, Lists*, Oxford 1984

C. Mooney, 'The Archives at Simancas as a Source for Irish Ecclesiastical History' in *Proceedings of the Irish Catholic Historical Committee*, Dublin 1955

—'The Irish Church in the Sixteenth Century' in *Proceedings of the Irish Catholic Historical Committee*, Dublin 1963

—'The First Impact of the Reformation' in P. J. Corish (ed.), *A History of Irish Catholicism*, iii, Dublin 1967

P. F. Moran, *History of the Catholic Archbishops of Dublin*, Dublin 1864

—'The See of Achonry in the Sixteenth Century' in *Irish Ecclesiastical Record*, 1 (1865)

—'The See of Elphin in the Sixteenth Century' in *Irish Ecclesiastical Record*, 2 (1866)

—(ed.), *Spicilegium Ossoriense: being a Collection of Original Letters and Papers Illustrative of the History of the Irish Church from the Reformation to the year 1800*, 3 vols, Dublin 1874–84

H. Morley, *Ireland under Elizabeth and James the First*, London 1890

G. Moroni (ed.), *Dizionario di Erudizione Storico-Ecclesiastico*, 103 vols, Venice, 1840–61; index, Venice 1878–9

T. Morrissey, *James Archer of Kilkenny*, Dublin 1979

D. A. Mortier, *Histoire des Maîtres Généraux de l'Ordre des Frères Prêcheurs*, 8 vols, Paris 1903–20

G. Morton, *Elizabethan Ireland*, London 1971

L. P. Murray and A. Gwynn, 'Archbishop Cromer's Register' in *Louth Archaeological Journal* (1932–8, 1942–3)

J. Nalson, *Foxes and Firebrands: or A Specimen of the Danger and Harmony of Popery and Separation: wherein is proved . . . that separation from the Church of England is, in the judgement of papists . . . found the most compendious way to introduce popery and to ruin the Protestant religion*, London 1680; 2nd ed., 2 pts, Dublin 1682 (the second part added by R. Ware); repr., 3 pts, London 1689 (the third part added by R. Ware)

J. da Natividade, *Additamento ao Agiologío Dominico*, v, Lisbon 1743

M. Ní Cheallacháin (ed.), *Filíocht Phádraigín Haicéad*, Dublin 1962

K. W. Nicholls, *Gaelic and Gaelicised Ireland in the Middle Ages*, Dublin 1972

—'A List of the Monasteries in Connacht, 1577' in *Journal of the Galway Archaeological and Historical Society*, 33 (1972–3)

—(ed.), *The O'Doyne (Ó Duinn) Manuscript*, Dublin 1983

J. O'Boyle, *The Irish Colleges on the Continent*, Dublin 1935

B. Ó Bric, 'Galway Townsmen as the Owners of Land in Connacht, 1585–1641' (unpublished M.A. thesis, University College, Galway, 1974)

S. O'Brien (ed.), *Measgra i gCuimhne Mhichíl Uí Chléirigh*, Dublin 1944

W. P. O'Brien, 'Two Sixteenth-Century Munster Primates: Donnchadh Ó Taidhg (1560–62) and Richard Creagh (1564–85)' in *Seanchas Ardmhacha*, 14 (1990)

M. Ó Cléirigh *et al.*, *Annála Ríoghachta Éireann: Annals of the Kingdom of Ireland by the Four Masters from the earliest period to the year 1616*, ed. and trans. J. O'Donovan, 7 vols, Dublin 1846–51; repr. New York 1966

W. D. O'Connell, 'The Cahil Propositions, 1629' in *Irish Ecclesiastical Record*, 5th ser., 62 (1943)

B. Ó Cuív, 'The Irish Language in the Early Modern Period' in *A New History of Ireland*, iii, Oxford 1976

D. O'Daly, *Initium, Incrementa, et Exitus Familiae Geraldinorum . . . ac Persecutionis Haereticorum Descriptio*, Lisbon 1655; ed. and trans. C. P. Meehan as *History of the Geraldines*, Dublin 1878

D. J. O'Doherty (ed.), 'Students of the Irish College, Salamanca' in *Archivium Hibernicum*, 2 (1913)

T. Ó Donnchadha, *An t-Athair Pádraigín Haicéad*, Dublin 1916

T. O'Donnell, *Franciscan Abbey of Multyfarnham*, Multyfarnham 1951

D. O'Donoghue, 'The Congregation of Irish Priests in Bordeaux (1602–1617)' in *Irish Ecclesiastical Record*, 4th ser., 5 (1899)

M. O'Dowd, 'Irish Concealed Lands Papers in the Hastings Manuscripts in the Huntingdon Library, San Marino, California' in *Analecta Hibernica*, 31 (1984)

—*Power, Politics and Land: Early Modern Sligo, 1568–1688*, Belfast 1991

P. O'Dwyer, *The Irish Carmelites*, Dublin 1988

S. H. O'Grady and R. Flower, *Catalogue of Irish Manuscripts in the British Museum*, 2 vols, London 1926–53; repr. Dublin 1992

J. O'Heyne, *Epilogus Chronologicus exponens succincte Conventus et Fundationes Sacri Ordinis Praedicatorum in Regno Hyberniae*, Louvain 1706; ed. and trans. by A. Coleman as *The Irish Dominicans of the Seventeenth Century*, Dundalk 1902

J. de Olarra Garmendia and M. L. de Larramendi (Olarra) (eds), *Correspondencia entre la Nunciatura en Espagna y la Santa Sede durante el reinado de Félipe* III *(1598–1621)*, 7 vols, Rome 1960–67

M. Olden, 'Episcopal Comments on the "Decreta pro Recto Regimine Ecclesiarum Hiberniae", 1635–6' in *Archivium Hibernicum*, 27 (1964)

—'Counter-Reformation Problems: Munster' in *Proceedings of the Irish Catholic Historical Committee*, Dublin 1967

S. A. O'Mahony, 'The Irish Discalced Carmelites, 1625–1653' (unpublished Ph.D. thesis, Trinity College, Dublin, 1976)

E. Ó Raghailligh, *A Genealogical History of the O'Reillys*, ed. J Carney, Dublin 1959

O'Rian, H., *Poema Encomiasticon de Adventu Excellentissimi Ducis Caroli de Crequi . . .*, Rome 1633

T. O'Rorke, *The History of Sligo*, 2 vols, Dublin 1889

B. O'Sullivan, 'Medieval Irish Dominican Studies' in *Irish Rosary* (Nov.–Dec. 1948 to Jan.–Feb. 1953)

M. D. O'Sullivan, *Old Galway: The History of a Norman Colony in Ireland*, Cambridge 1942; repr. Galway 1983

P. O'Sullivan Beare, *Historiae Catholicae Iberniae Compendium*, Lisbon, 1621; ed. M. Kelly, Dublin 1850

—*Ireland under Elizabeth . . . being a portion of The History of Catholic Ireland by Don Philip O'Sullivan Beare*, ed. and trans. M. J. Byrne, Dublin 1903

—*Selections from the Zoilomastix of Philip O'Sullivan Beare*, ed. and trans. T. J. O'Donnell, Dublin 1960

The Oxford Dictionary of the Christian Church, ed. F. L. Cross and E. A. Livingstone, Oxford 1974

G. M. Piò, *Delle Vite degli Huomini Illustri di S. Domenico*, pt 1, 2 vols, Bologna 1607–13

—*Delle Nobile e Generosa Progenie del P.S. Domenico in Italia libri due . . .*, Bologna 1615

A. de la Plaza Bores, *Archivo General de Simancas: Guia del Investigador*, Madrid 1980

D. D. C. Pochin Mould, *The Irish Dominicans*, Dublin 1957

J. Quétif and J. Echard, *Scriptores Ordinis Praedicatorum Recensiti, Notisque Historicis et Criticis Illustrati*, 2 vols, Paris 1719–21

A. Quiros, *Apuntes y Documentos para la Historia de la Provincia Dominicana de Andalucía*, 3 vols, Almagro 1915–33

J. Ranson, 'Irish Archives in Spain' in *Proceedings of the Irish Catholic Historical Committee*, Dublin 1955

H. Raposa, *Dona Luisa de Gusmão*, Lisbon 1946

W. Reeves, *Ecclesiastical Antiquities of Down, Connor, and Dromore*, Dublin 1847

B. M. Reichert (ed.), *Monumenta Ordinis Fratrum Praedicatorum Historica: Acta Capitulorum Generalium Ordinis Praedicatorum: 1220–1844*, 9 vols, Rome 1898–1904

L. F. Renehan, *Collections on Irish Church History*, ed D. McCarthy, 2 vols, Dublin 1861–74

E. Reusens and V. Barbier, *Analectes pour servir a l'Histoire Ecclésiastique de la Belgique*, 2ᵉ sér., vii, Louvain 1892

N. Robbins (ed.), *An Exact Abridgement of all the Irish Statutes*, Dublin 1736

A. M. Rodriguez Cruz, *Historia de las Universidades Hispanoamericanas: Périodo Hispánico*, 2 vols, Bogota 1973

M. V. Ronan, *The Reformation in Dublin, 1536–1668*, London 1925

—*The Reformation in Ireland under Elizabeth, 1558–1580*, London 1930

A. Ross, *Scottish Blackfriars in the Seventeenth Century*, Glasgow 1972

D. Rothe, *Analecta Sacra, Nova, et Mira de Rebus Catholicorum in Hibernia . . . Gestis . . .*, n.p. 1616; 2 vols, Cologne 1617–19; ed. P. F. Moran, Dublin 1884

J. P. Rushe, *Carmel in Ireland, with supplement*, Dublin/London 1903

C. W. Russell and J. P. Prendergast, *The Carte Manuscripts in the Bodleian Library . . . A Report presented to the Master of the Rolls*, London 1871

L. Sánchez Belda, *Guia del Archivo Histórico Nacional*, Madrid 1958

St J. D. Seymour, *The Diocese of Emly*, Dublin 1913

A. J. Sheehan, 'The Recusancy Revolt of 1603: A Reinterpretation' in *Archivium Hibernicum*, 38 (1983)

J. J. Silke, 'The Irish College, Seville' in *Archivium Hibernicum*, 24 (1961)

—*Ireland and Europe, 1559–1607*, Dundalk 1966

—*Kinsale: The Spanish Intervention in Ireland at the End of the Elizabethan Wars*, Liverpool 1970

—'The Irish Abroad, 1534–1691' in *A New History of Ireland*, iii, Oxford 1978

—'Some Aspects of the Reformation in Armagh Province' in *Clogher Record*, 11 (1984)

J. G. Simms, 'Seventeenth-Century Ireland, 1603–1702' in T. W. Moody (ed.), *Irish Historiography, 1936–70*, Dublin 1971

F. Soria Heredia, *El Santuario de Nuestra Señora de la Peña de Francia*, Salamanca 1982

[T. Stafford], *Pacata Hibernia*, London 1633; ed. S. H. O'Grady, 2 vols, Dublin 1896

Strafford, T. Wentworth, Earl of, *The Earl of Strafforde's Letters and Dispatches . . .*, ed. W. Knowler, 2 vols, Dublin 1739

I. Taurisano, 'Note Storiche sul Collegium Divi Thomae de Urbe e gli Studi Domenicani in Roma' in *Analecta Sacri Ordinis Praedicatorum*, 17 (1925–6)

M. A. Tierney (ed.), *Dodd's Church History of England*, 5 vols, London 1839–43

J. Toravel, *Nomenclature des Religieux de la Congrégation de Bretagne au XVIIème et XVIIIème siècles*, Angers 1964

A. Valkenburg, 'The Ven. Peter Higgins, Dominican, 1601?–1642' in *Journal of the Kildare Archaeological Society*, 15 (1973–4)

—'Pádraigín an Doiminiceach as Caiseal Mumhan' in *Feasta*, 36 (1983)

J. and J. A. Venn, *Alumni Cantabrigiensis*, 10 vols, Cambridge 1922–54

M. H. Vicaire, 'Frères Prêcheurs' in *Dictionnaire d'Histoire et de Géographie Ecclésiastique*, xviii, Paris 1977

Wadding Papers, 1614–1638, ed. B. Jennings, Dublin 1953

J. Wadsworth, *Further Observations of the English Spanish Pilgrim*, London 1630

K. Walsh, *A Fourteenth-Century Scholar and Primate: Richard FitzRalph in Oxford, Avignon and Armagh*, Oxford 1981

M. Walsh [Kerney Walsh] (ed.), *Spanish Knights of Irish Origin: Documents from Continental Archives*, 4 vols, Dublin 1960–78

—*'Destruction by Peace': Hugh O'Neill after Kinsale*, Monaghan 1986

P. Walsh, *The MacGeoghegans*, Mullingar 1938

—'Glimpses of the Penal Times' in *Irish Ecclesiastical Record*, 4th ser., 28 (1910)

R. Walsh, 'Some of Our Martyrs' in *Irish Ecclesiastical Record*, 3rd ser., 15 (1894)

—(ed.), 'A Memorial presented to the King of Spain on behalf of the Irish Catholics, 1619' in *Archivium Hibernicum*, 6 (1917)

T. J. Walsh, *The Irish Continental College Movement*, Dublin/Cork 1973

A. Walz, *Compendium Historiae Ordinis Praedicatorum*, Rome 1930; 2nd ed., Rome 1948

—*I Domenicani al Concilio di Trento*, Rome 1961

—*L'Università San Tommaso in Roma*, Rome 1966

J. Ware, *The Whole Works of Sir James Ware concerning Ireland, revised and improved*, ed. W. Harris, 3 vols in 2, Dublin 1739, 1746, 1764

—*De Hibernia et Antiquitatibus eius* . . ., London 1654; 2nd ed., 1658

R. Ware (ed.), *Foxes and Firebrands: or A Specimen of the Danger and Harmony of Popery and Separation: wherein is proved . . . that separation from the Church of England is, in the judgement of papists . . . found the most compendious way to introduce popery and to ruin the Protestant religion*, London 1680; 2nd ed., 2 pts, Dublin 1682 (the second part added by R. Ware); repr., 3 pts, London 1689 (the third part was added by R. Ware)

—*The Hunting of the Romish Fox and the Quenching of Sectarian Fire-Brands, being a Specimen of Popery, and Separation . . . collected by . . . Sir James Ware, . . . and now published for the publick good by Robert Ware* . . ., Dublin 1683

'Waterford Inquisitions' in *Journal of the Waterford and South-East of Ireland Archaeological Society*, 11 (Jan.–Mar. 1908)

J. A. Watt, *The Church and the Two Nations in Medieval Ireland*, Cambridge 1970

—*The Church in Medieval Ireland*, Dublin 1972

A. E. J. Went, 'Irish Monastic Fisheries' in *Journal of the Cork Historical and Archaeological Society*, 63 (1955)

T. J. Westropp, 'A Survey of the Ancient Churches in Co. Limerick' in *Proceedings of the Royal Irish Academy*, 25 (1905), sect. C

N. B. White (ed.), *Extents of Irish Monastic Possessions, 1540–1541, from Manuscripts in the Public Record Office, London*, Dublin 1943

P. Woulfe, *Sloinnte Gaedhael is Gall: Irish Names and Surnames*, Dublin 1923

A. Zucchi, *La S. Penitenzeria Apostolica e l'Ordine di S. Domenico*, Florence 1942

Index